THE LIFE OF
SIR HERSCH LAUTEI
QC, FBA, LLD

Hersch Lauterpacht, of whom this book is an intimate biography by his son, Elihu, was one of the most prolific and influential international lawyers of the first half of the twentieth century. Having come to England in the early 1920s, he first researched and taught at the London School of Economics before moving to Cambridge in 1937 to become Whewell Professor of International Law. He did valuable work to enhance relations with the United States during the Second World War, and was active after the war in the prosecution of William Joyce and the major Nazi war criminals. For ten years he was also involved in various significant items of professional work and in 1955 he was elected a judge of the International Court of Justice. The book contains many extracts from his correspondence, the interest of which will extend to lawyers, historians of the period and beyond.

SIR ELIHU LAUTERPACHT, CBE, QC has had a distinguished career in international law, combining teaching and practice on an extensive scale. He was called to the Bar in 1950, became a QC in 1970, and has practised extensively before the International Court of Justice and other international jurisdictions, as well as before the English courts. He was ad hoc judge in the Bosnia case before the International Court, has been an arbitrator in NAFTA, ICSID and other arbitrations, President of the East African Common Market Tribunal, of a Panel of the UN Compensation Commission, the World Bank and Asian Development Bank Administrative Tribunals and of the Eritrea–Ethiopia Boundary Commission.

THE LIFE OF SIR HERSCH LAUTERPACHT, QC, FBA, LLD

BY

SIR ELIHU LAUTERPACHT

CBE, QC
HONORARY PROFESSOR OF INTERNATIONAL LAW IN
THE UNIVERSITY OF CAMBRIDGE
MEMBER OF THE INSTITUT DE DROIT INTERNATIONAL
FELLOW OF TRINITY COLLEGE, CAMBRIDGE
BENCHER OF GRAY'S INN

CAMBRIDGE
UNIVERSITY PRESS

CAMBRIDGE UNIVERSITY PRESS
Cambridge, New York, Melbourne, Madrid, Cape Town,
Singapore, São Paulo, Delhi, Mexico City

Cambridge University Press
The Edinburgh Building, Cambridge CB2 8RU, UK

Published in the United States of America by Cambridge University Press, New York

www.cambridge.org
Information on this title: www.cambridge.org/9781107412897

© Cambridge University Press 2010

First published 2010
Reprinted 2011
First paperback edition 2012

A catalogue record for this publication is available from the British Library

ISBN 978-1-107-00041-4 Hardback
ISBN 978-1-107-41289-7 Paperback

To the memory of
Hersch Lauterpacht,
and of his parents, Aron and Deborah,
and the other members of his family who perished in the Holocaust;
and to the memory also of his devoted wife, Rachel Lauterpacht,
and her parents, Michael and Gittel Steinberg

CONTENTS

PLATES

The plates will be found between pages 372 and 373.

ACKNOWLEDGMENTS

In the preparation of this work I have received much assistance from a wide range of friends and scholars in the field. I list them in alphabetical order since, although their contributions have varied in scale, it would be invidious to weigh the value of one against another. I am immensely grateful to them all, though I need hardly add that they bear no responsibility for the product.

Those to whom I am indebted include Professor Philip Allott; the American Jewish Committee; Ms Mahnoush Arsanjani; Mr Daniel Bethlehem; Ms Michelle Bradfield; Professor Jonathan A. Bush; Dr and Mrs M. Cahn; Mr Jeremy Carver and Messrs Clifford Chance & Co.; Professor James Crawford; Mrs K. Das; Mrs Lesley Dingle; the late Mr W. Frankel; Ms Emanuela-Chiara Gillard; Ms Norah Gallagher; Dr Joanna Gomula; Dame Rosalyn Higgins; the late Sir Robert Jennings; Mr Tim Johnson; Mrs Inka Katz; Professor Martti Koskenniemi; the late Mr Vitaly Kutik; Ms Catherine Lammers; Ms Sarah Latimer; Ms Dinah Heller; the LSE archives; Ms Frances Meadows; Mr Tony Millett; Ms Amanda Morgan; Ms Penelope Nevill; Professor Shabtai Rosenne; Professor Christoph Schreuer; Judge Stephen M. Schwebel; Ms Merav Segal; Mr William Shawcross; Ms Karen von Hippel; Dr Michael Waibel; Mr Tony Weir; Mr Aureliusz Wlaz; and all those who sent their recollections to RL in 1960.

In addition, I must express my special thanks to the Leverhulme Trust and to Trinity College, Cambridge, for substantial grants towards meeting the costs of the preparation of this work. I appreciate also the consideration shown by Finola O'Sullivan, and her colleagues at Cambridge University Press. Nor can I fail to mention specifically the great contribution of Miss Maureen MacGlashan who has prepared the index, Mr Andrew Sanger, especially in the late stages of the work, and my personal assistant, Mrs Jenny Byford, who has shown great skill and patience in coping with my repeatedly changing drafts. To my wife, Catherine, and our children, who have been obliged to tolerate my virtual withdrawal from family life while this book was being written, I offer my loving thanks and blessings.

ABBREVIATIONS

AD	*Annual Digest and Reports of Public International Law Cases,* 1929–49 (continued as *ILR*)
AIOC	Anglo-Iranian Oil Company
AJC	American Jewish Committee
AJIL	*American Journal of International Law*
Annuaire	*Annuaire de l'Institut de Droit International*
Archive	Archive of HL-related papers
ASIL	American Society of International Law
BYIL	*British Year Book of International Law*
CLJ	*Cambridge Law Journal*
Collected Papers	*International Law – The Collected Papers of H. Lauterpacht,* ed. E. Lauterpacht, 5 vols. (Cambridge, Cambridge University Press, 1970–2004)
EJIL	*European Journal of International Law*
EL	Elihu Lauterpacht
Hague Academy	Academy of International Law, The Hague
HAZ	Organization of the Zionist Academics in Galicia
HL	Hersch Lauterpacht
ICJ	International Court of Justice
ICLQ	*International and Comparative Law Quarterly*
ILA	International Law Association
ILC	International Law Commission
ILO	International Labour Organization
ILR	*International Law Reports* (continuation of *AD* from 1950)
KB	Law Reports, King's Bench
KOC	Kuwait Oil Company
LQR	*Law Quarterly Review*
LSE	London School of Economics and Political Science
Oppenheim	*Oppenheim's International Law*
PCIJ	Permanent Court of International Justice
Private Law Sources	*Private Law Sources and Analogies of Public International Law* (London, Longmans, 1927)
RL	Rachel Lauterpacht

The Function of Law	*The Function of Law in the International Community* (Oxford, Clarendon Press, 1933)
UN	United Nations
UNESCO	United Nations Educational, Scientific and Cultural Organization
WUJS	World Union of Jewish Students

PROLOGUE AND INTRODUCTION

This is the life of Sir Hersch Lauterpacht, who lived from 1897 to 1960. In his time, he was regarded, and still is, as a pre-eminent international lawyer devoted to the advancement of peace between States on the basis of law. To that end, he rejected the unbridled assertion of sovereignty by States and emphasised the fundamental rights of the individual. He was a prolific legal writer whose works carried great authority. His life fell into four parts: his early years in Eastern Europe from 1897 to 1923, followed by his marriage and emigration to England where he began a distinguished academic career. After the end of the Second World War, he became more involved in the profession of international law in which he used his great knowledge and literary capacity to powerful effect. Finally, he spent five years as a judge of the International Court of Justice, dying in office at the early age of 62.

His life was one of almost unremitting labour, on his own behalf, on behalf of his students and on behalf of governments or other clients. And coupled with this was an intense devotion to his wife, Rachel, and his only child, the author of this book.

The biography draws heavily on a major accumulation of family correspondence exchanged between Hersch, Rachel and myself over a period of nearly thirty years. It is supported by consideration of his writings which tell us much about his attitude towards life. To a limited extent this material is supplemented by my own personal knowledge, but it must be realised that there are many facets of his life of which I can have no direct knowledge, having been too young or away from home. Nonetheless, I venture to believe that there is much in these pages that will interest not only lawyers but also non-lawyers who will perceive in them many wise thoughts.

Let me elaborate now on some of the matters touched upon in the preceding paragraphs.

The distinctive smell of mothballs for long pervaded my study. It came from the large cabin trunk left behind by Hersch's widow, my mother, Rachel, when she passed away in 1989 and which, regrettably, was not seriously examined until 2003. In it she stored a huge accumulation of family correspondence – mainly letters passing between Hersch, herself and me. Some go back to the 1920s, and the collection continues even beyond Hersch's death in 1960. Rachel had thrown nothing away that came from him or me or from some other members of the family. When

I

I was away in the United States as a schoolboy during part of the Second World War, my mother told me to keep and bring home all the letters that I received from her or from my father. Most of them were in the trunk – well preserved.

Much use has been made of excerpts from these letters; the facts gleaned from them contribute substantially to this narrative. I have limited myself, so far as possible, to those written by Hersch, using those written by Rachel and myself only where they provide detail relevant to the life of Hersch. As it is, the reader may possibly feel that there is too much that is unimportant in the passages that are quoted. But I venture to justify them as showing how the man lived and thought, particularly during the difficult period of the Second World War when he was separated from Rachel and myself. Even so, my mother's letters must not be completely overlooked. She was the most active correspondent, writing to me almost every day; my father wrote frequently but not so often. My mother's letters shed much light on domestic matters and the conditions under which she and Hersch lived, especially after her return to England in March 1943. They speak incidentally about what Hersch was doing. The excerpts evidence his preoccupations, some of which may seem unimportant to us, but were not to him. However, what matters is that he overcame the complications of life that these fragments evidence and succeeded in continuing with creative work during a period of terrible outside upheaval. Also, the extracts from his letters to me not only tell us quite a bit about what he was doing but also, more importantly, about his own character and ambitions as reflected largely in his ambitions and concern for me. I have considered carefully the propriety of including so much that is really part of my life, but have concluded that his letters to me provide us with a significant insight into his personal qualities and therefore cannot be neglected. They may also be of interest to other parents and their children who may gain much from the guidance and wisdom they contain.

The extensive use of these letters has led to some unevenness in the length of the chapters and some unavoidable lack of uniformity in their approach. For example, those covering the early years are relatively short when compared with those devoted to the 'War Years'. This reflects the differing quantities of original material available for the particular years. There is little on which one can draw for Hersch's background and early years. On the other hand, during the War period, 1939–44, when the family was separated, there is a large and revealing body of intra-family correspondence. In the period between the end of that War and Hersch's election to the International Court of Justice, there are a number of well-documented episodes, which are treated at length.

I have hesitated to call this work a 'biography', as in some sections it is little more than a bare recitation of facts in the nature almost of a deposition. I claim neither the skills nor the experience, beyond a half-century of preparing legal arguments and opinions, to write a text that by its presentation, ideas, imagination, vocabulary and general style can be called 'literature' or, more precisely, 'biography'. Yet there is here a story that must be told – or at least material that must be presented to reveal the story – of the life of a man not significantly in the public eye, but nonetheless a leading figure in the world of international law for nearly forty years and whose influence has long survived his death. This is the life of a man who was entirely dedicated to the exposition and development of international law, not as an abstract academic subject but as one which, inspired by deep convictions of international morality, he saw as playing an essential role in international society, in the maintenance of peace, in the resolution of disputes and in the furtherance of human rights. It does not seem right to allow filial modesty to prevent me from openly acknowledging his greatness as a lawyer and a man.

In the years when Hersch researched, taught, wrote and adjudicated – from 1920 to 1960 – international lawyers were barely aware of some of the important topics that have become so familiar in the half-century since his passing. Although he was a pioneer in the development of the international protection of human rights, publishing in 1945 the first systematic set of proposals on that subject, it was not one that then attracted the intense attention that is now reflected in the adoption and constant application of international conventions and national legislation such as the European Convention on Human Rights and Fundamental Freedoms 1950 and the Human Rights Act 1998 in the United Kingdom. Nor was the need for international protection of the environment more than barely recognised then; and the numerous declarations and treaties on the climate were yet to come. The concept of international criminal law, though understood, rested on a limited foundation; and the emergence of permanent international criminal tribunals beyond those that operated in the aftermath of the Second World War lay in the future. The use of force in international relations, though formally prohibited in the United Nations Charter in 1945, had not by 1960 become the commonplace of everyday conversation that it has in the wake of events in the last decades of the twentieth century and the first decades of the twenty-first.

But all the advances and changes in the subject notwithstanding, the details of Hersch's life may well be of interest to many – not only to international lawyers but also to those who find meaning in the story of the absorption into British society of a person born and bred in an entirely different one. The lives of many biography-worthy lawyers are, for the most part, written round the famous trials or political events in which they were involved. Hersch's life, though largely affected by various public and academic developments from 1919 till his death, reflects activity with a lower profile. He did not court publicity. Only occasionally did he write letters to the newspapers – and then only in relation to some major international legal occurrence. And there were many events – of greater importance – that did not engage his attention in this way. But he did play a significant, if not loudly bruited, role in relation to quite a number of important international legal developments which will be mentioned later.

His story has not been told in detail before. I have allowed myself to embark on it because such evidence as there is of what he did can usefully be supplemented by the first-hand knowledge of one who, as his only child, had close contact with him between 1928 (the year of my birth) and 1960 (the year of his death) and who, by reason of my own continuous involvement in the same subject for over sixty years, is well placed to provide additional information.

When my father passed away in May 1960, I decided to produce a memorial to him in the form of a collection of his articles presented systematically, with a view to providing some kind of substitute for the comprehensive treatise on international law that he intended to write but, alas, never did. The outcome has been the five volumes of *International Law – The Collected Papers*, which, together with editorial notes, were published respectively in 1970, 1975, 1977, 1978 and 2004. The long delay in the completion of the series is to be explained by my own deep and competing immersion in academic and professional work in the field. My father had considered producing such a collection during his life, but had been put off both by the size of the project and by the apprehension that he might have to subsidise the publication. He was right about the size, but wrong about the need for a subsidy. The original printing of the collection has sold sufficiently well to justify a reprint.[1]

As I prepared the final volume of the series, and especially the chapters reflecting Hersch's work during the Second World War on neutrality and the law of war, I was led to look more closely into the details of his life

---

[1] Reprinted by Cambridge University Press in paperback, 2009.

during that period. In so doing, I concluded that, though there have been a number of substantial articles that have provided some outline of his life as part of a consideration of his academic work, a fuller account of what, by any standard, was a remarkable career entirely dedicated to international law should not be foregone.

A number of scholars have contemplated writing such a biographical study, and I sincerely wish that at least one of them might have been able to do so. But they, like me, have felt the compelling press of other obligations. In consequence, I have reached, not without much hesitation, the conclusion that I ought myself to attempt the task. There are, of course, many good reasons why a son should not write the life of his father. The principal difficulty lies, of course, in approaching the subject with a sufficient degree of detachment and objectivity. But there are certain countervailing considerations of which the most important is my first-hand recollection of much of Hersch's activity (but regrettably by no means all) and, no less, of the major role played in his life by his devoted wife, my mother Rachel.[2]

Also, as I read the letters contained in the cabin trunk, particularly those exchanged when we were separated from each other during the Second World War, many struck me as being too personally intimate to fall in their entirety under the scrutiny of even the most benevolent stranger to the family. And so I concluded that their perusal and use was a task that I alone should undertake.

The pages that follow will, therefore, be more personal in form and content than would be those of a memoir written by another hand. Though not neglecting Hersch's substantive work, they will be less concerned with its content than would be an account penned by someone writing principally on the basis of his academic writings and judicial opinions. Such work has already been done on a significant scale in articles written by Lord McNair, Dr C. W. (Wilfred) Jenks, Sir Gerald Fitzmaurice, Ambassador Shabtai Rosenne and, more recently, in a detailed and illuminating manner by Professor Martti Koskenniemi.[3]

In approaching my task, I have thought it appropriate to include some detail about Hersch's family, friends, activities and condition of life – certain aspects of which may in places appear to be excessively detailed or to border on the trivial. However, I believe this exposition to

---

[2] One may be reminded of a line in a review of Edmund Gosse's *Father and Son*: 'Let no one suppose that the spirit of this book is unfilial. It could not have been written except by one to whom the filial relation was most dear and sacred.' Quoted by James Hepburn at p. xii of his Introduction to the edition of *Father and Son* published by Oxford University Press in 1974.

[3] See the list of works about Hersch in Appendix 2, p. 443, below.

be justified by the consideration that others may find value in anything that sheds light on the character, thought and activity of one who, being Jewish, came, with commendable prescience – these being pre-Nazi days – from Eastern Europe to settle in England in 1923; whose mother tongue was not English; who within fourteen years of his arrival here was elected to one of the two principal chairs of international law in the United Kingdom; who within a further seventeen years was selected as the British judge on the world's principal tribunal – the International Court of Justice; who throughout this period continuously produced international legal writing of the highest scholarly originality and calibre which has led to the widely held view that he was one of the most significant international lawyers of the twentieth century; who did all this while adhering openly, though not assertively, to his Jewish faith and Zionist convictions; and who during the Holocaust lost virtually the whole of the family that remained behind in Poland and whom he could not persuade to follow him to England.

A word may be said here about Hersch's Zionism. In his early years in Lwów, Vienna and London, the Zionism that meant so much to him was a reflection of the political Zionist movement in the late nineteenth century following the publication of Herzl's seminal work, *Der Judenstaat*.[4] The Zionism of the first decades of the twentieth century was rather different from the Zionism that describes the political ideals and activities of many Israeli 'Zionists' of today. Hersch supported the establishment in Palestine of a secular, liberal-democratic Jewish state. He spent many of his early years with fellow students who taught themselves without the aid of teachers, studying the history of Zionism, the geography of Israel and the Hebrew language. His application to the Zionist Executive Committee in London and the letter of support written by the Executive Committee of the Zionist Organization in Eastern Galicia both attest to the fact that Hersch was preparing himself for 'activity in Eretz Israel in the future by learning the work of the Zionist Organization and its practical administration. In addition, he would like to enrich his knowledge by studying the subjects of administration and sociology.'[5] The supporting letter also notes that 'ideological motives alone bring our comrade to seek a position in the central office in London'.

There is nothing to suggest that Hersch would have weakened in his support of Zionism once the State of Israel was established. Indeed, the contrary is manifested in the first of the two lectures that he gave

---

[4] See generally *Encyclopaedia Judaica*, sub. tit. 'Zionism', vol. 16, pp. 1031–182 (Jerusalem, 1978).
[5] Letter to the Central Zionist Executive Committee in London, 23 June 1920.

in Jerusalem in 1950 at the twenty-fifth anniversary celebration of the founding of the university there.[6] But it must be a matter of speculation as to whether he would have remained uncritical of the State in the events that have followed during the ensuing half-century. It must not be assumed that he would have felt comfortable with the recent changes, or accepted them without question. It can perhaps be said that Hersch's support of Zionism was driven by the need to protect the Jewish minority against anti-Semitism and individual discrimination. One of his earlier contemporaries recalls that Hersch 'was angered by the social inequality, opposed to chauvinism and dreamed of a Jewish Renaissance based on the spirit of social justice'.[7] This desire to 'protect minorities' and work towards social justice no doubt underpins Hersch's future work on human rights, where he maintained that it was the role of international law to protect individuals if the State fails. A Jewish State would protect the Jewish minorities; international human rights would protect all minorities from across the world.

Views may differ as to whether it is really necessary or desirable to present all the detail that appears in the pages that follow. But many of the letters reproduced will shed valuable light on the substantive topics covered that would not otherwise be available. I cannot assume that the present volume will be the last word about Hersch's life and that the material here presented will not be of value to others.[8]

These details will, I hope, prove interesting to readers who are not international lawyers. As will be seen from the extensive quotations from his letters, Hersch was a man of remarkable insight, balance, sensitivity and foresight, capable of great understanding and affection and of expressing himself delicately, directly and clearly. Moreover, his letters of advice to me, particularly about preparation for examinations and the technique of writing, may be studied with benefit by other young persons.

A number of examples of these qualities will be found in one particular source. This is the correspondence between Hersch and C. W. Jenks. They met in about 1934 when both were preparing for their Bar exams.

---

[6] *Collected Papers*, Vol. 2, p. 159.

[7] Dr Joseph Roth, in a letter sent to Rachel after Hersch's death.

[8] This approach coincides with the opinion expressed by Professor D. H. N. Johnson in a review of McNair's British Academy obituary of Hersch (*Proceedings of the British Academy*, vol. 47, pp. 371–85): 'Even if to the present generation the contributions of Hersch Lauterpacht to international law are so well known as scarcely to need recording, it should be remembered that to future generations it will be of interest to discover not merely what a man wrote – which may be easy enough – but also what were his origins, the various experiences that he underwent, and last but not least his influence upon, and standing with, his contemporaries.' (1964) 12 *ICLQ* 1063.

There then followed a friendship and correspondence extending over twenty-six years until Hersch's death. At the beginning, Jenks was a legal adviser in the ILO in Geneva. In due course he was promoted to become the principal Legal Adviser of the Organization and eventually was elected as its Director-General. Jenks was reputed never to throw anything away and he left behind him the originals or copies of most of the letters exchanged between him and Hersch. It is the correspondence of two giants of legal literature for Jenks, though heavily engaged in official duties, was consumed by an irresistible urge to write academic works on international law, something that he did with imagination and brilliance. The correspondence is preserved in the archives of the ILO and runs to over 300 pages. So far as Hersch's life is concerned, the letters reflect, amongst other matters, the vast amount of work on which he was engaged at any one time and his capacity for constructive friendship which took the form, amongst other things, of providing Jenks with constant and detailed criticism of his emergent writings and of telling him of the possibility of academic preferment, first in London and later in Cambridge – opportunities which Jenks felt unable to take because of his commitment to the work of the ILO.

One important issue has required a decision from the beginning: whether to present matters on a subject-by-subject basis or to do so in approximately chronological order. With the exception of Chapter 8 towards the end of the volume, devoted to Hersch's extensive work on human rights, the latter approach has seemed preferable, principally because it can convey more cogently the number of matters with which he was dealing at any one time. He was able to move from item to item with seeming ease, but worked on each with impressive concentration.

Time has proved to be both an encouragement and an impediment to the completion of this work. 2010 is the fiftieth year following Hersch's death and I felt it important that the volume should appear not later than this year. But, as one writes, additional material keeps coming to hand and, although it does not change the story materially, it requires mention for the assistance of others who may wish to go over parts of the same ground. There will, therefore, be many sections of the work that could have been improved and enlarged if this time constraint had not been so pressing. But I have felt that, even marked by imperfection, it would be better that the work should appear sooner rather than later.

CHAPTER I

BACKGROUND AND EARLY YEARS, 1897–1919

Hersch Lauterpacht was born on 16 August 1897 in the small town of Żółkiew in Eastern Galicia. At that time, Galicia was the easternmost province of the Austro-Hungarian Empire, having been acquired by Austria as a result of the Partitions of Poland in 1772–96. In 1919, it reverted to its previous status as Polish territory, only to pass to the Ukraine in the aftermath of the Second World War.[1]

Hersch's parents were Aron Lauterpacht and Deborah Turkenkopf. Although they had been married in a synagogue, this had not been accompanied by a civil process. As a result, Deborah was not officially 'Lauterpacht' and retained her maiden name. It is not known when she came to be known as 'Lauterpacht'. For the first few years of his life, therefore, Hersch's surname was that of his mother – 'Turkenkopf'. His given name at birth was 'Hersz', which was transliterated into 'Hersch'. This was the name by which he was known to all except his childhood family and friends and his wife, who called him 'Zvi'.[2]

Hersch's father, Aron, was in the timber trade. Much of his business was conducted in the northern Polish ports of Gdynia and Danzig. In the latter he managed a factory making plywood boxes. During the years of the First World War, he also managed a large sawmill in what was then known as Lemberg (later Lwów and now Lviv), the capital of the province of Galicia.[3] Though he was far from being a wealthy man, he was able to meet the costs not only of Hersch's primary and secondary education but also of his time at university, first in Lemberg and then in Vienna. Indeed, even after Hersch's marriage in 1923, some support was provided until the drastic economic crisis that hit Poland in 1929.

The family lived modestly, first in a small house in Żółkiew, and later initially in a six-room flat in Lemberg. Aron was a devout Jew,

---

[1] See p. 17 below.

[2] In fact, both names mean the same thing, 'deer' or 'gazelle', with 'Hersch' being the Yiddish and 'Zvi' the Hebrew word.

[3] References to the capacity in which he was involved in the trade vary. Some say he was a manager, others that he owned the factory, but it seems unlikely that he would have been affluent enough to have owned it.

performing his ritual prayers each morning and going to synagogue on Saturdays. Hersch's mother, Deborah, was likewise very observant of the Jewish faith and requirements. As can be seen in photographs, she was a fine-looking woman, reflecting a strong character. She dressed modestly and had her hair cut short and covered by a wig. She kept a strictly Kosher home, separating milk and meat products and excluding forbidden foods such as pork and shellfish. Yiddish was the language spoken in the home. She devoted herself entirely to her family, to their care, upbringing and education. But her house was not a dull place. There was a piano, in the playing of which Hersch was able to develop some skill. There were books and a general atmosphere conducive to reading and serious discussion, engendered also by reason of the family commitment to, and belief in, the Jewish faith and dominating respect for study and learning. The distractions of television and perhaps even of a wireless did not then exist. There was no encouragement to waste time and, as can be seen from the many activities in which Hersch engaged, he wasted none. There was a secure home atmosphere, even though there might be uncertainty and danger in the streets outside.

Not only were Aron and Deborah devoutly Jewish, they were also inspired by an intense Jewish nationalism, with which in due course Hersch was imbued. Though he did not follow his father in formal religious observance, he was throughout his student days active in defence of Jewish interests and in the promotion of the Zionist cause. In 1916, he revived the Zeirei Zion[4] movement in Lemberg and formed the Herzliah Society of Zionist Youth. Later, he became leader of the Zionist undergraduate association, HAZ. In November 1917, he was arrested for arranging a demonstration to celebrate the publication of the Balfour Declaration. As this demonstration was seen as a pro-British move at a time when Austria was at war with Britain, he was tried by a military court, but was acquitted. (The judge was Dr Israel Waldmann, a well-known Zionist.) His later attraction to Rachel, his future wife, was also, no doubt, influenced by the fact that she came from Palestine

[4] Meaning 'Young Men of Zion', Zeirei Zion was a Zionist and modern socialist labour movement dating from 1903. It supported practical, constructive Zionism based on personal fulfilment through *aliyah* (a Hebrew word meaning 'a Jew who returns to their homeland, Israel'), pioneering the use of Hebrew, supporting the interests of the working masses and engaging in practical activities (such as collecting funds for the Jewish National Fund). Although the movement was particularly active in Russia (supporting the struggle to liberate Russia from the czarist autocracy), it also had a presence in Poland and Lithuania, where it sought equal rights and national autonomy for the Jewish people. Zeirei Zion also played an important role in the organisation of Jewish self-defence units (especially in response to the increase in pogroms) and in other cooperative measures. See *Encyclopaedia Judaica*, *sub. tit. 'Zionism'*, vol. 16, pp. 1031–182 (Jerusalem, 1978).

and by the prospect that he could therefore make a new life for himself there when they were married – as appears from his letters to his future parents-in-law.

Hersch had an elder brother, David (familiarly called Dunek), and a younger sister, Sabina (familiarly called Sabka). Dunek was a lawyer, though not a particularly successful one. He married and had one daughter. Sabka married Marcele (familiarly called Celek) Gelbard, a lawyer, and had a daughter, Inka.

The family remained in Żółkiew till Hersch was about 13, when the decision was taken to move to Lemberg, the capital of the province, a substantial city some thirty miles west of Żółkiew, where there were larger and better schools. Hersch continued his education there, attending the Humanist Gymnasium. He also joined the 'Shahei', a group of Zionist school pupils which met almost daily. We are told by his contemporaries of that time that they studied Hebrew twice a week, Jewish and Zionist history once a week and the geography of Israel once a week. On Saturdays there were additional lectures. In the summer they used to meet at 8.30am in the park to study Hebrew vocabulary and test each other to see who had learned most words in an hour. Hersch's great ability was recognised by his friends who, in 1913, elected him chairman of the group. It was then that he began to develop the lecturing skills that came to be so highly thought of when he reached England. His contemporaries remembered for years afterwards his lectures on Jewish history and philosophy.[5]

The only direct evidence of Hersch's home environment is provided by a note that some years ago I persuaded Hersch's niece, Inka, the only member of his family to survive the Holocaust in Poland, to write. It was a task that understandably she found painful. The first part of her note is reproduced below; the second – and much unhappier – part, about the war years, follows later. I have not changed the original wording of the note, since the realism conveyed by its highly personal character and even imperfections of expression would be much reduced by any editorial restatement or intervention. In reading it, it must be borne in mind that the period of which Inka writes was nearly twenty years after Hersch had left Lwów, but it is unlikely that much had changed during the interval.

Inka Katz to EL, August 2001
It's years since you have asked me to tell you whatever I may know about our family. I suppose it's about the time to do it, before it becomes too late. Most

---

[5] Memorandum by Dr Fleisher. See p. 21 below.

of those who survived the 1939–1945 feel 'guilty' somehow. Why us, not the others?

I shall try to describe our lives the way I saw the facts at that time, at the age between nine and twelve. A child changes to an adult very quickly in that sort of 'situation'.

You may want to know the kind of life the family led in Poland. I never went to the ugly sections, nor to the Jewish quarters. (There must have been 25%–30% of Jews in Lwów.) About 250,000–300,000 inhabitants altogether.

There was a lot of anti-Jewish feeling: at the university, in the professional life and, if one looked Jewish or spoke a not correct enough Polish, everywhere. I could not realize that at that time.

My parents were 'assimilated', well established. On my Father's side two or three generations of lawyers or something in that field. On the Lauterpacht's side the first.

Our life was the classical life of the upper middle class. Frequent receptions, holidays etc.

The grandparents Aron and Deborah were wonderful people. Hard working, generous and very ambitious for their children. Born in the third part of the 19th century, I do not remember the dates. Grandfather in Belzec (Belzec became in 1942 one of those camps where the Germans 'helped' by the Ukrainians killed, gassed, most of the Jews from Lwów and the small towns and villages around). Grandmother was born probably in Żółkiew (about 60 km from Lwów).

I believe that after they married, they remained for some years there, where Grandfather directed a saw-mill. Their three children, David (Dunek), Hersch and Sabina, were born there.

Both Aron and Deborah were in some way related to each other.

After the death of our grandmother's sister, Henek, Max and Mundek Ufel remained alone. (I do not know what happened to their father.) Grandparents took care of the three boys.

Henek studied in France and became a successful gynaecologist in Lwów. Married and was killed as well as his wife. Max remained a very medium lawyer.

Mundek a dentist in Paris first. You know all about him and Amy.[6]

---

[6] Mundek, usually known as Mundig, having been in France at the outbreak of the Second World War, was able to come to England with the Polish army in exile. He served as a dentist in the army, stationed in Scotland, and there met and married a Scottish girl, Amy. After the war, he remained in England as a practising dentist until he died. There were no children of the marriage. Amy died in 2002.

I should explain why they had to study abroad; being slightly younger than the Lauterpacht's children, for them there was already the Numerus-Clausus[7] at the University in Poland.

I do admire how could our grandparents manage to bring up effectively and financially a family of six children.

With the 1926 crisis the material situation became more and more critical for grandfather. He had to change from one place to another. It remained always the saw-mill.

Grandfather moved frequently from one village to another (where the factory was placed). However, they lived permanently in Lwów. His last post was in Gdynia. He used to return home now and again for a few days, and that was great!

They were kind and generous and loving. Taking an enormous interest in their grand children, me most of all, because their beloved daughter's daughter.

Spoiling me every way they could, I loved them dearly. (I remember how we used to hide the Christmas tree when Grandma came.) She was very intelligent – she knew the way we lived and kept quiet about it.

There must have been quite a big family. Excepting the Melmans of whom I have heard, because of the marriage with Ida Kaminska, the great Jewish actress, I did not know anybody. The Melmans name should have been Lauterpacht. Their parents were married just in the synagogue.

My Mother's family had very deep Jewish feelings and were Zionists. Aron and Deborah spoke Yiddish between the two of them, switching into Polish the moment my Mother or me arrived.

Dunek, the eldest son, had a beautiful wife Ninsia (a law student) and a daughter Erica. (16 years old when killed while trying to escape, with her mother, to Hungary. Denounced and shot.)

Very sociable, full of sense of humour, Dunek was extremely popular. They met often with my Parents. Ninsia introduced my Father to my Mother. They married in 1926; I arrived in 1930.

Grandfather Gelbard was a civil servant; a consulting lawyer to the Austrian, later, the Polish Railway. A good part of his life was spent in Vienna, where my father attended the law-school while in the army – 1913–1918. He had an Uncle GP, General in the Austrian Army, who found him in too poor health to go to the front.

In 1915, Hersch was conscripted into the Austrian Army. He was able to perform his short period of military service in 1915–16 in the sawmill

---

[7] The limitations in the number of Jews admitted to the university.

managed by his father, though how this was arranged is not known. One version has it that he was actually in charge of the sawmill. If so, he must have had a very reliable workforce needing a minimum of supervision, for he actually put his time there to non-industrial use and read voluminously. A notebook that he began at that time records him as reading works in German, English, French and Italian.

The notebook is an intriguing document. Its existence, apart from its very compilation, obviously meant something special to Hersch because he took care to preserve it, carry it with him when he came to England in 1923 and then bring it to Cambridge in 1937. The most likely explanation of the detailed notes – all made in the language of the book he was reading – is that he was trying to improve by practice his knowledge of the language concerned. From the list of titles it would appear that Hersch was by then already a student at the university in Lemberg.

It begins with *Der Krieg und die Volkswirtschaft* by Professor Dr Julius Landesberger, noted as having been read on 15 October 1915. It was followed on 20 November by *Krieg und Wähung* by Walther Federn. Then, on 20–25 November, he wrote an extended note of twenty-three pages on *The Laws of Moses and the Code of Hammurabi* (1903) by Stanley Cook. From there he went straight to *Psychologie sociale contemporaine*, by J. Maxwell, which he read between 25 November and 5 December and noted in eighteen pages.

Next, between 5 and 15 December, he read the four volumes of Adam Smith, *The Wealth of Nations*, to which he devoted sixteen pages of notes. One can only speculate as to why Adam Smith should have been included in this rather heterogeneous list. The explanation may lie in the fact that his work had exercised a considerable influence in Poland in the 1770s and that this influence may have survived into the twentieth century.[8] Adam Smith was followed without a break between 15 and 30 December by Dr Emil Hammacher's *Das philosophisch-ökonomische System des Marxsismus*, noted in twelve pages. Between 30 December 1915 and 4 January 1916, he read Paul Pic's *Les assurances sociales en France et à l'étranger*, noted in eight pages. The next day he began L. Tanon's *L'evolution du droit et la conscience sociale*, which he noted in eleven pages and finished on 10 January 1916. Then, straight on to Dr Carl Czyhlaz's *Lehrbuch der Institutionen des romischen Rechts*, finished on 15 January 1916 and noted in eight pages.

---

[8] See Gieysztor *et al.*, *History of Poland* (2nd edn, 1979), p. 319.

At this point, the detailed notes are replaced for a while by a list of lighter reading, including a historical novel, *Julianus Apostata* by Mereschkowski, and Zangwill's *Das Komodun des Ghettos*. The notes were not resumed until December 1918. The gap is probably to be explained by the fact that, between 1916 and 1918, Hersch was a student in the university at Lemberg and no doubt was preoccupied by his studies there. When he started making notes again, it was with Maurice Bourquin's *Le système socialiste et l'évolution économique*, noted in seventy pages, read between 25 December 1918 and 8 January 1919. How inconceivable it was at that time that Hersch would forty years later meet Bourquin in the Institut de Droit International and that Rachel and Hersch would become close friends with Bourquin and his wife Jano! This was the last entry in the book.

At some point during 1916, Hersch began legal studies at the University of Lemberg, which he continued for eight semesters. Whether he actually obtained a degree is not clear. In the letter that he wrote to the Zionist Executive in London in June 1920 applying for a post, he said that he had not been 'able to take the final examinations because the University has been closed to Jews in Eastern Galicia'.[9] However, it is difficult to reconcile these words with the terms of a certificate issued by the University of Lwów on 26 April 1917 stating that he took on that day an examination in law and history before the Commission for State Examinations of the University. This exam, it was stated, included Roman Law, among other papers. He passed these examinations with a 'good' result, stated in the certificate to be equal to a second. Whether this led to graduation from the Faculty of Law is not clear. The fact that, in 1919, he decided to go to Vienna to get a higher degree suggests that there may have been a further 'final' examination in Lwów. But, whatever may have been the exact position, it must have been sometime in 1919 that he decided – as did many other Jewish students – to continue his studies abroad. Some went to Prague or Paris. Hersch chose Vienna. But his commitment to study there does not seem to have been unwavering for, on 10 June 1920, after he had been in Vienna for a year, he applied to the Zionist Executive in London for a job.

HL to the Zionist Executive in London, 10 June 1920
I have been told by Dr Heschless, the editor of the Lvov newspaper 'Churila', that when you were on a visit to Galicia you were looking for people who could be employed in the Central Zionist Office in London.

---

[9] See p. 16 below.

I hereby apply for a post in the Central Office in the department of Pioneering and Immigration or the department of Culture.

I am 23 years old (I was born in 1897). I have completed my studies in Law (8 semesters). I was unable to take my final examinations because the university closed its doors to the Jews of Eastern Galicia.

I know the following languages: Hebrew, Yiddish, Polish, German, English, French and Italian. I am in command of both spoken and written Hebrew. I have known English for three years and, after being in the capital for one month in order to learn the accent, I shall be able to use the language. As for my knowledge of French and Italian, it is difficult for me to speak because I have had little practice, but I think that for the purposes of the office, namely, translation from these languages to Hebrew, my knowledge would be sufficient.

I have worked for the Zionist Organisation for eight years. Lately, I was vice-president and general secretary of the Pioneer Organisation of Eastern Galicia. I was also a member of Zionist Executive Committee. During the War I was the leader of the 'Organisation of the Zionist Academics in Galicia' ('HAZ'), and recently president of the Eastern Galician branch.

Other information about me you can find in the letter attached to this application. In any case, I would ask you to acknowledge receipt of this letter.

Hersch's application was supported by the Executive Committee of the Zionist Organization in Eastern Galicia.

To the Central Zionist Executive Committee in London, 23 June 1920
I have the pleasure to send you the application of our friend Lauterpacht with the warmest recommendation.

We know the applicant personally as a hard worker with many talents, who has worked for many years in our organization in spite of his young age. In particular, our friend Lauterpacht distinguished himself as one of the leaders of the youth movement which he knows very well. We think it is our duty to emphasise that ideological motives alone bring our comrade to seek a position in the central office in London. He wishes to prepare himself for activity in Eretz Israel in the future by learning the work of the Zionist Organisation and its practical administration. In addition, he would like to enrich his knowledge by studying the subjects of administration and sociology.

We are certain that our friend Lauterpacht will excel in his abilities and diligence, as well as his sense of duty, as one of the best members of the Central Office, and that the opportunity will be given to him at the same time to prepare himself in an honest and precise way for his work in Eretz Israel to which he aspires.

A similar letter was written by the Central Committee of the Pioneers of Eastern Galicia in Lwów.

There is no record of the reply, if any, to this letter. But no job followed.

Hersch's departure for Vienna in 1919 at the age of 22 marked the effective end of his connection with Poland and to a large, and ultimately tragic, extent with his parents. When he became engaged to Rachel in 1922, he did not take her to visit his parents in Poland, nor did he ever take her there subsequently. It could not have been an easy decision to make. He maintained his relationship with his parents by correspondence, though they did attend his marriage, but none of his letters to them have survived. There is one touching letter to him from his mother when he obtained the Cambridge chair in 1937.[10] He also occasionally wrote articles on legal subjects for Polish newspapers, and in 1928 visited Poland when the International Law Association held a meeting there. His parents visited him and Rachel in England on two occasions, once in 1928 and the other in about 1935. On the latter occasion, he pleaded with them to remain in England but they felt bound to return to Poland because his brother and sister were both still there with their families. After 1935, he never saw them again.

So, for the nearly forty years from his marriage to Rachel in 1923 until his death in 1960, Hersch's family effectively comprised only Rachel and, after 1928, myself; and, additionally, after 1946, his niece, Inka.

Hersch has often been described as being 'Polish'. But this description requires some qualification on account of the complex history of the region in which he was born and lived his early years, as well as his own limited contact with that area. His birthplace, Żółkiew, was in 1897 a small town in the Austrian province of Galicia. Before the dissolution of the Kingdom of Poland in 1772–95, Galicia had been part of that Kingdom. Most of its inhabitants were Polish speaking and thought of themselves as Poles, though there were also many Ukrainians. When Poland was partitioned, Galicia became the easternmost province of the Austro-Hungarian Empire. Its principal city and capital was then called Lemberg. Later, under restored Polish rule, it was named Lwów and now, as part of the Ukraine, it is known as Lviv. So, at the time of Hersch's birth, Żółkiew was part of Austria, though many of its people adhered to their Ukrainian loyalty and spoke not German or Polish but Ukrainian. Lwów, to the west, was a largely Polish-speaking city and this was the language that Hersch habitually used outside the family home. When

---

[10] See p. 86 below.

his family moved there in about 1910, their nationality remained the same – Austrian. On his arrival in England in April 1923, the Certificate of Registration issued under the Aliens Order 1920 recorded his original nationality as 'Austrian'. The same certificate also notes that in 1915–16 he had been a private in the Austrian Army. His current nationality was stated to be Polish. The explanation of that description is that, when Galicia was separated from Austro-Hungary and became part of the restored Polish State, by operation of law those living in that area who had previously been Austrian became Polish.

Thus, Hersch's connection with Poland, as it was between the two World Wars, was limited. After leaving Lemberg for Vienna in 1919, he never again lived there. Although he subsequently paid two short visits to the country, his total contact with 'Poland' in the sense of manifesting any genuine personal connection with the country of that name was limited to the very short period from the formal transfer of the territory from Austria in 1919 until he left it to pursue his studies in Vienna in that same year. Nonetheless, the fact that he acknowledged the formal connection by applying for a Polish passport in July 1922, which he retained until he was naturalised as a British subject in 1931, does support the Polish attribution, as does the fact that, despite its subjection to Austrian sovereignty for all the time that he was there, Lemberg was a Polish-speaking city. Nor did he ever suggest that his origins were not Polish. As a preliminary to being naturalised as British, he obtained from the Polish Consulate General in London on 12 June 1931 a certificate of release from Polish nationality. He swore the oath of allegiance to the Crown on 6 July 1931.

EXCURSUS: RECOLLECTIONS OF YOUTHFUL CONTEMPORARIES[11]

Hersch's family background and early life were described soon after his death by a number of his contemporaries who knew him in Lwów and Vienna. As they are no longer living, it has not been possible to discuss any of their recollections with them. Although the messages, which were sent to Rachel, are not always consistent with each other and are in some minor respects evidently inaccurate, it has seemed worthwhile to reproduce them as first-hand, authentic accounts of Hersch's personality and as showing the high regard in which he was held by his contemporaries.

[11] These were all sent to Rachel after Hersch's death.

From Dr Joseph Roth[12]

We recognize in his life great characteristics and particularly his own, which make his life like a fairy story.

Hersch was born during a peaceful period in the Austrian Empire of 1897, in a small village, Żółkiew, near Lemberg. In this village there was a very active Jewish community. From his earliest days good literature and serious books were always available. The teaching in the village school was relatively simple and so, in 1910, the decision was taken to move to Lemberg, where his father, Aron, was able to continue in the timber trade. Hersch was sent to the Humanist Gymnasium where he imbibed Polish culture as well as the classical culture and tradition of Rome and Greece. He was at all times a brilliant student.

But his real characteristics were observed away from school. He played an active role in Jewish national circles. At the age of 15 he joined the Zionist students' organization, the Shahei (The Dawn). His elder brother David took him there first. This group was devoted to self-education – without teachers. The members of this group were graduates of the Gymnasium. Under the patronage of the academic organization Emon (Faith), he made friends in this circle with whom he discussed and debated social and national problems with the enthusiasm of youth. Every Saturday there were general meetings where lectures were delivered on Hebrew literature and Jewish history, followed by discussions. His part in these discussions revealed a wide culture and a very high intellect. Every day of the week he joined the Hebrew lessons on Jewish history and the geography of Israel. He also participated in the debates on social and economic problems. In most of these groups he was the leader.

In 1914, at the outbreak of World War I, profound changes took place in the life of the population of Eastern Galicia. Russia conquered most of the territory. All public life came to a standstill, schools closed down. But Hersch continued, even under these circumstances, with his work of learning and his experience of life widened.

In 1915 the Austrians reconquered Eastern Galicia and Hersch concluded his school studies. The question then was where he should go for his higher education. He was greatly attracted to the subjects of philosophy, sociology and history. But his parents urged him to study jurisprudence. He began to pursue these studies in Lemberg and finished them in Vienna.

At that time he was also especially interested in music and Beethoven was among his favourites. He did not get regular music lessons, but loved to listen to his only sister who was a good piano player. He had a phenomenally good ear and musical memory. He would play the Kreutzer Sonata (Beethoven) with two

---

[12] The version set out in the text was originally written in Hebrew on 10 July 1960. The English translation has been slightly edited.

fingers. While in Vienna he went to concerts at least once a week, usually on a Sunday. He was also attracted to dance music. His girl friends used to invite him to dance – but in dancing he did not do well – mediocre.

In the First World War he was mobilized into the Austrian army and served in the big sawmill at Polska, owned[13] by his father, but requisitioned by the army. I remember visiting him there once and finding him in the engine room reading a legal book oblivious – among the terrific noise of the engine – to all around him.[14] It was also at that time that his interest in languages awakened. He learned French and English, self-taught from books; though he never heard the language spoken, he achieved some knowledge of the language, thanks to his diligence and remarkable memory.

In 1918 – at the termination of the World War – a conflict arose in Galicia between Poles and Ukrainians. The Versailles Peace Committee sent a Commission to decide upon the frontier between the two peoples. This Committee, known as the Curzon Committee, was looking for an interpreter who knew the two languages and was well acquainted with the location of that territory. Hersch, then aged 21, was chosen as interpreter and fulfilled his task satisfactorily.[15]

In 1919 he studied Hebrew intensively. Our teacher, Millu (today a teacher in the Agricultural School in Pardess Hanna, Israel), gave us as homework the task of learning by heart Metei Midbar (The Dead of the Desert) by Bialik. I (Dr Roth) sweated for several hours. Hersch arrived in the middle of the lesson, read the poem through twice and recited it by heart without mistake.

In his relations with his friends he was always kind and ready to help; this was no mere artificial politeness, but genuine human inclination. He was already then well known in Zionistic academic circles, in Herzliah, in Lemberg in 1916 – together with his friends Rieger, Beickel, Freund, Winstock. The superficial tendencies of most of the students to express comradeship by drinking together (German habits) etc., he discarded very soon. He thought it was foreign to the Jewish spirit.

He was angered by the social inequality, opposed to chauvinism and dreamed of a Jewish Renaissance based on the spirit of social justice. These ideas found expression in his speeches and discourses. He wrote at that time a series of articles on literary, philosophical and social subjects. They were published in

[13] As noted above, it is likely that Hersch's father managed, rather than owned, the sawmill.
[14] The reference to finding Hersch 'in the engine room reading a legal book' is supported by the small black-covered exercise book, described earlier, that has survived from those days.
[15] The statements about Hersch's work for the Curzon Committee have been impossible to verify. The records of the Committee's work in the National Archive contain no reflection of it. There may be some element of exaggeration in Dr Roth's statement because we know from what Arnold McNair said about Hersch's spoken English at the time of his arrival in London in 1923 that even then it was limited.

the society journals.[16] They displayed a vast culture, an extraordinarily powerful style and clarity of thinking and exposition of ideas. He participated very often in Conventions and Conferences and very often stood at the head of the group.

Herzliah, as a group, was active amongst a wide public. To Herzliah were invited, very often, famous men. In 1918 we invited the Jewish philosopher Martin Buber who delivered three lectures on Judaism. After these lectures a party was held to which all the important leaders were invited. Hersch, in his speech at one such meeting said to Buber: 'Jesus needed many disciples to spread his ideas amongst the people – so Buber too needs disciples to help him spread his ideas and to materialize them amongst the Jewish people.' Buber was very moved by this suggestion coming from young Lauterpacht. Those who knew Martin Buber and the historic period when this was uttered will understand the full meaning of these words.

In the autumn of 1918 – although the War was ended – friction and conflict continued and the division of the Austrian Empire between the nations of conquest, the Poles and the Ukrainians, began. The Zionist leaders of Galicia declared their neutrality in these conflicts and put forward their own national aims. To protect the Jewish population a voluntary Jewish militia was organized. All the members of Herzliah – all of them – volunteered for service. Day and night we patrolled the Jewish quarters and Lauterpacht was with us. Often, during these conflicts, the Jewish population suffered greatly at the hands of hooligans; the Jewish organization was hampered and hindered by Polish legionnaires and by the police. There were many victims, but the Lauterpacht family remained intact.

In 1928 I met Hersch once again in Lemberg; he had come to visit his parents. He attended a Conference of International Law convened in Warsaw. He was a member of the British group. During this Conference, at a banquet held in the 'Palace of Kings', Hersch spoke in English and Polish. Afterwards Mr Marcowicz, the Polish Chief Justice, came up to Hersch and asked 'how comes it that you speak such good Polish and how do you come from England?' And Hersch answered 'Thanks to your *numerus clausus*'.

From Dr Fleisher

I knew Lauterpacht in 1910 when I joined the 'Shahai', a Zionist group of elementary school pupils in Lwów. Lauterpacht was then in the 4th form at the Gymnasium. We met almost daily. Twice a week we learned Hebrew, once a week Jewish and Zionist history, and once a week we studied the geography of Israel; on Saturdays there were meetings with lectures on Jewish and Zionist subjects. In the summer we used to meet at 6.30am in the Park and studied Hebrew words from a dictionary, then we would test each other and see who

---

[16] These cannot be traced.

had learned most words in an hour. Already then Lauterpacht's great ability became apparent. He was very diligent and much beloved by his comrades. In 1913 he was elected chairman of the 'Shahai', a position much respected and coveted. He delivered two lectures which are still remembered: (1) 'Not this is the way' by Ehad Hahar (Jewish National Philosopher), (2) 'Rome and Jerusalem' (Moshe Hess, Jewish historian).

We parted in 1914. I left for Vienna and he remained in Lwów under Russian rule. In 1915, when the Austrians returned to Lwów, I received a letter from Lauterpacht telling me all about life under Russian rule, and his activities amongst Jewish youth. When I came to Lwów in 1916 he was Chairman of a Zionist students group. He invited me to a meeting.

In 1919 Lauterpacht arrived in Vienna to pursue his legal studies. He spoke with much enthusiasm and admiration of Professor Kelsen. After a few months in Vienna he became very active amongst the Jewish students there. In 1921 he was elected Chairman of the Jewish Hochschulausschuss. At that time there were about 8–10,000 Jewish students in Vienna. In 1922 I was invited to meet Prof. Chayott, the Chief Rabbi of Austria. Lauterpacht was there too. Both pressed me to assume responsibility for the Jewish Menza (kitchens). Because of the constant friction and conflict between Jewish students and the anti-semitic elements among the students, it was decided to have a special kitchen for Jewish students. Although I was just facing my final exams I assumed responsibility for the management of the kitchen (or dining hall). As housekeeper for this kitchen we engaged a woman who turned out to be Adolf Hitler's sister!

Towards the end of 1922 Lauterpacht resigned the Chairmanship and I succeeded him.

The first meeting of the World Union of Jewish Students took place in 1922 under the patronage of Professor Chayott, the Chief Rabbi, attended by representatives from many European and American universities. I was Chairman of this meeting, but Lauterpacht laid the programme before the gathering. He was elected Chairman of the WUJS and Professor Albert Einstein was elected Honorary President. Parts of Lauterpacht's speeches were delivered in Hebrew. As it was known that he was going to London, London was chosen as the seat of the WUJS.

From Dr Lew Gilead, Tel Aviv

Dr Freund knew Lauterpacht at the age of 15 as a pupil of the Gymnasium and a member of the youth movement 'Zeirei Zion' (Young Zion). From his early youth he showed great ability both at school and as a leader of youth. He learned Hebrew and had a good command of the language. The home of his parents knew security and was free from the struggle for existence. His parents early recognised his ability and spared no effort to enable him to pursue his studies without hindrance.

During his University years in Lwów Lauterpacht was President of the Jewish students organization 'Herzliah' and showed great organizing ability. Already then, in his young years, he showed great logic and analytical power. In 1918, when the Austrian Empire crumbled, the Poles conquered Lemberg and it became Lwów. The Jewish students decided to boycott the Polish schools until they were given recognition as a Jewish national group and, as such, given rights. Lauterpacht was partly responsible for this decision.

He left for Vienna in 1919.

In 1923, when Lauterpacht was in Lwów, he used to contribute articles to a Polish Jewish paper, widely read, the *Nowy Dziennisk*,[17] which appeared in Cracow. His articles were of absorbing interest and dealt with topical subjects, mainly in the political and international fields. In 1922 Lauterpacht was in Carlsbad attending the Zionist Congress.

In 1919 Lauterpacht acted as interpreter to the Curzon International Committee. He knew quite a few languages then: French, Italian, Polish, Ukrainian. The Curzon Committee dealt with the task of settling the frontier between Russia, Poland and the Ukraine.

From David Horowitz (Later Director General of the Bank of Israel, Geneva)

I met Lauterpacht for the first time in 1918. It was after the anti-Jewish pogroms carried out in Lwów by the Polish army under Colonel Mousinski. We felt that it would be impossible for Jewish youths to continue to attend Polish schools and to sit on the same benches with those who participated in the pogroms against Jews, in which so many of them had lost their lives.

It was then that we founded a secret organization of the heads of the Jewish Youth Movements with the object of boycotting Polish schools, of bringing pressure to bear on the Polish population to convince them of the need for establishing Jewish elementary schools. On this Committee we met: Lauterpacht, who was the leader of the Jewish Academic Society 'Herzliah'; I. Reis who died from typhoid in the Warsaw Ghetto; Lauterpacht was the Chairman of the Committee and I (Horowitz) was responsible for the semi-military executive. I saw Lauterpacht everyday. We organized a watch on the Polish schools and constantly ran into trouble with the Polish police. We organized meetings of Jewish youths in order that they should support us in our demands. In the end, under great pressure, we succeeded in forcing the Jewish public to demand the foundation of a Jewish Gymnasium (High School) where Hebrew and Jewish history should be taught and where a Jewish spirit should prevail.

---

[17] 'New Daily'.

From then onwards we met frequently on Zionist platforms of the Jewish Youth Movements.

Lauterpacht excelled in his knowledge of Hebrew and in his devotion to Jewish matters; his speeches and lectures showed sound reason and a rational approach. He was also known as learned in many languages and possessed a wide culture in many fields. We parted in 1920 when I left for Israel and met again in 1921 in Vienna where Lauterpacht continued with his legal studies. He was a self-made man.

There is no doubt that in the years 1918–1920 he was one of the three outstanding leaders of Jewish youth in Lwów.

From Dr Gilead

I met Lauterpacht in 1921 when he was elected Chairman of the Juedische Hochschulausschuss. Through this contact I learned that he had studied law in Lemberg and was quite well known there for his great ability, his talents and his public activities amongst Zionists and university students. He was quite famous for his extraordinary talents already at the age of 16 when he was a pupil at the Gymnasium. They say that already at that age he knew what he wanted, that is, to pursue a course in a western European University. With this object in mind he devoted much time to learning languages diligently. His friends thought that he was especially singled out as a leader and possessed great qualities for public leadership, but Lauterpacht was always striving for real scholarly work of research.

At every meeting where I met him, whether amongst a few, or on a public platform, he was raising the standard of intellectual discussions to greater heights. This was known and expected of him amongst all the students.

He had especially good and happy relations with the Austrian Chief Rabbi, Professor Chayott, who was a scholar and a very cultured and civilized man. Lauterpacht displayed a biting humour that gave colour to his talks and speech. At the same time there was no familiarity between him and his friends – there was always a distance separating them, because he lived in a world of his own. He did not attach much importance to success in exams, but rather more to scholarly studies and research.

I saw him again at the World Jewish Students Organization (founded in 1922). At its first meeting, convened in 1924 in Antwerpen, students from many countries met and here too he was the natural leader, by his powers of reasoning and expression, by the careful measured exposition he would make of the position of Jewish students in the world. In Lemberg he studied law. In Vienna he studied political science. He was, at that time, writing on Mandates under the League of Nations.

From Professor Max Frankel (Hebrew University, Jerusalem), 1960

I met Lauterpacht in 1919 when we worked together for the Hochschule Auss-chuss in Vienna. He came from Galicia, was already a graduate, and the holder of a doctorate in law. He was immediately elected chairman of the Hochschule Ausschuss.

As Chairman of the Hochschule Ausschuss – an organization with many branches – dealing with the material and spiritual welfare of the 8–10,000 Jewish students in the Vienna of those days, Lauterpacht had to appear before the University authorities and the authorities of the high schools to present to them the position of the Jewish students in Vienna. In spite of the fact that he was an Eastern Jew (Ostjude) – for whom the authorities as a rule had little respect – he managed to gain the attention and respect of all circles, non-Jewish and anti-Jewish, with whom he came into contact in connection with his work. He strongly impressed them by his talents, his logic and he gained respect from others by the manner and the way in which he presented his case. As the champion of the Vienna student organization he had many responsibilities to shoulder, financial and others. He held in his hands many branches of the work and handled them most successfully.

Lauterpacht was then reading political science at the University and we met at the lectures given by Professor Hans Kelsen to whom I was much attached.

Lauterpacht was not a poor student – as some have reported. He never stood in need of financial help of any kind.

His closed and reserved nature was already then marked – for although he had warm and hearty relations with his friends, he guarded his private life, and separated the private from the public life.

I met him again in Berlin in 1922 when he was pursuing a course of lectures given by Professor Stammler.

CHAPTER 2

VIENNA: RESEARCH, ENGAGEMENT AND MARRIAGE, 1919–1923

Though there has been some confusion in the documents, it appears that Hersch began his studies in Vienna in 1919. The copy of his first residence registration card that still remains in the Vienna official archives is dated 16 July 1920 and records that he was travelling on a passport of the Lemberg Police Directorate issued on 7 May 1920, was a student of the University of Vienna and had a previous residence in Lemberg. However, there are other indications that he was already a student in Vienna in 1919. One is derived from the record in the University's archives of Hersch's academic progress.[1] The other is a statement in a note by a contemporary of his at the university saying that he had 'met Hersch in 1919'.[2]

Hersch first read law, attending lectures by Professor Hans Kelsen,[3] and graduated as 'Doctor jur' on 13 June 1921. Kelsen, in his note about Hersch,[4] recalls that international law at Vienna was taught not only by Professor Strisower[5] but also by Professor Alexander von Hold-Ferneck, and that, although Hersch spoke German fluently, he did so with:

---

[1] For some of the evidence on which this is based I am indebted to Professor Christoph Schreuer's investigations in the relevant archives.

[2] Note written in 1960 by Professor Max Frankel of the Hebrew University.

[3] Kelsen (1881–1973) had a long and distinguished career in the fields of international law, public law and legal philosophy. His teaching career began in Vienna, where he became a full professor in 1919. He was appointed to the Austrian Constitutional Court in 1921, from which he was dismissed in 1930 for political reasons. He moved immediately to the University of Cologne but was removed from his teaching post there in 1933 after the Nazis seized power. He then taught at the Institut Universitaire des Hautes Etudes Internationales in Geneva, but moved to the United States in 1940. He taught at the University of California, Berkeley, till his retirement in 1952. One of Hersch's earlier articles was on 'Kelsen's Pure Science of Law', published in 1933 in a volume entitled *Modern Theories of Law*, reprinted in *Collected Papers*, Vol. 2, p. 404. Kelsen's recollections of Hersch appeared in (1961) 10 *ICLQ*, and were reprinted in (1997) 8 *EJIL* 309–10.

[4] *Ibid.*

[5] Leo Strisower (1857–1931), born in Galicia, became a lecturer in international law at the University of Vienna in 1908 and a full professor in 1908. He was an active supporter of Jewish student organisations in Vienna. He was President of the Institut de Droit International in 1924. Kelsen observed (see (1997) 8 *EJIL* 309–10): '[T]hat not only Professor Strisower but Professor Hold-Ferneck, whose political attitude was not very favourable to men of Lauterpacht's origin, so highly appreciated his monograph is the best proof of his remarkable scientific standard.'

the unmistakable accent of his origin. This was, under the circumstances which actually existed in Vienna at that time, a serious handicap and may explain the fact that he, in spite of his profound knowledge in all the subject matters taught at the Law School, received the degree of Doctor of Law by no more than a passing mark from the majority of examining professors.[6]

Hersch was not discouraged by the mark that he received, though no record exists of his reaction at the time. He went straight on to become a candidate for a doctorate in political science and was approved for the degree of *Doctor rerum politicarum* on 15 July 1922 on the basis of a thesis entitled *Das völkerrechtliche Mandat in der Satzung des Völkerbundes. Zugleich ein Beitrag zur Frage der Anwendung von privatrechtlichen Begriffen im Völkerrecht*[7] (*The International Mandate in the Covenant of the League of Nations*). This was a substantial work of 116 typewritten foolscap pages accompanied by a slender volume containing basic documents. It is a remarkable reflection of the diligence of his examiners that, having received the dissertation dated 15 June 1922, they were able to approve it for the award of the doctorate no more than one month later.

Hersch had obviously researched the subject deeply. Much of it had been rehearsed in a 'Seminararbeit', or contribution to a seminar, prepared earlier in July 1921 – of which the thirty-six foolscap pages of manuscript text still survive. A printed copy from the library of the Peace Palace in The Hague shows him as having borrowed Lansing's *The Peace Negotiations* on 2 May 1922, thus indicating that he had the means and willingness to travel. The copy of the certificate attesting the award of the degree bears three signatures, two of which are of distinguished members of the Law Faculty of the University of Vienna at the time, Professor Ernest Schwind and Professor Leo Strisower.

During his time in Vienna, Hersch lived at a number of addresses, all of them in rather grim-looking apartment blocks – typical of middle-class Vienna of the time. One of them was in the building next to the residence of Sigmund Freud. His financial means, consisting of remittances from his father, were limited, but he still found time for extra-curricular activity, partly of a political and partly of a cultural kind. Money problems did not arise till later. As his friend Dr Roth recalled, Hersch:

was much enthralled and delighted by the beautiful surroundings of Vienna. He had so many subjects at heart and they all contributed to his fuller development.

---

[6] *Ibid.*   [7] A translation into English appears in *Collected Papers*, Vol. 3, pp. 29–84.

He was most active, however, in Jewish student matters. He became President of the 'Hochschulausschuss', the coordinating committee for the various organisations of Jewish students. His contemporary, Max Frankel, has provided a helpful account of these activities, as set out in the last extract in Chapter 1.

After taking his second degree, Hersch stayed in Vienna, possibly because he had by then (there is no clear indication of the date) met Rachel Steinberg, by whom he seems immediately to have been captivated. For some reason, nowhere explained, in August 1922 he applied for admission to the Philipps University in Marburg, but was informed that his admission was dependent upon the permission of the Ministry in Berlin and that if permission were granted he would need to deliver some papers that were still missing. There is nothing to show the outcome of this application. In any case, Hersch did not go to Marburg, but he spent some time in Berlin in 1922 attending a course of lectures by Professor Stammler.[8]

Rachel, then 22 years old, was a great beauty. She had been born in Palestine in 1900, her parents having emigrated there from Russia in 1882.[9] Her father, Michael, was one of the founders of the settlement of Hadera. Before the swamps there were drained, they were mosquito-infested, and he caught malaria. He was advised that, if he was to recover, he would need to leave the country. So he went to South Africa, where he spent a number of years, working mainly as a joiner. After his return to Palestine, he moved to the village of Motza, about seven miles from the centre of Jerusalem, where the road from Tel Aviv begins its ascent to the city. There he started a brick and tile factory, the tall chimney and principal structures of which, though twice burned down in Arab uprisings, still stand as a monument to his industry. Sadly, however, it has now been converted into a night club. His wife, Gittel, had also emigrated from Russia to join him in Palestine, living first near Haifa, then moving to Tel Aviv before going to Motza.

They had six children, three boys and three girls, all of whom achieved some prominence: two of the boys remained in Palestine in government service; one boy studied architecture in France and in the early 1930s moved to London to practise there. Rachel was the youngest of the three girls. Her eldest sister, Rivka (Rebecca), married a lawyer and remained in Jerusalem. The next sister, Leah, married an engineer who lived in

---

[8] Recorded by Hersch in the LSE registration form and mentioned by Professor Frankel.
[9] For Rachel's family background, see Suzy Eban, *A Sense of Purpose – Recollections* (2008), Chapters 2 and 3. Suzy Eban was Rachel's niece.

Tel Aviv, but soon moved to Egypt where, in due course, he became the chief engineer of the Suez Canal Company. Of their four children, two of the girls married men who were ultimately to reach high positions in Israel. The eldest, Suzy,[10] married Aubrey (later hebraicised to Abba) Eban, at the time an officer in the British Army stationed in Cairo, who after the Second World War entered the nascent Israeli Government Service. A Cambridge-educated scholar of the highest rank and a universally acknowledged orator of outstanding quality, he served as the representative of the Jewish Agency in New York during the difficult period, 1946–8, when the Palestinian problem was being considered in the United Nations. When Israel achieved independence in May 1948, he became the first Israeli Permanent Representative at the UN, then Ambassador to the United States and, later, on his return to Israel, he became Foreign Minister and Deputy Prime Minister. The second daughter, Aura, married an officer in the Irish Guards in the British Army, Vivian (later hebraicised to Chaim) Herzog, a son of the former Chief Rabbi of Ireland who subsequently became Chief Rabbi of Israel. Vivian had a distinguished career in the Israeli Army and, eventually, in 1983 was elected President of Israel.

At the time that Rachel met Hersch, she had already shown her talent as a pianist and was in Vienna for further study with a distinguished music teacher, Professor Richard Robert. It says something of her strength of character and independence that as a young woman of 22 she should have ventured alone into a foreign land, the language of which she did not know. She had not been there many months before she met Hersch. No exact date has been noted, but it was probably in the autumn of 1921.

The circumstances of their meeting are best presented in Rachel's own account of the episode (slightly edited), written many years later. She had heard much praise of Hersch and persuaded a friend, Dr Schaettenberg, to take her to a meeting at which Hersch was presiding:

We saw an attractive, intellectual looking young man of about 23 or thereabouts, speaking in German. The Hall was packed to the full, some students sitting on the floor. You could hear a pin drop – so quiet and absorbed was the audience in what the speaker said. I did not understand a word as I had no knowledge of German. At the end of the speech the audience broke out in tumultuous applause: 'Bravo Lauterpacht – Bravo Lauterpacht' they shouted. Groups formed round him, all spoke at once. There was much commotion

---

[10] *Ibid.*

about the speech. I felt most uncomfortable for I did not know what the speaker had said, what all the enthusiasm was about.

I said to Schaettenberg who brought me there 'Let us go out.' 'No', said he. 'I promised to introduce you to this young speaker, that's why I brought you here. He speaks Hebrew fluently – so you could converse with him.'

A number of students encircled us. Schaettenberg introduced Dr So and So a pupil of Sigmund Freud – it went on, and on, and I could not remember the names nor their merits. Suddenly silence fell over the group – as the speaker approached us. He was duly introduced to me as Lauterpacht, President of the Union of Jewish Students. He addressed me in Hebrew – which he spoke beautifully with a Sephardi accent – which astonished me greatly. I asked him where did you get this Israeli pronunciation – and he replied 'One learns – one need not be a "sabra" (native-born Palestinian) to speak Hebrew.'

A few of the students came up to me and said in German which had to be translated to me, 'We would like to call on you on Sunday' and I replied, 'I shall be delighted. Do come on Sunday afternoon. My hostess, Mrs T, loves entertaining for me, so do come.' On their disappearance Hersch came up to me and said that he too would very much like to see me. 'Please come too on Sunday.' 'No,' said he, 'I would like to come on Monday.' 'Really,' said I, 'why not on Sunday?' 'Because I would like to be alone with you.' So, when Monday came, Hersch arrived punctually at 8.30pm and left exactly at 10pm. His manners, his talk, so quiet, so gentle – not a movement of a hand – so unlike the other students from Eastern Europe.

He said: 'I hear that you are a pupil of Prof. Robert – so you must play well. Would you play something for me?' 'Yes, I will,' said I. 'What would you like me to play?' 'Anything you wish'. So I played the Beethoven Sonata which was set for me by Prof. Robert as my task. It was one of the early sonatas, very lovely but not too easy to execute, particularly since Prof. Robert expected and exacted a very clean technique and very orthodox interpretation. I was not brought up to play rigidly.

Hersch listened and said how lovely that Sonata was – and that he thought I played with rather great feeling. Indeed, it was just what Prof. Robert said to me only the day before.

I said to him: 'I did not know that you played the piano.'

'Oh! I do a little, I know a smattering. I would not be accepted by Prof. Robert.'

On leaving at 10pm he asked me whether he could see me again and take me out to a concert. I said 'Yes, but I really must work.' 'Yes, but a concert, that would help you a lot in your studies.' Well – he took me out to a concert. It was the first Symphony Orchestra I ever heard. In Palestine at that time they had only the music at school, an amateurish small orchestra. No Symphony. There were no records of music then either.

They played the Beethoven 7th Symphony. I was under the influence of the majestic music. I could not get over the beauty of this music. Unconsciously, I was hurrying the allegretto and so on. The mere rhythm fascinated me. 'So,' he says, 'you enjoyed it – that is exactly what I thought.' His demeanour was so different from all the other students I met. He was so polite, so correct, so immaculately dressed.

He came again and again. My hostess – Mrs T – said to me 'Be on your guard – I think you scorched him' which meant he is hot on me. 'Yet,' said I, 'he never shows any familiarity – he has not tried to kiss me – others did – he is just plain interested in me being a "Sabra" coming from Jerusalem.'

One day he said to me 'There would be a break in the studies during Christmas. Would you care to come to Berlin – where I am going to do research at the Berlin Library. I promise to look after you and take care of you.' 'How nice,' I replied. 'I might, I will ask my parents' permission to go to Berlin.' He said goodbye and left me, saying he would write to me if I would promise to spare him only one minute of my precious time, to answer him.

He had an acute sense of humour; I had none. Very often he puzzled me. I was never sure what he meant when he said something – whether he was serious and when he was not.

A short while later I received a very correct letter, not intimate, not a romantic letter. 'Well, are you coming? I will be so happy to take you round Berlin, act as your interpreter and this without any conditions.' He began to intrigue me. What sort of a young man is he? I knew that he was very brilliant – very greatly respected by his fellow students. That he had more money than the others – had a western air about him – although he was from the Eastern part of Europe. That he had gained two doctorates, one in Jurisprudence and one in political science of the Vienna University. That he mastered well the Polish language, German and Hebrew, knew Latin and Greek and also played the piano, wrote for one or two papers political articles and reviews. All the while I was corresponding with a few very eligible young men in Palestine. Was surrounded by a number of students, industrialists and bankers in Vienna who proposed marriage to me.

The Christmas vacation came. S the industrialist – on the suggestion of his mother – a great lady – took me to Berlin. He was hoping to have me to himself. Being a rich man we descended at the Excelsior Hotel – at that time one of the finest Berlin Hotels.

I sent an express note to L who was already installed in a room in a very fine house in Charlottenburg. He received the note on his return from the Library at 10pm – he turned up at once. I was already in bed and could not entertain him – so asked him to come the next morning.

He was always very punctual telling me that he gets up at 7am – and works long hours till late at night. Well – it was not anything like that after he took me out for the first time in Berlin to show me first the University and the Library. For three solid weeks we were together, inseparable. He came every morning to fetch me – brought me back every evening to the apartment.

I ran out of money; he supplied me with money – until I received my allowance from home. In short he acted as father, brother and guardian for me and he was only a little older than myself.

Vacation was up and I had to return to my studies in Vienna. The idea was that after a year I should go to London to the Royal College of Music to take my degree.

As the day of my departure was nearing – one day he stayed rather later than usual. He was teasing me a great deal – and I was quite disturbed – because I did not know how to interpret his behaviour. He took my hand, suddenly, and kissed me on my lips – I was most surprised. He said, 'You know, I think, it would be best if you stayed on here near me, instead of going to Vienna. I do love you so much. In three weeks I have not done a stroke of work. It is the first time in my life that I have given so much of my time to any other person. I do not regret it at all – for you mean a great deal to me. Let us get engaged, marry and go together to London. I have been playing with the idea of taking an English degree – an LLD in the London University, learning English, then I will take you back to Israel.'

I smiled and said 'I will think – you will see I did not say yes.' He kissed me again and again – and I became frightened. I said it was rather late – and he at once apologized – kissed me good night – and 'Sleep well my lovely daughter of Zion.'

Of course I did not sleep at all. I was suddenly awakened to all he said that evening. His unusually warm behaviour – I could not really connect it with this very correct fine young man. Was he really serious? I was not sure.

Next morning he came a little late and waved a telegram in his hand. It was a telegram from his parents, in Lwów to congratulate us on our engagement. I was most surprised. 'Did you not telegraph your parents?' he asked me. 'So you see that means we are engaged!'

I was thus engaged by surprise. But I was happy because I really liked him a lot.

He took me over, so to speak, arranged everything for me. Arrangements were to be made to explain the situation to Professor Robert. To communicate with my parents – who would be worried about this engagement because they knew not who this Dr L was.

All the young people with whom I corresponded in most affectionate terms wished to know whether I was really engaged to this Dr L.

Thus, on 18 December 1922, while still in Berlin, Hersch and Rachel became engaged to be married. In the circumstances, Hersch did not have an opportunity, nor, it seems, the inclination, to seek formally the consent of Rachel's parents who were in Palestine. Rachel must have written to them about it. They did not object. An announcement of the engagement appeared in the *Palestine Daily Mail* on Thursday, 2 January 1923.

How Hersch first communicated with Rachel's parents is not clear. The first family letter to survive is dated 17 January 1923, from which it appears that there must have been some previous letter that occasioned the following letter of felicitation to Rachel from her eldest brother, Zvi, in Jerusalem, written in English on 1 January 1923.

Zvi Hareven to RL, 1 January 1923
Heartiest congratulations on the occasion of your engagement. May God bestow his blessings on you and your chosen. Please convey our similar message to Dr Zwi Lauterpacht accompanied by our sincere expression of welcome into the family.

Although we are not as yet privileged to know him, still the very fact that you chose him – you, on your own accord, without the advice or counsel of any of those whom you so much love – your choice is sufficient! In your happiness we are happy; we feel that the man who succeeded in gaining your heart is worthy of it. Good luck to him!

Indeed, all good things do come unexpectedly. Who would have thought of it a fortnight ago? But in the works of Fate, in the Scheme of things ordained by God, who is he that can fathom his plans? . . . And now once again please accept our sincere wishes for your everlasting happiness, hoping that one fine day you shall with your beloved Zwi make your home in Israel . . .

I suppose your next letter will be followed by a photo of your young man with whom we would all like to get acquainted even though it be – on paper – for the time being.

Hersch's own communications with Rachel's parents took the form of two letters written in Hebrew (translated by Rachel many years later) that merit quotation in full, as reflecting both the strength of his convictions and his belief in the propriety of his conduct.

HL to RL's parents, 17 January 1923, from Berlin
Dear Parents

Please forgive me for not turning to you before your acceptance of our engagement. It is true, that Rachel, this last fortnight, was urging me to ask her hand from her parents – according to the accepted tradition. But I refused to do so. Why should I ask you to do something that was already decided? In spite of this I thank you from my heart for your acceptance and hearty agreement and for your good wishes.

I find it necessary to assure you one thing: I see from your letters, and know from what Rachel tells me, that she is like the apple of the eye to you. That you love her very much, and that it is difficult for you to hand over this dear daughter, to a stranger, whom you do not know. Dr Schmetterling, could not suppress the feeling of hate to the wolf that kidnapped her Rochalé [a diminutive of Rachel]. I assure you that my relation to Rachel will be not only of great love, but also of responsibility towards her parents and family. I understand that Rachel is not only mine but also yours.

Your wishes concerning marriage are very important in my eyes, especially as it is also the wish of Rachel. I have written about this to my parents, and hope that they will agree.

I thank you once again from my heart, and with greetings.

With much respect and great love.
Zvi

The replies from Rachel's parents have not survived, but on 7 February 1923 Hersch wrote again from Berlin.

HL to RL's parents, 7 February 1923
Dear Parents

Thank you for your letters full of love to Rachel and to me. I hope that this warm, hearty relation will continue and grow in strength, especially when we meet, and we get to know each other. Also from direct contact, and a life of work in Israel.

About our life here, and our plans for the future, Rachel, certainly writes to you with many details, so that I can immediately turn to the two points concerning which I wish to touch upon, in this letter:

I am asking you not to write more to Rachel about the thing called 'Nedouria' dowry etc. All this does not interest me at all and only worries the beloved girl. You ask her whether she mentioned anything about it to me on our engagement. Certainly not – she did not. She mentioned nothing, not because she has hidden it in her heart, but because this subject did not interest me at that time, nor does it interest me now. All this discussion – which is most unpleasant to me – and that I hope to finish with now – arose, undoubtedly, actually, because my parents must have written to you about it in their letter. I cannot forbid my parents from writing about it, but no one is bound to listen to them. I have the right quietly to ignore the whole thing. Please do the same. My parents think they have the privilege to meddle in this (they supported me until now and will continue to do so for another year or two). But do not parents forgo many of their rights for the sake of their children?

The promise that dear Abba [Rachel's father] will come to our wedding, which will take place middle of March, pleases me ever so much. I will then get to know not only Rachel's father but also one of the pioneers, the builders of Israel whose future is the future of all of us.

To the desire of getting to know you is added also another motive. I wish to consult you about my settling in Israel. I have no clear idea about the practical possibilities that await me there. It appears that from the general conditions in the land that it will not be easy to carry out my wish of getting a post in the administration. Accordingly I have to take into consideration the possibility of becoming a practicing lawyer. Officially, I am able to undertake one or the other of these two kinds of work. I have two doctorates – one in Law, the other in Political Science. Abba's counsel – as a practical man, who is acquainted with the conditions prevailing in the country – is bound to influence, and weigh greatly in, my decision and in shaping my plans for the future.

I thank you in anticipation for your promise of coming and am greatly looking forward, with much pleasure to meeting you.

I kiss both of you and send you greetings as well as to the dear family.

Yours,
Zvi

Following the engagement, Rachel stayed in Berlin. What she was doing there beyond keeping Hersch company is not known; Hersch was working in the library and attending lectures. They were still in Berlin on 4 March when Rachel received a telegram from her father saying that he would reach Vienna in time for the wedding. They returned to Vienna for the marriage on 20 March 1923. The ceremony was performed by Rabbi Feuchtwang. Hersch's parents were present, as was his elder brother, Dunek, together with his fiancée, Ninsia, and Hersch's sister, Sabka. On Rachel's side, only her father was there, having travelled specially from Palestine, presumably by boat to Italy and thence by train to Vienna, a journey that must have taken the best part of ten days – compared with the one hundred days that it took him to travel from Russia to Palestine when he emigrated in 1882. The best man at the wedding was Leon Steinig, an old friend of Hersch and a colleague in the Union of Jewish Students, who subsequently entered the service of the League of Nations, became first head of its drug control section and later of the corresponding unit of the United Nations. After the wedding, the couple stayed in Vienna for a few days, then travelled to Hamburg and took a boat to Grimsby.

The importance in Hersch's life of his marriage to Rachel cannot be overstated.[11] Although coming from very different backgrounds – he from Galicia, she from Palestine – they shared fundamental beliefs. Their religion was important as giving them a common outlook, even though formal observance played little part in their lives. But of great importance was Hersch's commitment to Zionism and the wish, which he maintained until he became fully established in England, to settle in Palestine. They also shared a love of music and books. Rachel gave him, without stint or reservation, and in total fidelity, the love and support that enabled him to produce his prodigious contribution to international law. She maintained their homes, first in Cricklewood in London, and then in Cambridge, on a low budget. She shopped, cooked, cleaned, laundered and entertained for him. At various periods, but by no means constantly, there was some domestic help – at a time when the wages of a live-in maid from Ireland or the North Country were between £1.00 and £1 10s a week. On a few occasions, in 1927, 1931 and 1937, Rachel went to visit her parents in Palestine. During the Second World War, there was a period from late 1940 to early 1943 when she was in the United States to be with me. Otherwise, she was with Hersch the whole time, except when he briefly went abroad to deliver lectures or take short holidays.

There were occasional episodes of tension. As Rachel subsequently recorded in a note that she prepared after Hersch's death:

we had a harmonious peaceful life together but one serious misunderstanding occurred on one of his parents' visits to us. His mother when she arrived had painted nails which Hersch could not bear, so the poor mother had to remove her nail varnish, while I said he had no right to interfere with his mother's toilet. A more serious conflict developed when his mother (whom he loved greatly) induced me to cut my hair in the fashionable crop of the period – just as she had her hair cut. Well, when I returned home and Hersch came back from the London School of Economics and saw me in my new hairdo he was terribly angry (he wanted me to remain all my life with a bun of my hair on my neck – like a bluestocking). He did not talk to me for 3 days. I was furious – so I decided to inform him that I made up my mind to return to my parents and intended to take the first boat home and take my child with me. Thereupon he asked,

---

[11] As observed by McNair in a note written after Hersch's death: 'It suffices to say that the marriage was ideal and that no man had a more inspiring and devoted partner in the battle of life – a fact which he readily recognized.' Originally published in (1961) 10 *ICLQ*, and reprinted in (1997) 8 *EJIL* 310–12.

'Why are you taking such a serious view?' I said to him it is very serious when my husband interferes with my most personal and private matters even more when he tries to punish me by ignoring me – so I cannot continue to be with him – there is no reason why I should stop on under the same roof with him. He realized that I really meant what I said – he approached me and tried to kiss me – but I would not have it – No, said I, you must apologise to me – [Hersch said] but you do things against my wishes – no said I, I can and must have my private harmless life without you bullying me. So he wanted to know how long my hair will take to grow – and I said I can not guarantee the length of time – in any case I will do my hair as I like and that is that. After that we had no serious conflicts – but I must confess that I submitted a great deal of my freedom to his wishes – and even today still wear my hair in a bun as he wanted. Now that he is not here with me – I do even more all the things he liked me to do.

He would have turned in his grave had I remarried after his death. I knew his opinion of widows remarrying when they lose their husbands. When I was asked to remarry I would not consider it at all – I said I am still married to my husband and people thought I was mad.

We had hard years together – but we also had good and very happy years together – it is wonderful to have had them with him. All his friends and pupils remained my friends to this day.

From time to time there were other flare-ups, happily none of them lasting, caused mainly by the severe and constant shortage of money that prevailed until the late 1940s. When particularly saddened, Rachel would turn to her piano and play a Beethoven sonata that I will always remember. But then harmony would return.

When Hersch became a member of the International Law Commission and then a judge of the International Court of Justice, Rachel accompanied him to Geneva, The Hague and on his other travels.

CHAPTER 3

ENGLAND AND THE LONDON SCHOOL
OF ECONOMICS, 1923–1937

Hersch and Rachel landed at Grimsby on 5 April 1923.[1] Hersch, as an alien, was issued with a certificate of registration at Bow Street Aliens Registration Office on 9 April 1923. His nationality was recorded as being Polish, evidenced by the Polish passport issued to him in Vienna on 20 July 1922. His previous Austrian nationality was also noted, as was the fact, under the heading 'Government Service', that he had been a private in the Austrian Army in 1915–16. His London residence was given as 19 Regent Square, WC, the first, it would seem, of a number of addresses that rapidly changed over the next few months. According to Rachel:

We moved into a bedsitting room in Regent Square – for which we paid 2 guineas a week exclusive of gas and electricity. The room was heated with gas which had a meter attached to it. A shilling in the slot heated the room for a few hours. If the hours ran out – and you were without a shilling to put in the slot – you remained in a cold room, which happened very often. Hersch was used to the cold but I, coming from a warmer climate, suffered a great deal especially from the dampness.[2]

By 24 April 1923, they had moved to 2 Hunter Street nearby; three months later, by 29 July, Hersch's residence was noted as being at 55 Hillmarton Road, a turning off the Caledonian Road, some distance northeast of King's Cross. Only two days later, on 1 August 1923, a new address was recorded at 78 Brondesbury Villas, a street leading off Kilburn High Road in northwest London. In the ensuing three years, there were no less than six changes of address before they moved to 103 Walm Lane in Cricklewood, there to settle for the next ten years until their move to Cambridge in 1938.

One may ask, why did they come to England when, in theory, they could equally well have gone to Germany, France, Spain, Italy or, indeed, any other country, including the United States or Canada? There is little in the documents to provide an answer, nor did the question ever come

---

[1] Endorsement in Aliens Order Certificate of Registration.   [2] RL's notes.

up in family correspondence. So one can do no more than make a partly informed guess. Of one thing one can be certain, namely, that Hersch was determined to leave the anti-Semitic atmosphere that prevailed in Lwów. He would have felt the same about Austria and, probably, even at that time, about Germany or France. Italy and Spain would have been possibilities, but language would initially have been a handicap. England would no doubt have commended itself as a politically stable country, where Jews could live in security and a tolerant atmosphere, and where he probably felt that he had the best chance of developing as an international lawyer. When he proposed to Rachel, he told her that he wanted to go to England for advanced work in international law and to take an English LLD, though he qualified this by saying: 'then I will take you back to Israel.' An additional factor may also have been that Rachel already possessed a British passport by reason of her residence in a British Mandated Territory. Even more to the point is the fact that Rachel had entered her studies in Vienna as a stepping stone on the way to the Royal College of Music in London.[3] Nonetheless, Hersch seems to have had in the back of his mind the possibility that he might eventually end up in Palestine. He wrote of it in his letter of 7 February 1923 to Rachel's parents.[4] Norman Bentwich remembers that, even in 1925, when in Jerusalem for the opening of the Hebrew University, Hersch asked him whether some position could be found for him there. But Bentwich could not find him one. In his memoirs, Bentwich commented:

Perhaps it was as well. He could not have made his immense contribution to the Law of Nations except in England.[5]

Why were there so many moves in the first years of their stay in the UK? Probably the controlling factor was cost – they had very little money. Rachel later wrote that:

Hardly had we settled into our new life when two things happened which nearly unsettled our lives. Firstly, my father's factory was burned down by the Arabs. The factory was not insured. My father was left with the skeleton of the factory. Secondly, the Polish zloty was devalued. Hersch's parents were impoverished overnight. Both these events affected our position in England.

The distress experienced at this time by Hersch's parents is reflected in the following letter:

---

[3] See her own account in Chapter 2, p. 32, above.   [4] See p. 34 above.
[5] N. Bentwich, *My 77 Years* (1962), p. 81.

HL's mother to HL and RL, 22 March 1926

My dearest and beloved children!

First of all best wishes for health and happiness for your wedding anniversary.

For the moment I can't send you anything else. Sabka has already written about everything. At home it's not too well for the moment.

We hope that God will help.

It is already three years since I have seen you. I miss you very much.

I pray God that Sabka marries.

Things are well with Dunek. Thank God the child is very sweet.

Have happy and good holidays.

We bless you and kiss you.

Your mother
Deborah

Proximity to the London School of Economics,[6] or access to easy means of transport to it, was no doubt important. But that does not really explain the choice of Brondesbury Villas, Cambridge Avenue or Burton Road, all of which were lengthy bus or underground rides from the LSE. At one time, Rachel recalled, they were in the same lodging house as Moshe Shertok who later, having Hebraicised his name to Sharett, became Prime Minister of Israel. It may have been that Palestinian schoolfriends of hers then studying in London were living in that neighbourhood. The area at that time had a quite substantial Jewish population.

Notwithstanding the unsettling effect of so many moves, Hersch quickly began to find his way around. He soon registered at the LSE for a full course of lectures in the 1922–3 session. But he was so impecunious that he fell into arrears with the payment of his fees to the LSE, at that time £5 15s 6d[7] per session. After his first payments in February and April 1923, he was obliged in June 1925 to ask for postponement, indicating that, if a delay could not be granted, he might have to terminate his research. Miss Evans, the Secretary of the School, noted that: 'McNair considers him a very brilliant student and is endeavouring to get him academic work.'[8] He eventually paid up on 11 November 1926. His reason for going to the LSE rather than to University College, which was just round the corner from Regent Square and Hunter Street, or to King's College in the Strand, was probably that at that time neither

---

[6] At that time, the LSE, founded in 1895, was a much smaller establishment than it is now. In 1923, its staff numbered 72 and the student body 2,239. The Director was Sir William Beveridge.

[7] Equivalent to £173 today.

[8] There is an indication that at the end of July 1925 someone was referred to Hersch for coaching in international law at the rate of fifteen shillings per hour, but there is nothing to show whether this contact materialised or for how long it may have lasted.

of the latter two institutions had anyone on their staff with any special expertise in international law, whereas the LSE had on its staff Arnold McNair, then in the early days of his involvement in the subject. Also at the LSE there was the specialist Fry Library of International Law, established in 1920 with a bequest from Lord Justice Fry, of which Hersch was to make much use during this period. He may, too, have found the Socialist spirit of the place congenial. It had been founded by Fabians with the aim of the betterment of society. He arrived there shortly after the move to the new building in Houghton Street.

MEETING ARNOLD McNAIR

Hersch's first academic contact at the LSE was with Arnold McNair. Meeting him was probably the most important event in Hersch's career. McNair (1885–1975) came from a significant family of Scottish intellectuals. One brother, William, was a barrister in The Temple, not far from the LSE, specialising in commercial law. He became a High Court judge in 1950. A sister, Dorothy, became an eminent gynaecologist. Arnold himself had first qualified as a solicitor, though he later changed to become a barrister and was called to the Bar by Gray's Inn, of which he subsequently became a Bencher and Treasurer.

McNair's earliest interest in international law was reflected in parts of his book on *Legal Effects of War*, the thesis for his Cambridge LLD. He joined the staff at the LSE where, in 1923, he was appointed a lecturer in international law and, in 1926, a reader in the same subject. He also developed a teaching connection with Cambridge on a part-time basis. In 1935, he was elected Whewell Professor of International Law at Cambridge, a chair that he held till 1937 when he accepted an invitation to become Vice-Chancellor of the University of Liverpool. Hersch followed him in the Cambridge chair. McNair remained in Liverpool till 1945 and then returned to Cambridge as Professor of Comparative Law, though shortly afterwards he was elected as the first British judge of the newly established International Court of Justice. He became President of the Court in 1952 and remained there until his nine-year tenure ended in 1955. Hersch was then elected to succeed him.

Such was McNair's generosity of spirit and support of Hersch that it has been suggested that he did not seek a second term in the ICJ in order to give Hersch, whom he regarded as the most suitable candidate, an early opportunity to succeed him. But McNair's active career did not end then. He was appointed a member of the European Court of Human Rights, of which he was President from 1959 to 1965. He also remained active in the field of international law, principally by the publication in 1956 of the three volumes of *Law Officers' Opinions*, by participation as the most senior consultant in the presentation of the case for Aramco in its arbitration with Saudi Arabia that concluded in 1958,[9] as well as by the completion in 1961 of a second edition of his major treatise on the *Law of Treaties*. McNair's reputation was that of a man of balance, moderation, wise judgment and independence of mind. He was not interested in the theory of law. As he said himself in a letter to Hersch: 'I have not an *anima naturaliter philosophica.*'[10]

He was financially generous too. There is a story, impossible to confirm, that when Hersch was running out of money (it might have been in about 1924) McNair lent him £100. This was a very large amount given that a lecturer's salary was only £500 a year.[11] Or it may have been about two years later in connection with the publication of *Private Law Sources*.[12] Another example is McNair's offer to 'help with the money' if, as he suggested, Hersch were to enter an Inn of Court.[13] Hersch did not do this until November 1928, when he joined Gray's Inn. He was not called to the Bar until 1936.

In later years, McNair recalled that, when Hersch first came to see him, they had difficulty in communicating because of the poor quality of Hersch's spoken English. This casts some doubt upon the statement made by Roth[14] that only three years previously Hersch had served as an interpreter for the Curzon Commission that had been charged with the solution of certain boundary questions on Poland's eastern frontier. McNair told Hersch to go away, study English and return when he spoke it better. Three weeks later, to McNair's amazement, Hersch was back speaking English relatively fluently. He had, in the meanwhile, spent eight hours each day in attending all the lectures he could. Although his English, both written and spoken, was soon to become perfect, he never entirely lost his continental accent which, though not guttural or heavy, was a sufficient indication that he was not a native-born Englishman.[15]

Rachel later recalled the relationship with the McNairs as follows:

Hersch must have made a great impression on him. He realized at once that Hersch was not an ordinary student – but an exceptional intellect. They soon developed a mutual liking and respect for each other, so much so that Hersch

---

[9] 27 *ILR* 116.   [10] See McNair to HL, 5 January 1927, p. 52 below.
[11] Very roughly, £1 in 1925 would be worth about £30 in the currency of 2010.
[12] See p. 56 below.   [13] See p. 51 below. McNair to HL, 4 January 1927.
[14] See p. 20 above.
[15] See p. 330 below for his reaction when, many years later, he heard himself speaking on the wireless.

said to me 'Would you like to see my professor?' 'Yes, indeed I would.' 'So please come to the LSE where and when McNair will talk about the coal crisis [1923].' I agreed to arrive before 5pm at the LSE for the lecture. But when I looked into my purse I could not find the six pence necessary to pay for my fare by the underground. I was in a great dilemma, knowing that it was quite a distance from London NW2 to the centre of town. But I was determined to meet or at least see Arnold McNair, so I walked all the way to the LSE. All would have been well but for the terrific shower of rain, it rained cats and dogs, as they say. When Hersch saw me arrive he was shocked – I looked terrible. I pacified him and said 'I will go down to the ladies room and make myself look presentable' and so I did. I liked McNair from the first moment I saw him and learned to love him to his last day. He was a great and loyal friend always and a great admirer of mine, so much so that Marjorie Lady McNair and I became great friends, and to this day all McNair's four children are my friends and their grand-children call me Auntie Rachel. After this first meeting we were invited to visit the McNairs in Cambridge for a weekend. In return I invited the McNairs, the whole family, to dine during their Christmas visit to London – when they stayed with Marjorie's family.

After Marjorie's death I used to see Arnold in my house frequently. I saw him a few hours before he died. He asked Oona[16] to phone me to come, although I saw him the day before – obviously he felt he was dying.

From that date we had close contact with the McNairs. Arnold and Hersch used to go out for walks together on the Coton Footpath in the afternoon in Cambridge. When they returned from their walks it was my great pleasure to entertain the two great international lawyers and I always made specially the lovely sandwiches McNair loved so that Hersch used to tell Arnold: 'Rachel does not make such sandwiches for me.'

I loved making them for them and enjoyed their delightful company. There was a real friendship between the three of us.

When Hersch was elected to the International Court of Justice and we came to The Hague by boat from Harwich to Hook of Holland early in the morning, the McNairs got up very early to await our arrival at the Wittebrug Hotel to have breakfast with us in their suite of rooms. After they had introduced us to most members of the Court they left The Hague and Holland, returning home.[17]

It is impossible to overstate the extent and quality of McNair's friendship with Hersch. McNair was a party to every step in Hersch's career, first at the LSE, then at Cambridge and ultimately at the ICJ. Hardly a week passed without letters passing between them. Unfortunately, Hersch's

[16] His eldest daughter.   [17] RL's notes.

letters to McNair have not survived, but McNair's letters to Hersch abound in the files and show the respect that McNair had for Hersch's views and the reliance that he placed on them. Hersch dedicated *The Function of Law* to McNair.[18]

He joined McNair's international law course for the 1923–4 session. It was evidently Hersch's intention to pursue research along the lines of the work that he had already begun in Vienna on private law analogies as sources of international law. To this end he prepared and presented a note to McNair sometime between August 1923 and March 1924 which he described as 'in place of a syllabus', setting out his approach to the subject:

I do not know, at present, what will be the structure or the conclusion of the thesis. I think only that a comprehensive and systematic exposition of the role and the influence of concepts of Private Law on the science of International Law would be of some use.

The problem appears not only in the *theory of treaties* (their character, conditions of their validity [immoral obligations, influence of duress, their termination (*clausula rebus sic stantibus*), participation of third states, interpretation]); and not only in these well-known questions of servitudes; succession; ratification; prescription; the modes of acquiring and of loss of territory (the much disputed leases!); the colonial mandates; but I think that even in such conceptions as 'Sovereignty' (also Sovereignty of the air) and the 'freedom of the sea' the influence of the concepts of private law can easily be traced. Some of these cases were treated – separately – by different writers (Jellinek, Nippold, Clauss, Keith, Huber, Wegmann, Heimburger, Roxburgh) but, as far as I know, no attempt has been made to deal in a systematic way with the whole question.

Is their constant use in International Law only a necessary sequel of its primitive undeveloped stage, or are they general concepts of law inherent to every system of law?

These questions have to be applied to every one of the above mentioned cases, but only by comparison with each other can the answer be found.

In the course of the research work other questions will, no doubt, arise.

I dealt with one part of this question (the interpretation of treaties) in my thesis presented to the faculty of laws of the University in Vienna.

Have the concepts of private law furthered or checked the growth of the Law of Nations as a positive service? How and why?

---

[18] See the note by Sir Robert Jennings in Appendix 2, p. 444, below.

When, in February 1924, Hersch applied for admission as a candidate for the LLD degree, he was confronted by a requirement that he first take four papers in the LLB Honours Qualifying Examination for Internal Students: the English Law of Contract and Tort; Comparative Jurisprudence; Public International Law; and either the Code Civil Français or the English Law of Real and Personal Property. Evidently, there had been some failure to appreciate the extent of his knowledge relative to all except the English law subjects. Following an intervention by McNair,[19] the matter was reconsidered, and, in July 1924, Hersch was informed that the earlier decision had been rescinded and that he was granted exemption from the LLB examination.

PRIVATE LAW SOURCES

From 1924 through to the first months of 1927, Hersch worked unremittingly on the preparation of *Private Law Sources*. In 1925, he submitted the developing work as a doctoral thesis and was approved for the degree of LLD in that year by the Faculty of Law at the University of London. On 18 March 1926, he became a member of the International Law Association. This enabled him to have contact with those lawyers in England most interested in international law and to participate in their activities. When the ILA had its biennial meetings, Hersch was able to attend – as he did the one held in Warsaw in 1928.

Hersch worked daily in the Fry Library at the LSE, initially walking to it from the various Bloomsbury addresses. When he moved in 1927 to Cricklewood, the journey was not so easy. It began with a walk up Walm Lane to Willesden Green station, from where he took a tube train journey on the Metropolitan Line to Baker Street station. There, he would change to the Central Line to go to Holborn station. The rest of the journey, on foot down Kingsway, would have taken about ten minutes. When I was old enough to go to kindergarten at King Alfred School, he would take me on the tram to Golders Green and we would then walk up the hill towards the school. Hersch would then continue on to the LSE. He must have spent one and a half to two hours a day in travel to and from the LSE.

---

[19] In his letter to Hersch on 10 April 1924 enclosing a statement in support of Hersch's application for exemption from these papers, McNair said: 'As you will see, I do not believe in superlatives in testimonials. They defeat the object and ensure a speedy end in the waste paper basket. I think you are quite right to apply and sincerely hope you may be successful, although I should be sorry to lose you ... I assume that you have sent a full statement of the courses you took at Vienna.'

During the whole of this time he kept in close touch with McNair, attending his seminars and taking a leading role in them. In October 1925, McNair asked Hersch to open a discussion on 'Westlake and International Law of To-day'.[20] As indicated in his outline for the discussion, Hersch intended 'to give an account of the fundamental principles of Westlake's teaching in the light of the present position of the theory and the practice of international law'. The subject was one on which he had already done some work for his first published English article in *Economica* in November 1925, entitled 'Westlake and Present Day International Law';[21] the outline of the discussion follows very closely the headings of the article. He was fortunate enough to make friends who corrected the English of his early writing. The first article on Westlake was corrected by Orby Mootham, later to pursue a judicial career in India and become Chief Justice of Allahabad.[22]

McNair to HL, 22 February 1926

Professor Noel-Baker asked me to enquire whether you would write something for publication on the general question of the legality of intervention to protect one's subjects – with special reference to the Chinese affairs upon which his party is much excited.

My private advice to you is do nothing of the kind. Anything that suited them would be quoted and would injure you who as a foreigner have no right to mix yourself up in our politics.

Don't you agree?

Hersch appears to have taken McNair's advice.

McNair to HL, 12 September 1926

This is not a letter but a mere string of ejaculations which call for no reply but merely reflection.

(1) <u>Research students class</u> At our dinner last June you spoke – for the second time thus wounding quite deservedly my hypersensitive conscience – of some scheme of making our research class more *organic*. What a man says after dinner is not evidence against him, but I don't think you were speaking merely post-prandially, and I should be grateful if you would turn this over in your mind and elaborate it when we meet next. I am anxious to make it more organic and

---

[20] John Westlake (1828–1913) was Whewell Professor of International Law at Cambridge for twenty years and was described by Oppenheim as one of Cambridge's 'most illustrious sons'.

[21] Reprinted in *Collected Papers*, Vol. 2, p. 385.

[22] Sir Orby Howell Mootham (1901–95), Honorary Bencher of the Inner Temple, 1958; Advocate and Judge of the Rangoon High Court, 1927–40 and 1945–6; Judge and Chief Justice of Allahabad, 1946–61; and Deputy Chairman of Quarter Sessions and a Recorder, 1964–72.

perhaps more productive, provided that we do not destroy its informality. Its very unofficial character has this advantage – that no one has a right to come: I can have whom I like; it appears on no programme of lectures; and no one can go to the Office and pay his fee and demand entry.

In this connection you might consider the following: (a) Economica Do we want to ask for a section of this for the publication of any of our Transactions? If so, clearly they must be of more than domestic interest. (b) Journal of the Society of Comparative Legislation Do we want to make use of this? (c) If you have not heard this, it is confidential. There is floating around the idea of forming at the LSE an Institute of International Studies – History, Politics, Administration, Law. Our Research Class would fit well into this, and any present organisation of the class should have this in view. I should very much like to see some post for you in any such Institute, and you may be certain that I shall keep my eyes skinned for any opportunity of bringing this about. But at present little more than the bare idea of an Institute exists.

(2) Your book I have told Mr Longman that you have been delayed over Oppenheim.[23] But the sooner the better.

(3) The Bar Have you thought at all seriously of being called to the English Bar? If you contemplate life in England, I think it is a very important and necessary step. Every teacher of law in England must have a professional qualification. It takes 3 years and costs about £45 on entry as a student and about £95 on call to the Bar. I might be able to help with the admission fees.

In February 1926, Hersch applied to the University of London Publications Fund Committee for a grant in aid of the publication of his LLD thesis. In June, he was notified that a grant of £50 would be made. By October, Hersch was in correspondence with Longmans Green & Co. Ltd regarding the agreement for the publication of the work. By that time, McNair had produced a subsidy of £100 from a source that cannot be traced[24] and which was referred to by Longmans in their letter of 18 October 1926 enclosing a draft of the agreement for publication. They suggested that, as the production of the book was rather more costly than they had anticipated, the profits should be shared equally between Longmans and Hersch. They proposed to make the price of the book one guinea.[25] There is no copy of Hersch's reply but, from Longmans' next letter, of 25 October 1926, it looks as if Hersch had suggested that

---

[23] By which McNair meant that HL's own work on *Private Law Sources* had been delayed by the help that he was giving McNair with the fourth edition of *Oppenheim*.

[24] Perhaps this is the £100 underlying the story that McNair made an advance of £100 to Hersch. See p. 42 above.

[25] Equal to £30 at 2010 prices.

part or all of his share of the profits should go to McNair. Mr Longman then reported that he had asked McNair 'whether any part of the profits should go to those who provided the subsidy, and his answer was "No". If you would like me to I will inform him of your suggestion, but I doubt if he will wish to accept it.'

In response to a request by Longmans for detailed information regarding the book for publicity purposes, Hersch supplied the following text:

This book deals with the problem of the influence of conceptions, rules and analogies of private law on international public law, with special reference to international arbitration. It examines the question whether that influence is solely a characteristic feature of the formative period of international law, or whether it is the inevitable result of the nature of international relations and the character of international law as a system of law. It deals, from this point of view, with the following subjects: treaties and their analogy to contracts of private law, acquisition and loss of territory, the international law of tort and the problem of state responsibility, the measure of damages, the question of interest, the theory of state succession, prescription, international servitudes, leases, international mandates under Article 22 of the Covenant, private law rules of procedure and evidence, especially those of estoppel and res iudicata. Special attention is paid to the interpretation of that provision of Article 38 of the Statute of the Permanent Court of International Justice which authorizes the Court to decide, inter alia, in accordance with general principles of law as recognized by civilized States. The meaning of 'general principles of law' and of 'conceptions of general jurisprudence' is discussed in detail. About one third of the book is devoted to an analysis of those numerous cases of international arbitration which illustrate the main problem of the treatise.

Hersch then sent Longmans the cheque for £50 received from the University of London and the book went to press in November 1926.

McNair to HL, 29 June 1926
I expect to be at the School between 11 and 1.00 tomorrow in case you should wish to see me. I am handing fascicles 3 & 4 to Longman tomorrow. The proofs have already begun to arrive but I shall not touch them until July 12.

As I am entitled to receive £50 disbursed from Longman on delivering the MS, I enclose a further £5 on account.

Gutteridge tells me the £50 grant for your book is now through.[26]

The book of which McNair was referring to the proofs was not *Private Law Sources* but the edition of *Oppenheim* that McNair was then preparing.

---

[26] In 1926, Hersch was also giving assistance to Gutteridge in the compilation of the International Survey of Labour Decisions for the ILO.

Evidently, he was paying Hersch for assistance in bringing the European continental literature up to date.[27] This is the first indication of Hersch's involvement in the editing of *Oppenheim*, to which we will return later.[28] A further example of his good will is the time that he devoted to reading Hersch's work and to commenting in detail on it as evidenced in the galley proofs of *Private Law Sources*. These still exist, with almost every page marked in McNair's clear hand. McNair's down-to-earth advice was reflected on the last page where he wrote:

Must you use the word 'norms', which strikes the ordinary British philistine as very highbrow? I would not recognize a norm if I met him in the street. Why not precept?

For the most part, Hersch adopted McNair's suggestions. After Hersch's death, the galley proof was bound in leather and given to McNair by Rachel and myself. McNair wrote, with characteristic modesty, inside the front cover:

These bound galley proofs ... contain a few comments by me when Hersch was my pupil – or had been – at the London School of Economics. It is clear that my contribution was trifling, which shows my good sense.[29]

ORIGINS OF THE ANNUAL DIGEST

The *Annual Digest*, renamed the *International Law Reports* in 1950, was – and still is – the only publication in the world entirely devoted to regular and systematic reporting in English of decisions of international tribunals, as well as judgments of national courts, coupled with summaries and extensive indexing. Since the *Annual Digest* began, over 10,000 cases have been reported in full or digest form.

Letters from McNair written in December 1926 and January 1927 show how close was his contact with Hersch and how encouraging McNair was.

McNair to HL, 26 December 1926
Many thanks for your letter and for your Christmas wishes for all of us. I sincerely hope that 1927 will bring to you through the publication of your book a measure of recognition which will compensate you in some degree for all the hard and good work you have done in international law and also open up the

---

[27] McNair to HL, 12 September 1926, p. 47 above.   [28] See p. 51 below.
[29] Annotations by McNair also appear in the galley proof of Hersch's article on 'The British Reservations to the Optional Clause' in *Economica*, June 1930, pp. 137–72, reprinted in *Collected Papers*, Vol. 5, p. 347.

way to something more substantial than mere recognition. I feel confident that if you can only hang on by the skin of your teeth to the scientific side of law instead of joining the practitioners' ranks something will open up. In one sense your choice of England is unfortunate, because in no country is International Law less recognized. In another sense it is a fortunate choice, I think, because as far as I am aware in none of the civilized, stabilized countries, does a foreigner and a Jew get a better reception. Do you think that this is an idle boast or not? There is a good deal of anti-foreign feeling in England <u>in bulk</u>, in Parliament, and in the Press. But I do not think that outside the sporting set and the Stock Exchange set there is very much feeling against <u>individual</u> foreigners.

You know how treacherous my memory is, so will understand me when I say that I cannot recall whether the proposal for a joint work as outlined on the reverse page is one of your own ideas, distorted by its passage through my brain, or is a Christmas brain-wave of my own.

With kindest regards to your wife and yourself,

Yours ever,

Arnold D. McNair

Annual Digest of International Case-Law

English, French and German in parallel columns like Internat. Code.

– First volume Quinquennial Digest 1922–1926 so as to [cover] Permanent Court cases.

– Method of treatment rather like [*illegible*] Annual Digest or any other English Annual Digest, i.e. same case referred to under numerous different headings.

e.g. The Wimbledon	– Neutrality
	Canals – Kiel, Suez, Panama
	Servitudes
	Civiliter uti, etc.
	Effect of treaties on third States etc.

– Each reference includes either a paraphrased statement of the relevant point and/or a verbatim extract, <u>plus</u> list of available sources AJIL, BY, RI etc., <u>plus</u> principal comments. No or little attempt at independent comment.

Jurisprudence to be digested: PCIJ, Hague Court of Arbitration, mixed claims, Commissions (probably <u>not</u> the mixed Tribunals under the Peace Treaties or not much of them), important decisions of national courts, other arbitrations, e.g. Taft's Tacna-Arica Award.

– ? where and who to publish? Cheaper abroad than Longmans.

– ? publish it under auspices of London School of Economics and so let our students have a hand in it.

McNair to HL, undated but probably during the winter months of 1926–7

I hope you have not interpreted my long silence as indicating any lack of appreciation of your comments and suggestions on Oppenheim. I need hardly say how valuable I find them.

I was very sorry to hear that your wife was not well. Indeed I did not know that she had come back to England, or my wife would have written to ask you both to come. I sincerely hope that once we get this cold spell of weather over she will improve. It is a beastly climate.

I have now reached p. 245 in Volume I and have turned back to grapple with Conciliation, upon which your notes and recent letters are very useful. I think I can see my way clear now through Chapters I and II and I expect to be able to leave a good deal of stuff with you on Tuesday. I am hopeful that you will concur in the classifications in those chapters, though I am certain that you will not be satisfied as to the amount I am content with.

I enclose a few queries.

McNair to HL, 4 January 1927[30]

1) Thank you for your letter of the 30th December, the spirit of which I heartily approve. You may be sure that I am not overlooking any opportunity of finding a foothold for you in this country. What you say causes me to revert to my earlier suggestion that you should at once enter an Inn of Court and that I would help with the money. I feel that it would improve your prospects here to be a student of an Inn and later a barrister. It helps, so to speak, to domicile you.

2) Will you please criticize the enclosed. The more I think of it, the more I like it, though I don't want any more work at present.

3) I have today received the Analogies and shall make a beginning at once. I shall put my suggestions on the clean copy so as not to complicate your revisions. My suggestions will be more in the form of queries than of positive amendments.

4) Life is further complicated by an Opinion I have to write in a question arising out of the Latin Monetary Union.

Many thanks also for the Oppenheim notes.

The item described in paragraph (2) as 'the enclosed' has not survived, but it may well have been the same as the attachment to McNair's

---

[30] In the original letter the year is given as 1926, but the content of the letter indicates that 1927 must have been meant.

letter of 26 December 1926,[31] concerning the idea of an annual digest of international case law.

McNair to HL, 5 January, 1927

I now return two copies of typescript up to p. [*illegible*]. I have read your revisions but put my suggestions in the numerised copy. I do not want you to feel under the slightest obligation to adopt any of them. It is your book and not mine. I know you will curse me (as I have many times cursed you) for making you reconsider some things which you thought you had finished and done with. But it will do neither of us any harm.

The book is going to be even better than I expected. I hope it will have a great success. I have not an *anima naturaliter philosophica* but I have read the philosophical parts with much greater interest and understanding than I usually do with such material. I hope to feel more at home in the later portions.

I wish you could split up some of these long paragraphs. A whole unbroken page is difficult for a weak stomach.

The English is remarkably good. I don't know how you can manage it.

I will certainly write a short preface as you wish it. May I keep your preface etc. until the end?

McNair wrote the foreword to the book, concluding thus:

It is difficult to be impartial in assessing the work of one who is a friend and was formerly a pupil; but I am hopeful that the reception of this book will confirm my opinion that Dr Lauterpacht is a valuable recruit in the field of international law, and may be expected to make further contributions of high quality to its literature.

There can be no better summary of what Hersch was seeking to achieve than his own words as best expressed in his preface to the work. Notwithstanding its length, it is convenient to reproduce it here in full.

PREFACE TO PRIVATE LAW SOURCES AND ANALOGIES OF
PUBLIC INTERNATIONAL LAW (1927)

It has become a custom with publicists writing on certain disputed questions of international law to base their argument on the assertion that the opinion with which they happen to disagree is nothing else than a misleading analogy to a conception of private law. It is now generally accepted that the recourse

---

[31] See p. 49 above.

to private law, which was, perhaps, justified in the formative period of international law owing to the then prevalent patrimonial conception of State, has subsequently impeded the growth of international law, and ought to be discouraged. The habit of falling back on private law is looked upon as betraying a regrettable tendency to imitation, as ignoring the special structure of international relations, and as threatening to thwart, by introducing technicalities and intricacies of municipal jurisprudence, every attempt at a fruitful and creative scientific activity in the domain of international law. And even in those rare cases in which an author is forced, by the sheer identity of the legal relations with which he has to deal, to adopt a solution suggested by a general principle of private law, the recourse to analogy is usually accompanied by embarrassed counsels of caution or by apologetic explanations.

Does this disparagement of private law receive confirmation from the practice of States and from the history of international law? This was the question which the author set himself to answer. The student who surveys in its entirety the whole field of application of private (and Roman) law must realize that the reliance upon it is not solely a characteristic feature of the formative period of international law, and that there is in the constant recourse to analogy something more than a peculiarity of one historical period. A critical examination shows that the use of private law exercised, in the great majority of cases, a beneficial influence upon the development of international law; that in other cases international law ultimately adopts solutions suggested by private law, without paying regard to the so-called special character of international relations; that it adopts, even now, notions of private law whenever exigencies of international life seem to demand such a solution; that in international arbitration the recourse to private law, on the part both of governments and of tribunals, is a frequent feature of the proceedings and of the decision: especially is this so in view of the fact that general principles of law, recognized by civilized States and adopted by customary and conventional international law as a source of decision in international disputes, are for the most part identical with generally recognized principles of private law.

The adoption, in Article 38(3) of the Statute of the Permanent Court of International Justice, of 'general principles of law recognized by civilized States' as a binding – although, it seems, only supplementary – source of decision in the judicial settlement of disputes signifies that that practice, hitherto unsupported by universal and authoritative international enactment, and regarded by many as derogating from the strictly judicial character of international arbitration, has now received formal approval on the part of practically the whole international community. There lies the outstanding and, to a certain extent, revolutionary contribution made by the Statute to international law as a whole. This book is, in a sense, a commentary on Article 38(3) of the Statute and a respectful acknowledgement of the great service rendered to the cause of international law by the Committee of Jurists assembled in 1920 at The Hague. As a result of earnest and prolonged discussions, they arrived at a compromise which honours equally the representatives of both Continental and British–American jurisprudence, and places the judicial function of the Court upon a solid foundation.

For it is especially in modern arbitration that the inadequacy of the positivist treatment of the problem comes clearly to light. Arbitral tribunals resort to private law because international relations demand such recourse to analogy, and because international law is not always developed enough to supply a solution itself. But the science of international law gives here no guidance to judges and arbitrators, because it rejects, under the influence of the positivist teaching, any analogy whatsoever. The same happens when in a treaty the parties resort to a conception of private law. It is not surprising, therefore, that publicists fall back upon political explanations of doubtful value.

It is the modern positivist doctrine which is chiefly responsible for the acceptance of the prevalent iconoclastic view. A true offspring of the doctrine of sovereignty, it could not countenance the intrusion, into the field of binding rules of international law, of notions and principles not directly derived from the will of the States. The same doctrine of sovereignty, with its conception of eternal and inalienable interests protected by the State and of their public and absolute character, was bound to reject any recourse to private law as concerned with interests deemed to be of an economic and lower order. It would have been an easy task, therefore, to criticize the current repudiation of private law from the point of view of the now so popular rejection of the doctrine of sovereignty. The author, however, decided not to avail himself of this method of approach. The international lawyer, if he wishes to assist in the searching investigation which is now taking place on the subject of external sovereignty, will be well employed if he confines himself to the examination of the question whether the doctrine of sovereignty is in accordance both with the practice of States as expressed in customary and conventional international law, and with a rational and consistent system of international law as developed by international publicists, positivist and non-positivist. If he succeeds in showing that certain widely spread notions, directly and demonstrably resulting from the doctrine of sovereignty, run counter to the practice of States and to the conception of international law as taught by the general body of writers, he has done his share. The doctrine of sovereignty as a legal conception cannot be shattered by well-meaning publicists and pacifists who denounce it as mischievous and as out of date. It will only disappear when notions usually associated with it are shown to be inconsistent both with the practice of States and with the science of international law in its individual branches.

It is necessary to point out at this stage that when referring here and elsewhere in this book to modern positivism, the author in no way alludes to that legitimate aspiration of the science of international law which regards custom and treaties as the primary sources, whose authority, so far as existing law is concerned, is higher than any conflicting rule of natural law or morality. What he has in mind is the uncompromising tendency which isolates international law from any outside influence, which obstructs the task of interpretation and the attempts at consciously developing international law, and which not infrequently goes to the length of disregarding the practice of States if the latter happens to run counter to positivist formulas.

There was, however, quite apart from the positivist teaching, another reason which tended to render difficult an unprejudiced treatment of the problem. When confronted with the question of application of private law, international lawyers are too apt to forget the maxim, *ab abusu ad usum non valet consequentia.* The recourse to private law has been so frequently abused by writers lacking in originality and falling back upon ready-made constructions, by unscrupulous lawyers and diplomats championing doubtful causes, and by skilful counsel at international arbitrations, that some prefer to dispense with it altogether. Such an impatient attitude can hardly be commended. For after all has been said on the dangers of analogy, and on the difference of interests protected by the two spheres of law, the fact remains that, with regard to some of the most essential and most urgent questions of international law, it is in the approximation to the analogous general rules of private law that we see embodied the principles of legal justice and of international progress. The author believes that, amongst others, it is also on the realization of this fact that the success of future attempts at creative juristic activity in the domain of international law depends.

It will be observed that the subject of this book is in no way connected with questions of international private law or with the relation between international and municipal law. It deals with problems of international public law only and exclusively. And even here its scope is restricted in so far as it is concerned with those relations only in which States appear as political entities and as subjects of public rights and duties. It is not concerned either with the bearing of international public law on private rights, or with the interpretation of treaties in which terms of private law are used for the purpose of defining private rights and duties, or with questions of private law arising out of the fact that States engage in trade or enter into purely financial or economic relations with one another.

However, considering the wide range of subjects covered by the problem of application of private law in international public law proper, the scope of this monograph approaches in many respects that of a treatise. On the other hand, the undertaking to illustrate the subject and to verify the propositions put forward in the monograph by reference to cases of judicial settlement of international disputes nearly resulted in a digest of international arbitration. The author is nevertheless but too conscious of the incompleteness of this attempt to deal in a comprehensive manner with his subject, and he only hopes that the very deficiencies of this attempt will prove useful as showing the necessity of a further detailed and independent study of this question.

In the first part of the book, Hersch considered the problem from a theoretical point of view. This still arouses the interest of legal philosophers, though it would engage much less attention today than it did then.[32] The second part of the book is much more practical, consisting of a review of State practice and international arbitral and juridical decisions in which recourse was had to private law analogies as a basis for the identification of a rule of international law. Hersch explained that it was common practice in international adjudication to examine and apply (either directly or by analogy) private law rules, many of which had their origins in Roman law and existed in municipal legal systems.

This explanation challenged the traditional positivist perceptions of the doctrine of sovereignty by demonstrating that international law, in the form of international adjudication, sometimes subjected 'the sovereign will of States to rules which have never received their express consent'.[33] Hersch also uses this examination of the use of private law sources where there was no clear international treaty or custom to demonstrate the 'completeness' of international law as a legal system and its similarity to municipal legal systems. This idea is also taken up later in *The Function of Law* where Hersch argues that there are no gaps in the international legal system because they are filled by 'the normal exercise of the international judicial activity' including general principles, judicial balancing and the observance of social purposes.

Longmans sent the volume to press in November 1926. The book appeared in May 1927 as part of a series published on behalf of the LSE under the general title of *Contributions to International Law and Diplomacy*. As soon as it appeared, McNair wrote to Hersch on 26 May 1927:

First let me congratulate you on the birth of your book, a copy of which I have received today. It looks splendid. You must forgive me a certain amount of grandfatherly pride in it, though no one knows better than you how entirely it is the fruit of your own work and how little I had to do with it. I should feel very

---

[32] See, for example, Koskenniemi, in: 'Lauterpacht: The Victorian Tradition in International Law' (1997) 2 *EJIL* 215–63; 'Hersch Lauterpacht (1897–1960)' in *Jurists Uprooted: German-Speaking Émigré Lawyers in Twentieth-Century Britain*, ed. Beatson and Zimmerman (Oxford: Oxford University Press, 2004), pp. 601–62; 'Hersch Lauterpacht and the Development of International Criminal Law' (2004) 2 *Journal of International Criminal Justice* 810–25; and 'Lauterpacht: The Victorian Tradition in International Law', in *The Gentle Civilizer of Nations: The Rise and Fall of International Law 1870–1970* (Cambridge: Cambridge University Press, 2001), pp. 353–412. See also Carty, 'Hersch Lauterpacht: A Powerful Eastern European Figure' (2007) 7 *Baltic Yearbook of International Law* 1–28.

[33] *Private Law Sources*, p. 44.

proud if I could produce a work of the same substance and originality. Now we leave it to God and the critics.

I have now had an opportunity of studying your revised classification which gets better in each edition. I have suggested some additions and changes which I should like to discuss with you some time on Monday if you are free. Butterworth's have turned us down, damn them, so we must turn again to Longmans.[34]

The work was well received. In a laudatory review in the *American Journal of International Law*, a leading American scholar of the day, James Brown Scott, spoke of it as 'a great and abiding contribution to international justice', said that he knew 'of no better defense of natural law' and declared that 'the volume is a model of what a monograph dealing with a question of international law should be'.[35]

Writing in the *British Year Book of International Law* under the pseudonym 'E', Eric Beckett, later to become the principal Legal Adviser of the Foreign Office, was equally approving though more restrained in his praise:

The work under review ... is a valuable contribution to the science of international law ... it is a first blazing of the trail on practically new ground and ... is a work which those who disagree as well as those who agree with the author's conclusions cannot fail to find useful.

Dr Lauterpacht comes from Vienna to teach and study international law in England and this promising beginning will evoke memories of Oppenheim who also came to England from the continent – *favete linguis*.[36]

For the period which the book covers, the book remains of lasting value.

ASSISTANT LECTURER

Following publication of *Private Law Sources*, Hersch soon reaped, in 1927, the first real reward for his hard work. He was appointed an assistant lecturer at the LSE. His application had strong support from McNair, Gutteridge and Laski. In a separate letter, Laski told Hersch: 'I will pull the School down if you do not get it.'[37] Hersch's excitement was reflected in a letter that he wrote to Rachel, then in Palestine, in fluent, cursive Hebrew script. This is her translation of it:

---

[34] This reference to the 'revised classification' is not to *Private Law Sources* but to the evolving structure of the *AD*.
[35] (1928) 22 *AJIL* 217–19.
[36] (1928) 9 *BYIL* 200–3. A comparably laudatory review, written by Dr Winfield, later to be one of the electors to the Whewell Chair when Hersch was a candidate, appeared in (1929) 3 *CLJ* 322.
[37] Laski to HL, 16 June 1927.

HL to RL, 7 July 1927

Yesterday evening I received the letter from the School in which they proposed to me the position. I answered at once and so legally the thing is finished. The salary (and that most interests you) £350[38] – (besides that, I think I can earn another £50 from the Digest).

The post as it is is better than assistantship in the Department of International Studies. The official name is Assistant Lecturer in International Law. My duties are to teach, to lecture, to conduct classes and to be editor of the Digest. This is more academic. It starts in the next term but the salary I will already get in August or September. Officially, the first year is a year on trial – and really it will be a very difficult year indeed.

Now come the worries of a home. I wish very much that we should have a <u>house</u> and not a flat. A house of our own with our own furniture. But I do not know how to do it. We need at least £250 – and the rest to pay by instalment. I could do the instalment from the salary but £250 is a difficult problem, but it is good that I can already think about it . . .

We must hope that the tide has turned, and that the good will come, although I know that a colossal work is awaiting me.

I think that while I write this letter, you have already received my telegram and that you are a little pleased.

If we have luck and you will be a help to me this day is only a beginning to better and more beautiful things and I will doubly repay <u>you</u> for the bad days.

Yours with love

Zvi

The appointment was soon followed by a request from Philip Noel-Baker, then the Professor of International Relations at the LSE, to the Director of the School, seeking authority to ask Hersch if he would assist in Noel-Baker's seminar on the pacific settlement of disputes. The Director agreed. Hersch was also elected to the LSE's Sociology Club, joining a distinguished membership that included Beveridge, Laski, Manning, Julian Huxley and Martin Wight. On 17 February 1932, he gave a lecture at the Club, entitled, 'Is International Law Different in Nature from Other Law?', and in 1940 he gave a paper on, 'Can Some Application of the Federal Principle Make Any Contribution to the Post-War Settlement, and, If So, What Form Should Its Application Assume?'.[39]

---

[38] Equivalent to about £10,500 in 2010.

By the time that his next – and most important – work, *The Function of Law in the International Community*, appeared in 1933, he had been promoted to lecturer. He was advanced to a readership in 1935.

Hersch entered upon his lecturing duties most seriously. Although he was in due course to become known as a lecturer who did not read from a prepared text but at the most referred to a few scraps of paper containing some brief headings, his LSE lectures were written out in full. Amongst the papers that he prepared are the typewritten texts of some 400 pages of lectures on the law of peace and a further 400 pages of lectures on disputes, war and neutrality. They may not have all been prepared at once, and may have taken the typewritten form some years later. But Hersch obviously attached importance to them since he took care to preserve them. I decided not to print them in the *Collected Papers* because Hersch would not have regarded them as suitable for publication in their original form. However, they show the range and depth of Hersch's knowledge of the subject; and they are very readable. The work that he was doing on the *AD* was of much help to him because extracts from the proofs of the *AD* volumes then already published were included in the boxes with the typed notes.[40] The forty lectures between them form a very clear elementary treatment of the whole subject. It has proved impossible, however, to relate specific lectures to the many unnumbered and undated scraps of paper scattered through the collections of typescript. In addition to lecturing law students, Hersch also gave lectures and supervised economics students (Bachelor of Science, Master of Science, and Certificate for International Studies) who took international law as one of their modules.

OTHER EARLY ARTICLES

From 1927 onwards, Hersch was preoccupied with the preparation of *The Function of Law*. Nonetheless, he still found time in August 1927 to accept an invitation from Professor A. J. Toynbee, the editor of the *Survey of International Affairs*, to contribute an article for the 1926 volume, then in preparation, on 'The United States and the Permanent Court of International Justice'.[41] The fee payable was £1 per printed page.

---

[39] See The Sociology Club, Minutes Book, 1923–1953, LSE Archives. See also: Koskenniemi, 'Hersch Lauterpacht (1897–1960)', in *Jurists Uprooted: German-Speaking Emigré Lawyers in Twentieth-Century Britain*, ed. Beatson and Zimmerman (Oxford: Oxford University Press, 2004), p. 615.

[40] These have now been placed in the Archive.

[41] See (1926) *Survey of International Affairs* 80–98. Reprinted in *Collected Papers*, Vol. 5, pp. 380–97.

And he went on to reciprocate Mootham's earlier kindness[42] by helping him complete in satisfactory form the latter's article on 'The Doctrine of Continuous Voyage, 1756–1815'.[43] He also sent to the *Journal of the Society of Public Teachers of Law* a short article on 'The Teaching of Law in Vienna'.[44] Then making progress with *The Function of Law*, in 1931 he gave a series of lectures in French at The Hague Academy on 'La Théorie des Differends Non-Justiciable en Droit International',[45] in which he presented a succinct exposition of the views that he was about to develop at length in *The Function of Law*. Though not published until 1933, this densely packed volume of some 470 pages had its origins in an earlier article that he published in 1928 under the title of 'The Doctrine of Non-Justiciable Disputes in International Law'.[46]

But his activity was not limited to the preparation of *The Function of Law*. In the same period, he produced a number of substantial contributions on other topics.

In May 1927 he submitted to the *American Journal of International Law* an article under the title of 'Fomenting and Preparing Revolutions in Foreign Countries'. Though the editor of the journal considered the article favourably, he indicated that it was about twice the acceptable length. Hersch then reduced it by half, mainly by omitting the section dealing with revolutionary activities originating from the government of a foreign State.[47] This part of the article he instead delivered, in July 1927, as a paper to the Grotius Society on 'Revolutionary Propaganda by Governments'.[48] This appears to have been the first time that he gave a talk outside the LSE. In it, he emphasised that the freedom of a State from foreign governmental propaganda was a right, not merely a political entitlement. He drew a clear distinction between the actions of foreign governmental agencies and those of private individuals, and observed that patient analysis was required when the responsibility of the foreign State and of the individuals within it tended to merge into one as the result of a dictatorship or another form of absolute government.

At the behest of Sir Cecil Hurst, then the Legal Adviser of the Foreign Office, in March 1927 Noel-Baker invited Hersch to produce an article for the *BYIL*. This led to Hersch's article on 'Spinoza and International

---

[42] See p. 46 above.

[43] (1927) 8 *BYIL* 62. Mootham was by then in Rangoon and evidently not quite happy there. Things improved for him in 1927 when he became a judge, first in Burma and then in India.

[44] Reprinted in *Collected Papers*, Vol. 5, pp. 711–14.

[45] Published in (1931) 34 *Hague Recueil* 499–653.   [46] (1928) *Economica* 277.

[47] The shortened article was published in (1928) 22 *AJIL* 105–30. Reprinted in *Collected Papers*, Vol. 3, pp. 251–78.

[48] (1928) 13 *Transactions of the Grotius Society* 143–63. Reprinted in *Collected Papers*, Vol. 3, pp. 279–96.

Law' in which he offered an explanation of 'why Spinoza, of all men, should have lent himself to preaching the doctrine of lawlessness in the relations of States': this was because Spinoza had failed 'to apply the method of which he and Hobbes were the precursors, namely, that of dealing with human relationships on a rational basis and by means of inductive inquiry'.[49]

CONTRIBUTIONS TO THE *ANNUAL SURVEY OF ENGLISH LAW*

In addition to these writings, Hersch participated in the initiation by the LSE in 1929 of an *Annual Survey of English Law* with contributions from members of the Departments of Law and of International Studies. Each annual volume included a chapter on international law, usually divided into two sections, one on case law prepared by Professor H. A. Smith, the Professor of International Law, and the other on the literature of the subject prepared by Hersch. The latter went beyond the mere listing of textbooks, treaties, general works, monographs and articles in periodicals that had appeared during the year under review; it extended in many instances to informative descriptions and critical comment amounting almost to short reviews. Hersch, who must have begun this task in 1928, continued with annual contributions, usually about twelve pages in length, until the volume for 1937, by which time he had become Whewell Professor in Cambridge.[50] The total number of pages of print covered by his work over ten years came to about 120. There can be little doubt that the detailed study of the current literature, even though limited to English-language material, coupled with the study of case law required for the *AD*, enabled him to acquire a rare knowledge of the subject which he was then able to put to good use when he first came to edit *Oppenheim*.

THE FUNCTION OF LAW IN THE INTERNATIONAL COMMUNITY

Notwithstanding all these diversions, if one may so call them, he eventually completed and published in 1933 *The Function of Law in the International Community*. This was an elaborate volume of some 450 pages. Such is the complex scope of the work that it does not lend itself readily to summarisation or simplification. Once again, therefore, it is better to allow Hersch to describe it in his own words as presented in the preface:

---

[49] (1927) 8 *BYIL* 89–107.   [50] See the volumes of the *Annual Survey of English Law*, 1928–37.

The plan of this book has undergone in the course of its preparation a series of substantial changes. It has grown out of an article, published in 1928 in *Economica* under the title 'The Doctrine of Non-Justiciable Disputes in International Law' and a course of lectures with a similar title given at the Academy of International Law at The Hague in 1930. Its original purpose was to examine the current doctrine – a doctrine accepted by most international lawyers and embodied in leading international conventions for pacific settlement – of the inherent limitations of the place of law and of the judicial process in the society of States. According to this doctrine, international disputes are, by virtue of the peculiar structure of international law and relations, necessarily divided into two categories variously described as 'legal' and 'political', as 'justiciable' and 'non-justiciable', or as disputes as to 'rights' and conflicts of 'interests'. In the opinion of the adherents of this doctrine, this distinction not only affords a satisfactory basis for scientific exposition, but also can, and ought to, be used in international treaties having for their object the creation of a legal duty of pacific settlement in all possible contingencies. This doctrine the writer believes to be juridically unsound, and the original object of the book was to substantiate this work.

As the work progressed, however, it became clear that a merely critical approach might fail to bring into relief the true implications of the scope of the judicial function in international society. As in any other system of law, so also in that which governs the relations of States *inter se*, the question of the limits of the rule of law is the central problem of jurisprudence. It may not be difficult to prove that there is no merit in a classification which is based on the opinion that certain categories of disputes are not amenable to judicial settlement on account of the absence of relevant rules of law. But even when this particular aspect of the doctrine has been disposed of, there still remain special problems confronting international tribunals on account of the shortcomings of the international legal system; for it is a system in which general principles have not always found specific expression in concrete rules, in which law frequently lags behind morals to an extent unknown to the law obtaining within the State, and in which the process of adapting the law to changed conditions is still in a rudimentary stage. It may be easy to demonstrate that the absence from international society of law-making machinery which might effect a compromise between legal stability and social change is neither a sufficient basis for the classification of international disputes nor a reason for urging any limitation of the rule of law among States. But when this has been done there still remains the task of examining how the dangers arising from the absence of an international legislature may be overcome, and what is the solution, in the international sphere, of the perennial conflict between security and justice. To refute a doctrine and to avoid an issue of practical urgency and abiding legal interest would be too rigidly academic. Thus it happens that what was originally intended as a criticism of the orthodox doctrine of the inherent limitations of the international judicial function has been subordinated to an attempt to examine underlying legal problems of a more general nature. Subsequently, the extension of the original plan of the work made it necessary to consider the problem of the limitation of the place of law as a general problem of jurisprudence with special reference to the so-called 'specific' character of international law.

These are the reasons why what was originally intended as a monograph written *cum ira et studio* has developed into an examination, with reference to the relations of States, of some of the persistent problems of legal philosophy, such as the place of law in society, the nature of the judicial function, the problem of judicial discretion, and the antinomies of stability and change. This book is thus no longer a plea in support of a definite doctrine or an argument against a particular theory. It is an attempt at an exposition, by reference to the problem of the international judicial function, of what are believed to be the principal issues of the philosophy of international law.[51]

In some respects, *The Function of Law* builds on *Private Law Sources*. In *The Function of Law*, Hersch argues that international rules do not have 'essential' or concrete meanings; but rather, they possess meaning only through judicial interpretation. International judges and arbitrators ultimately 'interpret' the meaning of these rules. *Private Law Sources* is replete with examples of judges performing this role when they use private law sources to 'fill the gap' and to resolve international disputes where international treaties or international custom were not available. According to Hersch, international judges play a substantial and essential role in international law – an idea emphasised in both *Private Law Sources* and *The Function of Law* (where Hersch dedicates an entire chapter to examining the impartiality of international tribunals) – as he explains:

The problem of the impartiality of the international judge is the Cape Horn of international judicial settlement. It has proved to be an important factor in the efforts to establish a permanent international tribunal and, generally, in the history of obligatory arbitration. Its urgency was clearly recognized in the course of The Hague Conferences. It has been a persistent theme of lawyers and political writers. It is undoubtedly one of the most urgent problems of the political organization of the international community, a problem the consideration of which requires a combination of conscientious abstention from imputation of motives with the determination not to avoid the issue because of the necessity of taking into account factors of a psychological and personal nature.[52]

Both *Private Law Sources* and *The Function of Law* present international law as a 'complete legal system', capable of relying on general principles of law (some of which are derived from private law sources) and judicial

---

[51] Preface, pp. vii–viii.   [52] *The Function of Law*, p. 203.

interpretation. Hersch thus challenges the positivist notion of absolute state sovereignty (i.e. the notion that states are the only source of, and only actors in, international law) and began to establish the legal arguments that he developed in his later works (both academic and professional) on international criminal law and human rights.

Hersch's editorial work on the *AD*, and later the *BYIL* and *Oppenheim*, can also be viewed as part of his project to present international law as a complete legal system and to take international law from its esoteric origins into an influential and important area of law.

The *AD*, for example, was a crucial development: not only did it include significant international cases but it also contained municipal law decisions that had a bearing on international law, further demonstrating the link between international and domestic law. The *BYIL* published only the highest quality work and *Oppenheim* became a standard international law text for academics, lawyers and the Foreign Office.

Hersch was involved in bringing articles, cases, commentary and literature reviews to international lawyers. This work illustrates the ways in which Hersch contributed – in a practical way – to his view of international law; if international jurists were to be the 'backbone' of an international legal system, they needed the proper tools with which to perform their essential role.

The book was very well received. The most substantial review appeared in the *Law Quarterly Review*,[53] again by Eric Beckett. The last paragraph of his review reads:

No greater mistake could be made than to consider this book merely as one of the many propagandist works by enthusiasts for international solidarity. It is a serious legal treatise produced as the result of great research. It is technical and addressed to lawyers only. It attacks by an array of scientific argument and legal material the position taken up by most international lawyers of the past and by many of the present time. Its value in no way depends on the acceptance of the author's conclusions. The present writer finds himself in agreement with the bulk, though not quite all, of the author's general argument and at variance with him on several points of detail. He would single out as of especial interest those chapters which deal with the objections to judicial settlement of international disputes put forward on the grounds of the insufficiency or incompleteness of international law and its rigidity in the absence of a Legislature, and those in which the possibilities of the future development of the law by judicial decision are explored (Chapters III–VI, IX–XIV). Most useful also are the copious collection of instances and references and the numerous summaries and quotations from writers of other countries with which the work abounds.

[53] (1933) 49 *LQR* 583.

Phillips Bradley, one of Hersch's friends at the LSE, reviewed the work fully in the *AJIL*.[54] Referring to Hersch's suggestion that the task incumbent upon international lawyers is to relate international law 'to higher legal principles or to the conception of international law as a whole', Bradley observed:

This creative function was perhaps never more needed, or more possible than it is to-day. As a contribution to this imperative, which he states with persuasiveness and cogency, Dr Lauterpacht's present study will rank high.

A more restrained assessment appeared in the *BYIL* over the signature of A. P. Fachiri. Though describing the book as 'an interesting, learned and earnest work designed to demonstrate that international law, rightly understood and applied, is capable of covering the whole field of international relations' and 'valuable ... as a storehouse of information', Fachiri was not convinced by the main thesis:

True, every dispute can be decided by the application of law, [but he criticised the thesis on the ground that if] states are to submit matters of life and death to a third party for decision they must at least be able to know in advance with reasonable certitude and precision the actual rules and principles governing the case.

Nonetheless,

whether one agrees or not with his central thesis, Dr Lauterpacht's book is a serious and weighty contribution to an important subject, which deserves to be read with respect and from which much is to be learned.[55]

Hersch's colleague at the LSE, Harold Laski, who though essentially a political scientist was a voracious reader in related subjects, on 13 June 1933 reported to Mr Justice Holmes, of the US Supreme Court, with whom Laski was in regular and extensive correspondence, that he had done 'a great deal of reading these days':

First and foremost, I place Lauterpacht's *Function of Law in the International Community* (Oxford), one of the ablest legal books I have read in many a day. It's a little long and a little heavy, but a grand piece of work.[56]

However, not everyone agreed with these reviews. E. H. Carr, in his book *The Twenty Years' Crisis, 1919–1939*, used *The Function of Law* as the basis

---

[54] (1934) 28 *AJIL* 197.

[55] (1934) 15 *BYIL* 206. A similarly restrained, but lengthy, argumentative review by an anonymous author also appeared in the *Times Literary Supplement* on 24 August 1933, p. 555.

[56] *Holmes–Laski Letters*, ed. Mark De Wolfe Howe (1953), vol. 2, p. 1443.

of his attack on what he perceived to be Hersch's 'utopian idealism', leading to what is sometimes referred to as the 'idealism' versus 'realism' debate.[57] This idealist/realist debate primarily expressed itself in four different forms: (a) questions of sovereignty (do states have to assent to all rules or are there some rules that can be derived by principle and with states bound by these rules?); (b) the role of international courts and judicial arbitration; (c) whether there is a 'harmony of interests' among all states; and (d) the failure of the League of Nations: did it fail because the very idea is too utopian or because the idea was badly executed?

In *The Twenty Years' Crisis, 1919–1939*, Carr takes Hersch's view of the unlimited nature of the judicial function put forward in *The Function of Law* as the best example of 'legalistic utopianism' that he believed to be meaningless and wholly incorrect. In the words of Carr himself:

No government has been willing to entrust to an international court the power to modify its legal rights ... Some theorists have, however, been more ready than practical statesmen to brush this difficulty aside, and are quite prepared to entrust to a so-called arbitral tribunal the task not only of applying existing rights, but of creating new ones ... [Such as] Professor Lauterpacht's belief that international 'conflicts of interests are due ... to the imperfections of international legal organization'.[58]

And:

It is a pity that Professor Lauterpacht, having brilliantly conducted his analysis up to the point where the unwillingness of states is recognized as the limiting factor in the justiciability of international disputes, should have been content to leave it there, treating this 'unwillingness', in true utopian fashion, as perverse and undeserving of the attention of an international lawyer.[59]

Carr further characterises Hersch's support of the League of Nations/international institutions as being too optimistic:

It is a meaningless evasion to pretend that we have witnessed, not the failure of the League of Nations, but only the failure of those who refused to make it work. The breakdown of the nineteen-thirties was too overwhelming to be explained merely in terms of individual action or inaction. Its downfall involved the bankruptcy of the postulates on which it was based. The foundations of nineteenth-century belief are themselves under suspicion. It may not be that

[57] This debate has been referred to as 'the first great debate of international relations': R. Jeffery, 'Hersch Lauterpacht, the Realist Challenge and the "Grotian Tradition" in 20th-Century International Relations' (2006) 12 *European Journal of International Relations* 232.

[58] *The Twenty Years' Crisis, 1919–1939*, p. 259; the extract quoted by Carr is from *The Function of Law*, p. 250.

[59] *Ibid.*, p. 249, n. 1.

men stupidly or wickedly failed to apply right principles, but that the principles themselves were false or inapplicable.[60]

It appears that Carr's criticism did not undermine either Hersch's work or good humour, when he wrote that 'practically everyone who disagrees with Professor Carr is Utopian'.[61]

The work has maintained its status in the years following. A substantial analysis of the book, as of Hersch's other writings, has been presented by Professor Martti Koskenniemi, a noted international legal philosopher, in his extended biographical essay on Hersch in the volume entitled *Jurists Uprooted*, published in 2004,[62] as also in a lecture in 2008:

I have said this before and I will say it again: *The Function of Law in the International Community* is the most important English-language book on international law in the 20th century.[63]

Once *The Function of Law* was completed early in 1933, Hersch immediately concentrated on the preparation of a series of five lectures to be delivered at the Graduate Institute of International Studies at Geneva in January 1934 on 'The Development of International Law by the Permanent Court of International Justice'. These were published by Longmans later in the same year and were the forerunner of the much larger volume on *The Development of International Law by the International Court* published in 1958.[64]

DEVELOPMENT OF THE ANNUAL DIGEST

In parallel with his work on *The Function of Law* and the aforementioned articles, Hersch had begun work on a series of digests of international law cases under the title of *Annual Digest and Reports of Public International Law Cases*. This was the series that McNair had referred to in the attachment to his letter to Hersch of 26 December 1926.[65] As McNair had indicated, it is not clear whether the idea for the series originated with McNair or

---

[60] E. H. Carr, *The Twenty Years' Crisis, 1919–1939*, p. 39.

[61] Lauterpacht, 'Professor Carr on International Morality'. Reprinted in *Collected Papers*, Vol. 2, p. 69.

[62] *Jurists Uprooted: German-Speaking Émigré Lawyers in Twentieth-Century Britain*, ed. Beatson and Zimmerman (Oxford: Oxford University Press, 2004), pp. 601–62.

[63] 'The Function of Law in the International Community: Seventy-Five Years After', keynote lecture by Professor Koskenniemi at the 25th Anniversary Symposium of the Lauterpacht Centre for International Law, 11 July 2008, www.lcil.cam.cc.uk/25th_anniversary/. The lecture has been reprinted as Koskenniemi, 'The Function of Law in the International Community: 75 Years After' (2008) 79 *BYIL* 353–67.

[64] See pp. 409–10 below.   [65] See p. 50 above.

Hersch. As Beckett had said in his review of *Private Law Sources*, the decisions of municipal courts on international law:

> are valuable sources of international law (the more valuable in proportion as the courts giving them are free to take into consideration all international authorities) ... This source of international law is also in great need of scientific treatment and collation, and Dr Lauterpacht (with Dr McNair, who wrote the foreword to this work) is shortly to add his services to the scientific development of international law by the editing of an annual digest of judicial decisions on questions of international law, which will be of great value to all students of the law of nations.[66]

The principal burden of editing the digest was actually borne by Hersch. The first volume in the series appeared in 1929 and covered the years 1925–6. It was followed a year later by the volume covering 1927–8. For these two volumes, the joint editor was McNair. In 1932, Sir John Fischer Williams,[67] a distinguished practitioner though with little academic involvement in the subject, took over from McNair and the series was extended backwards to 1919. For the fifth volume, covering 1929–30, published in 1935, Hersch was left on his own. He continued the series with great success for the rest of his time at the LSE, during his period at Cambridge and even while he was a judge at the International Court until his heart attack in 1959, at which time the twenty-fourth volume (for 1957) was being prepared and was, at Hersch's request, completed by me.[68] In 1956, with the volume for the year 1950 (being the seventeenth in the series), he changed the title from *Annual Digest* to *International Law Reports*. The work done by Hersch on the series was posthumously recognised by the American Society of International Law, which in 1972 awarded him its Certificate of Merit. The *Reports* are now a publication of the Lauterpacht Centre for International Law at Cambridge, a connection which ensures their continued publication as an enduring memorial to Hersch.

Hersch's approach to the business arrangements connected with the publication was relaxed to the point of naïveté. He was not concerned

---

[66] (1933) 49 *LQR* 583.

[67] Sir John Fischer Williams, KC (1897–1947); British Legal Representative on the Reparation Commission under the Treaty of Versailles, 1920–30; Member of the Permanent Court of Arbitration from 1936. Publications included *Chapters on Current International Law* and *Some Aspects of the Covenant of the League of Nations.*

[68] The series was then continued by me, initially with considerable assistance from Gillian White (later to become Professor of International Law at Manchester). In 1979, Christopher Greenwood, subsequently to become Professor of International Law at the LSE, and a judge of the ICJ, joined me, and, in 1990, became joint editor. By 2009, 135 volumes had been published.

with cost, price or numbers of copies sold. Fortunately, for many years the series was the beneficiary of grants from a number of sources, initially from the Carnegie Endowment for International Peace, the four Inns of Court, All Souls College, Oxford and the LSE. In later years, there was significant help from the Ford Foundation and the International Law Fund. Hersch, however, was content that the publishers should take the prepared volume, print it and sell it, retaining for themselves such meagre profits as it might generate and making a small contribution to editorial costs. The first volumes were published by Longmans as part of the LSE series in international law mentioned earlier. In 1938 Butterworths took over the publication. With the help of a shrewd publishing consultant, John Grant, a more commercial basis for the publication was established in 1972, which led to the receipt of an income sufficient for a while to cover the cost of editorial assistance. In 1978, Butterworths gave way to Grotius Publications Ltd, a small specialist international law publisher willing and able to give the series the attention it required. In 1993, Grotius Publications, having grown so much that it could not conveniently continue as the amateur 'cottage industry' publisher it was originally intended to be, was taken over by Cambridge University Press. It was a resting place that would have pleased Hersch.

The substantive preparation of the volumes of the *AD* was demanding. Albeit financially with little remuneration,[69] Hersch nonetheless found it rewarding in other respects. It involved the establishment and maintenance of links with contributors in a number of countries who sent in cases bearing on international law decided by the courts of their countries, as well as decisions of international tribunals. These contributions almost invariably required editing, sometimes considerable, especially in improving the English of versions prepared by non-English-speaking contributors. In this work, Hersch had no full-time assistance but was greatly aided by his former LSE secretary, Gladys Lyons, and occasionally by her husband, Bernard Lyons, an official of the Treasury Solicitor's Department. Also, Hersch himself contributed significantly to the content of each volume. For example, in the volume for 1931–2,[70] he was responsible for the digest of the cases decided by the PCIJ and all other international tribunals and arbitrations – some 44 entries out of a total of 233. The amount of correspondence involved in the process was

---

[69] There is mention in the letter that Hersch sent to Rachel announcing his appointment as an Assistant Lecturer at the LSE of the prospect of a £50 payment for the Digest, but nowhere else is there any reference to payment.

[70] This became Volume 6 when the series was numbered under the general title of *International Law Reports*.

considerable, but Hersch did not begrudge the time that he spent on it. He saw the series as a major development in the literature of international law, as indeed it was and still remains. Moreover, the whole exercise placed him in a unique position to keep abreast of the increasing case law in the field. However, he did not live to see the enormous expansion of the cases touching the subject decided by national and international courts; this has already led to an increase in the number of volumes published each year from one to four, which may soon require a further increase and has already led to the series going online.[71]

McNair and Hersch associated with the series an Advisory Committee consisting of international lawyers of standing from a number of countries, but their role was largely nominal. More important were some of the individual contributors. As the list of contributors to the first volume that Hersch edited on his own, covering 1929–30, shows, there were then twenty-six contributors covering the various jurisdictions. One of the later recruits on whom he came to rely greatly was Richard Baxter, an American who, as a career officer in the Judge Advocate General's Office of the United States Army, pursued research in Cambridge on the law of war under Hersch in 1950–1 and then went on to become a professor at the Harvard Law School, his initial research appointment there having been sponsored by Hersch. From there, he received the well-deserved nomination for election as a judge of the ICJ, on which he served from 1979 to 1980. Very sadly, he died within a year at the age of 59. He had been devoted to Hersch and was responsible for the United States cases. These he produced in immaculate form, with the facts perfectly summarised and the relevant parts of the decision clearly identified. The contribution of the United States cases was then continued for some years by Stephen M. Schwebel who, after Baxter's death, followed him to the ICJ.[72] Schwebel was also instrumental in obtaining from the Ford Foundation some financial support for the series.

<h2 style="text-align:center">LEAGUE OF NATIONS UNION</h2>

In January 1933, Hersch accepted an invitation to join the International Law Committee of the League of Nations Union. The Union was a

---

[71] Available at www.justis.com/ilr/ilr.html.

[72] Stephen M. Schwebel (born 1929), Judge of the ICJ, 1981–2000; President of the ICJ, 1997–2000; Assistant Professor at the Harvard Law School; Assistant, then Deputy, Legal Adviser at the US Department of State; Executive Director of the American Society of International Law; Burling Professor of International Law, Johns Hopkins University; Member of the ILC; President of the International Monetary Fund Administrative Tribunal; active international arbitrator.

non-governmental, non-party body formed in England to support the League of Nations. In the early 1930s it gained in popularity to the extent of having over 10,000 members, but interest waned as the weaknesses of the League became more apparent in the wake of the Italian invasion of Abyssinia and the failure of sanctions.

Within the Union a number of committees were formed dealing with various aspects of the work of the League. One of them was the International Law Committee, of which in 1932 Brierly was chairman and Fischer Williams, Pearce Higgins, McNair and Philip Noel-Baker were members. The committee met irregularly, barely twice a year.

When Hersch joined, he soon became an active participant in the committee's work. He had in fact already, in December 1932, provided the Committee with a memorandum on the equality of States in the League which the Committee resolved should be submitted to the sub-committee on the reform of the League. Its subsequent fate cannot be ascertained.

Amongst other matters, the Committee, in December 1932, had begun to consider the question of the responsibility of States for crimes against foreigners committed within their territory. The basis of its discussion was a draft resolution drawn up by a sub-committee of the International Federation for consideration by the Federation at its forthcoming meeting in February 1933. The draft resolution observed that such crimes 'are sometimes such as to disturb the good relations between States', went on to examine the suggestion that such cases should be submitted to a criminal section of the PCIJ, took the view that there were practical objections to such a suggestion, and concluded by expressing the wish that States would conclude conventions providing for such eventualities by some form of judicial cooperation. The draft resolution appears not to have been discussed by the International Law Committee till after Hersch had become a member. The Committee then concluded, however, that the proposals of the Federation's sub-committee 'cannot be reconciled with the British system of criminal law' and that such proposals should be opposed. Hersch seems to have been a sole dissenter from a related aspect of the discussion, taking the view that Members of the League were bound by the Covenant to accept the opinion of the Assembly or Council on the question whether or not a Member of the League was guilty of aggression or resort to war.

In October 1933, the Committee had before it a memorandum prepared by Hersch[73] on the question whether the League should provide

---

[73] SG 6223.

a definition of 'war' and whether the League should be empowered to declare when 'a situation constitutes a state of war'. At the meeting of the Committee on 24 October 1933, Noel-Baker and Hersch expressed willingness to prepare a memorandum on the definition of 'war', but the product of such work as they may have done cannot be found.

Hersch also undertook to prepare a paper on the question of whether the Optional Clause of the PCIJ could be invoked to secure an interpretation of the Covenant by the Court.[74]

THE PEACE ACT, 1933–4

The Committee then went on to consider a proposal that had been made by Arthur Henderson, in an October 1933 Labour Foreign Policy pamphlet, that Parliament should enact a statute that would add to the legal obligation accepted by the United Kingdom in relation to the conduct of war and the use of force. The government would be required as a matter of UK law to conform to its obligations under the Covenant of the League, the Kellogg–Briand Pact, the Geneva Act for the Pacific Settlement of Disputes and its declaration of acceptance of the Optional Clause of the Statute of the PCIJ. The idea of limiting in this way the otherwise unlimited prerogative powers of the Crown, i.e. of the government, was in 1934 entirely novel. If pursued, it would have represented a significant forward leap in the limitation of the prerogative that was not imagined until the United Kingdom became a member of the European Communities in 1973. Moreover, in substantive terms, the Act would have prohibited the government from resorting to force against a foreign nation in breach of the treaties mentioned above. Had the proposed Act been adopted and remained in force, it would have rendered even more controversial the so-called 'Suez action' in 1956[75] as well as the use of force in Iraq in 2003. Of course, those who promoted the initiative could not have foreseen these developments. Hersch's willingness to lend his skills to the formulation of the draft undoubtedly stemmed from his conviction of the importance of maintaining the integrity and effectiveness of the instruments covered by the draft. He would not have seen himself as siding with the Labour Party or any other party of the time. He would have been mindful of McNair's advice that he should not become involved in politics. On the other hand, he could not help

---

[74] This was produced as SG 6312, but cannot be traced.

[75] For McNair's speech in the House of Lords condemning the government's actions, see *Hansard*, HL Debates, 12 September 1956, vol. 199, cols. 657–63.

but be influenced by the predominantly Labour atmosphere at the LSE, not least by Noel-Baker, who was to become a government minister when the Labour Party was returned to power in 1945, and by Harold Laski, an eminent political scientist, who later became Chairman of the Labour Party. But, in the end, nothing came of the draft. As Hersch observed to Brierly in a note of 2 May 1936, by May 1936, '[t]his is now safely shelved.'

However, Hersch had in the meantime sent a copy of the draft to Dr Maxwell Garnett, the Secretary of the League of Nations Union, for his private and confidential use. Garnett responded by passing on to Hersch a suggestion by Sir Walter Layton that:

it would be wise, before the occasion arises, to examine the problem of economic sanctions under the Covenant with a view to spreading the incidence of pecuniary losses in the event of such sanctions being applied, for example, by this country.

Garnett wondered whether it might be worthwhile introducing a clause on this subject into the draft Peace Act. Hersch replied on 8 April 1935 that 'this is just the kind of suggestion that ought to be considered in connection with the Peace Act' and that he would 'try and see how it could best be expressed in the Act'. From then on, silence prevailed on this subject.

With others, Hersch was much interested in the treatment by the Council of the League of Nations of the dispute between Yugoslavia and Hungary regarding incidents on their common border, and the assassination of King Alexander of Yugoslavia on 8 October 1934 by Croat separatist terrorists. The parties agreed to submit the dispute to the Council of the League, which appointed Anthony Eden as Special Rapporteur. He concluded that it was the duty of all States to repress political terrorism. Hungary was requested to investigate the incident and submit a report to the League. This was eventually done and the matter did not arise again.[76]

At the same time, on the advice of McNair, Hersch took steps to be called to the Bar. He joined Gray's Inn. He had prepared for his Bar exams while still carrying on with his regular teaching at the LSE, squeezing the preparation into any spare time he could find. He took Part 1 of the Bar exams in 1934. During the summer of 1936, he joined Rachel and myself while we were on holiday in a rented house in Frinton-on-Sea. When we went to the beach each morning, Hersch stayed in

---

[76] See F. B. Walters, *A History of the League of Nations* (1952), vol. 2, pp. 599–605.

the house to continue with his studies for the Bar Finals. At about noon, he would pass by Sainsbury's, buy some cold cuts and carry them to the seaside hut for a family picnic. Then he would return to the house for more preparation.

In studying for the Bar exam, Hersch and Jenks[77] had entered into a friendly rivalry.

HL to C. W. Jenks, 20 December 1934
Before everything, let me congratulate you on beating me so handsomely in Elements of Contract and Tort. I was relieved to see my name in the list. As to Property there is not the slightest doubt about the soundness of the advice received by the two distinguished candidates. I have so far read only one hundred pages of Cheshire and found them delightful reading (considering the subject). But there is no chance of my doing anything on it until April. Shall we meet for the Finals in October? . . .

My interest in it is not merely esoteric as I am on the Labour Party Committee which has to submit a draft of the Article . . .

Everyone here is in self-congratulatory mood on account of the part of the Government in the Yugoslav–Hungarian affair. But is it the end of the matter? What will happen if Hungary issues the findings of the investigating authorities to the effect that there was no foundations at all? Frankly, I cannot quite understand it. If the question before the Council was one of fact – i.e. the guilt or innocence of the Hungarian authorities – how could it be settled by way of compromise?

Even so, Hersch found time in the course of 1935 to write a thirty-page article entitled 'Contract to Break a Contract'[78] dealing with the question of the validity of a contract which, to the knowledge of both parties, could not be performed without the breach of a prior contract binding upon one of them. To the main text of the article was appended a five-page note on French, German and international law considering the legal position of the second inconsistent contract. This is Hersch's only published work on English law. It shows a grasp of the authorities and of the techniques of common law reasoning that is striking in one whose time had until then been spent entirely in the study of international law. Hersch was particularly proud of the fact that in his Bar exam he was able to refer to his own article!

---

[77] C. W. Jenks (1909–73) was educated at Gonville and Caius College, University of Cambridge, and the Geneva School of International Studies. He joined the ILO in 1931, serving in turn as Legal Adviser, Assistant Director-General, Deputy Director-General, principal Deputy Director-General and, from 1 June 1970, Director-General.
[78] (1936) 208 *LQR* 494.

The two years leading up to Hersch's election to the Whewell Chair in Cambridge in 1937 were ones of unrelenting activity, even though it was not known till 1936 that McNair would be vacating the chair to become Vice-Chancellor of Liverpool University on 1 July 1937. So Hersch's efforts were not specifically directed towards the prospect of a Cambridge vacancy of which he was then quite unaware.

At the encouragement of McNair, Hersch was working hard on Volume II (*Disputes, War and Neutrality*) of the fifth edition of *Oppenheim*, during the early months of 1935, with a view to sending it to the printer in April. It was published in September 1935. In it, Hersch introduced some fifteen new sections, including over twenty pages devoted to the General Treaty for the Renunciation of War which he considered as having effected a fundamental change in the system of international law. In the preface, he set out at length the reasons for his view that the study and exposition of the laws of war must continue to be a legitimate object of the science of international law. 'Clashes of physical force on a large scale', he prophetically said, 'will not be absolutely eliminated even after the Federation of the World has become a reality.'[79]

EXTRACT FROM THE PREFACE TO VOLUME II OF THE
FIFTH EDITION (1935) OF *OPPENHEIM*

I have believed myself justified in devoting over twenty pages to the General Treaty for the Renunciation of War. For the reasons stated in the body of the volume, that Treaty must be considered to have effected a fundamental change in the system of International Law. The legal significance of that change is independent of the present political importance or prospects of the Treaty. In the long run the progress achieved by it will probably tend to become unreal unless, in addition to the necessary clarification of its terms and the adoption of obligations for its enforcement, it is supplemented by the gradual evolution of institutions for the discharge of a function which has hitherto been fulfilled by war. These include, in particular, agencies for enforcing the law as found by judicial or arbitral tribunals endowed with obligatory jurisdiction in disputes between States, and for altering territorial and political conditions in accordance with justice. But in an unorganized international society changes cannot always be affected *pari passu*, and it is probably more in keeping with true historical perspective to regard the Treaty as a positive contribution to international progress rendering further developments feasible than to underestimate its significance because these developments have not yet become law.

---

[79] *Oppenheim* (5th edn, 1935), pp. vii–viii. This penetrating assessment of the role of law in war and peace, of which the sentence quoted above is only a small part, merits fuller quotation, the more so now that the fifth edition occupies only a remote position on many library shelves.

I have also thought it necessary to indicate why the study and the exposition of the laws of war must continue to be a legitimate object of the science of International Law. Governments have not adopted the view that the General Treaty for the Renunciation of War has rendered laws of war unnecessary. In fact, most of them signed in 1929, and subsequently ratified or adhered to, important conventions on the treatment of the sick and wounded in armies in the field and on the treatment of prisoners of war. Having so far failed to abolish submarine warfare, they have formulated afresh the customary rules of International Law relating to the sinking of merchantmen. And attempts have since been made to lay down rules for the protection of non-combatants from the dangers of aerial bombardment in a manner more specific than that afforded by customary International Law. Clashes of physical force on a large scale will not be absolutely eliminated even after the Federation of the World has become a reality; they may assume then the form of a public and collective sanction against the law-breaker, or of a rebellion, comparable to a civil war within the State, against the constitution of the organized community of nations. It is obviously preferable that the use of force in such cases should be regulated and, if possible, humanized. Now a very considerable part of the laws of war, as distinguished from the laws of neutrality, is an attempt to mitigate the unscrupulousness and brutality of force by such considerations of humanity, morality and fairness as are possible and practicable in a relationship in which the triumph of physical violence is the supreme object and virtue. The net result of such rules of moderation may, even if they are observed, prove to be insignificant when compared with the devastation wrought by war. But they ought not on that account to be disregarded. The well-being of an individual is the ultimate object of all law, and whenever there is a chance of alleviating suffering by means of formulating and adopting legal rules, the law ought not to abdicate its function in deference to objections of apparent cogency and persuasiveness. One of the most persistent of these objections is that, by devoting attention to the laws of war, we not only create an unjustified belief in the possibility or likelihood of their observance, but also deny by implication the reality of the renunciation of war as an instrument of national policy. Another is that the more brutal war is allowed to become, the sooner will it be abolished.

However, these humanitarian rules constitute only one branch of the laws of war. With regard to others, and to rules of International Law in general, reference may here be made to the frequently quoted passage in the Preface, written in 1889, to the third edition of Hall's *International Law*. That distinguished lawyer confessed to doubts whether the next great war would be scrupulous, either on the part of belligerents or neutrals. But, he predicted, 'there can be very little doubt that if the next war is unscrupulously waged, it also will be followed by a reaction towards increased stringency of law.' He interpreted history as showing that, after periods of disregard of the law, the collective conscience of nations which, he thought, in this field exerts itself more surely than the individual conscience, 'has done penance by putting itself under straiter obligations than those which it before acknowledged.'

The first part of Hall's prophecy was undoubtedly fulfilled. The World War was great and was not scrupulously waged. Some of the most important rules of war and neutrality were thrown overboard, and lawyers were faced with the task of discovering whether the measures adopted by the belligerents amounted to a violation of International Law, to a lawful application of reprisals, or to a legitimate adaptation of the law to new conditions. But it is questionable whether the positive side of Hall's prophecy has been fulfilled in the domain either of the law of peace or of war. In both these fields the science of International Law is now confronted with tasks of particular significance.

So far as concerns war, the practice during the World War and the developments of modern warfare have created gaps, which still remain unfilled, in some of the most important branches of the law of war and neutrality. Some of these gaps were, in fact, revealed during the World War, but not created by it. The law of war as it existed at the beginning of the twentieth century, and the Hague Conferences which framed or codified some of these rules, failed to take into account the unprecedented extension of the scope of modern warfare and the resulting difficulty of confining the effects and incidents of the state of war to the belligerent State as such or to its armed forces. It is therefore not altogether surprising that the stringency of the law proved to be illusory. But there have been since the World War no signs of a deliberate effort to adjust the law to the changes in the modern conditions of war. Twenty years after the outbreak of the World War the dispute on the question of the relevancy of these changes is unsettled and opposing views are stoutly maintained. The attempts to regulate warfare in the air have so far proved abortive. There is a widespread doubt whether, taking into account the intervening changes, such rules can be framed, and whether, if framed, they will be observed. Such restraint on the part of belligerents as is anticipated is widely assumed as likely to come either from the fear of reprisals or from the realization that the ruthlessness of weapons which modern civilization has placed at the disposal of Governments may result in the destruction of that very civilization. Reliance on these negative factors may or may not be justified. For the science of International Law to rely on them would mean to abdicate its proper function. Its task is to assess the effect of the changes in the scope and instrumentalities of war and to assign to them their proper place and their proper limits in the law of war. At the same time the distinction, seemingly jeopardized by the new developments, between combatants and non-combatants must be rigorously upheld; for that distinction remains one of the bases of the legal regulation of war. The reconciliations of the consequences of the altered scope and instrumentalities of modern war with the continued existence of the distinction between combatants and non-combatants must therefore be regarded as justly claiming the attention of Governments and of the science of International Law. It is imperative to examine from this point of view the rules of war and neutrality accepted in the eighteenth and nineteenth centuries – just as an effort must be made to translate into terms of positive International Law the changes in the rules of neutrality which result by implication from the Covenant of the League and which have become necessary in consequence of the General Treaty for the Renunciation of War. Such efforts must not be frustrated or even influenced by the consideration that in a future war all rules of war and neutrality are likely to be exposed to the strain resulting from the fact that one at least of the belligerents has not hesitated to violate a solemn and fundamental treaty for the renunciation of war and thus may feel little hesitation in brushing aside any inconvenient restraints imposed by the law of war or neutrality.

No less clear or urgent is the task of International Law in the domain of the law of peace and the organization of peace. In this field the experience of the World War, and of the centuries which preceded it, ripened into the Covenant of the League – the fundamental charter of what was intended to be the organised community of nations. This instrument, whatever its imperfections, constituted in its terms a significant departure in International Law and, in some respects, a substantial diminution of the freedom of action hitherto enjoyed by the members of the League. But the subjection to 'straiter obligations' has not been maintained. The following years have witnessed the phenomenon of humanity recoiling before the boldness of its effort to translate into terms of law and order the lessons of history. The receptivity and continuity of the collective mind in matters affecting international relations have proved less potent then in other spheres. International Law can, it is believed, play an important part in strengthening and keeping alive these qualities of the collective conscience. The social consequences of legal rules and institutions may at times be fraught with danger inasmuch as they may tend to give undue stability to conditions which are essentially temporary and to obstruct progress. At the same time, however, the law serves the function of giving flesh and bones to social experience and of protecting it from the effects of opportunism and of passive acquiescence in retrogression. The science of International Law must, in the strict fulfillment of its function as exponent of existing law, study and interpret the new institutions of the international system not by way of generalizing the political conditions of any transient period of relapse, but in the light of the intentions of the individual and collective framers of these institutions as determined by overwhelming, and still enduring, historical experience.

In the last weeks of 1935 and the first of 1936, Hersch managed to write an article on 'The Covenant as Higher Law'. He had originally intended that this should be no more than a note in the *BYIL* but McNair thought it 'very important and very topical'. Fischer Williams took the view, with which McNair concurred, that it should be published as a full article, and so it was.[80] However, McNair, for reasons not stated, said 'I make all reserves as to whether I agree with you or not.'[81]

During that summer much time was spent on preparation for the Bar Final exam, which Hersch passed with a low second – but still well ahead of the long list of thirds! On the eve of the exam, he received the following words of encouragement from McNair:

This is merely to send you my best wishes for the Bar Final and to tell you that I shall be telepathing with intensity the small amount of English Law which I still retain in case there are any chinks in your armour. Not being an examiner I cannot do more. I hope that the work has been going well. I am sure the matter need give you no anxiety. You will probably get firsts in everything, but it does not really matter what you get.[82]

He must have been under great pressure during these months because when he went to Switzerland 'for a short holiday to recuperate' he wrote to Rachel that he felt much better and that his 'jaw had stopped trembling'. Even there, however, he had to spend two days on a memorandum for the Emperor of Abyssinia, of which no copy has been found. The precise subject is unknown and one can only speculate what it was. It was just after Emperor Haile Selassie left Addis Ababa to travel, via Jerusalem, to Europe to address the League of Nations. On 5 May, Addis Ababa was captured by Italian forces, and, on 7 May, Italy officially annexed Ethiopia; two days later, King Victor Emmanuel III of Italy was proclaimed Emperor of Abyssinia. Ethiopia was then merged with Eritrea and Italian Somaliland into a new State called 'Africa Orientale Italiano' (Italian East Africa). The Emperor Haile Selassie was eventually enabled to address the Assembly of the League of Nations on 30 June, and the Assembly then condemned the Italian action. But, on 4 July, the League dropped all sanctions against Italy – one of the most pathetic episodes in the life of the League. So possibly Hersch had been asked to advise the Emperor on the legal implications of these developments and in particular what might have been their effect on the status of the Emperor, or perhaps even to help the Emperor with the draft of his speech. Apart, of course, from the general references to the terms of the Covenant of the League, the speech contains only one mention of technical international law – an observation about the rules of neutrality prohibiting transport of arms for Italian forces by the railway from

---

[80] (1936) 17 *BYIL* 54–65. Regrettably, due to an oversight, this article does not appear to have been included in the *Collected Papers*.

[81] McNair to HL, 25 March 1936.   [82] McNair to HL, 21 September 1936.

Djibouti to Addis Ababa. But advising on this would have been unlikely to have taken Hersch two days. More likely is the possibility that he was asked to advise as to how to enable the Abyssinian representatives to take their seats in the League Assembly. This explanation is suggested by the appearance of a short note on this subject in the *BYIL* in the following year.[83] It would have been like Hersch to have suggested recourse to the PCIJ for an advisory opinion if a positive response from the Credentials Committee could not otherwise be obtained. But the suggestion was discarded because the Committee recommended the admission of the Abyssinian delegation.

Later in the year, Hersch was approached by Professor Paul Guggenheim, the Professor of International Law at Geneva, with a question relating to the German–Polish Convention on Minority Rights in Upper Silesia, 1922.

Professor Paul Guggenheim to HL, 23 November 1936

On instruction of the Executive Committee of the World Jewish Congress, I address a confidential request to you.

The German–Polish Convention on minority rights in Upper Silesia dated 15 May 1922, which to a large extent guaranteed minority rights to the Jews of Upper Silesia, will expire in July 1937. The Jews of Upper Silesia believe, and I think rightly so, that not all rights expire at that date, but rather that certain rights, for which no temporal limit was foreseen, continue to exist after that date. Above all, the rights in question are rights duly acquired in the zone of the referendum before the acquisition of Upper Silesia by Germany. These provisions will remain in force pursuant to the decision of the Ambassadorial Conference on 20 October 1922, under the guarantee and supervision of the major, formerly Allied Powers, in the first instance Great Britain, France and Italy.

The Jews of Upper Silesia have approached us in confidence. They would like to obtain the prolongation of the guarantees by diplomatic means. If this is not possible, they would like at a minimum to be allowed, similar to the Jews of the Saar region, to leave Germany with their personal wealth. Finally, they attach great importance to the presence of an international body at the local level in future, which guarantees and supervises those provisions of the Convention on Upper Silesia without time limit beyond 1937.

The Jews of Upper Silesia desire several legal opinions to be written by some renowned, non-Jewish, experts at the international level on the legal situation after expiry of the special minority protection rights. We have therefore thought

---

[83] 'Credentials of the Abyssinian Delegation', (1937) 18 *BYIL* 184–6. Reprinted in *Collected Papers*, Vol. 3, pp. 589–91.

of requesting a legal opinion from Professor Charles de Visscher. In addition, in our view it would be advisable to receive a legal opinion from an English lawyer in view of the fact that England is guarantor of the Convention on Upper Silesia by virtue of the decision of the Ambassadorial Conference. We thought above all of Fischer Williams and Brierly and we would be very grateful to you if you were to share your opinion with us whether either of these would be suitable and willing to write to such an opinion for us. We would be particularly interested to learn whether either one would have some influence in English public circles by writing a legal opinion.

We have also contemplated to ask an Italian instead of an English man, and I have thought of da Salvioli. It would be most kind of you if you could share your opinion with us whether the consultation of an Italian expert in present political conditions would be apt to create a favourable impression with the British government, the Foreign Office in particular, and if there is some hope of success with such an opinion, or whether a legal opinion by an English man would be preferable.

The text of Hersch's reply cannot be found, but the gist of it is reported in a letter from Guggenheim to the person who initiated the enquiry:

Professor Guggenheim to Ms Helene Heumann, 1 December 1936
Attached please find an exchange of letters with Professor H. Lauterpacht, London, on the subject of a legal opinion. Professor Lauterpacht, an absolutely trustworthy character, who will treat the matter in strict confidence, believes that requesting a legal opinion would not achieve the desired objective and would hardly influence the position of the British government at this point in time.

Personally – alongside the other men of Geneva – I share these concerns and fully agree with the opinion of Mr Lauterpacht.

I would be grateful if you could let me know whether, in spite of this, you insist on the creation of a legal opinion, or whether one should, to avoid unnecessary costs, wait for a point in time when a legal opinion becomes a critical ingredient to further our cause.

CHAPTER 4

CAMBRIDGE, 1937–1939:
THE WHEWELL CHAIR

Towards the end of 1936, McNair was appointed Vice-Chancellor of Liverpool University. He resigned the Whewell Chair of International Law with effect from the end of that year and ceased lecturing at Cambridge at the end of the Michaelmas term, 1936. He had it in mind that Hersch should succeed him and, no doubt to that end, he moved the Faculty to invite Hersch to teach in the Faculty at Cambridge once a week in the Lent Term, 1937, holding a weekly discussion class on Saturday morning for LLB students and a course of six lectures on the 'Legal Organisation of Peace' to be delivered at 5.20pm on Friday afternoons. The holding of the weekly discussion class was to be contingent on a sufficient number signing up for it. He was to be paid £70 if both the class and the lectures were held, but only £36 for the lectures alone.

Apart from his election to the ICJ in 1954, the most significant event in Hersch's career was his election in November 1937 to the Whewell Chair of International Law at Cambridge. The Chair had been established in 1867 under the will of William Whewell, Master of Trinity, 1841–66.[1] The Chair became one of the two principal chairs of the subject in England, the other being the Chichele Chair at Oxford held at the time of Hersch's election at Cambridge by Professor J. L. Brierly. The previous holders of the Cambridge Chair had been a diverse group and were not all dedicated international lawyers.[2] The first was Sir William

---

[1] William Whewell (1794–1866) was a polymath with a deep knowledge of astronomy, mathematics, geology, philosophy and divinity. He was also interested in international law, translating the treatise by Grotius entitled *Of the Law of Peace and War* from Latin into English. This interest was reflected in the provision of his will for the establishment of both a professorship in international law to be supported by the income from the properties in Cambridge adjacent to Trinity which he left to the College and a number of scholarships in the university 'to be obtained by proficiency in the subject of international law'. He added: 'And I enjoin the said Professor of International Law in his lectures and in all parts of his treatment of the subject of International Law to make it his aim to lay down such rules and to suggest such measures as may tend to diminish the evils of War and finally to extinguish War between Nations.' Arnold McNair gave Hersch a printed copy of the will inscribed 'You should have this. ADMcN'.

[2] See J. Crawford, 'Public International Law in Twentieth Century England', in *Jurists Uprooted: German-Speaking Emigré Lawyers in Twentieth-Century Britain*, ed. Beatson and Zimmerman (Oxford: Oxford University Press, 2004), pp. 681–704.

Harcourt, a distinguished Liberal politician, for whom international law was his 'passion, not profession', elected in 1869. His reputation as an international lawyer rested on the *Letters of Historicus* (published anonymously), a series of letters examining the subject of neutrality as practised by Britain during the American Civil War. So involved was he in national politics that, between 1883 and 1885, T. J. Lawrence[3] acted as his deputy while also serving as the vicar of Tadlow, Cambridgeshire. Harcourt was followed in 1887 by Henry Maine, a prodigious legal author, but with only a marginal interest in international law.[4] After Maine came John Westlake, described as 'the one major scholar to hold either the Oxford or Cambridge chairs in the nineteenth century'.[5] He remained as professor until he was 80.[6]

With the election in 1908 of Lassa Francis Lawrence Oppenheim,[7] an émigré from Germany via Switzerland, the chair came to be occupied by one whose name subsequently became a by-word for a comprehensive and systematic exposition of international law. He was followed by Pearce Higgins,[8] and then in 1935 by Arnold McNair.

Hersch's election to this distinguished succession within thirteen years of his arrival in England was an extraordinary achievement that did not go unnoticed. The principal alternative candidate appears to have been H. A. Smith, then Professor of International Law at the London School of Economics. His significant literary contribution to the subject by then was limited to a two-volume collection of materials, principally opinions

---

[3] Rev. Thomas Joseph Lawrence (1849–1920), Fellow and Tutor of Downing College, 1873–6; Honorary Fellow, 1908. Taught international law at Chicago, 1892–8, at the Royal Naval College, 1884–1909 and at Bristol University. Member of the Institut de Droit International. Also an ordained clergyman. Published a *Handbook of Public International Law*, 1885 and *Principles of International Law*, 1895.

[4] Sir Henry Sumner Maine (1822–88). Appointed Regius Professor of Civil Law at Cambridge in 1847, aged 25. Resigned in 1854. Published *Ancient Law* in 1861. Corpus Professor of Jurisprudence, Oxford, 1869–77. Whewell Professor, 1887–8. Lectures on *International Law*, published 1888.

[5] J. Crawford, 'Public International Law in Twentieth Century England', in *Jurists Uprooted: German-Speaking Émigré Lawyers in Twentieth-Century Britain*, ed. Beatson and Zimmerman (Oxford: Oxford University Press, 2004), p. 693.

[6] John Westlake (1828–1913). Practised at the Bar, 1854–88. Published *A Treatise on Private International Law* in 1888. Whewell Professor, 1888–1908. Published *Chapters on the Principles of International Law*, 1894, and *International Law, Part 1: Peace*, 1904, and *Part 2: War*, 1907.

[7] Oppenheim (1858–1919) was a renowned German jurist, and is regarded by many as the 'father of international law', especially with regards to the legal positivist school of thought. Oppenheim first lectured at the LSE, and, in 1908, became Whewell Professor of International Law at the University of Cambridge. He is the author of the seminal textbook, *Oppenheim's International Law: A Treatise*, published in 1905–6 (first edition).

[8] Alexander Pearce Higgins (1865–1935). Deputy Whewell Professor, 1908; Adviser on International Law in the Department of the Prosecutor-General and Treasury Solicitor, 1914–20; Lecturer in International Law at the LSE, 1908, and Professor in the University of London, 1918–23; Whewell Professor, 1920–35; Member of the Permanent Court of Arbitration, 1930.

of the Law Officers of the Crown, entitled *Great Britain and the Law of Nations*. As an objective matter, it could not stand comparison with Hersch's two major studies, *Private Law Sources* and *The Function of Law*. Some years later, Norman Bentwich told Hersch that he too had been a candidate, but was not at all distressed by his failure.

Hersch's success could hardly have been achieved without the loyal and active support of McNair, who guided and instructed him as to the form of application – even to the extent of going to some trouble to dig out and send him a copy of his own application for the chair. McNair also advised him to ask Gutteridge[9] and Fischer Williams[10] if he might give their names as referees. Gutteridge agreed, but Fischer Williams excused himself on the ground that the 'competitors will or may be personal friends'.[11] A friendly eye was kept on the process by Douglas Logan, a former colleague at the LSE who had recently become a teaching Fellow at Trinity and was on good terms with Professor Hollond, also a Fellow of Trinity and one of the electors to the chair. The other electors were Professor W. W. Buckland (the former Regius Professor of Civil Law),[12] Sir Cecil Hurst (former Legal Adviser of the Foreign Office and a judge of the Permanent Court of International Justice), Professor Percy Winfield (Professor of English Law), and three non-lawyers, Benions, Clapham and Reddaway (two of them were historians and the third was an economist). Other LSE colleagues – notably Ivor Jennings – sent encouragement: 'Don't let modesty interfere with your candidature ... even if a colleague of ours is a candidate too.'[13] Harold Laski, another LSE friend, wrote in similar terms.

Earlier, McNair had asked Hersch whether he would be interested in writing a book on recognition in international law.

McNair to HL, 8 March 1937

I am writing to you, with Gutteridge's approval, to know whether you would be so good as to give us a promise of a volume, and in particular whether you would consider sympathetically the suggestion of a volume on 'Recognition in

---

[9] Harold Cooke Gutteridge (1876–1953), Cassel Professor of Law, London University, 1919–30; Professor of Comparative Law, Cambridge University, 1930–41.

[10] See Chapter 3, n. 67, p. 68, above.   [11] Fischer Williams to HL, 10 September 1937.

[12] Buckland was Regius Professor of Civil Law and a close friend of McNair. An eminent lawyer who was a student of Buckland told the following story, which may well be apocryphal: He was waiting for a tutorial from Buckland who, when he arrived, told him that he was unable to give him any time as he was rushing to an Appointments Committee meeting for the Whewell Professorship. Buckland mentioned that there was one candidate, Lauterpacht, an Austrian and a Jew, to whom there was some opposition. Buckland said he was head and shoulders superior to any other candidate, and that, if he was not appointed, he (Buckland) intended to resign his Chair. But Hersch was elected.

[13] W. Ivor Jennings to HL, 1 July 1937.

International Law'. It seems to me that such a book would have a very considerable appeal for the following reasons: What before the war was considered a Recognition, namely, of new States, of new Governments and of belligerents, although the subject of a good deal of periodical literature, has never been comprehensively treated in a monograph in English. Moreover, since the war it has developed enormously in importance, and there have been a considerable number of decisions upon it. In addition, the whole question of Recognition and non-Recognition of situations, facts, treaties, etc., in the Stimsonian sense of the word is completely new, and practically nothing has been written except Fischer Williams' 'Hague Lectures' and articles in periodicals. What is really wanted now is some new Historicus to enlighten the public as was done in the 1860s. It occurs to me that once you get Oppenheim and the Annual Digest out of the way, you might be able to give time to this before you get on to your big text book.

Hersch accepted the invitation and began work on what was to become the fourth of his major contributions to international law. Though largely written in 1937–8 and completed by 1939, the outbreak of war prevented immediate publication. It was set aside to be revised and published after the war. It appeared in 1947 and then began to influence the British Government's views on the subject.[14]

In August 1937, Hersch gave a course of lectures at The Hague Academy and then went to Villars in Switzerland for a rest. Whilst on the train,

5 km before Lausanne my black hat flew out of the window and lay beautifully on the line. When I came to Lausanne I went to the Office d'Objets Trouvés. They telephoned to that post and there is a chance that they will send the thing to the railway station at Villars.[15]

There is no record of its recovery.

In the midst of all this, McNair added to Hersch's burden with the task of reading four heavy prize essays for which McNair could not find the time.

The appointment process dragged on, with Logan sending Hersch a telegram on 8 October, after his return from holiday, to say that no decision had yet been reached. This was followed almost immediately by a further telegram saying that the election 'had been postponed for a month'. McNair wrote sympathetic and supportive letters, reassuring Hersch, who had expressed some concern on the subject, that it would not occur to anyone to doubt his loyalty. It was not until 13 November 1937 that Hersch received the good news of his election that day. Hersch's

[14] See pp. 299–300 and 332–8 below.   [15] HL to RL, 25 April 1937.

85

appointment was to take effect from 1 January 1938. Before that date, however, he made a brief introductory visit to Cambridge.

HL to RL, November 1937
I have been having a very busy twenty-four hours. Discussed yesterday with King[16] for over five hours various business matters; dined at Pembroke; this morning I saw the Registrar and the Bursar at Trinity; saw Winfield; inspected the Library; lunched with Gutteridge and the Secretary of the Faculty; saw King again; and had interesting and instructive tea with the Goldsteins. I am dining to-night with Wade[17] and seeing Buckland and others to-morrow.

The question of the house will have to be gone into thoroughly. We must not do anything in a hurry.

A letter from Douglas Logan gave Hersch warning that he would be receiving an invitation from Harry Hollond to come to the Audit Feast in Trinity at the end of the month, and added that Hersch:

must come – it doesn't matter what you have to cut in order to attend. You will get an introduction to the Combination Room under Hollond's wing and that counts for something.[18]

The news of Hersch's election was followed by many letters of congratulation. The letter that meant most to him was from his mother.

Deborah Lauterpacht to HL, 17 November 1937
My dearest and beloved son!
For this piece of good news I thank you thousands of times. I congratulate you and send you my warmest wishes for many years of happiness and health. Let us all stay in good health. Now I can see that my tears and my prayers were not in vain because I prayed not only at Yom Kippur, but every Saturday when I was at synagogue selecting the Torah ... Thank God that he listened to me. My dear, you may imagine how happy we are. Dad is not in Lwów so we cannot be happy together but we immediately sent him a telegram to Gdynia so that he could be happy with this news. Please congratulate Rachel in my name. I hope you will be together for many, many years so that you can raise your beloved child in happiness. Stay healthy. I kiss you many times and Rachel and your dear Eli. I kiss you heartily.

Your happy mother,
Dora [Deborah]

---

[16] Brian King, Fellow of Pembroke College, Cambridge, who was also teaching International Law.
[17] E. C. S. Wade, Professor of English Law, principally constitutional law, not to be confused with H. W. R. Wade, a younger man and an expert in real property law who also became Professor at Oxford and then returned to Cambridge as Master of Gonville and Caius College.
[18] D. W. Logan to HL, 2 November 1937.

Another letter from his former teacher, Hans Kelsen, gave him special pleasure:

Hans Kelsen to HL, 3 December 1937
Esteemed and dear colleague!
Newspapers report your appointment to a chair in the University of Cambridge. I probably do not need to mention how much joy I experienced at these news. Please allow me to send you my heartfelt congratulations on this extraordinary achievement of yours. As you long ago became one of the leading teachers of international law, your appointment at one of the world's leading universities has only confirmed externally what is due to you on the basis of your brilliant scientific achievements. For all those who are interested in the advancement of science and therefore in the good spirit in the universities, this is a moment of great satisfaction, as universities still exist where merit is rewarded, in spite of all political prejudices.

Please do not regard it as a sign of immodesty, esteemed colleague, if I not only take great joy in your great and deserved success, but if I am also a bit proud. You will certainly understand, that I fondly remember at this particular point in time with inner satisfaction, that you have been my student and that your writings 'echo my own intellect'. Please let me thus thank you for raising my awareness that I have not worked in vain.

I remain with kindest regards.

Yours,
Hans Kelsen

The Legal Adviser of the Foreign Office, Sir William Malkin, said:

At least since the days of Oppenheim there has been a tradition that the Whewell Professor and the Foreign Office should help each other when they could, and I am sure that you will be ready to carry on the tradition.[19]

Hersch's former colleague at the LSE, Philip Noel-Baker, wrote:

It is the more important because of the other candidate whom you defeated. I am extremely happy to think that Cambridge is to have your eminent assistance, and that you will now have the additional authority conferred by the Whewell Chair. I hope the day will come when I shall be able to help you more effectively than I now can in labouring for the cause of real International Law.[20]

---

[19] Malkin to HL, 19 November 1937.   [20] Noel-Baker to HL, 19 November 1937.

One letter to which Hersch attached special importance was from Sir William Beveridge, the Director of the LSE.[21] Though brief, it occasioned a rather full reply from Hersch.

Sir William Beveridge to HL, 15 November 1937

My dear Lauterpacht,

Hearty congratulations on your thoroughly well deserved election at Cambridge. I am glad it has turned out this way in the end.

Yours very sincerely,
William Beveridge

HL to Sir William Beveridge, 16 November 1937

Dear Sir William,

It was kind of you to send me so promptly your wishes and congratulations.

There is – with the exception of McNair – no one whose message in this matter I value as highly as yours. You were very kind to me ever since I came to the School. You appointed me and you gave me an ample and most generous opportunity of work. You helped me with the publication of my own books and you made possible the publication of the Digest. My feeling towards you has always been one of profound gratitude and, since that Professorial Council when you put the case of the German refugees, of great affection.

I can quite imagine that you, Director, are glad about my appointment to the Whewell Chair. You have made it possible in many ways.

I feel that the Electors have been magnanimous and I am most anxious to justify their confidence.

May I use this opportunity for sending you personally my fervent wishes for your happiness and prosperity at Oxford.

Once more, with much gratitude.

Yours very sincerely,
H. Lauterpacht[22]

Others who wrote included McNair, Bentwich, Brierly, Kahn-Freund, Goodhart, Oppenheim's widow, Daube, Schwarzenberger and Wortley. Especially welcoming were the letters from his prospective Cambridge colleagues, Gutteridge, E. C. S. Wade, Winfield, King and Laffan. A number of his LSE colleagues added their good wishes, notably, Laski, Eileen Power and Gower.

---

[21] Sir William Beveridge (1879–1963), created 1st Baron Beveridge, 1946. Graduated from Oxford with first-class honours in *literae humaniores* and then embarked on a legal career; became a Law Fellow of University College, Oxford, 1902–9; was much involved in matters relating to labour and employment as chairman of various government committees; was a senior civil servant, 1915–19; Director of the LSE, 1919–37; and Master of University College, Oxford, 1937–45. His period at the LSE covered the time that Hersch was there.

[22] LSE archive, 2/B/37/4.

He left the LSE with regret. He had been happy and had made his mark there as an outstanding international lawyer. Many of the friendships that he had formed there survived for a long while. Although Hersch did not officially assume the duties of Whewell Professor until 1 January 1938, he was already inscribed, in the Lent and Easter Terms of 1937, as continuing McNair's course on State and diplomatic immunity. The first record of his giving lectures in his own right appears in the lecture list for the Michaelmas Term, 1938, when he was entered as giving two lectures a week on 'The General Principles of the Law of Peace' at the undergraduate level at 12 noon on Tuesdays and Thursdays. These were to be the times at which he lectured for the ensuing seventeen years of his tenure. He also gave classes on 'Recognition in International Law' to the LLB (now called the LLM) group on Mondays at 11am in the Michaelmas Term; and, in the Easter Term, 1939, he held four LLB discussion classes on 'Leading Prize Cases During the War of 1914–18'. In the academic year 1939–40, he continued both with undergraduate lectures and, for the LLB group, with his Monday classes on 'Problems and Disputed Points of International Law'.

His undergraduate lectures were presented under headings analogous to the private law concepts of persons, property, contract, tort, constitutional and administrative law and procedure.[23] In addition, during the Lent Term, 1938, he gave a course of six lectures on 'The Legal Organisation of Peace'. Though the printed syllabus for these lectures does not identify them as being for the graduate LLB students, their specialised character makes it likely that this was so. The topics covered were: 'Law and Force in the Settlement of International Disputes'; 'Settlement of Disputes by Conciliation'; 'Conference and Agreement'; 'Obligations of Arbitral and Judicial Settlement'; 'Enforcement of Pacific Settlement'; 'Collective Security'; and 'Revision of the Status Quo'. After his first lecture following the commencement of his tenure on 1 January 1938, he wrote to Rachel, who was at home in London:

It was delightful to receive your letter. It made all the difference to the lecture which, I believe, was a good one. There was a crowded room of over two hundred eager students, and I was quite eloquent. I cannot, of course, judge the effect, but I have received enthusiastic reports. The voice carried very well. I am now preparing the lecture for tomorrow afternoon. The hotel is not too bad, in any case, it is probable that I shall get my rooms at the end of the month.

---

[23] These appeared in a printed syllabus, now in the Squire Law Library.

He was at that time staying in a hotel as his rooms in Trinity were not yet available.

William Whewell had prescribed in his will that the Professor of International Law should be a member of the Foundation of Trinity College. This did not mean that he would be a Fellow, only that he would have many of the privileges of a Fellow, but without a say in the running of the College. Most of Hersch's predecessors had been, or soon became, Fellows of other colleges, thus making them independent of Trinity, though they received invitations to college feasts and to some extent participated in the social life of the college. Hersch was not immediately invited to become a Fellow – this did not happen until 1945. However, in May 1938, he was invited to become a Fellow of Downing College, a much smaller and poorer establishment than Trinity. He declined, explaining that he felt unable to divide his obligations between two colleges.

During the year of the move from London, and before the family moved into 6 Cranmer Road in Cambridge, he was assigned a set of rooms, L2 Nevile's Court, in Trinity, so that he had somewhere to stay in Cambridge. It was an agreeable set of rooms on the north side of Nevile's Court, with the two large windows of the sitting room and the one window of the study facing south over Nevile's Court. There was a small bedroom, but no bathroom. Washing facilities in College were then still fairly primitive. A wash basin and slop bucket were dealt with by a daily cleaning woman called a 'bedmaker' who attended every morning. Breakfast was sent up from the college kitchens, which enjoyed a high reputation for their cooking. The furniture in the room belonged not to the college, but to the previous occupant from whom Hersch bought it at a valuation. When he moved out of college, Hersch found it convenient to retain some of it to help furnish his new house.

Rachel did not immediately accompany Hersch to Cambridge but remained for the time being in London while the house there was disposed of and a home was found in Cambridge. However, in June 1938, Hersch bought, direct from Arnold McNair, the remaining years of the lease of 6 Cranmer Road for £1,800. This house was to be his home for the remainder of his life and that of Rachel who died there in 1989. The rest of 1938 was taken up with the redecoration of the house and the move from London.

By September 1938, the family was completely installed at 6 Cranmer Road – a road in those days regarded as a very 'professorial' one. At No. 4 lived the Regius Professor of Hebrew, D. Winton Thomas; at No. 8 there was Dr Brooks, an elderly former cleric; at No. 13 Professor Winfield, the author of a leading student text book on the law of tort; at No. 19 Professor A. B. Cook, Emeritus Professor of Classical Archaeology, whose daughter also ran a small elementary school there; at No. 17 Sir Ernest Barker, the Professor of Political Science; and at No. 23 Professor Frank Debenham, the Professor of Geography, who had accompanied Scott on his last expedition and who was Director of the Scott Polar Research Institute at Cambridge. Later on, Professor Hamson moved into No. 7 and Professor Radzinowicz into No. 21.

Though a reasonably large house, No. 6 was, in fact, only a semi-detached one, its conjoined neighbour being No. 8. Downstairs, there were the necessary reception rooms – a south-facing sitting room and a garden-facing dining room, together with a smaller sitting room always called 'the little study' in contrast to Hersch's larger study upstairs. There was a butler's pantry, connecting the dining room with the kitchen, and, beyond the kitchen a scullery where the cooking was done. When not entertaining, and if there was no resident domestic help, the family ate in the kitchen.

On the first floor, there were four rooms: Hersch's study, facing north, looking over the garden; Rachel's bedroom, facing south; Hersch's bedroom; and my own smaller room. There was one bathroom and a separate lavatory. This left two rooms on the top floor, for a maid or cook when there was one and for occasional guests or for the obligatory lodgers during the war – initially two students from the LSE, which had been evacuated to Cambridge, and later a distinguished and most welcome army officer, Colonel Tommy Robbins, and his wife.

There was no central heating until after 1951, when Hersch, as a result of his professional activity, could afford to install it. Till then, heating depended on gas fires in the bedrooms and 'cozy stoves', quite efficient closed anthracite-burning stoves, in the entrance hall, in the dining room and in the study. In the kitchen, there was a coke-burning 'Ideal' boiler which provided the domestic hot water. All these stoves required constant care – riddling at least twice a day to clear the grate of ash and clinker and replenishing with fuel. When there was no maid or daily help, this task fell to Rachel. Hersch did not concern himself with it save for putting more anthracite on the stove in his study. In this way, the house was kept moderately warm in winter – though it involved moving rapidly from one pool of warmth to another.

Economy remained an ever-present preoccupation in family life. Although Hersch's income was greater in Cambridge (the salary of a professor was £1,200 a year) than it had been in London where, as first a lecturer and then a reader, he had earned little more than £500 a year, money was always short. The cost of the move from London was considerable; much new furniture – principally for the sitting room and the dining room – had to be bought. Hersch allowed himself the indulgence of a fine new mahogany pedestal leather-topped desk costing £25, and an impressive walnut elbow chair costing £5 10s to go with it. The house in London had been a rented one, so there was no capital available upon giving it up. A mortgage helped to cover the cost of No. 6. But there was little to spare after paying for redecoration (the cost of which was kept helpfully low with the assistance of Rachel's brother, Maurice, an architect in London). Money was really the only subject on which Hersch and Rachel ever fell out – usually due to an occasional extravagant lapse on Rachel's part, perhaps in buying a new dress to play her part in supporting her husband in the Cambridge social scene.

The latter was not an easy task for her. Sometime during the 1920s or early 1930s, Rachel became quite deaf and had to resort to various types of hearing aid. Initially, these were heavy and cumbersome instruments in the form of a small box connected to an earphone. She tried to conceal the box in her bodice and the earphone by her hairdo, but their very presence was a source of strain for her. They often failed to perform satisfactorily. Sometimes, in the middle of a lunch or dinner conversation, the instrument would begin to emit a high-pitched whistle, of which Rachel did not immediately become aware – and there would be a moment of embarrassment. For her, it was a difficult period – only relieved in the early 1950s, and then imperfectly, by a fenestration operation on each ear, one performed in New York by the originator of the operation, Dr Lempert, the other in London. But deafness remained with her for the rest of her life, as did dependence upon one or another hearing aid. And, as they became smaller and more sophisticated, so did they become more difficult for an ageing lady to manipulate. However, during the active Cambridge years, 1937–54, Rachel dealt bravely with her affliction and enabled Hersch to provide necessary lunches, teas or dinners to his university colleagues or visitors from abroad, which had to be done with some frequency.

Soon after his appointment, Hersch invested £90 in a car – a second-hand Standard saloon, painted dark blue. He took driving lessons and passed the test, but was never a confident driver. On one occasion, so the story goes, when reaching a fork in the road between Stevenage and Graveley (those days were long before the present M11 motorway), he was so uncertain whether to turn left or right that he compromised, albeit at a very slow speed, by driving straight ahead and colliding with the signpost! The car remained in use until the outbreak of war and was later sold. It was not replaced until 1949 when a second-hand Riley sports saloon was purchased. It was used at least once to carry the family to Geneva, driven by myself and a friend of mine. But Hersch always insisted firmly from the rear seat that the speed should never exceed 50 mph.

For Hersch and Rachel, the rather formalised university social routine appropriate to a newly appointed professor soon began. At that time, there were only about forty-two professors in the university and there was a clear understanding of their hierarchical status. Between their wives, certain social conventions operated. The wives of existing professors called at 6 Cranmer Road, leaving their visiting cards with one corner turned up. Calls were in due course returned by Rachel, who would visit at the customary time – tea-time – for a cup of tea. In those days, the provision by the hostess of a Fitzbillies sponge cake, price 1s (alas, no longer available) was mandatory.

Most houses had resident domestic staff – usually a maid, often also a cook-housekeeper – and things remained that way till (and for some throughout) the war. However, Hersch and Rachel did not like the intrusion into their privacy involved in resident domestic staff and preferred to make use of regular daily help. Even so, for a while, they employed and gave a home to a mother and daughter, German refugees, but it was not a comfortable relationship and ended with the outbreak of the war.

Hersch found himself invited to dinner in various colleges by his professorial colleagues in the Law Faculty. Amongst the most prominent of these was Professor Winfield (later Sir Percy), a Fellow of St John's, who specialised in the law of torts, Professor S. J. Bailey, also of St John's, an expert in property law, Professor W. W. Buckland, the Regius Professor of Civil Law, Fellow of Gonville and Caius College, and Professor Harold Cooke Gutteridge, of Trinity Hall, the Professor of Comparative Law. Gutteridge, who had previously taught, and been a supporter of, Hersch at the LSE, also had a substantial commercial law practice at the Bar.

As Whewell Professor, Hersch was entitled to rooms in Trinity and to take meals in Hall (the college dining room). When the house at Cranmer Road was ready, he was able to give up his residential rooms in college. But he was then allocated a study in Whewell's Court in Trinity. In addition, he had a room of his own in the Squire Law Library (the library of the Faculty of Law). A benefactor, Rebecca Flower Squire, had originally left money for a law library at Downing Street in Cambridge. In 1935, when the main University Library moved to its new building off West Road, part of its former premises in the Old Schools was assigned to the Squire Law Library. This comprised the magnificent reading room in the upper part of the Cockerell Building, together with a smaller room at the side. Leading off the length of the main reading room were a number of small offices, their windows facing north over Senate House Passage and Gonville and Caius College. Room No. 7 became Hersch's room for his exclusive use, and there it was that he regularly saw most of his research students from 1938 to 1954. The room was sparsely furnished with an oak table and, more importantly, an oak chair, with an upholstered green velvet seat bearing a brass plaque indicating that it had been presented to the library by A. Pearce Higgins when he was Whewell Professor. Though, of course, not officially the 'Whewell Chair', it came to be regarded as the symbol of that position. The walls of this room were covered with framed photographs of many distinguished foreign international lawyers which had been collected by Oppenheim.[24]

At that time, the Squire Law Library was quite a small place. Its total number of books was probably no more than 130,000, and it subscribed to 50 periodicals. There were only two members of staff. The librarian formally designated by the Faculty was Dr T. Ellis Lewis, who began life as a coal miner in Wales, where he lost several fingers of his right hand. He had then, despite all the odds, studied law, qualified at the Bar and had been appointed an assistant lecturer in law, specialising in the law of torts. He was a kindly and gregarious man, generally known by his acronym 'TEL'. A Fellow of Trinity Hall, he spent many hours in the social company of the students he taught. As Librarian, he had a double-size room near the entrance of the Squire from which he supervised the work of the Library's very small staff. One was Mr Staines, tall, slender and bald, with gold-rimmed spectacles, who did all the administrative work of ordering and cataloguing books and keeping the Faculty's accounts. He was helped by the burly figure of Hill, one of the university 'bulldogs', who, when not working in the Library, accompanied the Proctors as they patrolled the streets at night on the lookout for undergraduates not wearing gowns or otherwise misbehaving. It was his job to keep the Library tidy and restack the books left on tables by the readers. The atmosphere in the Squire was tranquil and studious, in keeping with its furnishings of oak tables and chairs and the impressive impact of its magnificent barrel-vaulted ceiling.

---

[24] These photographs are now in the Lauterpacht Centre for International Law, 5 Cranmer Road, Cambridge.

The Law Faculty also had the use of five lecture rooms on the ground floor of the buildings known as the Old Schools of which the Squire was part. Even earlier, before the Old Schools became the University Library, law had been taught in the Old Schools (hence the name 'Old Schools') and there was, therefore, a certain historical continuity in the return there of the Law Faculty in 1935. It was a continuity of which many were unaware, among them, those who agreed to abandon the Old Schools site in 1995 for the move to the modern law school on the West Road site.

The principal lecture room was Room 3, a long room able to seat about 300, with windows on the south side facing onto King's College Chapel, formed out of a number of smaller rooms and given a sloping floor focusing on an elegant eighteenth-century pine lecturer's lectern (now in the entrance lobby of the new Law School). In this room, Hersch regularly gave his Law Tripos general course at 12 noon on Tuesdays and Thursdays. His lectures, although not compulsory, having gained a high reputation for substantive content as well as entertainment and good humour, retained throughout the year an audience not limited to students from the Law Faculty. A lecture review in *Varsity*, the undergraduate newspaper, had this to say in November 1947:

Professor Lauterpacht is a lecturer with only one fault. He window-gazes. Apart from this, he is a first-class lecturer, with a well practiced and polished technique. He uses his hands to good purpose – an unusual accomplishment among lecturers. The notes taken at his lectures are as comprehensive, clear and well-ordered as a book. His exposition of difficult points is lucid. There is a mystery about him, though. What private joke causes that little smile to hover eternally on his lips?

On the days when he gave his Tripos lectures, Hersch devoted the earlier part of the morning to their preparation. He did not lecture from elaborate and detailed notes (a significant advance from his practice at the LSE when he was still developing his lecturing technique and wrote out his lectures in full) but took into the room no more than two or three sheets of paper on which, in a sparse manner, he had jotted down a few headings. They were all that he needed to enable him to cover the ground in sufficient detail to justify his assertion that, if a student came regularly to his lectures, took careful notes and also read Brierly's *Law of Nations*, he would be able to get a good second in the exams. What a difference there is between the content of international law then and today![25]

The lecture being at noon, Hersch would leave home at about 11.15am to walk by an unvarying route down West Road, through the Backs of King's and up Senate House Passage. He considered that a lecturer owed it to his audience to dress in a respectable manner. Casual clothing was never contemplated. Instead, a dark grey suit, white shirt with stiff white collar, a suitably discreet and understated tie – all covered by a dark grey top coat, worn always with a black homburg hat. A briefcase would hold his few notes and a change of shirt for after the lecture. Despite his command of the subject, a certain nervousness underlay his performance – reflecting perhaps his awareness that his accent was obviously foreign, not distractingly so, but still not an English one, and he felt it to be a disadvantage. So the lecture was physically taxing. Afterwards, he would go up to his room, change and walk home for lunch. When I was an undergraduate reading international law, I went to his lectures and always walked home with him. On one occasion, when I was approaching the end of my fifth and postgraduate year in the university, my urge to move away from Cambridge and to get started professionally led me to quote to him George Bernard Shaw's observation that 'those who can, do, and those who can't, teach'. He replied, 'That may be, but let me tell you, it's a good life.' It was only much later, when I had spent many years trying to be both a good practitioner and a sufficient academic, that I recognised the profound truth of his reply. Though substantial exposure to practice enhances one's substantive knowledge of the subject in a way that enables one to be a more stimulating and effective teacher, there can be little doubt that the time and energy taken by heavy practice limit opportunities for the deep, disinterested and imaginative research and exploration which are the essential elements of significant academic work, so characteristic of Hersch's contribution.

On most days, after his lunch and a short rest, Hersch was free to pursue his other academic work. The exception was Wednesday when he held his weekly seminars on some pre-assigned topic of discussion. These would last one and a half hours. The participants, never numbering more than twenty, would be LLB students specialising in international law and most of the research students working in the field.

---

[25] In 1938, he produced a printed syllabus of 117 pages. See p. 89 above. But this practice lapsed during the war and was not revived afterwards.

To the latter, Hersch gave serious and devoted attention. Many of those whom he supervised during the period 1948–55 went on to play distinguished roles in the field.[26] Hersch was thus the father of what came to be known in the international legal community as 'the Cambridge Mafia' – a body of Cambridge-trained international lawyers which, even if all its members did not necessarily share his views, nonetheless adhered to his commitment to the subject and sought to maintain the high standards of technical excellence that he set.

In addition to his teaching and his guidance and care of his research students, from the time that he came to Cambridge until he took up his position in the ICJ, Hersch produced a steady stream of books, articles, and memoranda. These will be mentioned at appropriate places in the pages that follow.

Sometime in the autumn of 1938, in his capacity as editor of the *AD*, Hersch circulated to the Advisory Committee of that publication certain proposals, of which no record exists except a letter from one member,

---

[26] George Barton, from New Zealand (born 1926). Pursued a career at the Bar there, in which he earned the highest respect. Nico Bar-Yaacov (born 1926) came from Israel to work on dual nationality and returned to Jerusalem, later becoming Professor of International Law at the Hebrew University. Richard Baxter (1921–80), already mentioned as a most helpful contributor to the *International Law Reports*, returned to Harvard where he became Professor of International Law and, in 1979, judge of the ICJ. Hans Blix (born 1928), from Sweden, worked on the law of treaties, returned to Uppsala to become a Professor, then Legal Adviser of the Swedish Foreign Ministry, Foreign Minister of Sweden and Director-General of the International Atomic Energy Agency for sixteen years. After being Chairman of UNMOVIC, he acquired high international prominence as Chief Weapons Inspector for the UN in Iraq. Michael Brandon (born 1923), worked for a while in the UN Legal Division, then established a highly successful practice in Switzerland as a trust law adviser. Iain MacGibbon, who wrote two major articles on estoppel and acquiescence, proceeded to Edinburgh as Professor of International Law. Felice Morgenstern (1926–2000), of Newnham College, Cambridge, worked on problems of jurisdiction and procedural abuse and then in 1952 went as a lawyer to the ILO where she gained a reputation as an outstanding draftsman, and remained as deputy to the Legal Adviser until her retirement in 1982. Daniel O'Connell (1924–79), from New Zealand, wrote three major works, one on *State Succession*, the other a comprehensive two-volume treatise on international law and a treatise on the law of the sea. From being Professor of International Law at Adelaide, he moved to Oxford as Chichele Professor in 1972, over-extended himself by excessive work and travel and died in 1979 at the age of 55. Christopher Pinto (born 1931), from Sri Lanka, went as a legal adviser first to his Foreign Ministry at home, then to the World Bank followed by the International Atomic Energy Agency. He was a member of the ILC, 1973–81. After playing an important part in the negotiation of the UN Convention on the Law of the Sea, he became (in 1982) Secretary-General of the Iran–US Claims Tribunal. Stephen M. Schwebel (born 1929) came from the United States to read international law at Cambridge and, after working for some years in a major New York law firm, went first to Harvard as an Assistant Professor before moving on to the State Department as an Assistant Legal Adviser for United Nations Affairs and to the American Society of International Law as Executive Director and concurrently as Burling Professor of International Law at the School of Advanced International Studies of the Johns Hopkins University. He returned to the State Department in 1973, first as Counselor on International Law, then as a Deputy Legal Adviser, 1974–80. He was a member of the International Law Commission, 1977–81, was nominated for election to the seat on the ICJ left vacant by the early death of Richard Baxter and served as judge of the ICJ from 1981 until 2000, becoming President in 1997.

Professor Edwin D. Dickinson of the Boult Hill School of Law, Berkeley, California, dated 7 September 1938. From the enthusiastic response in this letter, it would appear that Hersch probably had consulted the members of the Advisory Committee on the idea of expanding the title of the *Annual Digest* to become *Annual Digest and Reports of Public International Law Cases*.[27] It was his intention to expand the *AD* into a proper series of reports, something which he eventually did in 1956.

In the course of 1938, Hersch, having been actively engaged in writing his monograph on *Recognition in International Law*, of which the publication was delayed until 1947 because of the war, became rather concerned with the case of *The Arantzazu Mendi* in the English courts, in which the status of the Nationalist authorities in Spain was in issue.[28] Did the Nationalist Government amount to a State entitled to state immunity in proceedings in the English courts? Although no direct trace has been found of Hersch's views, a letter to him from Mr Pilcher, KC,[29] leading counsel for the Republican Government, suggests that Hersch had given him some assistance in the form of a note supportive of the view that the Nationalist Government did not constitute a State and was not entitled to immunity. This view was not accepted by the House of Lords.[30] Subsequently, Hersch criticised the decision in Chapter XVII of his book on recognition.[31]

Brierly evidently shared Hersch's hostility to the Nationalist Government: 'I feel so bitter about the Spanish question that I can hardly trust myself to speak of it to anyone who takes a different view.' Commenting on an editorial in *The Times* supportive of the Nationalist position, Brierly reported that a junior member of the Government had recently described that paper as a 'pro-Nazi rag'.[32]

In February 1939, Hersch received a request from the Jewish Agency for Palestine for an opinion concerning Article 18 of the Palestine Mandate. To this he responded with a substantial opinion,[33] for which he charged a fee of 75 guineas. This was probably the first substantial professional opinion that he wrote. The question was whether the obligation placed upon the Mandatory by Article 18 of the Mandate to ensure that there was no discrimination in Palestine against the nationals of any Member of the League of Nations precluded the introduction of a system of differential tariffs on goods imported into Palestine so as to

---

[27] See the Preface to the volume of the *AD* for 1933 and 1934, now Vol. 7 of the *ILR*.
[28] See 9 *ILR* 60.   [29] 9 *ILR* 61.
[30] *Recognition in International Law*, pp. 279–94 and p. 368.
[31] *Ibid.*, pp. 278–94.   [32] J. L. Brierly to HL, 20 February 1939.
[33] Now printed in the *Collected Papers*, Vol. 3, pp. 85–100.

favour countries which took a correspondingly larger share of Palestinian goods. Hersch reached the conclusion that it did not. The subsequent use made of that opinion is not known. In August 1939, Hersch was also asked by the Jewish Agency whether the British Government's policy, as laid down in the White Paper, regarding immigration, the registration of land sales and constitutional changes was incompatible with the Palestinian Mandate. There is no document indicating what, if any, reply Hersch gave to this question.

Hersch retained strong feelings of affection for the LSE even many years after he had moved away. Having attended in July 1958 a dinner at the LSE for the Editorial Committee of the *Modern Law Review*, he was struck by the absence – with the exception of some fine pieces lent by Sir Alexander Carr-Saunders – of the silver table ornaments customary on such occasions. He was moved to write to the Director of the LSE:

The other day I handed over to Professor Gower a Georgian silver Cup and Cover and I asked him to be good enough to enquire whether it would be acceptable as a gift to mark my association – dating back to 1923 – with the School as one of its former students and teachers and my gratitude for the many kindnesses which I received from it and from friends and colleagues in the London School of Economics. I am now very pleased to learn that the presentation is acceptable. The date of the cup and cover is 1777; the maker is John Carter; the weight is 96 ozs 5 dwts ...

There is little – by way of external embellishment – which can be added to the intrinsic splendour of that great academic society of the LSE. But I thought then that, however non-essential, this is a factor of some slight importance in fostering the communal life of an institution such as the London School of Economics and in adding to the sense of occasion and to the pleasure of its present and past members invited to official functions, and I felt that a modest beginning might perhaps be made in that direction.[34]

34 HL to Sir Sydney Caine, 24 August 1958.

CHAPTER 5

THE WAR YEARS, PART I:
SEPTEMBER 1939–JANUARY 1941

In reading this chapter about Hersch's life during the Second World War, one may ask why it contains so little direct reference to the events of the war, for example, the fall of France, the Battle of Britain, the United States' entry into the war, and the invasion of Europe. This is not because Hersch was indifferent to such matters. Far from it. He was fully aware of them. Listening to the news on the wireless and reading *The Times* were part of his daily routine. He was too old – 42 at the outbreak of the War – for military service. Nonetheless, as will be seen, he was active in war-related matters. Important amongst these were his two missions to the United States in 1940–1 and 1942. Ostensibly, they were to give lectures, but actually they were intended to garner support in the American academic community for the British position, especially in the period before the United States entered the war. Also important in that earlier period was the assistance that he gave to the United States Attorney-General in developing the arguments supportive of the American position of qualified neutrality and in thus combating the hostility amongst some American academics. He was active also in the development from 1942 onwards of the procedures for the trial of German war criminals. Compared to these contributions, his roles in the Home Guard as a firewatcher were small though pertinent items. And most of this was done against an emotional background of separation from Rachel and myself and of distress about the fate of his family taken captive by the Germans in Poland and eventually murdered.[1]

The Second World War began on 1 September 1939 with the German invasion of Poland from the west, south and north and the Soviet Union's invasion from the east. By late September 1939, Soviet forces had occupied Lwów, where Hersch's parents lived. However, in June 1941, the Soviets were driven out of Lwów by the Germans. The removal of Jews, of whom there were some 160,000 in the city, did not begin until March 1942. It was still possible for Hersch's family to send out some letters.

---

[1] See Chapter 10 below.

Two were received in New York from Poland in March 1941 and were forwarded to him by sea, a thoughtless economy. The sender was 'D. Turkenkopf', the maiden name of his mother.[2] We do not know whether he received them. Such others as may have been sent to Hersch in Cambridge were not received. Nazi treatment of the Jews was sufficiently well known for Hersch to have been greatly concerned about the fate of his family, even though he had only seen his parents three times since he left for Vienna in 1919. After their last visit to England in 1935, when he tried but failed to persuade them to remain in England, he never saw them or any others of his family again, except his niece, Inka, whom he found in a displaced persons camp in Austria after the war and brought to Cambridge in 1946.[3]

Though he doubtless talked to Rachel about his worries, whatever he may have felt or said to her was never made known to me. He may have mentioned his concern to McNair who, in a letter in March 1940, expressed the hope that Hersch was not suffering from too much anxiety concerning his family. With two exceptions, on 13 July 1941 and 7 December 1942,[4] there is no mention of the Polish family in the many letters that he sent to Rachel and me between 1942 and 1944. This silence suggests a deliberate decision on his part to close himself off from their fate, not out of any lack of love or absence of distress, but simply out of a realisation that there was nothing that he could then do for them. When the opportunity came to rescue his niece, Inka, he seized it immediately and vigorously. To some extent, he may have sublimated his feelings in his work in assisting the United States administration in 1941 with legal arguments in support of qualified neutrality, in his participation in the prosecution of war criminals between 1942 and 1946 and in the preparation of his book on the international bill of human rights between 1942 and 1945. But he did not brood, at any rate not openly. He was constantly busy. Twice he travelled to the United States; he saw many people, wrote letters to Rachel and me and spent not a little time in maintaining 6 Cranmer Road, shopping, firewatching and training with the Home Guard.

Although he must have seen it coming, Hersch listened, together with Rachel and myself, to the broadcast of Chamberlain's declaration of war on Sunday morning, 3 September 1939. We sat in his study, Hersch in his high-backed desk chair, Rachel and I in the two deep, squarish, green

---

[2] EL to HL, 17 March 1941.
[3] In 1948, she married a distant relative, Maurice Katz, and went to live in France.
[4] See respectively p. 175 and p. 220 below.

armchairs, all of us facing the solidly built Pye radio in the corner. For me, an 11 year old, the development was exciting – I had no understanding of what it would mean in terms of human suffering. For Hersch and Rachel, it was, of course, entirely different. Just as Hersch was directly affected, so was Rachel. Her parents were living in Palestine. By then, her father, Michael, was already in his seventies, as was her mother, Gittel. Rachel must have realised that the war would keep her separated from them for an indefinite period and that Palestine might itself fall into enemy hands. Happily, it did not, even though there was much worry about her sister, Leah, who lived in Egypt, especially as German forces moved across North Africa. Nonetheless, Hersch and Rachel received the news of the declaration of war calmly, and preparations were begun to put the house on a war footing.

Within an hour of Chamberlain's broadcast, the siren on the top of the gatehouse of nearby Selwyn College sounded an air raid alarm. It was clearly a false one. There was no way in which a hostile aircraft could have reached England so quickly, nor any reason why Cambridge should be chosen as the first target. Still, it served as a reminder that preparations had to be made. A place in the house had to be chosen for refuge during an air raid. Consideration was given to the cellar, but this was rejected as too cold and damp. The dining room was preferred because it had a solid mahogany Victorian dining table on four sturdy legs. This, it was hoped, would protect those lying under it if the upper floors were to collapse. As instructed by the civil defence authorities, the insides of the windows were covered with a small mesh adhesive netting intended to prevent glass fragments from spreading into the room if the windows were blown in. Some reserves of food were laid in, particularly sugar, flour, rice and semolina. Blackout curtains were hung in all the rooms of the house and the blackout was strictly enforced. Street lights remained unlit. Cars had to have blackout shields fitted to their headlamps. Cambridge became, and remained until May 1945, a dark city. Rachel and I took the need for these precautions much more seriously than did Hersch, whose attitude remained rather detached.

Soon afterwards, identity cards and gas masks were issued – the latter in cardboard boxes with a string attached so that one could follow at all times the instruction to carry them slung over one's shoulder. A number of soldiers were billeted next door but, contrary to Hersch's worst anticipation, proved not as noisy as he had feared.

The even pace of life in Cambridge was, at any rate for the first twelve months of the war, little altered. University term began as usual in early October 1939, and Hersch continued his lectures and seminars as previously. Numbers were down a bit on previous years as students were conscripted or volunteered for military service. Nonetheless, Cambridge became a crowded town as host to the London School of Economics, the Imperial College of Science and Technology and University College, London, all evacuated from London. Two LSE students lodged in one of the top-floor rooms of No. 6, but they were agreeable tenants and Hersch was not unduly troubled. The other top-floor room was occupied by a former LSE colleague, Crotch, and his wife. Some LSE students attended Hersch's lectures. Trinity continued with its usual service of meals, and members of High Table, such as Hersch, who dined but once a week, were not required to provide ration coupons. So he continued to go into Hall regularly, and occasionally stayed on to 'go upstairs' to the Combination Room and drink port or, when supplies ran low, Constanzia, a sweet dessert wine from South Africa.

Apart from his lectures, Hersch was then engaged in the preparation of the seventh volume of the *AD* covering 1933 and 1934. He was also busy with Volume II of the sixth edition of *Oppenheim*.

In this connection, Hersch had to give special consideration to the interception by the Royal Navy in February 1940 of the *Altmark*, a German naval auxiliary vessel, while passing through Norwegian territorial waters. Norway then still being neutral, legally every vessel, even an enemy vessel, was protected while in its waters. The Norwegian Government protested against what it saw as a breach of its neutrality. The British Government justified its action on the ground that the *Altmark* was carrying to Germany British prisoners of war taken from the various vessels sunk by the German battleship, the *Graf Spee*, and was using the Norwegian territorial waters not for 'mere passage', as was permitted by Article 10 of the Hague Convention No. XIII, but as 'a device for gaining immunity by circuitous resort to the shelter of neutral waters in a manner involving a conspicuous prolongation of the voyage'. These were the words used by Hersch in the sixth edition of Volume II of *Oppenheim*.

Conscious of the sensitivity of the subject, Hersch sent a copy of the new section that he was drafting to the Foreign Office and received from Sir William Malkin, the Legal Adviser, an indication that 'there is . . . little or nothing in it with which I should want to quarrel'.[5] Hersch was allowed to see a copy of a British note to Norway of 15 March 1940, but was not allowed to quote or refer to it, though he was tactfully

---

[5] Malkin to HL, 1 April 1940 and 4 May 1940.

told that 'a knowledge of the line which we have taken should be of assistance to you in settling the text of the relevant passage in *Oppenheim*'. The correspondence was not published until 1950.[6]

But, despite the fact that his work on *Oppenheim* kept him quite busy, Hersch was evidently troubled by the fact that he was not making any direct contribution to the war effort. He must have expressed his discontent to McNair, who wrote on 14 June 1940:

I wish you could get something to do, but you must not be disappointed if you don't. My experience of this war is that it requires a tremendous amount of ingenuity for anybody over 40 to get anything to do at all, and in your case you cannot shut your eyes to the feeling of reluctance in regard to the employment of naturalized British subjects, whatever their origin may be.

So Hersch joined the Home Guard, a motley body recruited from all parts of the community. There he was reported by one of his colleagues as being enormously popular and enjoying the nickname 'Lumpersplash'! But the heavy khaki uniform and forage cap did not sit easily on him. He can be seen fifth from the right in the third row of Plate 13 in this volume. Because of his knowledge of German, he was assigned to the Intelligence Section. If German prisoners were taken, he would have had to interrogate them. Fortunately, his skills were never put to the test. His map of Cambridge, with pillboxes and other defences marked on it, still exists. With the fall of France and the evacuation of Dunkirk in June 1940, the risk of invasion was taken seriously. In a limited way, Hersch seemed to enjoy his involvement and the camaraderie, though he was far from being a man of military inclination.

FIRST VISIT TO THE UNITED STATES

In July 1940, a group of American university teachers centred on Yale University, supportive of Britain – and by no means all American academics were supportive – organised a scheme for the evacuation and reception in the United States of the children of British academics. Hersch and Rachel decided that I should go. In the meantime, Hersch had been invited by the Carnegie Endowment for International Peace to accept a visiting professorship and undertake a lecture tour during the first semester (the autumn of 1940) in the United States for an honorarium of $2,000. Initially hesitant to accept, he consulted his contacts in the Foreign Office, at that time, principally Sir William Malkin, the

---

[6] A full account of the episode is given by Waldock, 'The Release of the Altmark's Prisoners' (1947) 24 *BYIL* 216. See also British Parliamentary Papers, Norway, No. 1 (1950), Cmd 8012.

Legal Adviser, and Sir Stephen Gaselee, the Librarian and Keeper of the Papers. The latter, despite his title, played an important role in policy-making. Both advised Hersch to go. They took the view that his visit would be useful and approached the university authorities to obtain his release from his teaching duties. So it was decided that he and I should go and that Rachel should not be left behind. The Foreign Office and the Ministry of Information helped to obtain our passage by ship.

Hersch's decision to go was warmly approved of by the Vice-Chancellor, by his eminent colleague, W. W. Buckland, and by Harold Laski. The last provided Hersch with letters of introduction to Felix Frankfurter, a US Supreme Court Justice, and to Lord Lothian, the British Ambassador in Washington, saying that Hersch was 'one of the really first rate people I know'.

Laski to HL, 15 September 1940
Good luck in America. Give all my friends whom you see my warm affection and the assurance of our victory.

Of course, Felix is devoted to the British cause. How could you doubt it?

And, equally, of course, he bears nothing but goodwill to you. You must not fail to see him in Washington. I will tell him to expect you.

The enclosed letters may be of help.

We are all safe so far. A bomb fell 50 yards away, and smashed all our windows, but I find this only adds to one's sense of determination.

McNair took a very positive view:

I am very glad that you have decided to accept the Carnegie Professorship. I think it is the right thing to do. I think you just slightly misunderstood my attitude. My main object was to disabuse you of the feeling that you would be criticized for leaving the country at this stage. I think that Gaselee's attitude is decisive – much more important than that of the MOI.[7]

You will probably sail from Liverpool. I cannot offer you hospitality as in 10 days time we are moving into a flat which contains only 2 bedrooms, one for ourselves and one for the maid, but I will certainly find accommodation for you. I shall have various messages to give you. So if by any chance you are not sailing from Liverpool please let me know.[8]

On 21 September 1940, Hersch, Rachel and I boarded the SS *Scythia* at Liverpool docks in the late afternoon after a prolonged and grimy train

---

[7] Ministry of Information.   [8] McNair to HL, 10 August 1940.

journey from Cambridge. We were due to sail on the early morning tide the next day. We shared a small three-berth cabin with no toilet facilities except a wash basin. Ten days later, we disembarked in New York.

THE JOURNEY TO THE UNITED STATES AND THE FIRST DAYS THERE

Most unusually – for he was not a diary-keeping man – Hersch kept a record, albeit fragmentary, of the voyage and his first days in the US. The substantial body of family correspondence accumulated during the years 1940–4 includes thirty-four pages written in Hersch's hand on stationery of the Cunard White Star Line which he obviously picked up on board the ship.

The handwriting is often far from clear and there are, therefore, a number of gaps in the transcription that follows, but they do not affect the general flow of the story. The pages consist of jottings and keywords, apparently intended to remind him of larger impressions, but sufficient to provide even now a striking picture of what the journey from Cambridge to New York was like during the Blitz and the German U-boat campaign.

20 Sept, Thursday[9]
Left Cambridge at 9.30 (or rather – a bad omen – at 9.45). The Crotches and Registry at the station. Thinking with some reflection, of the crowds of 'seers-off' (e.g. the insignificant [*name omitted*]).

Bletchley $\frac{1}{2}$ h late, but 'no reason for anxiety' the London train one hour later – the luggage, after some anxiety, duly in the van – a first class compartment – two pleasant officers – the chatty lady asking the soldiers about London, are they coming back from South England – polite reticence – all fall asleep.

Crewe – only five minutes to spare – but the other train half an hour late – Liverpool – first 'scene'[10] with the luggage collector, but half a crown smoothes matters – Eli indignant.

The hotel – little politeness but Mrs McNair's roses in the room – difficulty about table for supper.

---

[9] 20 September 1940 was actually a Friday.
[10] 'Scene' was a well-known word in the family to describe Hersch's indignant and vocal reaction to something that displeased him, for example bad service in a restaurant. He knew that these scenes were highly embarrassing to Rachel and me: 'Please, Daddy, don't make a scene.' The plea sometimes worked.

McNair – tired, but polite as always – how is the family – Ruth menagerie – would Mrs McNair come to Cambridge – Oh no – she is tired of Ruth and Ruth's animals – 'Oxford sent 150 children, but Liverpool will send more!' – After dinner Rachel and Eli left – With McNair in the lounge smoking his thin cigars 'the only ones he can afford' – Discussing the powers of the belligerent occupant whom McNair, rather surprisingly, identifies with the *de facto* occupant – by the way, handed over the will to him – went out for a breath of fresh air – 'How long do you think this war will go on?' – 'I doubt whether we can stand the bombing of London for several years' – 'Oh, no, we could not, but then it will stop before that . . . Germany cannot stand industrially our bombing.' – Rockefeller and Carnegie, in connection with McNair's project to teach international law – It is getting cold – we bump into three drunken people – with difficulty we find the hotel in the darkness.

Went to bed – dressed in my little room – no siren – first quiet night in over three weeks.

21. Saturday
Up after a sleepless night – a pleasant breakfast – 9.30, Jenks – had to wait for his boat for weeks – had a 'private' talk after the family left – Jenks dutiful, confident, but not a born optimist – the ILO reduced to 50 – the London office nearly wrecked – his papers and memoranda can't be recovered.

Taxi to the docks – refusal of the luggage which goes out to the [*illegible*] – the formalities numerous, but courteous – the ration books go but the identity cards are charmingly restored – the military representative for passports – the customs man – big and polite – any jewels etc. – no – Eli's gold watch – small value – 'I am satisfied'. Any cameras? No – Oh yes, says Eli cheerfully. His 27/– Ensign camera; also a stamp collection – The big man becomes very alert. Interrogation as to stamps – Please, do not interfere, he says – I will ask him – What is the most expensive stamp – 8s 6d – how many, etc. – 'I am satisfied' – But as to the camera – Will you please show it to me – The tragedy – Where is it – In the small trunk, in the big one? – Out of 12 – Where are the trunks? – Eventually find the very big one – Unlock it with difficulty – Search it – Hot and perspiring – and not very kind to Rachel – who is responsible for the packing – Despair – *She* will go to the customs officer – She went and reports: The great man said 'I am satisfied'. He initials the passports – Still to pass the pretty censorship girl – She first examines a German refugee – Any cameras, photos, goods, etc. – She searches every piece of his wallet. (No-one dreams of searching any of the big trunks) – It seems interminable – But at the end she too is satisfied and charmingly invites the refugee to put in a coin for the Spitfire funds. Will mine take as long? – I produce some official letters – Works like magic – She gives me the 'white card' – I am not even invited to contribute to the fund – Back to the luggage – shall we ever find our 16 pieces of luggage? –

Unnecessary, a man hustles us out, impatiently, to go on the tender – we pass the Cunard ticket man – [on] the tender, a huddled, dispirited mass, an old Jewess nervously and fervently reads from her prayer book – after an hour we move – manoeuvring – what is going to be our ship – there are a number of big ships – eventually the Scythia – a good cabin – Eli's first rebuff – the porthole – our steward – tired? frightened? The boat generally? – The kind of service – Whittaker confirms – 'Scenes' – There is really no reason why they should make the life of passengers more intolerable – it is bad enough – the staff generally – refusal to answer innocent questions – our waiter – a nitwit – no knowledge of service – conversation with the Italian beauty at the other table – I propose to complain – tea arrangements – could not stand it – the main steward – little satisfaction – After tea writing letters to 'catch the last post'. Little we know that another two full days to elapse – But in the evening one of the old guard tells us we may undress – The boat does not sail during the night. We undress at 1am – the bang – the gongs – 4 of them – alarm – we dress in panic – Rachel in her slippers and green dressing gown – Eli bangs his head – I without collar – the two life belts – in the passage – our steward – our life belts wrong – refuses to untie Eli's – stay in the inside cabins – at 3 back to 'bed'.

22. Sunday
Waiting in port.

The beauty of the harbour – Lloyd's [Royal Liver] Insurance building – the enormous number of ships – still some ships left in the British Empire.

The service – bad – the steward – death incarnate – sulky, frightened, lazy, arrogant – the first alarm – scared as anyone – angrily pointing that life belts not properly adjusted – refuses to untie Eli's knot – ask him to bring beer while he is engaged in a long conversation with the occupant of the cabin opposite – the stewardess – vulgar but more friendly, in expectation of the tip – the steward does not seem to care – the same with the deck steward – not as much as thank you for the tip – the tea arrangements on deck – in the dining room – the sissy waiter – compared with Trinity waiting – waiter snatching the tea or coffee pot – only six for the whole room.

22/3
Complaint to superior – he himself scared of his subordinates – what is the explanation? – Difficult to obtain labour in war time – but this does not apply to higher staff – not always efficient – the last drill – no-one knows – a girl to me: 'Some Germans complained that. Inefficient.' – Yes, nothing to be proud about – another reason – strain – after all human – the musicians: haggard, unhappy – another reason – a large number of foreign refugees who are easily bullied – no competition – unpardonable – just in these times it ought to be the duty of the crew to make the life of passengers more tolerable.

The strain of waiting – after the news of *The City of Benares*[11] – many would drop out if given the opportunity – but none given.

23. Monday

7.30 – Eli – missed yet? go into smoking room and see – no – out of 'bed' – 'slept' 'in trousers and collar' – probably no sleep – In the morning bought deckchairs – read *Midpassage*[12] – afternoon – continue with *Midpassage*.

Spoke to the lady who is taking the little son to US – her two daughters and husband – hopes will return to him after six months – Played chess with Eli – full of praise for the boy – Tea – slow process – can't get it outside or inside – complaining to the steward – Eli indignant – another scene.

Watching the ships, sloops, barges in quiet autumn sunshine – lots of ships still left in England – Dutch, French – a convoy coming back, the Liverpool jail, Lloyd's.

23. Monday

After tea.

News of the torpedoing of the *City of London* liner.[13]

One woman – this is going to be a quick convoy.

The dear lady – cheerful – some of her friends knocked down in motor car accident – two German ladies – sobbing quietly – Six – the King's speech – unforgettable – nearly sunset – the news now spread – woman crying quietly – a big crowd – the King commiserating with the victims – a ship of death? Like day of atonement – the glowing sunset – God Save the King – Eli pulls himself together – hands out of pockets – the crowd sings – foreigners move their lips in solidarity – the random hooting – the siren – no-one moves – discipline has gone – greatness of the King's speech – the slight stutter has gone – 'we went into it with our eyes open' – 'I am speaking to you from Buckingham Palace' – winter is coming, cold, dark – with the honourable scars – reference to the wicked submarines – the lonely fight – Unforgettable – got hold of the tattered Sunday Express – a German refugee approaches me anxiously trying to see

[11] The *City of Benares*, which had sailed from Liverpool for Canada on 13 September 1940, was torpedoed by the German submarine U-48 on 17 September with the loss of 248 lives, including 77 evacuee children. The news did not reach the passengers on the *Scythia* until three days after they had embarked.

[12] *America in Midpassage* by Charles A. Beard and Mary R. Beard, published in 1939, a massive 950-page study of the state of America following the Great Depression and covering most of its then recent history, economics, politics and social and cultural structure. It was for Hersch an admirable introduction to the American scene with which over the coming months he was to become more closely acquainted at first-hand. He kept the book by him and, in due course, after Rachel had also read it, it came back to Cambridge.

[13] Clearly a mistaken reference to the *City of Benares*.

the newspaper – I suggest he better not – news of no interest – another raid on London.

The discipline has not deserted the waiter – 18 minutes – apologized – shall cut out the *hors d'oeuvre* – nice duckling, but strained supper – the head waiter appears to apologise – I feel ashamed – Eli is still indignant – I must positively promise not to make another scene – told Eli therefore next two days discipline relaxed – he may read the 'comic' – After supper a game of chess with Eli – a crowd of Cockney children under the American scheme watch eagerly – don't know the game at all but want to learn – after Eli duly beaten I am teaching the children – an intelligent lot – rough, not good looking, one lisps badly, the one with a badger hat – imbibe the lesson with alacrity – a bulb falls – a tornado? – promise another tomorrow – in the meantime they start their own – have to go down – the siren – out [*illegible*] – one of the boys reminds me of tomorrow's lesson – the smoke room is full – the lady who did her lips in the morning now appears much subdued [*illegible*] – except the American scheme which has personal discipline – the dance at 9.30 – will it be cancelled? – there is a tendency to congregate and one must not go to the outside cabins – Eli plays cards happily with a bunch of girls – Rachel knits, she cannot read – and she told me her doubts whether she can knit (in anxious time her maternal nature reveals itself) – how she tucked me into the blankets on the deck.

24. Tuesday. Sailing

A sleepless night but no alarms – the letterbox closed and this indicates sailing.

At 11.50 we are actually sailing – acting on advice we have a light lunch – it is a quiet affair as we want to see the sailing out – there is no motion as the river is small – we pass two or three wrecks – it is a stately bay – Blackpool tower on the left – North Wales and Anglesey on the right – we enter the sea which is as smooth as the river – here the procession unfolds itself – these four big ships altogether, one on the left but we are still looking for the escort – here it comes – A destroyer – the beauty of it – camouflaged – it was joined by the other to become a closer thing – it is about half a mile astern – as we proceed the protecting arm assumes the form of bombers – fly there and back very low – cheered by the passengers – they reply – the commotion – one, flying low drops something – smoke – submarine? – wreck? – armchair strategists – the sea calm – I relax in one with Scottish Colls on the other – to bed dressed.

25. [Wednesday]

We wake up – the convoy enlarged – two more ships – an enormous 30,000 old and clumsy, apparently without passengers – the other long painted grey – and another faithful destroyer on the left far in the distance.

These destroyers – graceful, quick, clever things like sheep dogs – darting about – signalling – we think of their hard life – the signalling by blast – zigzagging – we must be 300 miles off Ireland – and yet the faithful bombers appear again and again – flying low – inspecting the sea – summoned by blasts – very proud to have them – the atmosphere of a chase – we are not only the hunted ones – so is the submarine – the depth charge – the ramming – the heavy sea – the stately procession of these five ships – ours in the middle – the boss of the show – changing their relative position because of the zigzagging – but ours always in the middle – protected – why? – the children? – the American committee? HG Wells? – a defiant company – the drill at 11am – the same thing – action stations boat station – unsolved problems: mothers, children.

To bed, the most anxious night? – Dancing in the smoking room – but we do not stay up – one cannot sleep – at least let it be a long rest – long, the clock one hour back – rehearsals for the emergency – things put in order – protecting the passports from the water – as if it mattered – washing Eli's knees – having a sponge – quickly in case we are called.

26. [Thursday]
Nothing happened during the interminable night – the first thing to ascertain is whether the faithful convoy and the destroyers still here – yes, says Eli – Eli more and more surly – one cannot maintain discipline – preserve decorum.

The drill – the chief officer himself – not expert speaker – foreshadows the departure of the destroyers – have to rely on ourselves – we are not a fighting ship – we run away.

26. [Thursday]
In view of the serious possibilities – asthma attack – the quick changing of woollens for aertex.

The second thing – a bath – a quick, risky thing – but must be done – seven days without a bath – the attendant encouraging – 600 miles – I bother a change – a relief.

A sunny day – but the sea rough – the sea-sickness takes its hold – for the time being I act as the doctor – fairy godmother – a pill to the Hatchard girl who, until now, treated me with contempt – a pill for the boy – but then I do the cowardly thing and have cases of . . . – not too comfortable but

[*page missing*]

27. [Friday]
Wake up – convoy has gone – without goodbye – all to ourselves – only the sister ship – *Samaria* – still seen far ahead of us – she will probably be first in New York.

28. [Saturday]
Rewarded – the convoy of fifty ships back to England – like a fleet – an encouraging sight.

29 [September]–2 October [Sunday–Wednesday]
The journey – the routine – with pleasant weather and better service would be a rest – it is so – except little restful sleep – the porthole closed because of the black out – (the most rigid enforcement of blackout) – the sea water bath – refreshing – regularly after the fourth day – and at leisure.

The people–

Reverend Whittaker – Secretary of the Missions in India – a bit like Bradley – a St John's man – an excellent type – something 'Christian' about him in the best meaning of the word – courteous – willing and eager to meet people – his wife, the doctor – a splendid big lady – kind and sociable – and what a sea journey does! – painted her nails and even let her face done by the Russian wife of the Admiralty Officer – Dick, John.

Mrs Johnston – 36(?) – fat and painted – but kind (saved Rachel from the stewardess in the ironing room) – 20 years in England – no English – 'girls and womans' – daughter of the governor of Crimea – father and two brothers shot – first husband killed – her Russian cooking – fortune reading – entirely brainless.

Mrs Robbins – her tiger-like claws – off for one shilling in drinks.

Professor Loewe – the economist, his wife, and two pleasant daughters – (danger of too much politeness) – the outcome of the war – social reconstruction at the same time – (the young wives without their husbands – what will remain of their morals – or – paw-paws with the officers).

The Italian Jewish woman behind our table. Ben-Gurion – first class to Palestine – but as a Labour man very often in tourist and 3rd.

Mrs Hatchard with Anne (the cattish beauty who likes brandy, cigarettes etc.) and Pamela ('Pamela is very bad – touch wood').

The frail Scottish woman with her sister's boy opposite.

The East End big Jewess – the talkative Jewess who 'belongs to Liverpool'.

The children – not very representative – the vamp girls – Jean and Janet – the pretty escorts – the American beauty chief – rather inefficient and frightened of her responsibility – the song of the seavacuees.

3 October [Thursday]
New York – the morning – the peacefulness of the shore – the grey ships – the disappointing Statue of Liberty – the sky scrapers of Manhattan – the

immigration officers muddle – five hours of disorder – the procedure itself five minutes – only three officers for 800 tired passengers – at last out – the polite customs official – all pieces searched but perfunctorily – no sign of Bradleys[14] – meeting Herbert L accidentally – he telephoned for the Bradleys – the wait outside the dock – Eli visibly ill – no ham sandwiches – the Jewish poster on the New Year – two dollars – the station wagon with two flags – Wilkie – at last Bradley – three times as fat but efficient – how he packed the luggage! – the drive through New York – the *Normandie* and *Queen Elizabeth* – the beauty of the size – nothing comparable – Eli sick in Harlem, but immediately hot dogs – at last Bayside – like Hampstead Garden Suburb – uncut grass – new! – the pleasant Bradley house – but crowded upstairs – no wardrobe! – where to put the baggage – the fleshy humanity of Bradley – the helpful, disciplined children – the great cook, Pearl and the bad fish – early to bed – with an imminent cold.

Without delay, on the day following our arrival in New York, Hersch began to go about his business. The three remaining entries in his travel 'diary' record his activities over the next three days.

4 October [Friday]

Main business Jessup – 3 hours – pleasant, gentlemanly, business like, inscrutable – Mr Haskell – Deak & Jessup on neutrality – by 1 January – but no repeal of the Johnson Act – no repeal of the Neutrality Act.

The Columbia University – unbelievable – expansion – owners of Rockefeller Plaza! – the lunch in the refectory – looking down on roofs – the fork and knife business[15] – visit to the British Library of Information – the girl who attended my lectures.

Mr Dudley who saw me in the LSE 15 years ago – the gentle Mr Wilberforce as the great Mr Fletcher unobtainable – the Rockefeller Plaza – the sky scrapers.

---

[14] 'Bradley' was Phillips 'Phil' Bradley, a professor of political science at Queens College in Long Island. A large, rotund and jolly man, he had been a research student at the LSE during Hersch's time there and they had become good friends. Phil had written a laudatory review of *Private Law Sources* in the *American Journal of International Law* (see p. 65 above). He arrived in a large Ford station wagon, and we and all our luggage were bundled into it for the drive to Bayside, in Long Island, where Phil lived with his wife, Rebecca, and their children, Helen, Wendell and John. On the way we stopped for our first taste of America's classic food – a hot dog – a taste for which never left Hersch or myself. The Bradleys were very welcoming and hospitable. When Hersch went off on his lecture tour, Rachel and I remained with them for some weeks till I was placed as a boarder at the Horace Mann School, a highly regarded establishment in the Bronx where, as I subsequently learned, Richard Baxter had preceded me by a few years. As previously noted, Richard Baxter became one of Hersch's most prized research students and eventually the US judge at the ICJ.

[15] The reference to the 'fork and knife business' was to the American practice of usually employing the fork and knife together only for the purpose of cutting up the food prior to putting down the knife and using the fork alone, normally transferred to the right hand, to carry the food from plate to mouth.

Back home – with a cold all the time – the party in the evening – the Reynolds who put up Jennings – the intelligent Mrs Reynolds – to bed.

5 October, Saturday

Breakfast in bed – Hyde for lunch[16] – Folsom – Neutrality – Kellogg–Briand Pact a joke – but basing it on self-defence – peace overtures after the election – home – packing – early to bed – the practical talks with Bradley.

6 Oct Sunday

Hurried breakfast – taxi to station – 15 minutes for ticket – non-stop to Pennsylvania station – the Rockefeller Plaza – Fletcher – ? is there any international law? – Meeting the family – a pleasant surprise – Ethel Barnett – the splendid fellow Kahn – the 12.30 to Washington – comfortable coach – Washington – like Paris – the kind, informative, taxi man – the beauty of the simple big Government buildings – endless succession of parks – the Dearborne Park Hotel – the luxurious repast – meal for two – 'for your peace of mind' – absolutely private – bit too quiet at 8am – a lovely morning – cold, malted chocolate and apple – full advantage of the bath – cancelled appointment with the Ambassador.

The diary form ends at this point.

US LECTURE TOUR, OCTOBER–DECEMBER 1940

Of these meetings, the one with Jessup[17] on 4 October was the most important. At that time, Jessup was a Professor of International Law at Columbia University Law School, then, as now, one of the leading law schools in the United States. He was also the Director of the International Law Division of the Carnegie Endowment for International Peace, the organisation which sponsored Hersch's visit to the United States. Jessup was an urbane and friendly gentleman, of considerable presence and

---

[16] 'Hyde' was Professor Charles Cheney Hyde (1873–1952), the principal professor of international law at Columbia, who had for some years been the Solicitor of the State Department and was the author of a monumental three-volume general treatise on international law, full of knowledge and wise judgment, expressed in an elegant though complex and rather old-world style. Like Jessup, he was recognised by Hersch as a considerate and understanding friend, notwithstanding difficulties of conversation with him due to his deafness. He had a son, Jim, who later became a distinguished practising international lawyer in New York and a daughter, Betsy, who married Oliver Lissitzyn, an émigré from Russia, also a professor of international law at Columbia, for whose book on *The International Court of Justice* a decade later Hersch wrote a substantial foreword.

[17] Philip Jessup (1897–1986). From 1925 to 1946, he served as a lecturer at Columbia Law School. In 1946, he was elected to the position of Hamilton Fish Professor of International Law at Columbia Law School, a post he held until 1961. He served as an advisor at the United Nations Monetary and Financial Conference and to the US delegation to the United Nations Charter Conference at San Francisco in 1945.

ability, with a sufficiently liberal outlook to make him the victim in later years of attacks by the notorious Senator McCarthy as an alleged communist. Jessup was nothing of the sort. He served for a time as one of the United States Permanent Representatives to the UN and as an Ambassador at Large. Later, he became a judge of the ICJ. It was Jessup who planned Hersch's marathon journey of more than 4,000 miles, starting two days later, to visit nine law schools in the eastern, southern and mid-western States between then and December.

The scope and intensity of Hersch's tour between 7 October and 9 December is revealed in the report that he sent on 4 January 1941 to Dr Nicholas Murray Butler, the President of Columbia University and of the Carnegie Endowment.

HL to President Butler, 4 January 1941

I now beg to submit a report of my work as Visiting Carnegie Professor in the months October–December 1940.

I felt honoured by your invitation, which I received last July, to come to the United States for one semester as Visiting Carnegie Professor. I thought it necessary to consult the proper authorities as well as the Vice-Chancellor of the University of Cambridge and my own Law Faculty there as to the advisability of accepting, in time of war, an invitation involving temporary absence from the country. I was advised that, as a teacher of international law, I ought to avail myself of the opportunity, at a time when normal contacts were interrupted, of promoting the understanding of questions of international law, in particular as they affect both the relations between Great Britain and the United States in time of war and the wider issues of international law and organization in which these two countries have traditionally shown an active interest.

I arrived in the United States on October 3. I started on my tour on October 7. I visited the following universities:

University of Virginia, Charlottesville – October 8–14

Duke University, Durham, and

University of North Carolina, Chapel Hill – October 15–23

Tulane University, New Orleans – October 25–31

University of Kansas, Lawrence – November 3–9

University of Illinois, Urbana – November 11–18

University of Wisconsin, Madison – November 21–24

University of Minnesota, Minneapolis – November 25–30

Cornell University, Ithaca – December 4–8

Independently of my engagements as Visiting Carnegie Professor, I delivered single lectures in the following universities and institutions: University of Louisiana; University of Chicago; University of Michigan; Harvard Law School; Amherst College; Smith College; Queens College.

My work in the Universities which I visited as Carnegie Professor consisted mainly of lectures before classes of students of law, international relations and government; of public lectures to mixed audiences under the auspices of the University and the Law School; and of closed and more intimate talks to groups and clubs of faculty members. On occasions, at the invitation of my hosts, I delivered lectures before such audiences as the Kansas Bar Association or the Round Table Club at New Orleans. I was also available to graduate students for consultation concerning their advanced work. In addition, in all the Universities which I visited, I was invited by the Faculties of Law or Government, or both, to be their guest at a formal function – usually a luncheon or dinner – followed by a period of questions and answers on conditions in Great Britain in war time and the international situation as it affected Anglo-American relations. With regard to the latter, I invariably found a most helpful willingness to make allowance for the fact that I was a visitor from a belligerent country upon whom circumstances enjoined certain duties of restraint in the expression of opinion on matters of current political controversy.

In my lectures and classes I concentrated on the following subjects:

(1) *The Laws of Warfare in the Present War.* These were devoted to a survey of the laws of war in the light of the practice of the belligerents in the present war, to an examination of the reasons of the failure to observe rules of warfare in many of its major aspects, and to a discussion of the question of the extent to which the basic principles and the traditional rules of warfare admit of an adaptation to the changed conditions and the extended scope of modern war.

(2) *Neutrality in and between the Two World Wars.* In these lectures I traced the development of the notion and of the practice of neutrality as an institution of international law. I also examined the question of the extent to which neutrality is an institution whose character and content are determined by the legal admissibility of war at any given period.

(3) *The Place of Recognition in International Law and Relations.* These lectures on recognition of states, governments and belligerency as well as on the principle of non-recognition, were devoted to a survey of the practice of governments in so far as that practice has a bearing on the question, which has for a long time divided international lawyers, whether recognition in its various aspects is a matter governed by international law or whether it is within the exclusive orbit of politics.

(4) *The Problem of Post-War International Organization.* These lectures were, in part, an account of the recent discussion in Great Britain of the problem of post-war

international reconstruction; in part, they were devoted to re-statement of the essential purpose of the League of Nations conceived as the abiding political ideal of mankind; in part, they were concerned with a legal and political analysis of the notion of Federation in its relation to the problem of international organization. It was for me a pleasure to find in the Universities in the South and in the Middle West a keen interest in these subjects. I was only very seldom confronted with the objection that all discussion concerning the future progress of international organization is based on an assumption which must still be proved. In general, I felt that there was agreement that as human beings we must act on rational assumptions and that the rational assumption is that law and order and other no less valuable things will prevail.

(5) *The Reality of International Law. The Place of International Law in Jurisprudence. Private Law and the Law of Nations.* I attached importance to lecturing before law students and, occasionally, before wider audiences on these related aspects of international law at a time when it is assailed by many well-meaning but disappointed persons. The current criticism of international law in so far as it expresses itself in an impatient or cynical denial of its reality or usefulness is of very recent origin. International lawyers, it is true, have been frequently confronted with the view that the rules usually referred to as international law do not in fact deserve that name. But the adherents of the Austinian school of thought and others who have held that view have not denied that there exists and ought to exist a body of rules binding upon states in their mutual relations. They merely denied the legal nature of these rules. We must go back to Hobbes and Treitschke for a parallel of the view, now voiced by many, that power and not law must remain the enduring and decisive factor in the relations of States.

The reasons of that attitude are near at hand. In the first instance, there are many who while denouncing force have been unable to escape the disheartening influence of its temporary triumphs. Secondly, it is natural that law when repeatedly violated with impunity in things fundamental tends to fall into disrepute. And yet this is an attitude which ought to be combated even at the risk of engaging in polemics. My experience before and during my present visit has been that both the man in the street and the average lawyer are appreciative of the effort made to shake their cynicism. On occasions, they are prone to discard as unreal the plea that, normally, international law is as regularly observed as domestic law. But this is nevertheless a valid argument. So is the plea that international law is constantly administered as law by the judicial and executive organs of the State; that the strength of the present reaction against its continued violations is in itself an expression of its essential validity and vitality; and that the sad plight of a world in which violations of international law were for a long time allowed to occur with impunity is in itself a persuasive proof of its significance. Above all, the challenge of the critics of the shortcomings and of the ineffectiveness of international law must be met by the retort that, in the last analysis, international law is not an abstract entity; that it is endowed with as much power as peoples, acting through their representatives and governments, are willing to confer upon it; and that it often happens that the critics of international law are conspicuous in opposing measures calculated to secure its effectiveness, such as progressive restrictions of state sovereignty through the assumption of unequivocal legal duties to refrain from resort to war, to submit disputes with other states to compulsory judicial settlement, and to endow international institutions with coercive measures intended to insure the fulfilment of these obligations. In giving these lectures on the place of the law of nations in international relations and in jurisprudence I acted on the view that it is not inconsistent with the scientific character of the teaching of international law to discuss the reality of international law from the point of view of these considerations.

My tour of the Universities and Law Schools in this country has confirmed the view which I have formed in Great Britain that in both countries the development and the study of international law are to a large extent dependent upon the attitude of the Law Schools and professional organizations of lawyers. In none of the Universities and Law Schools which I visited is international law included as an obligatory subject in the curriculum. In some, as in the Law Schools in the Universities of Virginia or Minnesota or in Cornell University it is admitted as an elective subject, but even there it is taught intermittently and is taken by few students only. In some Law Schools the handful of students who select international law attend the lectures given on this subject in the department of government. In others still, international law has no place at all in the curriculum. There is agreement as to the reasons of this state of affairs in the United States and in Great Britain (in the latter the University of Cambridge is the only one in which international law is a compulsory subject in the Law Tripos). Law Schools feel bound to adapt themselves to the fact that international law is not recognized as one of the subjects in the professional examinations qualifying for admission to the Bar. But there are many, in and outside the Law Schools, who believe that it is of importance that international law should acquire a definite place in the academic and professional training of future members of a class of citizens wielding considerable influence upon the government and the policies of the nation. Any such change would be bound to have a beneficent effect in enhancing the understanding of international relations and in fostering an enlightened respect for the law of nations in one of the most influential sections of the community. Teachers of international law who are, in a sense, an interested party in the matter, cannot conveniently urge any such reform. However, from my conversations with Deans of Law Schools and members of Law Faculties I gained the impression that the time may not be altogether inopportune for a change in that direction. A number of Law Schools – like those of the Universities of Chicago, Minnesota and Wisconsin – are considering the broadening of the bases of legal education in the direction of emphasizing the philosophical and sociological approach to law as distinguished from purely vocational training. In any such scheme the insistence on a more thorough teaching of international law would probably not be out of place. It is a subject of admitted jurisprudential interest and in so far as – in the language of the Statute of the Permanent Court of International Justice – it is based on general principles of law recognized by civilized nations, it is not without significance for the study of comparative law. Neither is it irrelevant to note that American and English courts are frequently called upon to decide on matters involving the application of international law and that a more thorough and widespread training in that subject would tend to enhance the quality both of judicial decisions bearing on international law and their scientific criticism. For these reasons I am looking forward to the day on which international law will become an integral part of legal education in the United States and Great Britain – the two common law countries in which the doctrine that international law is part of the law of the land was first proclaimed and subsequently acted upon by courts with, on the whole, an inspiring consistency.

Professor Jessup, in his capacity as Director of the International Law Division of the Endowment, undertook the heavy task of making the detailed arrangements for my visit and of conducting the necessary correspondence with the Law Schools and Universities. I availed myself constantly of his advice and assistance, and I shall regard it as a favour if you will convey to him my expression of gratitude for his unfailing courtesy and thoughtfulness.

To you, Sir, I am much indebted for the invitation to come to the United States as a Visiting Carnegie Professor and for the consideration which you showed me throughout my visit. I enjoyed and benefited from my work under the auspices of the Endowment. From my hosts everywhere I received nothing but kindness and generous hospitality. I only hope that I have been able to contribute in some measure towards the object which you had in mind in extending your invitation. May I also say that I deeply appreciated the message of encouragement in the Christmas greetings which you very kindly sent me. I know it will be so appreciated in England.

Hersch's formal account of his marathon journey tells us little about the immense personal effort and frequent discomfort involved. This is revealed in the almost daily letters that he sent to Rachel and me. By Tuesday, 8 October, he was in Washington and reported on his time there in a letter to Rachel written on the train from Washington to Charlottesville, Virginia, the seat of the University of Virginia.

HL to RL, Tuesday, 8 October 1940

This has been a crowded day.

(1) I spent two hours in the morning in the Carnegie Endowment where I was very nicely and helpfully received and where I received the details of the journey

to Charlottesville. I also received from Dean Dillard a most charming letter. They will put me up and expect me in a car. The Carnegie Endowment also strongly urged that I should visit Ann Arbor, Michigan. I would not mind that as I rather liked your family (may God forgive me).

(2) I then went to the gorgeous building of the Supreme Court and saw Mr Justice Frankfurter for a while.

(3) From there to the Embassy. The ambassador was not in Washington, but I saw the Legal Adviser (whom I knew from London) and had a useful talk (among others he provisionally booked the Clipper[18] for me – it's 550 dollars not one thousand).

(4) I then went to lunch in the house of Mr Butler, the principal counsellor and the second man next to the ambassador. A splendid affair in one of the most beautiful houses I have seen. Butler (who was also private secretary to Baldwin and McDonald) was minister in Tehran and brought home from there an incredible collection of Bokhara carpets. The Legal Adviser was there too and also a man called McDougall (and his wife), formerly Legal Adviser to the Iraquian Government.

(5) After lunch, which left me a bit immobile, the McDougalls drove me in their car to the hotel where I collected the luggage, then they drove to see the town and to the station where I spent 25 cents in giving them a nice cup of tea.

It is getting dark. The country is a bit hilly and almost red in the autumn foliage. The train is very comfortable.

In his next letter,[19] written to me from the Colonnade Club of the University of Virginia in Charlottesville, he touches upon themes that were of constant concern to him and appear repeatedly in his letters – Rachel's welfare and my own schooling:

I am writing particularly to you to ask you to take special care of Mummy. She is now left by herself and she needs all your care and attention. I know that it will cheer her up very much – as indeed it will cheer me up – if you start going to school and try, with Mummy's help, to keep up your Hebrew and French. And you may try on your own to brush up your Latin so as not to forget what you know.

As Charlottesville was the first place at which he lectured, he was having to devote much time to the preparation of the lectures. 'I live in a hopeless rush. It will be easier next week', he wrote on Thursday, 10 October. By Friday, the first set of lectures was behind him.

---

[18] The Pan Am flying boat service across the Atlantic.   [19] 9 October 1940.

HL to RL, 12 October 1940
I have found this a most exacting week. The audiences are rather on a low level, and I simply could not adjust my lectures accordingly. Still, it could be worse. The place and the surroundings are simply beautiful.

He was comfortably lodged and anxious that Rachel should find a cheap but comfortable flat 'in not too low a part of New York'.

I am most confident that I shall be able to leave you at least the five hundred dollars of the big cheque which I left you – this will be all to the good and it will satisfy your urge for 'independence'. May you have a good (but not too good) time!

He spent the weekend in Charlottesville, writing 'about 25 letters' and going to a party, before moving on to Duke University at Durham, North Carolina, on 14 October.[20] It took him nine and a half hours, from 11.30am to 8pm, to cover the 200 miles in an uncomfortable train. But he was pleased when he got there.

This is a beautiful place. The University, which is right outside the town, is all together. It was built and endowed by the Duke family; it is built in the Gothic style. I am most comfortable. I have a special suite of rooms and an enormous bathroom. It will not cost me anything. (In Charlottesville I was put up privately and had to pay.) On the whole, this is a much more satisfactory place from every point of view. But they work one hard! I had to lecture this morning at 9am! But enough about me.

He was, however, troubled by having missed observance of the Day of Atonement. He wrote of:

the continuous rush in which I am living. The University is giving me a lunch today; the Political Science faculty tomorrow; and the lawyers after tomorrow. And on Saturday I have to go to a football match and sit in the same box with the Governor of the State![21]

While at Duke, he had to go over to Chapel Hill to give two lectures at the State University of North Carolina, ten miles from Durham, have a public lunch there and answer questions. On the Thursday, he was either lecturing or answering questions almost continuously from 2pm to 10pm. 'I hope', he wrote, 'when I get used to these things, the whole business will not be so tiring, but it is an ordeal now.'[22]

---

[20] HL to RL, 14 October 1940.   [21] HL to RL, 15 October 1940.
[22] HL to RL, 18 October 1940.

And, as so often, he was worried about money:

I am perturbed a bit – but not too much – by the amount of money which goes. But whatever it may be I want you not to hesitate to buy for yourself and the boy whenever you feel like it some extra fruit, ices and other good things to cheer yourselves up.[23]

The pressure began to take its toll. On Sunday, 20 October, he said:

I have not written for two days. The reason is that I live in a continuous rush and feel awfully tired. There is continuous preparation of lectures which I have to change and to adapt to varying audiences. Then there are various functions which would be interesting – like yesterday's football match – if I were not so tired. I hope I shall not have to give up the thing before the end. Also – the news from England is so depressing. Will there be a Cambridge to go back to?

On the next day he wrote:

I am still alive after a very rotten public lecture which I have just given. What a mess! Still – they clapped.[24]

The following day he went again to Chapel Hill. Writing to Rachel in the interval between his morning and evening lectures, he said:

[A]nd these poor people had to come here [Duke University] in the morning to fetch me, then bring me back for a short afternoon rest; they will fetch me again at 7 and will bring me back, probably dead, at about midnight. So that is that.

Things improved on the next day, 22 October:

I think yesterday was the first successful day. In the evening I had a crowd of about 300 and I think I did well.

The Wednesday was his first free morning, which he spent registering as an alien and having his fingerprints taken. He packed in the afternoon and at 6pm left by train for New Orleans, a twenty-six-hour train journey to cover 1,200 miles. There, he was to lecture at Tulane University.

They are preparing to grill me again. They have formed a special committee – bless them![25]

Before he left Durham, however, he received a cheering piece of news. Jessup wrote to tell him that the Carnegie Endowment had found it possible to increase his honorarium by an additional $1,500:

---

[23] *Ibid.*   [24] HL to RL, 21 October 1940.   [25] HL to RL, 20 October 1940.

122

We have all recognized that the honorarium originally suggested was quite inadequate and are glad that we can bring it closer to what I would consider an appropriate amount.

He added that, as regards my school fees at Horace Mann, 'if you can pay $300 the rest will be taken care of'.[26] Hersch was greatly relieved. He wrote to Rachel:

I am so glad. I can now go home in the knowledge that you and the boy are secure here for a year and a half.[27]

Hersch arrived in New Orleans on Thursday evening, 24 October – understandably tired and not a little fed up:

I arrived here last night after 26 hours journey. It seems to me a rotten place and the people very stupid, uninteresting and uninterested. Why I have come I really do not know. I have to give one lecture tonight and one tomorrow morning. I am playing with the idea of going off for a long weekend to the sea-side, especially seeing that the place where I am staying is rather uncomfortable. It is hot and the air is extremely sultry.[28]

The next day, however, saw him more cheerful:

New Orleans is proving a better place than I thought. My hosts are proving cordial and appreciative. I have given two successful lectures and there was no end to clapping. I am being taken on trips to see the city and if I am not careful I shall get indigestion from eating French food. I am stationed at Warren House, Newcombe College. This is – yes! – a girls college which has one or two rooms for male University visitors. They are extremely kind to me, and bring me my food to my room. I have established friendly relations with the principal dietician and she sent me, for instance, a breakfast as follows:

    i. An enormous glass of orange juice
    ii. Porridge and cream
    iii. Egg and bacon
    vi. Grapes
    v. Coffee – cream
    vi. A glass of milk
    vii. All kinds of toast, hot rolls, etc.

Don't tell Eli!

You must imagine me sitting practically naked and writing this letter. It is a tropical country. I am learning a great deal about the University and conditions generally.[29]

---

[26] P. C. Jessup to HL, 22 October 1940.   [27] HL to RL, 23 October 1940.
[28] HL to RL, 25 October 1940.   [29] HL to RL, 26 October 1940.

In a postscript, he mentioned that he had an enormous daily corre-spondence with the universities which he had visited and which he was about to visit; and 'I am using up seven vests a day'. He referred again to Jessup's letter:

I never expected that he would be so friendly and gentlemanly. He is the Director of the Int. Law Division of the Carnegie Endowment. I have heard that he may succeed President Butler. I suppose he is one of the most important in the field. In case you should have to meet him I think it is important that you should be very friendly and extremely reserved. In many ways he is like McNair. I spent two hours in drafting my answer of thanks to him.

In his next letter, Hersch told Rachel, in relation to the arrangements for my schooling, that:

the most important thing – and I hope you have done it – is in no way to offend or antagonize Jessup who is doing his best and whose help may prove vital for things much more important than Eli's school. He is more important here than McNair in England . . .

I have a terrible day today [Monday, 28 October]; lecture in the morning, official luncheon, lecture at 4, reception by the English Speaking Union at 5.30, official dinner at 7.

On 29 October, he was telling Rachel:

I feel washed out after the rush of yesterday. To walk from one function to another wet throughout – the collar getting as soft as paper – is no fun. I caught a bit of a cold and, apart from going to a short luncheon to Frieda Liebman, I am cancelling other things.

On Thursday I am going to Baton Rouge, the capital of Louisiana – 90 miles from here – to give a lecture to the State University of Louisiana. From there I am going straight to Kansas.

On the following day, he wrote:

Here I am in the capital of Louisiana for 36 hours. I am giving a lecture tonight and am going to Lawrence tomorrow (800 miles North, madam).

Two days later, he was on his way to Kansas, stopping off at Baton Rouge on Friday, 1 November, to lecture at the State University of Louisiana. Having stayed there overnight, he left in the evening for the long train journey northwards – a direction in which he said he was glad to go to escape the 'damned climate' of Louisiana. To fill the spare day in Baton

Rouge, he allowed himself a rare indulgence: 'I think I will fill the time by going to a cinema (if you don't mind).[30]

From there, he wrote to Rachel saying:

Today there is no lecture, but I had a 'luncheon' and a 'talk'. It is now six pm and I am left to myself after having been taken for a three hours drive to see the place. I am leaving at midnight for Kansas where I am due to arrive tomorrow night.

What a life! (By the way, my lecture last night was *rotten*.)

His continuing worry about money was reflected in his saying that: 'I will save tomorrow $10 by travelling coach instead of Pullman.' The journey to Kansas took twenty-four hours. In Kansas, Hersch was already trying to settle the arrangements for his return to England and booked the Clipper for 16 January 1941. The fare was $425.

In his correspondence with Rachel he still had time to ask for her accounts, which he scrutinised with care.

He reached Kansas City on Saturday 2 November, en route to Lawrence, thirty miles away. In Lawrence, he found the weather much more comfortable.

At least one does not have to change vests seven times a day. But it is not a very great University. They put me up in a hotel, moderately comfortable. This means that I shall have to pay for my board and lodging. It is a nuisance, but I shall have to economise in other ways. I am determined to return to New York without having exceeded the $300 which I took with me – even if I have to walk the last 200 miles.

The blighters here – they are extremely nice – expect me to work for the money. Among others I have to address on Friday a meeting of 300 lawyers including the Chief Justice of the Supreme Court of Kansas. And there are lectures and classes every day. You will be surprised, but I do not feel unduly tired.[31]

The first of his lectures was, he said:

not a bad one. There was a crowd of 250. There are all kinds of receptions and it is a most hectic life, but at least I can move ten yards without having to change my vest![32]

Despite Carnegie's increase in his honorarium, he still remained anxious about money, mainly in relation to my school fees and the prospect of Rachel getting a flat in New York.

---

[30] HL to RL, 1 November 1940.   [31] HL to RL, 3 November 1940.
[32] HL to RL, 11 November 1940.

On Monday, 4 November, he told Rachel that he was:

glad that things are settling down and that you have such a full engagements list. At least you are getting some fun and meeting people . . . There may be some disadvantages about 4002 221st Street[33] but you are sure there of company and of being in the centre of things. On the whole, matters have worked out very well indeed. How many people in England have been able to have their families provided for a year with American money (as I hope will be the case with you and Eli)! And how glad I am, with you, that the boy is at that School![34]

In a short letter to me the next day, he again exhorted me to read plentifully:

The more I think of it, the more I see how very lucky you and we are to have you in this School. The important thing now is to fulfill the expectations. I imagine history must bother you. I hope you are doing some extra reading on your own initiative in American history. A substantial part of the weekend ought to be devoted to that.[35]

He was planning to leave on Saturday for Chicago and, after sleeping there, to proceed on Sunday afternoon to his next stop, Urbana, Illinois. He turned down an invitation to visit Winnipeg, Canada, 'as they offered to pay expenses only'.

Hersch had a crowded day in Kansas – 'an official luncheon with the Chancellor of the University plus a "talk"; a tea; a supper; and a lecture thereafter'. In his letter, there was a rare reference to national politics: on 4 November, Roosevelt had been re-elected for a third term as President of the United States. 'Congratulations to the President. There must be great rejoicing at 4002.'[36] The Bradleys were a staunchly Democratic family.

Although it was a heavy week, it was

not too unpleasant. But it was an expensive week as they put me up in a hotel and I have to pay for it. However, I still hope not to exceed the $300 limit . . . Addressed last night 200 members of the Kansas Bar Association including the Chief Justice and the State Judges. I do not think I did it too well.[37]

On 9 November, he travelled to Chicago en route to the University of Michigan in Urbana, Illinois. Stopping in Chicago for the night, he wrote:

---

[33] The Bradley's house, where Rachel was still staying.   [34] Horace Mann.
[35] HL to EL, 5 November 1940.   [36] HL to RL, 6 November 1940.
[37] HL to RL, 7 November 1940.

I am here in this gorgeous but not too expensive hotel, and am leaving tomorrow for Urbana.

This *is* a great city. On the lake it is beautiful just now. But it is a noisy place.

I shall have to return here next Sunday because I am to give a public lecture in the University on Monday, the 18th.[38]

Still in Chicago on 10 November, he reported that:

It is foggy here and windy and rainy. One might be in Cambridge. I wish we were.[39]

By 11 November, he was in Urbana, in 'a highly uncomfortable hotel'. From the heat of the South he now found himself in freezing temperatures.

On 12 November, however, he had moved to Champaign, Illinois, a few miles from Urbana:

I have refused an invitation to a concert and to a reception this evening and I am having a quiet evening at last in the hotel writing letters, preparing my two performances for tomorrow, and eating two pounds of grapes (which I am sure you will not grudge me – especially if I ask you to go out with the boy and to buy some).

I enclose, registered, the two identity cards. They are for both of you more important than a passport and I hope you will take care of them. (By the way, I have been told that by going to Washington for a day I can obtain a re-entry permit which will enable me to return here, if necessary, without a new visa).[40]

He wrote his next letter on notepaper that he had picked up on the train from Chicago to Urbana. Writing to me on 13 November, he said:

This note paper is from the poshest train I have ever been on. I was on it only for one hour and a half, but I had to pay first class plus extra for Pullman plus excess fare (it takes the richest people from Chicago to Florida in the South) plus a supplement for a revolving chair (which I did not use because I sat all the time in the Observation Cab).

From Champaign, Illinois, he wrote to Rachel on 15 November 1940:

Here I am in a new hotel! (I think I am a genius. I have not so far forgotten a single thing in any of the places where I stayed.)

---

[38] HL to RL, 10 November 1940. [39] HL to RL, postmarked 12 November 1940.
[40] HL to RL, 12 November 1940.

I gave two good performances last night and this morning to big audiences and one after lunch talk. I am becoming a great piece of humbug. I will probably return to Chicago on Friday. You can write there to me: Professor HL, International House, The University, Chicago. I am lecturing there on Monday afternoon. Immediately after the lecture I am going to Madison, Wisconsin for three days, namely, from the 19th to 21 November. I will then return to Chicago for three days and then go 700 miles North-West to Minneapolis from November 25–30. So that is that.

It is absolutely freezing here. I bought ear-muffs.

You must now be busy with the flat – and may you have plenty of luck and . . . with it. I sincerely hope you will be able to share it and that the financial aspect of it will not therefore be too catastrophic. You will have your hands full of it and if I were you I would not accept any invitations to go out.

I have splendid news from the boy – except that he got unnecessarily upset about my suggestion that he ought to do well in history. He takes me very seriously – from the distance. How very lucky we are about his school!

From Minnesota, he wrote:

I arrived here last night with only a slight cold. Today I have not yet had a minute to myself. People are extremely kind here – I sat with the Law Faculty for luncheon from 12.30 to 4pm, but there is no time to breathe.

I am beginning to be quite proud of ourselves. University of Minnesota is the third greatest University in the country – 16,000 students. And you will be glad to hear that your husband has been a success. I have just delivered the first public lecture. The Hall was full, and I did a good job. Last night I addressed 80 professors, including the President of the University. It was a success too. These people are so appreciative! I have a comfortable room and am being constantly entertained for meals. I should be sorry to leave Minnesota, but I must go on Friday morning. I will spend a day in Carleton College, 60 miles from here. There I hope to pick up 25–50 dollars.

[Minnesota] was even better than Urbana. They spoke again and again of their gratitude for my coming to them and hoped that I would visit them again in the future. They meant every word of it. I had a busy time, but I did not regret it. They made me a member of this University and I had the privilege of inviting guests. I did entertain McKinnon Wood, former legal adviser of the League.[41]

By Friday he was at Northfields, apologising for not having written on the previous day:

---

[41] HL to RL, 24 November 1940.

I had no moment to spare. Two lectures, two other functions and things between. At 11pm I was driven here in a snow blizzard and arrived at 1am. It is a most beautiful college, 50 miles from Minneapolis. I have the most gorgeous suite of the trip, but also a bit of a cold. I have to address at 11.30 the whole body of students – about 800 (and fifty members of the staff). I shall be disappointed if I do not get $50. I am leaving in the evening by the night train to Chicago and from there to Detroit where I shall be expected by your family at 4.53.[42]

But Northfields did not live up to expectations. In his next letter, he reported:

Northfields proved to be a flop. I did not enjoy my address and – what is more important – they never paid a cent! It was a net loss.[43]

The 'family' of Rachel to which he referred was a branch of her mother's family which had emigrated from Russia at the end of the nineteenth century and had settled in Detroit under the name of 'Bennett'. Harry Bennett was a successful lawyer and was anxious to do what he could to help Rachel and me during our stay in the US. Of the visit, Hersch wrote on 30 November:

I arrived here two hours ago duly met at the station by Ethel, her son Richard and Harry Bennett. (He is a jolly hearty fellow.) I was driven to Ethel's house to meet her mother and your mother's sister. She is a nice lady and [I] was quite touched. They then fought as to with whom I have to stay and Harry won. He has a fine house. I first had a great shower bath and have to go shortly to town to dinner with them. At 8pm there is a great reception in Harry's house. I hope I will survive. In any case I like the people and am on excellent terms with them. Tomorrow I am going to Ann Arbor.[44]

Cold though he was in Champaign, where he stayed while lecturing in Urbana, a neighbouring town, he seemed more light-hearted. By then, the tour was more than half over.

Two days later, he gave his last lecture at Urbana and left for Chicago to spend the weekend there. He professed himself 'very comfortable' in the International House of the University of Chicago. Having lectured on Monday afternoon, he left immediately afterwards for Madison, Wisconsin, 200 miles north, where he was to spend three days before returning to Chicago for three days.

The pace was almost frenetic. In Chicago, on Wednesday, 20 November, he gave three lectures, one before what he describes as 'a very

[42] HL to RL, 29 November 1940.   [43] HL to RL, 30 November 1940 ('Saturday').
[44] HL to RL, 30 November 1940.

critical audience of an excellent University which is twice as large as Cambridge'.[45]

At about this time, he received an encouraging letter from Harold Laski, his former colleague at the LSE:

Felix [Frankfurter] wrote to me of your arrival; and it sounds like a really interesting itinerary. I know you will do good – for your sanity and tolerance will make Americans feel that the kind of society we are fighting for is one on which the inherent decencies of life depend.[46]

Moving eastwards again on 3 December, Hersch wrote to me on the train from Detroit to Buffalo:

Many thanks for your letter. I was so glad to have it. It arrived after I had given a lecture this afternoon at Ann Arbor (University of Michigan) before 600 people in an enormous lecture room in which there is room for another 600. I had to speak to two microphones. I did not like it at all and I hated the sight of the big audience. I am not an opera singer. The result was a rather indifferent lecture and a bad headache which I am having just now. How glad I shall be to have some days rest in New York with Mummy and you! I am not used to this mode of life. (But I was glad to go to Ann Arbor because I picked up an extra $75 for the lecture – I was running short of money.) I arrive at midnight at Buffalo and have to wait there overnight for a train to Ithaca (Cornell University).

You must not get conscious-stricken because of not writing for a week. Of course, I understand. You have so many new things. I am very glad that you are getting used to them and that you are abandoning the habit of worrying. This is an inherited habit for I, too, worry about things that never happen. Life is difficult enough with real difficulties and we ought not to add to them imaginary ones.[47]

He also wrote to Rachel:

All this, of course, is sheer waste of time and energy. The Ann Arbor lecture was, I think, a flop. Brierly was there and other dignitaries (including Ethel and four other members of the family). The Bennetts are most hospitable. I stayed with them. Reynold – who is a nice boy – collected me there and took me to Detroit where I lunched with his father, who just got a new car. I then went to their home; saw Mrs Bennett, whom I found very pleasant; went to dinner with all of them and Ethel and Bennett; and then did my duty of going to the family.[48]

---

45 HL to RL, 20 November 1940.   46 Laski to HL, 3 November 1940.
47 HL to EL, 2 December 1940.   48 HL to RL, 3 December 1940.

By the time he entered the last week of the marathon, he had clearly had enough of it. Writing to Rachel on the train between Buffalo and Ithaca, on his way to Cornell University, he exclaimed: 'Only *4* (!) more days of this damned business.' He spoke of his visit to the family in Detroit in unenthusiastic terms: 'They are a strange lot, but very pleasant for 24 hours and well-meaning', but then continued:

I am getting quite tired out, and shall be glad of a complete rest of several days at home. I hope I shall last out so long. In the meantime, please do not make any arrangements for meeting anyone; your invariable answer must be: 'I will let you know. I do not know what arrangements he has made. He will probably have to go to bed for a days rest.' *And this is true.*[49]

Again, a couple of days later:

I do not know whether you realize what these two months have meant in physical energy and mental strain.[50]

On reaching Ithaca, he wrote:

I arrived here two hours ago. The place seems to be in a state of disintegration. I was not met at the station and, apart from one public lecture and a luncheon, I have not heard of any arrangements. However, I am expecting to see them this evening.[51]

But some explanation was forthcoming the next day:

I have given a very good lecture at 12–1. I had a visit in the afternoon of the representative of the Law Faculty. They feel a bit guilty, but the fact is that they do not teach international law in any real sense and they are somewhat embarrassed about that.[52]

This was the last of that remarkable series of letters, though not of the burden of lecturing. He still had commitments at Smith College and at Harvard, as well as invitations from Phillips Bradley to lecture at Queens College and from myself and another student at Horace Mann to give a talk to the school. But he and Rachel were greatly pleased to be invited by the Jessups to a black-tie dinner at their apartment on East 86th Street on 17 December. By 23 December, he was able to write to Mr Robert H. Jackson, the United States Attorney-General, to whom he was introduced by a letter from Harold Laski, asking him if he might call on him when in Washington in the first week of the New Year. It was to be,

---

[49] HL to RL, December 1940, from Ann Arbor.
[50] HL to RL, December 1940 ('Wednesday'), from Ithaca.
[51] HL to RL, December 1940.   [52] HL to RL, December 1940.

as will be seen, an important meeting. From Nicholas Murray Butler, the Director of the Carnegie Endowment, he received an acknowledgment of his report,[53] which said:

We have received most enthusiastic letters from the institutions which you have visited and are confident that you have performed a very great service to the cause of international understanding. We rejoice that all has gone so well.[54]

What do we learn of Hersch from his report and his series of family letters? They reflect, first, his physical stamina. He travelled over 6,000 miles, always by train, on occasion for long distances in coach class rather than Pullman, and lectured in 15 different law schools and universities. He coped, though not always comfortably, with the difficulty he had in sleeping and overcame severe changes of climate with only an occasional cold. But it is hardly surprising that, by the end of the tour, he was desperate for a complete rest – though even then he took only four days before going on to his next appointment.

The letters are mainly concerned with six themes: where he is; his own doings; his accommodation and state of health; where he will be going next, so that letters may be appropriately addressed; his preoccupation with economy, both on his own part and Rachel's, so that sufficient funds should remain available for her and myself when he returned to England; and his concern about me and my schooling.

Surprisingly, perhaps, his letters give little if any indication of what substantive impact he thought his lectures might be having on his audiences. True, they were, on the whole, academic exercises in international law and, for that reason, were unlikely in themselves to have generated much support for the British cause. At the same time, he appears to have received a warm welcome everywhere he went, in no way suggestive of any animosity towards Britain. Still, it is curious that, other than in his letter to the Foreign Office,[55] he makes no mention of the effect of the lectures. Evidently, he was careful to avoid political discussion. At the beginning of his tour, Jessup had specifically warned him about this:

I am sure it is not necessary for me to say anything in your case because I remember when we talked that you had very much in mind your desire not to be enmeshed in public political discussions about the war. I have noticed, however, in the letters from some of the institutions which you are going to visit that they hope to have you speak to several public meetings and I am

---

[53] See pp. 115–19 above.   [54] Nicholas Murray Butler to HL, 10 January 1941.
[55] See pp. 141–4 below.

writing this merely to reinforce what I am sure is your own judgment. I think you can very properly say in regard to any such situation that you do not care to discuss the present war situation in any way which might be misinterpreted as implying an argument about the role of the United States. The reason why I put on this postscript is that my attention has recently been called to one or two unfortunate incidents where newspaper reports indicated that some of our English visitors had attracted attention by remarks that were construed in that way.[56]

And he took the warning seriously. Jessup was able to write to him on 19 November, while he was in Chicago, saying that he was glad to know that all was going well:

I know from what I have heard from the universities which you have already visited that from our point of view, the trip is going very well indeed.[57]

As to Hersch himself, the letters reveal a man of strong will, determination and the ability to cope with adverse circumstances – the loneliness of spending each night on his own and the absence of any familiars with whom he could share his feelings about the events of the day. He was immensely conscientious and meticulous in the preparation of his lectures even though, having regard to their limited range and his knowledge of the subject matter, he could quite easily have repeated the same lectures in one place after another. He wanted to perform well and was critical of himself if his lectures fell below the standard that he wanted to maintain. Equally, he clearly enjoyed the admiration and praise that his good lectures generated.

There are curious omissions from this intense correspondence. There is scarcely a reference to the presidential election campaign then being waged in the United States which culminated in the re-election of Roosevelt on 5 November, beyond the one sentence to Rachel in his letter of 6 November.

Nor did Hersch ever mention during the period of his lecture tour the subject matter of the lectures. Only from his letters of report, first to the President of the Carnegie Endowment[58] and then to Sir Stephen Gaselee at the Foreign Office[59] do we get some indication of their content. The notes or texts of the lectures have not survived.

---

[56] Jessup to HL, 22 October 1940.   [57] Jessup to HL, 19 November 1940.
[58] See pp. 115–19 above.   [59] See pp. 141–4 below.

His love and concern for Rachel and myself shines through all the letters and can be seen in the detail with which he concerned himself with her and my activities while he was a thousand miles away from New York. As already remarked, one of the recurrent themes in Hersch's letters, both at this period and later, is his concern for my welfare. As this is his biography, not mine, I forbear from setting out the detail of these letters, but to omit all reference to their content would give a false impression of what was so often on his mind. Three excerpts will suffice. In the course of a letter to me from New Orleans on 30 October 1940, he said:

I am writing to say three things:
  (1) that I am happy that you are going to be in one of the best schools in the country;
  (2) that this has been made possible as the result of Mummy's great efforts and at the cost of a financial sacrifice which we can hardly afford. This being so I know you will plunge immediately into most serious work – steady and concentrated and try to show your gratitude and appreciation. This is also extremely important because of what Professor Jessup has done;
  (3) that you may find it difficult at the beginning to get into the new atmosphere and to become acquainted with things with which the boys have been familiar since childhood. Let that not weigh on your mind. Do your best; be modest; try to win friends and keep their friendships.

Then, on 7 November, he wrote:

I do not want you to worry about money and to try to 'economise'. I do not mind at all if you spend on yourself a dime (what a word!) here and there. The most effective economy which you can make is to get the full value of the money which we – and probably others – are spending on the school for you. For instance, nothing would please me more than if as the result of private study on your own you would become top boy in American history!

Evidently, his encouragement to me to engage in 'private study' of American history did not please me, for, on 12 November, he wrote:

I am replying in the first instance to that about History. I am so sorry my suggestion has upset you. Of course, I did *not* mean for you to take it if it is inconvenient. What I had in mind was that in case you do take it in your form you should try to do well. That is all I had in mind. Now that you have explained what is the position I suggest you simply forget all about it. You must not get upset by such small things. So that finishes history.

I was extremely happy about the first letter in which you told me that the School is perfect in every respect and that you are happy there. I cannot tell you how glad I am about it. I feel now that my coming to the United States was justified.

There will probably be ups and downs in the School, but I am convinced that this is a splendid School and that you are determined to do well. That is quite enough for me. I know that when you are determined to do well, you will do that.

And now the last but not least important thing: Winter is coming and with it the danger of catching colds. Try, please, not to get overheated and when you are overheated on no account remain stationary outside. We must not spoil this wonderful opportunity by catching colds and being ill.

In the meantime, Rachel had found a small flat in a newish apartment block in Riverdale, a northwestern suburb of the Bronx, bounded on the west by the River Hudson. The area was not heavily built-up. The private houses had large gardens and there was a general air of tranquillity. One could have been many miles away from the hubbub of downtown Manhattan, though it was barely ten miles away. The flat was about ten minutes walk from the dormitory of the Horace Mann school, and a further ten minutes from the school itself. Although I began as a boarder at the school, soon after Rachel took the flat I moved in there with her. When Hersch returned from his lecture tour in early December, we were all reunited there.

1941 MEMORANDUM FOR THE US ATTORNEY-GENERAL ON 'QUALIFIED NEUTRALITY'

The first days of January 1941 were spent in Washington, initially in consultation with the Attorney-General, Robert H. Jackson, and then, ensconced in a hotel room, trying to draft a memorandum on what Jackson described as 'the philosophy in international law of the US policy of aiding the allies by all means short of war'.

For a few days Rachel was able to be with him. Even after she left, he found that the 'work was proceeding desperately slowly. And it is rotten work.'[60] Although, in the end, the work turned out well, it is hardly surprising that after the efforts of the previous three months he should have felt mentally drained. Nonetheless, by 15 January, he was able to send the memorandum to the Attorney-General.

---

[60] HL to RL, 13 January 1941.

It was a substantial document of some fifteen pages,[61] which developed the case for a doctrine of 'qualified neutrality', relieving a neutral of the duty of strict impartiality towards a belligerent which had commenced a war illegally. He argued that the United States was entitled to assert a right of discriminatory action by reason of the fact that, since the Kellogg–Briand Pact of 1928, the place of war and with it the place of neutrality in the international legal system were no longer the same as they were prior to that date. The prohibition of recourse to war contained in the Pact, to which Germany and Italy, in common with practically all nations, were parties, destroyed the historical and juridical foundation of the doctrine of neutrality conceived as an attitude of absolute impartiality in relation to a party engaged in an aggressive war. The aggressor derives no rights from its illegality. Additionally, departure from strict impartiality was justified both by the right of reprisal and as a measure of self-defence. The principal concepts set out in the memorandum were adopted by the Attorney-General in a major speech to the Inter-American Bar Association on 27 March 1941.[62]

This exposition of the law considerably advanced the rationalisation of United States partiality towards Britain. Previous justification, as reflected for example in an important letter written to the *New York Times* in August 1940 and signed by four distinguished lawyers, of whom Dean Acheson[63] was one, rested principally upon a more liberal interpretation of the Neutrality Act. The concepts developed by Hersch had not earlier entered into US legal thinking.

He was fortunate to secure a seat on a Clipper flying to Lisbon via Bermuda and the Azores. From Horta in the Azores, he wrote:

You got my telegram by now. They took me from Bermuda after all – although I was not sure until after the last moment. From Bermuda it became quite a small party of seven – all sitting in one room and talking to one another – Willkie or no Willkie. He is a fine fellow – in many respects still a boy.

---

[61] It is reprinted in *Collected Papers*, Vol. 5, pp. 645–58.

[62] The full text of the speech was printed in the *New York Times*, 28 March 1941. Jackson 'drew on' this for his speech on 'International Order' (delivered on his behalf) to the first meeting of the Inter-American Bar Association in Havana, 27 March 1941. Reprinted in the *American Bar Association Journal* (May 1941) and in the *AJIL* (1941). The text can be found at www.robertjackson.org/the-man/speeches-articles/speeches/speeches-by-robert-h-jackson/.

[63] Dean Acheson (1893–1971), American statesman and lawyer, became US Secretary of State in the Truman administration (1949–53) where he played a central role in defining US foreign policy during the Cold War.

The night was ghastly. The Clipper bumped up and down mercilessly. As the result I was actually once thoroughly sick in the morning. We just managed to get in, but we cannot get out. There is at least a day's delay, and that is all to the good. I shall have a good rest at the Pan-American Airways expense. They put us up in a nice and comfortable hotel. Accordingly, so far – apart from being sick – the trip is shaping nicely. And you make it easier for me by being brave. The journey from New York to Bermuda was very pleasant – almost like in a train – though more noisy. I do not know when we leave here and when I shall be able to get a connection in Lisbon.[64]

Wendell Willkie, who was one of his travelling companions, was the recently defeated Republican candidate in the November 1940 presidential election. The two got on well together, and when Hersch reached Cambridge he tried to arrange for Willkie to visit the university, but Willkie could not manage it.

So limited was the space available on the connecting flight from Lisbon to London that Hersch had to spend a number of rather uncertain days waiting there. On 25 January, he wrote to Rachel from Estoril:

It is possible – or rather likely – that before this reaches you you will receive a cable informing you of my arrival in England. The prospects are that I may go in about three days. The FO have written and this carries weight. But the Air Attaché whom I saw yesterday was sour like vinegar and would not look at me. But he has now reconsidered the matter in the light of various circumstances – including a strong word from the Commercial Attaché who is a former student of mine and who was full of enthusiasm when he saw me on Saturday in the Embassy hall. So that's that.

The journey from Horta – 7 hours – was very pleasant except for the last half-an-hour. I am staying now in a very pleasant spot – about 14 miles outside Lisbon. The latter is a typically Eastern city with narrow, hilly, filthy streets.

I have 'made friends' with Dr Cole who went with our Clipper from New York. He is Professor of Surgery and Head of the Orthopedic Department in Minneapolis and is going to England to become head of the American Hospital there.[65]

CAMBRIDGE, JANUARY 1941

Four days later, he was safely home and had resumed his normal routine. His first letter was to Rachel:

---

[64] HL to RL and EL, January 1941.   [65] HL to RL, 25 January 1941.

Here I am, writing at my desk, with a football game in front of me, with some of the yellow aconites peeping out under the tree. It is a cold, misty day, but the study is warm and pleasant. I have an enormous mess to clear up, but it is pleasant to write this first letter from home to you. You were so beautifully understanding in this last fortnight and the separation will therefore be specially difficult to bear.

We left Horta on Friday and arrived in Lisbon in the afternoon. The Air Attaché was there to meet Willkie. He showed no sign of enthusiasm when he saw me (I sent him a telegram from Horta). I thought that I should have to stay in Lisbon at least a fortnight, and I decided to take a room in a very pleasant hotel in Estoril. On Saturday morning I went to the Embassy and there I met by accident the Commercial Attaché who was a student of mine and who proved to be a grateful student. His good word and the telegram from Gaselee worked like magic, and I was told on Sunday that I may go on Monday morning. I duly appeared on Monday at the airport, but was told by the police that I cannot go because I had no exit permit from Portugal. You can imagine how I felt! However, the Air Attaché appeared in the last moment. The British word still counts in Portugal and I was allowed to go. In the afternoon I was in England after a very bumpy journey. I cannot tell you where we landed, but I may tell you that I was so tired that I spent the night there. I sent you a cable from the hotel. Next morning I went to London, saw Locker and Gaselee and went by the 4.45 to the good old Cambridge. The Crotches prepared a nice dinner – a very difficult thing in these days. I saw the Thomases. They are well, but they are feeling the effects of the food situation. This morning I saw my various colleagues. I am due to lecture tomorrow. The Vice-Chancellor will invite Willkie – the result of my journey with him and of Gaselee's advice.

It is very quiet here. There has not been a siren for days. You must have no apprehension on that account. Keep well, have a good rest, and think occasionally of a husband who thinks of you with much love.[66]

The understanding that he had reached with Rachel was that he would write her an airmail letter once a week, but even so he sent his next letter two days later:

If you don't mind, I feel that in the first week or two I ought to write more than one airmail letter a week. I am settling down slowly to work. Just now I am busy on the Digest in order to give the typist something to do. There are also three examination papers to be set. And there is the long report to Sir Stephen Gaselee to be written. I want it to be a long and useful report. Yesterday I gave my first lecture. The Class is smaller than last year – about 60. There will [be] very few before long because the 19 and 20 year olds will be called up. I dined

[66] HL to RL, 29 January 1941.

in College last night and talked to the new Master. I do not like him very much. The Vice-Master is a darling as usual. Hollond is extremely kind. There is no doubt that the journey has done good. The house is very quiet. Miss Isaacs and Miss Brown and Crotch's mother left about a fortnight ago. It is possible that Crotch will get a new job, and that they will go too. There will be no difficulty about tenants. The important thing is that Gladys is here – efficient, devoted, and quiet as usual. She is worth her weight in gold. The house is clean and well looked after. There is no scratch on the walls. There are fires in the two studies and in the dining room. We want them as there has been no sun here for weeks. It is cold and damp. People don't look too well. Gutteridge has aged; Turner is not too bright. I had a cordial letter from McNair waiting my arrival.

I do hope you will take things quietly now. You must not worry about me. I shan't go about hungry. I have a gas mask and am going to buy a steel helmet. And – Master Eli – I am becoming the Chief of the Fire Spotting and Fire Fighting Service in Cranmer Road! I want Eli to work, but not so as to make himself unhappy or nervous. I want you to go with the boy to the cinema once a week and yourself be as happy as circumstances permit. I should like to receive frequent letters from both of you.[67]

The 'new Master' of Trinity was the historian, G. M. Trevelyan, for whose best known books, *A History of England* and *English Social History*, Hersch had a high regard (and later insisted that I read them!) even though he found Trevelyan's austere and dour personal manner rather off-putting. There is a story, probably apocryphal, that, when a delegation of undergraduates went to see Trevelyan to complain about the food in Hall, he angrily ejected them from his study and virtually threw them down the steep flight of stairs into Great Court. The Vice-Master was Denys Winstanley, also a historian, but on a narrower scale than Trevelyan, his principal works being two volumes on the history of the university in the eighteenth and nineteenth centuries. He was a gentle soul, living a bachelor life in a set of rooms in Great Court, treasuring his antique china cups of which, when broken, the parts were stapled together. Hollond was the Dean of College, a legal historian who, although not academically very significant, was a powerful university politician and was credited with the consolidation of the university law teachers into an effective faculty of law. Gutteridge was the Professor of Comparative Law. Hersch had first met him during his days at the LSE and he was one of those who had written supportive references when Hersch applied for the Whewell Chair. Turner was a lecturer on criminal law who, despite his strong left-wing leanings, was a shrewd investor

[67] HL to RL, 31 January 1941.

and lived stylishly in a large house in Girton. His wife and children (six of them) had been evacuated to the United States at the same time as Hersch, Rachel and I went there in October 1940. As regards Hersch's mention of his own role as Chief of the Cranmer Road Fire Service, so little did his wife and son conceive of him as capable of discharging so practical a role that it elicited from me the comment in my next letter: 'Frankly speaking, it must be a farce.'[68]

---

[68] EL to HL, 17 February 1941.

CHAPTER 6

THE WAR YEARS, PART II:
FEBRUARY 1941–MARCH 1942

One of Hersch's first tasks after his return was to prepare a lengthy report to the Foreign Office on his US visit, focusing principally on his contact with the US authorities and his discussions with international lawyers. He also appended his report to the Carnegie Endowment.[1]

Hersch wrote to Sir Stephen Gaselee at the Foreign Office on 5 February 1941:

When, last September, I accepted the invitation to visit the United States, I was, to a large extent, guided by your advice. In fact, your letter to the Vice-Chancellor left me with no doubt that it was my duty to go. This being so, perhaps you will not regard it as inappropriate if I submit through you this report on some aspects of my visit which the authorities may find of interest.

In accepting the invitation I had three objects in mind:
  (1) I thought that I ought to avail myself of the opportunity of influencing opinion by lecturing on current topics of international law and relations and of establishing other kinds of contact with university faculties, law schools, foreign policy groups, associations of lawyers, and so on, especially in the part of the United States in which such contact appeared to me to be particularly necessary, namely, in the Middle West.
  (2) I believed that I ought to try to use the opportunity of having conversations with teachers of international law in the leading universities in the United States. For various reasons these have tended in recent years to assume a somewhat pronounced isolationist attitude, and it appeared to me that their standing justified an attempt to influence their attitude.
  (3) I envisaged the – then somewhat remote – possibility of being of assistance to the United States authorities in case they should require it in connection with any attempt to explain, from the point of view of international law, their policy of all help to the Allies short of war. As things have turned out, this proved feasible, and, with the full approval of our Chargé d'Affaires, I was engaged on this matter in Washington during the last fortnight of my visit to the United States. It will be convenient if I deal with this first.

---

[1] See pp. 115–19 above.

Contact with the United States Authorities

In the fulfillment of its policy of providing all aid to the Allies short of war, the Government of the United States have had to meet objections coming not only from the Axis countries but also from the opponents of the administration in the United States to the effect that that policy is contrary to international law. On occasions the spokesmen of the United States Government have tried to solve the difficulty by expressing the view that Germany, after having committed violations of the law of nations both against her adversaries and neutrals, was not entitled to rely on international law. At times, as in the matter of the transfer of destroyers, attempts have been made to present the action taken as being in accordance with the established rules of neutrality.

Both these courses were felt to be unsatisfactory, and when, early in January, I saw Mr Jackson, the Attorney-General, he told me that the Government felt the desirability of a statement of general principles of international law, as distinguished from specific rules, which could be invoked as explaining and justifying the action of the United States. 'What is wanted', he said, 'is a philosophy, in terms of international law, of our policy of all aid to the Allies short of war.' He told me that as he could not in this matter count on the assistance of the leading American international lawyers – like Professors Jessup, Hyde and Borchard – he would welcome a memorandum by a lawyer in my position for the use of himself and of the Cabinet. I answered that I would consider the matter and let him know. I then consulted our Chargé d'Affaires who, after considering the matter, told me next day that the opportunity was an excellent one and advised me to go ahead. This coincided with my view. I thought that only good could come out of the attempt to assist the Government of the United States by placing at their disposal an exposition of legal principles which made 'all aid short of war' appear to be fully consistent with international law and with formal neutral status as distinguished from specific rules of neutrality as practiced in the 19th Century and as codified in the Hague Conventions. I felt I could undertake this task conscientiously and without any imputation of special pleading, for I have for many years held the view that neutral duties are not immutable and that they are determined by the legal position of war at any given period.

Ten days later I gave the memorandum to the Attorney-General. For various reasons I declined the offer of a honorarium – one of the reasons being that the acceptance of it might have jeopardized the necessary anonymity of the authorship of the memorandum. Before leaving Washington I left a copy of the memorandum with the Chargé d'Affaires who suggested that I should leave another copy with the Foreign Office for the use of yourself, Sir William Malkin, and of Mr Scott. I enclose it herewith. I handed in the memorandum just before Mr Hull and Mr Stimson testified before the House Committee, and I believe I am right in saying that much of what they said on that occasion on the legal aspect of the question bore the impress of some sections of the memorandum. In a further conversation with the Attorney-General I advised him as to international lawyers who could usefully be called upon to testify before the Senate Committee. I recommended particularly Professor Quincy Wright and Professor Charles Fenwick.

Perhaps I ought also to mention that I had some discussions with Mr Justice Frankfurter and with Mr Hackworth, the Legal Adviser to the State Department. While on the Clipper and in the Azores I had talks with Mr Willkie and his party. You will have heard by now from the Vice-Chancellor that he was unable to accept the invitation to Cambridge, but, in view of the terms of his reply and on general grounds, I am very glad that you approved of the suggestion and that you communicated it so promptly to the Vice-Chancellor.

Contact with Teachers of International Law

In accepting the invitation to go to the United States I hoped to have conversations with my isolationist colleagues in the principal universities. I had discussions with Professors Borchard, Hyde and Jessup. I am doubtful whether I succeeded in making any impression upon Professor Borchard – a teacher and writer who was closely connected with the late Senator Borah and who still wields considerable influence with some senators. But I mentioned to him that Professor Hyde held strongly to the view that teachers of international law ought not in these matters to embarrass the State Department by adverse criticism in public. It remains to be seen whether he has taken the hint. Neither was Professor Hyde, former Legal Adviser to the State Department, amenable to persuasion on detailed questions of the law of neutrality. But he agreed with me, at the beginning of October, that unneutral action, of practically unlimited extent, might be made to rest on the broad basis of the doctrine of self-defence. In view of Professor Hyde's relations with the State Department I thought it proper to report to Mr Angus Fletcher as to the possible trend of the attitude of the State Department in that direction. Several weeks later I was interested to see that the Secretary of State relied on the principle of self-defence as a full justification of American policy of help to the Allies. Professor Jessup of Columbia – a distinguished scholar and administrator who was freely mentioned as a possible Secretary of State in a Republican administration – is still somewhat reserved, but I doubt whether he will say or write anything likely to embarrass the Administration. I may say, incidentally, that in my view it is advisable that British authorities in the United States should maintain with him as close a contact as is feasible in the circumstances.

Lecturing Activities

The enclosed report[2] which I submitted to President Nicholas Murray Butler gives a picture of part of my work in this field. I lectured before fifteen universities

[2] See pp. 115–19 above.

and law schools. I concentrated mainly on the Middle West. In my public lectures before large audiences I had to avoid anything in the nature of direct propaganda. But public functions were as a rule preliminary to a less formal exchange of views before private circles or limited audiences. I enclose President Butler's acknowledgement of my report – an acknowledgement which I thought showed a full understanding of the purport of my visit. He is most sincerely devoted to the cause for which Britain stands, and, in his capacity as President of the Trustees of the Carnegie Endowment, he was largely responsible for extending to me the invitation to visit the United States.

In the course of my visit I covered large portions of the country – over six thousand miles – and I had the opportunity of discussing with many well-disposed persons some aspects of British propaganda in the United States. It is possible that after I have got again into stride in Cambridge I may put down in writing the results of these discussions and of my own experience in the matter.

I am not, of course, a good judge of the results of this visit. In many respects there is little that is tangible about them. But I feel that the venture was worthwhile, and I wish to express my deep appreciation of your encouragement throughout and of your assistance at the various stages of the journey.

The report was well received in the Foreign Office, though part of Hersch's reasoning in the memorandum given to Jackson occasioned some expressions of doubt. Sir William Malkin, the Legal Adviser, noted:

The memorandum which Professor Lauterpacht wrote for the Attorney-General of the United States is extremely interesting. Apart from the argument based on 'self-defence', which strikes me as rather a dangerous one, it consists of an admirable statement of the argument that the position as regards neutrality has been profoundly modified by the Covenant and the Pact of Paris. We have always tried to push this argument in our own interests, and even did our best to keep it alive at the beginning and in the early months of the war, though considerations of policy, or one might say of fear, prevented the neutrals in general from accepting or acting upon it – a fact which some of them at any rate have already had cause to regret. It does not, however, seem beyond the bounds of possibility that circumstances after the war may be such that the argument may revive, and it is in any case of considerable interest that it should be being employed in the country which produced the Pact of Paris, and, it would appear, to some extent by spokesmen of the Administration.[3]

He recommended that parts of the letter and the whole of the memorandum should be printed for internal Foreign Office use. One Official, though acknowledging that 'the exposition of the elastic nature of the

---

[3] 22 February 1941, FO371/26215.

concept of neutrality under international law is valuable', trenchantly criticised the statement in paragraph 15 that 'there is no practical limit to state action which may be made to rest on the broad shoulders of self-defence', saying that 'it might well have emanated from Herr Hitler'.[4] Fortunately, this comment was not to see the light of day during Hersch's lifetime.

On the same day, Hersch wrote to Rachel.

HL to RL, 5 February 1941

I have been writing almost every day, and this must stop. But I feel that in these first weeks you will not mind receiving a letter or two in addition to the agreed programme.

It is 9am now, and I am sitting at the desk after breakfast. The study is cosy and warm. There is snow in the garden, but the tops of the daffodils and crocuses are already appearing.

I have dined twice in College, spoken to the Master and visited the Secretary-General who was extremely nice. Tomorrow I will see the Vice-Chancellor.

In the meantime, I had here yesterday for an hour and a half the Liverpool Vice-Chancellor [McNair]. He is tired, but looks well and does a great deal. He sends you both his warm regards. He appreciated very much what I have done for him in the matter of his Rockefeller project.

I have finished the report to Gaselee and in the light of his reactions I will see what is the best method to proceed about Wellesley.

Before his letter had reached her, Rachel had written at length to tell him how things were going in New York and mentioning, in particular, a visit from Hersch's uncle, Julius, whose presence in New York Hersch had entirely overlooked. 'I really forgot all about his existence.'[5]

RL to HL, 9 February 1941

The Lauterpachts came this afternoon. Uncle Julius, is an extremely nice and kind hearted man, he is like your dear father, but very much better looking, he is the image of your brother Dunek. He is about the same age as Dunek too. His wife quite nice and very friendly, but not exactly the type I love, but I respect her. She treats her husband like a baby, and that is very noticeable, I do not like it. The old man I love very much. He so reminds me of your father that the feelings towards him was quite natural. He cried when he came in, He controlled himself though at once. It must have brought back, to him his youth, his family etc. I felt it for him. They have two sons, most delightful boys, Robert

---

[4] R. Ashton (a Foreign Office Official), 12 March 1941.
[5] HL to RL, 28 February 1941.

the eldest is a dentist and will be fully qualified to practice on his own next June. The youngest one a boy of twenty is a civil engineer. The father seems to be doing very well. They drove up in a very posh car, and they tell me that they have a very large house and a large garden in Brooklyn. Of course we are invited to spend a week-end with them soon. We shall certainly go. Eli loves the younger boy, and they are great friends. Your Uncle can not forgive you for not trying to find him while on your visit here. He is a dear old man, and I am glad I have a real friend in him.

Subsequently, Rachel changed her views on 'Auntie Sarah', as Julius' wife came to be called. She was a very generous, kindly, hospitable and loving woman. I often visited her at her home, especially after Rachel had returned to the UK.

By the end of February, the Crotches had left Cranmer Road. In their place came a Colonel Robbins and his wife, accompanied by their Swiss housekeeper. They were particularly welcome as they were able to pay a better rent than their predecessors and the Colonel had a treble meat ration which made a big difference. He also had a batman, who offered to polish Hersch's shoes.

HL to RL, 28 February 1941
Life is hectic at No. 6. The Robbinses – delightful people – and their Swiss housekeeper moved in last Tuesday. On Thursday Gladys's foot got very bad and she is an absolute invalid at least for a week, if not permanently. The result is that I am landlord, housekeeper and <u>cook</u> – in addition to my other duties. But the Robbinses are sports. The Colonel makes a point of dining in Trinity in order to relieve the situation. Mrs Robbins is satisfied, if necessary, with cold ox-tongue and potato-crisps. But it is hard work. Yesterday, for instance, after having prepared supper I had to rush off to give a paper to the University of London Law Society. I hope they will stay. It is financially a great help.

Some of Hersch's letters of this period have been lost, but from Rachel's letters to him we can learn of his distress that Longmans, the publishers of *Oppenheim*, had been bombed and the stock of volumes destroyed. She was also sending him frequent food parcels. But he was able to write:

HL to RL, 5 March 1941
Term will finish next week. I am looking forward to that as I am beginning to feel slightly tired. I had to give extra lectures from last term. The Digest required a great deal of work. I had to write an article – not yet finished – from which I am expecting £8. And there was a great deal to do at home. Gladys was ill for five days just after the Robbinses moved in, and – with the help of the daily – I had to look after them and her. She is all right now. The lodgers are delightful. Their Swiss old housekeeper – for whom they pay – is a great help.

I could not have found better people in every respect. I only hope they will stay here long . . . The house is spotlessly clean and in order. My shoes shine for half a mile (the Colonel's batman asked my permission to shine them for me!).

The article which he mentioned was a review article for the *Political Quarterly* of Lord Cecil's autobiography, *A Great Experiment*.[6]

HL to RL, 10 March 1941
I just could not find the right <u>medium</u> between a journalistic article and something professional. The result, I think, is deplorable and probably will not be printed. If it is I will ask you to accept a copy with the author's love.

This is the last week of term. I still have two lectures to give. I have been giving three lectures instead of two to make up for the last term.

I received today <u>one</u> blue volume of Oppenheim which you sent. The other has not arrived. I was sorry you did not register it. I may send you a cable enquiring whether you sent the other half. It would take me many months of work if that part got lost somewhere . . .

When I was having tea to-day the Master of Trinity was announced. He brought with him Professor Nevins of Columbia, a very distinguished historian who is the guest of Trinity. He is here for a week. He is in England for six months on a good will mission. He is the author of that best seller – the book on Rockefeller. I took him out for a long walk in very foul weather – poor fellow. It is possible that Mrs Nevins will write to you.

Hersch's assessment of the article as 'deplorable' is entirely ill-founded. In fact, it is a declaration of the importance of the establishment after the war of an international organisation not subject to the same limitations and weaknesses as was the League of Nations. While not excluding the prospect of international confederations, Hersch concluded that:

Without the League of Nations . . . we must see ourselves deprived of that beacon of historic continuity, of universality, and of the unity of the human race without which all schemes of international organization must remain mere constitutions.[7]

Throughout this period, he was working on the *AD* and *Oppenheim*. He had left behind in the US the American contribution to the former, prepared by Lawrence Preuss, as well as the editor's interleaved copies of *Oppenheim* (the 'blue volume' to which he referred in his letter of 10

---

[6] 'Resurrection of the League', (1941) 12 *Political Quarterly* 121–33. Reprinted in *Collected Papers*, Vol. 3, p. 592.
[7] *Collected Papers*, Vol. 3, p. 601.

March, above) in which he had already made a number of changes. He had asked Rachel to send him these, but initially only one arrived.

On 11 March, he came down with a 'nasty 'flu'. He added:

[I]t is an unpleasant feeling to lie in bed with a 101½ temperature and hear the siren going – although in such a situation one does not care.[8]

But he was quickly up again and said he would be alright in a few days. The Robbinses sent him up food while he was ill, for which he thanked them in a card and received a cordial acknowledgment.

Mrs and Colonel Robbins

The Landlord hopes you are having a successful luncheon.

He begs to thank you for the very generous helping of the sweet.

HL

The Robbinses replied:

To the Whewell Professor of International Law, Cambridge

Lt Col. and Mrs Robbins return thanks for the kind enquiry. The lunch, from a gastronomic point, was most successful, but marred by the absence of the kind landlord, whose non-appearance cast a gloom over the feast. The sweet portion was a very small percentage of the lodger's feelings for their host.[9]

ARRANGEMENTS WITH WELLESLEY COLLEGE, JANUARY–MARCH 1941

Shortly before he left the United States in January 1941, he received an invitation from Wellesley College, Massachusetts, one of the leading eastern seaboard women's colleges, to become the Mary Whiton Calkins Visiting Professor in the Department of Political Science. His programme would include a half-year course in International Law, a year course in International Politics and a half-year course in either Law and the Administration of Justice or Modern Political Theory. The stipend would be $5,500. Hersch replied that he could not make a decision before he returned to England but managed to squeeze in a quick visit to Wellesley to discuss the matter in the days between finishing his work in Washington and his flight home.

---

[8] HL to RL, 14 March 1941.　　[9] 14 March 1941.

As he said to Rachel:

I feel I ought not to burn my bridges. One never knows in what way one may need it. Also – there are hundreds of girls there.[10]

He made a good impression there. Shortly afterwards, Louise Overacker, the head of the Political Science Department there, who later became my guardian when Rachel returned to England, wrote to Phillips Bradley:

I do not know how much Wellesley has to thank you for in the case of Lauter-pacht but I imagine a good deal. Whatever happens I shall always be glad that I had the opportunity to meet so rare a person. I have seldom met any one whom I liked as well and of whom I was so certain upon first acquaintance. Miss McAfee[11] and the others who met him felt exactly the same way. I know he would do a grand job here and I know that it would be a rare privilege, that he is worth much more than we can offer him, but it is the best we have and our location offers many very real advantages.[12]

At the meeting, Hersch had said that he hoped he could give a reply early in March. However, on 23 February, he felt obliged to write to Professor Overacker as follows:

HL to Louise Overacker, 23 February 1941
It is now clear that, barring unexpected developments, I shall not be at that time in the position to give an affirmative – or, for that matter – a negative answer. I have come to the conclusion that, in these days I cannot, consistently with my duty to you, accept definitely an undertaking to be fulfilled six months hence. For reasons which you will appreciate, the matter is not entirely in my hands. It is difficult for the authorities to sanction an arrangement lying so far ahead. There is no disposition to doubt the value of any work performed over there, but it is possible that during the period in question my services may be required for matters more directly connected with the national effort. I realize that you might agree that my acceptance should be made subject to contingencies lying outside my control, but I feel that the degree of uncertainty is such that I cannot conscientiously give an affirmative answer.

On the other hand, I think that both the cordiality of your invitation and the merits of the case justify me in making an alternative suggestion. If you could leave the matter open until the summer – say, June – I might then be able to give a definite answer. I can foresee that, subject to two points mentioned below, my answer will then probably be in the affirmative. So far as I am concerned there would be no objection to your saying in your prospectus or elsewhere, if

[10] HL to RL, 13 January, 1940.   [11] President of Wellesley College.
[12] Professor Overacker to Professor Bradley, 4 February, 1941.

you wish to do so, that there is a possibility of a professor of international law from England coming over for next year or for part of it as a Visiting Professor.

The two points are the following:

The first is that, having regard to the circumstances of a visit of mine to the United States, it is of importance for me that I should give my lectures on three consecutive days so that I should be free for the remainder of the week. You told me of the difficulties surrounding any such departure from your arrangements. I do not know to what extent you are in the position to reconsider the matter. I am mentioning it again because it is a major factor in the situation and because I would regard a concession in this matter as a particularly eloquent expression of your wish to give me the opportunity of an association with your College.

The second point is of a financial nature. The figure suggested by President McAfee is such that, after deducting the heavy cost of the return passage, the remuneration would not alone be adequate. It would not be possible for me to accept any subsidy from other sources. I do not regard this point in any sense as decisive, but you may be willing to reconsider that matter in the light of what I have said.

I realize that all this is very complicated and that you may prefer to make some other arrangement. I assure you that in that case I shall fully appreciate the reasons of your decision. Conversely, I very much hope that you will regard my present inability to give a definite answer not as showing any reluctance to accept a most flattering invitation, but as an expression of a disinclination to give a promise the probability of whose fulfillment seems to me at present too uncertain to warrant any definite undertaking on my part.

Professor Overacker replied warmly, saying that, although it would be difficult to hold their plans in abeyance until June, 'we have decided to do so rather than abandon all hope of having you here next year'.[13] Wellesley then offered an alternative appointment for the first semester at a salary of $3,000. Hersch eventually felt able to accept the offer, and in the ensuing months, in addition to fulfilling his university functions, the prospect of his next visit to the United States was much in his mind.

Just as his letters to me were full of paternal advice about the importance of working hard, being nice to people etc., so my letters to him were full of the filial counsel of a 12 year old: hurry up with the reply to the Wellesley invitation lest it expire; 'don't take needless risks'; 'don't forget to give the C [Colonel Robbins] a glass of very strong beer before he goes to courts martial. He can't sentence anybody very well under the influence of drink'; 'the loft ought to be cleared out and some day

---

[13] Professor Overacker to HL, 15 March 1941.

you had better finish scraping that dry, dead, ivy from the wall. It would flare up like gunpowder'; and 'carry your gas mask and steel helmet at all times'.

By 17 March, he had received and was correcting the proofs of the *Political Quarterly* article. The *Oppenheim* interleaved volumes arrived from America 'which means a saving of many months' work', but the Preuss contribution to the *AD* did not. Term being over, he was able to get on with his writing and do some gardening, devoting the flower bed on the east side of the garden entirely to vegetables. His neighbours, the Thomases, dug up half their lawn to grow potatoes. Rachel was sending them food parcels from time to time, notwithstanding Hersch's warnings to economise. The irregularity of the mail was troublesome – though understandable and accepted. Even airmail letters took three weeks to a month as flights could only carry limited loads. Outward mail was subject to censorship.

The house was in good order and relations with the Robbinses were cordial.

[T]hey are delightful people and ... financially very useful. Also he has some lovely liqueur.

In the same letter Hersch repeated his encouragement to Rachel to relax and enjoy herself:

I am delighted that now that you had news from your worse half you will gradually settle down to a quiet life. I want you to have a pleasant and interesting time while you are there. Whatever happens – and I am very confident both as to the immediate and more remote future – you have an opportunity of a restful and interesting time. There are many friends there who wish us well, and that too is a help. So, while I know that you would not mind us being together, I want you to be happy and contented. Opportunities of my coming over in the autumn (and late summer) I can not tell anything at present. It is not likely that I shall know before the beginning of June.

Each of them wrote particularly loving messages to the other on 20 March (their eighteenth wedding anniversary), and Rachel sent Hersch a telegram. Rachel, though, was suffering much discomfort from radical and debilitating dental treatment, news of which clearly troubled Hersch. But she still continued to write a letter nearly every day.

HL to RL, 23 March 1941
After the three letters which I received on the 17th and 18th (these were your letters of 20th and 23rd February) and the two telegrams the rest of the week was in the nature of an anti-climax. Still, I was glad I had all these.

I forgot to tell you that I was delighted to see that the boy is happy in the school. This is the most important step to making really good progress.

This has been the first week after Term. I have finished and corrected the proof of the article for the Political Quarterly. It appears on the 1st April and I will send you a copy. But for the American cases – which have not yet arrived (it is <u>not</u> your fault) I would be finished with the Digest. I have now started on Oppenheim. So you see that I have not been and am not likely to be idle.

In the relatively even flow of Cambridge life, he managed to resume relationships with some of his former LSE colleagues. Laski came to lunch and stayed for four hours.

Arrangements with Wellesley looked as if they might come to fruition.

HL to RL, 6 April 1941
The principal item of news is this: As I told you (I had to interrupt the letter because of the 6pm news on today in which Yugoslavia entered the war: Addis Ababa captured) the reception of my work and of the manner by the authorities justified me in thinking that another visit may be of much utility. I have, therefore, cabled to Wellesley to enquire whether they agree to my suggestions: (a) that it should be only for 4 months; (b) that they should wait with my final answer until May or June; (c) that I should give my lectures on three consecutive days so that I am free to go on with the writing. I received their reply yesterday. They approve of all my suggestions. This being so I have today written to the authorities asking for their views on the matter. I shall know in about 2 or 3 weeks. In January the chances of my coming were 5%; by the end of February 30%; today they stand 75%. I rather fancy you will like this piece of news, Great Lady – send much love to you!

Otherwise the news. With all this business Oppenheim is progressing slowly. The Digest is troublesome. Chandler [the gardener] is willing but has not got much time. However, Mrs Robbins puts in four hours a day and I do something. So the garden begins to look its best.

I see the Thomases quite often – usually for a glass of beer after dinner. The Vice Master has tea in my study: one biscuit! I had shown him the printed memo. I will give it to the Vice Chancellor too.

It is rather cold now, but we have plenty of coal. I am dining in College tonight; then fire-spotting duty.

I <u>do</u> hope you are writing often to my family. Their address: ml. Obrony Lwów 32, m.8, Lwów, Western Ukraine, Soviet Russia.

The mention of writing to his family in Poland is one of the only three times in the correspondence in which he mentions them specifically.[14] Seemingly, he could not write himself because no mail would pass from England to Soviet-occupied Poland,[15] though such transmission was possible from and to the US. There is one envelope from Lwów, addressed to New York (the contents having been sent on to Hersch), bearing a Soviet postmark, partly illegible, but probably 24 May 1941.

On the same day, Hersch wrote to Sir Stephen Gaselee at the Foreign Office.

Thank you for your letter of the 1st inst. And for the printed copy of my memorandum. I was delighted to see it in that form. On the same day I received a letter from Sir William Malkin telling me that the US Attorney-General used it recently for what the New York Times described as a historic declaration of policy!

He also wrote a brief note of condolence to Leonard Woolf, a former colleague at the LSE, on the death of Virginia Woolf.[16] The Passover came and went. Rachel and I celebrated it on our own in New York, despite a pressing invitation from Hersch's uncle Julius. In Cambridge, it was both 'Easter Sunday and Pesach, of which there is not much in this house this year'.[17] Hersch complained of 'not feeling too strong', but nonetheless said that 'on the whole I am very well and putting a lot of work into various things'.[18] He rarely went to London, but on occasion visited Ziedman, the grocer in Cricklewood with whom we dealt before the move to Cambridge:

He is a blessing. He gave me the other day all the frying oil I wanted and other things which are unobtainable here. I usually leave £3–4 with him. It would be difficult to manage the house without him.[19]

He added:

I would be rather lonely but for my lodgers who are a blessing. I did a very good piece of business by taking the Robbinses. They are very devoted and decent. She says she watches over me like an aunt (she <u>does</u> clean my razor blades every morning – by the way the cutler blades have <u>not</u> arrived, but I have not given

[14] More poignant are his letters of 13 July 1941 and 7 December 1942, p. 175 and p. 220 below.
[15] But see p. 215 above/below about sending food parcels to Poland.
[16] 6 April 1941, reprinted in a volume of condolence letters, *Afterwords: Letters on the Death of Virginia Woolf*, ed. Sybil Oldfield (Edinburgh: Edinburgh University Press, 2005), p. 123.
[17] HL to RL, 13 April 1941.   [18] *Ibid.*
[19] HL to RL, undated, but likely April 1941.

them up). (This letter has been interrupted as Miss Stanley came in to enlist me as a member of a saving group – an expenditure of five shillings per week.)[20]

At last, on 20 April, Hersch was able to send Rachel the good news about Wellesley.

HL to RL, 20 April 1941

It is possible that before you receive this letter you will have received a cable of mine telling you that I have accepted the Wellesley invitation. This I have done after putting the matter before the same authorities as last year and after receiving their considered opinions that they are 'strongly of the view' that I ought to go. The same facilities are eagerly – more eagerly – offered as last year plus the Clipper. If I do not cable it is because in these days nothing is certain and because it would be foolish of me to stir up vain hopes. However, barring unforeseen developments, I propose to arrive about the middle of July. I am looking so much forward to being with you again. My idea is that, to begin with, we should have a quiet holiday *à deux* for a fortnight somewhere at the seaside. I feel so tired after this continuous work of the last year and I should have a heavy time in front of me. However, it is premature to discuss details. Of one thing I am quite sure – that you will not mind looking after me for a while.

It will also be a satisfaction to see the boy again. I hope all this will materialize and that, in about ten weeks, the old gang will expect me again at La Guardia aerodrome.

In the meantime there will be a rush: I have to lecture; to examine; to send the Digest to the printer; to push on with Oppenheim; to prepare the paper for Chatham House; to deal with the passport, work permits, Clippers; to settle the problem of No. 6 (if only the Robbinses would remain! They are such a decent lot!) and so on, and so on. Still, you will look after me on that short holiday, won't you?

I sent a copy of the printed memorandum to the Vice-Chancellor and had a delightful letter from him. McNair begged me to give him a spare copy – which I did. I will keep one for you – here, for I must not take it out of the country. I have deposited one in a sealed envelope in the Squire Law Library and the other in the Trinity Library.

It has been a depressing fortnight and, for many reasons, I have not had much sleep. But, on the whole, I feel well. It is Sunday morning now, and I am looking at the garden from my desk. Our hyacinths bed must be the best in Cambridge. The daffodils at the far end semi-circles are a great show. The wild cherry tree is beginning to blossom. We put in potatoes yesterday – enough to keep a family

[20] *Ibid.*

for the winter. There is a pleasant smell of the joint of lamb coming through the kitchen window – so you must not think that I shall be hungry.

I shall dine in College tonight and hope to discuss with Hollond the visit to Trinity of Ben Cohen, Winant's[21] legal adviser. I hope to meet him before long and to ask him to Trinity.

This letter is in bad taste; for it is all about myself. But I know you will not mind that. Let me end with a big hug, and a kiss, and lots of love for both of you.

Rachel received the news with elation; but within days Hersch sent her a sobering letter.

HL to RL, 24 April 1941
You know by now from my cable – many thanks for your cabled reply – and from my last letter how matters stand. The position, in principle, is that I propose to come in the first half of July or in the third week. I was in London yesterday to see the British Airways and American Air Lines people, but they told me that they do not deal with individuals. The matter will have to be taken up altogether by the authorities. This, of course, is not the only difficulty (the process, I gather, is extremely complicated). We do not know what the position as to communications will be in July in relation to Portugal (I am determined not to go by boat). So, although the matter is decided in principle, it is as contingent and uncertain as many other things in the present circumstances.

This brings me to the financial position, and I know you will excuse me if I speak frankly. I was rather horrified to read that in a few months time you will have exhausted the money which you had and that you will have to draw on friends. I was even more startled to hear that in addition to your flat expenses (which you say are 1000 dollars a year) the other expenses will be 1500. The boy's fees will be 120. How you can spend 27 dollars a week I cannot see. In my view it is an impossible position. I am writing below about the prospects of your earning money. They are necessarily negligible . . .

There is no special reason for you to look for work which even if you get it will make of you a nervous wreck and a slave. If you will try to economise – I know you think of it, but you are too good to deny, for instance, your visitors a proper meal – you will be able to manage. If I do not come, I will take up the matter with the Yale Committee concerning the payment it sent and I will also do other things. But it is clearly impossible to do anything on the basis of you and the boy spending altogether 2500 dollars a year.

The times are worrying and full of anxiety all round. I hope therefore that you will agree that it is not quite fair that I should receive letters saying that you are getting tired of New York, etc. I live under great strain not only physically,

---

[21] Winant was the United States Ambassador in London.

but also on account of the pressure of various kinds of work, and so long as I know you are safe and reasonably provided for, I am sure you will try not to add to my anxieties. Summer is coming; it must be beautiful at 5444; join a good library; go out for walks; enjoy life quietly; do not make yourself miserable about non-earning (I know you are willing to do your bit, but circumstances are against you) . . . I know you will not mind this letter.

He was evidently in a censorious mood because three days later he wrote me a rather severe letter.

HL to EL, 27 April 1941
I have long promised myself to write to you a long letter all to yourself – and here it is.

In the first instance, I want to thank you for your numerous letters. I was very glad to have them – although I am still bothered by two things: The first is their external form. I think it is a sign both of respect and of internal discipline if they are written tidily and in good handwriting on proper paper. The other is more serious: I want you to be happy and cheerful but the tone of your letters occasionally struck me as being on too easy and carefree lines. It might be nice if you realized that your letters reach here people who live in a state of more immediate anxiety and worries of all kinds than people in the USA.

To Rachel he wrote on the same day.

HL to RL, 27 April 1941
I have put the question of the passage in the hands of the authorities and the matter will depend upon their willingness and eagerness – to some extent. But in view of the various possibilities, it may be outside their control. In any case, it is a long business. I will let you know as soon as I can. I am arriving at the first half of July.

To the President of Wellesley College, Miss McAfee, he wrote on 28 April 1941:

I sent you the other day a cable informing you that I have accepted, for a period of one semester, your kind invitation to be Visiting Professor at Wellesley College. This is the result of the decision taken by the authorities and, very eagerly, by myself. The only possible outstanding difficulty is not so much that of securing a place on the planes to and from Lisbon, but the availability in the summer of the existing lines of communication. Subject to that difficulty – which makes it, perhaps, advisable to postpone the announcement till June – I hope to be in Wellesley about a week before the beginning of the semester. I also hope that you will believe me if I say that I am intensely looking forward to the association with your College.

Your letter of April 4th gave me great satisfaction. It not only settles the financial aspect (perhaps I ought to add that I do not feel justified in expecting the College to provide for any increment in excess of the twelve hundred dollars required for the return passage by air). It gave me the complete assurance that you reciprocate my desire to be associated with the College. The same applies to Professor Overacker's letter of March 15th concerning the schedule of the lectures. I am writing to her separately.

Two days later, he was able to send good news to Rachel.

HL to RL, 30 April, 1941
I had a cable from Wellesley saying that they were delighted. The matter is now in the hands of the authorities and, perhaps, not quite in theirs. If I can fly, then probably I will be in New York in July and take you – and myself – out for a fortnight to some country place or the sea. I am so tired. The Digest gives more trouble than usual because, in the absence of contributors from various countries, I have to do correspondingly more. I have hardly the time to touch Oppenheim. Then there is the examination period and the paper for Chatham House.

Rachel's hopes of Hersch's return in early July were dashed when, on 14 May, he wrote:

HL to RL, 14 May 1941
This letter does not, I am afraid, bring pleasant news. I heard today from the authorities that while it will be possible to secure a passage by sea, it will <u>not</u> be possible to secure passage by plane which is henceforth reserved for urgent official business. This has come as a great disappointment, and the journey has now become very doubtful. There is, first, the fact that unless the authorities feel that the journey is of urgent importance I cannot feel justified in going. The second is that, with my ignorance of swimming, a journey by sea now and especially the return journey are extremely risky, and I hesitate to undertake it. All this means that the chances of my going have been reduced to very little. I can imagine that this letter will be a shock to you, but you ought to know the position.

I am not informing the authorities that I do not propose to go, and I am going on with Wellesley as if nothing happened. This being so you must not let Wellesley know in any way that the chances of my coming have dwindled. But Phil may know, but, naturally, I do not wish him to do anything in other matters.

This also means that you ought to accept, in principle, Goldberg's offer of the job of which you wrote to me. It may make it possible to keep the flat – and, as I told you, that makes all the difference. Frankly, I do not think that there is much chance of your getting work as a shorthand-typist. I am pushing on with the Yale Committee's contribution. I most fervently hope that you will not feel unduly depressed by this letter. Not all the chances have disappeared. I will see the authorities next week, and I will consult McNair next month. But we have to plan ahead and be prepared for a longer separation than we thought. It is a dull prospect, but I have not given up hope. No one knows what the conditions will be like in July or August. So, sweet lady, cheer up and tell me that you are not depressed.

On 14 May too, Rachel asked Hersch if he had heard from his parents, but Hersch had 'heard nothing more'.

He wrote to Rachel again on 18 May.

HL to RL, 18 May 1941
You must feel very disappointed – to say the least – after my last letter about the very greatly reduced chances of my going over. I have not yet quite recovered from the unpleasant shock. I have not yet given up all hope, and I am doing a thing or two, but the chances are smaller unless unforeseen developments happen. I would not rule them out, and I am writing today to Wellesley authorizing them to publish my appointment on June 10. One never knows what will be the position in July or August. For all we know, American convoys may then be in full swing. And there are other possibilities. For this reason I do not want you to tell anyone of the change – except Phil (and it is particularly important that he should not mention it to anyone).

You can imagine that I am not in too happy a state of mind. I was making such interesting plans for both of us for July and August! I feel that, from the national point of view, it would be very useful if I went – and McNair fully agrees – and I am therefore grieved that the department concerned does not see the point. But if they do not see it, then I must interpret their attitude as indicating that the journey is not, for me, of sufficient importance to run the risks of a sea journey. (Jennings waited 8 months for a place on the plane for his journey to Ceylon. Mrs Jennings and the two girls followed by sea. Their ship was bombed and sunk; they escaped in a lifeboat and were brought back to England, but one of the girls is now wounded, in hospital!)

As I said, there may be a change. For this reason I do not think you ought to make any changes in your plans. It is clear to me: (a) that the flat must be kept; (b) that otherwise you must devise a plan of rigid economies; (c) that you ought to consider the Goldberg job as the only practicable probability; (d) that there is a probability of help from the Yale Committee (I shall be dealing with the matter); (e) that there is a probability, a distant one, of relaxations in the exchange regulations so that money may be sent (the H suggestion clearly involves a criminal offence under the existing law and it must not be touched);[22] (f) that on no account must you get despondent about the money position.

---

[22] See p. 164 below.

I sent off the Digest to the printer, and am preparing the paper for Chatham House. I gave yesterday the last lecture (applause, as usual); examinations are beginning this week. I am going to London on Wednesday. One returns from there heartbroken at the sight of devastation but inspired and strengthened by the courage of the people.

And, troubled by remorse over his earlier critical letter, he wrote a further letter the next day.

HL to RL, 19 May 1941

I wrote yesterday, and this extra letter is an unwarranted expenditure of 1/3d in these days of economy. But I got your letter of 7 May[23] just now, and I feel I must write and say that I am grateful for it. It is the reply to my rather quarrelsome and reproachful letter of 24 April in which I lectured you about economy (almost exhorting you and the boy to eat less!) and accused you of unfairness in bothering me with your restlessness and discouraged you about your shorthand-typing course (which, I am sure, must cost you a lot of labour). I felt very unhappy about having written this mean letter. It was noble and lovely of you not to argue and to take the blame. I feel so grateful that I am almost inclined to take the sea route!

However, I am clear that it would be foolish to do so. I have not given up the matter yet, and the second reason of this extra letter is to ask you seriously not to worry unduly about it – because not all is lost. I am consulting people and doing what is necessary.

He also wrote to me on the same day.

HL to EL, 19 May 1941

I got your beautifully written letter of May 7 (Question marks are still missing, and I do not understand why you should not be able to produce your best handwriting in pen – but it was a delight to have all the news from you).

Your questions:
  i. The bicycle: I am afraid I am making no progress. I simply have not got the time.
  ii. My generalship in fire-spotting: I grant you that one could imagine better generals, but I am trying to do my best . . .
  iii. My gas mask: Yes, I do wear it occasionally. I shall have to bring it when I invigilate at the examination.
My main reason for writing is to express the hope that you are specially thoughtful and considerate to Mummy just now. She must be worrying about the diminished chances of my coming, and she will need all your kindness.

[23] This letter has not been found.

He also told Louise Overacker that Wellesley might announce his appointment, as they wished to do on 10 June, but might 'find it advisable to qualify the announcement, for instance, by referring to the exigencies of the war situation or to contingencies which may be outside their control'.[24]

Within a few days, the situation began to look a bit brighter.

HL to RL, 23 May 1941

I can imagine how very much depressed you are by the recent news from here – because I had somehow the impression that you really wanted me to come – and I hope, therefore, that you will forgive another extra letter. Your recent letters have been so sweet (the painted nails being the only fly in the ointment – I trust you washed the thing off before you went to Wellesley) that I, a hard-boiled egg, was getting sentimental.

As I told you, not all is lost. I was in London last Wednesday, and I saw both Malkin and Gaselee. The latter, who is dealing with the matter, will try again. He was most charming – not his usual detached self. I may hear in another fortnight or so. I am still against the sea passage. People, of course, are using it. In the near future Barbara Debenham, of No. 23, will proceed there by sea as one of the secretarial assistants in the Purchasing Commission . . .

I also think that Bentwich recently went by sea. Of course, he is an expert swimmer. I am not. (I told Gaselee: 'I do not want you to think that I am funking the sea – because I do'. He smiled.)

The passport (I am getting a new one – with the enclosed photo) and the exit permit business is proceeding smoothly.

Otherwise there is no news. I sent the Digest to the printer. I am now preparing the paper for Chatham House for next Tuesday.[25] The exams have started. I am paying fortnightly visits to Ziedman – it is a blessing (he gave me the other day 8 pints of frying oil – an unheard of thing in Cambridge!) . . .

The Robbinses are still here and – thank God – there is not yet a sign of their going away.

Rachel received his letter of 14 May ten days later. She was, understandably distressed.

RL to HL, 24 May 1941

Your letter of the 14th arrived this morning. Although I read it and re-read it several times, I can just see, amongst my tears: 'It will not be possible to secure passage by plane'. 'The chances of my going have been reduced to very little.'!!

[24] HL to Louise Overacker, 19 May 1941.   [25] See p. 168 below.

It came like a bomb shell. I wish I could tell you that I am not unduly depressed. But, you don't expect me, really, to say this.

Darling, my sweet darling, in very critical moments of my life – such as: before Eli's birth, before my operation. I always trusted myself completely to God – and I put my life and my destiny into his will. Today, too, I turned to him, and while I look up to him, I can only say: God, I trust thee to do the right thing of my husband, Zvi Ben Aron – I know you will help us – as you always do – and won't let us down.

No, my darling, I have not lost hope. I am looking forward to having you here in July. I am praying for it with all my heart and soul. God has always helped me, and I trust he will help us this time too.

It is a shock to me, and I try and face it bravely. It is right of you to acquaint me with the position. But I still cling fast to my hopes of having you with us here very soon.

I can not, just now, think of a long separation. No, my dear, it won't go on like this. If you won't come – I will try – by hook or crook – to come back to you. I think I have come to the conclusion that we need each other, much more than we care to admit. I must be with you, whatever happens.

I want you, my sweet, not to worry over us here, we are well – and have for some months all we want. I mean, in so far as necessities of food etc. but the heart and soul are empty – the mind is yearning, thinking, praying for the one so much beloved, so much adored. My darling, I hope for better times, and with this hope and determination I shall face life with courage and to the best of my ability.

Don't worry over us, we are well – but only wish to hear that you are well, and if possible of good cheer . . .

But I want to assure you that if you will face it bravely – we will too.

I was distressed too, but offered him some constructive advice.

EL to HL, 24 May 1941
We have just received your letter of the 14th. In which we received the unwelcome news about the Clipper. I think they must be crazy. There is one other alternative. Plane to Lisbon and then an American Export Liner. Incidentally, now that the hot, summer weather is here, it would not be a bad idea, if you went down to the river, and asked the custodian of the bathing place, or a friend, to give you a few elementary lessons in swimming. You should then practice each day, till you can stay afloat for at least three hours <u>without</u> a lifebelt. If you do come by ship, we will send you a life-jacket to you. (You must not come by ship. R.)

You do not send us much news about the home etc. If you want to sell the car, do not do so for a long time. No more cars are being made, there will soon be a demand for them. Till then you ought to lease it to the Army, for about 5/– per day. Speak to the Colonel about that.

Then, on 26 May, for the first time he indicated that he was considering crossing by sea.

HL to RL, 26 May 1941
I received today your letter of the 15th May. The mail is getting really much better.

You are asking about the flat. My answer is very clearly that you ought to keep it. There is no other solution half as presentable or practical.

I can well imagine that you are not just now in too happy a mood in view of the uncertainty surrounding the coming of your other half. There is a very small chance that an exception may be made. If not – I feel I ought not to exclude altogether the possibility of going by sea. If the authorities decide – as they have – that it is useful that I should go, I may find it difficult to say that I do not wish to go because of the dangers of the Atlantic. I think I ought to tell you that I am considering the possibility.

I am going tomorrow to London to read a short paper before the Institute of International Affairs on – guess what! – the Reality of the Law of Nations.[26] I will probably see Moshe[27] and Ziedman!

The weather is dismal. I do not think we have had three days of sunshine in the last month. But the garden looks lovely. The plums have been killed by the frost, but there may be the greengages – this probably does make your mouth water – and plenty of apples. Mrs Robbins is getting 'housemaid's knee' by taking out the weeds from the lawn. She is putting in 4 hours a day (by the way: she tells me that £20 a year for dresses is a ridiculously small sum and that I owe you therefore a lot of money retrospectively. It will please me if you tell me that you have made a nice dress for yourself – belated repentance!).

The house is in order. We are doing spring-cleaning now. There is not a scratch on the wall-paper. Gladys continues to be a good girl.

In conclusion – I want you to tell me that you are not worrying and that you are having a quiet, pleasant time.

For the rest of May the uncertainty remained, but Hersch carried on as normal a life as he could.

---

[26] Reprinted in *Collected Papers*, Vol. 2, p. 22. See p. 165 below.
[27] Rachel's brother, an architect.

HL to EL, 30 May 1941

I am writing this letter while invigilating, between $1\frac{1}{2}$–$4\frac{1}{2}$, in the Law School (the big room No. 3), at the Tripos examination. There are about sixty boys taking International Law this year – much more than I expected. It is a rather squally afternoon – it has been raining for two days – and this, as well as the boredom of invigilating and the thought that I should have to correct sixty papers, makes me rather sleepy. It is wonderfully quiet. The organ from King's College Chapel is playing gently and sadly. I feel rather warm in my gown and hood.

The rains of the last week have had an excellent effect on the gardens and the backs. There is a fresh, deep green everywhere. Cambridge looks its best. They will sing madrigals under the bridge next Tuesday. On June 8 the Musical Society is performing Beethoven's Missa Solemnis in the Chapel, and I am in the mood of going.

The house looks nice and tidy. When you return – and I trust and hope it may be soon – you will hardly believe that so much time has elapsed since you left. Your room is practically unchanged. I am using it now as a bedroom. I put in there my 'patent' electric lamp from the Study. It is a good lamp to have in the bedroom; it does not get easily upset . . .

I sent the Digest to the printer last week; next week I shall be receiving proofs. Together with the examination papers, it keeps me quite busy. Also, I have to revise the paper which I read last Tuesday before the Royal Institute for International Affairs.

All this is rather difficult because as you know my personal position is so unsettled. I am writing to Mummy constantly about it. She, bless her, must be rather worried about this sudden complication, and I am quite sure that you are a comfort to her and a good friend.

The principal object of this letter is: (a) to wish you a happy time in your camp; (b) to utter one very serious warning, namely, to remember all the time that your health is the most important matter in the situation. You know of your inclination to catch colds. This means that whatever other boys may do, however ridiculous you may seem to them, you have to take utmost precautions in the matter. Never expose yourself to cold when you are hot and perspiring; never wear wet things. Above all, swimming or no swimming – safety first. Never show off in this respect and do not take any risks.

And now – enough lecturing! Have a happy time and be sure of the warm wishes of your Dad.

At no point did he arouse in me any real opposition to his positive encouragement and advice, even though then and for long afterwards it was insistently repeated.

During this period, much of the space in the letters between Hersch and Rachel was taken up with two themes. One was whether, and on what terms, Rachel should keep the flat in Riverdale. Hersch was strongly in favour of her doing so even though the cost seriously stretched the available funds. The other was how Rachel might earn some money. She did some Hebrew teaching, but the schools were far away and she found it too exhausting to be done on a full-time basis. The alternative was secretarial work, for which she was not trained. She took a typing and shorthand course. While she was able to master the typing easily, she found the shorthand very difficult and did not persevere. Hersch all along took the line that she should never have started it. There was concern about Rachel's health – she had much painful trouble with her teeth and her dental treatment proved very expensive.

Money was also a persistent theme because money could not be sent from England, so we were entirely dependent on what Hersch could leave behind after his lecture tours. A suggestion made by an American friend for circumventing the exchange controls and increasing the funds available to Rachel in the US (by an arrangement in which equal sums could be credited to an account in England) was passed on by Rachel to Hersch. He immediately rejected it, telling her that it was illegal and that it should never have been made by a friend who should have known better. But the matter was picked up by the postal censors and Hersch was required to provide an explanation, which he did, and eventually the enquiry was dropped.

Rachel's letters were full of expressions of love and concern for Hersch, which he reciprocated though in rather less flowery terms. For his part, after his return to Cambridge, Hersch described living conditions there, the care of the house, access to food supplies and his comfortable relationship with his lodgers, the Robbinses. There was also a certain amount about the neighbours in Cranmer Road, especially the Thomas family next door, whose lives were dogged by illness and limitations of income.

What did not appear in the letters was any elaboration of the reasons for, and content of, the various matters on which Hersch was working. There was no need, of course, to explain why he continued with the *AD* or *Oppenheim*. Though the former produced no income, it was an enterprise in the establishment of which he had played a leading role and to the continuance of which he felt committed. As to *Oppenheim*, its continuance was important, not only as a demonstration of the range and depth of his knowledge in the field, but also because he received a share of the royalties, which made a significant contribution to his income. But there is no mention of why he undertook the article in the *Political Quarterly* on Lord Cecil's autobiography,[28] unless it was the payment of £8.

On 27 May 1941, he delivered a paper at the Royal Institute of International Affairs on 'The Reality of the Law of Nations'.[29] There is no indication of why he agreed to do this, but it was probably because he felt that, in the course of a war which was being fought to uphold the foundations of international law, it was important to remind people of what the subject was about and of the critical role that it had to play in international life.

The paper as delivered was not printed, but Hersch spent some time afterwards in expanding it into what, when eventually printed thirty-four years later in his *Collected Papers*, became a fervently expressed, tightly argued and critical text of twenty-nine pages, so closely woven that it cannot readily be summarised but must be read as a whole. It began thus:

Anyone who, in these days, chooses to speak of 'The Reality of the Law of Nations' lays himself open to the charge of untimely simplicity or even audacity. For the reality of international law has become, for many, a byword; and mention of it has often been used as an occasion for recrimination. However, in this as in other matters, despondency or cynicism may be a cloak for facile thinking, and the time is perhaps ripe for facing the issue squarely on a not purely technical ground. Nor is it sufficient – although it may be legitimate and necessary to do so – to stress the fact that the sad plight of the world, which for a long time tolerated grievous violations of the Law of Nations, provides impressive evidence of its significance, or that the World War which began in 1939 is in itself a vindication of its vitality. The problem of international law and of its reality is, in essence, identical with the problem of world order in general and of the post-war World Order in particular. This being so, it is proper that a discussion of it should not be confined to a limited circle of experts.[30]

He then developed the theme that the 'shortcomings of international law are not a quality inherent in the very nature of the international legal system . . . but a transitory stage in the rational progression towards a full and effective system of law among nations'.[31] He concluded his analysis of the reality of international law in relation to State sovereignty, the law of war, changing concepts of neutrality and the development of international institutions, with this observation:

---

[28] See *Collected Papers*. Vol. 3, p. 592.
[29] 'The Reality of the Law of Nations', reprinted in *Collected Papers*, Vol. 2, pp. 22–51.
[30] Reprinted in *Collected Papers*, Vol. 2, p. 22.   [31] *Ibid.*, p. 33.

If we fix our gaze on the enduring purposes of the Law of Nations and if we bear in mind that they are identical with the issues which are now being decided on the field of battle, we shall neither get despondent in times of adversity nor succumb to the temptation of gauging the reality of international law by the ignoble test of temporary triumphs of force wielded by lawless States or to the craving to adapt international law to other manifestations of their inferior statehood. Above all, we shall then be in a better position to remember that the degree of the reality of the Law of Nations is in the last resort determined not by Governments, nor, even less so, by international lawyers, but by the will and the exertion of the citizen. Westlake's insistence that the rights and duties of States are the rights and duties of man expresses a profound truth in more senses than one. The cause with which the Law of Nations is totally identified is being defended, in this Second World War, by the common effort and suffering of the individual citizen to a higher degree than at any previous period in history. It is therefore legitimate to hope that the individual will succeed henceforth in giving to that experience – superadded to the lessons of the First World War and of the preceding centuries of international anarchy – an expression commensurate with the magnitude of the greatest political task which has confronted mankind since the inception of history; that by the action of his Governments, he will revive and strengthen the existing institutions of international order; and that, by dint of his own municipal law and of precise international obligations, he will safeguard these achievements from the vicissitudes inherent in the fallibility of Governments and in the imperfections of collective memory.[32]

He wrote to Rachel on 30 May:

From the letter to Master Elihu you will see that I am now invigilating in the soporific atmosphere of a warm, sultry afternoon.

I had yesterday your letter of the 20 May – another record. I was very glad to get it. You sound so cheerful, touch wood (I nearly said touch food – of course, you will supply a Freudian explanation) and quite in love with your appearance (it is not fair to remind me of it just now!) That extra inch of height is the result of the new hair – which must make all the difference! I was so delighted to hear that Mrs Nevins is still friendly, and that she introduces you to others. I think Professor Nevins is one of the most charming and most able people in the United States I met.

Still you are probably getting impatient in reading this letter waiting for the more substantial news from me. There is no news at present. Such as there is is not too encouraging. When I was in London last Tuesday to read the paper to the Royal Institute I phoned Mrs Bentwich to ask whether she had news from her husband. He left by boat a week before; she did not expect any news

---

[32] *Ibid.*, pp. 50–1.

for another fortnight. He found it quite impossible to get the Clipper. Most important people cannot get it, for instance, Wedgwood or – although I do not believe it – Sir Arthur Salter. That is what she told me. As I wrote to you, I do not intend to turn down definitely the boat suggestion although I may postpone it until August. One cannot know what the position will be then.

It is surprising that I can write so composedly about it, but I am getting slowly used to the idea. I am not giving up yet! . . .

. . . Things here are quiet although no one is too happy. America is still the crux of the matter.

At home everything is all right. The chances of the Robbinses staying on have improved. It was a stroke of luck to get them. I must have the best lodgers in Cambridge. They are like a family.

Well, darling, I hope you have not written to me wretched letters which will make me full of unhappiness because of your disappointment. There is no reason for it. I feel, somehow, that I shall be there. I am corresponding with Wellesley on these lines.

He received a notification from the Passport Office that a passport and an exit permit would be sent to him if he would sign an undertaking that he would return to the United Kingdom if and when required to do so by His Majesty's Ambassador in Washington. 'This undertaking', the Passport Office assured him, 'is required of all persons proceeding to the United States of America for lecture purposes.'[33] This gave him some encouragement, but he remained uncertain.

HL to RL, 2 June 1941

I received today your letter of May 22. It is still a cheerful letter (I do not believe you that you were pulling my leg about the painted nails, because if you did, you succeeded – for the first time!) but I dread your letter which is due to come in a day or two after you had heard about the hitch in the journey. I repeat: there is as yet no reason for giving up hope: (1) I still may get the plane; (2) I may decide to go by sea. As to the latter I do not want to ask your advice for this is not a matter with regard to which one wishes to saddle someone else with responsibility – even one's wife. I may decide that if the authorities wish me to go, it is my duty to go. However, there is no immediate hurry about the decision. I received today my new passport with the exit permit valid until 31 August. So I do not want you to be too miserable. There is plenty of time (you will need all of it for washing off that paint from the nails).

---

[33] Passport Office to HL, 26 May 1941.

In the meantime we have had a quiet fortnight. I need it as I am snowed under with examination papers. Also, I have to revise my Chatham House paper. The lecture itself went off very well. Noel-Baker was there; Lord Hailey; and others. I may publish it in their World Order papers . . . [34]

You may ask Phil what he thinks of the ship journey. The trouble with the matter is that the decision is not so much with the British authorities as with the US Department of State which allocates the priorities on the Clipper. Our authorities cannot possibly say that I am going on an official mission . . .

The boy *must be made* to take regular strenuous exercise with long walks. It will be disastrous for his future if he becomes a fat boy – for various reasons, one reason being that he is so susceptible to the danger of looking ridiculous. He must not have any starchy food. But it is exercise that matters and about that your constant vigilance would be decisive. Medicines are a mere palliative.

I saw McNair the other day. He looked worried. The son of Cameron, the Master of Caius, died in a German prison camp. Sheila had an operation for appendicitis and immediately afterwards, almost still under anaesthetic, she had to be moved into a shelter basement because of an air-raid. She is now well in the Wales Cottage. I was in London last week and I returned depressed. Gray's Inn – my Inn – is in ruins. In the Temple I literally walked in ruins. Cambridge is almost indecently quiet; the garden is lovely. Next week we shall eat our first garden lettuces. And with this bright prospect I am sending to my lovely wife and the great boy lots of love and kisses and hugs.

Rachel, cut off in New York and lonely, was very troubled by the situation and poured out her heart to him.

RL to HL, 2 June 1941
Your letters of the 23rd and 26th [May], the latter only 8 days on the way, received today. Both of them moved me and made me very thoughtful. I have a certain satisfaction in realizing some of the opinions you have, only lately, acquired or formed of me. The proverb says 'Better late than never'. If you repent now, some of your misdemeanours towards me, in such trifles as dresses and pocket money, it is gratifying to know that you have at last realized that I am not always wrong, and extravagant in my demands. But, I must confess that it hurt slightly that you had to be convinced of my just necessities by Mrs Robbins or such another one.

I have reached a stage in my life, that I am above all these things now. I do not say that I do not care for nice clothes and well cared, and trimmed hair, and

---

[34] The lecture was expanded into a substantial paper which when eventually printed in his *Collected Papers*, Vol. 2, pp. 22–52, came to twenty-nine pages.

face etc (and I assure you, my dear Sir, I look a million times more attractive even in my old clothes as long as my <u>heart</u> and soul are fed properly).

There is <u>one</u> thing that matters to me now – and only this <u>one thing</u> has my <u>whole thoughts</u> and <u>attention</u>. The love and care of one man, to whom I am married and to whom I dedicated my life – irrespective of what his attitude towards me would be – at times. From this deep rooted wish to help and serve this great man – by love and by devotion, and by <u>blind</u> submission – <u>I drew the strength</u> that I needed very often, to combat the differences in our approaching day by day life. Who cares now about such trifles. It is true that such trifles bring a lot of misery and sometimes are capable to wreck and undermine that sacred structure of married life and love. But, if it is deep rooted – and solid as a rock, nothing will shake it in its depth – although it may ruffle the surface sometimes.

I am now in this respect serene and calm. I know the chaff from the grain. The chaff may fly into your life and hurt you, and blind you – but it is really the grain that counts.

So, my dear, great, <u>obstinate</u> darling, forget about these things of slight importance. I assure you, my great darling, that I will <u>try</u> to look my best when you come. I will don my best dress and perhaps I may buy a new one, especially in your honour. I will meet you, with paint off my nails, and with lipstick off my lips – but will bring hearts full of love and deep devotion, and lips ready to be sweetened and moistened by yours and only by yours. I hope, my dear 'hard boiled egg' this meets with your approval, but kindly sir, would you please tell me when and where shall I meet my love? Will it be at La Guardia airport? Or will it be a different place? You know, I am getting more excited but even more worried over the approaching journey.

It is for you to decide what is right to do. May God guide you in the right path. I have not written for 4 days. I was tipped over by a wave of depression. I feel better now, and it is so good, so kind of you to write often now. I feel such a void, empty, feeling round my heart – it so aches and pains. The anxiety and worry over <u>you</u> occupies my very being.

God bless you my darling better half. Thank you for the snap. It is not a too good one – but still dear to me.

The exchanges about the journey continued.

HL to RL, 10 June 1941
I received today your letter of 27 May with Phil Bradley's letter. I am so sorry you are going through this worry and anxiety and uncertainty. I am rather concerned about that, but I feel that it would have been a mistake not to let you know.

I agree with Phil that the absence of plane accommodation is in no way an expression of change of the views of the authorities as to the usefulness of my visit. I was expressly assured that this was not so, and, on my part, I thought it necessary to emphasise that I would not go unless I were assured that, in their view, I ought to go. I am still waiting for the result of their second demarche. For the time being there is no use speculating as to what decision I will eventually make – except that I feel that if the authorities are convinced that my journey may do good I shall have to take that very seriously into account even if the journey involves considerable danger. No more about it for the present except that I do not want you to worry.

The Tripos examination is over, and I can breathe more freely. But the Digest proofs are arriving, and the revisions for the Chatham House paper take more time than I thought it would take.

The weather is ghastly. We have not had two consecutive days of sunshine for weeks. But, in the homely phrase, it does the garden good.

But, a few days later, Hersch was able to send some good news tending in the right direction.

HL to RL, 13 June 1941
This letter is written two days earlier than the schedule, but you will be pleased to know – unless in the meantime you get even more definite news by cable – that the authorities have decided to put through a kind of request to the State Department about the Clipper. I rather liked this piece of news both for its own sake and also as an indication that the authorities realize the usefulness of the journey. In view of this I feel that even if the plane does not materialize I ought to consider seriously the boat question (Mrs Bentwich told me yesterday that the husband has arrived safely by boat).

I spent yesterday in London and arrived home at 10.45pm – still daylight. What a paradise Cambridge is both absolutely and in comparison with London! . . .

In the afternoon I had a very long meeting in the Grotius Society. At 5pm Oxford Street was full; it does not look quite normal; imagine, for instance, the John Lewis block razed to the ground and a heap of ruins (but the other building remains and they are selling cheerfully porcelain and other things of utility!) I had a quite good supper of smoked Scotch salmon. In general the food situation in London is much better than in the provinces . . .

The Robbinses are still here, with no sign of going. If they only will stay on while I am away (Madam, I am writing to the Portuguese consul about the transit visa!!).

This had not reached Rachel by 15 June. She was getting so desperate at the absence for 12 days of any news from Hersch that she sent him a cable asking about his health. Hersch replied on 17 June:

I was surprised when I received your telegram telling me that you had not received any news from me for 12 days. The letters have been so regular recently! However, in comparison with what used to happen: February, when letters took 5 weeks by air mail, even the present position is not unsatisfactory.

I told you in my answer that I am perfectly well and that the chances of my coming have rather increased. I am waiting for the results of the efforts of the authorities in the matter of the Clipper. But even if these do not succeed, I shall seriously consider the journey by boat. I have now evidence that the authorities wish me to go, and at a time when so many people face dangers I shall find it difficult to refuse to go on a journey which I am assured is useful and of importance. Neither do I feel like refusing.

I had yesterday as my guest in College (and today at home for breakfast) Professor Cole, Head of the American Hospital in Britain, who arrived with me in the Clipper last January. He is a delightful man, passionately – although critically – devoted to England; he left his family in the USA and has come here for 6 months. He will be going back at the end of July and we both thought that it would be great fun if we repeated the return journey! (He is a professor of surgery and while we were on the plane he bandaged Willkie's arm after the inoculations. Willkie, who did not know that he was the professor, wondered whether he was a good enough man to change the bandage!)

The other visitor last week was Professor Carr. He is still as wicked as before in his international outlook, but we are great friends and we had a great time . . .

Another visitor, to tea, was Miss Evans of the LSE. She has gone rather old, but is very friendly . . .

But enough about me. I hope that my cable put your mind at rest to some extent and that you are less worried. I am rather glad that you have no job now; it must be dreadful in New York in the summer in any case, but to travel in the subway is specially unpleasant. I could not stand it. (We have had the first two warm days this year. The peonies are in full bloom; so are the lupins of which there is a lot; the potatoes are coming up very promisingly, and we are actually eating our own lettuces!)

Still no change. On 21 June, he wrote:

There has been no change in the situation since I wrote last. I am still waiting for an answer concerning the Clipper. But in any case, as I told you before, my mind is almost made up. The authorities have done their best, and I have no doubt about their attitude. This being so, it is my plain duty to go. There is little I can do here. The services of international lawyers are not required just now. Smith is doing some menial work in a quite different field; Brierly is writing innocuous memoranda. Over there I can be useful.

I have been busy in the last fortnight in enlarging – almost into a small book – my paper which I read in Chatham House. I am considering whether I ought to publish it in the World Order Series. The proofs of the Digest are arriving; there are almost 200 pages of them. I have been doing the work almost exclusively at home. It has become too hot to go out. The garden is lovely. We have had our first lettuces and spinach.

He was ever concerned with my development. Replying to a long letter that I had sent him, he said on 29 June:

I received only yesterday your big letter of 2 June written on thick paper with the result that there was a delay and Mummy had to pay 60 cents – a terrific expense in these days. But otherwise I was delighted with the letter. I liked not only its tidyness (or tidiness?), but the style. I have the impression that you are reading a great deal and carefully with excellent results. My own experience as a reader has been that no book is worth reading unless it is worth reading twice or even thrice. I should like you to read a great deal of Macaulay, Burke, Kingsley, Jane Austen, Hardy and try to see the excellence of their style.

It is splendid that you are interested in Librarianship. It stimulates a critical approach to books and it stimulates reading. By all means catalogue your books here according to your system. With great regret, I am not sure that I want my books catalogued. I know where to find them. But my pamphlets are not so tidy.

And now – this letter will reach you about July 13th. Very many happy returns to you and very much love, darling boy. I hear from Mummy that you are growing not only in years, but also in mind, and that, with very occasional lapses you no longer regard yourself as the centre of things, bless you. This being so I went to the Bank yesterday and I applied for permission to send you £10 in dollars. I have been told that each evacuee child can be sent that sum once a year for his (or her) birthday. We shall see.

I trust this letter will find you in camp. Remember my warnings a propos, but otherwise enjoy yourself.

I do not think you can reply to this letter, for I shall be leaving in your direction about the end of the month. So, good boy, much love to you and once more, lots of happy returns.

To the United States again

At long last, a seat was found on the Clipper. Hersch received a letter from Gaselee telling him that he had a flight to Lisbon on 29 July and an onward flight to the United States on 31 July.[35] Rachel was 'very happy indeed'. The Foreign Office also wrote to the Vice-Chancellor of Cambridge supporting Hersch's application for leave of absence for the Michaelmas Term. This was duly granted. Hersch was still to receive two-thirds of his stipend since the payment from Wellesley would only be sufficient to provide for his expenses in America including the cost of his passage by Clipper. The arrangement would be subject to reconsideration if Hersch received additional payment for special lectures or any other work he might undertake.[36]

Meanwhile, Professor Manley O. Hudson, the Professor of International Law at the Harvard Law School who had been a judge of the Permanent Court of International Justice, told Louise Overacker that, if Hersch were making Wellesley his headquarters during his stay, there would probably be a place for him to work in the Harvard Law Library.[37]

Virtually the whole of July was taken up with preparations for the journey, including completing the *AD* volume for press and securing a letter from his doctor testifying to his vaccination.

HL to RL, 5 July 1941
I have not written for about five or six days. I have been busy settling the details of and the hitches over the journey. You have no idea what problems all this involves in these days. For instance, I am now held up because the London office of the United States Lines has not yet received confirmation of the passage having been booked for me. I shall actually get the ticket from England to Lisbon, but I am still waiting for confirmation of the Clipper passage. Without that I cannot do anything about the Portuguese visa for which, as last December, they have to have authorization from Lisbon. I spent two days in London trying to expedite matters, but I am still waiting. There is no reason to assume that anything has gone wrong, but all this is so unsettling! It is of importance that the journey should not be delayed, and I do not think that it will be delayed . . .

I have now received the entire Digest proof, and it is now clear that I shall be able to see the volume through the press before I go. The paper at Chatham House was not a flop – I assure you. After I read it I devoted another three

[35] Sir Stephen Gaselee to HL, 25 June 1941.
[36] Secretary General of the Faculties to HL, 23 July 1941.
[37] Louise Overacker to HL, 23 June 1941.

weeks to revising it, and it is now a piece of work which does credit to the family. I was glad that you liked my review of Lord Cecil's book. Noel-Baker wanted to reprint it as a separate pamphlet, and perhaps it will be done.

HL to RL, 8 July 1941

I have just had – at last – the confirmation of the Lisbon–New York passage. In these days one cannot be too definite or too certain that there will be no hitches of various descriptions, but if all goes well if I were you I would stay at home on August 1 and 2 in case there is a telegram. I do not think that there is time for you to answer this letter. They take now about a fortnight each way.

You can imagine that I am having a rather busy time. There are immeasurable details of the journey – and the omission of any of them may mean a lot of trouble. I am getting along nicely with the final stages of the Digest and with the completion of that article on International Law in the War which I started last year.

Luckily the details of handing over the house to the tenants are much less troublesome than last year. I could not hope for better tenants. The Colonel is a perfect gentleman with a great sense of humour. Mrs Robbins is a housewife who knows how to treat furniture. In fact, you would be astounded to see how little the house has changed. The walls show no scratch; the lovely carpet on the stairs wears quite well. The garden is a joy. This week is the best for roses, and it is a delight to be in the garden.

A card from Buckland, written in his minuscule hand, replies to a question, not repeated, that Hersch had put to him when sending him a typescript, not identified in the card but probably related to *The Reality of the Law of Nations*:[38]

Many thanks for the typescript. The question of whether I.L. is law or not seems to me idle: it depends how you choose to define 'law'. But it wants all the support it can get and the very name counts for something. Hall's introduction to his 3rd edition is painful reading. Only the pessimistic part of his prophesy has been realized. I am not very hopeful of surrender of part of sovereignty. I have the League of Nations in mind. It was possible only with the unanimity clause which destroyed 9/10 of its value. And it had no power. It is obvious that few of the nations were in good faith. They joined for what they could get and wouldn't stay when things went against them. I do not believe in international police. It could not be so constituted that I would trust it.

---

[38] *Collected Papers*, Vol. 2, pp. 22–52.

Whether the English-speaking peoples could make a strong enough League of Nations to enforce peace I do not know – I fear not.

But I know nothing about the matter.

HL to RL, 13 July 1941

This is Eli's thirteenth birthday – and you know what I feel for you and him – bless him on this occasion. I sent him a cable yesterday. Today I am in thoughts with both of you.

This is probably the last letter I am writing before leaving. I calculate that letters take 16–17 days. So will you hold your thumb up on the 29th and then on the 31st! Also – expect a cable on the 31st or 1st. Also prepare some bread and salt to greet the visitor!

There is nothing, in these days of coupons, that I can bring you by way of clothing. But I have set my mind on a lovely Waterman pen which you badly need.

Subject to the Portuguese visa, everything is settled. In these days a fortnight is a long time, but if there are no unexpected developments, the original plan will be adhered to.

I have practically finished with the Digest, and I have finished with the article on the war of 1939 and with the revised Chatham House paper (I am sending you a copy). I must now find time to sketch out my lecture programme – it is a terrific one – on the subjects about which I know only little. I shall have to do the necessary reading in New York. There is no time to do it here. You know how many things must be seen to.

McNair was here for three days. He looks much better. He is preparing for the printer the second edition of his book on Legal Effects of War . . .

You know all about Lwów. I do not like to express my sentiments, but the thing is constantly with me like a nightmare. It is astonishing how a human being can split his personality! I am perfectly normal in my intercourse with people. I did, for instance, my job very well in helping the other night the Vice Master and Robbins to entertain in Trinity two generals and two colonels.

This is the first of the only two occasions of which I am aware on which Hersch referred so directly to the fate of his family in Poland and is the key to the absence of any further mention of his family in his correspondence.

Just before leaving for the United States, Hersch was a signatory of a message of support for the Russians, which was reported in the *Manchester Guardian* of 22 July 1941 in the following terms:

CAMBRIDGE AND RUSSIA

Greetings and Support

The Tass Agency has received a copy of the following cable sent to the Academy of Sciences of the USSR from Cambridge University:

Warmest greetings and support for your country's heroic fight against the common foe.

The signatories are as follows:

EA Benians, Vice-Chancellor of the University;
Rev GA Chase, Master of Selwyn College;
Professor GM Trevelyan, OM, CBE, Master of Trinity College;
ED Adrian, FRS, Professor of Physiology;
FM Cornford, Professor of Greek Philosophy;
EJ Dent, Professor of Music;
Sir AS Eddington, OM, FRS, Professor of Astronomy and Experimental Philosophy;
Professor Admiral Sir HW Richmond, KCB, Master of Downing College;
HA Harris, Professor of Anatomy;
J Hilton, Professor of Industrial Relations;
Sir FG Hopkins, OM, FRS, Professor of Biochemistry;
H Lauterpacht, Professor of International Law;
DS Robertson, Professor of Greek;
GI Taylor, FRS, Yarrow Professor of the Royal Society;
CE Tilley, FRS, Professor of Mineralogy and Petrology;
Elizabeth Hill, Reader in Slavonic Languages;
J Needham, FRS, Fellow of Gonville and Caius;
Sir William Dunn, Reader in Biochemistry;
HF Stewart, DD, Fellow of Trinity College, Reader in French

The distinction of the nineteen signatories was such as to exclude any suggestion that they were in any way Communist sympathisers. It will be recalled that, in breach of the Non-Aggression Pact concluded between Germany and the Soviet Union in 1939, Germany attacked Russia on 22 June 1941.

Hersch eventually reached the United States on 2 August 1941. The plan had been that he and Rachel would immediately travel to New Hampshire to visit me at summer camp, but he had a number of things to attend to in New York, principally preparation of the lectures that he was to give at Wellesley. As he had previously warned Rachel, the international law lectures were not a problem, but he also had to give a course on international relations, a subject to which he had only been marginally exposed. So he almost immediately began reading in the library at Columbia University. Their visit to me at camp was postponed till 29 August. In the meantime, Hersch was not slow to complain about the dearth of letters from me.

HL to EL, 6 August 1941
When Randolph Hearst sent his boy to a camp and did not receive letters from him he sent the following wire: 'If you write I hope you are hugely enjoying yourself. If you do not write I hope you are having a most rotten time'. However, I am not Hearst.

I am very eager to see you as soon as possible, but things are rather in a tangle here. They may disentangle themselves in a day or two. I will write in any case. It is clear to me that – tangle or no tangle – I must see you by the 15th at the latest. There are so many things we must discuss – including the question of the school.

In the meantime, can you find out reliably and in some detail about a decent boarding house or something similar in the neighbourhood of the camp.

It is quite warm here, but nothing like the usual New York heat wave. In any case I do not mind it very much as I sit in the room very scantily dressed.

I hope your tooth trouble is over and that you are not allowing anything to interfere with your enjoyment of the holiday.

However, as the August days went by, Hersch became increasingly disinclined to leave New York. Preparation for Wellesley was on his mind; the expense of the journey to New Hampshire and the prospect of fatigue troubled him. Rachel indulged him ('a duck for dinner and blackberry jelly') and he was reasonably comfortable in Riverdale, though the heat was oppressive.

They were reassured that I was happy at camp and not missing them. So the visit to see me was put off and eventually made unnecessary by the conclusion of camp at the end of August.

Robert Jackson, who had been Attorney-General during Hersch's first visit, had in the meantime been appointed a Justice of the US Supreme Court. Hersch wrote him a congratulatory letter before he left England and Jackson, unaware that Hersch had already reached the US, replied on 13 August:

Robert H. Jackson to HL, 13 August 1941
I greatly appreciate your letter. I am confident that I shall like the work of the Supreme Court which is something of a relief from administrative duties which make the office of Attorney-General a good deal of a burden.

Following your visit, I made some adaptations of the material you suggested to me and used it in an address to the Inter-American Bar Association at Havana. I have no doubt it has come to your attention, but I enclose a reprint. It has had the rather wholesome effect of turning discussion to what International Law can do for mankind rather than toward the cynical view that it was dead, which had been all too prevalent . . .

Should you be on this side of the Atlantic again, do not fail to let me know so that we may get together.

Later in the month, Hersch and Rachel went to Washington for a couple of days.

The semester began at Wellesley on 22 September 1941. Hersch was given accommodation at Cazenove Hall, but tried to get back to New York at weekends to see Rachel, even though it was a five-hour train journey from Boston to New York. He made occasional visits to the Harvard Law School Library and saw something of Manley Hudson. But it was not smooth going.

HL to RL, September 1941
I am having a nerve-wracking and uncomfortable time, and I often regret that I undertook the thing (in addition – I was told today that Uncle Sam will retain 27% of the salary as income tax!). I cannot recall anything as unpleasant.

The reduction in net income was as painful as it was unexpected and added to his basic unhappiness, stemming no doubt from his thoughts about his family in Poland, as well as from having to lecture systematically on an unfamiliar subject.

McNair kept in touch with him. Writing from Liverpool on 14 September, he said:

Arnold McNair to HL, 14 September 1941
Many thanks for your letter of 5 August from which I was glad to hear of your safe arrival. I expect that you are now overwhelmed by the American tempo of life but I hope that you have had some kind of holiday and are feeling equal to the next few months. American public opinion seems to be moving very rapidly and is being watched here with great interest. The President is obviously asking Hitler to declare war – thus saving him the considerable trouble of doing so.

I had a fortnight's holiday in August of which I spent the first week at the cottage. For the second my wife and I went to Cambridge and had a most enjoyable time. We had rooms in Eltisley Avenue. It was exactly the holiday she needed – complete rest from domestic work and many friends to see. I got a fair amount of work done in the library. Mrs Brockhouse gave me the proofs of the AD to read. It is an interesting volume. The usefulness of that work increases with every volume. We must try to go back to 1900. In 50 years time it will have profoundly affected the corpus juris by the introduction of so much judicial matter into fields where writers – unaware of the decisions – have been forced to speculate.

I am making slow but steady progress with my book [the second edition of *Legal Effects of War*] and am anxious to push on before the winter raids begin. I am hopeful that within 6 or 8 weeks I shall have covered the ground and shall then be able to settle down to the final polishing. I have already re-written the main chapter 'General Principles of the Effect of War on Contracts' twice.

Russia is putting up a superb resistance and it is galling that we are not able to give her more help. It looks as if Hitler will be unable to strike a mortal blow at her this year, and after 6 months I am hopeful that British and American supplies coupled with the enormous Russian power will make her invulnerable. If the war is fought to a military conclusion I cannot see an end within less than 2 years, but I think the political factors are more important and more uncertain in this war than in any previous war, and I should never be surprised any morning to read of some kaleidoscopic change such as the Army taking control in Germany . . .

I am sending a paper to the Grotius Society towards the end of this month on Effect of War on Contracts (including Frustration). I think that after the war you and I might be able to help Hurst to improve the ILA and the Grotius. I feel however that we shall never get the study of international law in this country into a really healthy state unless we can break down the rigid bar between the teacher and the practitioner. It would improve the teacher enormously to have a little practice as his Continental confrère has, and it would enhance his standing . . . [*the rest of the letter is missing*]

Eric Beckett, then the Deputy Legal Adviser in the Foreign Office, also wrote to him, telling him of the *Trail Smelter* arbitral decision[39] and enclosing a note about the case. Beckett added in handwriting:

I hear you have had a great success in the US with your papers and addresses. I hope to see you sometime.[40]

He received a number of invitations to lecture elsewhere. One was from Yale to take over Frederick Dunn's course on international law and diplomacy during the second semester (the first weeks of 1942) which would, if it had materialised, have brought him in a further $2,000. Another was from the University of Illinois for the same period. But he could not accept either since he was due to return to England by the beginning of 1942.

---

[39] 9 *ILR* 935.   [40] E. Beckett to HL, 26 September 1941.

At Wellesley, he was kept busy not only with his regular courses but also with additional public lectures, two of which, on 'The Present Position and the Future of the Law of Nations', he gave on 15 and 23 October. Sandwiched between them was a trip to Washington to see the Attorney-General, Francis Biddle, returning to Wellesley the evening before the second lecture. Even then, he had to begin giving thought to his return journey to England. He received a letter from the British Embassy in Washington reminding him of the need to apply for a Portuguese visa and warning him that, in view of the congestion on the Lisbon–London air service, he would be well advised to allow for a certain delay in Lisbon.[41]

He had to make another trip to Washington in November in connection with the work that he was doing for the Attorney-General. He also saw Justice Jackson, who invited him to Thanksgiving dinner on 20 November, but Hersch could not accept this because he was due to leave Washington that afternoon to get back to his teaching at Wellesley. He was a bit unhappy, telling Rachel, who had been to the Bradleys for Thanksgiving dinner, that:

I was rather sorry for myself that I did not have turkey this year. It would be a nice thing to have a hot turkey from Schmidt one day when I am back – what do you think?

I am now in the midst of correcting exam papers. I have also started on the RHJ[42] stuff. This will take me about three weeks. On Monday I propose to be in the Harvard Library for the whole day.

The 'RHJ stuff' was a memorandum that he was preparing for Justice Jackson who was going to address the New York Bar Association in January.[43]

HL to RL, 21 November 1941
Back again in Wellesley – after ten hours in the train. Within four minutes of entering my room I had a bath. And how I needed it!

I hope that you are much better and that you were able to go to the thanksgiving dinner at the Bradleys. If you are not quite better, do not hesitate to put off Mrs Miller.

---

[41] British Embassy, Washington, to HL, 23 October 1941.   [42] Robert H. Jackson.
[43] See Robert H. Jackson, 'Our American Legal Philosophy: Mechanisms and Techniques to End International Lawlessness', presented at the Annual Banquet of the New York State Bar Association, Waldorf-Astoria Hotel, New York, 24 January 1941.

As I wired you – (it was a night letter for 33 cents so you need not get alarmed that I am squandering your inheritance!) – the interview was very successful. I stayed an hour. He has accepted the invitation to address the New York Bar Association in January and I shall be the discreet first fiddle. The thing is working well. <u>Also</u>, I just had time to pay a visit to Internal Revenue Department, and this, I am now quite sure, will rescue at least $300 from the clutches of the Wellesley Treasurer.

And now to work for RHJ and much love to you and the boy.

The work that he was doing for Justice Jackson evidently troubled him – though the cause of the worry is not clear. He wrote to Jackson on 13 December:

In the last ten days I had occasional moments of hesitation, but I am quite convinced now that I was right in going on with the matter. I hope to send you the notes on the 15th of this month.

But it reached a satisfactory conclusion. There is no copy of Jackson's acknowledgment, but, on 21 December, Hersch wrote to Jackson:

I am very pleased to hear that you have found the memorandum useful. I was specially glad to learn of the way you intend to use it. Parts III and IV – and, possibly, Part I – will be useful for the New York meeting. I say 'and, possibly, Part I' for it seems to me that the question of the legality of the conduct of the United States is one which, for reasons stated in the memorandum, is of general interest. This would also be a good opportunity for administering a public rebuke to Borchard and for mentioning that he is receiving a proper reply elsewhere. Some, though not many, of those present may have read his article, and they may like to know that it will not pass unanswered.

I have little doubt that the American Journal of International Law will publish your reply to Borchard. For that you may be able to use the material in Part II of the memorandum. Part I might provide a suitable introduction. The first two or three pages of Part III are also relevant.

I agree that the recent practice of the Latin-American States is of importance. It might, of course, be objected that in so far as their action is based on the Kellogg–Briand Pact they ought to grant favourable treatment to all members of the Axis. However, as the discriminatory treatment is a right – as distinguished from accruing from the Pact, it is for the Latin States to decide to which extent they wish these consequences from it.

I propose to be in Washington on the 2nd and 3rd. Perhaps you will let me know when you would like me to call. If in the meantime you would like to have some material on any special point which may occur to you, I hope you will not hesitate to tell me.

Notwithstanding the pressure under which he was placed by the work he was doing for Justice Jackson, Hersch added to his burdens by concerning himself with the choice of a boarding school for me, principally so that Rachel would be free to return to England when she could get a passage. Manley Hudson put him in touch with Phillips Academy, Exeter. He also corresponded with Phillips Academy, Andover. These two schools were (and remain) two of the most prominent boarding schools in New England, having been established even before the American War of Independence. He visited the Headmaster of Andover on 16 December and it was then decided that I should start there in January 1942. It was an extraordinarily good school and I remained there until I graduated in June 1944 and soon thereafter returned to England.

Christmas and the New Year were spent in New York with Rachel and me before he returned to Wellesley to resume his lecturing there. In addition, he was still working on the memorandum for Justice Jackson. By 21 January, he was approaching the end of his Wellesley stay and was much troubled, to the point of boredom, by the uncertainty regarding his travel back to England and he resorted to the unusual, for him, activity of reading novels. Some enjoyment was got from a tea-time visit to Judge Lehman, the former Chief Judge of the New York Court of Appeals, whose palatial home made a considerable impression on both Hersch and Rachel. Hersch's letters to me were full of good advice about the study of geometry and participation in the French play.

The days dragged on.

I am not going tomorrow. In fact, I do not know when I am going. The Embassy sends me promising telegrams, but the Pan-American Air Lines are obstructive . . .

I gave my last lecture today – the best of all I have given. There was a terrific ovation – and there were tears. It is as well that I go for I am acquiring a collective affection for these young things. They are so grateful!

I lunched with Miss Overacker . . . I dined in Tower where again I was touched by their genuine sadness about my going.[44]

Bad war news, especially the fall of Singapore, added to his gloom. He cabled Sir Stephen Gaselee at the Foreign Office in London in the hope that a place might be found for him on a bomber. But nothing came of it. On 13 February, he wrote to me:

44 HL to RL, 21 January 1942.

I am still here [New York] – without any definite date of departure. It is a position which would get on anyone's nerves. One is condemned to inactivity and writing – a very demoralizing business. This explains the laconic character of my writing. But I will write you a long letter before I go – dealing largely with your studies. Now that the rush and the novelty are over, it will be time to take stock and to plan for the future. Your mid-term report was good, but leaving room for much improvement – which, of course, is natural at the very beginning. One of the most important things is to acquire the habit of reading a great deal of good books. Your rest ought to be devoted either to exercise, like walking, or reading in your armchair.

I am slightly depressed also because of the war news. We are passing through a very bad period. I am assuming that you are reading regularly the newspapers. It is very important that you should.

The delay became so long that he was obliged to register for the selection draft. This meant he had to have special permission to leave the country, but he obtained this on 18 February. None of the associated anxiety, however, prevented him from adding a postscript to his letter to me of 16 February: 'I should like you to acquire the habit of reading two books a week and of skipping through about ten'!

The boredom was briefly alleviated by a request from the British Embassy in Washington on 18 February to write an urgent Opinion, within the day, but there is no record of what it was about, and by a brief visit to Albany, the capital of New York State, during which he met the Governor, Mr Herbert H. Lehman. And still he was kept waiting. On 22 February, he wrote that he would definitely know on the coming Wednesday.

HL to EL, 22 February 1942
I am having a quiet day reading the Sunday Times and Commager and Morrison's History of the USA. What a well written book it is! It is American history at its best . . .

If I do not go home during the first week of March by plane, I will take a boat. There is an element of risk everywhere. There is nothing which weighs me down more than inactivity.

Recourse was had to playing chess by post. The game started on 21 February.

This chess business is a charming idea but I am not sure that it is practicable (also, I <u>hope</u> it is not practicable for I am most anxious, for very important reasons, to go away as soon as possible). In the meantime, I shall mark my moves with a pencil. You mark yours in ink.

There were five pairs of marks, but on 5 March Hersch gave up:

Suppose we call it a draw and begin a contest of five games, over a coca-cola, when you come home.

HL to EL, 23 February 1942

I am very glad you have taken out Commager's and Nevins' anthology. I would like you to have a shot at all the writings of Nevins and Commager (and possibly also of Morrison). You need not read everything in them. But it is useful that you should know what is in them. Later on I want you to study the works of Trevelyan and Macaulay.

I am playing some chess with Mummy. I show her how to beat me, and she thinks she is beating me!

At last the waiting came to an end. On 24 February, he heard from Pan Am that the State Department had given him a definite priority on 14 March. His spirits were lifted. In the interval he was able to attend a conference on legal problems in post-war planning in Atlantic City organised by the Carnegie Endowment, all expenses paid.

HL to EL, 1 March 1942

A rather dull business, but it is a change from New York... This place [Atlantic City] is a cross between Frinton and Brighton. The hotel [Chalfonte-Haddon Hall] is A1...

I am writing this listening to a speech of a dull but vigorous speaker who is looking all the time at me – damn him!

He relaxed sufficiently to add to a letter to me from Rachel the words 'Cheerio, old lunatic!' He and Rachel went to the cinema a few times. 'The Man Who Came To Dinner' bored them, but they enjoyed Leslie Howard in 'Mr V'. They were able to have dinner with their good friends, the Louries. They were the parents of Arthur Lourie, an old friend from London days, who was an official of the Jewish Agency and who, after Israel became independent, served for a while as the Israeli Ambassador to London.

HERSCH'S RETURN TO ENGLAND, MARCH 1942

But Hersch's departure was once again postponed. On 12 March, he was told that he would have to wait until 1 April, principally because decisions on seating in flights rested with the military authorities and even the State Department could not override them. However, some vacancy must have occurred because on 23 March Hersch was able to cable from England that he had arrived home 'perfectly fit'. Then began a year-long separation from Rachel who was unable to return to England until March 1943. It was a hard period for both of them.

The regular trans-Atlantic correspondence started again, with Hersch writing regularly to Rachel and me, the two of us exchanging the letters we got from him, and each of us writing separately to him.

His first letter was sent on 28 March 1942:

I think that in the first month or so you must allow me to write twice a week. There is such a lot to tell.

The Faculty Everyone is most understanding and full of sympathy for the predicament in which I found myself in these seven weeks. I had a letter today from Saunders the Secretary General of the Faculties ending with a post-script: 'What an awful time you must have had waiting!' The Vice-Master, who was most kind, told me that during the last war he had to wait in Cairo five weeks for a boat and that that was the worst time he had in his life. The same night I dined in College. The Master, who was told by the Vice-Master, came up to me most cordially and shook me by the hand. He asked me to sit next to him. (That, of course, was the beginning of the trouble. We soon started a discussion on international matters and there was a disagreement – quite a violent one. When we were walking up to the Combination Room Hollond whispered to the Vice-Master: Don't let him sit next to the Master: It is fatal! However, he was most pleasant in the Combination Room and dumped port on me with the result that I was very jolly when I was walking home. Apart from drinks, the dinner in Trinity is now a mere shadow of its former self.)

Fortunately, there is the vacation now, and I have time to pick up the threads at my leisure. I have four examinations papers to set and to start the Digest. Also, I am preparing a report for Gaselee.

I had a cordial letter from McNair who is coming up here for a week on the 11th.

At home everything is all right. I have altogether abandoned house-keeping. It is a physical impossibility. The food situation is worse, but the main trouble is that shops no longer deliver anything. You have to get everything yourself. (Nothing is delivered. When you 'send' a suit to the cleaner you must bring it there and must collect it.) You cannot buy anything, presently, without coupons or so-called 'points'. You get twenty points a month for tinned food. One tin of canned fruit is 12 points! This being so Mrs Robbins manages everything. It is a full time job. She goes out at 9 in the morning and comes at 12.30 from the various queues. But there is a very good old cook – and this is much more than anyone else has. Mrs Winfield has neither cook nor maid. Mrs Thomas only a half-daily! I will continue that sorry tale some other time.

I have applied for the permission to send 62 dollars per month. It is likely that I shall get it as from 1 January which means that I may be able to send you half the money for the three months of the first semester and for the three months of the next: 312 dollars!

You may register at your leisure for going home, but you must do absolutely nothing decisive. In July we should know more clearly how we stand.

In two or three days I will write again – via Andover.

Two days later, after chastising Rachel for having taken on an over-demanding job for $5 a week and urging her to drop it, he continued:

Please do <u>not</u> send any parcels with vitamins or chocolate. I have more than enough to eat. Take an example: The Winfields[45] are coming to tea in about half-an-hour and I am giving them the famous asparagus rolls, two cakes, biscuits, jam, etc! I had my two eggs and bacon and honey for breakfast to-day, and I am dining in College! You <u>must not</u> worry about my food.

He lost no time in resuming his normal pattern of work. He was 'deep in Oppenheim', that is, the preparation of the revised sixth edition of Volume II (*The Law of Disputes, War and Neutrality*), which appeared in 1944. But the urgency of this was diminished when Longmans said that they were not going to reprint Volume I for the time being on account of shortages of paper and that as there were 400 copies of Volume II still in stock a new edition was unnecessary. He started again on the research for the *AD*, of which Volume 9, for 1938–40, was completed in September. Examination papers had to be set on the Law of Peace for the Law Tripos Part I and on Peace and War for the LLB.

But his first substantial task was to send Sir Stephen Gaselee at the Foreign Office a report on his visit to the United States.

HL to Sir Stephen Gaselee, 30 March 1942
On the occasion of my first visit to the United States in the autumn of 1940, I was guided by your advice in accepting the invitation to go there as Carnegie Visiting Professor. This was also the case when a similar invitation was extended to me in 1941. The contacts which I had already established in the United States and the apparent results of my first visit left me with no doubt that I ought to act on your view, and that of the Ministry of Information, that it was desirable that I should accept the invitation.

---

45 Percy Winfield was Professor of English Law at Cambridge.

My work as lecturer was confined largely to New England. I acted as Mary Whiton Calkins Visiting Professor at Wellesley College, Massachusetts, one of the largest and most important women's Colleges in the country. I gave also occasional lectures at other Colleges in New England. I maintained contact with the Boston Foreign Policy Association and attended as their guest at their meetings. I soon found that this part of New England, because of the numerical strength and the influence of the American-born Irish section of its population, provided a useful field of activity. After my arrival I agreed to read a paper on the Future of Neutrality before the American Political Science Association at the Annual Meeting in December, 1941. When the time came, I decided that, notwithstanding the change in the political situation, it was advisable to proceed with a suitably adapted paper bearing on this subject.[46]

As on the occasion of my first visit, I regarded lecturing as the secondary object of my work in the United States. Accordingly, I devoted a great deal of my time to maintaining contact with those of my fellow teachers of international law – like Professor Jessup, Professor Hyde and Judge Hudson – whose attitude in the matter of active assistance to the Allies or of the participation by the United States in the war was critical or negative. I also agreed to take part in the Conference on legal studies of post-war problems convened in Atlantic City at the end of February, 1942, by the International Law Division of the Carnegie Endowment for International Peace. I visited from time to time members of the office of the Legal Adviser in the State Department with whom I was personally acquainted. I attached importance to being in touch with some of the higher judicial officers who wield political importance in the United States. Particular reference to Mr Justice Jackson and Mr Justice Frankfurter is made in a subsequent part of this report.

I had hoped that after having established, in the course of my first visit, some advantageous contact with Mr Jackson, the then Attorney-General, it might be possible for me to be of some use to his successor, Mr Francis Biddle, who, I believe, is as sincere a friend of this country as Mr Jackson. When I saw Mr Biddle early in October, the United States had just embarked upon the third crucial step of the period of pre-belligerency (the transfer of destroyers to Great Britain and the Lend-Lease Act being the first two landmarks), namely, direct offensive action against German submarine and surface naval forces. The President and some other governmental spokesmen had occasionally described the activities of these German forces as piratical. The Attorney-General and I agreed that it would be useful if it could be shown that the designation of these acts as piratical, far from being a mere manner of speech or mere abuse of an unfriendly State, was warranted by international practice and that its practical implications, namely, the summary suppression of the vessels engaged

---

[46] See *Collected Papers*, Vol. 5, pp. 675–83.

in these activities, was in accordance with international law. This view of the legal position coincided with the opinion which I had expressed before the war in connection with the Nyon Agreements of September, 1937. The Attorney-General asked me to prepare a memorandum on these lines. I enclose a copy of it.[47] As on the occasion of my memorandum to Mr Jackson in January of 1941, on the subject of the Lend-Lease Bill, I was of the view that it is desirable, having regard both to American public opinion at large and to its isolationist element, to assist the American authorities in the presentation of their action as being in accordance with international law.

For the same reason, I attached importance to maintaining close contact throughout with Mr Justice Jackson, the former Attorney-General and now one of the Associate Justices of the Supreme Court. He has the ear of the Administration and is often spoken of as a future Presidential candidate. He is actively interested in the promotion of Anglo-American relations, especially from the point of view of post-war reconstruction and of international orga-nization. In addition, we both agreed that it was important to use available opportunities for discouraging and refuting the recurring isolationist attempts to malign the conduct of the Administration as being in clear violation of international law. The enclosed memorandum which I submitted to him at his request in January of this year served two purposes. The first was to assist him in putting before the Annual Meeting of the New York State Bar Association a picture, based largely on a historical survey of the political relations between the United States and Great Britain and of the contributions made by them jointly to the cause of international arbitration and organization, of the possibilities of closer Anglo-American cooperation in the future. The address, which was also broadcast on the wireless, was delivered before an audience of fifteen hundred members at the annual dinner of the Association. It was a practically literal reproduction of the last part of the enclosed memorandum. I was present as Mr Justice Jackson's guest.

The object of the first part of the memorandum was to help Mr Justice Jackson to answer a somewhat virulent criticism, made by Professor Borchard of Yale, one of the leading isolationist lawyers in the United States, of the address which Mr Jackson made at Havana in April, 1941, at a time when he was Attorney-General, and in which he formulated the legal bases, from the point of view of international law, of the Lend-Lease Bill. I had assisted in the preparation of that address and for this, as well as for other reasons, I felt it proper to offer my services to Mr Justice Jackson in drafting a document containing a reply to Professor Borchard and setting forth, in a comprehensive manner, the theory of international law on which the United States acted before they entered the war. This aspect of the matter is covered by Parts I and II of the enclosed

---

[47] *Collected Papers*, Vol. 5, pp. 665–74.

memorandum. I also enclose two letters of Mr Justice Jackson bearing on the matter. Before submitting the first draft, I consulted Sir Ronald Campbell, in particular with regard to the part referring to the bases of Anglo-American relations. I was told that both he and the Ambassador were of the opinion that I ought to go ahead.

In this connection, reference may be made to the memorandum which, after discussion with some American friends, I submitted at his request in September, 1941, to Sir Ronald Campbell, then acting Ambassador, in the matter of the agitation then current in the American press and in American commercial circles to the effect that British authorities and British business men were taking unfair advantage of the Lease-Lend materials and of the war situation generally for promoting British commercial interests to the disadvantage of American trade. In this memorandum, a copy of which I enclose, I set forth certain proposals concerning the legal machinery for dealing with this important problem which was, and still is, a factor of significance in Anglo-American relations. When in February of this year, at the invitation of some lawyers associated with the New York State Legislature, I visited Albany to study the state of opinion there, I was struck, in my conversations with the Governor and the leaders of both parties, with the disquieting persistence of that problem.

The question of the political and psychological aspects of Anglo-American relations is one outside the purpose for which I undertook the journey to the United States. I hesitate, therefore, to make any observations on this matter with regard to which the authorities are very likely being overwhelmed with various kinds of advice. But as during my visit I had the opportunity of studying American public opinion both prior to and after the entry of the United States into the war, and as I discussed this question with a number of American friends, I feel that it may be pertinent if I make two observations, in the nature of suggestions, on this subject.

It is generally agreed that the relations between the peoples of the United States and Great Britain, as distinguished from the relations of the two governments, constitute a vital factor both in the conduct of the war and in the post-war period of reconstruction, and that in this respect the situation has deteriorated, in a substantial sense, since the United States have entered the war. There is no single cause to which the present situation can be attributed. Some of these causes existed before the United States entered the war; others have accrued since. It cannot be part of this report to survey them or to analyse them. But I venture to submit two specific suggestions: (1) It might be useful if the department responsible were to make it a practice of asking persons, who are not necessarily government officials and who have returned from the United States from a prolonged stay, say, four months or over, to report on their experience in this matter in some detail and to submit concrete proposals for action or organization best calculated to meet the situation; (2) The authorities might take into consideration the advisability of immediate and concerted action aiming at inviting, or facilitating the invitation, through Universities or other bodies, of a considerable number of University teachers and other professional men and women for the purpose of lecturing or generally working in this country for periods of not less than six months. The value of such visits, if adequate steps could be taken to make the stay of the guests in this country both pleasant and fruitful, would be immeasurable. From the practical point of view, it would, I believe, exceed the value of any British efforts made in this direction in the United States. I know that this also is the opinion of distinguished Americans who are devoted friends of this country. They are perturbed by the present trend of affairs. For example, at the beginning of this month, Mr Justice Frankfurter asked me urgently to deliver a personal message to Professor HJ Laski begging him, out of consideration for American public opinion, to refrain from expatiating on the theme of this war heralding a social revolution.

All the enclosed memoranda are for your use. Please do not trouble to return them.

I should not like to conclude this report without thanking you warmly for the trouble you took in order to secure for me a speedy passage to the United States and, in face of exceptional difficulties, on the return journey. I ought also to add that the Vice-Chancellor and the General Board of the Faculties of the Cambridge University have fully co-operated in making my journey possible.[48]

Hersch, as requested by Justice Frankfurter, promptly sought Laski out to convey Frankfurter's admonition. It was not well received.[49]

[48] *Collected Papers*, Vol. 5, pp. 640-3.   [49] HL to RL, 8 April 1942.

CHAPTER 7

THE WAR YEARS, PART III: APRIL 1942–DECEMBER 1944

Hersch having returned to England, he wrote to Rachel on 1 April 1942:

I wrote yesterday a long letter to the boy, but to-day is Passover eve and, as I am sure you will be thinking a great deal of your husband, it gives me pleasure to write this letter to send you my love and all my warm wishes.

I have now been here for a week and I have done quite useful work – including the writing of immeasurable letters and of a long report to Sir Stephen. I will now take two days off and then settle down to the Digest, to lectures, and to more serious work. I am so happy that this nightmare has passed and I am grateful that I escaped many a danger.

I received to-day permission to send you the allowed sum of money retrospectively from 1 January. I went to the bank and arranged that you will receive, through a bank, £78, which means about 310 dollars. This is for the first two quarters. The next installment of 156 dollars will follow about 1 July. Until then, although you may take all precautionary steps, you must do nothing definitive either about the apartment or about your return. I was extremely grateful that there was no necessity for you to go by boat in March. It would have been a terrific risk. I will discuss the whole thing slowly with Turner and others. I asked the Bank Manager to-day and he told me that there is no movement for any large scale return. I will consult McNair and others . . .

McNair is coming here on the 11th for a week – I am much looking forward to seeing him. I shall not go to London for some time. I hate travelling.

I am spending the seder to-night with the Daubes.

HL to RL, 4 April 1942

It is a Saturday afternoon – like the many Saturday afternoons you have known: rather sultry weather; raining intermittently; rather mild; Chandler doing the usual stuff in the garden: cutting the hedges, tidying up the shed, putting in potatoes (he does it slightly better than before for I gave him a rise of 3d an hour. All people get rises these days except University professors.) I am doing work in the study, but as usual from time to time I go into the garden to do my bit.

Everything is in order in the house. The wall-paper is as nice and clean as when I left. I have not noticed any deterioration in the carpets or furniture. The kitchen looks shabby where the cooking is done, but Agnes, the cook, is quite happy there. She is an austere woman of about fifty-five and is of the opinion that in war-time one ought not to paint the kitchen. The same applies to the various places where the white paint is coming off with the result that the green one is showing. Everyone agrees that this is not a time for embellishing things.

We have now excellent neighbours in No. 8. They are officers and are very quiet indeed. We could not wish for better neighbours.

I am going to London on Tuesday – to see Laski and others . . . I am so sick of travelling that I am going to reduce my London expeditions to a minimum. Also they are too expensive.

I was invited to-day by Lady Thomson[1] to lunch with them tomorrow, but it is Easter Sunday and I promised to be at home as Mrs Robbins is making preparations for the occasion.

I am assuming that it is quite and abundantly clear that you are staying on in the apartment. There cannot be any discussion about it. I should feel unhappy if you left it.

HL to RL, 8 April 1942

These two enclosures will please you: (1) is the first violet of the garden – rightfully belonging to the first (absent) Lady of the House, bless her; (2) is a cutting from the Times of 5 March. In the 7th line of the obituary notice about Politis you will notice a reference to your husband which will please you.[2] (You may show, if there is an opportunity, to Segal[3] who is a great believer in me. Do not show it to Elizabeth Hyde who thinks that her father is <u>the</u> man. You <u>may</u> show it to a boastful fellow called Elihu Lauterpacht.) . . .

There is no startling news. I went to London yesterday, mainly in order to have a heart-to-heart talk with Laski in conformity with Frankfurter's request to ask Laski to talk less about a revolution. Laski did not take it kindly, but we had a very cordial and pleasant time. He is very devoted – subject to his limitations . . .

Otherwise London is a nuisance. I came home quite exhausted. But I must be there on the 22nd for the Annual meeting of the Grotius Society and, possibly, also in order to see Gaselee.

---

[1] Lady Thomson was the wife of Sir Joseph John Thomson, Master of Trinity 1918–40.
[2] See p. 195, below.
[3] Simon Segal was a member of the foreign affairs staff of the American Jewish Committee and eventually its Director. He initiated the proposal to Hersch to write his book on human rights (see Chapter 8, p. 251, below). He was present at the San Francisco Conference in 1945 when the Charter of the UN was drawn up and successfully pressed for the inclusion in it of the human rights provisions that had not been included in the Dumbarton Oaks proposals.

McNair is coming on the 11th. I will dine with him in Caius and go for a walk in the afternoon.

Rachel, on her own in the apartment in Riverdale, was far from happy. She saw a few friends, but was oppressed by her loneliness. She made enquiries about the possibility of our both returning to England, but was told that space was very short. Also, many ships were being lost at the height of the U-boat campaign. She foresaw the possibility of a teaching post opening up in September, but much depended on where it would be and how much daily travelling it would involve. Hersch's view was that if he could find a place for me at an English public school in September 1943, I should stay at Andover till the end of the academic year 1942–3.

In April 1942, he wrote that he was:

studying the question of so-called War Crimes, i.e. the question of punishing the Germans guilty of various violations of international law during this war, especially in territories occupied by them. I have also resumed the study of the problems of post-war reconstruction . . . I feel better now than in New York, but my sleep has not yet quite returned.[4]

HL to RL, 18 April 1942
I wrote to the boy on Wednesday. Today is your day. (Incidentally, your letters have now begun to arrive regularly. It usually takes about 12 days.) There is nothing special to report except that the garden has been enriched by eight standard roses. I feel all right except for sleep the irregularity of which makes me rather tired. In the house everything is normal. I am not troubled with house keeping. This means that occasionally I do not get exactly what I would like, but this is a very small matter. Mrs Robbins does her best in difficult circumstances. (One has to calculate so carefully: In addition to rationed food, a person is entitled to 24 'points' a month; a tin of salmon is 32 points! There are no such things as tunny fish!)

The advice to me was constant:

HL to EL, 19 April 1942
Very many thanks for your several letters (the last being of March 27) which I received yesterday. The last one specially cheered me up; it was long, carefully written, with a sense of form <u>and</u> with interrogation marks and commas and full stops in the right place. You <u>almost</u> reached the Hall stage! (I really think that the principal drawback of KCC school[5] was that they neglected your handwriting and the form of your expressions.)

---

[4] HL to EL, 15 April 1942. See pp. 212–13 and Chapter 8 below for the substance of this work.
[5] King's College Choir School, Cambridge.

I did not mind at all that you took a full week off and had a short term. I am now quite convinced that you are acquiring a proper understanding of time in the matter of examinations and of looking far ahead. (You remember the old silly days when you thought of the examination only a week before it was due!) Above all, it is excellent news that you are doing good reading. It would please me very much if you were to go to one or two of your teachers or to Professor Bradley and ask them for a list of ten or twenty best books, mainly historical novels.

There is no special news from Cambridge. The garden is lovely. The daffodils are a glorious show. In a day or two the wild red cherry trees at the far end will begin to blossom. (Yes, the garden chairs are in danger. The Colonel – bless him – weighs 17 stone.)

The next day, he sent Rachel a copy of the menu for Hall in Trinity a few days earlier.

HL to RL, 20 April 1942

The enclosed is the usual Trinity dinner these days. It is less gorgeous than it reads – that 'mushrooms and bacon on toast' is an object worthy of a microscope – but it shows you that no one is starving.

DINNER
Madras
Grilled Fillet of Cod, Parsley Sauce
Mashed Potatoes
French Beans
Rhubarb Tart and Custard
Mushroom and Bacon on Toast

On 22 April, he went up to London for the first time since his return.

HL to RL, 22 April 1942

I have just returned from a tiring day in London devoted to a great variety of things. The annual meeting of the Grotius Society; visit to Gaselee and Beckett; visit to Howard Bros., visit to Leonard Stein;[6] supper with Stella Cornes;[7] buying a wedding present for John McNair;[8] luncheon with Colombos;[9] seeing Jenks and fetching the keys; buying some chocolates.

---

[6] Leonard Stein was a barrister having studied at Balliol College, Oxford. He was also Political Secretary of the World Zionist Organization (1920), President of the Anglo-Jewish Association (1939–49), was active in the League of Nations and, in 1953, was awarded an OBE for political and public services.

[7] Stella Cornes was the fiancée of Rachel's nephew, Nachman Ambache. They had met as undergraduates at Cambridge, both studying medicine. They married in September 1942.

[8] John McNair was Arnold McNair's son.

[9] Colombos was a practising international lawyer in London, of Maltese origin. He wrote two notable books, *The Law of the Sea* and *The Law of Prize*.

The FO are still studying my report. I have not noticed any obvious enthusiasm but that does not matter – The Legal Advisers are studying it . . .

My lectures begin tomorrow and will last five weeks.

I was delighted to hear that Miss Overacker visited you and sent flowers. But I was sad to hear that you are lonely in the evenings in that apartment. I quite understand it. I felt miserable when I was there alone one day only! I do not know what to suggest – except that you should try to be with someone every second evening either by going out or by having someone visit you.

Some development was in the air regarding Hersch's movements. On 24 April, he cabled Rachel to say 'Chances reunion substantially increased', but gave no indication of what they might be. On 26 April, he wrote at length:

HL to RL, 26 April 1942
I feel I ought to be more helpful with my advice about your coming home. My feeling is that if by the end of May there is no appreciable change in the situation then you ought to feel free to come home. I do not say that you ought to come – this is a matter upon which you must decide – but I say that if you decide to come I shall not discourage you and I shall be very glad indeed of your decision . . .

I have started lecturing. It is a small and dull class. The examiners' meetings have begun, and that takes some time . . .

I saw Rappard in London the other day, and I have now induced the Faculty to invite him to give a lecture. I shall be rather busy if he accepts the invitation. Tonight I am entertaining in Trinity – HA Smith! I got a cable from New York today from the Jewish Committee. They want me to do the job and ask about the fee. I am writing to them. In the meantime, if you have an inconspicuous opportunity of showing Segal the Politis note[10] – do it. I am getting loquacious.

Rappard was the Director of the Institut des Hautes Etudes Internationales in Geneva, at which Hersch had lectured in 1935, and was in London attached to the Swiss Legation. Rappard gave his lecture on 'Some Tentative Lessons from Swiss Federal Experience' on 7 May. In sending Rachel the notes of the lecture, Hersch said:

He was a great success. People said that his English was better than that of an Englishman! The Master made a great fuss of him and he enjoyed

---

[10] Extract from the obituary of Nicholas Politis, in *The Times*, 5 March 1942: 'Politis, who died at Cannes on Tuesday night, was a statesman with a wide international outlook and strong democratic sympathies, and one of the highest modern authorities on international law. In this field, indeed . . . only Lauterpacht and Oppenheim were his equals in our generation.'

himself thoroughly. But I had a very hectic 24 hours. He was on my hands all the time.[11]

H. A. Smith was the Professor of International Law at the LSE, which had been evacuated to Cambridge early in the war, and was one of Hersch's competitors in the election to the Whewell Chair. They were not on good terms, hence the exclamation mark at the end of the sentence.

The reference to the 'Jewish Committee' wanting him to 'do the job' is the first indication of what developed into the agreement for Hersch to write his book on *The International Bill of Human Rights*. Because his treatment of this subject was spread over a long period of time, it will be more convenient to deal with the topic from beginning to end in a separate chapter without interruption by other matters.[12]

Hersch's constant concern with the details of my welfare is well illustrated by his letter to me of 29 April, written on the back of a copy of a letter he had sent to Shrewsbury School asking what prospects there might be of admitting me if I came home in 1943:

This is merely (1) to confirm your letter of April 3rd which pleases me no end; (2) to express my satisfaction with your determination about geometry; (3) to impress upon you the necessity of putting a question mark at the end of sentences containing questions; (4) to assure you that although there has been a recrudescence of bombing, Cambridge has had none of it; (5) – last but not least – to tell you that I bought a beautiful <u>ivory</u> chess set – a hundred years old in red and white.

The chess set which he mentions was one of a number that he bought from time to time from Mr W. S. Adie, a former Fellow of Trinity, who had retired from the position of Auditor-General of India and, living in Cambridge, occasionally, like Hersch, came in to dinner in college. As the collection grew, it was housed in a glass-fronted mahogany bookcase in Hersch's study. He became very proud of it and occasionally he would select a set with which we could play a game.

That same evening – 29 April – he took Laski into Hall. On the menu which Hersch sent to Rachel (bean soup, fillet of plaice, asparagus and chocolate pudding), he wrote:

A memorable evening with Laski in Trinity. He refused to eat the asparagus (perhaps a protest). But what he might have been protesting against is not

---

[11] HL to RL, 9 May 1941.   [12] See Chapter 8 below.

recorded, unless it was the rather cool reception that he had from several Fellows.

HL to RL, 29 April 1942

Your letter was specially welcome because you were cheerful. It was good to learn that you are going out for walks and doing exercises and, generally, getting into shape again. I read with interest of the prospects of the job. It you have an assured job of $1,500–2,000 a year for only 4 hours a day for five days in not unpleasant circumstances, that would be a substantial factor in making up my mind. And it is a factor to which I would attach great importance in making up your mind. I want to have you here, but I see some advantages in not taking the risk of the journey, in remaining in comparative safety, and in being near the boy . . .

I am very well. I am sleeping much better than at any time in the last ten months . . .

The food at home is excellent. Everything runs smoothly. There are not many households which have a cook! I sleep every Friday in the Old Schools – fire 'watching'!

HL to EL, 3 May 1942

I think I have now settled to work properly, and I have started writing a long article. My class is much smaller than usual and the boys are not so bright. I dine in College twice a week and I sleep once a week in the Registry as a fire-watcher. I go out practically every day before dinner for a long walk through the rifle range in the direction of Coton. Cranmer Road is rather quiet in the last fortnight as the martial neighbours have left. The garden looks pretty although the weather has been cold and dry. Yesterday Chandler spent the whole afternoon in trying to put up the gate-post which has been knocked down some months ago. The Robbinses are pleasant and I am very lucky to have them in the house . . . Trinity is as usual except that the quality of dinners – and the quantity – has come down. There is no white wine, but there is still some claret and a bit of port – enough for twenty years.

You will be sorry to hear that both my trunks, which you took so much trouble to send, are now at the bottom of the sea. I received the notification yesterday. They were insured for £82 (328 dollars). This is not enough but will go some way towards replacing my wardrobe – if I can get the coupons. I will get some for there is special provision for people whose belongings have been lost by enemy acts. How clever it was of you and Mummy to forget all about the things in the blue suitcase which contained the more important notes! I very much hope that neither Mummy nor you will worry about it. My first thought was: It is as well that I was not with those two trunks!

I cannot tell you how pleased I am that you are trying to win various kinds of prizes. It is not so much the money that matters – although this has its obvious uses. It is the <u>habit</u> of winning prizes; it is the frame of mind of a scholar; it is the desire of not being satisfied with anything but the top place – this is why I was so glad to learn about it.

At about that time, a large house in Grange Road that had been built by Oppenheim when he was Whewell Professor and was called Whewell House came on the market. 'Are you interested?', he asked Rachel. She was not, and they remained at 6 Cranmer Road.[13] Generally, he was feeling very well. He had the energy to go to his tailor in London to get a new suit. The house was 'in perfect order'. He had friends to tea. He could afford to buy another antique ivory chess set.[14]

HL to RL, 17 May 1942
Nothing special has happened since I wrote after my visit to London. I am marking quite well and lecturing five or six times a week. The Digest is troublesome and causes a lot of work; the trouble is that I do not know whether it will be possible to publish it owing to the shortage of paper. My longish article on War Crimes is progressing slowly but well . . . [15]

The enclosed petal of lilac is to remind you of the dear husband.

He was reminded of his origins by an enquiry from Professor Winiarski, a Polish professor who later became a judge and President of the ICJ, who was working with the Polish Government in exile in London, as to whether Hersch had certain Polish international legal texts that he could lend Winiarski. Hersch was able to provide four titles, saying that there was no hurry about returning them. Winiarski had written in Polish. Hersch replied in English, saying:

I hope you will forgive my writing to you in English. I have not been in Poland for over twenty-four years, and I find it rather difficult to write or speak Polish.[16]

HL to RL, 25 May 1942
I am well. The lectures are now over, and I shall have time to do some serious work. I do not intend to go anywhere for the vacation. It is so uncomfortable. The Robbinses went away for a week to Cornwall, and they write that they are hungry. And as the weather is rotten, they will be glad to be home. I had Jenks to dinner in Trinity last night. He is returning to Canada soon. Laski is dining with me on Friday in College. I wonder how he will get on with people.

---

[13] HL to RL, 13 May 1942.   [14] *Ibid.*
[15] Eventually published as 'The Law of Nations and the Punishment of War Crimes' (1944) 21 *BYIL* 58. Reprinted in *Collected Papers*, Vol. 5, p. 491.
[16] HL to Winiarski, 20 May 1942.

Bentwich is my guest on 7 June and EH Carr on the 17th. So I am making use of Trinity.

HL to RL, 30 May 1942

Everything is well here – except that there will be changes in No. 6 before long. The Robbinses are leaving Cambridge. It is possible that before you receive this letter you will have even more up to date news. I am genuinely sorry to lose them. I have been looked after very well by them, and they were splendid company. I must begin to think of new lodgers. It will be difficult to find anyone even remotely as attractive – as you will probably see – and as convenient. I may be able to keep their cook. She is slow and about 55 and rather deaf, but the best cook and the most decent we have ever had. As to the future lodgers I do not know. There is the danger of billets.

The examinations have started, but they will not keep me busy for more than a fortnight. I had an exciting evening in Trinity the other night. I asked Laski to dine with me in Trinity. How they hate him there! There was a gloom over the table. The Vice Master did <u>not</u> invite us to his room. And Harold, for once, was shy! McNair told me that <u>I</u> was perfectly right in asking him.

On 3 June, he wrote:

Our letters necessarily cross one another and cause the confusion in the exchange of ideas about your return. To summarise my view once more: (1) Eli is definitely staying on; (2) You ought to stay on and make arrangements accordingly. I do not want you to undertake the risks of the journey. At the same time, in case there should be a rather radical improvement in the situation, you ought to make arrangements for returning early in September. This is all clear. In the meantime, unless you feel very lonely, try to avoid a rush of engagements.

I am well – although mentally feeling the strain of work. You will not believe it but the Digest actually goes to the printer after a month – only three months after my arrival. I am writing a long memorandum on War Crimes.[17] There are the examinations. And before long I will start on the book for the Jewish Committee on the International Bill of the Rights of the Individual (or something like that) with special application to the Jewish question. I received today a cable from them agreeing to my terms. This ought to have a good effect on the financial situation.

As the above letters illustrate, Hersch was concerned with the departure of Colonel and Mrs Robbins, to whom he had become much attached. He gave Rachel detailed instructions as to what to feed the Colonel when he visited her in New York:

---

[17] See n. 15 above.

I hope you will give him a meal. His teeth are not too good. Some tender brisket beef (in the Jewish fashion) as you cooked for me will be appreciated. Some soft creamy cheese (the Jewish one in the blue cartons) he will like. Nothing elaborate. If you want to give him some salmon caviar (please do not send me any) he may like it. But do not prepare anything which requires a lot of cooking. He must come to the apartment. I told him how to come. No more about the Lodger. The war news is good and 90% of people here think it will end soon.[18]

A week later, he was still troubled by the prospective departure of the Robbinses:

I may be slightly embarrassed by the difficulty of finding suitable lodgers. It is not quite easy these days because there is absolutely no domestic help available. The Gasters would have liked to come, but she is not too strong and she cannot take a house without domestic help. Mrs Robbins has postponed her departure until July 15 and, because of the dangers of billeting, I must find someone until then. It is a misfortune that they are going. They were so friendly and I was looked after very well and very regularly. This business is especially annoying as I have to start on that book for the American Committee – which means financially a great deal – and I ought not to waste time. You will be delighted to meet the lodger. He is a simple and fine man, most decent – and very good looking! Don't get frightened by his martial appearance. He is the jolliest fellow imaginable. I miss him much.

The examinations are over, and I am grappling with the memorandum on war criminals. I am slowly starting on the preparations for the book for the American Committee. They are paying well, but half of it will go in income tax.

The jar of tobacco – 1lb – arrived today. I paid 25 shillings duty, but it is worth it. It is a splendid gift and most useful. Please thank Sam very much.[19]

On 11 June, he again gave voice to his preoccupation with the necessity for me to work hard and get good results:

Mummy was very proud of the way you are shaping. I could have had no better news. It is good to be quite certain, as I am, that you know what you owe to yourself and your name.[20]

Norman Bentwich called on him in Cambridge in early June and persuaded him to join in establishing in Cambridge a branch of the Friends

---

[18] HL to RL, 3 June 1942. The war in Europe lasted another three years.
[19] HL to RL, 11 June 1942. 'Sam' was Sam Kahn, an old and devoted family friend, a lawyer in New York.
[20] HL to EL, 7 June 1942.

of the Hebrew University of Jerusalem – a task which Hersch undertook out of a sense of duty and with little enthusiasm. He had had no experience of raising money for good causes and did not find the task congenial.

In mid-June, McNair paid a short visit to Cambridge:

I have just returned from a long walk with McNair. We did eleven miles in three hours. We went to Comberton, about 5 miles from here, to inspect a farm house with 50 acres which he thinks of buying. He is still as vigorous as ever, piling one job on top of the other. He has become Chairman of a Government committee on Education, and last week he became member of the National Commission for Miners' Wages. At the same time he is Chairman of the Committee on War Crimes, and so on. I gave him luncheon at home, and Mrs Robbins was on her most respectful behaviour.[21]

On 18 June, he wrote:

There is nothing new here. I have not been feeling too well – with my old complaint,[22] little sleep, lots of work and the additional worry about the house. I could let it furnished if I were not here. But otherwise it is difficult in view of the position in the domestic service market. I can not, while remaining here and having to rely on being looked after, take any people without domestic help. And such are not available. For this reason, the Gasters had to drop out. Mrs Robbins, who understands the difficulty, has postponed her leaving until July 15 and there is a prospect that she may delay it beyond that. Otherwise, I shall be a bit in a mess. Her cook does not want to stay on . . . Jenks has now left for Canada. I had EH Carr for dinner in College last night. I think they have already forgiven me bringing in Laski.

HL to RL, 26 June 1942

I can imagine what a worrying time you must have had when she [Mrs Turner] was leaving and how torn you were between various feelings and considerations. I am glad your passport was not ready. In any case I did not want you to consider coming before September. Perhaps you ought to have the papers ready for then. In the meantime you must try to weigh the various conflicting factors and feelings. The separation from the boy will be a hard blow, and so will be the continuous absence from him – one does not know for how long. There is also the danger of the journey. (I do not want him to come in any case. He is already late for Shrewsbury or any other scholarship. When he comes home next year, he will have to come as an ordinary boy, but with his sense of responsibility and his intellect, it will not matter.) On the other point, you must consider the inconvenience of your position in America and the effect upon your health. Of

---

[21] HL to RL, 14 June 1942. [22] 'Old complaint' was with his waterworks.

course, I want you back for obvious reasons. But I do not want that desire of mine to influence your decision. It must be entirely your decision ...

Of the parcels, the usual one from Macy's, and the macaroni, and the ham plus tunney [*sic*] fish have arrived. But I do not want you to send any more. I do not need them. I think with warm gratitude of the trouble you take to send them and to that extent it is pleasant to open the parcel but, again, I do not want you, absolutely, to send any ...

I am, on the whole, all right. The house is in perfect order and from the point of view of food and service I am looked after well and regularly. But what an anxious life it is! Fortunately there are no money worries.

On 29 June, he wrote:

I feel much better than a week ago. What apparently happened was that I caught an internal chill and that made my ordinary troubles rather acute. I felt most miserable – with, in addition, all the work and the house troubles hanging over me. As to the latter, the situation has improved as Mrs Robbins's projected job in London has not yet materialized. This means that she will stay on for another six weeks or two months or perhaps more. But it is an uncertainty. It is rather difficult to find satisfactory people now. (By the way, we just had a letter from Robbins giving an account of the short visit to Riverdale. He was enchanted with Mrs Lauterpacht and Master Eli.) ...

I am having a visitor next Friday and Saturday: Professor James Mackintosh of the Glasgow University. He was with me on the Clipper and we have become great friends. I was rather anxious about the way the Vice-Master will receive him after the Laski episode, but the Vice-Master is as sweet as ever. They cannot [stand] Laski, but they will forgive me many things.[23]

On 1 July, Hersch wrote to Rachel:

I received today your letter of 29 May! It was rather heavy, and I suppose it must have gone by boat. However, I found it both welcome and illuminating. In this letter you gave me a detailed account of the interview at the consulate of yourself and Mrs Turner (she is not yet here!). I was much impressed by what he said about the undesirability of leaving the boy by himself and also of what you told me of the great mental stress which a separation from him will cause you. In view of this; of the shipping situation; and of the general situation I think that there ought to be little doubt as to the decision. If you decide to stay on, you will have my full approval, and I will think that it is a wise decision. The situation here has improved in so far as Mrs Robbins has decided not to leave yet for some months. This will relieve me of a great problem of finding lodgers – a difficult problem for various reasons. As it is, the house is very well looked

---

[23] HL to RL, 29 June 1942.

after by three women in addition to the woman who comes once a week to do my socks etc. The food is good and the house is beautifully clean.

There will still remain the problem as to how you will manage on the £13 per month plus the remnants of what you had. I dislike the idea of your moving every two months to new relatives. It will make you miserable. From what you tell me of your being compelled to give up the Hebrew job because you could not stand the strain, I see that there is little chance of your being able to earn much. I know that you do not spend an unnecessary amount – except for my parcels, which <u>must</u> stop, and stockings for Stella (which was a pleasure which you could not afford) – but I hate the idea of your having to live in a stuffy room in town. You <u>need</u> fresh air and lots of it. I will make an effort and try to release, through the Foreign Exchange control, about five hundred dollars, on compassionate grounds, from my future earnings from the American Committee – I am starting on the work today! – but I understand that this is hopeless.

So, although I think that it is wise to assume that you will stay on, you might have the papers ready for September and some appearance of a place on a boat. I feel with you so much in all that anxiety and indecision. And I am glad that you are going out to families and are seeing people, and that you had a pleasant time in Detroit. (I received your two picture cards from there; they came <u>before</u> the airmail letter; I can imagine you did not look ugly with the rose in your hair.)

I feel much better. In fact, I am well. I am sunbathing a bit, and that does one good. I sent off yesterday the memorandum on War Crimes. I am putting the finishing touches on the Digest and I am starting today on the International Bill of the Rights of the Individual. If I am lucky, I shall have it ready in December.

I bought today a thin summer coat for fourteen and six pence (and six coupons!). This shows that I am perfectly all right so far as wardrobe goes. You <u>must</u> not send any thing in addition to what you sent with Mrs Turner.

On 6 July, he gave some indication of how much time he spent working:

I am still busy on the Digest (which goes to the printer in about a week), but I am starting slowly on the book. I put in about 8 hours a day, but otherwise I do not feel too energetic. The heat does not affect me too well – although it is nothing comparable with New York.

On 9 July, Hersch wrote to Rachel:

Things are quiet at home. There is no sign of Mrs Robbins moving yet, and I think I have a respite until September which is a good thing with that book hanging over me. It will be a terrific sweat, but I dare not drop it with the financial situation being what it is. The fact is that one gets these days only one half of one's salary.

On 10 July, he wrote to me:

I hope it is nice and sunny this afternoon in Andover – in contrast with the weather in Cambridge which is dull like ditchwater. I have had to take to artificial sunbathing (I bought a sunlight lamp last winter, but I have not used it much.)

I got hold of the Entrance Examination papers for 1940/1 and shall be sending them in a day or two. They cover also other Colleges, and it is as well that you should have a look at them. On looking through them I was impressed, once more, by the fact that what is expected is maturity of judgment, wide reading and good style (which does not necessarily mean a flowery style. It certainly means good punctuation, but, subject to occasional lapses, you are good at it.)

Have I told you that Chandler has given me notice – after the war? This is one of the reasons why I hope that it will end soon. Today, invasion day of Sicily, is a fateful day, and when this letter reaches you we shall be much wiser . . .

Yesterday there were meetings for the whole day of the War Crimes Committee. I got quite swollen headed for my memorandum was in the centre of the stage and the whole work of the Committee will be modelled after it. I also established useful contacts with the legal advisers of the various Foreign Offices and with Presidents of military tribunals . . .

Today in the morning I did some necessary shopping and then came to luncheon by the Polish lawyers of which I was the guest of honour. It was a delightful affair – specially delightful because they did not expect me to make a speech. They gave me Polish vodka and Polish sausage (without gherkin) and the food was altogether excellent. There were some members of the government, the legal adviser to the Polish Foreign Office (yesterday I lunched with Kaeckenbeeck, the Advisor for the Belgian FO, the consul general (who offered to be helpful about sending parcels to my parents), the President of the Bench for Tribunals, the President of the Military Tribunals etc.). I am rather glad of the whole thing. I think I shall have an opportunity to do much good in this way for the minorities of eastern Poland. I shall have some of them in Cambridge . . .

I am now back at home in the peace of Cambridge. I will send the Digest to the printer on Saturday . . .

On Monday I start reading – and a bit of thinking – on the Order on the Bill of Rights.

On 20 July, he wrote again to me:

Mummy may decide to return home late in September – it is a matter on which she must make a decision – and in that case there is an additional reason why you should be together for a fortnight. In any case, it is a wise thing. I know that I need not tell you that when you are with her you will not be slow in showing all your affection and respect – no Mother has deserved it better – by helping her in every respect and not letting her do a thing which you might do for her. In the school I think you have done well, but perhaps not so well as I expected. I am slightly apprehensive about the tone and the implications of Dr Fuess's letter. He is making the continuance of the scholarship dependent upon your maintaining a very high standard. This is a matter which cannot be the result of any spasmodic decisions and ups and down in energy and industry, but of a steady resolution, of a mature and steady frame of mind. You know what is at stake. For this reason, although I want you to have a good time in Camp, I rather welcomed the news that you will devote part of the vacation to filling the gaps in geometry and other subjects. No-one has a holiday in England these days, and I think that it is therefore proper that you should devote part of yours, however small, to making sure of a high degree of scholarship.

Things are quiet here – at least on the surface. The garden, as I see it now from my study window, is beautifully green after the rains. The second crop of roses is coming up, and the place is a mass of colour (and, occasionally, when I am slack, of weeds).[24]

To Rachel he wrote on the same day:

There is nothing new here. The day's routine is normal from day to day. I work in the morning in the Squire; in the afternoon at home. I go out for a walk either in the afternoon or before supper. I fire-watched Friday night (which means sleeping fully dressed on a camp bed). I play twice a week chess with Winton and dine in College two or three times a week – which is satisfactory both for me and for the lodger who likes to have her supper on a tray by herself whenever she has a chance. She is very considerate – especially after your letter. Nothing has been said about leaving recently. The Digest has gone to the printer – thank God. I have now started reading on the book. If I only could finish it by the end of the year!

Eventually, an acknowledgment was received from Sir Stephen Gaselee at the Foreign Office of Hersch's letter of 30 March.

---

[24] HL to EL, 20 July 1942. Dr Fuess was the Headmaster of Andover.

Sir Stephen Gaselee to HL, 23 July 1942
I find with great regret that your letter of the 30th March has gone unanswered and that we have never offered you any expression of thanks for the valuable memoranda which you sent us at that time.

These papers have all been read with keen interest by Malkin and our legal staff as well as by the various departments of the Office concerned with the subjects to which the papers relate.

Malkin is particularly interested in the memorandum mentioned in paragraph 3 of your letter, rebutting criticism of the Administration's action in the period between September 1940 and December 1941. He would be most grateful if should you have a spare copy of this paper, you would kindly let him have it for his own records.

You will be interested to know that some steps to promote the kind of contacts suggested in paragraph 9 of your letter are being taken.

Your visit to the United States has I am sure been very fruitful and I am most grateful for your report.

On 25 July, Hersch wrote to Rachel:

I have now started reading, general reading, for the book. This will take me two or three months. For the time being the thing is a blank. But it will become clearer. The house is, on the whole, quiet. David Robbins is joining up tomorrow and that is creating a slight commotion, but otherwise everything is regular like a clock. It is not difficult when three women do the work. I shiver at the idea that one day the lodger will tell me that she has decided to leave. However, she must give me at least a month's notice. And of this there is no sign yet. I am going to London on the 5 and 6 August to attend Committee meetings, to see your dear brother and his dearest wife, and to buy a thing or two. I also have to dine with Brodetsky and Stein. I can see that in the coming days and months I may be able to be useful – just as you would like me to be. The Poles will be the principal factor in the post-war settlement of the minorities in question, and I am therefore glad that I have established with them very promising contact. I am entertaining some of them and some other allied statesmen, one after another, in Trinity. It is expensive, but not too expensive and very worth while. Next week I am having Dr [*illegible*], the President of the Polish Military Tribunals and a distinguished member of the Polish National Council.

A rare alarm in Cambridge was reflected in Hersch's letter to Rachel of 30 July:

HL to RL, 30 July 1942
We had a disturbed night and I feel slightly groggy – so you will understand if this letter is not too intelligent . . .

During the disturbed night I felt grateful that you and the boy were not here (Marion had to take the children to the hall downstairs). She must have had an unpleasant time as Winton was out that night fire-watching in the University. Friday is my night, but I have been lucky so far. All this means that I am rather relieved that you – or we – have not taken yet any decision. On the whole, as previously suggested, we must budget for two alternative contingencies.

I am quite well – in fact as well as can be expected in these days. People are getting tired, mentally. Winton has had to fortify himself with a tonic of strychnine for the last four weeks. I have not been reduced to that, and I have not touched the medicinal since I arrived here . . .

I am due to lunch today at the Vice-Chancellor's to meet Mr McLeish, the Librarian of the US Congress, who is going to deliver a lecture in the afternoon. I am afraid I shall have to go to the lecture – although I am slightly sleepy. But I am taking things easy this morning.

HL to RL, 2 August 1942
Things are quiet here and uneventful except that the nights have become more disturbed. Otherwise most of my time is devoted to reading (and practically no writing). It will take 2–3 months to get into the subject which is very much connected with political science. I find that the library in my study is much better equipped for the purposes than I expected. And the University library is within five minutes! Compare it with New York! Last Thursday was a busy day for Mr McLeish, the Librarian of US Congress and Assistant Minister of Information came here to deliver the Rede Lecture. The Vice-Chancellor gave him an official luncheon. There were four people invited: The former Vice-Chancellor, the next Vice-Chancellor, the Librarian of the University and your husband. It was a good and pleasant luncheon, but the lecture in the afternoon was a poor show. There was an enormous audience, but he had not prepared his lecture properly. This is a great pity, for it is important that any inferiority of an American performance should not stimulate what they call British superiority . . .

We have to get up – or be awake – practically every night. (I am fire-watching in the Old Schools the whole night tonight.)

HL to RL, 7 August 1942
Yesterday there arrived three lovely studio photos of you and I was tremendously glad to receive them. I liked the black, serious one most and the brighter one, with the summer blouse next. They seem to be fairly recent, and you seem to look well. I may be extravagant and frame the 'black serious' one. It is an exquisite photo. The household – from the principal lodger to the cook – went mad over it.

Today I received parcel No 11 (the dried stuff). Very many thanks, but on no account do I want you to do it again. In any case the parcels will be stopped –

except perhaps the one pound ones like tobacco. I am not opening anything, but for my birthday dinner I will open one thing because I will like it and I know you will like me to do it. Mrs Robbins – she supplies all the food now – will be delighted to agree.

I spent two days in London . . .

In the evening I dined with Brodetsky and the Secretary of the Joint Foreign Committee, and spent five hours with them. I am so glad I can be useful for a cause which is dear to me and of which you will approve. I spent the morning with General de Baer, President of the Belgian Military Court, in connection with the War Crimes Committee. The afternoon, on the same matter, I spent with the President of the Dutch Maritime Court. Next day I spent an hour viewing the house which belongs to the Robbinses in South Kensington. What a mansion! There are at least eighteen rooms. I can now understand why before the war they spent six thousand a year.

I am back at my study now – busy with the same business: War Crimes, Digest (the proofs have started arriving) and the book. I know that I ought to be envied in comparison with the uncertainty and the precariousness of your own position.

HL to RL, 12 August 1942
Your letters are again very irregular. It is more than a week since I received one. (In the meantime, you will be interested to hear, Parcel No 1 has arrived. No 11 arrived last week. In No 1 there was the salmon caviar and I opened it immediately and had a grand time. For my birthday I am going to open a tunny fish tin. Thank you very, very much.)

There is nothing new to report since my last letter. I am doing quiet reading and trying to do some writing, but it is a slow business. I feel somehow so tired. However, August is not, as a rule, a very pleasant period in Cambridge. There is not the slightest hope of a holiday. There is simply nowhere to go . . .

There is, of course, no honey here. There are no servants. The cook will go with Mrs Robbins. It is a hard existence, but forty million people live like that . . .

Winfield was here the other day playing chess with me and admiring my ivory sets.

Although Hersch did not know it at the time, it was round about now that his sister and brother-in-law were taken by the German occupation forces in Lwów and were never seen again.

While it is not easy to find the appropriate place in which to fit the second part of Inka's narrative, of which the first part is quoted in

Chapter I above,[25] the tragedy of the fate of the family in Lwów may best be set out here:

The year 1939

1st September the first bombs fell on Lwów and on Gdynia, where Grand-father Aron was at that time. I remember my mother rushing to be with Grand-mother, alone. We lived not very far away, just the Parc to cross, 20 minutes' walk, perhaps.

Grand-Father returned safely. There was more bombing and 10 days later the first Russian Soldiers entered Lwów. (The pact between Stalin and Hitler).

What should I say about that period? On the whole, the Jews as such, were not particularly bothered. Except if one was wealthier than the average, or well known professionally or otherwise. Lived in too nice a place etc.

My father had the privilege to correspond to that profile. My father was not a lawyer any more, became a sort of secretary. The flat, excepting two rooms at the back was taken by an NKVD general. The man was very fond of my mother and helped us a lot. My parents had to take care of the man, the flat, his visitors. Finished the life they were used to, finished my exclusive school, and the piano lessons. (This I did appreciate.) Grand-Father Aron managed quite well, Dunek and Ninsia seemed OK. Jewellery was worth lots of money – Maman had plenty – and we always managed to have enough of everything.

The year 1941

The war with Germany from June 21st, a few days later, the Germans were in Lwów.

Many fled to Russia following the Russian troops. My parents would not. They did not want to leave their family and they hated the communists. 'After all, cultivated as they were, the Germans could not be much worse than the Russians.'

A day or two later the German soldiers, officers, the Ukrainians started going from apartment to apartment: 'Are Jews living here?' If yes, they come in (armed military) and took whatever they liked . . .

Again our flat became 'free' and the Germans settled in, except for one room left for us.

My mother was supposed to do everything for them, but she was so unused to the hard house-work that after work my father used to wash piles of dishes and took care of the fire. Everybody had to work. My father got a 'certificate of work' for my mother. Himself, worked (for nothing) as 'a secretary', really as a

---

lawyer for the people who took our flat. Correct enough, my Parents became quite friendly with them.

Grand-Parents had Ukrainians in their apartment – they managed at that time.

There were days when anybody could be arrested on the street, or at home.

The year 1942
On January 31st my Grandfather Gelbard was arrested. He was a high civil servant and was used to saying what he thought. When the Jewish police came to arrest him, he chased them away, so he did with the Ukrainians. The Gestapo threw him into a lorry downstairs, probably still alive. His wife (it was not my grand-mother Seraphine, dead very young) was arrested. For three weeks I used to bring parcels to prison (less dangerous for me), then I was told, 'no use any more'.

More and more people got arrested. Grand-parents Aron and Deborah, left their apartment, too dangerous because of the presence of the Ukrainians.

Grand-Pa went to Dunek and Nunsia. Grand-Ma to us.

In August 15th or 16th, hidden in the bath-room, in a wardrobe, he was found and taken away.

I will never forget Grand-Mother fainting and dropping on the floor when she learned it.

Two days later, August 18th, the police came to us. That day they were supposed to arrest 'only' the old useless people and the children. Grand-Mother was hidden in a closet and me in the German part of the apartment.

That day was the very end for us. From the second floor window I saw my Mother rushed by the Ukrainians and Soldiers. My Father must have been told what was happening, I saw him running after her.

(I can still visualize the scene: the dress and the high heels my mother was wearing, my Father's dark grey suit. I never saw her again . . .)

I never believed, but that day I try to pray to any and every God that could exist. Never again.

I let Grand-Mother out of the closet. Did we talk, did we cry. I do not remember.

The day after, Dunek (already alone) came to take us to the Jewish Section. It was not yet the Ghetto. Grand-Mother went, I did not. Could not imagine myself in the proximity of that place. I felt guilty about it immediately.

I decided to poison myself with my little dog. The mixture of all I could put hands on, gave only a very unpleasant passing effect. I tried to offer my dog, providing quite a big dowry; he came back.

I left my home for ever.

My parents must have been separated at once. Several months later, my Father managed to escape, paying his way, from the Janowski Camp in Lwów.

We were again together for a few months. My father paying a great deal of money. Going out at night he was arrested and me kicked away the next morning.

Months later, (I was a maid) washing up, I could smell the Ghetto burning, a horrible smell.

Why did you cry said 'the lady'. 'The Jews are grilling, so what?' My tooth is aching, Madam, said I. I lost my job.

You know more or less the rest, then the convent. I should be very grateful, but have had souvenirs. The Melmans were more than loving to me.

Then came in your Parents, Eli. I aspired to leave the displaced person's camp, as soon as possible. Just to learn to become again a normal human being. I wanted much more than that...

Your Parents were ever so patient with me. We soon learned to love and respect each other, I do believe so. All the rest you know.

HL to RL, 16 August 1942

I have had no letter from you for almost a fortnight, but today your birthday telegram[26] – for which very many thanks – has arrived and I hope therefore that all is well. I am delighted to have your cable; and I did not think for a moment of the expense. Here I was touched by the warmth with which my birthday was received by Mrs Robbins. She and the Colonel have given me an ivory chess set – a lovely Chinese set – for my collection and some other presents. There was a birthday cake with candles and other pleasant things including paté-de-fois-gras for luncheon (for supper there is going to be a Rachel menu – consisting almost entirely of things which you sent me from the USA). Stella sent me two handkerchiefs.

I would enjoy it all, but for the fact that I am not too well. The old trouble has come back with a fresh ferocity, and I get very little sleep. Neither, as some of the neighbours have remarked, do I look too well. As the result, I get only little work done. I shall probably put myself into the hands of the doctors next week. It is a blessing that there are friendly people at home. I am writing all this not because I want you to regard it as a decisive factor in your decision as to coming home. But it would be silly of me not to tell you this – even if, as I hope, it is only a temporary setback...

---

[26] It was Hersch's forty-fifth birthday.

The Digest proofs are arriving in prolific numbers. I have re-engaged Mrs Lyons for two months to relieve me of the donkey work of the Index etc. She has a quite agreeable boy of 18 months.

HL to EL, 16 August 1942

This is my birthday and – as you have only one Dad and I have only one boy (and also for other reasons) I feel very much like writing this short note to you. Its main purpose is to wish you a very happy and very successful year in the School. How things change! It seems ages since I gave you a whacking and I cannot imagine myself doing it again. (I suppose I would have to take a ladder for the upper regions!) Neither can I imagine myself lecturing you upon your duties. For, and this fills me with great satisfaction, you have a pronounced sense of duty to yourself and your parents. And you have also the feeling that you must not let certain people down – e.g. Professor Nevins and Dr Fuess. All this is to the good. But I do want you to ask me from time to time – not for lectures, but for such advice as I can give.

I do not know how long Mummy will be with you. So long as you are with her or near her give her all the affection and care you can afford – and that is a lot.

There is another ivory set – good boy – a gift from the Robbinses. We shall have the best collection . . . in England.

HL to RL, 19 August 1942

What a waste of postage! I am writing the third day in succession . . .

There is at least some sunshine here, and I feel correspondingly better. Our road is being properly organized for fire-watching and this takes some time.

By 17 August, Hersch had completed the memorandum on 'Crimes against International Public Order and the Punishment of War Crimes'. He sent a copy to George Finch, the Secretary of the American Society of International Law, perhaps with a view to publication in the *AJIL*. But it was not published there.

His work on war crimes was being done within the framework of the International Commission for Penal Reconstruction and Development, within which there was a committee 'concerned with crimes against international public order', and within that committee there was a sub-committee on the 'Defence of Superior Orders'. Within that sub-committee, a request was circulated on 18 August 1942 requesting information from its various members on the law of their countries on the following matters:

(1) To what extent does the criminal law of your country recognise the plea of superior orders as a justification for illegal acts?

(2) To what extent, if any, does your military law differ in this respect from the general criminal law of your country?

(3) What qualifications, if any, with reference to the lawfulness of superior orders, does the law of your country recognise with regard to the duty of the soldier to obey the orders of superior officers?

(4) Is there any information available with regard to the practice, during the first World War, of the military courts of your country with respect to the plea of superior orders put forward by members of enemy armed forces accused of a war crime?[27]

Hersch was asked to produce the answers for England.

During the university's summer break, G. Kitson Clark, one of the Tutors of Trinity, asked Hersch whether he would feel up to taking small classes in international law for young officers in training in Cambridge.[28] There is no record of Hersch's answer, but it seems likely that he agreed to do so.

At long last, Rachel took the plunge and in late August 1942 sent Hersch a cable announcing that she was returning in October.[29] Hersch was obviously pleased by her decision:

I received your cable yesterday and answered immediately – not without some feeling of guilt. Apparently you received my letter of the middle of August, a time when I felt rather down and out, and, with your famous determination, made up your mind. But I have been much better since. The 'water works' trouble has largely subsided. (I have now given up alcohol altogether.) In any case, I have just been for a thorough check up at Richards and he told me that there is nothing wrong. He gave me thyroid (yes, thyroid!) and prescribed a slimming cure! But I may have another opinion. In any case, as I cabled to you there is nothing which gives reason for apprehension or for making up your mind in a way other than you intended . . .

I am now at the Index stage of the Digest and shall finish with the thing after a fortnight! I shall then have time to do more serious work on the book.[30]

In September, Hersch showed distinct signs of perking up – no doubt at the prospect of Rachel's return.

HL to RL, 4 September 1942
It is Friday before dinner (at Trinity). From there I have to go to spend a night fire-watching. And I am now going to fill the interval pleasantly by writing a letter to you.

---

[27] J. M. de Moor to HL, 19 August 1942.   [28] G. Kitson Clark to HL, 22 August 1942.
[29] RL to HL, 28 August 1942.   [30] HL to RL, 31 August 1942.

First of all, I feel well. As I told you I had a 'check up' by Richards who did not find anything wrong. Probably I did not have enough exercise – among other things – and I am now spending 45 minutes before breakfast on a walk and run on the rifle range and on the Coton footpath. This being so, I hope you will dismiss from your mind any anxiety on this account.

My work on the Digest is nearly over, and I am now doing quiet reading – but not yet writing – on the International Bill of Rights. I let myself in for a difficult thing, but I do not regret it for a moment. The 'dough' will be useful in due course.

I am also spending some time in trying not to eat too many of our lovely greengages. There is an abundance of them.

HL to EL, 5 September 1942

I feel I have not written to you recently as much as I would have liked to. One of the reasons was that the volume of the Digest for the years 1938–1940 was being printed at an unusually great speed and I had to do a great deal of proof reading and other donkey work like supervising the preparation of the Index and of the Table of Cases. Things are easier now. It is a Saturday afternoon and I am taking matters leisurely. Chandler is in the garden making a new rose pergola near the kitchen. He is also doing some more shelves for my study for the book bays and the black shelf where the dogs stood . . . The lawn is slightly patchy with lawn seed, but the tomatoes are beginning to ripen and the second crop of roses is turning up. The greengages on the far end tree are a delight. I am having a visitor to tea.

HL to EL, 21 September 1942

In case Mummy has left or is leaving – I hope that while feeling a pang at the parting you will not otherwise feel too lonely or miserable. Many boys have been sent away in peace or wartime for a year or so from their parents' house, and rather liked it. It gives them a feeling of independence and an increased sense of responsibility. You are not lonely or friendless in the USA. There are people, both our friends and relations, to whom you are very dear and who would do a lot for you. They are not a substitute for a Mother – especially one like yours – but they will give you a very clear reassurance that you are not by yourself and unbefriended. We thought that we ought to let you get the very best from that lucky chance of Phillips Academy – one of the best schools in the USA – being willing to have you. You will make us very happy – and you will serve your own future in a worthy manner – if we get excellent reports about your progress and if I get the conviction that my son is a scholar. I want you to have some fun, but I know that you will realize that your own situation, your own future, and the unhappy state of the world impose definite limits upon what a boy of your age could otherwise legitimately have.

I want you to write to me very often. Make it a habit to jot down every day half a page of what you are doing, of what is worrying you, and of what has made you happy. All this will greatly interest both of us. I have known a boy who has written to his parents only when he wanted something – and he was a miserable specimen.

It is just after the fast of the Day of Atonement. I made a point of spending practically the whole day in the students' Synagogue in Thompson's Lane. Last night I went to the Synagogue of the German refugees as a sign of my feeling of solidarity with their sufferings.

The printers are in the finishing stages of the Digest. I am doing good work on my reading for the book on the International Bill of Rights of the Individual. The lectures start in about a fortnight.[31]

HL to RL, 27 September 1942

Autumn has arrived and Cambridge is looking at its best. But I am rather restless and cannot do much work. It is an upsetting business altogether. I went out for a short walk with McNair today, but one of his legs got slightly lame and he was not too much good of it. (He expects you to telephone when you arrive in case there is any difficulty. Cross-country journey is such a horror these days that it might be better to go to London – first class – and from there to Cambridge. I will meet you in London.)

Winton was laid up with bad tonsillitis, but he is up now slightly emaciated. I wasted three hours yesterday sitting for a sketch portrait by a good refugee artist. The result is excellent and will be exhibited.

In late September, Hersch asked the Polish Consulate in London if it could arrange to send food parcels to his brother, Dunek. Apparently, there existed some system of communication with occupied Poland, for the Consulate replied that parcels would be sent and that, as soon as the Ministry of Labour received confirmation that the parcels had arrived, Hersch would be informed of the cost – a maximum amount of 16 shillings per month was mentioned.[32]

In anticipation of her return to England, at the end of September 1942, Rachel gave up the apartment in Riverdale and moved in with Hersch's uncle and aunt in Brooklyn. From then on, Hersch addressed all letters to me as he could not know whether Rachel had left the United States. Knowing that Rachel's return was imminent, their tone was much more cheerful. However, they were both in for a long delay and considerable

---

[31] HL to EL, 21 September 1942.
[32] Consulate General of Poland, London, to HL, 29 September 1942.

disappointment. After this, there are fewer of Hersch's letters (possibly because Rachel may have mislaid them) and they are principally concerned with the arrangements for Rachel's crossing. Even as early as 15 October, he was saying:

This correspondence is very disjointed and haphazard not only because I do not know whether these letters will reach you, but also because recently the airmail letters have taken more than three weeks. It takes nearly two months to receive a reply.[33]

He proposed sending a cable once a month, with a prepaid reply, to keep ahead of developments.

The upbeat tone continued through October:

I am well and enjoying my morning walk before breakfast. I have given up coffee and, as a result, I sleep much better.

The garden is improving rapidly. I had a great number of hardy perennials put in as a gift from the Robbinses garden in London.[34]

On 23 October, he wrote to Rachel:

I hope this letter will not find [you] in the USA but if it does I hope you will know how very much I feel with you in this anxious and upsetting period of waiting. The important thing is not to be unduly disturbed. Don't let the waiting interfere with your normal life or health. It is possible that you may not go for another two months. On the other hand, it is possible that you may get only two days notice. I am glad you are buying a coat. As to the preparations in connection with collecting your valuables etc. I would not hesitate to avail myself of the Bradley's help. If the worst comes to the worst, Nevins will help. He offered to do so (by the way, Professor Commager is here. He is sleeping in Emmanuel College. I called on him today and he is dining with me in Trinity next week.)

I am very well – much better than for many months. The reason is that I have given up Richards (unofficially) and I have put myself in the hands of Silberstein . . . [He] is a very good man. For the last fortnight I have slept excellently. As soon as you come, I will have you properly examined by him.

I laughed loudly at yours – and Eli's – suggestion that instead of buying chess sets I ought to get interested in Whewell House. The chess men cost me £35 or slightly more. They are worth £200. I simply get them practically for nothing from a Trinity man – a retired judge from India.[35] They look beautiful. But Whewell House is beyond dreams – with half the salary going to Income Tax

---

[33] HL to RL, 15 October 1942.   [34] HL to EL, 15 October 1942.   [35] W. S. Adie.

and most of the rest for the rates, payment for the house, the bank loan etc. It is merciful that I can live at home for nothing.

He returned to the Home Guard.

HL to EL, 23 October 1942
I am now a Home Guard with full battle dress, steel helmet and all. If you could see me! I am afraid you would not be as complimentary as a good boy ought to be to his Daddy. It takes a lot of my time, but I am glad to do it.

HL to RL, 1 November 1942
My Home Guarding is not too strenuous. But I am snowed under with other work. Yesterday I entertained Brodetsky, who is President of the Board of Deputies, and that will result in work. My War Crimes Committee means work. I have to read a paper this week before the London University Law Society and next week before the Grotius Society. The book is progressing slowly.

HL to RL, 4 November 1942
I am well, and my sleep has recently improved very much. The only trouble is that I am taking on all kinds of unnecessary jobs like papers, committees, etc. In addition, the Home Guard – people say that I look grand in battle dress – takes up a great deal of time. Still, half of the Term is nearly over.

The stove is already on in the study. I think we should have enough coal for the winter. I also bought half a ton of wood. So you will not freeze.

HL to EL, 11 November 1942
I am going to London [tomorrow] to lunch with the Yugoslav Prime Minister and probably with King Peter. In my next letter I may be able to tell you what it is all about; on the other hand I may have to be silent about it.

The winter frosts and fogs have arrived, but my study is warm and pleasant. There is a good crop of chrysanthemums in the garden, and I have just cut a lot of spinach for luncheon.

The Home Guard is taking up a great deal of time, but I am glad to do it. Mummy (to whom you may send this letter) too would love to see me in uniform.

HL to RL, 15 November 1942
Next Term I shall probably be responsible for the international education (once a week!) of King Peter. I lunched with their Prime Minister, their Minister for Justice and the Chief of the King's Court. The matter must still be confirmed by the full Council of Ministers, and the King, who is more interested in mechanical things than in humanities, may have to say a word, but I hope that for his good and that of the cause he will be amenable. I was pleasantly surprised to learn that the Ministers were anxious that he should receive a progressive education

with emphasis on the League and so on. I am seeing the King on the 2nd of December when I am due to read a paper before the Grotius Society. He will be coming in Term time to our house. They are poor and will pay very little but it does not matter.

HL to RL, 22 November 1942

Your letters are arriving in a frivolous way. Some take four weeks, others a fortnight. But on the whole it is good to see that you are bearing up amidst that period of waiting. Perhaps it is a blessing in disguise. A bit later on the weather may improve and the journey may become safer. You need not tell me – a sufferer of last February and March – what this waiting must be. I can also imagine that you suffer from lack of privacy more than of other things. But I hope that you are taking them philosophically. There are advantages and disadvantages in every situation. The important thing is not to show any one any impatience for after all it is all well meant. You might find it wise to invite yourself elsewhere for a fortnight or so.

Another parcel arrived yesterday – 3 tunas and corn on the cob! Very many thanks, sweet lady. But, please, on no account and absolutely ought you to send me any more of these parcels. I do not use the stuff. It simply goes in the cupboard to await your pleasure when you return. Also please do not send me any chocolate, or butter, or Walnut tobacco. (*A propos* the latter, the first thing that McNair said when he entered my study unexpectedly yesterday was 'Can you give me a bit of your delicious Walnut?') I regret now that I have not got a full tin to give him as a Xmas present. He is such a friend. By the way: when you arrive, his Tel. Number is Royal 5460 and in the evenings Allerton 2413. The Royal 5460 is the number for the Liverpool University. If he is not in Liverpool, please ask for his secretary and tell him where you are. He will give you money. The hotel in which we stayed last was Shaftesbury Hotel. There is in the morning an excellent train via Bletchley to Cambridge, the only good train across country. It will bring you to Cambridge at 2.30. But I will come to Bletchley. It is a horrid station, but it will be worth it.

HL to EL, 22 November 1942

I have received your various letters, and I was glad to have them. I hope the small setbacks are now a matter of the past and that you are forging full steam ahead. Perhaps Mummy's arrival was in the right psychological moment. I thought for a while that it might have been better if you had faced the adversities of school life by yourself, but you are the kind of boy who is likely to be made soft by excess of maternal (or parental!) help. And, also, you can brave the pangs of repeated partings. Algebra is a worry, but so long as I know that you are doing your best – and a bit extra – I am not prepared to blame you for that. I wish my royal pupil of next term were as conscientious. I have been told that I have to call him simply Peter. I have arranged to see him and his ministers on the 2nd of December. I have been told that according to the Yugoslav constitution he is an absolute monarch and can dismiss all his ministers at will. On the other hand, his mother is very firm with him.

I was glad that Mummy bought you the coat, but I was not at all happy about the dinner jacket. It was an unwarranted expense in your circumstances. I am not blaming you for not having prevented it, but the fact is that money will be getting extremely scarce for professional people like University professors and there is little hope of being able to repay debts from current income. Still – as you have it already, may you flourish in it.

I am writing on Sunday afternoon after three hours of Home Guarding in the battle dress and heavy boots. I cannot tell you which Section I am in, but, apart from the unavoidable rifle and foot drill, it is interesting work. But it takes such an awful lot of time. I have little time left for writing.

HL to RL, 26 November 1942

I am very well – especially when I compare my present Term with the most exacting time which I had in the two preceding winters. It is almost a holiday – but for the fact that we are not together. I am fully occupied now with various things, including the Home Guard, but it is not physically and mentally so exhausting as the double jobs of the previous years . . .

Since this letter has begun, news came through that the Lodgers will most probably stay on as they are not going to leave Cambridge. We shall know for certain within the next two or three days. It is in any case good to know that I shall not be left in the house by myself or with billeted soldiers without domestic service.

The Term is coming to an end next week during which I have to be in London on Wednesday to read my paper to the Grotius Society and to see Peter. During the vacation I hope to put some work into the book as time is getting short. And I have not started yet! But I must do it – one reason being that I want to keep my mind off the news about extermination in occupied territories.

HL to RL, 3 December 1942

I went to town yesterday to read the paper to the Grotius Society.[36] As you see the title is a solemn one: there was an atmosphere of solemnity and, you will like to hear it, of some embarrassing worship of your husband. Hurst was in the chair. In the morning I saw the Yugoslav Prime Minister about Peter. I will probably begin in the first week of January; the Vice-Master of Trinity[37] will probably be the other person to take him. I came home tired, but quite satisfied with the day. I got a good dinner and an enthusiastic reception. They [the Robbinses] are a loyal lot. I will know in a day or two whether they are

---

staying on. It changes from day to day. They will probably remain in any case until after Xmas.

Knowledge about the implementation of the German policy of exterminating the Jews had been accumulating throughout 1940, 1941 and 1942. There were many reports in *The Times*, which Hersch read every day. On 30 October 1942, there was a demonstration of protest at the Albert Hall against Nazi atrocities. The Archbishop of Canterbury said:

Upon these people – the Jews – the fury of the Nazi evil has concentrated its destructive energy. It is hard to resist the conclusion that there is a settled purpose to exterminate the Jewish people if it can be done.

On 7 December 1942, the Chief Rabbi ordained that,

in view of the catastrophic situation facing Jews in Europe, next Sunday (December 13) should be observed by Anglo-Jewry as a day of mourning and fast. Services will be held ... No entertainments are to be held, and no meetings, except in relation to this solemn occasion.

On that day, Hersch wrote to Rachel:

I am writing this letter in a slightly sentimental mood. It is 6pm on a Sunday and I have been fasting all day. It is the Day of Fast and Intercession for the murdered Jews in Poland, and I felt I would like to join in. My very dear ones are there, and I do not know whether they are alive. And the situation there is so terrible that it is quite conceivable that they may prefer death to life. I have been thinking the whole day about them.

In an undated fragment at around December 1942, Hersch wrote to Rachel:

[I]f they refuse to give you a passage or a definite date, you should send me a cable. I will then undertake some steps here. I will cable to the Consul and I will take up the matter through appropriate channels. It does not seem to me that they have treated you with sufficient consideration and impartiality. So darling, you must not worry or spoil your eyes by crying.

The Robbinses will be here over Christmas and, most probably, over January and February if not longer. You will be mighty glad if they stay on and if you come home to a clean and warm house, with friendly people, and with the principal domestic problems settled. Yesterday I received the parcel which he sent me when he was in Montreal. Also a big store of his own foodstuffs arrived – including two large Virginia hams! There will be some eating here at Christmas! Yesterday we had Camembert cheese.

The boy's pictures arrived yesterday. It is good to have them. One of them is being framed and will be hung up in the study, together with your own recent photo. I am also having framed my own life drawing (this reminds me: I look rather sad and worn out in that drawing. I hope you will not think that I am not well. The idea was to accentuate such spiritual features as may be found in a plump face).

HL to RL, 21 December 1942

I am busy with all kind of work including the Home Guard which is taking a great deal of time. I am rather worried about the slow progress of my work on the Rights of Man. It is more than International Law and I find that I have a great deal of reading to do. To expedite matters and to prompt myself to produce something tangible, I have announced three public lectures in the University in the last three weeks of February on 'The Law of Nations, the Law of Nature, and the Rights of Man'. I wonder whether the darling wife will be there to listen to the dull business.[38]

The University Press is reconsidering the question of the publications of the series in which my book on Recognition was due to appear. If they decide in the affirmative that will mean a terrific rush in the summer.

HL to RL, 28 December 1942

The Christmas festivities here are over. It was jolly in the house and I was not too lonely. The food was excellent: turkey, goose, and venison. I got a Dunhill pipe and tobacco bowl from the Robbinses. I played a lot of chess with Tommy. I now must start on some work – the Home Guard permitting . . .

I am well although not too bright. Silberstein keeps on saying slyly that Mrs Lauterpacht ought to come home, but I want you back for many other reasons. How I shall pray for a safe journey! You must not get terrified if you get into a small craft. They are the safest and the pleasantest.

I went to the Thomases for tea on Christmas day. They are slightly depressed by the economic difficulties. Their house looks terribly untidy and rather poor. They had no turkey, and not even a chicken. I gave them a large tin of ham which I got from Miss Patterson and a tin of sardines and tunny fish. Also, I brought gifts for the boys.

HL to RL, 4 January 1943

Today your letter of 29 November arrived, and it was good to see that, at that time, all was well – in particular that you are seeing various people, that you are entertained by them, attend meetings and do your work for Groat. It is excellent. I am sure that when you return you will think with great satisfaction

---

[38] Lecture eventually delivered on 2 December 1942 and published as 'The Law of Nations, the Law of Nature and the Rights of Man' (1944) 29 *Transactions of the Grotius Society* 1–33.

of these times and that you will not mind that life here is dull and monotonous in comparison. You are seeing more people in a week than Marion in a year. I am so delighted about it – especially about what you say in your enjoying conversation without difficulty. Your various parcels have been arriving in profusion. They have been most gratefully received and put away for your use when you come home. I am not touching them. Yesterday the lovely box of Suchard chocolates arrived – a most useful box. But if you are going to stay here for some time yet – I really do not want you to send any more. I would hate to think that you have to borrow money in order to send parcels for me. It would be different if I were going about hungry here. The opposite is the case: yesterday, for instance, the 3rd of January – a certain Lady's birthday – (bless her) – Tommy appeared in full uniform at luncheon. Nora was suitably dressed, there was an enormous goose (!) on the table, and an ancient bottle of wine – and they drank, very touchingly, to the Lady's health. There was a lovely sweet, three kinds of cheese, cognac, and other delicacies.

I would feel very lonely without them – especially that I am not always too well: the old trouble. I was examined in London by one specialist last week and I am going next week for a thorough X-ray examination and so on for two days into a private ward in a hospital. I must try and get fit. The idea that I could be left in the house with some unfriendly lodgers, without service, and ordinary amenities fills me with terror. I hope to be able to induce them to stay until February or March. It is inconvenient for Tommy because he has to come here from London where he works.

HL to RL, 7 January 1943
I am worried about your money position. I should have thought that with the very little I send you and with your earnings from Groat you should, as you do not have to pay rent, be able to keep ends meet. I was rather shocked to read that you bought a present for $25 for Teddy. You cannot afford it and they ought to understand it. A token present of $2 (two) dollars would have been enough in the circumstances. In England no one buys these days a present for £6; it means, in effect, a present for £12 seeing that for every ten shillings we spend we must pay ten shillings in income tax. Neither is there any justification for inviting the Bradley family – or any one else – to restaurants. You are not in the position to return hospitality. For the same reason I want you definitely to stop sending any parcels. (Although a monthly Walnut message is appreciated.) You cannot afford 3 dollars a week for parcels to me – not to mention the entirely unnecessary parcels for Nachman or Moshe. It would be wicked to borrow money for such purposes.

But enough of money. There are no changes in the house yet – thank God. I would not be temperamentally fit to deal with them. My silly trouble has been pulling me down, and I have arranged to go to a private ward in University

College Hospital and be thoroughly examined by Harley Street specialists. I must try, if possible, to get rid of the thing.

HL to EL, 7 January 1943

There is no news here. It is a January at its worst: wet and cold. But there is plenty of coal in the house. Also I cut down (or, rather, Chandler did) a very big branch of a tree and that supplied us with about $\frac{1}{4}$ ton of wood. The garden is tidy; so is the shed.

HL to EL, 8 January 1943

This is only a hasty note after a tiring day in London when I went down with Nachman. I must be getting very provincial for a day in London makes me quite exhausted, and I sigh with relief when I am back in our garden once more. And it is a lovely garden just now.

I went to London to see my doctor in connection with my recent illness. He found nothing very wrong, but recommended some exercises and also impressed upon me the importance of some good sleep which I have not had for years.

HL to EL, 8 January 1943

I cabled yesterday Mummy's passage money, and, all being well, she ought to be on the way home by the time this letter reaches you. She will be accompanied on the journey by the prayers of both of us and – I know – of many others. You will, of course, receive a cable as soon as she has safely arrived here. But it may be a long journey and you must not get impatient.

I can imagine that you will feel very lonely and rather at a loss within a week or so of her sailing. She has been such a selfless friend to you and such a companion in the ups and downs of life. I know how much you realized it. But I am sure that that feeling of loneliness will pass soon. To begin with it, there is hardly a boy from England in the USA who will be looked after by so many 'friends and relations'. In Louise Overacker – I am proud that during my short stay at Wellesley I succeeded in gaining her friendship – you have an affectionate and wise protector and counsellor. I know that you will do your best to justify her faith in you. (It is an inspiring thing in life that the possession of noble friends is a constant stimulus to live up to the nobility of their personality.) There are many other friends in New York, Wellesley, and elsewhere. The important thing is that you should regard yourself as fortunate in having them and not take anything for granted.

Write home very often by ordinary mail. It does not take longer than air mail, and if you write often it does not matter if one gets lost. It is possible that if we feel affluent in money (which is not likely) we may stand ourselves a cable to you plus a prepaid reply. This will not happen often.

The Term has started and the spring has almost arrived. The yellow aconites in the garden are out and some violets have appeared. All this is in keeping with the good news from the various war fronts. I am rather optimistic. The fact that the Germans are everywhere on the run seems to suggest that something is beginning to crack. One must not indulge in wishful thinking, but I can see that the end may be nearer than we have been expecting.

The Robbinses are still here, but will be leaving before long – I hope not before Mummy comes.

Write often boy and remember that in addition to all the friends enumerated above, you have a very good one – with much love – in your Dad.

Sir Cecil Hurst to HL, 26 January 1943
I am so sorry to hear you are laid up with the 'flu. Please take great care of yourself. Good men are precious in these days.

HL to EL, 28 January 1943
I just received your letter about Mrs Miniver. It is curious how the same film impresses differently various people. I thought that it did not really give an adequate picture of the hard and difficult daily life of an ordinary housewife in England. Mrs Miniver was too pretty for the purpose. (And I disliked her appearing in her nighty with her new hat before her husband! It was a cheap trick.) I thought that 'Mr V' which Mummy, you and I saw in New York was a much better film.

In any case I was glad to see that the principal lesson which you derived from it was that it is your business to continue with your studies in a most proficient way and to get honours in all of them. We can best serve the common purpose by doing our duty in our restricted sphere.

HL to EL, 5 February 1943
I am entering an anxious stage of waiting for news about Mummy, and I find that writing a line or two to you relieves the anxiety. I do not know whether she has started; most probably she has. But in these months secrecy is of the essence of the business and any enquiries are discouraged.

I have had my share of colds and had several days in bed. This was a disappointment for the reason, among others, that I had made arrangements to see King Peter, to whom I have agreed to give some talks on my subject. This had now to be postponed for a week or so. I will tell you something about it later on, but you must not talk about it to boys.

I am receiving numerous letters from Wellesley. There was also last week a parcel of various foodstuffs from Miss Overacker and a lovely coloured photo of the central building. I am being glutted with food parcels, but I make good use of them and give some articles to less fortunately situated people. Thus for Christmas I gave the Thomases a large tin of ham and various sardines etc. The only thing they do <u>not</u> send me, alas, is the lovely Walnut tobacco which I used to smoke over there.

February is now at its worst. I should think it is the most dismal month in England. But the snowdrops and the aconites have appeared and the crocuses are peeping out.

The Colonel was here yesterday for his fiftieth birthday, and there was a jolly party. (Speaking of parties, if all goes well and Mummy is back we are going to have on March 20 a big party to celebrate the 20th anniversary of our wedding. If you write immediately a message of congratulations, I am sure it will [give] Mummy – and myself – great pleasure. It will arrive just in time.)

HL to EL, 9 February 1943
Another four days of waiting. It is not a pleasant time, but I shall not be surprised if another ten days elapse before I hear Mummy's voice. I have made arrangements for McNair to meet her. There is a very good train from Liverpool which will bring her to Cambridge within six hours.

The house is being prepared for receiving the head of the house. Mummy is very lucky to be able to return to a well-run house with the best cook we have ever had here – a fat, jovial woman of about 55 of unusual decency and honesty – and with a family who have become the best friends we have in this country. The trouble is that their stay must shortly come to an end. Robbins is already working in London and Mrs Robbins is really staying out of kindness to Mummy and myself so that there should be no interregnum. It is such a stroke of good fortune that I took them in two years ago. Cambridge is such a friendless place and it has made all the difference in the world to have that devoted family with me.

I hope that you are happy and not at all lonely. You will find that writing home will relieve much of any anxiety you may feel. There may be matters on which you may prefer to write to me, and I hope that you will not hesitate to do so. In any case write often and with great care to Miss Overacker. You may not have time to write often to others but when you do write, do it with great care in the matter of form and style.

The war news is very excellent. If things go on in the present tempo, you may well be able to return home 'under your own steam', as it were, without special protection. You will be pleased and surprised to find your books and things in perfect order. I wonder whether you will feel like reading Henty[39] again.

---

[39] G. A. Henty, prolific early twentieth-century author of historical novels for young people.

HL to EL, 15 February 1943

This is now the third week of waiting and it is getting more unpleasant as time goes on – and with a stroke of luck Mummy ought to be here after ten days or so. The journey must be an ordeal – much more than when we did the trip together. For then we were together (although, little blighter, I remember how difficult it was to get hold of you on occasions, not to mention the fact that I just could not make you read Morrison's History of the United States).

We are already planning the festivities of the reception and the kind of dinner she will get on arrival. How glad she will be to be in her own home again. Chandler has been specially good and has tidied up the approaches to No. 6. It is difficult to keep the place tidy in these days; last Monday a military lorry tried to back out and made a ditch three feet long in a border in which I had put my best crocuses.

Your detailed letter, in the form of a diary, was received with great approval and your statement that it took you 55 minutes to write it did not get as much sympathy as it deserved. I hope that you will continue with the diary arrangement as long as you are away from us. It makes the thing much easier.

My royal pupil failed to put in an appearance and has not sent an apology. As a reprisal, I informed him that I could not see him on the second appointed time. So the matter is now in the nature of a deadlock. Mrs Robbins does not like him for he nearly knocked her down in his racing car in which he drives about round Cambridge. His Ministers dare not stop him from driving, for according to the Constitution of his country he is an absolute monarch and can dismiss the whole lot of them. His mother lives in a very modest cottage in the neighbourhood.

The next letter, from Hersch to Rachel, which bears only the incomplete date of 'February 1943', must have been sent to the shipping company or to McNair to be delivered to her on her arrival there:

Welcome, welcome, welcome home! You must feel as I did when I landed – like kissing the ground.

As I told you, I hope you will get in touch with McNair as soon as you land. If he is not in Liverpool, the Secretary will be helpful.

Do not go to London or Cambridge on the same day. Have a rest and then take next morning – at 8.20 – the train which will take you without changing to Bletchley. You can get breakfast on that train. I will most probably come to Bletchley. I may not be able to come if I still have to take special care after a complicated flu which kept me in bed for quite a while. I will tell you when you telephone home from the Liverpool hotel. You must telephone.[40]

---

[40] HL to RL, February 1943.

During this whole period (1940–2), Hersch managed to make progress with his draft on *Recognition in International Law*. He asked Rachel to deposit the manuscript with George A. Finch, the Secretary of the American Society of International Law. This formed one of several instructions that he sent her regarding things that she should bring back with her.

HL to EL, 2 April 1943

I was going to begin this letter by expressing the hope that you are leading a more exciting life in Andover than me in Cambridge – for there is not much variety here and you must be getting rather tired of my telling you of the progress (or lack of progress) of the famous Rights of Man – but then I thought that the less excitement you have the better it will be for you . . .

You will have noticed that the preceding page was composed of one sentence – not a good example to set to one's son.

HL to EL, 3 April 1943

We have not had letters from you for ten days (17 days [in Rachel's case]), but parents are not revengeful and they do not retaliate. On the contrary, they remember that the post plays ugly tricks these days and that you are most certainly living up to your high reputation as an excellent letter writer.

All is well here. Today is a lovely sunny Sunday. The spring is looking its best. So does Mummy who has put on her new (the 20th anniversary) brooch and a fine pair of ear-rings.

I am well too – although slightly despondent over my failure to buy a new chess set yesterday. But my usual seller wanted a price which I could not afford. Still the collection as a whole is lovely as ever (except for the dust).

HL to EL, 6 April 1943

I was glad to hear that the volume of the Digest arrived from Butterworth. It is an expensive volume; the Library will have to pay $20 for it. I had to get special permission from the Treasury to send it. Because of the exchange no-one is allowed to send complimentary copies. I will make a point of sending to your Library all my publications. For you I will send one or two nice old prints of Cambridge.

HL to EL, 11 April 1943

Imagine the study, with the windows open on a warm spring afternoon, with the lovely exhibition of chessmen at the back with the garden beginning to look its very best, and with the moving strains of Bach's St Matthew's Passion filling the room – and you will have an idea of the atmosphere from which this message of much love and affection is written.

HL to EL, 12 April 1943

I am sending you three rather new and good prints. I should like you to keep the Chapel. Of the other two you may like to give one to Louise, and I leave it to you to choose which. But if you are greedy, you may keep both. However, I should not like you to be greedy in relation to Louise. She has been touchingly good to you and us. Will you please acknowledge these as soon as you get them.

May will be a heavy month for you, and although we want you to write often, you need not make a point of being too detailed if it means a great drain upon your time and your inventive powers.

HL to EL, 15 April 1943

It was good to learn from LO that you have not done badly in the second Term notwithstanding the illness and that you will get the scholarship for the Summer Session. I congratulate you. But I am pinning my hope to the Summer Term as your *chef d'oeuvre*. It will decide so many things. On the other hand, I do not want you to get panicky about it or unduly anxious. Do your best, but do not worry. This worrying complex is in the family, and it must be overcome.

Summer Term begins next week. My lecture programme is rather short. I shall not give more than ten lectures. But I will probably give three public lectures on 'The Law of Nations, the Law of Nature, and the Rights of Man'. I intended giving them last Term, but illness intervened. I may also have King Peter again, if he is still here. He has proved to be a rather disappointing student. Also, he has not returned a number of books which I lent him. As English courts have no jurisdiction over a foreign Sovereign, I may be left without a remedy!

In the first three weeks of May 1943, Hersch gave three public lectures in the university on 'The Law of Nations, the Law of Nature and the Rights of Man'. These, together with the paper that he had delivered to the Grotius Society on 2 December 1942, were the first fruits of his preparation of the book on the *International Bill of Rights* and subsequently formed the basis of Part 1 of the work.

HL to EL, 23 April 1943

This is only to tell you that I have now taken in hand entirely the question of your Cambridge studies. What matters in your case is, of course, I have been told, your entrance scholarship, i.e. a College scholarship. The University is not concerned with this. It is the business of the Colleges. I saw one tutor today, and I am seeing another tomorrow. I am going to see the principal tutor of Trinity. I have ascertained that it is quite proper for you to enter Trinity notwithstanding my association with the College. Mr Duff, the Trinity Tutor, is a friend of mine, and I shall be safe in relying on his advice. In the meantime, much love to you, good boy, and my best wishes for a successful conclusion of the Term (notwithstanding your forgetfulness about Walnut).

RL to EL, 4 May 1943

We have just returned from Daddy's first public lecture on the Rights of Man. He had a very large audience. It was a great occasion. Daddy was in good form and the lecture was a most enlightening exposition. It strikes me though as if it was slightly above the heads of the younger students.

HL to EL, 15 May 1943

Here I am in the study one lovely Sunday afternoon preparing my third public lecture and smoking the Walnut, the gift of Master Elihu. I had just run out of my store and had been wondering what I was going to do when the consignment arrived (the glass jar was broken, but the contents were none the worse for it). But I was even more pleased with the fact that amongst all the hustle of Detroit you did not forget about it. I used to be occasionally slightly worried by some manifestations of what I thought was your self-centred disposition. But this is passing. Very many thanks.

All is quiet at home after the lodgers have gone. I am again tasting Mummy's food, and it tastes 'fine'. She is very happy housekeeping, but I wish she could do less of it. However, there is little hope of any satisfactory help.

HL to EL, 26 May 1943

I am doing quite good work, and I hope to finish it in July. But it is heavy going. My public lectures on the subject were a great success, and someone told me that after I had read out solemnly the draft of the International Bill of Rights of Man people thought that it was a historic occasion.

HL to EL, 16 June 1943

I am deep in my draft and comment on the International Bill of Rights of Man. Sometimes I regret that I have taken it on. For it is a difficult subject. If that Bill of Rights were merely a declaration of principle like the Atlantic Charter, then there would be no difficulty. We could cram into that Bill of Rights all kinds of things including the so-called social and economic rights like the right to work, to social security, to equal opportunity in education, and so on. But the Bill of Rights, if it is to be effective, must be enforced not only by the authorities of the State, but also by international actors if necessary. How shall we do that? Shall we allow any individual whose rights, as guaranteed in the International Bill, have been violated to go to an international court and appeal against his own State and its courts? This would mean an international court flooded with thousands of cases on matters of which a tribunal of foreign judges has little knowledge. And would States agree to entrust to a foreign tribunal such questions touching the most essential aspects of their sovereignty? However, I must deal with the matter somehow.

I have other jobs: The Digest, of which we are now going to publish another volume, and the British Yearbook of International Law, of which I have now become editor in succession to Sir Cecil Hurst. <u>Also</u>, I have to make breakfast, cut spinach in the garden, wash up occasionally etc. etc. All this is fun, but it takes time.

HL to EL, 7 July 1943

Life is proceeding here in a very uneventful fashion. I am working steadily, though slowly, on my book. In about a week I hope to give to Mrs Lyons – née Bloch – the first batch for typing. (This is really more than the first batch for the introductory part is half-ready having been delivered in the form of three public lectures and having been typed by that expert typist, your Mummy.)

There will be an excitement next Saturday when the Electors will elect the successor to the Chair of English Law now occupied by Professor Winfield who, being 65, is retiring because of the statutory age limit. It is difficult to know who will be elected. One of the candidates is Mr Jennings who is now Principal of the University in Ceylon. He did not know anything about the vacancy. After consulting Sir Arnold McNair I cabled him telling him of the vacancy, and he applied by cable.

HL to EL, 25 July 1943

I am working hard, but the results are rather slow – although I am not wasting a day. Sometimes I wish I were less anxious to be thorough. Still, I hope that I shall feel differently when I have finished this Bill of Rights. So will be Mrs Lyons – for my handwriting has not improved. When I finish with the Bill of Rights I will have a go at my Wellesley Lectures for I have promised Miss Overacker to have them published by Wellesley and Yale. Then I have to tackle my big book on Recognition. Then there is the Year Book for which I have to write an article and which I have to edit. And finally, the Digest. I hope that you will be less busy.

There is no further reference to the Wellesley Lectures, and Hersch appears not to have returned to them.

HL to EL, 30 July 1943

This is my writing day – for a change. The reasons are many: (1) I want to have an innings. Mummy has been monopolizing the writing recently; on occasion she has even excluded me from the privilege of the post-script; (2) I want to show off the new writing paper in my capacity as editor of the Year Book; (3) Mummy is more than usually busy. We had visitors to luncheon – Professor Brodetsky (who is President of the Jewish Board of Deputies), his wife, and their boy (who is doing applied mathematics in Queens. His father, who is a Professor of mathematics, approved very much of his son following in the footsteps of his Dad. The same here, i.e., Elihu L following into his Dad's footsteps.)

HL to EL, 31 July 1943

In the meantime – I am longing to see you and am thinking a great deal of you. Not that I regret that you are for one year left to yourself – it is good for you altogether – but it is pure paternal selfishness, which even rational professors cannot control, to have one's boy at home. I am taking it for granted that you are never sorry for yourself about being alone. For you are certainly in our thoughts.

I smiled about the Walnut incident. I am looking forward to it not only because I prefer it to anything else but because it will remind me of you so terribly.

I am sleeping better than I have slept for many months and am feeling alright. One reason is that I have the unpleasant part of the book behind me. There is still a lot to do but at least I know now what I am going to say. I did not know it five months ago.

I was in London last Wednesday to attend another inconclusive meeting on War Crimes. It was so hot that I left the meeting in the middle. I saw Mrs Lyons, who is again my Secretary, and some other people. I also inspected a lovely set of chess men, but the price was above my means. In the morning I had a conference with Sir Arnold and Sir Cecil Hurst. Both are coming here to a meeting, which will take place at 6 Cranmer Road, on the 21st.

The study is lovely and clean. Above all, it is cool. I am sitting in my old shorts and a very light sports shirt. It is unusually hot and I fear for the grass. This is parched. But the plantains thrive on the heat!!

HL to EL, 6 August 1943
This is an ordinary letter (not air-mail), and I feel very ordinary for I have just returned from town where I had to buy meat for the cat. This is a great rarity and people have to queue up for it. Luckily I met on the way a colleague, a Fellow of Trinity, and we both went to the shop . . .

I am working steadily at my desk – with the wireless on my left. I am listening many times during the day. It is a crucial time for the happenings [in] Italy mean not only, in all probability, the quick elimination of Italy from the war. They are important as giving a cue to German generals in case they decide one day to dispose of Hitler as Badoglio disposed of Mussolini.

HL to EL, 9 August 1943
You will have to make a number of decisions.

(1) You have to decide not to worry either about what has happened or may happen. Worry is no substitute for determined effort. Although you will no doubt do your best to avoid the humiliation and problems of my interference with your scholarship, you must not get panicky about it. You can only do your best (and this, I am convinced, is a lot).

(2) You must try and get very fit in the second half of the vacation. Drink milk and eat fruit and other things . . . Have a good rest and do not overdo things.

(3) You must not think too much of the Trinity Scholarship. When you come here next year, you will have about a year to prepare for it, and that will be plenty. I would not bother your teachers in Andover with the matter. Between the Commons and the determination to get honours in all six subjects in Andover you will have plenty to do.

(4) It will be necessary for you to curtail your correspondence and outside activities. Do not touch plays and similar things with a barge pole. Preparation for plays takes a lot of time. The important thing in your Andover studies – as in other matters – is concentration and avoidance of dispersion of effort. You will show the Scholarship Committee and others that they were wrong and that you are worth the Scholarship. You must not let down Miss Overacker who has great faith and affection for you.

(5) Subject to that, you must not forget that however important Andover is, it is only an episode in your life. Next year you will be here, among us, and have tangible signs of love which now works through distance. You must never feel lonely because, literally, there is not an hour during the day in which either Mummy or I do not think of you.

HL to EL, 15 August 1943
I wish you could be with us after tomorrow to share in the festivities – including a chicken and salmon (both rarities in these days) – of my birthday. But I am sure that you will be in spirit with us. We certainly shall think of you not a little.

I was delighted with your letter in the matter of the Commons. This is just the way I wanted you to take it. It is a bit humiliating to be treated as a privileged person and I am glad you are looking at it that way. Undoubtedly, this will take a bit of a time which you would otherwise devote to study and exercise, but my experience is that if one does not want to waste time one has time for everything. In any case, I want you to promise me that you will tell me truthfully, without concealing anything, whether you find it tiring and tiresome.

Has Mummy told you that I am contemplating selling the car? This is not because of any financial stress, but because I want in due course to have something smaller and easier to manage. I hope you will approve. I am not selling my chessmen.

HL to EL, 22 August 1943
We are having a quiet Sunday after a rather hectic two days of a meeting with Sir Cecil Hurst, Dr Arnold McNair and Professor Brierly. Hurst was my guest in Trinity and we had to put up Brierly at home. There was a big tea-party at home. And I had my full share of meetings. Today I breakfasted with him (Hurst) for nearly two hours. He told me a great deal of amusing stories of the various State conferences he has attended. One of them was this: Before the Peace Conference of 1919 an official of the Foreign Office – of high rank, but with no sense of humour – read somewhere that during the Vienna

Congress Metternich obtained a great deal of useful information by ransacking the wastepaper baskets of the various delegations for torn-up drafts, discarded blotting paper etc. That high official decided that we must guard against any such danger and he therefore arranged that we brought over to Paris a dozen or so British char-women! They soon got drunk on cheap French wine and had to be sent home.

I am considering going for a holiday with Mummy before finishing the book. McNair may be able to find for us a place in the Lake District (which I have never seen before). I shall be much more useful <u>after</u> I have a rest and a change.

HL to EL, 26 August 1943
I notice from one of your recent letters that you enquire why I am writing so little. I hope you are not judging me very harshly. In the first instance, Mummy tells you every shred of news that it is possible to extract from our uneventful life in a quiet place like Cambridge. I am left to supply you with such tit-bits as she has forgotten – and that is not much. Secondly, writing or no writing, you are every day – and more – in our thoughts.

I was delighted that you have established friendly relations with a number of boys. The difficulty is that friendly relations may mean a lot of time which you will not be able to afford easily next year. But I am sure that you will find the appropriate middle way.

We may be going for a short holiday which I need rather badly. I have not had one for years. And this silly book has exhausted me.[41] I do want to begin the new Term as rested as possible.

HL to EL, 1 September 1943
With the next airmail letter you will get a rather long 'Statement of principles' for your next year in Andover. I am slightly perturbed by the report of the Summer Session. It is not a bad report, but I do not want us to get into the habit of 'not so bad' reports. They must be excellent. However, as mentioned, [more] about this in the next letter.

Today I feel on the lighter side for I have sent off to the typist the last big Part of the book and I am beginning, on the sly, to think of a future effort. However, there is still a lot to do on the 'Rights of Man'.

HL to EL, 6 September 1943
I have just been beaten in chess by the farmer friend of mine from Swavesey.[42] The explanation is that I am in need of a holiday which has now happily been arranged. I am rather looking forward to it for the Lake District is renowned

---

[41] This must have been *The International Bill of Rights of Man*, which he had in the previous years undertaken to write. See p. 251 below.
[42] Sam Berger. He visited Hersch frequently and kindly supplied farm produce.

for its beauty. I hope we shall visit it together one day. I shall then have the advantage of being able to tell you where are the best places to see. (I have never viewed with favour the spectacle of young brats telling Professors where to go on the walks.)

HL to EL, 8 September 1943

To-day – the day after the capitulation of Italy – is a day of elation and no one, even if he wanted to, can shake off that feeling. One feels that it is good to be alive and to witness the downfall of evil and a tangible sign of the triumph of the forces of progress. We are often so pre-occupied with the labours of the day and its small and big worries that we tend to forget what was at stake in 1940 and how very near the abyss we were. For us, personally, our very physical existence was at stake – although I wondered then whether you were conscious of it. But, of course, much bigger things were in the scales, namely, the fate of human progress. I feel very strongly that in reason – apart from religion – the best of progress and the faith in it are the only justification of suffering and the only thing that makes suffering tolerable. If matters had turned out differently in 1940 that faith would have gone by the board. The fall and the fate of Italy make certain what until now was highly improbable. No wonder that I spent a restless – though certainly not unhappy – night.

As bad luck had it, I missed the 6 o'clock news which first brought the good tidings. I took a day off and went to St Ives, a charming little town about twelve miles away. There I went to an antique shop and bought for £1 a nice box of incomplete sets of ivory chess-men (not carved ones). When I came home I completed them with the help of my collection of oddments. I sold, as a favour, one of these sets to my farmer friend for one pound. So I remained, as net profit, with another set (which I am giving to Pipsy), with lots of odd pieces and a good box. And people say that Professors are not good business men!

HL to EL, 12 September 1943

I worked hard during the morning to finish my last section of the work [Human Rights]. Mrs Lyons will finish with it at the end of the week. I hope to send it off to the USA before we go on holiday. But I will ask them not to publish it yet, but to send me their comments so that I can revise it properly in the meantime. The secret of such reputation as one has is not the writing of books – any one can do it – but the devotion of patience to revising the stuff again and again. A book which has not had at least three drafts is not worth the paper on which it is written.

HL to EL, 14 September 1943

This is not yet the big letter which I intended to write to you. This will come before very long. For, at last, I can see light in my work. The first draft of the book on the Rights of Man will go off to the USA next week – just before we go to Windermere. Then I have to do a good many jobs, not to mention the teaching in the University. But none I think will give me as much of a headache as the Rights of Man.

HL to EL, 21 September 1943

I have still not written the long letter. The explanation is that I have received from Mrs Lyons the typescript of the Bill of Rights and that I am revising it prior to sending it to the USA. I am not too happy with it. However, I am asking the Committee for comments – so that I should have plenty of time to go over it, after receiving their comments, before I send them the final thing in December or January.

While I was sitting this afternoon revising the thing and listening to quiet strains of music from the wireless there came through – the Nut-Cracker Suite of Tchaikovsky, which we both know so well. Would you trot after me now as in days of old?[43]

HL to EL, 15 October 1943

I was delighted to hear that you followed my advice about reading and that you have tackled Macaulay's Essays, amongst others. He and others whom I mentioned will do a great deal for your style – which is already most promising. It is possible that, when this letter reaches you, you will be so busy with the ordinary work and the Commons that you will have little time for this kind of reading. Do not worry if this is so. And, generally, do not get alarmed if your present knowledge falls considerably short of what is required for the Scholarship. You will have plenty of time – at least eight months – when you return to supplement any gaps . . .

Term has started. It is not a very exciting Term in point of lectures. My class of hundred and twenty before the War has now been reduced to twelve – a dismal business. But there is other work to do. I have laid aside the Bill of Rights, the MS of which has gone to the US. I am now starting on a draft of post-war international organisations for a Committee which has been set up for the purpose. And there is the Year Book and the Digest.

HL to EL, 21 October 1943

Yesterday your Walnut arrived beautifully packed with the glass unbroken. Thank you very much. I have now considerably reduced my smoking for reasons of expense (I have to pay £2 duty on a pound of tobacco) and health, and I shall therefore keep your pretty receptacle unopened for two months. I have lots of the stuff from another source which I am also stopping for a while.

The term is in full swing, but students are few. I am working on a Report on post-war international organisation and am finding it rather difficult to compress

---

[43] This refers to a game that Hersch, Rachel and I played when I was very little and we still lived in Cricklewood.

within forty printed pages the results of much study. I have made good progress with editing the British Year Book of International Law. I hope to have the material ready by the end of the year. I am myself writing a longish article on Recognition. (By the way: the book on Recognition which I put in cold storage three years ago will now be taken out from the drawer and put into shape. Professor Gutteridge and I have started a Cambridge Series of International and Comparative Law and we hope to send to the printer in the spring three books: my own on Recognition; Gutteridge's on Comparative Law; and Mervyn Jones's on Ratification and Full Powers in the Conclusion of Treaties.) . . .

I spent some time to-day in putting new tulips in the far end of the garden. They grow very well under the trees. But in the summer nothing will grow there and as soon as you are here we shall decide whether one or two of them ought not to go. I do not want to take the major decisions without consulting you. In the meantime the garden is snowed under with autumn leaves. I have to remove lots of them myself for Chandler is getting lazier and lazier. I cannot dismiss him for there is absolutely no gardener to be got for love and money. The same applies to the field of domestic service. Mummy is now without any help, and we are not too happy about it.

HL to EL, 28 October 1943

You say you are worrying about the amount of house work Mummy is doing. It is a lot, but she is bearing it cheerfully. The amount of visitors has been reduced practically to nothing except those of the family, actual and potential . . . Also, you must not forget that your Dad is an A1 cook and altogether a handy man about the house (hear, hear, Mummy).

I was interested in your offer – which is gratefully accepted – to contribute your new history book to our joint library. As a matter of legal interest I would like to know whether thereby you have established a partnership in regard to my entire library or whether this book is a nucleus of a joint library in addition to our respective private libraries. However, we shall discuss this personally at leisure – as well as the question of the chess-men about which I fear you will be as keen as about the books.

The Bill of Rights is on the high seas – although I have certainly not finished the thing. In the meantime I am preparing a report of post-war international organisation for a British Committee of International lawyers set up for the purpose. It is all going to be based on the principle of universality, i.e. on the idea that any future political organisation of States must embrace all States, that membership should be compulsory and that no withdrawal is possible. Only thus can we have an international organisation which is effective and which expresses adequately the fact of the unity of the human race and of the political and economic interdependence of States. But if I judge the temper of politicians in the USA aright, we shall see no participation of the USA in an effective international organisation worthy of that name. This is a tragedy, but we must be ready to meet the situation . . .

I am writing to-day to Mr Steinig[44] (who is writing a short note for the British Year Book). I shall ask him, quite plainly, to invite you for a week to Washington during the Christmas vacation. It would be a pity if you did not see the capital and the Kapitol before leaving the USA.

I occasionally like to do things in the last moment, but in the matter of your return I am doing some preparatory work in order not to leave anything to chance. I shall be disappointed if I do not beat you in chess in July.

Be of good cheer . . . in case you should have passing moments of home sickness (and it is natural that you should have them) remember that you are very much at home with us.

HL to EL, 31 October 1943
I can see that you are having a busy and, probably, a difficult term. The amount of hours in the day is limited and there is little left for leisure after the Commons, the towels, the lessons, the study, the rehearsals for the play etc. You do not say that you like all this and probably, but for your desire not to make us anxious, you would say that you dislike it. I can well imagine that. You know my views on the subject. You try your best, but not more than your best. I do not want you to worry or to impair your health. It is important that you should do well at school, but it is also important that you should not make yourself miserable. But perhaps you will consider whether it is necessary for you to take part in such extraneous activities like singing in the choir or taking part in the plays. Of course, if you must do it, this is the end of the matter. Also, if you like doing it, no one will grudge you that. But if it is a question of being firm and telling people who ask you to join these things: 'I am sorry, but I have the Commons and with my ordinary work, I find it as much as I can manage' – then, I hope, you will show that firmness. I have constantly to do it and to turn down invitations to give lectures, address College societies etc. It is unpleasant to say 'No', but it is wiser in the long run . . .

Mummy and I have adopted the custom of having our morning tea together (before breakfast). We were discussing to-day whether you will care to join us in these ceremonies in the bedroom in the morning.

HL to EL, 6 November 1943
Your letters from the beginning of the Term in Andover have been very welcome and, on the whole, comforting – including those in which you ticked us off for interfering with the arrangements for your holidays.

---

[44] He had been best man at the wedding of Hersch and Rachel on 20 March 1923.

It is possible that you minimise the discomforts of the Commons in order to relieve any apprehension on our part, but I really think that they are working out better than we thought. Mind you – there will be ups and downs in the matter and you may reasonably feel that the burden is very great (in which case, off you go and stand yourself a coca-cola and drink our joint health), but, generally speaking, I feel that the worst has not materialized. And if you can really make it a *cum laude* year, I shall be happy . . .

I want you to tell me: (1) that you have bought an expensive packet of Abdol vitamins and that you are having one a day; (2) that you are feeding wisely and are having no less than two pints of milk a day.

HL to EL, 13 November 1943
There are only three weeks to go to the end of term. The winter is already upon us. Which reminds me that we are slightly anxious about the prospect of your remembering to take precautions against catching colds. You <u>must</u> remember not to go out when you are hot and perspiring, or when you have to go out to keep moving and not to stand in the same place.

We shall most probably stay at home during the Christmas vacation. It is too uncomfortable these days to go anywhere.

Have I told you that in addition to other troubles, I have to start now on a new edition of the War volume of Oppenheim? The stock is exhausted.

HL to EL, 16 November 1943
This is the first really wintry day and I have given up the ritual of going for my afternoon walk (it is surprising how Cambridge walking is lacking in variety: it is either the Coton footpath or the Grantchester footpath. I ought to try the tow-path from Chesterton Road to Ely.)

Also, I am recovering from a tooth extraction which went off yesterday very satisfactorily. In about five weeks I shall have a set of false teeth which will make your Dad look much prettier.

HL to EL, 23 November 1943
The Term ends next week. It passed rather quickly. My lecturing duties are not too onerous. My LLB course did not materialize for there were no students taking the subject. The ordinary Tripos course began with ten, and is finishing with fifteen. Still it is a dull business compared with 130 before the War.

The Term has passed quickly. There have been no illnesses – apart from two tooth extractions preparatory to a nice set of artificial teeth which, following Mummy's strong feelings about my attractiveness, I am standing myself as a New Year present.

But I have had plenty of work to do. Last year the American international lawyers appointed an enormous Committee (including your friend Judge

Hudson) to draft projects of post-war international organisation. They held various meetings in distant parts of the USA and eventually produced an elaborate report which they sent here to the British international lawyers. We decided thereupon to produce our own report. I have undertaken the principal part of it. The thing has now kept me busy for six weeks and has slightly worried me. It has to be short and this makes it more difficult. However, I have now broken the back of it and I hope to be ready in about a fortnight.[45]

Then there was the Digest of which a new volume covering the years 1941–1942 we hope to publish next summer. None of the numerous packages from America has been lost on the way. I have been lucky to arrange with Professor Rappard, who was here last year, that the cases from Italy and Germany will be prepared by a Swiss contributor. The Swiss Legation has agreed to including the correspondence in their diplomatic bag (after it has been censored) and this has expedited matters.

Then there is the British Yearbook which I hoped to have ready for the printer by February. But I doubt now whether this will be possible. One prospective contributor after another is backing out. Last week I had a call from [one] telling me that he must postpone his article. And there have been other defaulters.

Then there is my book on Recognition in International Law. I finished it three years ago and put it into cold storage. Now it is being dug out and tackled again. We have decided to publish here a series called Contributions to International Law and Comparative Law and edited by Professor Gutteridge and myself. My book will go into that Series. I promised to have it ready by Easter, but it is unlikely that I shall be able to do so.

For, finally, I have received a peremptory request from Longmans to prepare as soon as possible a revised edition of the War Volume of Oppenheim. The present stock is exhausted – one reason being that practically every new American warship has it in its Library! If the American navy grows at the present rate, we shall have to have yet another edition in 1945!

The book on the Bill of Rights is now due to reach New York any day. I do not know yet how and by whom it will be published. I will insist on reading the proof here. In the USA they do it rather negligently. Moreover, I will try to have the major part of it published here separately.

---

[45] This work, to which Hersch refers several times in his letters during the latter part of 1943, is evidently the one that was printed in his *Collected Papers*, Vol. 3, pp. 461–503, under the title 'The Principles of International Organisation'. Some of the speculation as to the circumstances in which the work was prepared, which appears in the editorial note at pp. 461–2, can now be seen to be not entirely accurate. The paper was prepared by Hersch as a member of the British Committee for the Consideration of the Principles of International Law and Organization and followed the transmission to England of a paper prepared by an American committee of international lawyers of which the membership and terms of reference cannot now be traced. However, Hersch makes no reference to the American work in the text. It has not been possible to find further information about the British committee.

Next Sunday I am reading a paper to the Cambridge Jewish Students Society on 'Some Problems of the Law of War in Jewish Law'. I have not sweated a great deal over it. (In confidence, I gave a similar lecture, which has not been published, about ten years ago and I am dishing it up now.)[46]

As you see, this has not been an idle Term. Nonetheless, I decided to re-join the Home Guard which I had to give up owing to my illness last year. I have now been to two parades. Mummy thinks that I look quite becoming – though she thinks that I ought to be at least a corporal. She does not know that in the HG the best people are privates.

This has been a very egocentric letter. But I have not been writing at length recently and you ought to have, at least once a Term, a detailed account of my doings.

HL to EL, 4 December 1943
Do not worry about your style. It has good potentialities. You are a bit rushed now and you may not have time to read a great deal of the right literature. But you will have at least a year for thorough unhurried reading and this will make a great difference.

HL to EL, 9 December 1943
[A]ssuming that the question of your essay on Civil Rights under the Bill of Rights is still topical, you may find the following advice useful: Begin your work by reading and taking notes. Go to the Library and find the most recent things. Do not rely on little pamphlets. In your case, I would look up: Willoughby, *The Constitutional Law of the United States* (1929 edition), vol. II, pp. 1184–1208; Willis, *Constitutional Law of the US* (1936), pp. 487–513; and above all, Chafee's *Freedom of Speech in War* (an excellent book). I would also try and find out any interesting decisions of the Supreme Court on the subject in the last 2 or 3 years.

Do not rely on small, secondary, sources. In writing on blockade, you could have gone straight to Lauterpacht's edition of Oppenheim, instead of being irritated by Goodhart.

Of course, all this may be a counsel of perfection seeing that your time is so limited. But remember it for the future. Above all, try to form your own opinion about things. You may say what others think, but that cannot be a substitute for your own thinking.

HL to EL, 16 December 1943
As to the joint use of our respective libraries, your suggestion sounds most reasonable. My ambition is that you should have a study of your own at No. 6. I am keeping carefully the upright boards for the shelves, and I do not see why before long you should not have a room full of books – with a wireless of your

---

[46] Subsequently published in the *Collected Papers*, Vol. 5, pp. 715–27.

own (I hope you will bring your set and your pick up. I have here a set of the whole 9th Beethoven symphony).

We have decided not to go away for Christmas. Home is in these days the best place. I am beginning to see light in my work. In a day or two I am dispatching to the typist a piece of work which has kept me busy for a Term – I appreciate what you say about Oppenheim. After the war, the whole position will be reviewed and it is probable that I shall start writing a text book and then a big treatise of my own.

HL to EL, 22 December 1943
Here, for a change, is a letter for you on the Digest note-paper. This is also a good opportunity for telling you that the volume for 1941–1942 is well on the way. It will probably be published in the autumn of 1944. It will be the tenth volume and if there is a peace at that time we may have a celebration in the form of a dinner. The Digest has become an indispensable instrument of work for any serious students of the subject. But it is a dull business editing it – especially when one has to deal occasionally with lazy or unintelligent contributors.

HL to EL, 26 December 1943
It is Christmas Sunday afternoon and we are about to go out for a walk to the Daube's to present little Jonathan with a Chanukah present – $\frac{1}{4}$ lb of good chocolate which he will no doubt fancy very much. Since lunch I have been busy on the revision of the sixth edition of Oppenheim's War Volume. I am going to devote very little time to it – one reason being that the work is going to be reprinted from the standing type. This means that, so far as possible, I must not disturb the page to the point of trespassing on the next page. It is a ticklish job. I have just been doing a note on the US Selective Service Act, 1941, which, you will recall, has caused me some anxiety.

HL to EL, 18 January 1944
I am going to London to-morrow, and I ought therefore to 'do' my weekly air-mail letter to-day.

Why am I going to London? There is a meeting of the Publications Committee, of which I am a member, of the Royal Institute of International Affairs. Its business is mainly to decide what books shall be published under the auspices of the Institute. The main decisions are usually taken by the secretaries before the meeting. But I feel it my duty to attend some of these Committees – especially in view of the fact that the Year Book is associated with the Institute. Otherwise a trip to London is a nuisance these days quite apart from the question of expense. The trains are crowded and on return to Cambridge there is no taxi available. It is not pleasant to walk home from the station in the black-out.

However, a visit to London is a good opportunity for seeing a number of people. Thus to-morrow I hope to see, among others, Professor Lawrence Preuss who is a member of the USA delegation in connection with the punishment of war crimes. In peace time he is Professor in Ann Arbor, Michigan. He has been having colds since his arrival in this country. Recently he smashed his glasses and his nose in the black-out. He also complained that British liquor is expensive and very weak. There is little I can do about that.

I also hope to see Professor EH Carr who is now one of the leader writers in The Times. He may be a candidate for the Professorship of Modern History left vacant after the death of Professor Temperley. Most Professorships are now being filled; the policy of waiting for the end of the war has been abandoned. Thus we recently filled the Regius Professorship of History. It has been given to Professor Clark who left his Oxford Professorship in order to come here – a great compliment to Cambridge.

I have written to-day to Longman to tell him that my revised edition of vol. II of Oppenheim will probably be ready at the beginning of February – a month earlier than I expected. I can now start on my article for the Year Book on 'Implied Recognition'. It is part of the book which I prepared on Recognition generally but which I find is very much in need of revision. I am very glad I have not published it two years ago.

Sir Neville Butler to HL, 26 January 1944

You will remember that on the 23rd July, 1942, the late Sir Stephen Gaselee wrote to you about the most useful memoranda which you had sent to the Foreign Office earlier that year. In your second memorandum you made the interesting suggestion that some permanent machinery should be set up in the form of a joint board for investigating complaints of injuries to British or American commercial interests by the administration of war economy.

This suggestion has been the subject of considerable interdepartmental discussion both here and in Washington. Official opinion has been divided on the practicability of such a proposal and I am therefore writing to you to give you in outline some of the questions that have been raised in connexion with this proposed scheme.

It has been objected that this tribunal would not in fact provide a solution of the difficulties with which it would be intended to deal because it would either not be able to get at all the facts and details of the complaints or else it would have to cross-examine government departments and ultimately have to come to a conclusion on matters of public policy. It is admitted that such an organization might be well suited for dealing with malicious rumours or groundless complaints but it would seem that where the questions raised involved complicated matters of administrative policy the tribunal would not be in a position either to investigate the matter thoroughly or to prescribe an effective remedy.

For all these difficulties, which seem to us real, we have felt that a scheme such as yours would be of great value if it could be made to work. I would not, of course, ask you to go to the trouble of trying to find solutions to these problems: but if the foregoing recital should suggest to your mind some alternative procedures whereby these obstacles might be avoided I need not say that we should be very ready to examine the proposal again in conjunction with the other interested departments. For the present, please accept our sincere thanks for the thought you have already devoted to the problem.

RL to EL, 29 January 1944

I do not remember whether I mentioned to you that Daddy wrote an article on the International organisation (of the World, after the War). Sir Arnold read the article typewritten. He says that he thinks this article is the most powerful Dad has written – 'If someone came and told me in 1924 that you will be writing such articles – I would have said it is impossible . . . How could you absorb the best in English thought and style so rapidly.' I quote from memory, for I can not lay hands on the letter just now. I was delighted to read Arnold's letter. I suppose Dad was pleased too – but he does not care much what people say – it is what he himself thinks of his work that matters to him most. I know this bit of news will please you.

Dad says he would like to have a <u>really</u> good serious game of chess <u>with you</u> and <u>me</u> looking on, he wants to know whose part I am going to take. I really would like to see you both equal strength in the game. But I know Dad is very formidable and good in beating others – but <u>not</u> so good in taking himself a beating. I think you take after your Dad – so it will be a tough game.

HL to EL, 30 January 1944

This is Sunday, air-mail letter day, and you are in for a long letter.

The setting is this: Your Dad is at the desk in the study quite satisfied with the garden below in which a loud profusion of future tulips, hyacinths and daffodils shows its promising tops. It is surprising that this garden looks so well. For Chandler is getting more – and not less – lazy and bored with his job. But one has to stick to him for you simply cannot get anyone else. On my side, on the left, there is a pile of letters either already written or envelopes indicating letters to be written. On my right there is the MS of the revised Sixth Edition of Oppenheim which I will send to the printer this week. One has to be firm in these matters and draw a line and say 'no more'. Which means that if any new material comes to hand, I am going to disregard it. Otherwise, there is no end to it. Yesterday, for instance, Sir Arnold brought me the page proof of his book on the Legal Effects of War, and I shall have now to devote several days in incorporating new stuff.

At the same time I am getting on with the Digest and the British Year Book. On Wednesday I am going to London to lunch with Mr Noel-Baker, the

Parliamentary Secretary to the Ministry of War Transport... and to see a number of persons on various matters, including Professor Lawrence Preuss of Michigan who is now attached to the USA delegation in the Commission on War Crimes. I am spending the evening with him and shall be staying in the Strand Palace Hotel. I have to leave early on Thursday in time to give my lecture in Cambridge at 12.

Referring to an essay that I was writing on freedom of speech, he observed:

But the proper method is, after you have decided on which aspect of the matter you are going to concentrate, to read a great deal about this particular aspect. You may have for that purpose to look at ten big books and ten articles. But in these books what you have to look at is only the particular chapter – or perhaps only a page or two – in which you are interested. It is only so that you can hope to form an independent and mature judgment...

I sent off yesterday to the printer the revised edition of vol. II of Oppenheim. I have sent it all in my hand-writing and I do not envy the printer. This coming week I am going to devote to revising Part I of my book on Recognition (Part I is on Recognition of States) which I intend to send to Miriam Lashly, Editor-in-Chief of the Yale Law Journal! It will be an article of about one hundred pages.

I had a busy day in London last Wednesday. I lunched with Noel Baker and found him as delightful as ever. He is now a member of the Government and he told me many interesting things.

HL to EL, 14 February 1944
I am a day late with my weekly air-mail letter. The reason is not laziness. For I have been working hard trying to have ready for Mrs Lyons my very long article – which may come to one hundred pages in print – for the Yale Law Journal on Recognition of States. It is in part an adaptation of Part I of my future book on Recognition which I wrote three years ago and put away in cold storage. This was a good thing to do. For I think that the book needs substantial improvements. Every writer – a good one, I mean – has often to make up his mind in relation to two conflicting principles: One is that it is never too late to send a book to the printer; that it is a mistake to rush matters; and that every subsequent draft is an improvement. All this is true. The other principle is that as there is no limit to improvement, one reaches, after a time, a stage when additional effort yields very little and when caution and conscientiousness become a sign of laziness and lack of courage. There must be a limit to improvements. (Have you heard of the Cambridge Professor who was preparing for ten years his inaugural lecture and died without having given it?)

However, I must not chatter about myself.

HL to EL, 9 March 1944

The Term here is over. I gave my last lecture yesterday. There were three American officers present. All American officers and men have received permission to attend any University lectures they like, and they make frequent use of that permission. I felt slightly guilty because after having finished the lecture I walked out of the room as usual without coming to them and saying a word or two. But I usually feel tired after a lecture and long for a rest in my room. It is interesting that I find lecturing to fifteen people more tiring than to hundred and fifty before the war. The reason, I suppose, is that one has a bit of a sense of futility in talking to a small and rather non-descript class of boys of not too high intelligence.

I sent off last week my long article on Recognition of States. I am working now on a biggish article on War Crimes. The vacation will be largely devoted to completing the work on the Annual Digest and the British Year Book of International Law – both of which are long overdue.

HL to EL, 17 March 1944

This has been a strenuous afternoon (a Saturday) devoted largely to gardening with Mummy acting as chief assistant. Fortunately, Chandler was unable to come and we have been able to do some useful work. The plot we chose was the famous one at the far end of the garden on the right which I once gave to you for your own use. (I still remember your express stipulation: 'You must not tell me what to do'). We put in a lot of peas, called English Wonder, which ought to be ready just about June or July. I think you like them sweet, straight from the pods. Mummy is very efficient once she can be persuaded to join in the work. Otherwise, with Chandler being really of no use, I find that I can not cope with it. Recently I have been devoting hours to scraping moss off the lawn – a tiring job. However, there must be an end to the garden . . .

I am working hard to finish the article, which is a biggish one, on war crimes. The proofs of the revised sixth edition of Oppenheim may be coming any day. Also, I am putting a great deal of work into the Digest, and I hope to have it ready for the printer in about a month. This will be the tenth volume of the Digest. We are going to have a cumulative index.[47] In normal times, we would celebrate the occasion by a dinner of the Advisory Committee. It is possible that we may have that dinner, for the volume will not appear before October. By then, the thing may be over. For I am an optimist with regard to the military prospects. I am not so optimistic about the political aspect of things. The Russians are a very gallant ally, but they are very trying and unpredictable. The bad thing is that a dictatorship – and they are one – can change its policy overnight. You never know how you stand about them.

---

[47] For an account of the cumulative indexing of the *Annual Digest/ILR* up to Volume 137, see Maureen MacGlashan, 'Indexing the International Law Reports (ILR)' (2010) 10(2) *Legal Information Management*.

RL to EL, 19 March 1944

Twenty one years ago today – I was rather an excited girl, staying in a big hotel in Vienna – waiting to be married the next day. In the same hotel were your Dad, my Dad, and the grandparents from Poland et famille. I was happy and sad. Happy to marry the man I loved, sad to marry him in a foreign land, away from my mother and family. On April 5th we shall have resided 21 years in England. Life is like a dream – but thank God it is a good life.

HL to EL, 20 March 1944

It is vacation time – so to speak – and I am able to finish some of my work including the article on War Crimes (for the publication of which, however, I have to obtain the permission of the authorities)... Most of the vacation will be devoted to the Digest and the British Year Book. The latter is a nuisance. One half of the prospective contributors have defaulted; some have sent in such imbecile stuff that I shall have to use all my diplomacy not to offend them while rejecting what they have sent in. But the upshot of it will be that I shall have to do a lot of supplementary writing myself.

I wish I were writing less and reading more. The University Library is within seven minutes walk, and such a lot of good stuff there.

HL to EL, 6 April 1944

I have been in London twice last week. On Saturday I went to a meeting of a Committee of international lawyers on the future of international organisation. It was an annoying meeting. Some of my colleagues are what they believe to be very realistic. This means that in making proposals they do not wish to consider what is sound and rational, but what the Governments are likely to accept. What they forget is that what Governments will think will to some extent be influenced by what we think is the right course.

On Wednesday I went to see the people of the World Jewish Congress in connection with the Inter-Allied Commission for the investigation of war crimes. The Jewish Congress wish, very properly, that a special Committee of the Allied Commission should investigate the terrible war crimes which Germany has perpetrated against the Jews. I have promised to assist them. This will involve me in extra work, but there is no option.

HL to EL, 20 April 1944

I am in arrears even with my weekly air mail letter. It is no use arguing that you seem to be slightly in arrears too. Two blacks do not make one white. The explanation, if any, is that as soon as I finish with one piece of work there crops up another. I had finished with the article on Implied Recognition – a lengthy thing – and I have now to tackle and presently to re-write an article sent in by a rather highly placed but not too conscientious man on Consular Immunities. It tires me to do it – not only because it is a troublesome thing, but also because it makes me angry to have to do donkey work for others. But I promised to bring out that volume of the Year Book and it is now clear that I will do it – and it will be quite a good volume (with about one-third contributed by myself). The proofs of the revised edition of Oppenheim are pouring in but I have had no time yet to look at them. I am dreading the moment when the proofs of the Bill of Rights will begin to arrive from the USA. The Annual Digest work is all the time with me. And I have to start shortly on a kind of memorandum which I have promised the World Jewish Congress on the War Crimes against the Jews. Moreover, the Term has started – with lectures, meetings and examinations. You will realise now that I am not lazy or unemployed.

HL to EL, 1 May 1944
My weekly airmail letter to you is long overdue. I was rushed last week with many things including a week-end conference in London. It was a conference of international lawyers organised by the Grotius Society. Personally I think that these functions are of very little value, but my colleagues believe that they foster international understanding. In any case, there was a tea for ladies at the concluding session and Mummy arrived there very resplendent. I was glad to be back in Cambridge after a standing journey on a crowded train . . .

I am working very hard these days, and the examinations period will not make things easier. The Oppenheim proofs are coming in, and I am expecting any day the proofs of the book on the International Bill of the Rights of Man which is being published by Columbia University Press. I have insisted on having the proof for our common experience here is that proof-reading in the USA tends to be rather perfunctory. I hope to send the British Year Book of International Law to the printer next week, and the Annual Digest some time this month. There is a lot of donkey work in both. In addition I have been busy writing a memorandum for the World Jewish Congress in connection with the work of the United Nations Commission for the Investigation of War Crimes. The Jews have been the greatest victim of the German crimes and it is proper that these anti-Jewish atrocities should be the subject of a special investigation and report. But it is difficult to make the various Jewish bodies move together.

HL to EL, 10 May 1944
The summer has come at last after some frosts which have spoiled a great deal of the apple crop. But there will be some left for you. The garden looks lovely. There are more flowers than ever. The vegetables are doing well and we have enough cabbages to last us till the autumn.

I have sent off to the printer the British Year Book of International Law, and thus there is, provisionally, one less load to carry. I hope to send the Annual Digest to the printer next week. I suppose that by that time the proofs of the book on the Bill of Rights will begin to arrive. The Oppenheim proof is coming in steadily. The examinations begin in about a fortnight. I am examining in three of these, but the number of students is small. My lectures finish next week. It was an easy lecturing Term – nine lectures! In addition there are all kinds of odd jobs (not to mention the Home Guard). Thus, for instance, I have been asked by solicitors to give an opinion as to whether the British Government is bound to admit to England a lady, a member of the Czechoslovak Red Cross, who escaped from France in 1940! The reason for the rather silly question is that according to the Geneva Convention of 1929 a belligerent is bound to send back captured Red Cross personnel. From this the client wants to deduce the right of the Czech lady to be admitted to England!

The remarkable correspondence between Hersch, Rachel and myself, extending over hundreds of letters, diminished after June 1944 as a result of my return to Cambridge upon graduation from school in the United States. In the three months following, Hersch corresponded frequently with McNair and others attempting to find me a place at an English school in order, as McNair observed, 'to undo the effect of his American education'! Hersch was then confronted by the need to find the fees to send me to Harrow, but, notwithstanding his limited income, did so with great grace and eventually took me there himself at the beginning of the autumn term in September 1944.

Sir Neville Butler to HL, 10 July 1944
As I told you in my letter of the 28th February we have been thinking over the further suggestions which you so kindly offered me on your proposal for a combined organisation for dealing with complaints about British wartime economic administration.

I hope it will not disappoint you to hear that we have come to the conclusion that the hope of progress along these lines is not great enough to justify our pursuing the matter further with the hard-worked departments concerned. The root of the problem lies, as I am sure you will agree, in the bias of the American mind against giving the British the benefit of any doubt that may be raised against our words or acts or policies. Time, I think, is slowly correcting that bias: but it is a slow and uncertain process and it has not yet gone far enough, I fear, to respond much to treatment by the sort of method we have been examining together.

Thank you again for all your trouble.

HL to EL, 30 October 1944
I am extremely satisfied – in fact, happy – about what you say as to being immersed in history reading. Reading, reading, and again, reading, is the decisive thing. Its fruits are not immediate, but as to its long range significance there is no doubt. I agree with you about novels – except, perhaps, historical novels by good writers and authors like Austen, Trollope, and others of similar standing. Also, they are important from the point of view of learning to write (Allen Nevins and Commager are voracious readers of good historical novels).

I am flattered by your reference to the results of 'three months reading under Daddy'. I wish they had been three full months! But, on the whole, I am very satisfied with the way things are shaping.

I fully approve of your idea of wishing to read Joad. The book is at home. But I will urge you strongly to read some other easy philosophy. Nothing is more conducive to elegance of expression and the proper development of the intellect.

I certainly approve of your taking part in the debates – after mature preparation. You will receive some pamphlets which will help you for the agriculture debate. Your seconding of five minutes ought to take about four pages of quarto size. Write them out in light (not too heavy) language; introduce two or three humorous passages if possible; and learn the thing by heart. You must speak freely.

I am giving some thought to coaching during the vacation. A junior lecturer would be a good idea, but a Cambridge Professor is a better one. There is one in Cranmer Road.

In 1944, Hersch began a decade of additional labour as editor of the *British Year Book of International Law*. The *BYIL* was the leading British periodical in the field of public international law from its inception in 1922 under the editorship of Sir Cecil Hurst. Its publication had been suspended in 1939 due to the outbreak of the war which led to depletion in the ranks of contributors by their absence on various forms of national service, coupled with the shortage of paper and difficulties of printing.

As the end of the war came in sight, the Editorial Committee, of which Hersch had become a member in 1936, decided that the series should be revived. Hersch was invited to become Editor. There then began under Hersch's guidance a period of ten years during which the series regained authority as one of the two leading international law periodicals in the world. Hersch remained as Editor until 1955 when, being elected as a judge of the ICJ, he resigned and was succeeded by Sir Humphrey Waldock.

Hersch insisted on the originality and literary quality of the articles submitted for publication. He wielded a ruthless editorial pen and, indeed, spent much time doing so. He himself contributed significantly. Nine of the eleven volumes that appeared under his editorship between 1944 and 1954 included articles by himself, each of them on a subject of major importance: recognition, the Grotian tradition in international law,[48] the punishment of war criminals, interpretation of

---

[48] The 'Grotian Tradition in International Law' has been described as 'the most comprehensive expression of the "Grotian Tradition" to date': see R. Jeffery, 'Hersch Lauterpacht, the Realist

treaties, sovereignty over submarine areas, State immunity and the law of war. He insisted that where possible his former students should reflect their work in articles in the *BYIL*. The dimensions of the editorial burden that he placed upon himself are illustrated by the fact that during his editorship the size of the volumes increased from a little over 300 pages to well over 500 pages.

Challenge and the "Grotian Tradition" in 20th-Century International Relations' (2006) 12 *European Journal of International Relations* 224.

CHAPTER 8

HUMAN RIGHTS

As can be seen from earlier chapters, the position of the individual in international law was long a matter of major concern to Hersch. From the earliest days of his research in Vienna, he rejected the view that States alone are subjects of international law. In due course, his thinking developed into a direct and deep involvement in what became the most important facet of the decline of absolute State sovereignty, namely, the international protection of the rights of man. In the present chapter, this aspect of his work will be set out as a whole; to approach it simply in chronological terms interspersed with other matters would lead to an unacceptably fragmented presentation.

In April 1942, Hersch received from the American Jewish Committee (AJC), one of the foremost American Jewish organisations, an invitation to write a book on the international law of human rights. The arrangement was concluded in May 1942 when the Committee agreed to pay him a fee of $2,500, plus $800 for secretarial and other expenses.[1] The Committee foresaw that it would take Hersch about a year to complete the study but urged him to do so as soon as possible because the same subject was currently being examined by the American Law Institute and the American Bar Association. From the beginning, it was made clear that the study should not be limited to the substantive content of a Bill of Rights but should extend to discussion of the means of enforcing such rights.

Hersch did not begin work on the book immediately because he was busy with the volume of the *AD* for 1938–40 and the preparation of a long memorandum on war crimes. He began his reading for it in July with a view to finishing it by the end of December. He reckoned that he would need to read for three months before being ready to start writing. In a letter to Rachel in September 1942, he acknowledged that he had let himself 'in for a difficult thing, but I do not regret it for a

---

[1] Letter of 27 May 1942 from the Director of the Committee to HL. At the then exchange rate of $4 to £1, this amounted to £625 – a very significant sum to one whose professorial salary was £1,200 a year with half going in income tax. The leading role in this initiative of the committee was played by Simon Segal (see p. 192 above).

moment'.[2] By 2 December, he had progressed sufficiently to be able to present as the first fruits of his research a paper to the Grotius Society on 'The Law of Nations, the Law of Nature and the Rights of Man', the substance of which was in due course to form the first part of the book. He summarised the essence of his message as follows:

[W]hat has been said here about the part which the law of nature has played in the matter in the past is not of mere historical interest. If we are to face with any hope of success the bewildering and seemingly insoluble problems of an International Charter of Human Rights, it is proper that we should seek assistance in the contemplation of the continuity of human thought on this matter and on the true objects of international law. Statesmanship may recoil from the revolutionary immensity of the task. It is certainly the duty of the student of international law to bring into relief the complexities of any such innovation in the constitutional law of States and of mankind. At the same time it is within his province to show that any such departure in the law would not be in the nature of a break with what is truly permanent in the legal tradition of western civilization but that it would be in accordance with the purpose of the law of nations. That purpose cannot be permanently divorced from the fact that the individual human being – his welfare and the freedom of his personality in its manifold manifestations – is the ultimate unit of all law.[3]

The completion of the manuscript, subject to other competing claims on his time, occupied the rest of 1943. By the beginning of 1944, he was able to submit to Columbia University Press, with which the AJC had arranged publication, a text carrying an opening section forming the doctrinal and jurisprudential basis of the practical proposals that formed the second part of the book. The first part was an elaboration of the Grotius Society paper of December 1942 and of a series of lectures that he then gave in Cambridge in the summer of 1943. The second part contained a series of specific proposals both for the substantive content of an international bill of the rights of man and for the international enforcement of such a bill. In his preface, he fully recognised that he was entering into a controversial subject which would invite 'outspoken and impartial' criticism. He continued:

[I]t is incumbent upon the student of the subject to put forward concrete proposals as a starting point for deliberation and discussion aiming at the incorporation of the International Bill of the Rights of Man as an integral part of the law of nations. In leaving the safer path of expounding the existing law and choosing to propound schemes involving fundamental legal changes, the

---

[2] HL to RL, 4 September 1942. See p. 213 above.
[3] (1943) 29 *Transactions of the Grotius Society* 1–34.

lawyer cannot legitimately complain of any trenchant criticism by the expert and the layman alike. I have deemed it my duty to incur that risk.[4]

While the doctrinal part of the work eventually occupied some 68 pages of print, the substantive proposals took up 100 pages and were followed by 55 pages relating to enforcement. The substantive proposals consisted of a draft International Bill of the Rights of Man presented in a preamble of eleven paragraphs and twenty operative articles.[5] The latter provided, in Part 1, for personal rights: for the liberty of the person; the prohibition of slavery; freedom of religion, of speech and of association and assembly; the sanctity of the home; equality before the law; entitlement to nationality; and the right of emigration and expatriation. A second part dealt with political rights: the right of citizens to choose their governments in free elections; territories which had not reached full political independence should be subject to the supervision of an international authority; minorities were to have the right to maintain their own schools and cultural institutions out of public funds; States were to make effective provision for the right to work and for securing just and humane conditions of work. A third part contained what at that time were relatively novel provisions for making the Bill of Rights part of the domestic law of States, overriding any inconsistent internal rules of law and granting to the highest courts of States jurisdiction to pronounce upon the conformity of legislative, judicial or executive action with the provisions of Part 1 of the Bill of Rights. In addition, the Bill was declared to be an integral part of the Law of Nations.[6] There was to be a High Commission within the framework of 'the United Nations of the World' to supervise the observance of the Bill. (It must be remembered that the Bill was drafted in 1943 at a time before there were any developed proposals for what became the United Nations.) The Commission was to have the power to receive petitions from individuals and organisations. The 'Council of the United Nations', not then even contemplated, was to be the supreme agency for securing the observance of the Bill of Rights. If it found that there had been an infraction of the Bill, the Council could make a pronouncement to that effect. If the State in question persisted in its refusal to remedy the violation the Council was required to 'take or order such political, economic, or military action as may be deemed necessary to protect the rights of man'.

---

[4] Preface, p. vi.

[5] The text of the International Bill of Rights appears in Hersch's book at pp. 69–74.

[6] These were ideas that Hersch had in mind at least a decade previously when he prepared a draft of the Peace Act. See p. 72 above.

The version originally submitted to the publishers also contained a substantial appendix of extracts from various national Bills of Rights. But, some months later, Hersch decided to withdraw this appendix on the basis that it 'is not in keeping with the character of the book and is, to a substantial extent, misleading'. He was firm in his position: 'I fear I cannot reconsider my decision in this matter.'[7]

When the draft reached the AJC, the Director of its Overseas Department, Max Gottschalk, sent Hersch several pages of detailed suggestions[8] to which Hersch replied on 11 December 1944 when revising the proofs, accepting some but not all.[9] In the end, the published text of the Bill of Rights differed little from the text produced by Hersch at the end of 1943. The book was published in June 1945 but not before Hersch was obliged to make strong representations to the AJC over 'the liberties' which the editor at Columbia University Press took with the text:

The Reader (or Editor) is entitled to his views in the matter of elegance or clarity of style – these are often a matter of taste – but it is clear that the author cannot delegate to another person any part of what must be his own – the author's responsibility. I have now had to expend a great deal of time and patience in restoring many passages of the book to their original wording. In view of what has taken place I should make it clear that it is a condition of the publication of the book that all the corrections which I have made in the galley proof should be rigidly adhered to.[10]

Hersch remained, however, disturbed by a sentence in the publisher's blurb on the dust jacket stating that 'the book leaves no stone unturned in stating the case for establishing' an international bill of rights. Hersch protested that:

Such a sentence is, of course, the very thing that ought to have been avoided. It suggests that the book is propaganda and not an impartial inquiry.

He suggested that, if the book was sent to England, a new dust jacket should be printed and offered to bear the expenses of the new cover.[11] Hersch thought it necessary to add in a separate letter:

[7] HL to Dr Gottschalk of the AJC, 11 December 1944.
[8] Gottschalk to HL, 4 May 1944.
[9] In the meantime, Hersch had been in touch with H. G. Wells, noting that Wells had given a talk at the Churchill Club on the Natural Rights of Man and asking whether Wells might lend him a copy (18 April 1944, University of Iowa Library, Iowa City). No reply has been found. Wells had been interested in the subject for a number of years, having participated in a meeting sponsored by the National Peace Council held on 12 March 1940 on 'The Basic Principles of a New World Order' (*ibid.*).
[10] HL to Dr Gottschalk, 12 December 1944.
[11] HL to Dr Simon Segal, Acting Director of Overseas Department of the AJC, 17 July 1945.

Perhaps I ought to warn you that this is a kind of book which draws upon itself almost uniformly adverse criticism. It will be assailed by the orthodox as going too far; by the progressive as being too conservative and evasive; by the lawyers as being revolutionary; by the laymen as being too legalistic; and so on. I will take all this philosophically and I hope that you will do the same.[12]

The AJC enlisted the help of a public relations firm to give the work publicity in the American media. And, of course, the book was soon reviewed in major legal periodicals.

The *AJIL* carried a major review by Philip Jessup. He began by drawing attention to the fact that the manuscript of the book was completed in the autumn of 1943, which permitted only a page reference to the Dumbarton Oaks proposals and meant that the significant advances in the recognition of human rights in the Charter of the United Nations were 'not then even on the schedule of future international events'.[13] Jessup continued:

This reviewer penitently acknowledges that if he had had the opportunity to review this gallant book before the San Francisco Conference of the United Nations, he would have classified it among the patterns of Utopia; today it is a useful hand book for officials of foreign offices and governmental representatives on the Preparatory Commissions which, as this review is written, is preparing in London the agenda for the first session of the General Assembly of the United Nations . . . [I]t is not too pessimistic to assert that Professor Lauterpacht's proposals still extend into the future and will not be realised all at once, but he is dealing with a vital current issue. Though one must be on one's guard against millennial relaxation, one can be inspired by the anticipation of revolutionary development . . .

Professor Lauterpacht's great contribution lies in the fact that he has brought the idea [of an international bill of rights] into focus and has elaborated his plan . . . with a quiet and moderate assurance which, in the light of developments, makes the book particularly persuasive.[14]

But Jessup had some critical comments on Hersch's omission of any attempt to redress the legal inferiority of women and the inequalities of aliens. Jessup commented that:

it is perhaps the greatest weakness in the book, being weak by the very effort to lean strongly on the rock of practicality . . . The author's own yielding on certain basic problems in the field of human rights inevitably subjects to attack by the same arguments, the assertion of those rights upon which he thinks there should be no yielding despite political opposition.[15]

---

[12] HL to Dr S. Segal, 17 July 1944.   [13] (1945) 39 *AJIL* 847.   [14] *Ibid.*   [15] *Ibid.*

In the *Harvard Law Review*, there appeared a similarly positive review by another distinguished American international lawyer, Quincy Wright, which concluded thus:

Lauterpacht's volume is a penetrating study recalling in its philosophical breadth and historical learning the classical seventeenth century treatises on the subject. It presents much food for judicial thought, perhaps blazing a pathway from the sterility of nineteenth century positivism.[16]

More critical, but ultimately and equally approving, were the observations of Herbert Briggs, Professor at Cornell Law School:

It is to be feared that the author's attempt to revivify the thoroughly discredited concepts and terminology of natural law and inherent natural rights of man will deny him the wide hearing his proposals should have.

Briggs' view was that:

no concepts of natural rights are necessary to justify the proposals of the author... the rights [in question] will stand or fall on their merits – or, perhaps, their feasibility.[17]

The book appeared at almost the same time as the drafting of the United Nations Charter was completed at the San Francisco Conference on 26 June 1945. This document contained important provisions on human rights to which Hersch ascribed a fundamental law-creating role. The Preamble spoke of reaffirming 'faith in fundamental human rights'; the purposes included the promotion and encouragement of 'respect for human rights and for fundamental freedom for all without distinction as to race, sex, language or religion'; the General Assembly was required to assist 'in the realisation of human rights and fundamental freedoms for all without distinction as to race, sex, language, or religion';[18] the UN was to 'promote . . . universal respect for and observance of human rights and fundamental freedoms for all';[19] the Members pledged themselves to take joint and separate action 'for the achievement of these purposes';[20] the Economic and Social Council was specifically authorised to make 'recommendations for the purpose of promoting respect for, and observance of, human rights and fundamental freedom for all and to prepare draft conventions for submission to the General Assembly with respect to matters falling within its competence';[21] an international trusteeship system was to be established, one of the objectives of which

---

[16] (1944–5) 58 *Harvard Law Review* 1266–7.   [17] (1945–6) 31 *Cornell Law Review* 255–6.
[18] Article 13.   [19] Article 55.   [20] Article 56.   [21] Article 62.

was to encourage respect for human rights and fundamental treaties within such territories.[22]

An anonymous reviewer in the *American Bar Association Journal* had concluded by observing that Hersch 'could render a vast service by re-surveying the whole subject in the present tense with the Charter and the Statute before him'.[23] Within a very few months of the publication of the book, Hersch was at work on a revised second edition to take into account the developments that had occurred in the meantime, principally with the UN Charter. However, Columbia University Press was not willing to move so soon to a second edition without a further subsidy and the AJC was not prepared to give it. Hersch dropped the idea for the time being.[24]

Under the umbrella of the Economic and Social Council, there was soon set up a Commission on Human Rights to be assisted by a Division of Human Rights. A drafting committee of the Commission was charged with the preparation of a preliminary draft of an International Bill of Rights on the basis of a documented outline prepared by the Division. From then on, Hersch appears to have been left out of the many activities in the UN and the British Government. These, he felt, were not going in the direction he favoured. He took the view that attention should be given first to the development of machinery for the enforcement of the basic rights. He felt that further elaboration of the actual rights could follow later. So it was that he was left to assert his own views through non-governmental means. Even so, in the opinion of Professor Brian Simpson, the author of the most substantial history of the evolution of international protection of human rights:

[T]he real importance of Lauterpacht's Bill and his commentary upon it lies not so much in the particular proposals he made, but in his skilful and realistic analysis of the problems involved in the enterprise, and in the intellectual quality of the discussion. The American movement certainly produced, as the American Law Institute's *Statement of Essential Human Rights*, an impressive draft Bill, but nothing produced in the USA provided anything comparable in quality to Lauterpacht's analytical treatment of the subject.[25]

When it came, from 1946 onwards, to selecting a British representative to sit on the UN Human Rights Commission, Hersch's name was amongst those being considered – most of them distinguished academics, but only

---

[22] Article 76.   [23] (1945) 31 *American Bar Association Journal* 531.
[24] See also pp. 262–4 below.
[25] A. W. B. Simpson, *Human Rights and the End of Empire* (Oxford: Oxford University Press, 2001), p. 207.

four of them international lawyers. Beckett, the then Legal Adviser of the Foreign Office, firmly opposed Hersch's appointment in a minute of quite surprising content:

I think Professor Lauterpacht would be a very bad candidate . . . It would be disastrous, I think, to make him the delegate. Professor Lauterpacht, though a distinguished and industrious international lawyer, is, when all is said and done, a Jew recently come from Vienna. Emphatically, I think that the representative of HMG on human rights must be a very English Englishman imbued throughout his life and hereditary [*sic*] to the real meaning of human rights as we understand this in this country.[26]

The minute was regrettable both in content and in tone. The reference to Hersch being Jewish was most likely intended to pander to the known anti-Semitism of the then Foreign Secretary, Ernest Bevin. The statement that Hersch was 'recently come from Vienna' was wrong. Hersch had by then already been in England for twenty-three years and had been naturalised some fifteen years previously. The suggestion that Hersch was not 'imbued to the real meaning of human rights as we understand this in this country' entirely disregarded the fact that Hersch was the only person who had up till then surveyed British constitutional law and practice in terms of the protection of human rights in the form of a substantial chapter in *The International Bill of Human Rights*.[27]

The end result of excluding Hersch and the several other respectable lawyers who could have been chosen in his stead was that the selection fell upon one of Bevin's cronies, Charles Dukes, a former trade union organiser who had been General Secretary of the National Union of General and Municipal Workers, a Chairman of the Trades Union Congress and for a while a Member of Parliament, but who had had no experience of international negotiations. As Professor Simpson, who has set out the lamentable story in detail, has observed:

So it was that the United Kingdom came to be represented by a retired trade unionist, whose mind was unencumbered by the least knowledge of international law . . . Thus did the Foreign Office exhibit its commitment to the cult of the gifted amateur.[28]

---

[26] Quoted in *ibid.*, p. 350.
[27] Chapter v on 'National Rights in British Constitutional Law and Political Theory', pp. 54–65.
[28] A. W. B. Simpson, *Human Rights and the End of Empire* (Oxford: Oxford University Press, 2001), pp. 350–2.

From the outset, the Foreign Office approached the work of the UN Human Rights Commission in restrictive terms. It opposed the suggestion that the Commission had any power to consider and react positively to the many petitions regarding violation of human rights that were soon sent to it – this for the reason that it read Article 2(7) of the Charter, which prohibited intervention in matters falling within the domestic jurisdiction of members, as excluding any action by the Commission in the absence of a convention specifically authorising such action. For the Foreign Office (and Beckett in particular), elaboration of the substantive content of a bill of rights must precede any consideration of modes of supervision and enforcement.

Hersch's contrary view was asserted from unofficial sidelines, through active participation in the work of the International Law Association and lectures at The Hague Academy[29] in the summer of 1947.[30] In September, he opened the discussion on human rights at the ILA Conference in Prague.[31] He was appointed *rapporteur* of a committee under the chairmanship of Lord Porter to report on the legal effects of the Charter on human rights, on the powers and constitution of the Human Rights Commission and on the content and enforcement of an international bill of rights. A draft of his report was available by February 1948, and was discussed within the Foreign Office; the UN Secretariat circulated the preliminary Report in May and the final version was discussed at the ILA Conference in Brussels on 31 August 1948.

Hersch's argument was that the UN Charter by itself was sufficient to place legal obligations upon Members and the UN itself, thus taking the subject out of the limitations imposed by Article 2(7) of the Charter. Human rights did not need to be further defined before being open to enforcement by the Human Rights Commission. He was emphatic in opposing the production of a mere declaration which he saw as a 'retrogressive step'. He had, indeed, already written to *The Times* in June 1947 opposing the idea of a declaration and urging that more time should be taken over the drafting of the Bill itself:

HL to the Editor of *The Times*, 26 July 1947
During the greater part of June a committee of the United Nations Commission on Human Rights were engaged in drafting an International Bill of Human Rights.

---

[29] Described in detail by Simpson, *ibid.*, pp. 354–7.   [30] (1947) 70 *Hague Recueil* 5–105.
[31] ILA, *Report of the Forty-Second Conference, September 1947* (London, 1948), pp. 13–63.

The present intention of the majority of the drafting committee seems to be that, after the Governments of all the United Nations have been given the opportunity to submit observations, a Declaration of Human Rights should be laid in 1948 for adoption by the General Assembly; that the declaration should be in the nature of a manifesto as distinguished from a binding and enforceable legal obligation; and that, if agreement can be reached at some future date, it should be followed by more specific conventions. I venture, Sir, to express the hope that careful consideration will be given to the matter before the organs of the United Nations commit themselves either to the substance of these proposals or to the date of their execution. It is doubtful whether an adequate Bill of Rights can be produced within the time contemplated. For this is not only a most difficult subject of codification of existing law. It is to a large extent a piece of international legislation. Unless the Bill is to be a mere statement of generalities or unless its clauses are to be reduced to the lowest common denominator, it must imply some changes, voluntarily consented to, in the law and practice of States.

The discussions held so far have revealed the vast complexity of the problems involved. There is agreement that the Bill must include personal rights of freedom and of equality before the law – such as security from arbitrary arrest, fair trial before independent courts, and freedom of speech, religion, association, and assembly. However, the extent to which most of these rights may be regarded as general principles of law is controversial. They all raise wider questions of jurisprudence and political philosophy, in particular the necessity of the limitation of all rights by the rights of other members of the community and by considerations of the welfare of the State, including the temporary suspension of the ordinary law. They also raise the question whether the Bill of Rights ought to remain a one-sided declaration of the claims of the individual without any reference to the duties which he owes to the State. These are not questions which can be rapidly solved by mere competence of drafting. They involve the weighty issue of the relation of man and State – the abiding problem of all law and government.

There is even less agreement with regard to another category of rights – the right to government by the consent of the governed, a right without which all the others tend to become precarious and illusory. To what extent shall that right to political freedom be recognised and endowed with safeguards which, upon final analysis, amount to an international guarantee of constitutional government? The implications of a proposal of this kind are alarming, and many will dismiss it as wholly impracticable. Yet there are others who regard some such guarantee as the hard core of the Bill.

No less intricate are the problems raised by the economic and social rights. These include the right to work under proper conditions, to education, to equality of economic opportunity, and to social security. They are a subject of some novelty when contrasted with the French Declaration of 1789 or with the American Bill of Rights. But claims to 'freedom from want' are widely considered to be no less compelling than rights of personal freedom and of political liberty. The interest of Soviet Russia in the International Bill of Human Rights has been stated to lie particularly in this sphere. How far is it feasible to incorporate these claims in an enforceable Bill of Rights?

These questions cannot be readily solved by the art of skilful compromise at meetings of committees. The same applies to the no less crucial problem of enforcement. There will be objection in many quarters to the idea of fulfilling the promise of a Bill of Rights by means of a declaration binding only in the sphere of conscience. In so far as the existing provisions of the Charter amount to some – though controversial – measure of legal obligation and enforcement, a mere declaration of principles would be in the nature of a retrogression.

It is surely desirable that no attempt should be made, in this period of uncertainty and turmoil, to hasten unduly the drafting and the adoption of the Bill of Human Rights of Man and that ample time should be left for further discussion and study. This is pre-eminently an enactment in relation to which bodies other than Governments should be given the opportunity of forming and expressing their views. The Bill should be the product of the best efforts of statesmen and scholars in the fields of jurisprudence and of the political and social sciences. It might be greater in historic achievement if it materializes in 1950 rather than in 1948.[32]

His letter was supported by one signed on behalf of the ILA by Lord Porter[33] who urged the appointment of a full-time Human Rights Council to investigate petitions, make enquiries on the spot, publish the results of its investigations and, if violations were found, to make recommendations to the State concerned.

In August Hersch was in Czechoslovakia, at Mariánské Lázně, having a rest before going on to Prague for the meeting of the ILA. Even so, he wrote that he was feeling:

physically and mentally very down and out. The cumulative result of sleeplessness is beginning to tell – I simply dread the night . . . Psychologically I am in danger of reaching a stage of doubting whether all this was – or is – worth while, but I shall not give up without a fight![34]

The 'all this' to which he was referring was his struggle to secure recognition for his approach to human rights, on which he was about to present

[32] *The Times*, 26 July 1947.   [33] *The Times*, 29 July 1947.
[34] HL to EL, 30 August 1947.

261

a report to the Prague session of the ILA. On the whole, he did not find Czechoslovakia comfortable, rationing was still prevalent, the cost of living was high, and the hotels were badly run and very expensive.[35]

Hersch pressed his case further, for example, at the conference of the European Movement held in Brussels in 1949 and again when he read a paper on 'The Proposed European Court of Human Rights' at a meeting of the Grotius Society in February 1949. But the fact remained that he was left out of the mainstream discussions and developments of a subject that he had made specially his own; and this was undoubtedly a disappointment to him.

In the meantime, he pressed on with the preparation of a revised and enlarged version of the 1945 book which eventually appeared in 1950 under the title of *International Law and Human Rights*.[36] During the autumn of 1947, there was some discussion between him and the AJC about the possibility of further sponsorship of the book by the Committee. Hersch's work continued intermittently during 1948. (As can be seen in other chapters, in 1948 he was heavily involved in a number of other matters.) He observed, however, to Kamal Das, one of his former research students at Cambridge, by then employed in the Human Rights Division of the UN, that:

I fear the book which I am writing will not be to the liking of the Human Rights Commission because it is rather critical of some of its decisions and of the Declaration of Human Rights which is about to be adopted.[37]

In December, when thanking Das for his help in sending documents from New York, he said:

One must be very careful in disapproving of the work to which many devoted years of hard effort, but it is clear to me that the Declaration does not carry things further and that in some important respects it has put the clock back. We shall have to make a new start.[38]

Despite the detailed discussions between Hersch and the AJC about further sponsorship by the AJC of the new book, which had come close to agreement, all of a sudden he had a change of mind and wrote to Dr Segal of the AJC suggesting that it should no longer be involved with the book.

---

[35] As reported by RL to EL, 3 September 1947.
[36] It was published by Stevens & Sons in England, and was reprinted in the US in 1968 by Archon Books.
[37] HL to K. Das, 21 November 1948.   [38] HL to K Das, 16 December 1948.

HL to Dr S. Segal, 23 December 1949

I feel now that I ought to suggest to you that we ought to abandon the project. The book has assumed a form and a character very much different from what was originally intended. Apparently it will be a treatise covering about six or seven hundred pages. Moreover, in particular with regard to the Universal Declaration of Human Rights, it is highly controversial and very much outspoken. For that reason it will be certainly frowned upon by the Commission on Human Rights and by the Human Rights Division. Undoubtedly, the AJC could not be held to be responsible for what is said in the book. But, clearly, it would have some responsibility for the publication and that fact might make its relations with the organs of the United Nations somewhat difficult in the future.

Dr Segal replied on 3 July 1950 regretting the change in plan but expressing understanding of the reasons which prompted Hersch's decision. But in April Hersch, having by then learned that the book would not exceed 480 pages and having re-read the passages concerning the United States, said that he was not as sure as he was before that they would embarrass the Committee:

I do not want you to think that I attempted, without good reason, to get out of an agreement as to which we mutually agreed.

So he renewed the offer to the AJC to have the book published under its auspices. But the Committee did not respond, and, when the book appeared in May, the preface contained no reference to the Committee.

International Law and Human Rights, as it appeared in 1950, was much more than a second edition of the 1945 book. The new book, as stated in its preface, had three purposes: first, to analyse the legal effects of the human rights provisions in the UN Charter and the relevant practice of its organs; secondly, to re-examine the question of an international bill of rights of man in light of the initial efforts of the UN to give substance to the idea; and, thirdly, to present afresh the wider problem of the subjects of international law. This third aspect drew heavily upon the 1945 volume. He also thought it desirable to discuss in a general way development of a regional solution in the form of the proposed European Court and Commission of Human Rights.

This is not the place to pursue Hersch's detailed analysis of the UN Declaration and of the emerging European instruments. The outcome of both initiatives lay in the future in the European Convention for the Protection of Human Rights which, though signed in 1950, did not enter into force until September 1953, and in the two UN Conventions on Economic, Social and Cultural Rights and on Civil and Political Rights of 1966.

Hersch did not live to see the emergence of the two UN Conventions or to observe the development of the procedures for their implementation. Nor could he have foreseen the extent to which the European development as it already appeared in 1950 would subsequently grow in character and scale. But the role which Hersch's pioneering work in 1945 and then in 1950 played in these developments was clearly considerable and was recognised, notably by Lord Kilmuir (formerly Sir David Maxwell Fyfe) who, as Lord Chancellor, said in his letter of condolence to me: 'I had the good fortune to have your father's personal help when I was preparing the European Convention of Human Rights.'[39]

[39] Lord Kilmuir to EL, 9 May 1960.

CHAPTER 9

THE YEARS OF PRACTICE, 1945–1950

1945

With the ending of the war, Hersch moved on to what may be called his 'years of practice' – activity that occupied much of his time until 1950 when, for tax reasons, he formally retired from the Bar. As will be seen, the addition of practice did not involve any lessening of his academic work in the university or in writing. It simply put him under greater pressure, to much of which he responded eagerly. The idea of being called on to provide specialist advice on important matters and to give a practical slant to his work gave him great satisfaction. And he was also able to turn much of the practical output into published material.

In the early months of 1945, Hersch was busy on Volume 1 of the sixth edition of *Oppenheim*,[1] on taking his book on recognition out of cold storage and on editing the *BYIL*. There also seems to have been quite a bit of social activity. In acknowledging the gift of a book, Figgis, *From Gerson to Grotius*, he indicated that he intended to give a public lecture in the university to mark the tercentenary of the death of Grotius – 'a lecture which will be to a very large extent a comparison of the Grotian and Machiavellian traditions.'[2]

HL to EL, 21 February 1945
I found Figgis slightly superficial – plausible is perhaps the right word – in his remarks on the immorality of statesmen. He reproves Lord Acton for being too dogmatic in the matter. He, Figgis, does not condone that immorality, but, he says, we must never forget that statesmen are exposed to very great temptations! Still, it is a scholarly book and a most useful one. Many thanks.

In other letters, he showed increasing concern over the Trinity entrance scholarship examination that I was to take in March.

HL to EL, 15 February 1945
I also hope that you are not getting unduly worried about the exam. In my experience the only justifiable cause for worry is the consciousness that we are

---

[1] *Oppenheim*, vol. 1 (6th edn, 1947) (preface dated October 1946).
[2] This eventually developed into his major article on 'The Grotian Tradition in International Law' (1946) 23 *BYIL* 1–53. Reprinted in *Collected Papers*, Vol. 2, pp. 307–65.

not doing our best. But I am sure that you do and that you remember not only the famous adage about 'you can not serve etc.' but also the equally important one: *tempus fugit*. The next four weeks and the amount of concentration and persistence you can muster will decide many things.

HL to EL, 26 February 1945

One piece of advice (which I think I have already given you . . .): remember that they judge scholarship candidates not only on the amount of knowledge they show, but also – perhaps mainly – on what they call 'promise'. The latter means the grasp of the general rather than of the particular. So, Sir, concentrate on the general aspect – if you know what I mean.

The outcome was obviously of great importance to him.

HL to EL, 2 March 1945

I have to go to the commemoration dinner on the 16th.[3] I am already glorying in the vision of you and I proceeding <u>together</u> to the commemoration dinner in March 1946. This is the feast to which scholars are invited.

HL to EL, 4 March 1945

I want you to remember that this is a <u>trial</u> run. You are doing your best not to make it a bad failure which reflects badly on the family name. But you must not treat it as if it were the real thing. Relax, boy; take it easy; stay loose. Above all, keep your temper and [do] not risk another rooming.[4]

By the end of March, the crisis was over – the scholarship was won. Hersch relaxed and, with Rachel, went off to Sidmouth for a few days of recuperation, of course much cheered by the approaching end of the war with Germany.

As the hostilities in Europe drew to an end and the full scale of the Holocaust became increasingly apparent, Hersch came to accept that there was little hope of the survival of his family in Poland. Of this, Rachel wrote in a letter to me dated 12 May 1945: 'Daddy does not say much. He never displays much emotion.' But, as will be seen, 1946 brought him some more cheering news – that his niece, Inka, the only daughter of his sister, Sabka, was alive.

In May Hersch was expressing his pleasure at the fact that I would be receiving an additional leaving scholarship from Harrow and would thus be reducing the extent of his contribution to my first year expenses. However, his letter included the admonition that 'we must have a long talk when you are here about your work next year. I am not sure that

---

[3] The annual commemoration of benefactors in Trinity.
[4] Confinement to one's room – a punishment for a minor infraction of discipline at Harrow.

we have thrashed it out thoroughly. Yet I feel strongly that it is that first year which will be decisive in many ways.' He never let up! For him, life was an unending series of mountain ranges; no sooner was one scaled than others, higher, appeared on the horizon, each to be conquered in its turn.

The same letter gave some indication of his future plans:

HL to EL, 20 May 1945

My lectures are now over. The examinations will begin this week, and I shall be busy with them for three weeks. I must then get on with Recognition and have it ready for the printer in August. And I must get rid by that time of Oppenheim. In a sense next year will be also of importance for me for I shall start then on my own text-book. If I am lucky, I ought to finish it in two years – so that I can start later on the bigger treatise in 2–3 volumes.

Of course, he could not at that moment have foreseen the amount of time that he would have to spend during the rest of the year on assistance to the Attorney-General in the Nuremberg trial and the Joyce case. Very sadly, he never got round to the writing of his own text book.[5]

He returned six days later to his series of instructions for me. I had expressed some interest in the Elizabethan Parliamentarian, Peter Wentworth:

HL to EL, 26 May 1945

As to Peter Wentworth. Nothing would please me more than an article by you, while you are still an undergraduate, on this subject. I suggest:
  (a) read Neale's article twice or thrice, study his method, and his article at your finger tips.
  (b) read similarly everything else on PW.
  (c) make a note of any points which occur to you.
  (d) make yourself as familiar as possible with the period.
  (e) when you are in Cambridge read as much as possible in the Univ. Library of the literature of, and on, the period with the view to discovering all that is relevant.
  (f) go out for long walks and think about it.

This is enough for the time being.

HL to EL, 3 June 1945

I am writing in connection with your intended Essay for the Illustrated News or whatever it may be. By all means do it. <u>But</u> do not prejudice your chances by sending it something in a hurry. If the first attempt is rejected by the Editor you

---

[5] But see the *Collected Papers*, which reprint his articles according to the scheme that he had prepared for the book.

will find it difficult to make him look at your things again. Accordingly, treat what you thought is the final thing as a mere draft. Improve it and rewrite it even if it means a week's delay.

Even during the darkest days of the war, Hersch had been applying himself to the question of responsibility for war crimes and the punishment of war criminals. Some of this work was originally academic in character. He had taken over from McNair the editing of the second volume of *Oppenheim*, and had produced the fifth edition already in 1935. In 1940, he published the sixth edition, and in 1944 the seventh edition. Part of his preface to this latter edition may be recalled here:

The last edition – the sixth revised edition – of this volume appeared in 1944. As I pointed out in the Preface to that edition, the latter was in a sense of a provisional nature for the reason that it was not feasible at that time to incorporate in the volume the developments which had taken place during the Second World War. These developments, as well as those which occurred after the War, I have attempted to embody in the present volume. They include, especially in the first Part – which covers the subject of disputes – the changes necessitated by the establishment of the United Nations. In the part devoted to rules of warfare, the account and analysis of the new developments are based, to a considerable extent, on the record of the violations of the law of war by Germany and her allies and of the decisions of the various war crimes tribunals which were called upon to adjudicate upon them. The stature of those tribunals is bound to grow with the passage of time and their judgments will be increasingly regarded as a weighty contribution to International Law and justice. These judgments – perhaps more than anything else – give a complexion of reality to any attempt at a scientific exposition of the law of war, which never before in history was so widely and so ruthlessly disregarded as in the Second World War. In that perspective the occasional criticisms of these courts as having been tribunals set up by the victor acting as judge in his own cause must be deemed to be of limited importance. Finally, both the practice of that War and the fundamental international instruments and enactments have necessitated alterations in and additions to the exposition of the law of neutrality.[6]

In January 1942, a semi-official body was initiated by nine of the governments of the States occupied by Germany in Europe which came to be known as the Inter-Allied Commission on the Punishment of War

---

[6] *Oppenheim*, vol. II (7th edn, 1952), p. vi.

Crimes.[7] They also then set up the Cambridge 'International Commission for Penal Reconstruction and Development' of which McNair was made chairman. Hersch, a member of this Commission, prepared a report for it on superior orders,[8] which was the most controversial part of its work.

During the First World War, the rule, as expressed in Chapter 14 ('The Laws and Usages of War on Land') of the British *Manual of Military Law*, was that military personnel acting upon superior orders were not criminally liable for offences committed under such orders with that liability falling only on the superior. Hersch questioned the rule, observing that it was at variance both with the principle proclaimed by the 1919 Commission on Responsibilities and with the corresponding principles of English criminal and constitutional law. He set out two principles: one was that the clearly illegal nature of the orders as intelligible to any person of ordinary understanding by reference to generally acknowledged principles of international law should render the fact of superior orders irrelevant; on the other hand, such a degree of compulsion as must be deemed to exist in the case of a soldier or officer exposing himself to danger of death as the result of a refusal to obey an order, should exclude *pro tanto* the responsibility of the accused. In Hersch's view,

> the result of the combination of those two principles will be, at the one end, that a person obeying an obviously unlawful order the refusal to obey which would not put him in immediate jeopardy, will not be able to shield himself behind the excuse of superior orders. At the other end, a person obeying an illegal order which is not on the face of it unlawful and disobedience to which would expose him to the full rigours of military discipline, may fully rely on the plea of superior orders. There will be a variety of intermediate situations between these two extremes.[9]

The *History of the UN War Crimes Commission* notes that:

> the above consideration met with the general approval of the Commission and of the various Governments.[10]

This led to the revision in 1944 of paragraph 443 of the *Manual of Military Law* to read:

---

[7] See UN War Crimes Commission, *The History of the United Nations War Crimes Commission* (London: United Nations War Crimes Commission, 1948), p. 89.

[8] *Ibid.*, pp. 266–7. The report was subsequently published as 'The Law of Nations and the Punishment of War Crimes' (1944) 21 *BYIL* 58–95.

[9] See (1944) 21 *BYIL* 73.

[10] UN War Crimes Commission, *The History of the United Nations War Crimes Commission* (London: United Nations War Crimes Commission, 1948), p. 277.

The fact that a rule of warfare has been violated in pursuance of an order of the belligerent Government or of an individual belligerent commander does not deprive the act in question of its character as a war crime; neither does it in principle confer upon the perpetrator immunity from punishment by the injured belligerent. Undoubtedly, a court confronted with the plea of superior orders adduced in justification of a war crime is bound to take into consideration the fact that the obedience to military orders, not obviously unlawful, is the duty of every member of the armed forces, and that the latter cannot, in conditions of war discipline, be expected to weigh scrupulously the legal merits of the order received. The question, however, is governed by the major principle that members of the armed forces are bound to obey lawful orders only and that they cannot therefore escape liability if, in obedience to a command, they commit acts which both violate unchallenged rules of warfare and outrage the general sentiment of humanity.

This change was followed by the appearance of similar provisions in the rules set out by other countries.[11] It was reflected in Article 8 of the Nuremberg Charter for the Trial of the Major War Criminals:

The fact that the defendant acted pursuant to the orders of his Government or of a superior shall not free him from responsibility, but may be considered in mitigation of punishment if the tribunal determines that justice so requires.[12]

However, the reflection is not complete, being limited to mitigation of punishment and not extending to acquittal. The Nuremberg Tribunal referred to the effect of this provision as follows:

The provisions of this Article are in conformity with the law of all nations. That a soldier was ordered to kill or torture in violation of the international law of war has never been recognised as a defence to such acts of brutality, though, as the Charter here provides, the order may be urged in mitigation of the punishment. The true test, which is found in varying degrees in the criminal law of most nations, is not the existence of the order, but whether moral choice was in fact possible.[13]

Following the capitulation of Germany on 8 May 1945, increasingly urgent thought began to be given in many governmental quarters to arrangements for the start of the trials of the major German war criminals. The matter was not being approached for the first time. As early as December 1939, the British Cabinet had decided that evidence should be collected of German breaches of international law.[14] By February 1942, the Law Officers had been authorised to begin investigating the

---

[11] *Ibid.*, p. 282.   [12] 18 *ILR* 222.   [13] *Ibid.*
[14] FO/371/25163, 23 February 1940.

question of German war crimes with a view to assisting the government to decide in due course on its policy and the best method of carrying it out.[15] Between July and December 1942, the Cabinet decided to set up a ministerial committee on the subject. This, in turn, proposed the setting up of a fact-finding commission later in the year. In October 1943, the commission was eventually set up by a resolution of the Allied governments.[16] In these governmental developments Hersch had no direct part, though in August 1942 he had prepared a paper on the defence of superior orders, and his memorandum on 'The Law of Nations and Punishment of War Criminals' was known to the Foreign Office.

Amongst others prominently active in the field were American Jewish organisations anxious to promote the idea that at the trial there should be some Jewish representation and specific, high-level evidence of the manner in which the Nazis had treated the Jews. The idea was canvassed that Dr Weizmann, as the acknowledged leader of the Jewish community worldwide, should be called to give evidence of these atrocities, and attempts were made to persuade Justice Jackson, by then a Justice of the US Supreme Court and previously the US Attorney-General,[17] who had been appointed by President Roosevelt as the chief US prosecutor at Nuremberg, of the desirability of this. Because Hersch had a good relationship with him, he was directly involved in the discussions. But, although Jackson initially accepted the idea, by the time of the opening of the trial it had been dropped. Nonetheless, Jackson devoted a substantial part of his opening speech on 21 November 1945 to a harrowing account of the Nazi conduct and of the personal role of the defendants in it.

On 1 and 29 July 1945, Jackson was in touch with Hersch and visited him to discuss the formulation of the indictment to be presented at the Nuremberg trial.[18]

---

[15] FO/371/30914, 7 February 1942.

[16] For a detailed history of developments, see *The History of the United Nations War Crimes Commission and the Development of the Law of War* (London: United Nations War Crimes Commission, 1948).

[17] See pp. 135-6 above for reference to Hersch's assistance to Jackson in 1941. On 2 January, Jackson wrote to Hersch thanking him for 'the many courtesies of yesterday'.

[18] Jackson was accompanied by his son, his aide, two secretaries and a chauffeur. Rachel gave them all tea, which she was pleased to do because Jackson was 'so delightful'. His son, William E. Jackson, also wrote to Judge Stephen M. Schwebel on 5 May 1999: 'While my memory is far from precise, I can confirm that during the Four Power Negotiations in London in June 1945 concerning the Agreement and Charter for an International Military Tribunal, my father did consult with Professor Lauterpacht in Cambridge and I accompanied him. The subject of discussion, as I recall, was whether a war of aggression was a crime under international law (which was central to my father's position during the London negotiations). I believe that Professor Lauterpacht shared and supported my father's position.'

Robert H. Jackson to HL, 30 May 1945

I have been but briefly in London and hoped to have an opportunity to get in touch with you. I find today that I must leave hurriedly for the States for the closing sessions of the Court, but in something like three weeks I expect to return. I do hope that we can get together and that I can have the benefit of your good judgment and learning on the difficult subjects with which we must deal.

Robert H. Jackson to HL, 23 August 1945

You have been extremely generous in extending courtesies and help to me in sending me your revision of Volume II of Oppenheim and in giving me such a painstaking memorandum on the subject of Definition of War Crimes. As you have probably observed, not all of your suggestions were heeded for various reasons which sometime I hope to have opportunity to discuss with you. But they were at least all considered and all helped to clarify our own thinking on the subject.

After a short trip to the Continent, I shall go back to the United States for a few days and probably then to Nuremberg until the trials are over. But I shall be in London from time to time and will be seeing you again.

It was at these meetings that Hersch put forward the idea of presenting the case against the major war criminals under three principal headings: crimes against the peace; war crimes; and crimes against humanity. Jackson subsequently attributed this formulation to 'an eminent scholar of international law'[19] whom Jackson's son later identified as Hersch.[20]

In August 1945, British officials were considering the composition of the British War Crimes Executive – the body in the UK charged with the preparation and presentation of the prosecution of German war criminals. Two academic names were being considered, Arthur Goodhart, Professor of Jurisprudence at Oxford, and Hersch. The Foreign Office proposed to the Attorney-General, Sir Hartley Shawcross, KC, the selection of Hersch, and this recommendation was accepted. The

[19] See *Report of Robert H. Jackson, United States Representative to the International Conference on Military Trials, London, 1945* (Department of State Publications 3080, Washington DC, 1949), p. 416. In a letter to Jackson of 17 June, 1945, Hersch said: 'I had the opportunity to read the full text of your Report to the President of 7 June. It is, if I may say so, an historic and inspiring document. I hope that it will be acted upon and that the judgments of the Tribunal will be a contribution of enduring value to the cause of justice and of the authority of the law.'

[20] See letter from William E. Jackson, who had been present at the meetings between Justice Jackson and Hersch, to Jacob Robinson, 31 May 1961, HL Archive. The concept of 'crimes against humanity' was not new, but the inclusion of it in the Nuremberg indictment attracted considerable discussion. See also Jacob Robinson, 'Lauterpacht's Contribution to the Development of International Criminal Law', in *Studies in Public International Law in Memory of Sir Hersch Lauterpacht* (Jerusalem, 1961), pp. 84–91 (in Hebrew).

composition of the Executive was eventually announced on 15 September 1945. It included Sir David Maxwell Fyfe, who had been Attorney-General in the previous government, as well as Sir Frank Soskice, KC, the Solicitor-General.[21]

The Agreement for the prosecution of the major war criminals had already been concluded on 8 August 1945. Shortly afterwards, Hersch wrote in some detail to Patrick Dean, one of the Foreign Office legal advisers, enclosing an extract from the forthcoming edition of Volume I of *Oppenheim*, on the criminal responsibility of states, that was intended to anticipate and rebut any suggestion that the terms of Article 6 of the Charter of the International Military Tribunal were an innovation.

HL to Patrick Dean, 20 August 1945
I am a bit late in sending you the paragraph on Criminal Responsibility of States from the forthcoming edition of volume I of Oppenheim. As you will see, it has a direct bearing on Article 6 of the Charter of the International Military Tribunal. Its purpose is to show: (a) that there is in international law such a thing as criminal responsibility of States; (b) that the criminal responsibility of States means criminal responsibility of the individuals who are the organs of the State; and (c) that the initiation of a war of aggression can properly be regarded as the principal instance of an international criminal act.

The main criticism which the Government may have to meet in this matter will be that (c) – as accepted in Article 6(a) of the Agreement – is an innovation. The paragraph which I am sending you shows that it is not so (see, in particular, footnote 2 on p. 1). The General Treaty for the Renunciation of War not only rendered aggressive war unlawful; it condemned it and thus created the basis for a declaration that aggressive war is not only unlawful, but also criminal. It is very important that full use should be made in this connection of the General Treaty for the Renunciation of War – a universal treaty solemnly subscribed to by Germany, Italy and Japan. The legislative character, if any, of the Agreement of August 8, 1945, consists in the acceptance of the principle – which is an unavoidable principle if the law is not to be reduced to an absurdity – that the agency which commits a criminal act is not the abstract mystical entity of the State; but human beings who plan and execute the crime. There is, therefore, on sound principle no element of retroactivity either in expressly declaring an aggressive war to be a criminal act or in fixing that responsibility upon the individual human agents. Undoubtedly, as there is no legislature or obligatory judiciary in international society, these principles do not partake of

---

[21] See *The Times*, 15 September 1945, p. 2. The other members of the Executive besides Hersch were Mr G. D. Roberts, KC; Major Elwyn Jones, KC; Mr E. G. Robey; Major-General Lord Bridgeman; Mr E. J. Passant; Mr P. Dean; Mr George Coldstream; Mr M. E. Reed; Mr R. A. Clyde; and Colonel H. Phillimore.

the clarity or of the finality of an Act of Parliament or of a decision of the House of Lords. Thus you will find occasionally writers who maintain that as the State is sovereign in international law it cannot be criminally responsible – as if there existed any good reason why sovereignty should shield the State from criminal as distinguished from contractual or tortious liability. In so far as the Agreement of August 8, 1945, helps to remove these principles from the realm of controversy, it is a wise and necessary legislative act of a declaratory character.

Paragraph (c) of Article 6 of the Agreement – Crimes against humanity – is clearly an innovation. It is a fundamental piece of international legislation affirming that international law is not only the law between States but also the law of mankind and that those who transgress against it cannot shield themselves behind the law of their State or the procedural limitations of international law. The principal part of paragraph (c), namely, its first sentence is very wide indeed; it is not limited by the somewhat vague qualifications to which the crimes enumerated in the second sentence are subject. It will be as well if the four Governments frankly admit that – notwithstanding the doctrine and the various historical instances of humanitarian intervention – all this is an innovation which the outraged conscience of the world and an enlightened conception of the true purposes of the law of nations impel them to make immediately operative.[22]

Once appointed to the British War Crimes Executive, Hersch began to participate actively in its work. On 26 September 1945, he attended a meeting of the Executive in London to consider a number of administrative matters, for example, who were to be admitted to the trial at Nuremberg as observers. The preparation had to be carried out under some pressure. On 4 October 1945, the Attorney-General, when writing to Hersch about the Joyce case,[23] also commented on the difficulties arising in connection with securing agreement on the indictment, and expressed the hope that Hersch could be present at the opening of the case.

Sir Hartley Shawcross to HL, 4 October 1945

May I take the opportunity of referring to the War Criminal trials? We have had very great difficulty in securing agreement on the Indictment, but I think that we have at last done so. I gave instructions that a copy of the last draft should be sent to you for any comments that you might wish to make, but we are having to agree the thing in its final form today. It is not a document that I like at all, and some of the allegations in it will, I think, hardly pass the test of

---

[22] HL to Patrick Dean, 20 August 1945, FO371/51034.
[23] See p. 280 below.

history or, indeed, of any serious legal examination. The difficulties, however, of securing agreement between the four delegations were immense, and we shall just have to make the best of this rather unsatisfactory document. The present time schedule is for the trials to start at Nuremberg on the 10th November. If you could find it possible to be there for a few days at the commencement, I am sure it will be of great assistance to us. I am afraid, however, that I am not in a position to offer any financial remuneration, although the trip would involve no expense so far as you are concerned. I appreciate, also, that the date is in the middle of term, and that you might find it inconvenient to attend. Perhaps you would think it over and let me know in due course.

Hersch had already met Sir Hartley, having on 21 August received a telegram asking him to call on Sir Hartley at the House of Commons. The subject of the meeting was not indicated in the telegram but in fact it was principally concerned with the assistance that Hersch might give in connection with the Joyce case.[24] It probably also touched on Hersch's views on the approaching Nuremberg trial. From then until the Attorney-General eventually delivered his closing speech at Nuremberg on 26–27 July 1946, Hersch was much taken up with the preparation of drafts for him.

The trial began at Nuremberg on 20 November 1945. The first speech for the prosecution was made by Justice Jackson on 21 November. Hersch was there for the opening,[25] having already assisted Sir Hartley in the drafting of the legal part of his opening speech, but returned to Cambridge on 22–23 November before Sir Hartley gave his speech on 4 December. The return journey was not free of hazards.

HL to RL, 29 November 1945

We had to go from Nuremberg by car to Frankfurt; from there we flew to Brussels in order to go by sea to England. For the weather made flying impossible. In the last moment we were told that we can fly. When we arrived from Brussels over England we could not come down because of the fog. We circled for another [hour] over various places in low cloud, nearly hit a hill, and eventually landed

---

[24] See p. 280 below.

[25] Hersch's presence in Court at the opening of the case was reported in *The Times*, which spoke of the Attorney-General being at the head of 'a remarkably young group of British barristers, strongly reinforced by Professor Lauterpacht, of Cambridge University, an eminent authority on international law'. On 17 December, Hersch sent Rachel a photograph clipped from the *Illustrated London News* showing the Nuremberg defendants in the dock, but including also some of the members of the Executive, Hersch amongst them: 'In case you do not recognise your husband, he is on p. 633, in the bottom left hand picture, seated in the extreme left. You never expected your husband to be photographed with Goering.'

in a small aerodrome near Croydon. But our stomachs and hearts were upset – at least mine – and I had to go to Richards.[26] I think I am all right now.

But that was not the main trouble. Just as I was leaving Nuremberg, I was shown the British case which the Attorney-General was to put next Monday, December 3, and I saw immediately that it was bad to the point of being ridiculous. I told him that immediately – he apparently wrote part of it himself – and he agreed with me and asked me to prepare a new draft. This I have been doing for the last five days and I finished only an hour ago. They sent Mrs Lyons by car here yesterday; I put her up at Miss Cooks; but slaved her there since 9am and they just [fetched] her by car with the finished document. I feel quite exhausted and I am going to drink port tonight in Trinity to celebrate the deliverance.[27]

Sir Hartley Shawcross to HL, 27 November 1945

Many thanks for your letter of the 26th November. I am sorry to hear that you have been seedy. I realise the very heavy pressure under which you are working, and that you may not be able to complete the draft until Thursday. Reed, of my office here, will, if necessary, arrange to meet your secretary at Liverpool Street, so that the draft may be brought straight to me, and I will work on it all Thursday night.

I have already made a complete redraft of Part 2, cutting out practically all the quotations and many of the references to documents altogether. This morning I have had a talk with Passant about the redraft, and he is kindly working on it and will provide me with his own emendations by tomorrow evening, so that I can work on the final draft tomorrow night.

We do not yet quite see how we are going to cope with the mechanical problem of translating and duplicating the speech, but no doubt we shall manage somehow.

Meanwhile, my very best thanks for all that you are doing.

Sir Hartley Shawcross to HL, 30 November 1945

Thank you so much for the drafts which you sent me of Parts 1 and 3 for the Nuremberg speech. With some changes of language to avoid too obvious a change of styles between the middle and the beginning and end of the speech, I have embodied most of your material in the opening, although a good deal of your Part 3 I have brought forward to Part 1. What I have not used, mainly because of the time factor, and some matters which I wished to introduce myself, we shall employ in the final speech. I want to tell you how very greatly I appreciate all the help you have so generously given in this matter.

---

[26] Dr Harry Richards was at that time his Cambridge physician.

[27] Rachel had by then left for Palestine to visit her ageing parents. Due to various difficulties regarding return travel, she did not return to Cambridge till March 1946.

HL to RL, 30 November 1945
Nuremberg was an unforgettable experience. The day of Jackson's opening speech was packed with emotion. It was a great satisfaction to watch the faces of the accused when Jackson was unfolding the story of the Jewish atrocities. It was a historic speech which lasted a day and a great personal triumph for Jackson. I shook [him] by the hand for a long minute. My table was at a distance of about 15 yards from the accused. The Times gave me a good 'write up'. It said: The British team of prosecutors has been strongly reinforced by Professor Lauterpacht, of Cambridge University, an eminent authority on international law. It was an unforgettable experience to see, for the first time in history, a sovereign State in the dock.

On 4 December 1945, Sir Hartley Shawcross, as the chief prosecutor for the United Kingdom, delivered his opening speech at Nuremberg on the second count of the indictment – the count dealing with the planning and waging of a war of aggression. The first part of the speech was largely legal in content, devoted principally to showing that not only was war outlawed, but that to initiate aggressive war was criminal. To assist Sir Hartley in the preparation of this part of his speech, Hersch had been asked to prepare a draft. Amongst Hersch's papers there are some fifty pages of manuscript, which were evidently the basis of the draft that was laid before Sir Hartley.[28] Not all of Hersch's draft was adopted, but it is clear from the text of Sir Hartley's speech as delivered that not only was use made of the legal material in Hersch's draft, but also of many of the phrases. A line-by-line comparison of Hersch's draft with what Shawcross actually said shows that, of the fifteen printed pages of the legal argument, twelve were drawn almost verbatim from Hersch's draft.[29]

On the same day in Cambridge, Hersch gave an open lecture on the trial.

HL to RL, 4 December 1945
I feel rather tired now, but quite satisfied with myself for I gave this morning my public lecture to about 250 law students on the 'Nuremberg Trial. The International Law Aspect'. It was a rather interesting coincidence that exactly about that time the Attorney-General was delivering his speech at Nuremberg and that on many matters we were saying the same thing for I simply used in Cambridge parts of the speech which I prepared for him. Your son was in the audience and I gather that he was pleased. Professor Wade was there;

---

[28] Hersch retained amongst his papers the manuscript draft referred to in this letter. The document remains in the Archive.
[29] The texts of the opening and closing speeches of the four Chief Prosecutors were printed by His Majesty's Stationery Office in 1946 under the authority of the Attorney-General.

Dr Jones from Girton; and other dons. For the time being I am glad I am free of Nuremberg for a spell.

Hersch was particularly pleased by the letter that he received from Dr Ellis Lewis, a Fellow of Trinity Hall and a lecturer in the Law Faculty, who had cancelled his own supervision class in order to be able to attend.

T. Ellis Lewis to HL, 4 December 1945
It is now 11.30pm and time I should be going home, but I feel I cannot leave my rooms here without telling you how much I enjoyed and appreciated your most instructive and interesting lecture of this morning . . .

It was a capital performance, you spoke with conviction, from your head and your heart and with the fairness one expects from a lawyer who knows his subject.

In his closing speech in July 1946, Sir Hartley devoted only sixteen pages to the law and sixty-one pages to the horrific facts of the atrocities committed by the defendants or under their orders. Of the legal part, twelve pages (three-quarters) were drawn from Hersch's draft. It is not difficult to imagine how Hersch must have felt as he read the remaining sixty-one pages reciting facts which included the murder of his own parents, brother and sister. It says a good deal for the strength of his character that he never spoke of it to me, though he may have said something to Rachel, and he never committed his feelings to paper. But his involvement in the proceedings did leave a mark on him. Rachel later recalled that, after his return to Cambridge, he used to cry out awfully in his sleep at the recollection of the bestialities he had heard described.

HL to RL, 13 December 1945
My rush work is over. To-day is the third day of William Joyce's week before the House of Lords and the Attorney-General is helping himself very generously to my three memoranda, and I am settling down to the more prosaic task of dealing with the arrears of the Digest and of the Year Book and of clearing the decks for starting on my own book. However, I have still to deal with Oppenheim.[30]

The same letter illustrated yet again the concern and ambition that Hersch had for my future. It must be borne in mind that at that date I was not yet seventeen and a half!

---

[30] This would have been the sixth edition of Volume 1, published in 1947 (preface dated October 1946).

He has not really settled to work since he came to Trinity and I am much worried about his future. He has done enough work for an ordinary undergraduate, but if he is to continue to be a scholar thinking of an academic career, this is grossly inadequate. If he creates for himself the reputation of an ordinary undergraduate, then he is doomed so far as Trinity is concerned. And I do not know what we shall do with him – or he with himself – if he does not succeed in obtaining some footing in the academic teaching world. The time and the opportunity which he loses are irretrievable. It might be a good thing if you wrote him a long and serious letter on these lines. You might tell him that I am profoundly worried and disappointed.

His assumption that the only career that lay ahead of me was an academic one – though in part prophetic – reflects little awareness of my human right to determine for myself the direction in which I was to go!

During all this time – November and December 1945 – and extending to March 1946, when Rachel was away visiting her elderly parents in Palestine, Hersch was left on his own in the house, doing all the shopping, cooking and even some housework because of the prolonged absence of the daily help. He took it quite cheerfully. On most days, though then living in college, I visited him and we ate together. There was a constant flow of letters to and from Rachel, with Hersch, as usual, giving long-distance advice upon the timing and method of her return home.

HL to RL, 15 December 1945
I am so glad that the parents are well and happy with your visit. I rather compliment myself about having given you the decisive push in the direction of going in November. You – and they – have all my sympathy for the moment when you have to say good-bye to them. But in justice and in reason, it might not be a moment of regret or complaint, but rather of thanksgiving for the way fate has treated them. Please give them my love and respect.

At Christmas, Rachel was still in Palestine. Nonetheless, the holiday was suitably celebrated at Cranmer Road. The lunch was based on a turkey that his farmer friend, Sam Berger, produced. As the neighbours, the Thomases, had no turkey, Hersch insisted on sharing it with them; there was plenty for all.

On the last day of the year, Hersch wrote that he was working on an article to mark the tercentenary of the death of Grotius. This appeared in the *BYIL* in 1946 as 'The Grotian Tradition in International Law'. It was a remarkably rich, learned and perceptive piece that came to be widely acclaimed. Hersch thought it the best thing that he had ever written. He also said that he was preparing shortly to start on his own book, but he never got very far – not because he didn't want to, but simply because too many other demands were made on him that he felt he could not refuse. His hopes that someone in his family in Poland might have survived were briefly revived by a telegram he received from someone in Romania whom he did not know offering to give him some information about his brother's family and asking for his address. In telling Rachel of this, he said: 'I hope that at least the child is alive.'

The closing weeks of 1945, and the opening weeks of 1946, were much taken up with providing Shawcross with assistance in the prosecution of William Joyce for treason. Joyce, who was by origin a US national, had applied for and obtained a British passport with which he had travelled to Germany. There he became an adherent of the Nazis and during the war broadcast Nazi propaganda to Britain. After the end of hostilities, he was captured and indicted in England for treason in that 'owing allegiance to the Crown, he had adhered to the King's enemies'. The basis on which it was claimed that he owed allegiance was his request for a British passport, the holding of it and the consequent entitlement to British protection which it gave him.

On 27 August 1945, Shawcross sent Hersch a note of the position in the case saying that 'he would be most grateful for any assistance which you may be able to give in regard to it'. Hersch responded immediately with a memorandum dated 4 September 1945, of which the manuscript is in the Archive and runs to some twenty-three foolscap pages. Its sections deal with the grant of a passport, the duty of protection and the duty of allegiance; the duty of allegiance of an alien outside the country but leaving here his dependants; locality of the offence and treason; the Treachery Act; the law of England and criminal jurisdiction with regard to acts originating abroad and consummated in England; broadcasting and the locality of the crime; and consequences of the proposed application of the Treachery Act with regard to (a) the potentially large numbers of offenders under the proposed construction of the Act, and (b) international law and the proposed construction of the Act.

The memorandum concluded with a discussion of the possibility of prosecuting Joyce as a major war criminal under the Agreement of 9 August 1945, should the prosecution for treason or under the Treachery Act fail. This idea was not pursued in view of the outcome of the prosecution for treason. The memorandum was acknowledged by Shawcross on 7 September.

Sir Hartley Shawcross to HL, 7 September 1945

I have just received the Memorandum on Joyce which you so kindly prepared for me and I must tell you at once how very grateful I am to you for having gone to such very great trouble in this matter.

I have been so overwhelmed with other work myself that I have simply had no opportunity of getting down to any proper research into the law and your paper will be the greatest possible assistance to me.

The trial is on Thursday. If it should interest you to be present at any part of it please let me know.

This was followed by a further seventeen-page typed memorandum from Hersch dated 1 October 1945 dealing with protective jurisdiction, locality of broadcasting, the issue of a passport to a non-national, diplomatic protection of non-nationals and the duty of allegiance of protected persons.

The following letter from Shawcross to Hersch summarises the situation as it stood after Joyce's conviction at first instance.

Sir Hartley Shawcross to HL, 19 September 1945

As you will have seen from the newspapers, the Judge in the Joyce trial ruled that Joyce was under a duty of allegiance on the 24th August, 1939, when he applied for a British passport, and that nothing that occurred since had terminated that duty. In other words, he held that the allegiance arising from residence was continued by the operation of the passport until the period for which the passport had been issued came to an end.

The case turned mainly upon the nature of the extraterritorial protection resulting from the issue of a passport, and upon this, apart from the Brailsford case, there appears to be almost nothing in the books. When the matter reaches the Court of Criminal Appeal I shall have, if I can, to try to trace the history of passports, the circumstances in which they can be challenged by foreign powers and the extent of the protection which is accorded under them in more detail. In particular, I shall have to establish from the books, if I can, what the situation will be if a person travelling, say, in Spain, under a British passport was denounced by the Spanish as being an American and not a British citizen. In such a case, could he continue to rely upon the British passport, and would the Ambassador and diplomatic officials continue to protect him until the passport had been revoked by the Secretary of State? There is, as far as I have been able to find, extraordinarily little in the books in regard to the position and practice as to passports. The matter was not one on which I thought it would be wise to call evidence, and, in the result, the whole subject is left in a rather vague state.

The defence also took the point that there was, apart from express statutory provision, no jurisdiction to try a foreigner for an offence committed abroad, and they relied upon the Jameson case. It was suggested that it would be an affront to the comity of nations for a State to exercise such a jurisdiction. It seemed to me that this was really begging the question, which must eventually be one of construction of the particular Statute concerned, but I am anxious to find as much authority as I can in regard to the principles underlying the protective jurisdiction which States have exercised over foreigners committing offences abroad which strike at the safety or security of the State.

I did not run the point that the act of broadcasting could be said to have taken place in England, since I came to the conclusion that even if that were so, one would still have to establish that a duty of allegiance was owed by the actor, and I felt that, on the whole, the better course was to rely strongly on the protection theory.

The matter is going to the Court of Criminal Appeal, where I think it will be argued more fully than it was at the Old Bailey, and it may eventually have to go to the Lords. I hesitate to ask again for your assistance, for I know how busy you will be, but if any further ideas occur to you, or if you could suggest any useful lines of research which I might pursue I should be most grateful for your help. The case does, of course, raise an exceedingly difficult, but also, I think, a most important question of municipal law with considerable international repercussions.

P.S. There is, of course, also the important point whether a State has jurisdiction to issue a passport to a non-national?

Hersch responded promptly with a memorandum of which it has not been possible to find the text. It elicited a reply from Shawcross as follows:

Sir Hartley Shawcross to HL, 4 October 1945

Thank you very much for the further memorandum which you have sent me about the Joyce case. The points you raise are formidable ones, and I shall give them very careful consideration. Your memorandum will be a great help in preparing for the next round.

There is one point in regard to which I think my letter of the 19th September to you was not clearly expressed. You refer to it on page 3 of your memorandum. When I said that I felt that 'the better course was to rely strongly on the protection theory', I meant not the protective theory of jurisdiction, but the theory that the duty of allegiance itself depended on the protection of the Crown. I shall, however, develop the points as to the locality of the crime in argument at the appeal.

A further memorandum by Hersch of the same date commented in some detail on some of the cases relied on by the defence at first instance.

Both in the Court of Criminal Appeal and in the House of Lords, Joyce's conviction was upheld.[31] With Shawcross's approval, Hersch gave a lecture on the case in Cambridge in the Lent Term, 1946, which he subsequently published in the *Cambridge Law Journal*.[32] As a final footnote to this article, Hersch added an interesting and, at that time, novel suggestion as follows:

It would be in accordance with an enlightened principle of justice – a principle which has not as yet become part of the law of nations – if, in the absence of effective extradition, the Courts of a State were to assume jurisdiction over common crimes, by whomsoever and wherever committed, of a heinous character. Territoriality of jurisdiction is a rule of convenience in the sphere of the law of evidence. It is not a requirement of justice or even a necessary postulate of the sovereignty of the State.[33]

When the proceedings were printed in the *Famous Trials* series, Shawcross, on 1 July 1946, sent Hersch a copy inscribed on the flyleaf: 'To Professor Lauterpacht, whose assistance contributed so largely to the success of the legal argument.'

1946

Hersch started 1946 feeling worn out – as well he might have been. Although he needed a change and would have liked to go to Hunstanton in January, the weather was too unpleasant and the days too short. Instead, he began drafting the plan for his own text book: 'but I feel tired and the work is very slow.'[34] He continued feeling under the weather: 'I have been trying to do some writing, but I am not making any headway. I feel tired all the time.'[35] But by 12 January he was in Hunstanton, writing to congratulate McNair on his nomination as a candidate for election to the ICJ: 'This is a good thing for the Court and a source of great satisfaction to many.'[36] From there he wrote to Rachel that he

---

[31] The House of Lords decision is reported in [1946] AC 347 and in 15 *ILR* 91.

[32] 'Allegiance, Diplomatic Protection and Criminal Jurisdiction over Aliens' (1945–7) 9 *CLJ* 330. Reprinted in *Collected Papers*, Vol. 3, pp. 221–42. It occasioned a reply by Professor Glanville Williams, a noted criminal lawyer: 'The Correlation of Allegiance and Protection' (1948–50) 10 *CLJ* 54. Hersch had argued that Joyce obtained diplomatic protection by his own voluntary act; this was sufficient to create a duty of allegiance based on the request for and the retention of a British passport. Glanville Williams considered this to be false, arguing that Joyce merely asked for a passport to leave for Germany; 'one can ask for a passport without asking for protection. In Joyce's case, no occasion for protection had arisen, so there was no need for Joyce to ask for it. To say otherwise is to 'create a fiction.'

[33] *Ibid.*, p. 348.   [34] HL to RL, 5 January 1946.   [35] HL to RL, 10 January 1946.
[36] HL to McNair, 12 January 1946.

simply felt 'tired and rather dismal' and contemplated putting himself in the doctor's hands on his return home. 'I cannot go on like this.'[37] But he was pleased to have been elected a member of the Athenaeum. He welcomed a visit from Green H. Hackworth, the Legal Adviser of the US State Department, who later became a judge and President of the ICJ. In his letters to Rachel, Hersch refers constantly to my frequent visits to the house, which made him feel less lonely. But in one of them he shows signs of concern over his financial situation; joining the Athenaeum 'accentuated his "bankrupt situation"'.

By then, Hersch was also able to say that he was getting along well with his work, 'not too energetically, but I am getting by'. Quite a bit of time was being spent trying to deal with housekeeping matters. His anxiety about his health continued.

HL to RL, 4 February 1946
I must do something about my health. Not only have I no sleep at night but recently I am in constant discomfort during the day. I cannot go on much longer like that.

There were additional demands on his time. In the spring he sent the 1945 volume of the *BYIL* to the printer with a view to publication by the end of November. It contained eleven major articles, including one of his own. A little later, McNair commented as follows:

McNair to HL, 31 December 1946
I have read a good deal of the new Year Book. It is as full of meat as an egg. The quality is high, but I am wondering whether we might not try in each number to have one or two entries of high quality but readable by those who without being lawyers follow international affairs with an educated mind.

McNair did not elaborate on this suggestion. There is little reflection in the tables of contents of subsequent volumes of any marked attempt by Hersch to implement it. Indeed, the suggestion ran rather contrary to Hersch's policy of producing a series containing material of high technical quality. He would not have been inclined to pander to the limitations of the layman. The one exception may have been Hersch's own article in the 1946 volume, 'The Grotian Tradition in International Law'. Hersch regarded it as the most important article that he ever wrote, not, I believe, so much because of its strictly legal content but because it was written in terms that would be understood by the non-lawyer, especially as Grotius, regarded as the father of international law,

[37] HL to RL, 4 February 1946.

also affected many areas of international relations. Hersch summarised his analysis in the concluding paragraphs of the article, which are quoted verbatim:

These intrusions of opportunism and realism did not decisively influence the character of *De Jure Belli ac Pacis*. But they are symbolic of the perennial problem with which the science of international law has been confronted almost from the outset. It has been exposed to the inducement to supply a rationalisation of inferior and irrational practices; to confuse, in the name of realism, the function of chronicling events with that of a critical exposition of rules of conduct worthy of the name of law; to furnish a philosophy of second best; and to represent the transient manifestations of immaturity and anarchy in international relations as resulting necessarily and permanently from the nature of States the mutual relations of which, it is said, may be regulated by voluntary co-operation but not by a rule of law imposed and enforced from above. Grotius did not succumb to that tendency. This fact explains much of the influence which he has wielded. For, in the history of political ideals and human progress, it will be found that the attraction of the short cuts of sound realism is matched – and surpassed – by the appeal to faith and to principle.

These then are the principal features of what has here been called the Grotian tradition in international law. They may be conveniently enumerated by way of conclusion. They are: the subjection of the totality of international relations to the rule of law; the acceptance of the law of nature as an independent source of international law; the affirmation of the social nature of man as the basis of the law of nature; the recognition of the essential identity of States and individuals; the rejection of 'reason of State'; the distinction between just and unjust war; the doctrine of qualified neutrality; the binding force of promises; the fundamental rights and freedoms of the individual; the idea of peace; and the tradition of idealism and progress. Some of these elements of the Grotian tradition have now become part of the positive law; others are still an aspiration. But they all explain why Grotius's work has remained an abiding force and not merely an episode, however important, in the literature of international law. They explain why writers and statesmen have turned to Grotius not only as a source of evidence of the law as it is, but also a well-spring of faith in the law as it ought to be. Grotius did not create international law. Law is not made by writers. What Grotius did was to endow international law with unprecedented dignity and authority by making it part not only of a general system of jurisprudence but also of a universal moral code. To many, indeed, it may appear that *De Jure Belli ac Pacis* is more a system of ethics applied to States than a system of law. This would not inevitably imply a condemnation of the work. For it may be held that at that time – as, indeed, at any time – it was important that the relations of States should be conceived and taught as part of ethics as well as part of law. Grotius's great merit is that he performed both tasks in one work. This combination of functions resulted in much methodological confusion offensive to the purist, who is in danger of forgetting that in the seventeenth century eclecticism was as important as systematic accuracy. *De Jure Belli ac Pacis* is pre-eminently a treatise which must be judged by reference to its method, but by its influence of the doctrine and on the practice of the Law of Nations. It satisfied the craving, in jurist and layman alike, for a moral content in the law. In stressing and, on the whole, maintaining the distinction between law and morality, it vindicated the place of the Law of Nations in legal science. Last – but not least – it became identified with the idea of progress in international law.

These considerations may help to answer, to a large extent, the question whether *De Jure Belli ac Pacis* is still a proper medium of study and instruction in international law. The reply is clearly in the negative if what we have in mind is assistance in the search for a legal rule which we may assume an international court would now apply in a case before it. From this point of view most textbooks and treatises are obsolete. But *De Jure Belli ac Pacis* may nevertheless have its uses not only for the legal historian or for the writer or advocate anxious to embellish a quotation or strengthen an argument by reference to a passage from Grotius. It cannot be rewritten or modernised by the simple device of committing quotations from the ancient authorities.[38] To do that, as Whewell did in the abridged version of his translation, is to run the risk of depriving the treatise of one of its characteristic features by reducing it to a body of dry propositions unsupported by the ripe wisdom of antiquity. It is not necessary for the average student to examine the whole of *De Jure Belli ac Pacis*, which ought to disappear, as a mere ornamental item, from reading-lists. But selected portions of the treatise may still be read with advantage as an instance of juridical method typical of the seventeenth century; as a fairly accurate statement, on any given subject, of international law in its formative period; and, above all, as expressive of the various aspects of the Grotian tradition. However, the significance of the subject transcends that of one item in the educational curriculum of international lawyers. In gaining an understanding of the Grotian tradition as a whole – this has been the main object of the present article – we may not only fathom the secret of its influence upon generations of scholars and men of affairs. We may, and that is no less important, obtain an insight into the persistent problems of international law in the past, in the present, and, probably for some long time to come, in the future. It is a measure of the greatness of the work of Grotius that all these questions should have found a place in his teaching and that he should have answered them in a spirit upon the acceptance of which depends the ultimate reality of the Law of Nations as a 'law properly so called'.

With this major contribution out of the way, Hersch then went straight on to complete the *BYIL* volume for 1946. There was much correspondence

---

[38] For an interesting discussion of this and cognate questions, see Sandifer in (1940) 34 *AJIL* 459–72.

between him and S. W. Rowson (later to be known as Rosenne)[39] regarding the latter's work on prize law.

As he and Rachel approached their twenty-third wedding anniversary on 20 March 1946, Rachel, who was visiting her parents in Palestine, wrote him a supportive, rather emotional, letter:

> I have time to think of you and the boy... I have been weighing things in my mind and life has been good to us and we have to be grateful... for the things that have come our way...

> Don't worry about the work. You must not let this work affect your heart and nerves...

> This letter will most probably reach you on 20 March. It is a great day in our partnership. You have all my love and devotion, and I send you my warmest and best wishes for great happiness, good health and yet a greater contribution, if possible, to International Law... I know your work means far more to you than lots of things... more to you than to many men. May you enjoy your work for many, many years and may I stand by you in the future as I did in the past.

Hersch's generosity of spirit is shown by his attitude to A. P. Sereni, a Jewish Italian international lawyer who wanted to leave Italy for the United States. Sereni had written two articles supporting the Italian war against Ethiopia. These led Jenks to be critical of him.

HL to C. W. Jenks, 29 March [1946][40]

Thank you for your letter concerning Sereni. He wrote to me two months ago. I advised him what he has to do and I promised him every possible help by way of introduction etc. to the US. At that time I had read his articles in the Rivista and in the Vienna Zeitschrift OR about the Ethiopian conquest.

I regretted the articles, but I did not think it ought to make the slightest difference to my desire to help him. Other international lawyers have written patriotic articles; many have written 'opinions', for substantial remuneration, in defence of causes which you and I dislike. It did not occur to us to show them our displeasure in unmistakable terms. Ought we to do it with regard to a man who is now faced with a tragedy whose implications few of us can visualize? It is just possible that he wrote the articles thinking of the impending doom and trying to save himself and his family. I am very willing to forgive him that. I would feel unhappy if, placed as I am by accident in a secure and pleasant post,

---

[39] Rosenne went on to produce much notable writing in international law of which the most important has been his four volumes on *The Law and Practice of the International Court, 1920–1966* (3rd edn, The Hague: Martinus Nijhoff Publishers, 1997).

[40] The year of this letter is uncertain.

I were to refuse to help an unfortunate man because he was a patriot or an opportunist.

I hope you will not think that I am indirectly criticizing you. I have good reasons for being more charitable in this matter than others.

In April, Hersch was contacted by the professor of international law at the Hebrew University and asked whether he would join the Editorial Committee of a proposed *Jewish Yearbook of International Law* and be prepared also to provide an article for publication in it.[41] Hersch, while approving of the idea in general, advised against limiting the content of the yearbook to questions of international law that are of interest only to Jews and Palestinians. He excused himself from joining the Editorial Committee on the ground that he was already fully occupied, particularly with editing the *BYIL* and the *AD*, but said that, if their yearbook materialised, he would be prepared to submit an article. In November, he offered the editor an article on 'The Subjects of the Law of Nations' that would not be ready till the end of the following March, but in April 1947 he replaced this with an article on the recognition by foreign States of German denationalisation decrees and the effect of the legislation of the Allied authorities in Germany abolishing these decrees. Then, in June 1947, Hersch reverted to his original idea of an article on 'The Subjects of the Law of Nations',[42] but eventually deferred to a request to adhere to the denationalisation title.[43] The article, entitled 'The Nationality of Denationalized Persons', was sent to Israel in October and appeared at pp. 163–85 of the 1948 volume of the *Jewish Yearbook of International Law*.

Hersch was approached for legal assistance or opinions on several occasions. Early in March 1946, he was asked by the Intergovernmental Committee for Refugees to give an opinion on the effect of certain laws issued by the Allied Military Government (AMG) and by the Allied Control Council (ACC) in Germany upon the status of persons, within and outside Germany, who had been deprived of their German nationality by virtue of certain Nazi laws and decrees. The AMG and ACC laws repealed these laws on the ground of their political and discriminatory nature. One such law was the Nazi decree of September 1935 and a decree made under it prescribing that a Jew who had his ordinary place of residence abroad could not be a German national. The decree also provided for the confiscation of property of Jews who thus became

---

[41] Professor Stoyanovsky to HL, 8 April 1946.   [42] HL to Professor Feinberg, 29 June 1947.
[43] HL to Professor Feinberg, 16 July 1947.

stateless. The French Government interpreted the Allied legislation as meaning that refugees who had previously been regarded by France as 'stateless' and under the protection of the Intergovernmental Committee on Refugees should henceforth be treated as German nationals – a view which had disadvantages for many and which troubled the Committee.

Hersch's interpretation of the Allied legislation was that it was not retroactive and was not intended to restore German nationality to persons previously deprived of it. To achieve such a result would require special legislation. Though he took the view that the position was so clear that the Opinion could well stop at that point, he thought it desirable, because the question had an international legal aspect, to enquire also what would be the effect of the legislation were it actually intended to have retroactive effect upon stateless persons of German origin whether residing in Germany or abroad.

As to this, he stated as a clear rule of international law that no law issued by the German State or by the Allied authorities could properly re-impose German nationality upon persons who had, in accordance with German law valid at the time of its promulgation, ceased to be German nationals and were at the time stateless or had acquired another nationality. 'There is no legal tie which connects these persons with Germany; any links which existed have been broken by their denationalisation.' Moreover, individuals should not, if possible, be compelled to acquire or retain a nationality against their will. Further, the State in which such persons were resident was entitled and bound 'in law and equity' to refuse to give effect to an attempt to re-impose upon them the nationality of which they had been deprived. This duty 'is also imposed upon [such States] by the as yet imperfect but increasingly recognised right of human personality not to be compulsorily afflicted with an odious nationality not based on residence'.[44] This duty was reinforced by considerations of international morality. Hersch noted particularly the fact that the persons concerned were originally deprived of their nationality in the course of religious and racial persecution unprecedented in history. 'The deprivation of nationality was a link in the chain of that ruthless persecution.' He mentioned a British case of 1945 which had refused to recognise the German decree of 1941 and thus treated the person concerned as remaining an enemy alien, and submitted that this approach would no longer be followed.

---

[44] Para. 12.

As regards persons who remained in or returned to Germany, 'the – so far imperfect – right of human personality not to be burdened by an unwelcome nationality is one enjoyed also by stateless persons'.

He concluded the Opinion with suggestions as to how the legal issues could be clarified by recourse to the ICJ.[45] The Opinion was forwarded by the Intergovernmental Committee on Refugees to the Foreign Office. There is no record of what action, if any, the Foreign Office subsequently took on the matter. But the question was never referred to the ICJ.

A quite different legal question arose in the case of the *Adelaide Star*, submitted to Hersch for an opinion in June 1946. The *Adelaide Star* was in 1939 a ship under construction in Denmark by Burmeister and Wain under a contract with a British company, Blue Star Line. When Germany invaded Denmark, the German occupation forces took over the contract as being an enemy asset, the ship was completed and passed under German control. After the war, Blue Star Line claimed that the shipbuilders were responsible for repayment of the sums that the company had paid towards the vessel's construction.

Hersch was initially asked to provide an opinion for use in the Court of First Instance, the Maritime and Commercial Court in Copenhagen, on three questions:

(a) Whether the seizure by the German authorities in Denmark in August 1940 of the *Adelaide Star*, then under construction, was, according to international law, a lawful seizure?

(b) Whether the action of the Danish Government in connection with the seizure was consistent with the international obligations of Denmark?

(c) If the answer to (b) was 'No', what remedies might be open to the Blue Star Line through international channels?

Hersch produced a substantial thirty-nine-page Opinion based on the fact that, at the relevant date, Denmark, though occupied territory, remained neutral and was not belligerent occupied territory. He concluded that the seizure could not be justified under the law of prize, or under the law of belligerent occupation, nor under the law of angary. He expressed the view that the matter was governed by the principle of law according to which, having regard to the illegality and criminality of the

[45] It was this opinion on which Hersch within a year based his article 'The Nationality of Denationalized Persons' (1948) *Jewish Yearbook of International Law* 163–85. Reprinted in *Collected Papers*, Vol. 3, pp. 383–404. See also p. 288 above, for Hersch's correspondence with the editors of the *Jewish Yearbook*.

German invasion of Denmark, no rights could be derived by Germany consequent upon and in connection with its illegal conduct.

Hersch's view, particularly on the effect of the illegal invasion, was not accepted by the Maritime and Commercial Court.[46] The Court found the invasion to be analogous to an unlawful war and so bound to carry with it legal effects of war – and not so as to limit the German right to seize the shipbuilding contract.

On appeal, the Supreme Court absolved the shipyard and the Danish Government from responsibility, on the ground that, in the conditions prevailing at the time, the requisitioning could not have been prevented. The effect of the Supreme Court decision was to place the liability to meet the Blue Star Line's claim on the insurance companies concerned.

In connection with the appeal, which was not concluded until October 1948, Hersch produced in June 1948 a further Opinion commenting on the view of the Court of First Instance. He returned to the subject in an article on 'The Limits of the Operation of the Law of War' that he published some years later in the *BYIL*,[47] in which, in his own words, 'in several respects [he] revised his views and considerably amplified their exposition in the light of practice and further reflection'. He qualified his earlier views by limiting the effect of the illegality of the war to the acquisition of title to property. '[T]here appears to be grave objection to the aggressor being allowed to retain after the war, any profit that may have accrued to him from his illegality. The same applies to those who go out of their way to lend him support by acquiring from him property of which he had dispossessed the victim of aggression or his nationals.'[48]

In May he declined an invitation from Carr Saunders, the Director of the LSE, to return to the School to take up the chair vacated by the retirement of H. A. Smith. A year later, Laski, in writing to Hersch about his *Recognition in International Law* book, added the following paragraph:

H. J. Laski to HL, 18 July 1947

I have only one complaint to make and it is that you did not, when we asked you to come back here, accept our invitation. What are the somnolent joys of Cambridge, even with its long low lawns and the constant peals of those intolerable bells, compared to the vivid and exciting life of London where people talk of other things than the college port and do not live by malignant

---

[46] See the brief report in 15 *ILR* 421.   [47] (1953) 30 *BYIL* 206–43.
[48] *Ibid.*, p. 226. At *ibid.*, p. 227, there is a long footnote offering an explanation of the decision in the *Adelaide Star.*

gossip of other peoples' eccentricities? Here you would have had the world at your feet: there you gaze down upon it from a cracked ivory tower.

As a reflection of Laski's character, this paragraph largely explains why Laski was not well received when Hersch had taken him into Hall in Trinity in 1942.[49]

In March, the Attorney-General returned with a request for assistance on another matter.

Sir Hartley Shawcross to HL, 29 March 1946

I wonder if you could help me on a rather unusual point which I shall have to argue before the Lord Chief on Wednesday and on which I simply am going to have no time to do any research myself as I am in the Lords on Monday and Tuesday and also doing the Trade Disputes bill in the Commons – probably all night on both those days. The point is one to which you may immediately know the answer. If you do not, please do not trouble to spend any time on it, but I thought you would not mind my writing in case you could point to where I should find the answer.

The question is whether Germany has, owing to the Allied occupation and the absence of any kind of German Government, so far ceased to be any kind of enemy State as to remove from German nationals the quality of enemy aliens capable of being detained by the British Crown. There is of course a lot of authority showing that residents in neutral territory occupied by one belligerent power may be treated as enemy nationals by the other belligerent for purposes of trading with the enemy, legislation, and so forth. These however do not really cover the point whether as between the occupying power and the nationals of the occupied enemy territory those nationals cease to possess an enemy character. The general position in regard to subjugation is of course dealt with at page 466 of the second volume of Oppenheim.

I hope you will forgive my writing you about this, but the case is one which must, I think, go to the Lords if we lose since it raises issues with very far reaching importance.

The case in question was *R. v. Bottrill, ex parte Kuechenmeister*.[50]

Hersch responded promptly, though the terms of his advice cannot be found. But he received the following letter.

Sir Hartley Shawcross to HL, 1 April 1946

I really am much indebted to you for the very useful note you have sent me – and sent me so quickly. It will be of the greatest help in what is really a

---

[49] See p. 196 above.   [50] [1947] 1 KB 41; 13 *ILR* 312.

very important matter since it will, I suppose, affect our detention of ordinary Prisoners of War.

Thank you also very much for saying that I may call on you in this way for advice. It is most kind and helpful of you.

This was quickly followed by another.

Sir Hartley Shawcross to HL, 3 April 1946

Many thanks for your further letter on the *habeas corpus* case. I shall try to argue, if necessary, that there is a distinction between the civilian internee and the soldier prisoner of war, but my main line will have to be that the detention is an act of State, and that the status of Germany is to be settled by the Foreign Secretary, *ipse dixit*, which is that Germany continues to exist as a State. I shall look up Chamberlain's statement on the release of the South African prisoners . . .

P.S. Since dictating this note the Divisional Court have dismissed this application on the ground of Act of State. It now goes to the [Court of Appeal].

In the meantime, the Nuremberg trial was proceeding. Hersch's assistance was again enlisted.

Sir Hartley Shawcross to HL, 17 May 1946

I am sorry to bother you again in the matter of the Nuremberg Trial, in which you were of such tremendous help to me in the earlier stages. The time has, however, now come for the preparation of the final speech, which I expect to make next month. To some extent it will involve a review (I hope a very short one) of the evidence against the individual defendants, but in the main the plan is that my speech should be devoted to the legal aspects of the case. It ought, of course, really to be a reply to the speech on these matters which will be made by German counsel representing all the defendants, but the difficulty of this unfortunately is that the speech has to be prepared in advance, and we are therefore in the position of having to try and anticipate, and as far as may be refute, the arguments which are likely to be raised. I wondered whether, in the light of the comments which have been made in the papers recently, any points might occur to you which I could usefully develop. As you know, I did not embody the whole of your previous paper in my first speech, and I think it may well be that I could appropriately use the rest of it in the final speech, but I should in any event be most grateful for your advice.

Hersch's reply cannot be found.

Sir Hartley Shawcross to HL, 21 May 1946

Many thanks for your letter of the 20th May, which I was very glad to have. I am in entire agreement with the general views you indicate, and I think our final speech, which is intended to cover the legal aspects of all the counts in the Indictment, is a matter of very great importance. I am afraid, however, that, as before, it will have to be prepared in a very hurried manner, because, as you can imagine, I am not only snowed under with my ordinary work here, but during the Whitsun Vacation I have to go to Poland and France. I am sending you herewith a copy of my opening speech at the trial. Sinclair, of the British War Crimes Executive, has a shorthand note of the proceedings from day to day, and some of the documents will be available there.

It would be very useful if we could have a talk together about the matter. If you are in London in the near future, this would be the most convenient for me. If, however, you are not coming up in the course of the next week or two, I will try and arrange to come down to Cambridge one evening. It is exceedingly kind of you to ask me, and I should very much like to come, but for the fact that while Parliament is sitting it is increasingly difficult to get away.

Sir Hartley Shawcross to HL, 27 May 1946

Many thanks for your letter of 23rd May. I am very glad to know that you will be able to go out to Nuremberg on Thursday. I wrote to Fyfe on Friday, telling him of the discussion we had had, and saying that you would wish to come out in order to confer with him about the line to be taken on the legal argument, and whilst I have not yet had a reply from him, I am sure he will be very glad to see you. It really is extraordinarily good of you to put everything else aside in this way in order to help in this very important matter. If I get any further news from Nuremberg before you leave, I will of course pass it on to you.

Hersch flew to Nuremberg on 29 May to consult with Sir David Maxwell Fyfe and then reported to Sir Hartley on 3 June.

Sir Hartley Shawcross to HL, 6 June 1946

Many thanks for your letter of the 3rd June. I am very glad that you were able to go to Nuremberg, and I am sure that the consultations there will be most useful.

I have now heard from Fyfe that the speech is likely to have to be delivered about the end of the first week in July, and this does not leave us a great deal of time. I shall, if I can, try and get out to Nuremberg about a week in advance for last moment consultations there, and in order to put the speech in its final form. In the circumstances, I think the most useful thing would be to divide our labours as far as possible: for Nuremberg to concentrate on the factual aspects against the individual Defendants, and for you to deal with the legal and historical part of the case, which I want to make the main feature of the speech. We could then marry the two drafts together in the final form. I expect to be in chambers most of Friday, and perhaps you will telephone and let me know when it would be convenient to you to come in.

Hersch then visited Shawcross and immediately prepared a draft of parts of the final speech.

HL to Sir Hartley Shawcross, 10 July 1946

I now enclose the draft of the Introduction and of Parts I and III (Part II being the contribution from Nuremberg).

I am naturally inclined to think that what I wrote is relevant and necessary. But I feel that delicacy ought not to prevent me from suggesting that, as this is not going to be the only and principal speech for the Prosecution, there is, in my view, no imperative reason to cover fully the 'Facts' (which cannot in any case be covered adequately) and that the much more important thing is to deal with the legal and general issues which are likely to be read by and influence both the Tribunal and the world at large.

Perhaps you may care to explore the possibility of putting in a full speech for the purpose of record and publications and reading such selected portions as can be read in the time at your disposal.

Hersch's draft came to 76 pages of typed foolscap. Hersch retained the manuscript, which is 109 foolscap pages and is in the Archive.

Shawcross replied in detail the next day.

Sir Hartley Shawcross to HL, 11 July 1946

Very many thanks for your letter of the 10th July and your draft for the Nuremberg speech. I need hardly say how very grateful I am to you for the enormous trouble which you have taken in preparing this admirable and careful argument. It really has been most good of you to help in this way.

I am, however, now faced with some considerable difficulty in regard to the whole matter. You have, I think, had sent to you the draft speech which has been prepared at Nuremberg and which, without allowing at all for the legal argument, is already longer than I feel any speech we now make can properly be. In sending the draft to me, Phillimore has written as follows:

> We have tried in the first three pages to put the essential facts and arguments as bluntly as possible at the expense of any sort of oratory and to compress the rise to power and the domestic government in the years 1933 to 1939 to the minimum. Please regard the figures on page 1 as tentative: we are, I hope, getting comprehensive figures and should be able to substantiate any figure quoted by the end of next week. Aggression is so hackneyed – it has been gone over again and again ad nauseam – that we have tried to compress to the minimum at the same time developing a new line at the finish.

> We are very apprehensive over the way the Judges are talking about conviction and sentence. Informally at dinner, etc., they have indicated that they may acquit two or three and that quite a number may not get the death sentence. Whilst their views now must necessarily be very tentative and what they say may not be intended very seriously, we all feel that the value of the trial in international law will be largely stultified if the results are regarded

as ridiculous by the people of Europe. Sir David asked me particularly to emphasise that he felt you could not put the matter too strongly. We can conceive of one or two escaping the death penalty on the evidence but the acquittal of any of these men and sentences such as five years for Raeder will reduce the crime of aggressive war to a farce.[51]

From this you will see that the view taken at Nuremberg is that there is real danger of some acquittals, the effect of which would be to discredit the trial, and that they feel, therefore, that we must concentrate on the facts rather than the law. Had it not been for this strong expression of opinion, I should entirely have agreed with you that the proper course now was to address the Tribunal on the law, and to have left the facts to be dealt with by our colleagues. This, indeed, had been my own plan for the speech. In view, however, of Fyfe's attitude, I think that I am compelled to attempt an address which covers both the legal and the factual aspects of the matter, although, I am afraid, not as adequately as could have been done had one or other aspect been substantially the sole purpose of the speech. If I fail to be guided by Fyfe's advice and anything went wrong, it would obviously be said that it was my fault for coming in at the last moment and taking a line which differed from that of those who have been responsible for the conduct of the trial during the greater part of the proceedings. Political opponents are always ready to try and make capital out of matters of this kind, and already in the House of Commons, Lennox Boyd made the following observation: 'Rumour has it that the Attorney-General is going shortly to Nuremberg to make the winding up speech at the trial there. Let us hope that he will not spoil all the good work done by Sir David Maxwell Fyfe.'

I do not think there is any possibility of putting in a full speech for the purposes of the record and only reading part of it in open Court. That possibility was, as a matter of fact, discussed in another connection and objected to. I am, however, committed to writing the introduction to an authoritative report of the whole proceedings, and in that I shall be able, with your permission, to make use of such of the material in your draft as I do not embody in the present speech.

I am going to have a talk with Lord Wright about the whole matter today, and I rather think from a letter that I have received from him that he would also like to have a chat with you about the matter.

Shawcross delivered his final speech on 26 and 27 July 1946.

H. J. Phillimore to HL, 29 July 1946
I am afraid that the Attorney must have been very much rushed in the end in compiling his speech but the result was very good and I am only sorry you were not here to hear its delivery as he did it magnificently and the effect was very considerable.

[51] Harry Phillimore was a member of the team working with Maxwell Fyfe in Nuremberg.

In late September, Hersch returned to Nuremberg to be present when the final judgment was delivered on 1 October. Three defendants were acquitted altogether (against the dissent of the Soviet member of the Tribunal); seven were sentenced to long terms of imprisonment; and twelve were sentenced to death by hanging.

Sir Hartley Shawcross to HL, 8 October 1946
Now that the Nuremberg trial is finally over I should like, both officially and personally, to thank you for the important part which you played in it. For your help to me personally, in regard to the speeches and other matters, I shall always remain most grateful.

I hope that you will always feel some satisfaction in having had this leading hand in something which may have a real influence on the future conduct of international relations, and I am looking forward to see how you deal with the judgment.

With the Nuremberg trial over, the pace of life slowed down a bit. In the autumn, Hersch was asked by the Imperial Continental Gas Association (ICGA) for an opinion in connection with the nationalisation by France of two utility companies owned by them. His guidance was sought in particular on the international remedies that might be open to ICGA, and he replied in a relatively short opinion explaining the limitations on the compulsory jurisdiction of the ICJ. He noted, though, that the question of the treatment of the property of aliens is not one which would fall within the reservation of matters solely within the domestic jurisdiction of States.

Another item on which Hersch's assistance was sought was the question of the treatment of the property of the Prince of Liechtenstein in Czechoslovakia. Here again Hersch had to advise that there was no possibility of compulsory recourse to an international tribunal. He limited himself to giving advice on the prospects – rather limited – of recourse to the General Assembly of the UN.

The year 1946 was marked by another development – a personal one of great importance for Hersch. In March, he heard from his niece, Inka Gelbard, the daughter of his sister, Sabka, that she (Inka) had survived. When her parents were seized by the Germans, she had been given refuge in a convent in Lwów. After the Germans were driven out, she succeeded in making contact with some distant relatives who had also managed to survive and, with them, was by then in a displaced persons camp in Austria. Hersch immediately urged her to come to England. Through his contacts in the Polish Embassy, he was able to get her a

Polish passport. Inka was initially reluctant to leave her relatives to whom she had become very attached and who wanted to go on to Palestine. She eventually decided, however, that she would be better off in England and so came to join Hersch and Rachel at Cranmer Road in late 1946. For a year she went to school in Cambridge. Subsequently, she married a distant cousin in Paris and went to live there, though keeping in close touch with Hersch and Rachel.

1947

With limited exceptions, 1947 was not marked by as many highlights as 1946 or 1948. Hersch continued with his university teaching and with his writing. He spent much time and effort in the preparation of a major report on the international protection of human rights for the ILA conference to be held in Brussels in September 1948.[52]

Despite the fact that earlier in the year Hersch received the Attorney-General's approval and encouragement to publish articles about the Joyce case and the Nuremberg trial, he only published a paper on the former (based on his lecture at Cambridge).[53] Hersch did not get round to writing an article on the Nuremberg trial. It may be that his health was troubling him. In January he had a thorough medical check-up by a leading Cambridge consultant, who found nothing seriously wrong with him except a tendency to anxiety to which was added his difficulty in sleeping.

Within the university, he felt obliged to present a strong argument to the Faculty Board of Economics for the retention of international law as an optional subject in Part II of the Economics Tripos. As an *ex officio* member of the Board, he was entitled to express an opinion. Part of the memorandum that he sent to the Chairman of the Board explains that:

There are many who believe that the subject covered by the teaching of International Law is of great importance to every citizen and that it is imperative that we should increase rather than reduce the numbers of those who are able to take an informed and intelligent interest in it. I suppose that this is probably one of the reasons why in the proposed revision of the Law Tripos International Law is the only compulsory subject in the Law Qualifying II and one of the two compulsory subjects in Part I of the Tripos. It seems to me that, unless more convincing reasons than those given can be adduced for the proposed step, it

---

[52] See Chapter 11 below. [53] See pp. 280–3 below; and *Collected Papers*, Vol. 3, p. 221.

would make a false impression, if the Board of Economics were to depart from what has become in Cambridge a traditional association.

I am not sure whether if I were not a less nominal member of the Board of Economics than I am entitled to be, I would not be prepared to urge that for those who pursue in this University a normal course of economic studies for three years International Law, with an economic bias, should be made one of the fourteen or fifteen compulsory subjects. This, I would urge, would be in keeping both with the conception of the study of economics as a science allied to humanities in their wider sense and with some distinctly practical needs of the present time. I would suggest that the greatest benefit – from the intellectual, vocational and civic points of view – can be derived from the study of international law with special reference to its economic aspects such as international regulation of foreign trade, the vast network of international commodity agreements, international control and exploitation of new materials, foreign investment and its diplomatic protection, international regulation of conditions of work in conjunction with the entire field of the diverse activities of the International Labour Organisation, international protection of industrial and literary property, problems of migration, international civil aviation, freedom of navigation on international rivers, international protection of fisheries and other resources of the high seas, international cooperation and administration in the field of transit and communications (including tele-communications), and a host of other matters which come within the scope of the Economic and Financial Organisation of the League of Nations and which are now being taken over by the United Nations. After all, it is in the economic sphere that the interdependence of the world is most real.[54]

The considerations which Hersch advanced for the study of international law have become increasingly pertinent with the passage of years. For a while, his arguments were accepted but international law eventually disappeared from the Economics Tripos.

In April, he received another request from the Attorney-General also relating to the effect of the German denationalisation law of 1941.[55] There is no record of Hersch's reply to this letter, but it seems unlikely that it would have differed substantially from the opinion that he wrote in 1945 for the Intergovernmental Committee on Refugees.[56]

Recognition in International Law appeared early in the year and was well reviewed,[57] though not all agreed with the basic thesis. Professor Winfield, reviewing it in *The Times Literary Supplement*,[58] said:

---

[54] HL to Robertson, Chairman of the Faculty Board of Economics, 24 February 1947.
[55] Sir Hartley Shawcross to HL, 9 April 1947.
[56] See p. 288 above.
[57] See, for example, a review by Norman Bentwich in the *Manchester Guardian*, 29 July 1947, p. 3.
[58] 30 August 1947.

It is one more testimony to the high reputation of its learned author and is an important addition to the literature of international law . . . It may be taken for granted that every international lawyer will include it in his library and it can be recommended to any layman interested in the topic.

A long letter from Quincy Wright, a professor of international law at the University of Chicago, entered a number of reservations, but was generally supportive of Hersch's views.[59] A less critical view of his opinions was taken in the Foreign Office.

Hersch returned to Cambridge on 15 September and gradually recovered from the strain of the Prague visit.[60]

In October, Hersch received a telegram from Eban saying that Dr Weizmann would welcome an Opinion on two points. The first was whether a resolution by the General Assembly on the partition of Palestine required a two-thirds majority. Hersch advised that it did not. The other was whether the General Assembly was legally competent to recommend a partition of Palestine. Hersch advised that it was. The elaboration in twelve pages of those views was much used in discussions with various UN delegates in the ensuing months.

The rest of the year was taken up with university teaching and with editing the *AD*, the *BYIL* and *Oppenheim*.

1948

Busy though 1947 had been, 1948 was to be even more so, an exceptionally varied and demanding year. During the year, Hersch added to his usual Cambridge lectures participation in the first stages of the *Corfu Channel* case, a four-week visit to New York connected with the work of the Codification Division of the UN, nearly three months as a visiting professor at the University of Colorado and three months of intensive assistance to Hyderabad, which was faced by the prospect of invasion from India.

THE CORFU CHANNEL CASE

In October 1946, two British destroyers struck mines in the Corfu Channel, a strait which lies between the mainland of Albania and the island of Corfu and is part of international waters through which there is

---

[59] Quincy Wright to HL, 24 September 1947.   [60] See Chapter 11 below.

freedom of passage. The warships suffered damage and there was a heavy loss of life. Claiming that Albania was responsible, the British Government immediately took the matter to the UN Security Council, which recommended that the British and Albanian Governments should refer the dispute to the ICJ. Britain then unilaterally started proceedings, contending that the action of the Security Council was a 'decision' which, under Article 25 of the Charter, was binding upon Albania. Albania responded by observing that it was not a party to any instrument conferring compulsory jurisdiction upon the Court and that the implementation of the Council's recommendation required a special agreement between the two sides. Nonetheless, Albania said that it was prepared, 'notwithstanding this irregularity in the action taken by the Government of the United Kingdom', to appear before the Court. This cooperative attitude of Albania was no doubt due to the fact that at that time Albania's application for membership was pending before the UN and Albania wished to make a favourable impression. The Court then fixed dates for the filing of the British Memorial and the Albanian Counter-Memorial. However, between the date of the Court's Order and the date fixed for the filing of the Albanian Counter-Memorial, Albania's application for membership of the UN was rejected as part of the Cold War tension then prevailing between the Western and Eastern blocs in the UN. In consequence, Albania changed its position and raised an objection to the Court's jurisdiction. This came before the Court for hearing from 26 February to 5 March 1948.

Hersch was a member of the British team that appeared before the Court, led by the Attorney-General, Sir Hartley Shawcross, and Mr (later Sir) Eric Beckett, Legal Adviser of the Foreign Office. Amongst the other members were Professor (later Sir) Humphrey Waldock, Professor of International Law at Oxford, Richard Wilberforce, who later achieved the highest prominence as a most distinguished Law Lord, and J. Mervyn Jones.

Hersch obtained leave from Cambridge to go to The Hague for the last week of the Lent Term and there participated in the flurry of discussion and drafting that marks the preparation for every oral hearing. What exactly his role was has not been possible to ascertain.

The Court found that it had jurisdiction and the case then proceeded on its merits, with further written pleadings being exchanged in the course of 1948. Hersch, largely because of his other commitments during the year, ceased to be involved at this stage. The case was eventually decided in 1949 in Britain's favour and damages were awarded.

UN SURVEY OF INTERNATIONAL LAW: NEW YORK, APRIL–MAY 1948

The background to Hersch's time in New York was the establishment by the UN of an International Law Commission charged with the codification and progressive development of international law. In 1945, when structuring the new international community, the draftsmen of the United Nations Charter referred to what they described as 'the codification and progressive development of international law'. No such idea had been included in the Covenant of the League of Nations, the precursor of the UN. To the draftsmen of 1945, the absence in the 1930s of suitable procedures for reviewing the nature and extent of the deficiencies in particular legal relationships was still a vivid memory. The spate of volumes in the 1930s recording the need for change and the means of achieving it evidenced the degree of concern.[61] For some the inter-war deficiency was largely a matter of lack of suitable machinery. Hersch's approach, for example, was primarily in terms of judicial or arbitral determination of disputes, all of which, in his opinion, were capable of being resolved by reference to existing legal rules. He was not preoccupied – though others were – by the thought that what was required was machinery to effect change in the content of the legal rules rather than procedures for applying them. In his own contribution on 'Peaceful Change – The Legal Aspect', a particularly thoughtful essay published in 1937,[62] Hersch does not advert at all to the idea of an institutional approach to the codification and progressive development of international law.

As a contribution towards the solution of the need for change, the Charter went no further than to include in the part relating to the General Assembly a provision (Article 13(a)) requesting the General Assembly, amongst other things, to initiate studies and make recommendations for

---

[61] Salvador De Madariaga, *The World's Design* (1938), p. 80: 'A Court of Justice is an inevitable necessity on the road to real peace. Unless all members of a community have agreed to bring before the Court all their differences without exception, the first and most elementary condition for peace within that community has not been achieved. World affairs are no exception: for the world the road to peace passes by The Hague. Without a World Court, no real peace [is possible] . . . Peace means justice. Justice depends on time and on space. This implies that justice can only be secured by means of permanent institutions with unlimited jurisdiction over the whole community and with unrestricted jurisdiction over all the conflicts between members of the community. This conclusion has been reached, not by heroically climbing to idealistic peaks, but by keeping to the modest and homely paths of the empirical valley. If we do want real world peace, we must create, strengthen, respect and obey world institutions.' See also H. G. Wells, *The New World Order* (1940); Clarence K. Streit, *Union Now: A Proposal for a Federal Union of the Leading Democracies* (1939); and Gerhart Niemeyer, *Law Without Force: The Function of Politics in International Law* (1941).

[62] Reprinted in *Collected Papers*, Vol. 5, pp. 7–25.

'encouraging the progressive development of international law and its codification'.

The distinction between codification and progressive development cannot be drawn precisely. In general terms, the function of codification is to bring together and restate the essential content, even in some detail, of a section of the existing law. This process inevitably leads to some reassessment and rationalisation of the current state of the law and thus to its change and hence to its 'progressive development'. Once the possibility of the 'progressive development' of international law was acknowledged, it became necessary to consider whether the law to be so developed was limited to the traditional and technical content of international law relating to such matters as the definition of statehood, the extent of state jurisdiction, the law relating to the acquisition of territory, the use of the seas, the position of diplomats and the law of treaties, or whether it extended more broadly to the political aspects of the law – as to how in various matters the relations of States to one another were to be governed. As Hersch was himself to observe later, after he had ceased to be a member of the ILC:

unlike codification in other fields, the codification of international law must be substantively legislative in nature. It must consist essentially in inducing Governments (or some Governments) to accept new law.[63]

Article 13 of the UN Charter did not grapple with these issues. This was left to the General Assembly itself. One of its first steps was to establish, early in 1947, a Committee on the Progressive Development of International Law and its Codification, which soon proposed the establishment of an International Law Commission. The General Assembly promptly adopted the necessary Statute for a commission of fifteen members, to be elected by the General Assembly, having as its object 'the promotion of the progressive development of international law and its codification'. The members were to act in their individual capacities and not as representatives of their national States.

Within the growing UN Secretariat, a Division of Codification was established as part of the Legal Department. The first Director of the Division was the former legal adviser of the Chinese (Nationalist) Government, Dr Yuen Li-Liang. One of his first steps was to recruit Hersch to undertake, initially in New York, the preparation of an assessment of contemporary international law with a view to identifying topics suitable

---

[63] 'Codification and Development of International Law' (1955) 49 *AJIL* 16. Reprinted in *Collected Papers*, Vol. 2, p. 285.

for consideration by the ILC, and suggesting some order of priority in which they might be examined.

Having obtained leave from Cambridge to begin this task, Hersch left for New York in April 1948 and worked in the Legal Department of the UN at Lake Success for four weeks. But, as he wrote to Beckett after his return, 'it soon became clear to me that my main work for codification will have to be done in Cambridge. The atmosphere of the UN is not conducive to concentrated work.'[64] He completed the survey on codification after much discussion with Liang; the final document appeared under the anonymous authorship of the UN Secretary-General and was entitled 'Survey of International Law in Relation to the Work of Codification of the International Law Commission'. Subsequently, authorship of the work was publicly attributed to Hersch,[65] thus enabling the full text to be reprinted as part of his writings in the *Collected Papers*.[66]

Within the space of some seventy closely printed pages, Hersch succeeded in reviewing the whole of the then traditional customary law of peace and identifying those aspects of it suitable for consideration by the ILC. The final chapter contained a discussion of the method that the Commission might use to select topics, continued with a consideration of the character of the work of the Commission and concluded with an examination of the procedure that the Commission might follow. Each of these sections was carefully drafted to raise the questions that the Commission needed to consider, rather than to propose solutions. When the Commission came to choose subjects for treatment, it based itself largely upon the Survey.[67] In fact, the Commission's agenda was for decades largely comprised of topics proposed by Hersch, such as the law of treaties, the law of the sea, state responsibility and diplomatic and consular relations. The influence of the Survey was felt for some fifty years.

While he was in New York, Hersch put forward to Dr Liang a proposal that the Codification Division should undertake responsibility for carrying the *AD* back into the period before 1919. This would be in implementation of Article 24 of the Statute of the ILC which called upon the Commission to consider ways and means of making customary international law more readily available by the collection and publication, amongst other things, of decisions of national and international courts

---

[64] HL to Beckett, 18 August 1948.

[65] This was done by Dr Liang at the 535th meeting of the ILC on 9 May 1960. See *Yearbook of the International Law Commission* (1960), vol. 1, p. 52.

[66] *Collected Papers*, Vol. 1, pp. 447–530 (and see Editor's Note, p. 446).

[67] Briggs, *The International Law Commission* (1965), pp. 27 and 171.

on questions of international law. Although the Division initiated and carried forward a series of *Reports of International Arbitral Awards*, of which the first three volumes were published in 1948, Hersch's suggestion for the publication of national decisions was not taken up, probably because of the considerable expense foreseen.[68]

ISRAELI DECLARATION OF INDEPENDENCE, MAY 1948

Hersch's period in New York in February and March 1948 coincided with developments in the UN leading to the end of the British Mandate for Palestine and to the creation in May of the State of Israel. Until Israel actually became a State, its diplomacy in the United States was in the hands of the Jewish Agency for Palestine. Its representative in New York was Aubrey (later Hebraicised to Abba) Eban, a former Fellow of Pembroke College, Cambridge, who had served as a major in the British Army. He was a specialist in Middle East matters, spoke fluently both Hebrew and Arabic and was a brilliant orator. He was married to Rachel's niece, Suzy, so Hersch saw something of him socially during his time in New York.

Sometime in March 1948, Eban asked Hersch to draft a document that could serve as a Declaration of Independence for the new State. Amongst the relatively few papers that Hersch thought sufficiently important to preserve are two manuscript documents written on yellow American foolscap legal paper. One, consisting of six sheets, is headed 'An Act of Independence'; the other, consisting of fifteen sheets of similar paper, is headed 'Declaration on the Assumption of Power by the Provisional Government of the Jewish Republic'. These were then sent by Eban to Palestine. Exactly what happened to them there cannot be ascertained with any certainty. Following the decision taken by Britain that the Mandate should be terminated on 15 May, some six weeks before the date proposed in the UN General Assembly partition resolution, there was considerable debate in the Zionist General Council in Tel Aviv as to how to proceed. Two bodies were set up. One was the National Administration, with thirteen members. This later became the National Provisional Government. The other was the People's Council, with thirty-seven members, which included the members of the National Administration. This later became the Provisional Council of State. On 12 May, Hersch's draft came before the National Administration and was about to

---

[68] HL to Yuen Li-Liang, 31 March 1948.

be read out in Hebrew by Moshe Shertok, when he was interrupted by Ben-Gurion, the chairman, who insisted that decisions should first be taken about the creation of the State, its Provisional Government and a Provisional Council of State. The content of the Declaration of Independence was then referred to a committee. Five drafts were before the committee. Hersch's was one of them. Though it was not adopted, its spirit infused the final text that was prepared by Shertok and revised by Ben-Gurion. Subsequently, it was incorrectly rumoured that Hersch had drafted the Declaration of Independence. Though he would have been proud if he had, it appears that this was not so.[69]

Soon afterwards, Hersch's views were again sought in connection with the American decision to accord no more than *de facto* recognition to the Government of Israel because it described itself as only 'provisional'. Hersch's opinion, of which there is only secondary evidence, was that there was no basis in law or precedent for this limited approach to the recognition of the new State.[70]

COLORADO, JUNE–AUGUST 1948

In November 1947, Hersch received from the Dean of the Law School at the University of Colorado an invitation to visit Boulder between June and August 1948 to deliver a course of about thirty lectures. The invitation was couched in flattering terms:

At a meeting of our faculty held yesterday, we decided that you most nearly fill the description of the world's leading authority on International Law.

The university would pay Hersch's travel expenses and provide him without charge with living quarters and an honorarium of 'about $2,000.00'. Hersch was pleased by the invitation and minded to accept it, subject to some qualifications about dates and a possible increase in payment to cover the cost of Rachel's fares.

The arrangements were suitably concluded, and, at the beginning of June 1948, Hersch and Rachel sailed to New York on the *Queen Elizabeth* en route to Boulder. By then, he had virtually completed his work for

[69] This account is largely derived from a detailed narrative by Moshe Z. Gurary in the *Jerusalem Post Supplement*, 10 May 1978, p. 20. See also (1987–8) *Palestine Yearbook of International Law* 265–93 for the Minutes of the Meetings of the National Administration, 12 and 13 May 1948. For comment, see Yoram Schacher, 'Jefferson Goes East: The American Origins of the Israeli Declaration of Independence' (2009) 10 *Theoretical Inquiries in Law* 589–618, esp. pp. 597–8.

[70] Letter from Aubrey S. Eban to Dr C. Weizmann, 29 July 1948, held in the Weizmann Archive, Rehovot, Israel.

the UN Codification Division, though while in New York for a few days he had several meetings with Liang. He also attended a meeting of the UN Human Rights Commission.

Once they arrived in Boulder, they quickly settled into what Rachel described as a 'luxurious cottage' and Hersch entered upon his series of lectures. They were made very welcome and greatly enjoyed the constant round of entertainment, the more so because of the easy informality of relationships. Having received a telegram from me telling them of my examination results, Hersch tendered further advice:

HL to EL, 21 June 1948
What is most important is that the result will put you in the right psychological frame of making absolutely sure of a good first in Part II. Large parts of that battle will be won or lost during this long vacation. Start at once. Put yourself into your situation next April or May. If you get a good first – possibly a Star – then probably you will get a research scholarship from the College for the LLB which when crowned with a Whewell Scholarship will be a practicable starting point – at your option – for a Humanist Trust Scholarship or Commonwealth Scholarship, or UN Post (which I do not fancy) or a teaching post (Jennings may be going in two years or so to London. Would it not be grand if you took his place!) For all this the next year will be decisive. It will be a year of drudgery and hard work. But will lay down firmly the foundations of your future – in any way you like. So good luck to you, boy.

Other letters of advice followed.

Between 22 and 26 July Hersch left Boulder to lecture at the Universities of Michigan and Illinois; 'Only one thousand miles', as he put it. Rachel regularly attended most of Hersch's lectures in Boulder. She wrote that he used to test her to see whether she had really followed what he was saying. In addition to his regular course, he gave three public lectures on 'Human Rights', as well as addressing the local Rotary Club. His valedictory lecture on 'Realism in International Law' generated a great ovation.

In July, he was elected a Fellow of the British Academy.

He remained in Boulder till 17 August, then left for New York to sail home on the *Queen Elizabeth* on 21 August.

THE EFFECT OF SECURITY COUNCIL RECOMMENDATIONS

Soon after his arrival in Boulder, Hersch received from Beckett a long letter on the question of whether recommendations made by the UN

Security Council under Chapters VI and VII of the Charter are binding on members of the UN.[71] To this Hersch replied on 20 July as follows:

The enclosed contains my reply to the three questions put in your letter of 29th June. As you will see, I am substantially in agreement with your tentative answers except that: (1) as to question iii, I do not think that the decisions which are enforceable are limited to the restoration of the *status quo*, and (2) as to question ii, I think that the last sentence of your answer rather begs the question (or, at least, it looks like it).

My answers to the questions formulated in paragraph 6 of the letter of 29 June 1948 are as follows:

(1) Question: Can it be held that the word 'recommendations' in Article 39 of the Charter does not exclude recommendations of 'terms of settlement'?

Answer: The word 'recommendations' in Article 2 of the Charter does *not* exclude recommendations of 'terms of settlement'.

(2) Question: If so, if the Security Council recommends terms of settlement under Article 39, are such terms of settlement enforceable?

Answer: 'Recommendations' of terms of settlement, whether under Article 37(2) or Article 39, are not, as such, enforceable. (I am using the term 'enforceable' in the sense of conferring upon the Security Council a legal power to enforce the recommendations by measures binding both upon the parties to the dispute and upon the members of the United Nations.)

(3) Question: If terms of settlement so recommended are not enforceable does it follow that the Security Council has the power to decide what should be done to maintain or restore international peace and security, but no power to see that in fact it is done?

Answer: The substantive terms of recommendations under Article 39 – with regard *both* to terms and modes of settlement – are enforceable if subsequently made to form part of a decision laying down measures to be taken in accordance with Articles 41 and 42 and aiming at maintaining or restoring international peace and security. They are not limited to decisions aiming at the restoration of the *status quo*.

The following comment will explain some of the reasons underlying my answers:

Answer 1

Neither the logical argument in Annex B nor the argument based on preparatory work have convinced me that recommendations under Article 39 cannot

---

[71] Beckett to HL, 29 June 1948.

include terms of settlement. It is true that Article 37(2) already empowers the Security Council to recommend terms of settlement. But this does not preclude the Security Council from recommending terms of settlement under Article 39 – even if the terms of settlement thus recommended are identical with those previously recommended under Article 37(2) – just as there is nothing to prevent it from embodying in a decision taken under the second part of Article 39 terms of settlement which formed part of the recommendations under Articles 37 and 39 (first part) and which have not been accepted by one or both parties. The legal possibility and admissibility of such repeated formulation of terms of settlement is of the essence of the scheme of pacific settlement under Chapters VI and VII. That scheme envisages a series of recommendations which, while they may be identical in substance, differ in authority – though perhaps only in political authority. They are recommendations in an ascending order of political authority. (For this reason I am not impressed by the argument in paragraph 1 of Annex B to the effect it would not be reasonable to assume that recommendations under Article 39 refer to terms of settlement seeing that the Security Council has power to make such recommendations under Article 37(2). For these are not recommendations of the same kind of authority. A recommendation of terms of settlement under Article 37(2) is not enforceable or, what is essentially the same, is not 'binding'.) Similarly, recommendation of the same terms of settlement under Article 39 is not binding. But it is a more authoritative and more compelling recommendation. For it has been made after the Security Council has determined the existence of a 'threat to peace, breach of the peace, or act of aggression'. It has been made under the provisions of a chapter concerned with 'enforcement action'. The parties are still legally free to disregard it but they can do so only at their peril. They run the risk of the recommendation being embodied in a decision, which *is* legally binding and enforceable, in conformity with the second part of Article 39.

If this reasoning is accepted, then the American thesis is perhaps less objectionable than appears at first sight (though the somewhat superficial reference to the dangers of the Security Council assuming the attributes of a World Government could have with advantage been omitted). For while the Security Council cannot enforce a political settlement in pursuance of its own recommendation or that of the General Assembly, it can enforce its terms as part of its own decision taken in order to maintain international peace and security after it has determined the existence of a threat to peace, breach of the peace, or act of aggression. To that extent the Charter does in fact confer upon the Security Council the powers of World Government, in conformity with the principles of the Charter – though the proposition is not so formidable as it appears at first sight seeing that such powers cannot adversely affect a permanent member of the Security Council against its will.

For the same reason the difference between the American thesis and that propounded by Mr Jebb[72] is not as fundamental as may appear at first sight. For although 'terms of settlement' may not be enforceable under Article 37(2) they may be, in substance, enforceable under the second part of Article 39. There is really nothing anomalous – or even strange – about it. Under Chapter vi there is as yet no determination of a threat to peace, etc.; under Chapter vii there is. Even then the Security Council may in the first instance be satisfied with a non-enforceable recommendation. It is only when that recommendation is not acted upon that its terms may become embodied – no longer as a recommendation – in the decision under the second part of Article 39. The American thesis becomes dangerous – and unacceptable – only if it is pushed to the extreme of the assertion that the terms of a decision under the second part of Article 39 are in no case enforceable for the mere reason that they previously formed part of a recommendation under Article 37(2) or under the first part of Article 39. There is no reason for assuming that they wished to go to that length – though it would have been better if they had qualified their statement. On the other hand, Mr Jebb's thesis that recommendations under Article 37(2) are enforceable as such – I am not sure that he goes to that length – cannot be accepted. For that thesis in fact amounts to making these recommendations binding and this – for reasons stated above and below – cannot be admitted. If recommendations under Chapter vi were enforceable, then that might indeed constitute the Security Council a World Government also as against the permanent members of the Security Council – for under Chapter vi these do not vote in decisions on disputes to which they are a party (a decision in this context includes 'recommendations'). This might be a very good thing, but it is not the Charter as it stands at present (I do not know whether Mr Jebb would suggest that although a recommendation of the Security Council under Chapter vi becomes enforceable against a permanent member regardless of his dissent, it can in fact be enforced only under Chapter vii where the veto does apply).

Answer 2

The above comment explains to some extent the answer to Question 2. It is, I think, of importance not to give countenance to the view that recommendations of the Security Council, whether under Chapter vi or vii, are as such 'enforceable' (i.e. binding). This is contrary to the natural meaning of the word and to the evidence of preparatory work (though the latter is not quite so relevant to recommendations under Chapter vii). Once we begin to take liberties with the natural meaning of words, we cannot tell where we shall end. For this reason – and also because of the preparatory work – I was not in favour of our

---

[72] Hubert Miles Gladwyn Jebb, GCMG, GCVO, CB (1900–96), 1st Baron Gladwyn, known as Gladwyn Jebb, was a prominent diplomat and politician. In August 1945, he was appointed as Executive Secretary of the Preparatory Commission of the United Nations, and was later appointed Acting Secretary-General of the United Nations from October 1945 to February 1946.

contention, advanced in the Corfu case, that recommendations of the Security Council under Chapter VI are binding. After it had been decided to go ahead with that contention, I felt it my duty to find arguments in support of it. One of them was the argument based on the distinction between recommendations embodying terms of settlement and those embodying modes of settlement. But it was a laboured distinction and, as you know, I did not think much of it.

Question 3
    Some of the comments relevant to my answer to question 3 are contained in the comments under (1) and (2).

If the view is accepted (a) that the word 'recommendations' in Article 39 does not exclude the terms of settlement and (b) that the substance of the recommendations (though not the recommendations as such) is enforceable in pursuance of decisions made under the second part of Article 39 – then it is not possible to accept the view that these decisions are limited to a restoration of the *status quo*. There are a number of additional reasons which make it difficult to accept that limitation. In the first instance the restoration of the *status quo* may be affected to a large extent under Article 40 (provisional measures). This, in fact, seems to be the normal kind of action to take in cases of violation of frontiers and acute territorial disputes. Thus, in the Greek–Bulgarian dispute the Council of the League of Nations recommended that the parties should withdraw their troops to their respective territories. After the invasion of Manchuria, the Council adopted – ineffectually, because of the Japanese vote – a similar recommendation. Probably the *situs materiae* for the restoration of the *status quo* is in Article 40 rather than in Article 39. Secondly, if recommendations under Chapter VII refer only – or mainly – to the restoration of the *status quo*, it is not easy to see what is the object of the qualifying clause of Article 2(7) which lays down that the exception of domestic jurisdiction does not apply to the application of enforcement measures under Chapter VII. Unless the recommendations of Article 39 can in fact cover measures interfering with domestic jurisdiction – restoration of the *status quo* cannot, as a rule, interfere with matters which are essentially within the domestic jurisdiction of a state – Article 2(7) has little or no meaning (it is, of course, possible to say that Article 2(7) has no meaning, and for various reasons – but not for the one connected with Article 39 – I incline to that view). Thirdly, in many cases a decision aiming merely at restoring the *status quo* is impracticable or irrelevant; in such cases international peace and security cannot be secured merely be restoring the *status quo*. Take, for instance, the Corfu cases and suppose that the injury which has been inflicted upon us was much greater than it was – for example, that a number of big warships had been sunk and thousands of lives lost. It is clear that in that case international peace and security could not be maintained by a decision aiming at restoring the *status quo*. (In this connection I do not follow that part of the reasoning in paragraph 6 of Annex B in which it is suggested that 'it is difficult to see how terms of settlement can be enforced'. There is no difficulty in visualizing a situation in which the Security Council compels a State, through various means of pressure available to it under Articles 41 and 42, to execute the terms of settlement. I think also that the conclusion of paragraph 4 of Annex B is a non-sequitur in relation to paragraph 3. The latter does not seem to me to substantiate the view that the recommendations of Article 39 are intended to cover specifically recommendations for 'the prevention of an immediate outbreak of hostilities'.) With regard to the possibility of enforcement, I do not altogether follow Mr Jebb in his difficulty concerning the enforcement of decisions under Article 39 on account of the fact that the agreements between the Security Council and the members of the United Nations have not yet been concluded. For that difficulty applies only to enforcement action under Article 42. It does not apply to the various measures of enforcement under Article 41, not involving the use of armed force. I am in general agreement with the reasoning, in this matter, of paragraph 9 of Annex B.

HYDERABAD, JUNE–OCTOBER 1948

Early in June 1948, Hersch received a letter from Christopher Brunyate,[73] a senior partner in one of the leading firms of solicitors in London, Coward, Chance & Co., asking for his help in connection with the developing dispute between Hyderabad and India. This was to be the first major contention in which Hersch was to play a significant role, and he responded to the challenge with enthusiasm and vigour.

The problem arose out of the termination of British rule in India by the Indian Independence Act 1947. India, which had been the jewel of the Imperial Crown, was divided into two parts, India and Pakistan, the first predominantly Hindu, the second overwhelmingly Muslim. The border between them was to be determined by a British judge of great eminence, Lord Radcliffe. His task was the difficult and unenviable one of attempting to separate peacefully the Hindu and Muslim populations of the border areas. In the event, it could not be done peacefully; between 500,000 and 1 million people perished in the ensuing bloodbath, and 10 to 12 million people migrated across the new boundaries.

In the days of Imperial rule the territory of India was governed in two ways. Some areas were directly administered by Britain and were known as British India. The remainder consisted of the so-called 'Princely States' which were administered by their own Maharajahs, or, in the

---

[73] Christopher Brunyate to HL, 31 May 1948. Christopher Brunyate was a partner in the firm from 1931 till his death in 1956 and had been advising the Nizam since the early 1930s. I am much indebted to Mr Jeremy Carver CBE, solicitor, of Clifford Chance (successors to Coward, Chance), for his help in obtaining the letters covering the period.

case of Hyderabad, a Nizam, who were subject only to the advice of British Residents. Their position was governed by treaties, most of them made in the eighteenth century between their rulers, who regarded themselves as otherwise independent, and the East India Company, as the representative in India of the British Crown. As part of the arrangements for independence, Britain brought these agreements to an end and gave the rulers the choice of adhering to either India or Pakistan. For the most part, each ruler adhered to the new State within which his own territory lay. The principal exception was Hyderabad, the largest of the Princely States. Its ruler, the Nizam, was a Muslim; its population was 85 per cent Hindu. The Nizam was reputed to be the wealthiest person in the world. He took the view that, as the treaty binding Hyderabad to the British Crown had been terminated, it reverted to its former condition as a fully independent State in its own right and was therefore entitled to refrain from opting for one or other of the two new States and was free to negotiate an acceptable accommodation with India.

The difficulty was that Hyderabad was located in the very centre of India and was surrounded on all sides by Indian territory. Its existence as an independent State was seen by India as anomalous and unacceptable, the more so because of the Hindu character of the majority of its people. If the Nizam did not of his own choice adhere to India, it was made plain that India would exercise its power and incorporate Hyderabad into India by force. As the Indian Prime Minister, Nehru, said, 'it is impossible for an independent State to have foreign territory right at its heart'. India did not accept that the termination of the treaty between the Nizam and Britain left the Nizam free to assert independence. In India's view, the relationship between Hyderabad and the central authorities in India then reverted to what it had originally been, a relationship of dependence based on the concept of 'paramountcy' derived from the days of Moghul rule under which all the Maharajahs were subject to the overriding, though sparsely exercised, authority of Delhi.

Anticipating the prospect of the end of his relationship with Britain, the Nizam sought the help of an eminent British lawyer, Sir Walter Monckton,[74] to negotiate a new arrangement with the Indian authorities. A one-year 'Standstill Agreement' was concluded in November 1947 which, contemplating the continuation of negotiations towards the

---

[74] Sir Walter Monckton, KCMG, KCVO, MC, KC (1891–1965) was a leading KC for many years. He is best known for his role as adviser to King Edward VIII, particularly at the time of the latter's abdication. He became Minister of Labour in Churchill's 1951 government but resigned in disagreement with British policy over Suez in 1956.

conclusion of a final agreement as to the form and nature of the relationship between Hyderabad and India, provided that the arrangements
that had existed between Hyderabad and Britain prior to the date of
the Indian Independence Act, including the conduct of external affairs,
would continue, insofar as may be appropriate between Hyderabad and
India. The Standstill Agreement also contained an arbitration clause to
cover any dispute arising out of it.

Negotiations continued, but by May 1948 it looked as if India was
about to take unilateral action to resolve the matter. The Nizam
instructed his solicitors in London to obtain additional help to preserve
his legal position. Recognising that the situation involved international
legal questions, the firm turned to Hersch for advice. At very short
notice, and with little background information, he attended a consultation in London in early June 1948 at which a number of questions were
canvassed: whether it could be argued that Hyderabad really was an
independent State and had the capacity to initiate proceedings in the
UN; if not, what State could act on its behalf; whether an invasion by
India would be a violation of Article 2(4) of the UN Charter which prohibited the use of force against the territorial integrity or independence
of any State; if so, to what organ of the UN could Hyderabad appeal, the
General Assembly or the Security Council, or both, and when and how
such an appeal could be lodged; the composition of any delegation to be
sent to the UN, and whether Hyderabad could commence proceedings
in the ICJ.

Hersch was due to leave on 8 June for his visit to the University
of Colorado for seven weeks. Despite the short notice, he yielded to
the temptation to be involved in so important a matter. He could not
decline the opportunity and indicated that he was prepared to work on
the matter while he was in Colorado.

Another consultation on the same matter was squeezed in before his
departure. Monckton, who was in India continuing negotiations with
the Indian authorities, was kept informed and he suggested that John
Foster[75] should be added to the team. But later in June the negotiations
broke down, India intensified the blockade of Hyderabad, a number of
border incursions took place and the Nizam began to fear the risk of
imminent Indian invasion. Hersch, by then in Colorado, was constantly

---

[75] Monckton to Brunyate, 25 June 1948. John Galway Foster (1904–82), barrister and politician;
Fellow of All Souls College, Oxford, 1924–82; Legal Adviser, British Embassy, Washington, 1939–43;
Legal Adviser to the Supreme Headquarters Allied Expeditionary Force, 1944–5; highly regarded
for his intellectual brilliance and imaginative approach to legal questions.

consulted by letter and telephone. In particular, on 28 June he was asked to produce a summary of the arguments for and against the proposition that Hyderabad was a 'State'.[76]

In the meantime, Monckton, who was a significant political figure as well as being a pre-eminent lawyer, had been discussing the situation with Winston Churchill, who was sympathetic to the Hyderabad case, and with Lord Mountbatten, the Governor-General of India. On 5 July Hersch sent a nine-page memorandum dealing with a number of mainly procedural issues, including the effect of Articles 35(2) and 11(2) of the UN Charter and the questions whether Hyderabad was a State and whether it could apply to become a party to the Statute of the ICJ. This was followed within four days by a letter emphasising in detail the need for preparation for recourse to the UN at the meetings that were to take place in Paris in September.[77] On 13 July, Hersch sent to London the summary argument on the status of Hyderabad. He was then asked to prepare a full version for inclusion in Hyderabad's appeal to the UN. In reply to a question as to whether Hyderabad should apply for membership of the UN, Hersch advised that there might be some tactical advantage in so doing, but only after appeal had been made to the Security Council under Article 35 of the UN Charter. He also advised that a further indirect way of asserting the statehood of Hyderabad would be to apply to become a party to the Statute of the ICJ,[78] but this was not done. On 19 July, Hersch again reverted to the importance of readying the material required for submission to the UN. He also raised the possibility that when in New York on his way home he should consult with the UN Secretary-General as to the best procedure to follow.[79] Eventually, he saw not the Secretary-General but some of the lawyers in the UN with whom he was acquainted.

On 21 July, he wrote:

I have now considered your suggestion that I should prepare a full version of the Summary Argument on the question of statehood. My feeling is that it would be a mistake to deal very fully with this question in our first communication lodging the appeal. We can deal with the matter briefly and say that if this question should create any doubts in the minds of the Meeting or the Committee, we are ready to develop this particular issue in detail. But by pleading the matter at length in our first communication we might create the impression that we have grave doubts on the subject. However, it is clear that we shall have to have ready

[76] Brunyate to HL., 28 June 1948.   [77] HL to Brunyate, 9 July 1948.
[78] HL to Brunyate, 16 July 1948.   [79] HL to Brunyate, 19 July 1948.

a more detailed argument on the matter sooner or later, and I am therefore proceeding as suggested.

At the same time as Hersch was at work on the various contributions asked of him, Brunyate and the team at Coward, Chance were preparing drafts of the factual part of the submission to be made to the UN, though by 26 July Brunyate was expressing privately his doubt about what the UN could actually do to help Hyderabad.[80] Further detailed letters of advice from Hersch followed on 29 and 30 July and 1 August. In the last, Hersch commented on Brunyate's doubts as follows:

> The larger issue of the effectiveness of the approach to the United Nations:
> My opinion is that whatever the United Nations may decide and whatever may be the respect which India will pay to a favourable decision, if any, of the United Nations, Hyderabad has nothing to lose – except, on a substantial scale, in the matter of expense – and has a great deal to gain. Possibly she may achieve an international recognition of her right to independent Statehood – a great asset in her negotiations with India even if eventually she consents to be satisfied, or is forced to be satisfied, with something less than full international sovereignty. Even if she does not achieve that, she may obtain an international pronouncement calling upon India to desist from hostile or aggressive action, economic or other. This, too, would be a valuable gain even if India does not comply with that pronouncement. Undoubtedly, a vital interest of India is involved in the controversy. But the force of international opinion will be a powerful factor in determining whether India will press that vital interest to the point of coercion pure and simple or whether she will be willing to accept a solution based on a compromise. At the same time it is clear that a vital principle of the Charter of the United Nations is involved, and I do not think that it is likely that the General Assembly – or the Security Council – will refrain from taking action for fear that its recommendation may be disregarded.[81]

Brunyate was by this time experiencing some difficulties with the Hyderabad representatives in London, whose attitude to the preparations for recourse to the UN was ambivalent. They appeared to be uncertain as to whether they wanted to keep the conduct of the whole matter to themselves or wished to rely upon the advice and help of Coward, Chance. In seeking some guidance from a former British official in London who knew Hyderabad well, Brunyate had occasion to observe:

---

[80] Brunyate to HL, 26 July 1948.
[81] HL to Brunyate, 1 August 1948.

They do not even want to have Professor Lauterpacht with them at the UNO. Yet he is one of the leading international lawyers of the day and he has thrown his skill into this job more whole-heartedly than I could possibly have expected from any such man. He is in America and has little knowledge of Hyderabad and no opportunity of consultation. Nonetheless he has sent us what I consider to be some of the most brilliant advice that I have ever seen in my professional career. To leave him off their staff would be folly.[82]

Eventually, Brunyate was led to tell Monckton of the difficulties he was experiencing and to conclude that if Hyderabad

genuinely wishes for our aid, we will give it... either we cease full-blooded assistance when the documentary case is prepared, or we continue at the work and in the confidence of the Hyderabad Government and in the determination to win the case. It is for them to say.[83]

Hersch was by then approaching the end of his stay in Colorado. It was arranged that John Foster would fly out to New York to consult with him and to provide support in the talks with the UN officials. On 20 August, Hersch and Foster advised by cable that there should not be a simultaneous approach to the Security Council and the General Assembly lest it make an 'unfavourable impression'. Hersch then started back to England on the *Queen Elizabeth*, arrived on 26 August and attended a consultation on 27 August. He followed this by going straight to Brussels for two days to attend a meeting of the International Law Association.

Zahir Ahmed, the Secretary of the Ministry of Foreign Affairs of Hyderabad, present in London, had received instructions from Hyderabad to apply simultaneously to the General Assembly and the Security Council. Following the advice of the lawyers in London, he took the decision to apply only to the Security Council and on 21 August a formal message on behalf of the Government of Hyderabad was cabled to the UN Secretary-General asking him to bring to the attention of the Security Council 'the grave dispute which had arisen between Hyderabad and India'. More than three weeks were to pass before 16 September when the Hyderabad communication eventually came before the Council. By then it was already too late to save Hyderabad. India had occupied the State on 13 September and, in the Security Council, took the position that Hyderabad was not an independent State and could not invoke the Security Council's aid.

[82] Brunyate to Sir Wilfrid Grigson, 9 August 1948.
[83] Brunyate to Monckton, 10 August 1948. Brunyate also gave Hersch some indication of the difficulties in a letter of the same date.

Meanwhile, activity continued in London. On 31 August Hersch had circulated a detailed note setting out, as a matter of urgency, the details for an application by Hyderabad to adhere to the Statute of the ICJ with a view to enabling Hyderabad to commence proceedings against India on the basis of India's acceptance of the compulsory jurisdiction of the Court.[84] This was followed on 2 September by a further note from Hersch developing the idea that Hyderabad might submit a unilateral declaration to the ICJ as a non-party to the Statute, accepting the Court's jurisdiction.[85] But Hersch recognised that such a declaration would be mainly of political significance. He then went on to prepare an elaboration of his summary of the case which was ready by 6 September. He was 'hacking about'[86] the main memorandum that had been prepared by Coward, Chance.

One idea that was not canvassed in the documents filed by Hyderabad with the UN was that of a plebiscite, notwithstanding that Monckton had at an early stage taken the view that Hyderabad's case would be strengthened if it contained an offer of a plebiscite to determine the views of the Hyderabad population. But the Nizam and his officials did not adopt the suggestion even though it was one that Hersch supported.[87]

A team arrived in London from Hyderabad on 12 September before moving on to Paris on 14 September. The question of Hersch's fees for all his work was discussed between Brunyate and Hersch's clerk; the latter proposed a fee of 5,000 guineas to cover all Hersch's work from the beginning through Paris. Coward, Chance thought this reasonable, though eventually a reduced fee was agreed.

The delegation, having arrived in Paris, presented to the Secretary-General the two volumes of Hyderabad's case that had been prepared over the previous weeks by the team in London. This included the parts on which Hersch had been working. There followed from Hersch a number of internal notes regarding preparations for the meeting of the Security Council, the need for an interview with the Secretary-General and the need to consider whether Article 39 of the Charter (requiring the Security Council to determine whether an act of aggression had occurred) should be invoked.[88] Hersch also began preparing the opening speech for Moin Nawaz Jung, the Minister who had arrived from

---

[84] HL to Brunyate, 31 August 1948. [85] HL to Brunyate, 2 September 1948.
[86] Brunyate's words, in a letter to Monckton, 6 September 1948. Some of Hersch's proposed changes are set out in HL to Brunyate, 8 September 1948. See also Brunyate to Zahir Ahmed, 10 September 1948.
[87] Brunyate to Zahir Ahmed, 10 September 1948. [88] HL draft, 15 September 1948.

Hyderabad and who was leading the delegation. Brunyate did not initially know of this and wrote to Monckton expressing his surprise that Hersch was proceeding on his own. Brunyate also told Hersch's secretary that Hersch must show the draft to John Foster before showing it to the client.[89] This was the beginning of some tension between Brunyate and Hersch. In his letter to Monckton, Brunyate said:

There have been other minor incidents, which show the value of observing some of the ordinary routine; for example there was a complete muddle yesterday, when the draftsman of the Speech made his own arrangements for its duplication, with the result that practically no copies were available when they were urgently wanted. When I pointed out in the evening, perhaps too gently, that I ought to have been called in for this, the Professor replied to John Foster and me, that he could not very well do that because he would have been told that we were not needed here any way. In brief, the Professor is a man of great knowledge of International Law under the United Nations, and in many ways a beautiful draftsman. I think too, that he has two thirds of a kindly heart, but he has no knowledge of organisations or of the requirements for successful work amongst a group of lawyers, and he is much too confident that he is quick to understand the mentality of the individuals with whom we are dealing, and that our difficulties would not occur with a man of his sweet reasonableness. The truth is, that he has an academic disdain for practical men of affairs. I should have been sorry not to have had him, I think he is a definite acquisition, but it is a great misfortune in most ways that you were unable to be here.[90]

The Security Council met on 16 September. During the meeting, India's doubts were shared by a number of members. No conclusion was reached on that day. When the Council met again on 20 September, the Hyderabad representative said that he had not received any instructions emanating from the Nizam, but the Indian representative informed the Council that he had received a telegram containing the Nizam's instructions to the head of the Hyderabad delegation to withdraw the complaint from the Council. After a brief discussion, the Council did no more than decide to keep the case on the agenda. On 22 September, the Nizam informed the Secretary-General directly that he had instructed the Hyderabad delegation to withdraw the case from the Security Council and the delegation no longer had authority to represent him or the State. Even so, the Hyderabad delegation transmitted a further note

---

[89] Brunyate to Monckton, 17 September 1948.
[90] Brunyate to Monckton. Monckton had been laid low with a serious attack of neuritis and was unable to come to Paris.

on 24 September reviewing recent developments in Hyderabad and asserting, in effect, that the Nizam was acting under duress.

On 25 and 27 September, the situation was the subject of speeches by India and Pakistan in the General Assembly, India justifying its action by reference to the need to maintain order in Hyderabad and Pakistan asserting that India had committed an act of aggression.

At the request of the Hyderabad delegation, Hersch was in Paris during these developments, giving such aid and counsel as he could.

On 18 September, Brunyate wrote to Hersch telling him that Monckton and Foster considered that the delegation ought to ask for a week's adjournment, but nothing was to be done until it had been discussed with Zahir Ahmed. Brunyate also indirectly raised the possibility that Hersch might wish to leave the team, saying:

I shall be grateful if you will discuss the position with me before you take any definite action as regards your own position either as regards the extent to which you can continue to advise or as regards returning to London.

He emphasised that, because of Monckton's close friendship with the Nizam, 'we ought to be sure that Sir Walter's views are fully taken into account'.[91]

Hersch seems to have taken some exception to this letter for he spoke on the telephone to Brunyate who, in a letter the next day, referred to the fact that Hersch had said he found the letter embarrassing. In acknowledging that:

inevitably problems will arise. Brunyate said they would need discussion. For instance, Counsel would not usually withdraw without first seeing the instructing solicitor who might have views to represent and so on.

At the same time, Hersch was preparing a draft of a speech for Moin Nawaz in which he included the suggestion that the Council should retain the matter on its agenda so that it might deal with it on its own initiative. But both Monckton and Foster thought that this would be going beyond Ahmed's brief.[92] Hersch then wrote on the same day to Brunyate saying that nothing in their telephone conversation 'could properly be interpreted as intimating a possibility, on my part, of withdrawing from the case'.

---

[91] Brunyate to HL, 18 September 1948.
[92] Brunyate reporting to Zahir Ahmed, 19 September 1948.

A further indication of the deterioration in the relationship between Hersch and Brunyate is to be seen in the latter's letter to Hersch of 19 September:

Earlier in these proceedings we allowed the ordinary rules of procedure and etiquette as between Counsel, Solicitor and Client to be relaxed. It seemed to us better that it should be so. We have now reached a stage of critical importance to our Client HEH the Nizam of Hyderabad and his Government, and we ask of all our Hyderabad Counsel that the rules of procedure and etiquette be now strictly observed, so that my firm, of which two partners are now in Paris (today), may exercise its proper coordinating function in the interests of the client and so that advice given may be fully recorded.

We shall of course keep you fully informed of all information which reaches us and we rely on you to reciprocate.

I am writing in similar terms to our other Counsel.[93]

The nub of the disagreement was recorded in a letter from Brunyate to his partner, Tim Tylor, on 23 September, as follows:

I can see that quite a number of difficult questions may arise before we are through with Hyderabad. One such question will be the extent to which Professor Lauterpacht is free to continue advising Zahir Ahmed or the late, present or future Hyderabad Governments. This was briefly discussed at the consultation on Tuesday between Mr John Foster, Professor Lauterpacht and myself. Mr John Foster said that in Walter Monckton's view the lawyers must scrupulously refrain from doing anything which is contrary to the Nizam's ostensible instructions; that is to say, if the Nizam directs that the UNO Appeal be withdrawn the lawyers must accept that direction and not seek to promote the Appeal further and they are not entitled to argue that the Nizam has acted under duress. Professor Lauterpacht appeared disposed to think that he could retain some freedom of action and that he could, if he wished, support Nawab Moin Nawaz Jung and Mr Zahir Ahmed in the steps taken to press the Hyderabad case with the United Nations. When Mr Foster pointed out that Professor Lauterpacht could not advise direct, the Professor replied that he had always considered himself free to take briefs direct from a Government. Mr John Foster replied that Professor Lauterpacht is of course free to take instructions direct from a government, but not where he has already been instructed by solicitors. The Professor did not wholly agree, but he said that he would not take direct instructions except after telling us.

There is to my mind a further point which we must safeguard. We have all been advising the Nizam and the Nizam's Government and none of us are free

---

[93] Brunyate to HL, 19 September 1948.

to advise another client on the same subject matter. For this reason alone I feel sure that our firm would not consider itself free to advise individuals such as Mr Zahir Ahmed or an émigré government and we should not, I think, free any Counsel without the consent of the Hyderabad Government or at any rate without the most careful consideration with Sir Walter Monckton. The restriction on our ability to advise other persons is something which enures for the benefit of the client and we must not give away what belongs to the client. We may indeed have to enforce our clients' rights against Professor Lauterpacht if he insists on advising others.

One factor contributing to this estrangement may have been simply logistical. Hersch was staying in the rather luxurious Plaza Athénée Hotel, in the Avenue George V, in the company of the Hyderabad delegation, while, because of the difficulty of securing hotel accommodation in Paris at that period, Brunyate and the Coward, Chance team were staying in the Hotel Lutetia on the other side of the river and less grand. So there was not the close neighbourly proximity between all concerned that it is desirable to maintain, and is usually maintained, in such proceedings – as demonstrated by the fact that so many letters needed to be exchanged at that time.

Hersch remained in Paris where he received a letter from Tim Tylor about fees. Tylor noted that, though Hersch had originally asked for 5,000 guineas, 'he had said that he would not expect this figure in the events that had happened'. Instead, Tylor proposed that Hersch should be put down for 3,500 guineas and asked him if he would find this acceptable. Tylor added that the firm's accounts showed that it was short of funds by about £4,100.[94]

Hersch's instructions, according to a letter from him to Tylor of 16 October (by which time Hersch was back in Cambridge), were terminated on 21 September. He then wrote to say:

I note that your accounts show a deficiency of £4,100. I have reason to believe that the Hyderabad Government will make good that deficiency. Should that not be the case I feel that the entire loss should not fall on your firm and that, in due course, Solicitors and Counsel should have a conference and try to apportion the loss on an equitable basis. You can regard this suggestion as a formal undertaking on my part. There were inevitable differences, in this somewhat novel case, between the various parties concerned, but we all tried to do our best in difficult circumstances and, so far as I am concerned, I would like to contribute to a fair settlement, should such become necessary, of the financial aspect of the matter.

[94] Tylor to HL, 4 October 1948.

In passing this reply to Monckton, Tylor observed that it was 'very civil',[95] a description with which Monckton agreed.[96] Hersch's suggestion was accepted and the fee of 3,000 guineas was paid, plus the customary clerk's fees of 2.5 per cent. And that is the end of the matter as it appears from the correspondence.

The balance of the large sums that the Nizam had sent to London to fund his effort to maintain his independence were subsequently the subject of extended litigation in the English courts.[97] The item has remained on the Security Council agenda to this day.

Hersch was saddened by the whole affair. The excitement and stimulus of his role in Paris were not sufficient to balance his disappointment at the outcome. Also, he had made the mistake of becoming too emotionally involved in the case, having developed warm personal relations with both Moin Nawaz and Zahir Ahmed. He was distressed by the falling out with his instructing solicitors. The fact that he became so embroiled reflects his relative inexperience at that time in the practice and etiquette of the Bar. He did not make the same mistake again.

This case produced his first substantial earnings at the Bar, as the work that he had done in connection with both the Nuremberg and the Joyce trials was unremunerated. His previous financial discomfort that figured so largely in his wartime correspondence with Rachel and occasionally recurred in domestic matters even after that period was much eased. He was never to become wealthy, but from then on he was sufficiently comfortably off to install central heating in Cranmer Road and to indulge himself and Rachel in occasional forays to Christie's and Sotheby's in London where he bought a few minor paintings and some pieces of silver and furniture. He was not a collector in the real sense of the word, never developing any specialist knowledge about the items he acquired. Nonetheless, these excursions to London and his purchases gave him much pleasure. The day usually included lunch at the Ladies' Annex of the Athenaeum, then very agreeably housed in No. 6 Carlton Gardens.

1949

The excessive workload of 1948 led to a bad start to 1949. Rachel had gone to Palestine in December 1948 to be with her father in his last

---

[95] L. P. Tylor to Monckton, 18 October 1948.   [96] Monckton to Tylor, 19 October 1948.
[97] *Nizam of Hyderabad* v. *Jung*, 23 *ILR* 173, subsequently appealed to the House of Lords, sub. nom. *Rahimtoola* v. *Nizam of Hyderabad*, 24 *ILR* 175.

days. He died on 4 January 1949. Hersch was on his own at Cranmer Road suffering from a sinus infection. He was confined to bed for some twelve days, followed by a short spell in the Evelyn Nursing Home in Cambridge to have his antrum drained. For a while, he was quite depressed. Although it was term time, I spent most of my days looking after him. When his health improved sufficiently, he went to Hove for a few days to get the benefit of some sea air. Rachel returned in late January.

As he regained strength, he followed Arnold McNair's advice to apply for 'silk', that is, to be appointed a King's Counsel. McNair guided him as to the form and content of his application, for which he sought and obtained the support of two Law Lords: Lord Porter, who had worked with him on the question of human rights, and Lord Wright, who had been chairman of the War Crimes Commission. McNair was active in promoting his candidature, and Shawcross who, as Attorney-General, was always consulted by the Lord Chancellor when considering the appointments, also put in a good word for him.

In April, the new appointments were announced, Hersch's name amongst them, and on 26 April he attended the ceremony at the House of Lords when, attired in formal court dress including a full-bottomed wig, silk gown and knee breeches, and in the company of the other successful applicants, he made the necessary formal declaration. This was followed by the traditional visit to the Royal Courts of Justice in the Strand when the new silks circulated from court room to court room, taking it in turn to bow to each judge and by so doing responding silently but affirmatively to the judge's question: 'Do you move, Mr Lauterpacht?' This quaint ceremony over, Hersch, Rachel and I enjoyed a celebratory lunch at the Athenaeum.

Serious work had been resumed in February, when he prepared and delivered a paper to the Grotius Society on 'The Proposed European Court of Human Rights'.[98] This was followed by a spate of professional work.

Rights under oil concessions in the Persian Gulf

Soon he became involved in the first of three matters relating to the interpretation and application of oil concessions in the Persian Gulf. Following the end of the Second World War, technical advances in oil exploration and production led to attempts in many areas to extend

---

[98] (1949) 35 *Transactions of the Grotius Society* 25.

activities into the offshore seabed and subsoil of the continental shelf. In 1945, President Truman issued a proclamation claiming jurisdiction and control over such areas adjacent to the coasts of the United States. The British Government and the oil companies operating in the territories around the Gulf began to consider how these developments might affect the rights of the companies granted in concession agreements dating from the mid-1930s.

The first item that came before Hersch in early 1949 was a request by the Kuwait Oil Company (KOC) (owned in equal shares by the Anglo-Iranian Oil Company and the Gulf Oil Corporation) for advice on two questions. One was whether the concession granted to the company on 23 December 1934 included the island of Quaruh and a number of other islands in the Gulf claimed by Kuwait but not appearing on the map attached to the concession ('the islands question'). The other was whether any subsequent accession to the jurisdiction or sovereignty of Kuwait in pursuance of an effective assertion of claims to the continental shelf would automatically be included in the concession ('the continental shelf question').

The words in the concession agreement defining the concession's area of operation were 'within the State of Kuwait including all islands and territorial waters appertaining to Kuwait as shown generally on the map annexed hereto'.

Hersch's Opinion, dated 14 March 1949, began by considering the law that would be applicable to the interpretation of the concession. He took the view that, in the absence of any express choice of law, English law and general principles of law would apply to the question of title; and that international law would determine the legal status of the continental shelf. As to the islands question, Hersch regarded the words '*all* the islands as shown *generally*[99] on the map' as sufficient to cover the islands in question. He noted that the concession agreement did not refer to 'such islands as are shown on the map'. As the right to explore for and produce petroleum was granted exclusively to KOC, no construction of the concession agreement could be countenanced that left any part of the territory of Kuwait outside the purview of the agreement.

As to the question of whether the company's claim extended to the continental shelf, Hersch opined that it was likely to be recognised by an impartial arbitrator adjudicating on the basis of international law and

[99] Emphasis added.

equity. He concluded that, even though Kuwait had not at that time proclaimed its authority over the continental shelf, the doctrine of the continental shelf had, on the basis of its application by numerous States, 'come to stay'. He expressly qualified his view by saying that the doctrine of the continental shelf was not part of international law at the time the concession agreement was granted, 'it is a valid affirmation of a claim to a title which is not prohibited by international law'.

Hersch discussed in some detail whether the rights under the 1934 concession agreement extended to 'after-acquired' territory, and concluded that they did, partly because the agreement applied to 'the State of Kuwait' without limitation and partly because the concession agreement was an exclusive concession, thus indicating that no rights could be granted to another company in respect of such 'after-acquired' territory.

There then followed internal discussions in which Hersch was closely involved, together with consultations in March and April 1949, as to how to present the company's case to the Sheikh of Kuwait. In the course of the discussions, Hersch and Godfrey Phillips, a partner in Linklaters and Paines, the instructing solicitors, became good friends.[100] Inserted in Hersch's papers there is a scrap of paper, evidently passed by Phillips to Hersch during a consultation: 'Don't tell your clerk to be modest re fee!'

Hersch followed up the March Opinion with a brief note on 16 May 1949 saying that 'further study of and reflection on the matter have confirmed me in the view that the case is a strong one'. He emphasised that the company's claim was not in respect of territory newly acquired by the Sheikh. The claim was in respect of the submerged coastal part of the territory of the State. He concluded:

It is, in my view, a good proposition of law that when a State grants an exclusive concession governing the whole of its territory and its territorial waters and that State subsequently claims control over a contiguous area on the ground of its organic connection with its main territory (e.g. on the ground of its being a submerged coastal part of its territory) then the concession covers the contiguous area thus claimed.

Subject to some limited qualifications, Hersch's views were accepted by the Legal Adviser of the Foreign Office.

On 12 June 1949, the Sheikh of Kuwait proclaimed that the seabed and subsoil adjoining the territorial waters of Kuwait 'become part

---

[100] Hersch's relationship with Linklaters became quite cordial and he worked with them closely in other matters.

of the principality of Kuwait and are subject to its administration and authority'.[101] The company then requested the Foreign Office to forward to the Sheikh Hersch's opinion to the effect that the seabed and subsoil in question are covered by the 1934 concession agreement. There appears to be no record of the reaction of the Sheikh to the opinion, beyond the fact that the Sheikh did not thereafter deny to the company the right to treat the continental shelf as included within its concession area.

The second item, relating to similar questions arising in connection with concessions granted by Qatar, Dubai and Abu Dhabi, overlapped with much of Hersch's work on the Kuwait concession. He was instructed, on 25 April 1949, to advise in company with Sir Walter Monckton, KC, and the Hon. H. L. Parker (later to become Lord Chief Justice of England), on the extent of the concessions granted by these three sheikhdoms. Advice was initially given in consultation on 3 May 1949. To the limited extent that it differed from the advice already given by Hersch in relation to Kuwait, this was because of the different wording of the relevant concession agreements. It probably also reflected the more traditional thinking of Monckton and Parker.

Hersch's opinion on the inherent adhesion of the continental shelf to the adjacent land territory, and on the basis of which the companies claimed to be entitled to rights in the continental shelf, was soon sorely tested in two arbitrations, in both of which Hersch participated.

The first was the case of the *Petroleum Development (Qatar) Ltd v. Ruler of Qatar*, decided by Lord Radcliffe in April 1950.[102] He held, without giving reasons, that the concession included the islands over which the Sheikh ruled at the date of the concession, whether or not shown on the map, as well as their seabed and subsoil, but did not include the seabed or the subsoil beneath the high seas contiguous with the territorial waters.[103]

---

[101] A translation into English appears in the *Laws and Regulations in the Regions of the High Seas*, UN Legislative Series, vol. 1 (1951), p. 26. As printed in this series, the Kuwait proclamation differs from all the others in that it states that 'the seabed and subsoil ... *become* part of the principality of Kuwait' (emphasis added). The other proclamations used the verb 'appertain' to the particular sheikhdom. 'Appertain' supports the view that the seabed was already part of the territory of the State, while 'become' could be taken as suggesting that the assertion of title was something new. The discrepancy does not appear in any of the other documents and was not adverted to in the Foreign Office documents or Hersch's opinions. Nor was any reference to it made in Professor Humphrey Waldock's analysis of the Gulf proclamations in his speech in the *Abu Dhabi* case.

[102] 18 *ILR* 161.

[103] *Ibid.*, p. 163. In November 1949, Hersch, jointly with Professor Kahn-Freund, Professor of Comparative Law at the LSE, had been asked to advise Petroleum Development (Qatar) Ltd as to which parts of the Kuwait Opinion could usefully be applied in the pending case against Qatar. This joint Opinion was generally in line with the earlier joint Opinion.

The second case was *Petroleum Development (Trucial Coast)* v. *Sheikh of Abu Dhabi*, decided by Lord Asquith in September 1951.[104] Here, too, though on a reasoned basis, Lord Asquith held that the concession did not cover the continental shelf because

in no form can the doctrine claim as yet to have assumed hitherto the hard lineaments or the definitive status of an established rule of international law.[105]

In a footnote to his decision, Lord Asquith acknowledged that he had derived instruction from Hersch's article in the *BYIL* on 'Sovereignty over Submarine Areas',[106] as also from Professor Waldock's article on 'The Legal Basis of Claims to the Continental Shelf'.[107] But evidently Lord Asquith was more persuaded by Waldock's article. In both cases, Hersch played a major role in the preparation of the written pleadings and of the oral argument of his leader, Sir Walter Monckton. Moreover, in the *Abu Dhabi* case, Monckton insisted that Hersch should present part of the oral argument. His contribution covers thirty-seven single-spaced foolscap pages of the transcript. So far as it has been possible to ascertain, this was the only occasion on which Hersch ever argued before an international tribunal.

However, the non-acceptance at that time of Hersch's presentation of the so-called '*ipso jure* argument' was not carried over into either the 1958 Continental Shelf Convention or the 1982 UN Convention on the Law of the Sea. Moreover, in 1969, the ICJ had already said in its judgment in the *North Sea Continental Shelf* cases:

[T]he rights of the coastal State in respect of the area of continental shelf that constitutes a natural promulgation of its land territory into and under the sea exists *ipso facto* and *ab initio*, by virtue of its sovereignty over the land, and as an extension of it in exercise of sovereign rights for the purpose of exploring the seabed and exploring its natural resources. *In short, there is here an inherent right.*[108]

There could have been no more explicit acceptance of Hersch's initial views.

Towards the end of April 1949, Hersch was asked by the Swiss Government for an opinion on its handling of the case of a Romanian national, Solvan Vitianu, who had been appointed as an economic counsellor to the Romanian Legation in Berne, but had been arrested and charged

---

[104] *Ibid.*, p. 144.   [105] *Ibid.*, p. 155.   [106] (1950) 27 *BYIL* 376–433.

[107] (1950) 36 *Transactions of the Grotius Society*. Although this had not yet appeared at the time of the Award, it had been submitted in draft as part of the argument for the respondent.

[108] ICJ Reports 1969, p. 3, para. 23 (emphasis added).

by the Swiss authorities with usury, bribery and economic espionage.[109] The question was whether Vitianu was entitled to diplomatic immunity despite the fact that, though his appointment by the Romanian Government had been notified to the Swiss authorities, it had not been accepted by the time that he was arrested. Hersch advised that, in the circumstances, Vitianu was not entitled to diplomatic immunity, but at the same time observed that the manner in which the Swiss Government had acted could convey an impression of 'lack of respect . . . for the authority . . . of the principle of diplomatic immunity'. He spelt this comment out at some length, saying that the Swiss authorities had 'laid themselves open to the reproach of a questionable practice in a matter of fundamental significance in international law'. He continued:

The Swiss authorities may feel inclined, by a statesmanlike act of clemency, to terminate an incident in which they successfully asserted the correct legal position in circumstances which may have given rise to plausible criticism of the manner in which they exercised their judicial right.

He suggested that, if Vitianu should be convicted, 'the legal position of Switzerland . . . would not be prejudiced' if the Swiss authorities were to consider whether the circumstances of the case might warrant remission or mitigation of the sentence. Vitianu was deported from Switzerland six months later.

In June, there was a pleasing domestic event. His niece, Inka, whom he had brought to Cambridge in 1946, got married at 6 Cranmer Road to a distant relative, Maurice Katz, a talented engineer, and went to live in Paris.

At about this time, the Lord Chancellor, Lord Jowitt, asked Hersch to provide him with some suggestions for a talk that the Lord Chancellor was to deliver. Hersch sent him a complete draft which occasioned the following acknowledgment from the Lord Chancellor:

I find it difficult to express my thanks adequately to you for your kindness in sending me suggestions for a speech on the future of international law. I have read your notes and find them most interesting, and I have determined to make the speech on the lines which you have suggested.

I feel sorry to think that I am appropriating as my own the work which you have done. I only hope you will derive satisfaction from two thoughts. The first

---

[109] The opinion is reprinted in *Collected Papers*, Vol. 3, pp. 433–57.

that imitation is the sincerest form of flattery. The second that by adopting your notes I may advance the cause which you and I both have at heart.

If, hereafter, I am acclaimed as the greatest living master of international law, I shall have an uneasy feeling that I am basking in the glory that ought to be yours.

I should, however, infer from your notes that you can spare me a little bit of your glory.

I am, however, most grateful to you for the work you have done.

In October, he was asked if he would care to send a message of congratulation to the Hebrew University on the occasion of the opening of its Faculty of Law. He replied as follows:

Enclosure in a letter from HL to Dr Zander, 20 October 1949
I consider it a privilege to be allowed to send a message of congratulations and warm wishes to the Hebrew University of Jerusalem on the occasion of the opening of its Faculty of Laws. As in other countries so also in Israel the study of law has a proper and indispensable place in the political life of the community and in the administration of justice. In addition, there are not many countries in which the study of jurisprudence in its wider sense, of legal history and of comparative law is based on deeper foundations of past achievement and native genius. As an international lawyer I am thinking with great hopes of my own subject which has so fittingly been given a definite place in the legal curriculum of the University in the City of the Prophets.

Whenever he could, Hersch returned to the revision and expansion of *International Law and Human Rights*, which he eventually finished in late September and sent off to the printers on 5 October. On this same subject, he was asked by the BBC to give a talk on the Third Programme entitled 'Towards an International Bill of Rights'.[110] On 12 October, he went to Broadcasting House to record the talk which was transmitted later in October. Hersch was at home to listen to it. He had never before heard a recording of his voice and was considerably mortified by what he heard. He vowed that he would never give a broadcast again!

HL to RL, 27 October 1949
We listened last night to my broadcast. What a flop! I had a cold when I was recording it and the voice sounded even more foreign than usually. I did not recognise myself. I do not think I will go down to posterity as a great broadcaster.

[110] The text is reprinted in the *Collected Papers*, Vol. 3, pp. 411–15.

For nearly two months, from September until November, Hersch was distracted by Rachel's absence in New York for an operation by a leading American ear specialist to relieve her deafness. She was very brave about going there on her own for a difficult and painful procedure with an uncertain outcome. She faced up to the prospect courageously and within a few days of the operation she was writing reassuring letters to Hersch.

CHAPTER 10

1950–1954

1950

Recognition

The year 1950 began with a rare venture into letter-writing to a newspaper. This was in connection with the change in the British Government's attitude towards the position of the Nationalist Government of China and the associated recognition of the Communist People's Republic of China. The change was announced on 6 January 1950, and on that same day, at the instigation of the Foreign Office, Hersch published in *The Times* an extended restatement of the law relating to recognition:

It may be helpful, at a time when His Majesty's Government is faced [in China] with the necessity of taking a decision of great moment, to state the rule of international law in the matter of recognition of Governments. Such action as is about to be taken must be based on legal principles capable of general application and rooted in the practice of this and other States. It must not be open to the charge that it is being adopted exclusively for the sake of advantages which may be immediate and tangible but which are insignificant when weighed in the balance of the enduring interests of this country and of the peace of the world.

The problem of recognition of Governments is one of the crucial issues of international law. It touches the independence of States at one of its most vital points. To decline to recognise a Government is to withhold from the community which it governs most of the advantages of international law. It involves, among other things, a refusal to acknowledge the validity of its legislative and judicial acts; and the denial to it and its organs of the ordinary jurisdictional immunities. On the other side, it involves the Government refusing recognition in a series of difficulties since *ex hypothesi* it is unable to use the ordinary international methods of protecting its own nationals and interests in territory controlled by the Governments which it refuses to recognise.

There are some who maintain that, all this notwithstanding, recognition is a purely discretionary act of policy – act of grace which may be withheld at pleasure and may legitimately be used as a weapon of political intervention or of economic pressure. There is no support for any such view in the bulk of the practice of this and other countries. On the contrary, overwhelming authority points to the view that, provided that the conditions presented by international law are fulfilled, there is a legal duty to recognise.

The principles of international law, which, in the absence of an international authority, States have by and large observed, are, stated as briefly as the subject permits, as follows:

(1) Recognition is a declaration of an existing fact. Whenever the requisite conditions of governmental capacity exist recognition is due as a matter of right. Once the revolutionary Government may fairly be held to enjoy, with a reasonable prospect of permanency, the obedience of the mass of the population, and once it is in effective control of the bulk of the national territory, it is entitled to recognition. Its revolutionary origin or the method of the revolutionary change is irrelevant.

The United States of America, which more than any other country has had occasion to formulate an attitude on the subject, has given emphatic and repeated expression to that view. As President van Buren said in 1829, 'that which is the Government *de facto* is equally so *de jure*' or, as Secretary of State Fish said in 1875, 'the practice of the United States in recognising that Government of a people which is a *de facto* one, is founded on the only true and wise principle and policy'.

(2) International law prohibits premature recognition of the revolutionary Government. So long as the lawful Government has a reasonable prospect of reasserting its authority, recognition is an unfriendly act and a violation of international law. The presumption is in favour of the established Government. As Sir William Harcourt, who was the first Whewell Professor of International Law in the University of Cambridge, put it in a letter to *The Times* during the American Civil War, 'a friendly State is bound to exact very conclusive and indisputable evidence that sovereignty of a Government with which it has existing relations over any part of its former dominions has been finally and permanently divested'. On the other hand, if I may quote from my book written in 1947, 'to maintain that the lawful Government holding out in one isolated fortress is entitled to continued recognition *de jure* is to strain to breaking point an otherwise unimpeachable rule'. It is a question of fact, to be ascertained in good faith, whether the authority of the lawful Government has become purely nominal.

(3) Can recognition properly be given to a revolutionary Government the support of which by the people is not evidenced by, to use a phrase of Jefferson's 'the will of the nation substantially decreed'? Is effectiveness pure and simple the decisive test or is a subsequent legitimation of the revolutionary change by a freely expressed popular approval an essential requirement of recognition?

That was a condition of recognition sometimes insisted upon by Great Britain until the First World War. That was also the practice of the United States, especially under President Wilson. But that practice, rational and desirable as it may be, was abandoned after the First World War and is not at present part of the law. It may be revived when the right of man to government by consent has become part of the positive law of nations suitably guaranteed and enforced. That day is not as yet.

In the meantime, constitutional legitimation through democratic process as understood by the western nations is not a condition of recognition according to existing international law. Professor Hyde, the leading American authority, has summarized in the following words the recent attitude of his country: 'It [the United States] does not seek by the withholding of acknowledgement of the achievements of insurgents to invoke a fiction that would identify a technically existing Government, however decrepit, with the foreign State concerned, so as to succour that Government in its extremity. In a word, the policy of the United States in relation to the recognition of new Governments appears to be no longer associated with, or made the handmaiden of, intervention.' (*International Law*, 2nd ed. (1945), 2, 182.)

(4) There is, finally, the question of the willingness to fulfil international obligations and of assurances to be given to that effect by the Government recognition of which is under consideration. That particular test of recognition has been often resorted to, and has recently loomed large in public discussion, including leading articles in *The Times*. But it is extremely doubtful whether it is a sound test and whether it forms part of international law. It was absent from British practice in the nineteenth century. It is a condition of recognition which has often been abused, in relation to weak Governments, for the purpose of extracting unilateral advantages and concessions. In relation to the Government of a large State its futility is obvious, for it is a clear rule of international law that a newly recognised Government is bound by the obligations of its predecessor and of international law generally.

No special assurances are required. Neither can it be expected that the Government of a great State will be induced to give them unless on a basis of mutuality and equality. The value of any such assurance, if not accompanied by good will, is insignificant. The proper course is to assume that the Government of a sovereign State will fulfil its obligations in good faith. Failing that, it is open to other States to adapt such methods of persuasion as circumstances and international law permit.

The distinction must be asserted between recognising a Government and entering into diplomatic relations with it. No State is legally obliged to enter into and maintain diplomatic relations with a State or Government which it recognises. On the other hand, it cannot enter into full and normal diplomatic relations with a State or Government which it does not recognise.

Recognition of a new governmental authority, accompanied as it must be by automatic withdrawal of recognition from its predecessor, necessitates an invidious decision which, in relation to old friends, may be distasteful and not free from anxiety. But decisions of this nature are unavoidable. They do not become easier by dint of being postponed. It may be of importance, in the case now before His Majesty's Government, to reassure public opinion that the decision at which they have arrived is not arbitrary or intended to minister to what may be a transient advantage, but that it is in accordance with principle and with the practice of enlightened nations, including that of our closest friend and ally.

Foreign Office to HL, 4 January 1950
Beckett has asked me to write to you about your letter on the subject of recognition. We are most grateful for what you have written. It meets our points admirably.

A representative of The Times called at the Foreign Office today and was given your original letter containing Beckett's manuscript alterations and a re-typed copy of the altered version. I am enclosing a carbon of the altered document.

As you feared, The Times representative was a little horrified at the length of the letter, but after we had pointed out the importance of the subject matter and the difficulty of condensing it, he thought that he could persuade the editorial staff to accept it without change. He has, however, made a note of your address and telephone number in case it is necessary to get in touch directly with you.

It appears that The Times will be willing to publish the letter (subject to the problem of length) on the material which I have given them. They would, however, like to receive from you as soon as possible, preferably before Friday, a signed copy of the final version of your letter.

Very soon afterwards, Hersch wrote to the Ambassador of Nationalist China in London:

HL to the Chinese Ambassador, 8 January 1950
I feel that I have a special reason – in addition to your kindness to me in the past – to write and say how very deeply I feel with you in the present situation. I thought it my duty to respond to an invitation to write an article in The Times in which, in accordance with the views which I put forward many years ago, I expressed opinions of which you cannot at present approve. But I hope that you will permit me to assure you that nothing which I wrote could possibly detract from the very high esteem and – if I may say so – from the affection and admiration to you personally. I fervently hope that my Chinese friends, of whom I am proud to have many, will understand the position.

Chinese Ambassador to HL, 11 January 1950
Many thanks for your letter dated the 6th January. It is very good of you to have written to me in the way you did. I can quite understand your position. In fact I presumed that you had written the article on invitation.

Your kind personal words to me are especially appreciated.

There was further detailed correspondence with the Foreign Office later in the year.

Beckett to HL, 14 June 1950
I am sending you a copy of a confidential circular despatch which the Foreign Office is sending out to all Missions abroad . . .

You will see that this despatch about recognition quotes you as authority for a portion of the things it says. I hope that, in so far as it purports to quote you, it does so correctly. In another portion, however, it goes beyond anything you have ever said (see particularly paragraph 7 *et seq.*). This portion of the despatch represents our conviction here that there is not really a half-way house in this matter, and that recognition is not appropriate as a method of any sort of policy, not even a policy ostensibly in support of law and legal order.

In any case, I think you would be interested in this despatch. In the second place, I would be very glad, at your leisure, to have your candid opinion on it. Lastly, in so far as it agrees with your views as an international lawyer, we should naturally be glad if, in your writings or statements, you support the principles which it enunciates, while not, of course, in any way referring to it.

HL to Beckett, 4 July 1950
The United States, of course, have refused recognition either *de facto* or *de jure*. The doctrine of non-recognition is a constant feature of unanimous pronouncements of the Conferences of American States. I doubt whether we are right in coupling the defence of our action in recognising the Communist Government in China with an attack upon the doctrine of non-recognition. Unless we are quite sure that we shall invariably succeed by other means in dealing with aggression, we ought not to make the recognition of the fruits of aggression a matter of legal duty. Suppose that the United States and other countries had not acted in Korea (or that that action will not in the end be successful) and that Southern Korea is overrun, will it be our duty to recognise the conquest? (Incidentally, are you quite sure that Great Britain recognised the annexation of Austria *de jure*? I have expressed a different, though hesitating, view on pp. 399, 400 of *Recognition*.)

The readers of the last sentence of paragraph 15 of the Circular may gain the impression that my views as propounded in the letter to *The Times* are in agreement with the other two points raised in the Circular and covered by my present letter. In that they would be mistaken. However, that does not matter much.

I come now to a different matter which is only very remotely connected with the question of the recognition of the Communist government, namely, the announcement made by the United States, in connection with the action in Korea, with regard to the operations of the Chinese Communist Government against Formosa. The action of the United States in Korea is, I think, in conformity with the Charter and with international law generally. Its action in relation to Formosa is not. As formulated so far, it is an act of intervention without justification in law. No State is entitled to intervene in a civil war to the extent of preventing a rebel government, which it does not recognise, from overthrowing the established government – though it is entitled to assist, to a very limited extent, the government which it continues to recognise. The action of the United States may have an unfortunate effect upon public opinion inasmuch as it will affect adversely the confidence in the legality and propriety of the action taken by reference to the Charter. This is bound to happen when the vindication of the Charter is being combined with strong action – which, to say the least, has no support in law – against communism in general. I do not know whether the United States consulted other governments before making that announcement. Obviously I cannot say anything about it in public but I can mention it to you. I am disturbed about the matter for the announcement about Formosa seems to me doubly regrettable: it is illegal in itself and its illegality is bound to infect the undoubted legality of the action taken in Korea. I realise that you cannot be expected to reply to this. The only way in which, in my view, the United States can make it clear, at an early suitable opportunity, that its action in relation to Formosa was a temporary measure prompted by the necessity of preventing military and naval operations in an area in which the United States and other countries were engaged in complicated operations is in the fulfilment of their duty under the Charter.

Beckett to HL, 6 July 1950
Many thanks for your letter of the 4th July about recognition. I only return a hurried and sketchy reply.

In the first place, our circular on recognition goes beyond anything you have ever said. Indeed, part of it is contrary to views which you have put in your book. I hope that this was clear in the circular because, after all, we quote your letter in full and everybody can see what you have said and what you have not said.

I am not surprised that you do not agree (at any rate at present) with what the circular says when it goes beyond anything you have said. In fact, I do not think many outside lawyers would go as far as the circular goes. It is in fact founded on my practical experience sitting here. I venture to think that if you had been sitting in my chair all these years, quite likely you would take the same view that I do. In a sentence, my view is that there are many things which the international community could and should to with regard to situations brought about in an illegal manner, but if they are not prepared to put the situation right they only bring international law into confusion and contempt if they adopt the line of not recognising the situation which they allow to establish itself. Perhaps you do not know the chicanery which accompanied the application of the Stimson doctrine. You would not know that the position under it was that the Governments said one thing while all their actions were contrary to what they said. This was not deliberate dishonesty. It was merely due to the fact that barren non-recognition is not practicable or workable. They virtually had to do what they did. Further, I have found that where you get non-recognition of something which is established, you get endless legal complications to which there is no real answer at all – a series of complications and artificialities which really can do nothing else but bring international law into contempt. I personally cannot help reacting strongly against a position where there is no possible means of giving a sensible legal answer or where one has to reconcile the irreconcilable by a series of artificialities which can only bring a contemptuous smile to the lips of anybody when you then try and say that international law is really a law at all. I should say a special word about the practice of the United States Government. First of all, recently at any rate, they have been really proceeding on the basis that recognition is pure policy. Secondly, they do not appear to mind saying one thing and acting in a manner which is not consistent with what they say in this respect. They pretend they did not recognise the incorporation of Austria into Germany, yet their actual conduct was absolutely inconsistent with that view. In fact, as far as I can see, in this as in so many questions their lawyers are rather divorced from those people who conduct policy, and they are hardly aware themselves of the extent to which their deeds contradict their words. I cannot pursue this now, but it is considerations such as this which led me to give the advice which I did.

Formosa. I will only say this about the matter. Remember that Formosa is not legally Chinese territory yet. Technically, it is still Japanese territory occupied by the Allies, and the Chinese were permitted or invited to go and administer the territory pending the peace settlement with Japan, and the United States is broadly permitted to act for the Allies generally with regard to Japan and the Far East. I think that thought may enable you to do what I have not time to do now, make out some justification for American action which, I admit, is not altogether easy to justify legally, and in any case is grossly inconsistent with their view about the recognition of the Chinese Governments.[1]

---

[1] It is difficult to identify to what Hersch and Beckett were each referring in the last paragraphs of their respective letters, the more so as the United States made it plain in their statements by the President and the Secretary of State on 5 January 1950 that 'we are not going to get involved militarily in any way on the Island of Formosa'. See *American Foreign Policy, 1950–1955, Basic Documents*, vol. II, p. 2451.

Lectures in Jerusalem

In February, Hersch received an invitation from the Hebrew University to attend its jubilee anniversary on 5 May (the university had been founded in 1925) and to deliver a guest lecture. Hersch informed the Council of the Senate of Cambridge University which indicated that it would wish to send an informal expression of its good wishes. This took the form of the following message from the Vice-Chancellor:

It gives me great pleasure to ask Professor Lauterpacht to take with him, to the celebrations of the twenty-fifth anniversary of the foundation of your University, this message of good will. The twenty-five years now brought to a close have been years of great trial and difficulty, and I trust that you may now enjoy a period of tranquillity in which your University may take its rightful place in the life of your nation.

As requested, Hersch delivered two lectures – one in English entitled 'International Law after the Second World War',[2] the other in Hebrew on 'Sovereignty and the Rights of Man'.[3] Its delivery in Hebrew elicited the remark from a member of the audience: 'What good Hebrew he speaks for a Goy [a Christian]!'

State immunity, 1950–1951

In January 1950, Hersch was invited to become a member of a British Government interdepartmental committee to consider in detail the law of State and diplomatic immunity. As developed in British practice over more than two centuries, the law of State immunity had come to accord to foreign States an absolute immunity from proceedings instituted in British courts, regardless of the subject matter of the actions.

In 1949, in a libel action brought by Mr Krajina against the Tass News Agency, an agency of the Soviet Government, the defendant's claim to immunity from jurisdiction was upheld on the ground that it was entitled to shelter under the cloak of that government. The decision of the Court of Appeal[4] gave rise to public outcry, vigorously taken up by Lord Vansittart in the House of Lords, and in November 1949 an interdepartmental committee was set up to consider whether the law of the United Kingdom afforded to foreign States, their agents and their diplomats a wider immunity than is desirable or is required by international law. Lord Justice Somervell, a former Attorney-General, was appointed as chairman and the committee was composed for the

---

[2] *Collected Papers*, Vol. 2, pp. 159–70.   [3] *Collected Papers*, Vol. 3, pp. 416–30.
[4] 27 June 1949, [1949] 2 All ER 274.

most part of very senior lawyers in the several government departments affected by the subject, to whom were added Hersch and C. J. Hamson, a comparative lawyer from Cambridge, to provide academic support.

In the course of 1950, Hersch prepared for the committee a substantial memorandum on State immunity, large parts of which formed the basis of an article subsequently published in the *BYIL*.[5] In it, he pointed out that, in contrast to the British approach, many foreign States granted only qualified immunity, distinguishing between acts *jure gestionis* (acts of an essentially private law nature), to which immunity did not attach, and acts *jure imperii* (acts of a sovereign nature), to which it did. Although the committee concluded that the law of the United Kingdom as prevailing in 1950 granted a greater immunity than was granted by a large number of other States, and some members took the view that international law does not strictly require absolute immunity, the committee as a whole could not agree on a suitable alternative approach. Rather than formulate their views individually, the Committee produced an interim report, which was not published, suggesting certain possible alternative principles but not committing itself to any. Hersch was not entirely happy with this outcome and appended a note of reservation in the following terms:

I understand that this Interim Report is in the nature of an analysis of the views expressed and solutions suggested by the members of the Committee, and I sign it as such. In general the deliberations of the Committee and the various memoranda submitted to it have confirmed me in the view, which I expressed in my own memorandum, that in so far as English law adheres to the rule of absolute immunity of foreign Governments it grants to them a degree of immunity wider than that accorded by most States; that the rule of absolute immunity of foreign States and Governments has become obsolete and out of keeping with modern developments in the economic sphere and with the progressive subjection of the State to the rule of law; that there is no warrant for it in any basic principle of international law; and that the proper solution of the problem would be to assimilate, in the matter of immunity, the position of foreign States to that of the Crown under recent legislation – subject to specific exceptions such as in the matter of diplomatic representatives, warships, and the like. I am in agreement with the Interim Report in so far as it embodies suggestions in that direction. As I interpret it, it does so to a considerable extent.

---

[5] (1951) 28 *BYIL* 220–92. Reprinted in *Collected Papers*, Vol. 3, pp. 315–73. The subject was then also being considered by the Institut de Droit International. Hersch was a member of the Institute's commission dealing with the matter. His comments on the rapporteur's (Ernest Lemoire) report appear in (1952-1) 44 *Annuaire* 111–24.

Nearly a score of years later, however, international discussion of the subject led to the adoption in 1972 of the European Convention on State Immunity and to the enactment in the United Kingdom of the State Immunity Act 1978. Both these instruments abandoned the doctrine of strict immunity and adopted a distinction between commercial and other transactions. Subject to certain qualifications, immunity would not be available in cases arising out of commercial transactions. The essentials of Hersch's views were thus vindicated.

On diplomatic immunity, however, the committee was able to reach agreement. It recommended no change in the law on that subject with the exception of a proposal that the government should be empowered to reduce immunities at present accorded to the mission of any foreign country so that they should correspond with the immunities granted by that foreign country to British missions there. The report was subsequently published[6] and led to the enactment of its recommendation in the Diplomatic Immunities Restriction Act 1955.

Hersch was elected an associate of the Institut de Droit International in 1947, followed by advancement to full membership in 1952. The Institut is an organisation devoted to the study and development of international law, with its membership comprising some 120 leading public international lawyers. It meets biennially.

Hersch was immediately appointed *rapporteur* of the Institute's working commission on the interpretation of treaties. This involved him in deep study of the subject, beginning in October 1949, and the preparation of a questionnaire for circulation amongst the members of the commission. Taking their responses into consideration he was required to produce a report on the subject. This was then circulated amongst the members and, again considering their responses, he then prepared a final report which was circulated to the full membership of the Institut for discussion at the session that was held in Siena in Italy in April 1952.[7]

The Cambridge term began once again in early October, as did his lectures. The work on the interpretation of treaties was demanding. He soon felt the need for a weekend in Hove and also planned to go for an extended stay as soon as term was over. Rachel would then be home and could go with him.

Atomic weapons

Towards the end of the year, Hersch was in touch with Beckett about a potentially controversial aspect of the edition of Volume II of *Oppenheim*

---

[6] As Cmd 8460, January 1952.   [7] (1952-1) 44 *Annuaire* 197–223.

then in preparation, namely, the question of the legality of the use of nuclear weapons. No copy of Hersch's letter to Beckett can be found, but part of the treatment of the matter as it ultimately appeared in *Oppenheim*, as expressing Hersch's opinion, is quoted below, followed by Beckett's non-committal reply of 2 December 1950.

After discussing the legality of the use of nuclear weapons by reference:

(a) to existing international instruments relating to the limits of the use of violence in war; (b) to the distinction, which many believe to be fundamental, between combatants and non-combatants; and (c) to the principles of humanity, which to some degree, must be regarded as forming part of the law of war.

Hersch concluded:

For these reasons it is difficult to express a clear view as to whether an explicit prohibition of the use of the atomic weapon in warfare would be merely declaratory of existing principles of International Law. In any case, so long as the production of the atomic bomb has not been prevented in practice by international agreement and supervision, there must be envisaged the possibility of its being resorted to in contingencies not amounting to a breach of International Law. In the first instance, its use must be regarded as permissible as a reprisal for its actual prior use by the enemy or his allies. Secondly, recourse to the atomic weapon may be justified against an enemy who violates rules of the law of war on a scale so vast as to put himself altogether outside the orbit of considerations of humanity and compassion. Thus if during the Second World War it had become established beyond all reasonable doubt that Germany was engaged in a systematic plan of putting to death millions of civilians in occupied territory, the use of the atomic bomb might have been justifiable as a deterrent instrument of punishment.

The effective prohibition of the production of the atomic bomb, coupled as it must be with strict international supervision and a resulting substantial sacrifice of State sovereignty in important spheres, would in itself be a manifestation of significant progress in the integration of international society. In the meantime, it may be doubtful whether the condemnation and renunciation, in a solemn international treaty, of the use of the atomic weapon would constitute a beneficent addition to International Law unless accompanied by previous agreement forbidding the production of atomic weapons and providing for international supervision and control in order to render such prohibition effective.[8]

Hersch added a significant footnote at the end of the first paragraph of the quotation:

---

[8] *Oppenheim*, vol. II (6th edn, 1952), pp. 350–2.

Moreover, as laws are made not only for the protection of human life but also for the preservation of ultimate values of society, it is possible that should those values be imperilled by an aggressor intent upon dominating the world the nations thus threatened might consider themselves bound to assume the responsibility of exercising the supreme right of self-preservation in a manner which, while contrary to a specific prohibition of International Law, they alone deem to be decisive for the ultimate vindication of the law of nations. The use of the atomic weapon in a contingency of that nature would still be contrary to the principle that the rules of International Law apply even in relation to an aggressor in an unlawful war. However, there is no decisive reason for assuming that, in the extreme contingency of the nature described above, that particular principle would or could be scrupulously adhered to.

Beckett to HL, 2 December 1950

As regards the section of Oppenheim on the legality of the atomic weapon, I am grateful to you for giving us a chance to make any suggestions on your draft if we want to. I do not know at the moment whether we shall want to do so or not. If we do send you observations, of course you will read them but it will be entirely a matter for you to what extent you choose to make use of them. May I trespass on your kindness to this further extent, that if you have had no further communication from us on this subject, you would send a line saying that you now had to go ahead with this and if we want to send any observations which could be considered they must be in by a certain time. The machine is apt to work slowly.

The difficulty experienced by Hersch is reflected in the inconclusive manner in which the ICJ dealt with the problem in the Advisory Opinion on the *Legality of the Threat or Use of Nuclear Weapons* (1996).[9]

Korea

On 25 June 1950, the Republic of Korea was invaded by the armed forces of North Korea. On the same day, the UN Security Council determined that this action constituted a breach of the peace and called for the immediate cessation of hostilities. Two days later, it recommended that the members of the UN should furnish such assistance to the Republic of Korea as may be necessary to repel the armed attack and to restore international peace and security in the area. Extensive military aid was then provided to the Republic of Korea by thirty-nine members of the UN, including the United Kingdom and the United States. The hostilities lasted until an armistice was signed on 27 July 1953.

[9] ICJ Reports 1996, p. 226; 110 *ILR* 163.

On 18 August 1950, the Attorney-General asked Hersch for advice regarding the legal status of the hostilities in Korea.

Sir Hartley Shawcross to HL, 18 August 1950

I am now rather urgently concerned with a matter to which I expect you – as I – have been giving some thought these last few weeks, namely, the international status of the events in Korea.

It can hardly be said that we are at Peace with North Korea: our warships are already involved and we are to send a land force. But if we are not at Peace, must we not be at War? Is there any midway position. Are the North Koreans enemies? You will at once see the implications from these questions. There is §189(1) of the Army Act – very important – the law of Treason, Foreign Enlistment and so on.

If you have written anything, or have formed views on these matters I should be most grateful for your advice privately. The matter is, of course, highly confidential.

Hersch was away on holiday in Switzerland when Shawcross's letter reached him. His reply cannot be found, but Shawcross sent him a telegram thanking him for his 'most useful memorandum'. The matter came up for consideration in the Cabinet on 18 September, when the discussion was briefly recorded under the heading 'Legal Implications of Korean Conflict'.

Att.G.: J thinks it's war. But Truman and St Laurent have said it isn't. I have sugg'd a half-way house – wh. Beckett and Lauterpacht approve.'[10]

Though it spent some time discussing the issue, the Cabinet did not reach a formal conclusion.[11]

Hersch's view was soon reflected in his seventh edition of Volume II of *Oppenheim*, which was published in 1952 and of which the relevant paragraph must have been written soon after Shawcross's letter:

Although hostilities waged for the collective enforcement of International Law – in particular, of the Charter of the United Nations – are calculated to exhibit the normal characteristics and manifestations of war, it is probably inaccurate and undesirable to describe them as war in the accepted sense of the word. Thus when in 1950 the forces of the United Nations were engaged,

---

[10] 'Att.G.' was Shawcross.
[11] For example, in the following papers and letters: note by the Chairman (Sir Robert Makins) of the inter-departmental committee established to report on the practical aspects of the international status of the Korean conflict, 17 November 1950; Report of the Inter-Departmental Committee on the Practical Aspects of the International Status of the Korean Conflict, November 1950; Letter from E. W. Bevin to the Lord Chancellor, 23 February 1951.

in pursuance of a decision of the Security Council, in repelling the invasion of South Korea by North Korea, there was no disposition on the part either of the United Nations as a whole or of the participating States to treat as war in the formal sense of the word what Chapter VII of the Charter describes as enforcement action. There was no declaration of war upon North Korea. It is consonant with the dignity and the purpose of the collective enforcement of the basic instrument of organised international society that it should rank in a category different from war as traditionally understood in International Law. The object of the latter – whether it be lawful or unlawful and whether it be aggressive or defensive – is to secure the interests of the individual State. The object of the former is comparable, in the municipal sphere, to the enforcement of the law against the law-breaker. Undoubtedly, as in an unlawful war – but certainly not to a larger extent, the rules of warfare must, for the reasons stated above, apply to hostilities conducted collectively for the enforcement of International Law. This was the case in the hostilities conducted by and on behalf of the United Nations in Korea when declarations to that effect – in particular, with regard to humanitarian rules of war such as those embodied in the Geneva Conventions of 1949 – were made by the authorities commanding the forces of the United Nations. It is also possible that in due course international society may develop a body of appropriate rules and principles governing the collective use of force. There is nothing to prevent the States taking part in the collective enforcement of the law from enacting legislation enabling them to take measures which their municipal law normally makes dependent upon the existence of a formal state of war.[12]

It is in this last sentence, and in the accompanying footnote, that the reply to Shawcross's question may be found.[13]

Stephen M. Schwebel

In October, Hersch wrote in warm terms about a young visiting scholar from the United States who had been educated at Harvard but who had not yet attended the Yale Law School:

HL to Dr S. Segal, 14 October 1950

I think I ought to tell you that I have never had a better, more able, or more charming student. This is also the impression of my colleagues, and we are

---

[12] *Oppenheim* (7th edn, 1952), pp. 224–5.

[13] The footnote reads as follows: 'Thus, in order to render applicable the relevant provisions of the Trading with the Enemy Act, of the Army Act, of the Foreign Enlistment Act, of the law relating to treason, and others, it might be possible to enact in Great Britain a United Nations (Enforcement of Peace) Act assimilating, in relation to municipal law, hostilities conducted for the purpose of enforcing the Charter to war in the technical sense of the term.' But no such steps appear to have been taken.

going to treat him in many ways as if he had already been through the Harvard Law School.

Of course, he will do very well in the academic sphere – indeed so well that I shall often have doubts whether he is not too good to be a mere academic person. In any case I am delighted to have him.

1951

The year 1951 was, if anything, even busier than the previous year.

Early release of convicted war criminals

Early in 1951, Hersch became seriously concerned about rumours that the United States might give early release to some of the war criminals convicted and imprisoned after Nuremberg. He contemplated writing to Robert H. Jackson, the former American chief prosecutor, who had returned to the US Supreme Court, and sent a draft to Shawcross who replied as follows:

Sir Hartley Shawcross to HL, 13 February 1951
Many thanks for your letter of the 12th February with the draft of one which you propose sending to Mr Justice Jackson.

I would certainly send it if I were you. The Government considered this matter yesterday when I took up a very strong line, indeed, in regard to it (this for your private information) and, as you may have seen in the 'Times', I made a speech on Friday stating that it was no part of Government policy to initiate any revision of the Nuremberg sentences. Moreover, I think our policy now will be to hesitate very much in making any remissions of the sentences imposed by our own War Crimes Courts. I am afraid the release of Von Krupp at the very moment that we are embarking upon a policy of re-arming Germany and the suggestions in other quarters that a policy of leniency might be adopted in regard to other war criminals has created a most unfortunate impression. I have been having a big battle on it but have met with almost unanimous support. I should tell you perhaps that I have been in correspondence with Biddle who was the American senior Judge and he agrees with my point of view.

Hersch thereupon sent the following letter to Jackson.

HL to Robert H. Jackson, 16 February 1951
I have been very distressed by the recent policy of the authorities of the United States in Germany in the matter of releasing war criminals.

The United States is now bearing in the Far East the main burden of the resolute refusal to bow to and to appease aggression. The stature of its action there will grow with the passage of years, and there is no doubt in the minds of many that it has been foremost in Korea in upholding, against heavy odds, the principles of international law and order. On the other hand the policy of authorizing the release of individuals found by its own tribunals to have been guilty of war crimes and crimes against humanity seems to be in patent and disquieting contrast to the principles which underlie its attitude in the Far East. Any denunciation, within the United States, of what is there regarded as appeasement of aggression can carry no conviction if it is accompanied by what appears to be appeasement of crime. That policy tends to deprive the world of the significant and beneficent gain achieved by the trials of war criminals after the Second World War. By acting as if they were treating as a matter of political expediency the continued enforcement of judicial sentences passed upon war criminals, the authorities of the United States lend colour to the otherwise utterly false accusation that these sentences were no more than vengeance wreaked by the victors upon the defeated. The policy of the United States in liberating war criminals must, if persisted in, weaken the cause of the free nations in any future struggle by reducing it, as it must do in the result, to the level of a mere contest for power wholly divorced from principle. That policy must impair the deterrent power of international law and of the very notion of effective individual responsibility for war crimes. It may thus, in any future hostilities, contribute to the loosening and to the abandonment of those restraints which, it was hoped, would result from the trial and punishment of those responsible for war crimes.

The policy of releasing war criminals appears to many to be so much at variance with the maintenance of the authority of international law and public morality that it renders altogether irrelevant the question whether it is likely to bring some particular advantage by securing the support of the German people in any emergency that may arise. Decent opinion in Germany – that opinion whose feelings, to quote the leaders of the German church, are those of guilt, shame, repentance and responsibility – will not acclaim these releases. The support of others is worthless even if judged by the realistic policy of moral shortcuts. Such, most questionable, advantage as that action may possess saps at the very vitals of your – and our – cause. It cannot endure. Many – very many – will interpret the recent action of the authorities of the United States as an indignity inflicted upon the memory of those who suffered death and martyrdom at the hands of the released war criminals. This applies also to released persons who were convicted on what uninformed opinion may consider to be political charges. Thus Herr Krupp was sentenced largely on account of his active participation in the crime of deportation for slave labour – a crime the direct and incidental cruelties of which were exposed by the International Military Tribunal and other courts. You will, of course, have noticed that some of the released war criminals were involved in the horrors of the concentration and extermination camps.

I hope – in fact, I believe – that you will agree with the sentiment which has prompted this letter. For I had occasion to see the fervour and the zeal of your efforts before, during and after the trial at Nuremberg. Much of the harm caused by the recent releases cannot be undone. But much can be done, even now, to restore the moral balance and to prevent such occurrences in the future. Not unnaturally, many will look to you for leadership in this weighty matter.

Jackson replied on 20 February 1951:

Robert H. Jackson to HL, 20 February 1951
I have never put in writing my feeling about the change of American policy which is resulting in the release of the war criminals, but I could not so perfectly express it myself as you have done in your letter of 16 February. I do not think the United States could have handed the Kremlin a better propaganda issue, certainly in those countries which the Nazis occupied, than in the release of Krupp.

This is not a sudden change. The change here began when Mr Stimson's influence left the Department of the Army and Secretary Royal came in. It has proceeded rather insidiously ever since. I could give you many illustrations of the change in attitude which now comes to the surface in these concrete acts.

To date I have held my tongue. My position makes it difficult to engage in a controversial discussion of public affairs. I would, however, be inclined to pass those considerations if it would avail anything. This country is so worked up about Communism at the present moment that the public temper identifies as a friend of the United States any person who is [a] foe of Stalin. It figures that Nazis were his foes, entirely forgetting that they did not hesitate to become his allies when they thought they would gain by it. General Eisenhower has pretty effectively stopped the movement which was in full swing to virtually rearm them. I hope a saner outlook will arrive here, but at the moment the scene is rather depressing. The spring will probably turn the tide one way or the other. I hope to God we will regain our senses.

Hersch let Shawcross see a copy of Jackson's letter. Shawcross replied:

Sir Hartley Shawcross to HL, 19 March, 1951
Thank you very much for letting me see the reply which Jackson has sent to you. I have taken a copy of this and I am retaining the copy of your own letter to Jackson. I hope to make a speech in the next week or so about this matter and I shall, if I may, use some of the points contained in the letters although, of course, without attributing them to Jackson or yourself.

In April 1951, in response to an invitation from the President of the Carnegie Endowment for International Peace, Hersch agreed to write a foreword to a book then being written by Oliver J. Lissitzyn on *The International Court of Justice – Its Role in the Maintenance of International Peace and Security.*

HL to Professor Joseph E. Johnson, 16 April 1951

Thank you for your letter of the 13th April and the invitation to write a preface to Professor Lissitzyn's book. The invitation, which I value, comes at a particularly busy time and normally I would hesitate to accept it. However, the subject of the book and – I am confident – the book itself is of importance; I know personally Professor Lissitzyn who is a scholar of distinction; and his father-in-law is a dear and respected friend of mine. In the circumstances I am very glad to accept your invitation and I shall be waiting for the proof. I am assuming that you do not desire a long preface, but perhaps you will consider it convenient to indicate its desired approximate length.

I hope you will not interpret it as showing any lack of appreciation of the final sentence of your letter if I say that an honorarium is neither expected nor desired.

THE ANGLO-IRANIAN OIL COMPANY CASE

The most time-consuming episode during the year was the aftermath of the Iranian nationalisation of the Anglo-Iranian Oil Company (AIOC). On 1 May 1951, the Government of Iran nationalised the assets of AIOC in Iran. These consisted of a concession granted to the company in 1933 giving it the exclusive right to explore for and produce oil in Iran and to export it, as well as associated facilities such as a refinery and pipelines. Provision for compensation was included but limited to 25 per cent of current revenue after deduction of exploitation expenses. This was regarded at the time as tantamount to confiscation. Hersch was soon involved in giving advice to the company on a number of the legal questions arising in this connection.

Faced by the prospect of nationalisation, AIOC began in March 1950 to consider what remedies might be open to it. The concession agreement contained, in its Article 22, a provision for the settlement of disputes by an arbitral tribunal consisting of three arbitrators, one to be nominated by each party and the third to be chosen by the two party-appointed arbitrators. If one of the parties failed to nominate its arbitrator, the other might request the President of the Permanent Court of International Justice to make the appointment. The PCIJ was replaced in 1945 by the ICJ, so the question arose as to whether the power vested in the President of the PCIJ had devolved on the President of the ICJ. This question was put to Mr V. Idelson, KC[14] and Hersch for a joint Opinion.

In an Opinion drafted mainly by Hersch, they concluded that, on a proper interpretation of the arbitration clause in the concession agreement, 'and having regard to procedures already established', the President of the ICJ is entitled to exercise the power of appointment therein contemplated. However, all the precedents they referred to related to the continuity of rights under treaties and they acknowledged that the concession agreement was not a treaty. They qualified their conclusion in an important respect:

If the Iranian Government were to challenge the right of the President of the International Court of Justice to make the appointment on the ground that he is not the President of the Permanent Court of International Justice, it would not necessarily be bound to accept either his finding on his right to make the appointment or to recognise the arbitrator or Umpire appointed by him. However, the Iranian Government would be entitled to consider itself not so bound only if it were willing to abide by some other impartial procedure for determining that preliminary issue. Failing that, it would be in effect denying the Company legal redress against a violation of its rights under the Concession. To that extent, as well as for other purposes, His Majesty's Government would be entitled to take up the case of the Company under the provisions of the Optional Clause of Article 36 of the Statute of the Court and to bring about a judicial determination either of the preliminary question at issue or of the substance of any complaint arising from a violation of the rights of the Company under the Concession.

Although we cannot advise that Iran would be legally bound by the action of the President of the International Court of Justice, it does not follow that she would refuse to accept an interpretation of Article 22 which is in full conformity with the 'reasonable interpretation' of the Agreement as provided in Article 21. It would be a serious matter, having regard to public opinion, to flout a decision of the President. Similarly, it is not at all certain that Iran will raise at all what may be generally regarded a specious issue hardly consistent with the dignity of a Government. However, these are questions of political probabilities with which we are not directly concerned.

Sir Eric Beckett, the Legal Adviser of the Foreign Office, commented on the Opinion, saying: 'I have read this Opinion, which is interesting and

---

[14] V. Idelson, KC (1881–1954), practised law in Russia, was legal adviser to the Russian Ministry of Finance during the Kerensky regime, but had to flee in 1918 and decided to go to England. He was called to the Bar at Gray's Inn in 1926 and became a KC in 1943. Among his clients was the Anglo-Persian Oil Company (later the Anglo-Iranian Oil Company). He drafted the 1933 concession agreement and was actively involved in legal matters following the nationalisation of the company in 1951.

helpful, and it seems to me to be right.'[15] In the end, they were all proved wrong. The President of the ICJ turned down AIOC's request for the appointment of an arbitrator,[16] principally on the ground that the continuity provisions in the Statute of the Court covered only commitments under treaties and not agreements, such as concession agreements, that were not treaties.

It was then decided that the British Government should file a substantive claim against Iran before the ICJ; an application was filed on 26 May 1951 complaining of a violation of international law by reason of the breach of the 1933 concession agreement and a denial of justice following from the Iranian refusal to accept arbitration in accordance with the agreement. Four weeks later, on 22 June, the British Government requested interim measures of protection calling on Iran to take no further steps against the company in violation of its rights under the agreement. Hersch participated in the preparation for, and appeared as one of the counsel in, these proceedings. Within two weeks, on 5 July, the Court made an order to this effect.[17]

The case then proceeded to its next stage, consideration of a preliminary objection to the jurisdiction of the Court raised by Iran on a number of grounds, principally that its own declaration accepting the jurisdiction of the Court was limited to situations or facts relating to the application of treaties, and this was not such a case. On 22 July 1952, the Court upheld this objection and the case thus came to an end.[18]

In all these proceedings, Hersch was much involved. Moreover, in the period following the initial application, when preparations were being made for the submission of the substance of the case to the Court, Hersch was asked by the company to assist the Foreign Office in the preparation of the legal part of the substantive British Memorial. This he did in the space of ten days, producing a draft which, when printed, came to sixty-six pages. The text, as it appears in the *Collected Papers*, is introduced by the following editorial note:

The draft was prepared by Lauterpacht under extraordinary pressure. My personal recollection is that he was asked to complete it in about ten days – and did so. I have thought it right to include it here because it is the only extended work on the treatment of alien property rights which Lauterpacht wrote. It is, moreover, an outstanding elaboration of the traditional view of the

---

[15] 9 April 1951, FO 371/9152.
[16] For a detailed consideration of the episode, see D. H. N. Johnson, 'The Constitution of an Arbitral Tribunal' (1953) 30 *BYIL* 153–8.
[17] ICJ Reports 1951, p. 89.   [18] ICJ Reports 1952, p. 93; 19 *ILR* 507.

sanctity of foreign property rights in international law as it stood before the period of challenge heralded by the post-Second World War nationalizations in Europe, encouraged by this very episode of nationalization and furthered by the first General Assembly resolution on 'Permanent Sovereignty over Natural Resources'.

Whether Lauterpacht, in his academic capacity, fully shared the views which he here developed in his professional capacity is open to some doubt. Some of the statements in this chapter may be compared with his brief observations in the next chapter. Also, in his eighth edition of Volume 1 of Oppenheim's *International Law* he qualified the statement of the rule that alien property is entitled to respect by the following observation (at p. 352): '[A] modification must be recognized in cases in which fundamental changes in the political system and economic structure of the State or far-reaching social reforms entail interference, on a large scale, with private property. In such cases neither the principle of absolute respect for alien private property nor rigid equality with the dispossessed nationals offers a satisfactory solution of the difficulty. It is probable that, consistently with legal principle, such solution must be sought in the granting of partial compensation.'

The same requirements of forensic presentation which explain the fact that some statements in the draft Memorial go some way beyond Lauterpacht's own academic views also explain the divergences between Lauterpacht's draft and the final text as eventually presented to the Court by the British Government. The Government were clearly and properly entitled to amend Lauterpacht's draft so as to present to the Court as cogent an argument as possible. For this reason it would be unwise and might well be misleading to attach any particular significance to differences between the two texts. Only the Memorial, as finally submitted to the Court, can be read as an authoritative statement of the views of the British Government at that time.[19]

In the event, though the British Government filed a Memorial incorporating with some amendment much of what Hersch had written, there was no occasion to argue the merits of the case before the Court. This was because Iran raised an objection to the jurisdiction of the Court, contending that the case did not fall within the limited terms of its acceptance of the Court's jurisdiction. This preliminary objection was heard by the Court during the last three weeks of June 1952. Hersch could not be part of the British team because he had to be in Geneva for the ILC session. On 22 July 1952, the Court upheld the Iranian objection.[20] On 30 and 31 July, even while busy with the ILC, Hersch published in *The*

---

[19] Reprinted in *Collected Papers*, Vol. 4, pp. 23–89.
[20] ICJ Reports 1952, p. 93. The majority included Sir Arnold McNair, who wrote an individual Opinion.

Times a 'turn-over' article in two parts commenting on the judgment. The first part of the article described the background to the judgment without seriously criticising it; the second part examined the alternative legal remedies which might be open to AIOC, in particular the practicality of proceedings in national courts.

This is what, in the meantime, the company had been considering, namely, what other measures could be taken to prevent Iran taking advantage of the nationalisation. The solution appeared to lie in proceedings in various foreign courts against any person acquiring or transporting oil from Iran (a process that has since acquired the name of 'pursuit litigation'). Idelson and Hersch first advised to this effect in May 1951. They presented a draft of a warning notice, in the form of an advertisement to be published in newspapers worldwide, to serve as a deterrent to would-be purchasers of Iranian oil. On 12 July 1951, Hersch, together with Idelson, advised that:

(a) municipal courts of the Members of the United Nations are bound to treat as unlawful any dealings with the oil in question pending the final decision of the International Court of Justice or subsequent to any decision of that Court declaring the action of the Government of Iran to have been or to be contrary to international law;

(b) that consideration now be given to making an announcement to that effect.

AIOC subsequently initiated proceedings in Aden,[21] Japan[22] and Italy.[23] Though only the first was successful, the existence of the warning notices was nonetheless effective to achieve a general embargo on trade in Iranian oil.

The AIOC matter was not the only one to require Hersch's attention in the summer of 1951. Towards the end of June, he gave a substantial Opinion to a leading English private bank that was apprehensive about its position in the event that England were ever invaded and occupied. Consideration was given to the possibility that a power of attorney might be issued to certain bank officials who, being abroad, could on this basis continue to administer the bank's overseas affairs. The difficulties associated with this course were set out, but the opinion did not conclusively reject the idea. The idea of a transfer of residence was also mentioned, as were the difficulties associated with it.

---

[21] *Anglo-Iranian Oil Company* v. *Jaffrate (The Rose Mary)*, 20 *ILR* 316.
[22] *Anglo-Iranian Oil Company* v. *Idemitsu Kosan Kabushiki Kaisha*, 20 *ILR* 305.
[23] *Anglo-Iranian Oil Company* v. *Supor*, 22 *ILR* 19 and 23.

Hersch's involvement in practice did not lead to any reduction in his attachment to his academic obligations. To the fulfilment of his duties as a lecturer and as a supervisor of an important cohort of research students, he added the chairmanship of the Faculty Board of Law. He held this post – comparable to that of a dean of a law school – for three years till 1954; and performed its duties efficiently and understandingly; somewhat to the surprise of some of his colleagues.

1952

At the beginning of 1952, Hersch was moved to write a 'turn-over' article in *The Times*[24] on the judgment of the ICJ delivered on 18 December 1951 in the *Norwegian Fisheries* case between Britain and Norway.[25] The case arose out of the Norwegian claim to be entitled to construct as baselines, from which its territorial sea was to be measured, straight lines enclosing its irregular coast, but following the general direction of the coast. By a majority of ten votes to two, the Court upheld the legality of the method advanced by Norway and, by a majority of eight votes to four, that the lines actually fixed by that method were not contrary to international law. Hersch, while pointing to the elements of novelty and subjectivity in the decision, did not condemn it outright, and concluded that:

there is perhaps no sufficient reason for the assumption that the judgment has caused irreparable injury to the principle of the freedom of the sea or that it has left the door wide open to exorbitant claims in the future.

It is to be recalled that the essence of the judgment was subsequently incorporated with little change into the 1956 Convention on the Territorial Sea and, thereafter, into the 1982 UN Convention on the Law of the Sea.

In February, he took ill again with what he described as 'bronchitis of a protracted kind'. This lasted into March and Hersch went to Dudley to recover. Despite this, on 4 March, he spoke in Cambridge at a meeting organised by the *Cambridge Daily News* to promote interest in human rights and was one of the judges in an essay competition sponsored by the paper. Together with Rachel, he then took a two-week holiday in the south of France and in Florence before going on to Siena for the biennial session of the Institut de Droit International.

---

[24] 'Freedom of the Seas: Implications of the Norwegian Fisheries Case', *The Times*, 8 January 1952.
[25] ICJ Reports 1951, p. 116.

At that time, he received letters from the French and Swedish Ambassadors in London inviting him to become President of the French–Swedish Permanent Conciliation Commission, of which he was already a member. Due to his impending absence at the ILC, he was obliged to decline an invitation from the University of Cambridge to give two lectures at a conference honouring Hans Kelsen on his retirement. He also had to miss the hearings in the ICJ on the preliminary objections raised by Iran at the proceedings brought by Britain in the *Anglo-Iranian Oil Company* case.

In June 1952, he was twice visited by Jacob Robinson, the Israeli Government lawyer engaged in the negotiations with Germany for the payment of reparations and who wanted some help: 'I had not only to advise him, but also to feed him!'[26] The Agreement was signed on 10 September 1952.

INTERNATIONAL LAW COMMISSION, 1952–1956

Mention has already been made of the Commission in connection with the preparation by Hersch in 1948 of the 'Survey of International Law in Relation to the Work of Codification of the International Law Commission'.[27] Now Hersch was to become much more closely associated with that body.

The first session of the Commission was held in 1949. Its composition reflected the already established custom in UN bodies of including nationals of the Permanent Members of the Security Council. The first British nominee was Professor J. L. Brierly, the Chichele Professor of International Law at Oxford, whose experience, apart from his membership of the 1947 preparatory committee, had been almost exclusively academic. His reputation rested principally on a small but very readable student's textbook, *The Law of Nations*, first published in 1937. A lawyer of conservative temperament who had expressed doubts about the prospects of the UN system, Brierly could not have found the atmosphere and methods of the Commission congenial, although he accepted appointment as Rapporteur on the Law of Treaties, a position which made him responsible for the preparation of a draft on that subject. In July 1951, he indicated his intention to resign after the end of the session.

The filling of casual vacancies, such as those occasioned by death or resignation, was a matter entrusted to the Commission itself, as opposed

---

to regular elections which were a matter for the UN General Assembly. When it became known that Hersch would be the candidate selected to replace Brierly, Liang was able to report, on 16 August, that 'most members of the Commission are delighted at the prospect' of Hersch joining them. Hersch wrote to Liang in September, saying:

I have told the authorities here that I am willing to step into the breach [left by the resignation of Brierly]. In fact this is the kind of work which appeals to me – so much so that, if the matter materialises, I shall most probably abandon my practice entirely to the work of the Commission. It is a great opportunity to do a thing of enduring value and I do not think that any material considerations ought to stand in the way.

The 'material considerations' to which Hersch was referring were the fact that no salary was paid in respect of the work on the Commission, apart from a daily subsistence allowance barely sufficient to cover the cost of living in Geneva. He would also be giving up the prospect of professional income. McNair offered prudent advice. Writing from the ICJ on 20 November 1951, he said:

As to the ILC I venture to make two comments:

1. Do not formally abandon practice until you are appointed to the Commission...

2. When you do decide to abandon your practice, take the best advice in the Temple and in Cambridge as to the most tactful way of making it known. It would be a pity to give people in Cambridge a wrong impression as to the extent of your practice and the amount of time that you have been devoting to it. It is sometimes better to let such information leak out accidentally.

So, on the day following the opening of the 1952 session, Hersch was elected by the Commission for the remainder of Brierly's term. He immediately went to Geneva for the first of the ten-week sessions that he was to spend there over the ensuing three years. For him, this was a major advance. It was the first time that he had an opportunity to step onto the international stage in his own right and to influence the development of international law in directions and to a standard that he thought appropriate. He had every intention of contributing fully to the work of the Commission.

Geneva was a city already well known to him. One of his closest friends, Wilfred Jenks, occupied a prominent position as Legal Adviser of the International Labour Office. Other friends there included Paul

Guggenheim, the Professor of International Law at the University of Geneva. He already had good friends amongst other members of the Commission, notably Georges Scelle from Paris.

After staying with Liang for a short while, Hersch took a flat in the Rue Henry Spiess, where he was able, when Rachel was not with him, to look after himself quite comfortably. He enjoyed the social relations with the other members of the Commission and established an efficient daily work routine: the meetings of the Commission in the morning and meetings of sub-committees or preparation of drafts in the afternoon.

From the beginning he was an active participant, but exposure to the work of the Commission led him to qualify his initial enthusiasm. In a letter to Rachel in May, he wondered whether he would be participating in the next session of the Commission.

I am not sure whether I will wish to remain with them. I am much respected, and people are very friendly, but it is an egregious bit of humbug; the majority do not know any international law; and the method of work is bad. The result is that after three hours – this is the normal period of the daily meeting – I am quite exhausted and have a splitting headache. There is really no reason for me to expose myself to that.

However, his views changed and within two weeks he was writing to Rachel as follows:

I have now fully entered into the work of the Commission and my presence seems to be appreciated. I speak a great deal and practically all my proposals are accepted.

On 16 June, he commented again, still in the same vein. This mood did not last long. On 19 June, he wrote to Rachel:

They are an ignorant lot. Sometimes I think that they appreciate what I am doing. Sometimes it seems that they are angry at being treated like members of my seminar. However, members of my class are much better.

To Stephen Schwebel, he conveyed a more positive message.

HL to Stephen Schwebel, 24 June 1952
The work on the International Law Commission is fatiguing, but provided that I can make an impression in the right direction, it will be worth while. I have a comfortable apartment and that means a great deal.

HL to RL, 16 June 1952
The Commission is not much good, but I have decided not to quarrel with anyone.

HL to RL, 28 June 1952

And we shall spend some time making plans for a holiday – for I shall need it. The Commission means continuous work. There are the meetings in the morning and the preparations in the afternoon, for the next meeting. I am much less miserable about it than I was at the beginning for I feel that I have made an impression on the Commission and that I may do even more. I have certainly displaced Manley Hudson from his position as the tyrant and boss of the Commission. On all major issues I have beaten him, and he has taken it more or less gracefully – though I know that he hates it. But matters require careful handling in the political atmosphere which prevails here. Also it requires work – for, political as they are, they appreciate work done by others. One must also be prepared to encounter some anti-semitism – not only on the part of El-Khoury, the Syrian, but also from Amado, the Brazilian. Of course, they do not show it directly. Again, one must be friendly with them for the Arab and Latin-American blocks in the Assembly have nearly one half of the votes.

The meetings, in a big hall with ear-phones and simultaneous translations, have an air of formality and stiffness . . . However, you will see it and listen to it.

Towards the end of his first session, he was appointed as *rapporteur* to take over the work begun by Brierly on the codification of the law of treaties. After some discussion in the Commission, Hersch was requested to take into account the work already done by the Commission and by Brierly, and to present 'in any manner he might deem fit, a report to the Commission at its next session'.[28] Brierly's approach had been marked by a stylistic terseness, limited commentary and a much broader approach. Hersch was determined to make a fresh start. As it turned out, because he was elected to the ICJ after the 1954 session, he got no further than the topics of the definition of treaties, their conclusion and the conditions of their validity.[29] On these, McNair makes the following comment:

McNair to HL, 12 June 1953

I have now read your Report on Treaties. It is full of meat and full of interest, and I congratulate you upon it. It is easily the best document connected with the International Law Commission that I have yet seen. I do not doubt that your draft Articles will be pulled to pieces and that you will have to exercise the greatest patience and self-control. I hope however, and support that when the complete draft Articles on the subject of Treatise are embodied in the form of a

[28] *Yearbook of the International Law Commission* (1952), vol. 2, p. 69.
[29] See his 'First and Second Reports on the Law of Treaties', UN Docs. A/CN.4/63 (24 March 1953) and A/CN. 4/87 (6 July 1954).

Report for the Assembly, you will be able to attach the text of your commentary upon them, either in its present form or in an amended form. I say this for two reasons, firstly, because it is important that your commentary should be preserved and, secondly, because without it, it would not be possible for the proposed Articles to be fully understood and appreciated.

In an undated letter, McNair added a footnote:

I heard you referred to as McLauterpacht by someone who seems to think that 'Mc' is a patronymic appurtenant to the Whewell Chair.

His successor, Sir Gerald Fitzmaurice, then started all over again with a very elaborate structure which he was unable to complete in the ensuing five years. It remained for Sir Humphrey Waldock, Fitzmaurice's successor, to adopt a much more pragmatic approach and to carry it through to a successful conclusion in 1978. Nonetheless, Hersch's work stands as an important contribution to the literature on the topics that he covered. As Wilfred Jenks said:

His comments on each of the articles of his draft . . . set a standard of thoroughness for such work which . . . is now widely regarded as a model for the future.[30]

On 2 February 1953, Hersch delivered a lecture on the 'Revision of the Laws of War' at the LSE. In addition, Hersch was in 1953 elected *rapporteur* of the Commission, that is, the member charged with preparing and steering through the Commission a report to be submitted by the Commission to the UN General Assembly for their consideration. The burden of the *rapporteur*'s work varies according to the inclination and capacity of the individual. Some prefer to leave much of the substantive drafting to the Secretariat, while others, of which Hersch was one, prefer to do most of that work themselves. In 1953, the Commission was, for the first time, exploring the law of the sea on the basis of reports on the subject by the Dutch member, Professor J. A. P. Francois. The particular aspects covered were the continental shelf, fisheries and the contiguous zone. To a large extent, the work of Professor Francois was developed in detail and style in the Commission's report,[31] under the guidance of Hersch, into a text which encapsulated the main elements subsequently reflected in the 1956 draft Articles on the Law of the Sea.

---

[30] C. W. Jenks, 'Hersch Lauterpacht – The Scholar as Prophet' (1960) 39 *BYIL* 89.
[31] See *Yearbook of the International Law Commission* (1953), vol. 2, pp. 200 *et seq.*

In October 1953, Brierly's term having expired, Hersch came up for re-election by the UN General Assembly and he was re-elected, though only in fifth place. However, the next session (1954) proved to be his last because, in November of that year, he was elected to the ICJ and took his seat there in February 1955.

MANUAL OF MILITARY LAW

In addition to all his work in Cambridge and Geneva, Hersch remained actively involved in the revision of Chapter 14 of Part III ('The Laws and Usages of War on Land') of the British *Manual of Military Law*. This was a task that the War Office had invited him to undertake as far back as 1950. Indeed, it was then decided that the War Office should 'receive the greatest help available and from the most authoritative source',[32] which, after consideration, was agreed to be Hersch. The work occupied a good deal of his time between 1951 and 1956, when he went to the ICJ. It was a substantial undertaking, involving the revision of a chapter that had last been revised in 1936,[33] since when there had been major developments in the law, principally, but not limited to, the conclusion of the Geneva Conventions in 1949 and the development in the jurisprudence of the laws of war as a result of the Second World War. Although much of the work drew upon the material that Hersch had prepared for the seventh edition of Volume II (*Disputes, War and Neutrality*) of *Oppenheim*, nonetheless assistance was given by Colonel (later Professor) G. I. A. D. Draper of the Directorate of Army Legal Services, an experienced army officer who had seen active service during the Second World War. He was also a meticulous lawyer with whom Hersch appreciated working, as he did also with Colonel Richard Baxter (Hersch's former research student, a reserve officer in the United States Army and by then a professor at the Harvard Law School) with whom official consultations were held, at a conference in Cambridge in May 1953.[34]

There was some unpleasantness during the preparation of this work. First, in July 1950 and then again in May 1952, the Earl of Cork and Orrery (a former admiral in the Royal Navy) raised in the House of Lords the question of the wording of the provision in the Manual on the effect of superior orders. He expressed concern about the fact that, in 1944, the

---

[32] War Office Minutes, 18 August 1950, LH 618.
[33] *Manual of Military Law* (1929), Amendments No. 12, 31 January 1936, as changed by Amendments No. 34, April 1944, which dealt with the doctrine of superior orders.
[34] See note by R. R. Baxter, 'The Cambridge Conference on the Revision of the Law of War' (1953) 47 *AJIL* 702–3.

Manual had been altered so that the plea of superior orders would not serve as a defence to a charge of the commission of war crimes.[35] Neither initiative came to anything, but Hersch, who was known to be editing Chapter 14 of the Manual, was referred to by Lord Cork in unattractive and sarcastic terms:

I do not think that rules as revised by him will be warmly received. I very much doubt if he is the right man to be employed for this work. No doubt the Professor has performed, and performs, valuable service for his adopted country, but we have to face things as they are, and I am sure that as a rewriter of the rules governing the actions of the British Forces under active service conditions he is out of place. If we want the Services to accept the new version of their duties and representatives, I think those ought to be presented to them over names that they know and trust. I should have thought that it was perfectly possible to get a British or Dominion international lawyer to look after the interests of the British people.[36]

It appears that the Earl of Cork and Orrery was more disturbed by a foreign-sounding name and the fact that Hersch had only 'adopted' Britain, than he was by any knowledge that Hersch, having been naturalised in 1931, was by 1952 already a British subject of twenty years' standing and thus as much to be trusted as the majority of members of the armed forces who, though being born British subjects, were no more than twenty years of age. It was not the only time that prejudice of this

---

[35] Before Amendment No. 34 of April 1944, the Manual contained the following provision: 'Members of the armed forces who commit such violations of the recognised rules of warfare as are ordered by their Government, or their commander, are not war criminals and cannot therefore be punished by the enemy.' After Amendment No. 34, para. 443 of the Manual read: '[T]he fact that a rule of warfare has been violated in pursuance of an order of the belligerent Government or of any individual belligerent commander does not deprive the act in question of its character of a war crime; neither does it, in principle, confer upon the perpetrator immunity from punishment by the injured belligerent.' Hersch's draft copy of Chapter XIV of the Manual contained the following: '[T]he fact that a rule of warfare has been violated in pursuance of an order of the belligerent Government or of an individual belligerent commander does not deprive the act in question of its character as a war crime; neither does it, in principle, confer upon the perpetrator immunity from punishment by the injured belligerent. Undoubtedly, a court confronted with the plea of superior orders adduced in justification of a war-crime is bound to take into consideration the fact that obedience to military orders, not obviously unlawful, is the duty of every member of the armed forces and that the latter cannot, in conditions of war discipline, be expected to weigh scrupulously the legal merits of the order received. The question, however, is governed by the major principle that members of the armed forces are bound to obey lawful orders only and that they cannot therefore escape liability if, in obedience to a command, they commit acts which both violate unchallenged rules of warfare and outrage the general sentiment of humanity.' The Manual drafted by Hersch and eventually printed in 1958 contained, in paragraph 627, the following statement: '[O]bedience to the order of a government or of a superior, whether military or civil, or to a national law or regulation, affords no defence to a charge of committing a war crime but may be considered in mitigation of punishment.'
[36] *Hansard*, HL [House of Lords] Debates, vol. 176, col. 961, 14 May 1952.

kind was reflected in official circles,[37] but Hersch seems to have been able to cope with it.

There was also some difficulty regarding a suitable statement of international law concerning the use of nuclear weapons. In Volume II of the seventh edition of *Oppenheim*, published some five years earlier, Hersch explained that:

While the permanency of the contamination caused by the atomic bomb within a defined area is controversial there is weighty evidence of the protracted and perhaps inevitably fatal suffering which it inflicts on the injured. Moreover, in view of the as yet incalculable nature of the indirect physical consequences to human beings far beyond the immediate range of its explosion, it is possible that the use of the atomic bomb on a larger scale may bring it within the orbit of biological warfare which has been condemned by the conscience of mankind. If these are in fact the consequences of the use of the atomic weapon – a matter on which it would seem premature to express an opinion – then there is room for the view that it is contrary to International Law even if it is directed against undoubted military objectives – such as battle-ships or large accumulations of troops – which contain or are composed of human beings.[38]

The Deputy Legal Advisor of the Foreign Office, F. A. Vallat, noted on 3 June 1957 that:

It may be, however, that the law is not accurately or correctly stated in Oppenheim and it may be that if we are to maintain the draft text in the *Manual of Military Law*, we shall have to be prepared to criticise this passage in Oppenheim. This may be a little awkward because in the main Oppenheim is the authority for the draft text.

At that time, the developing draft of the relevant paragraph of the Manual read:

In the absence of any rule of international law forbidding the use of land atomic and similar weapons, the legality of their use in any particular instance must be determined by the nature of the target against which they are directed and by taking into account whether the effects will be such as to infringe any existing provision of conventional or customary international law.[39]

---

[37] See p. 258 above for the observation of Sir Eric Beckett in 1946; and p. 376 below for those of Sir Lionel Heald as Attorney-General.

[38] *Oppenheim*, vol. II (7th edn, 1952), p. 348.

[39] Hersch's 'The Problem of the Revision of the Law of War' (1952) 29 *BYIL* 360–82 at 369–73 and *Oppenheim*, vol. II, pp. 347–52, are cited in support of this proposition.

G. G. Brown of the Foreign Office, in a letter marked 'Top Secret' to H. E. Smith at the War Office, remarked that this disagreement had been given full consideration and:

It is considered that if the omission of any reference to nuclear land weapons were challenged it could be defended on the grounds that the topic of nuclear warfare is one in respect of which there can at present be said to be no agreed law... Moreover, it can be maintained that as the rule which paragraph 113 lays down is, in principle, not peculiar to atomic or similar weapons, there is no necessity that it should be specifically stated in relation to such weapons.

It was eventually decided that it would be better to omit paragraph 113 from the Manual; as noted in a letter from G. E. Dudman, Legal Secretary at the Law Officers Department at the Royal Courts of Justice to the Directorate of Army Legal Services at the War Office,

the Attorney-General is agreeable to the omission of paragraph 113 of the revised draft of Part III of the *Manual of Military Law*, but he thinks you should substitute a passage pointing out that, in the absence of any rule of international law dealing expressly with a particular weapon, it falls to be dealt with in accordance with the ordinary rules.

After discussion between the Attorney-General, the Foreign Office and other service departments, it was agreed that the proposed draft paragraph 113 should be omitted and replaced with a footnote to paragraph 107 of the Manual that read as follows:

In the absence of any rule of international law dealing expressly with it, the use which may be made of a particular weapon will be governed by the ordinary rules and the question of the legality of its use in any individual case will, therefore, involve merely the application of the recognised principles of international law, as to which, see Oppenheim, vol. II, pp. 346–352.

However, even this compromise caused some concern, as noted in a briefing for the Secretary of State dated 30 April 1958:

The Foreign Office at official level are prepared to accept the draft, subject to the Committee's approval, although they do not much like the reference to 'Oppenheim's International Law' even in an oblique form, since although he does not take up any definite position on the legality of nuclear weapons, he suggests only two cases in which they are definitely permissible, neither of which take account of Her Majesty's Government's deterrent policy which is clearly based on the threat of massive retaliation in the event of an aggression, without necessarily waiting for the enemy to use nuclear weapons first. The Foreign

Office recognise that the Oppenheim statements are widely known and will be read whether we refer to them in the Manual or not.[40]

Hersch's discussion on the use of nuclear weapons in Volume II of the seventh edition of *Oppenheim* also prompted a critical reaction from Schwarzenberger,[41] who disagreed with the contents of the following footnote:

Moreover, as laws are made not only for the protection of human life but also for the preservation of ultimate values of society, it is possible that should those values be imperilled by an aggressor intent upon dominating the world the nations thus threatened might consider themselves bound to assume the responsibility of exercising the supreme right of self-preservation in a manner which, while contrary to specific prohibition of International Law, they alone deem to be decisive for ultimate vindication of the law of nations. The use of the atomic weapon in a contingency of that nature would still be contrary to the principle . . . that the rules of International Law apply even in relation to an aggressor in an unlawful war.[42]

As the following letters show, Schwarzenberger and Hersch in fact held similar opinions about the use of nuclear weapons: generally, they believed their use was contrary to international law. Schwarzenberger, however, considered that this footnote – in particular the first sentence; he conveniently overlooked the second – suggested that their use might be permitted by international law, asserting that *Oppenheim* (and therefore Hersch) 'supplies, in advance, the legal advisers of Service departments east and west of the world frontiers with the most obvious ex post arguments'.[43] Hersch was hurt by this accusation and believed that Schwarzenberger had misrepresented the views expressed in *Oppenheim*.

HL to Schwarzenberger, 2 April 1958:

You have been very prompt in acknowledging the receipt of my book of the Court. I fear I have been rather remiss in doing the same with regard to your

---

[40] Page 2, para. 6.

[41] An account is provided in German in Stephanie Steinle, *Völkerrecht und Machtpolitik, Georg Schwarzenberger (1908–1991)* (Baden-Baden: Nomos, 2002), pp. 216–18. Georg Schwarzenberger (1908–91) was born in Heilbronn, Germany, and educated at the Universities of Heidelberg, Frankfurt, Berlin, Tübingen, Paris and London. He arrived in England in 1934 and was appointed part-time lecturer in international law and relations at University College London in 1938, remaining there until his retirement in 1975. Schwarzenberger was appointed Professor of International Law in 1963. His most significant contribution to international law is the four-volume study *International Law as Applied by International Courts and Tribunals* (1945–86).

[42] *Oppenheim*, Vol. II (1951), p. 352, n. 2.

[43] See Schwarzenberger, 'The Legality of Nuclear Weapons' (1958) 11 *Current Legal Problems* 258.

lecture on 'The Legality of Nuclear Weapons'. I read it with much interest. I was also glad to see that, with regard to the essential aspects of the matter, we arrive at the same conclusion. We both think that while the use of that weapon may be, and is, from various points of view, contrary to international law, the more effective solution of the problem lies not in any mere legal condemnation of a declaratory or constitutive nature but in the conventional prohibition of its use coupled with a substantial measure of international control and supervision at all stages.

This is clearly set out at some length in the relevant section of my edition of Oppenheim to which you refer.

In view of this I was rather shocked to see that in your recent lecture you give repeated expression, with some emphasis, to the interpretation which you put on my views in your lecture in the Current Legal Problems of 1955 (pp. 231–232). You say there that it is my footnote on page 357 of Oppenheim which provides my 'real argument' and that it supplies in advance the Legal Advisers of the Foreign Officers with a justification for the use of the nuclear weapon. You thought it necessary to support that assertion by elaborating the theme that, often, it is the footnote that matters and not the text.

However, even that footnote provides no justification for what you say. I am not suggesting there that governments would be justified, in circumstances envisaged in that footnote, in using the atomic weapon. What I have said there is that they 'may consider themselves bound to assume the responsibility for exercising the supreme right of self-preservation in a manner which, while contrary to a specific prohibition of international law, they alone deem to be decisive for the ultimate vindication of the law of nations'. I deliberately refrained from saying that they would be entitled to act in that way. If there were any doubt about it, the next sentence of that footnote, which you did not quote, makes the matter quite clear. In that sentence I state that 'the use of the atomic weapon in a contingency of that nature would still be contrary to the principle – suggested above . . . – that the rules of international law apply even in relation to an aggressor in an unlawful war'. I added, as pointing to the limited effectiveness of a mere statement of the law in that matter, that there was no decisive reason for assuming that, in extreme contingencies there envisaged, governments would adhere to the legal principles in question.

The statement in the footnote is no more than the expression of an apprehension, which you share, that a mere legal prohibition, either by way of stating the existing law or of a treaty, is not sufficient and that, in the nature of things, it is highly uncertain in its effect. Essentially, that footnote does no more than to draw attention to some, non-legal, aspects of the main statement of the law on the subject in the text, namely, its doubtful effectiveness in a situation like that. The statement of the law in the texts leaves no room for doubt. It is that, except with regard to purely military objectives and except in case of reprisals against the state first resorting to it, the use of the atomic weapon is illegal whether by reference to existing international agreements, or to the distinction between combatants, and non-combatants or to the principles of humanity (which, unlike you, I consider to be part of international law). Moreover, even with regard to purely military objectives, such as battleships or concentrations of troops which contain or are composed of human beings, I pointed out that there is room for the view that the use of the atomic weapon is contrary to international law.

I remember having given anxious thought to the drafting of that section, which underwent a number of revisions before I sent it to the printer and even after that. It was drafted with care and with a sense of responsibility. It does not differ in any material respect, or even in emphasis, from your own conclusions. In view of this I am puzzled to know why you have written as you have done. Your recent lecture makes things worse, if possible. That footnote, which you misconstrued and inadequately quoted and which emphasises the danger of mere legal prohibition, unless supported by constructive international measures, you now describe on page 42 as a justification for the use of nuclear weapons and as my 'crowning argument' on the subject.

You know that, in all the circumstances, I cannot engage in public controversy. But I must draw your attention to this matter in the interests of scholarship and in the hope that you will see how misleading and unjust your misrepresentations are and that you will take adequate steps to remedy them.

I am leaving for The Hague on the 8th April. So if you were to write perhaps you will kindly address your letter there.

Schwarzenberger replied, still critical of the footnote in *Oppenheim*.

Schwarzenberger to HL, 10 April 1958
Thank you for your letter of the 2nd inst., which awaited me when we returned last night from a short Easter vacation in Cornwall. Admittedly, I was somewhat astonished that in the concluding paragraphs, you should accuse me of having 'misconstrued and inadequately quoted' your footnote and, beyond this, of, 'misrepresentations' which are supposed to be both 'misleading' and 'unjust'. At the same time, you appeal to me in the 'interest of scholarship' and to my sense of fairness as, even in relation to matters written by you before your election to the Court, you consider yourself precluded from engaging in public controversy.

I propose to respond to your letter on the double basis which you have invoked. If you should find that some of my remarks are perhaps somewhat forthright, I shall at least do my best to keep them within the bounds of academic courtesy and, having said that, in view of your letter, I fear needs saying, you will find that this letter does not have its sting in the end. On the contrary, I shall reserve for this portion the constructive proposals which I would like to make.

I have read again in the light of the commentary of your letter the relevant paragraphs of the last edition of Vol. II of Oppenheim. If this footnote were to refer merely to metalegal considerations, why should you then have added it exactly at the end of a paragraph which deals exclusively with 'contingencies not amounting to a breach of International Law'? Moreover, you – and not the hypothetical belligerents – make yourself responsible for the introductory statement in this footnote on the purpose of law on which the hypothetical argument that follows hinges. Finally, you state at the end of this footnote not only that, in the extreme contingency referred to, the prohibition would not, but also that it could not be scrupulously adhered to. As in the second sentence of this footnote, the qualification contained in the previous sentence is merely elaborated, it can hardly be said that the full quotation of the first sentence amounts to an 'inadequate' quotation.

What you say about the number of revisions of the 'nuclear' passage before and after they went to the printer is no news to me. Awareness of the sources which encouraged you to revise your original draft, if I remember rightly, three or four times formed the travaux préparatoires which, in a language of the International Court to which we both, I am happy to think, object, confirmed to me the 'natural' meaning of the words used in this footnote.

I might also mention that the passage in 'The Legality of Nuclear Weapons' to which you objected is merely a mild and condensed restatement of views which, as you rightly say, I have expressed more fully – and considerably more strongly – in Current Legal Problems 1955, and even before then in my review of Oppenheim's Vol. II in Year Book of World Affairs (1954), at p. 341. In these circumstances, I would consider anybody estopped even by the most lenient standards of Equity from raising this question at so late a stage and, in particular after our extended talk at the Athenaeum in the Spring of 1957.

You will probably be even more astonished to hear that in a review published at about the same time as my own review, and under your own editorship, a reviewer whom I have always regarded as one of your most uncritical followers, expressed exactly the same views as I did on the argument . . . [where he noted that the] footnote being so important a part of your argumentation that this remark 'might well have found a place in the text'. Moreover, Dr Mann took it for granted as much as I did that this footnote could not mean anything but a legal justification of the use of nuclear weapons in the contingency mentioned. He referred expressly to the victim as then 'entitled' to exercise the alleged right of self-preservation (British Year Book of International Law 1952, at p. 516).

If, as I refrained from doing, I had attempted to contrast the views which you had expressed in Oppenheim with those in your paper in the BYIL 1952, at pp. 369–370, this would really have been unkind.

Thus, while I must make it clear beyond any doubt that I do think you have accused me very unjustly of having misrepresented you in any way, I am quite willing to overlook this. Although I cannot accept any responsibility for wrong impressions which you own formulations may have caused, I am very willing to be helpful in the correction of any misunderstandings.

Am I then right in assuming that, reprisals apart, <u>you</u>, as distinct from the hypothetical belligerents mentioned in the footnote, consider the use of nuclear weapons in any circumstances as illegal? If this is so, will you please confirm that at the above private address at 4 Bowers Way, Harpenden, Herts, at your <u>earliest</u> convenience. I shall then take all steps in my power to point this out in the <u>Current Legal Problems</u> version of the paper and in the German and Spanish translations which are just going through the press. I think I could also persuade Messrs Stevens to add in loose form a note to the same effect to the copies of the pamphlet and book edition which they still have in stock.

I am very anxious that not only full justice is done to you in this matter – as I feel sure it has – but also that this is clearly apparent. It, therefore, occurred to me that, with your consent, we might publish in full this exchange of letters. As it refers to editorial activities of yours prior to your appointment to the Court, I am sure that you could obtain the Court's permission for such a joint effort. Who knows whether the implementation of this proposal might not even lead to another 'summit' meeting.

As I want to make quite sure that this letter does not get into any wrong hands, I send it by registered post. In this connection, you may want to know that, although your own letter was dated April 2nd, it was only posted in the evening of April 6.

Hersch considered the publication of the letters to be impossible, presumably because, despite the fact that it refers to work done before he was elected to the ICJ, it would conflict with his present position as a judge.

HL to Schwarzenberger, 11 April 1958
As you think it's beyond any doubt that I have very unjustly accused you of misrepresenting my views, that, I fear, must be the end of the controversy. In the circumstances I do not wish to take any further steps in the matter. I certainly cannot consent to the publication, in any way, of the two letters – although possibly, I may send a copy of them, for information but not for any action, to Professor Keeton in his capacity as joint editor of Current Legal Problems.

Schwarzenberger replied a few days later.

Schwarzenberger to HL, 17 April 1958
As your letter does not deal with the substance of my answers to your charges, I hope that, at your early convenience, you will either favour me with a reasoned

reply or withdraw unreservedly what I can only describe as completely unwarranted attacks on the professional honour and competence of an academic colleague and a member of the Inn of which you are a Bencher.

As you had asked me in the interest of scholarship and fairness to take adequate steps to bring your real views as <u>now</u> explained to me to the attention of my own readers, and I had to pass the German version for press on Friday last, I did so in what I hope you will consider not only a fair but also a generous way, and, to attain uniformity, I made the same additions to the Spanish translation. As <u>Current Legal Problems</u> 1958 was already in page proof I had to proceed there in a more summary way. Finally, I asked Messrs Steven at the same time to add at my own expense insertions corresponding to those made in the German and Spanish translations to all copies which they have still in stock of their pamphlet and book editions. Unfortunately, as I heard just now over the phone, they did not consider this proposal practicable as it would have involved too much work at their end.

In view of the seriousness of your attacks, I had no choice but to send at the same time when I wrote to you, copies of our two letters to all those who, in the various ways in which, these days, our paths happen to cross, are directly concerned with knowing about this matter. Naturally, Professor Keeton was one of these.

Hersch replied, not giving in to Schwarzenberger's claims, but offering a diplomatic – and understanding – end to the disagreement.

HL to Schwarzenberger, 19 April 1958
Thank you for your letter of the 17th April.

As you may have gathered from my letter of the 11th I do not agree with the interpretation which you have put on what I said in my edition of Oppenheim. I still think that it was an unjust interpretation. However, on these questions views may legitimately differ. There was, of course, no intention to attack on that account your professional honour or academic competence, and I am very sorry if anything said in my letter has created with you that impression or has given you cause for worry.

I am much obliged to you for what you say about the additions which you have now made in the proof.

It may be mentioned at this point that Hersch and Schwarzenberger had not had an easy relationship and this disagreement over the footnote in *Oppenheim* was not the first instance of it. The two had fundamentally different views on legal matters – Schwarzenberger saw Hersch as 'utopian' and 'romantic' and Hersch viewed Schwarzenberger as engaged in power politics – and these differences extended to personal matters, such as religion and politics. Hersch had previously disagreed with Schwarzenberger's work on the British Mandate in Palestine,[44] while Schwarzenberger was opposed to the use of private law analogies in international law.[45]

These views, and the insensitive and confrontational manner in which Schwarzenberger conducted himself, led to several clashes with the so-called 'Cambridge Group'. Although Hersch – and others, such as Fitzmaurice – initially declined to support Schwarzenberger for a professorial position,[46] it appears that he did eventually retract his opposition, as the following letters show.

HL to the Provost of University College, London, 15 January 1958

With regard to the subject of our discussion I am writing to say that should you, after any further consultation decide to go ahead with the proposal I shall feel, regardless of the attitude which I may formally take up in the meeting of the Advisors, that you are justified in your decision.

Keeton to the Provost of University College, London, 20 January 1958

It looks as though we did a great deal of good at the Athenaeum lunch. I too have had a most friendly letter from Lauterpacht, in which he writes: 'You must not worry unduly about the matter, which we discussed. I am sure that all will be well in the end. After you and the Provost have thought further about the matter – and, perhaps, after you have taken a view to advancing or clarifying matters' . . .

However, Schwarzenberger's critical attack on the footnote in *Oppenheim* relating to nuclear weapons led Hersch – and other British international lawyers – to retract their support for Schwarzenberger's appointment. In his letter to Keeton, in which Hersch enclosed copies of his correspondence with Schwarzenberger, he explained that 'in all the circumstances, I feel that I must withdraw the offer which I made some time ago to have a talk with Schwarzenberger'.[47]

A note in the archive files (dated 10 June 1958) explains that the Provost met with Professor Keeton on 9 June 1958 about the proposed application for Schwarzenberger's professorial position, and that Keeton:

---

[44] It is noted by Steinle, *Völkerrecht und Machtpolitik*, pp. 16–17, that Schwarzenberger opposed the recognition of a legal personality to the Jewish people under international law.

[45] *Ibid.* Steinle notes that 'this fundamental difference about the validity of private law analogies in international law remained a constant source of friction between the two international lawyers'.

[46] Keeton to Provost, 25 November, 1957, Personal File 29/1/19, Bl. 218, University College, London Archives.

[47] HL to Keeton, 14 April 1958.

has seen Sir David Hughes Parry, who has seen Sir Hersch Lauterpacht. Lauterpacht has seen McNair, Jennings, Goodhart and Fitzmaurice and the answers in all quarters seems to be that there would be no support.[48]

It was only in 1963, three years after Hersch's death, that Schwarzenberger received a professorship.

Despite having completed a first revised draft of the *Manual of Military Law* in 1951, as a result of internal difficulties and the desire to have the 1949 Geneva Conventions ratified before publication the final draft was not published until 1958. After completion, some awkwardness arose regarding recognition of Hersch's work. Sir Edward Playfair wrote the following letter to Hersch:

Sir E. W. Playfair to HL, 24 November 1958
I am commanded by the Army Council to convey to you, on the publication of Part III of the Manual of Military Law (the Law of War on Land), their warm appreciation of your assistance in the preparation of this work.

I ask you to accept the enclosed copy of the work.

The word 'assistance' hardly reflected the level of work and commitment Hersch had put into the revised text from 1950 to 1958. He responded with unusual sharpness, displaying a clear disinclination to see his role belittled.

HL to Sir E. W. Playfair, 5 December 1958
I beg to thank you for your letter of the 24th November, expressing the appreciation of the Army Council for my assistance in the preparation of Part III of the Manual of Military Law (The Law of War on Land). As the question of responsibility and authorship for this work is involved, I feel that perhaps I ought to point out that there is no question here of my assistance in the preparation of this work. I assumed the responsibility for its preparation, subject to the assistance of the Department of the Legal Services of the War Office, and I devoted several years to that work. Although the new edition is based to some extent on the former editions, it is in scope and size largely a new work.

There is, of course, no question here of a suggestion of any lack of generosity in the expression of their appreciation on the part of the Army Council. However, seeing that the question of responsibility and authorship is involved I think that I ought to draw your attention to this aspect of the matter.

It will perhaps be convenient if the subject is now regarded as closed.

---

[48] Memo to files of the Provost, 10 June 1958, Personal File 29/1/19, Bl. 266, University College, London Archives.

I beg to thank you for the copy of the work, which, I am told, has now arrived in Cambridge.

Hersch received the following response:

Sir E. W. Playfair to HL, 15 December 1958
I must take some personal responsibility for the phrasing of the Army Council letter of the 20th November. I drew the word 'assistance', which of course greatly underestimates your part in the work, from the note in the introduction which you had approved, and pitched the note no higher in order to avoid any confusion between your past help to us and your present international and judicial position . . .

May we, as you suggest, treat the subject as closed, on the understanding that the gratitude of the Army Council remains open and that the formal words of their official letter were never meant to imply any limitation of the real responsibility which you have borne, and consequently of the substantial service which you have rendered to them?

Despite the justification for Hersch's initial letter, he still felt uncomfortable about it as the final letter in this exchange demonstrates:

HL to Sir E. W. Playfair, 21 December 1958
Many thanks for the letter of the 15th concerning the Military Manual (Law of War). Your letter closes the subject not only formally but also most generously and to my entire satisfaction. I am very much obliged to you. Also, I am rather sorry about any unnecessary trouble I may have occasioned.

Plate 1 1902, Lauterpacht family portrait. From left, HL, with his arm through his father's, his father, his mother, Deborah (née Turkenkopf), his sister, Sabka, and his brother, Dunek.

Plate 2 1913, HL at 16, early in the First World War, taken in Lemberg (Lwów).

Plate 3 1920 c., RL, aged 20.

Plate 4 1922, HL.

Plate 5 1922, HL with Jewish students in Vienna, Leon Steinig seated on his right.

Plate 6 1922, 18 December, HL and RL in Berlin on the day of their engagement.

Plate 7 1922, 18 December, HL and RL in Berlin on the day of their engagement.

Plate 8 1923–4, LSE, International Law class. HL second from right, front row; Arnold McNair in centre of front row.

Plate 9 1932, HL and EL on Hampstead Heath, London.

Plate 10 1933 c., HL's mother and father, HL behind his father, RL on the right, EL in front.

Plate 11 1933, RL, HL and EL outside their home at 103 Walm Lane, Cricklewood, London.

Plate 12 1935, HL on holiday in Switzerland.

Plate 13 1942 c., HL in the Cambridge Home Guard. HL is in the third row from the front, fifth from the right.

Plate 14 1945, Members of the British prosecution team at Nuremberg. Front row, left to right: HL; the Rt Hon. Sir David Maxwell Fyfe, KC, MP; HM Attorney-General Sir Hartley Shawcross, KC, MP; Mr G. D. Roberts, KC; and Mr Patrick Dean of the Foreign Office. Back row, left to right: Major J. H. Barrington; Major Elwyn Jones MP; Mr E. G. Robey; Lt-Col. M. Griffith Jones MC; Col. H. J. Phillimore; Mr Maurice Read; and Mr Bashford.

Plate 15 1945 c., HL in the garden at 6 Cranmer Road, Cambridge.

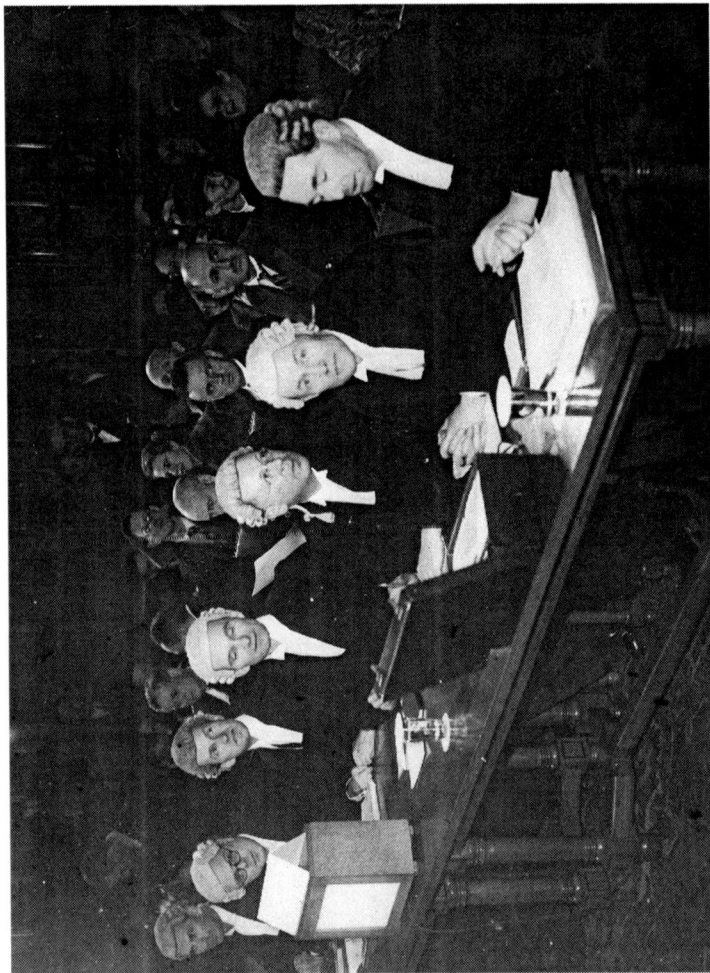

Plate 16 1946, The British team at the ICJ in the *Corfu Channel* hearings. From the right, Sir Hartley Shawcross (Attorney-General), Sir Eric Beckett (Legal Adviser of the Foreign Office), HL, Humphrey Waldock, Richard Wilberforce, J. Mervyn Jones.

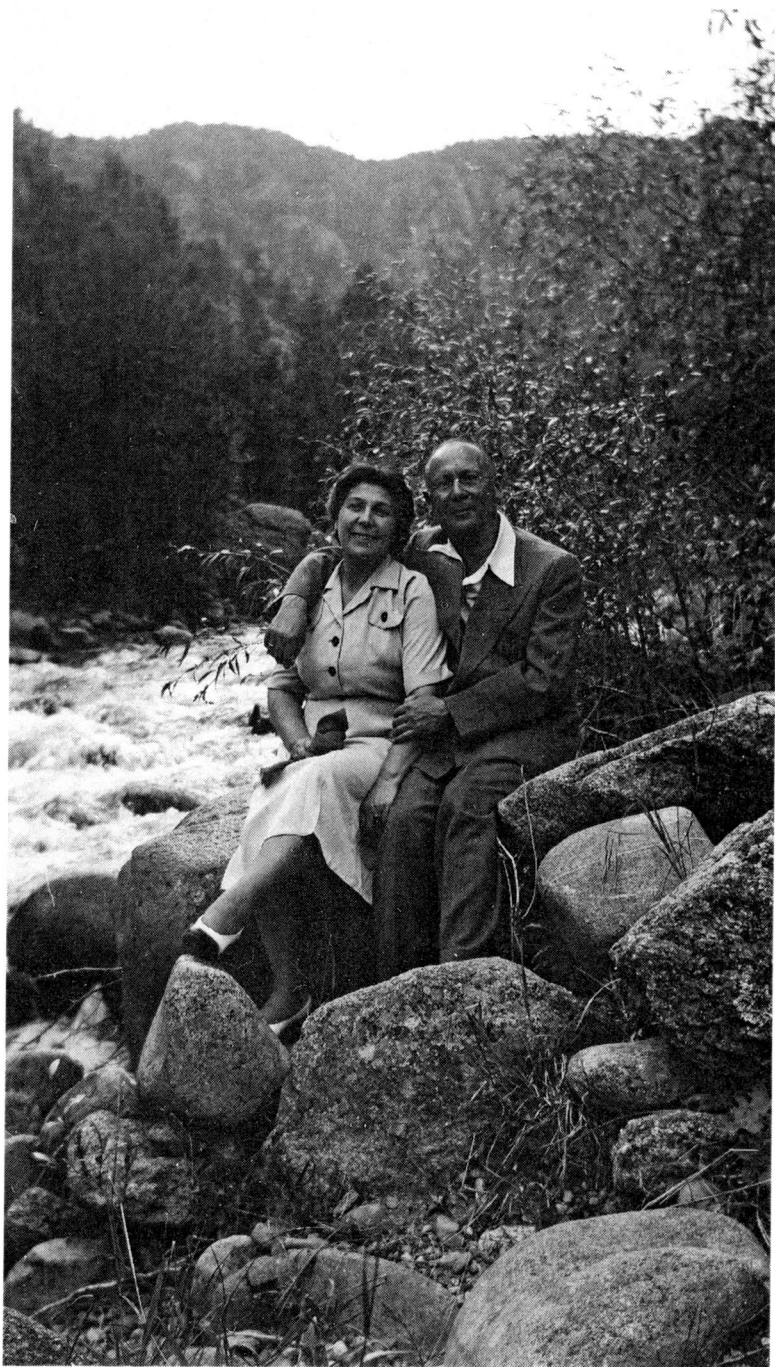

Plate 17 1948, HL and RL in Boulder, Colorado.

Plate 18 1949, 26 April, HL upon taking silk. From left to right: Reynold Bennett
(second cousin of RL), RL, HL, Inka.

Plate 19 1950, HL and RL with Lord and Lady McNair at Cranmer Road, Cambridge.

Plate 20 1952, HL with some of his research students. From the left, Iain McGibbon, Ruth Goldstein, Arthur Albrecht, Felice Morgenstern, HL, D. P. O'Connell, Alan Philip.

Plate 21 1952, HL and RL at the session of the Institut de droit international in Siena, Italy, 17–26 April 1952. HL and RL are in the third and fourth rows from the front, third and fourth from the right.

Plate 22 1953, HL in Geneva during the session of the International Law Commission.

Plate 23 1954, HL and EL in Brighton.

Plate 24 1955, HL at the ICJ.

Plate 25 1956, The ICJ in session, HL at the right-hand end of the row.

Plate 26 1956, 14 February, HL and RL, following his investiture as a Knight at Buckingham Palace.

CHAPTER 11

THE INTERNATIONAL COURT OF JUSTICE, 1955–1960

On 7 October 1954, Hersch was elected a judge of the International Court of Justice as successor to Sir Arnold McNair who was reaching the end of his nine-year term and did not wish to stand for re-election.[1] This ushered in the last and in some ways the most significant period of Hersch's life. Great as his reputation was by then, on the basis of his four major books, his editions of *Oppenheim*, editorship of the *British Year Book of International Law* and membership of the International Law Commission, it is to his separate and dissenting opinions as a judge of the Court that one looks for the ultimate practical implementation of his scholarship.

The ICJ was at that time regarded as the most important international tribunal in the world. Indeed, with the possible exception of the European Court and the European Commission of Human Rights, in its limited sphere, it had no competitor. It was described in Chapter XIV of the Charter of the United Nations as 'the principal judicial organ' of that body. Its jurisdiction extended to any dispute between States that they might agree, in one or another form, to submit to it. It did not have, and still has not, any jurisdiction over cases initiated by individuals. But it also possessed, and still possesses, the competence to give advisory opinions at the request of various organs of the UN and its specialised agencies – requests most often made by the General Assembly or the Security Council.

The role of the ICJ in the international judicial scene has altered somewhat in the ensuing fifty years. A number of other international tribunals have appeared, some dealing with important issues that transcend many of those that come to the Court. Notable examples are the European Court of Justice and the Appellate Body of the World Trade Organization, which handles appeals in trade disputes of considerable complexity arising between members of that organisation. The significance of these cases, in terms of impact upon the economies and finances of the parties to them is, it must be acknowledged, as great as the general

---

[1] McNair was among the first group of judges elected to the ICJ in 1945. He served as President from 1952 to 1955.

373

run of decisions of the ICJ. That is not to say that the ICJ no longer has the highest standing in the informal hierarchy of international tribunals. Moreover, the range of cases submitted to it remains wide, being related not only to territorial and maritime issues and questions of state responsibility, but also occasionally involving serious political issues such as the legality of the use of nuclear weapons and the legal consequences of the construction by Israel of the security barrier between it and the Palestinian West Bank areas. In addition, international jurisprudence is today the beneficiary of decisions by the International Tribunal on the Law of the Sea, the International Criminal Tribunal for the former Yugoslavia (established in 1993), the International Criminal Tribunal for Rwanda (established in 1994), the International Criminal Court (set up in 2002), and the various courts of human rights, European, inter-American and African. The criminal courts, in particular, represent the recognition in international law of a growing concern with the criminal behaviour of individuals that had previously been the subject only of intermittent war crimes trials following the First and Second World Wars.

Additionally, the development of international arbitration, whether within an institutional framework such as the World Bank's International Centre for the Settlement of Investment Disputes or on an *ad hoc* basis, in which individuals and corporations are directly involved, has meant that many cases, especially in the investment field, that might previously have been thought of as appropriate for settlement by the ICJ if it had not been limited by Article 34 of its Statute to hearing only cases in which States are parties, can now be compulsorily and impartially resolved by other bodies.

Of what was to develop in the next half-century Hersch of course knew nothing in 1955, though, as an active proponent of international protection of human rights and of the responsibility of individuals for war crimes and crimes against humanity, he might have dreamed of some of the changes that were to come. For him, the ICJ was of stellar significance and his election to it was the greatest recognition that he could have hoped for of the much acclaimed work he had already done. The Court was to provide him with an opportunity – shortened by his premature death – for the application and growth of his views on a number of important issues of contemporary international law.

The ICJ then, as now, consisted of fifteen 'titular'[2] judges, elected by the Security Council and the General Assembly of the UN, sitting

---

[2] As opposed to 'ad hoc' judges nominated by a party to a case if it did not already have on the bench a 'titular judge' of its nationality.

separately but simultaneously, from a list of candidates presented by the National Groups of the States parties to the Statute of the Court – nearly all Members of the UN. In the period 1953–4, the members of the British National Group were: Sir Arnold McNair, Sir Hartley Shawcross, Sir Francis Hodson (a Lord Justice of Appeal) and Sir Raymond Evershed (the Master of the Rolls). In theory, the National Group is quite independent in making its nomination. In practice, however, the British Government, especially the Foreign Office, exercises significant influence by providing the Group with information – though, even so, the final decision is the Group's and need not necessarily conform to the Government's view, though it usually does.[3]

As Sir Arnold McNair approached the end of his tenure, he consulted actively with the Foreign Office, especially the Minister of State, Mr Selwyn Lloyd, and Sir Gerald Fitzmaurice, then the principal Legal Adviser. McNair was strongly of the view that Hersch should be nominated for election as his successor, and in this he secured the support of both these influential persons. However, there was some opposition to the nomination, especially from the Lord Chancellor, Lord Simonds, and from the then Attorney-General, Sir Lionel Heald. Approaches were made to a number of British judges including Lord Justice Sellers and Lord Denning, but none of them was interested. Eventually, on 25 May 1954, the Minister of State wrote to the Lord Chancellor noting that very few English judges had experience of international law and that their ability or willingness to learn the subject was 'hardly a satisfactory basis on which to make an appointment that must, I think, certainly rank as one of the major international appointments'. The continuation of Selwyn Lloyd's letter deserves to be quoted in full:

In academic circles, on the other hand, there are persons who have all the necessary previous knowledge and experience of international law as a subject. Of these, by far the most eminent is Professor H. Lauterpacht QC of Trinity College, Cambridge, who at present holds the Whewell Professorship there. He has a very great reputation internationally, and probably ranks amongst the two or three recognized authorities on the subject. We have reason to believe, although we have naturally not approached him, that he would be willing to be nominated, and we believe that such a nomination would meet with universal approval internationally. We also have reason to believe that it would be welcome to the Court itself, and that, for all these reasons, Professor

---

[3] This account of Hersch's nomination draws heavily on an (unpublished) memorandum prepared by Mr D. L. Bethlehem in 1989. Bethlehem subsequently became the Legal Adviser of the Foreign and Commonwealth Office, and received a knighthood in the Queen's Birthday Honours list, 2010.

Lauterpacht might be expected to have more influence over his colleagues on the Court than most other persons would.

He is not British by origin, but he has been naturalized for more than 20 years, and continuously resident in this country for upwards of 30. He is very much liked by all those who know him, and, despite his continental origins, his outlook on legal matters reflects mainly the Anglo-Saxon approach. He is extremely conscientious. Owing to his origins, he would not perhaps be what we should regard as entirely sound from our point of view on matters of Human Rights; that is to say, his bias would be to take perhaps too wide a view of the topic. However, irrespective of the character of the British Judge, this is a subject on which we should as always wish to keep away from the Court, in any event. Therefore I doubt whether the point matters.

The nomination of Hersch was followed promptly by some acerbic criticism from the Attorney-General, Sir Lionel Heald. The Attorney-General's letter is surprising both in its insularity and its tone. It is an open question whether the English Bench and Bar would even then have felt as strongly as did Sir Lionel, and it is inconceivable that such views would be held or expressed at the time that this biography is being written. However, the full text of the letter should be seen:

Sir Lionel Heald to Mr Selwyn Lloyd, 27 July 1954

A week or two ago, you told me there was an idea of putting Lauterpacht in Sir Arnold McNair's place at The Hague Court on the latter's impending retirement. I said I thought this appointment would be badly received both by the legal profession and in the House and I gathered that you had got the same reaction from others. I was therefore surprised to hear in the Temple at the end of last week that Lauterpacht is actually in the course of being nominated for the vacancy, and I have since confirmed from the Foreign Office that this is so.

The Solicitor-General and I both feel strongly that this proposed nomination would be a mistake. Already we have had queries about it both at our respective Benches and also from legal colleagues in the House, and I feel sure that there will be strong criticism of the Government if Lauterpacht's name appears. He has of course the highest academic qualifications as an international lawyer, but he has never practiced and he has no standing at the Bar. Moreover, it has been impressed on me that, in these days, when the International Court touches British interests as to many points, public confidence in it is more than essential. It is therefore surely desirable that our representative at The Hague both be and be seen to be thoroughly British, whereas Lauterpacht cannot help the fact that he does not qualify in this way either by birth, by name or by education. I know that there are difficulties about getting anyone of suitable legal standing and experience to take the post, but I believe that, if a little more time were given to the matter and potential candidates given fuller information as to the conditions, it would be possible to get someone much more suitable.

From the experience we have had of conducting three important cases before the Court, it is abundantly clear, as I know Fitzmaurice will confirm, that the personality and influence of the Judges play an outstanding part in the result, since the Court proceeds on quite different lines from those familiar to us, in that the deliberations, which take place in private after the arguments are concluded, are lengthy and detailed, with the result that the weight and standing of the respective Judges are often decisive factors.

I am sorry to raise the matter at this late time, but I am sure you will not mind my saying that, after our conversation, it did not occur to me that we should not have a further opportunity of discussing the matter, particularly in view of our close association with the Court, and I did not therefore think it necessary to trouble you with any further reasons or arguments until you asked for them. I feel now, however, that there is no alternative but to put our considered opinion on record, in view of what I can only describe as the virtual certainty that the appointment will cause trouble if it is made.

I am sending a copy of this letter to the Lord Chancellor and, in view of the possible repercussions I have mentioned, I am arranging for a copy to be sent to No. 10 Downing Street.[4]

The ensuing election was almost a foregone conclusion. No candidate proposed by a permanent Member of the Security Council had ever been rejected. On 7 October 1954, Hersch received eight Security Council votes (at a time when the Council had only eleven members) and thirty-nine votes on the first ballot in the General Assembly, and was declared elected. On the same day, the Secretary-General of the United Nations, Dag Hammarskjöld, notified Hersch that he had been elected a judge for a period of nine years beginning 6 February 1955.

News of the election spread rapidly and dozens of congratulatory letters followed from colleagues and former students all over the world praising Hersch for his good work and personal kindness. Only one contained a sour note; an English lawyer, working on the margins of international law, qualified his no doubt well meant remarks with the following:

[B]eing a candid friend . . . I confess to you that I do not think that I should myself have made the appointment! I have been distressed by what I judge – on somewhat cursory impressions perhaps – to be examples of 'trimming' in recent examples of your work.

---

4 Foreign Office File: 112419-225/52.

No details were given. Hersch showed the letter to McNair, who reacted with unusual emphasis:

The letter is intolerable. I should feel very angry if I was accused of trimming . . . It is a disgraceful letter.[5]

The election was followed by a series of notes of practical advice from McNair: accommodation in The Hague; travel from England; bank accounts; pension arrangements; timing of resignation from the Whewell Chair; the undesirability of driving himself in The Hague, coupled with the offer of a loan of his car and driver; and the need to bring a bottle of Rose's Lime Juice if he likes lime with his gin as it is impossible to buy it in Holland. But McNair did not regard the giving of advice as a one-way matter. Having consulted Hersch about an invitation to take up an American appointment, McNair wrote:

I need hardly tell you that I shall always welcome your counsel, whether solicited or unsolicited, and that I value it greatly.[6]

In March 1955, Jenks sent a letter to Hersch offering his 'heartfelt good wishes':

C. W. Jenks to Hersch, 2 March 1955

I had meant to have a letter waiting for you in The Hague to send you our warmest good wishes for a long, happy and most successful term of office on the Court. Though I am now a little belated in saying this, you will, I know, forgive me, as the primary reason for the delay has been the difficulty of finding words to express it at all adequately. I feel so strongly that the future, not only of the Court but of international law, depends so largely on the extent to which some of the qualities which you analysed 20 years ago in *The Development of International Law* are present in the Court itself. It is all too difficult to find them in high judicial office, and much more difficult to find them there internationally now than it was a generation ago. We send you our heartfelt good wishes. There may be a rather barren period for a little while until the normal flow of cases to the Court is fully resumed, but blank spots of this type occur in the development of every international organisation and none of us need to be discouraged by them . . .

I have, in an unsympathetic kind of way, sampled fairly widely the 1953 *Yearbook*. It continues to maintain an extraordinarily high level of quality. While recognising that it may have been necessary to bow to the weight of opinion, I can only regret that you will be relinquishing the editorship, and hope the new editor, or editors, will be able to maintain both the standard and the comprehensiveness

---

[5] McNair to HL, 19 October 1954.   [6] McNair to HL, 28 October 1954.

of the last ten years, for which it would be difficult to find a parallel in any other international law yearbook or journal at any period.

Shortly afterwards, Hersch resigned from his position as Whewell Professor of International Law at Cambridge.[7] He and Rachel made plans for extensive redecoration at Cranmer Road. One may well ask why Rachel accompanied Hersch in these circumstances, but the answer must be that it would never have crossed her mind to leave him to face the new challenges of The Hague on his own. So it was that on 3 February 1955, having received a telegram of good wishes from the Fitzmaurices, Hersch and Rachel were driven from Cambridge to Harwich, thence to embark on the night boat to Hook of Holland. This was the first of many such journeys that they were to make in a leisurely fashion over the next five years. He and Rachel enjoyed taking their time and stopping for tea *en route* to Harwich as they also revelled in the comfort of a *de luxe* cabin on the SS *Amsterdam* with a large bathroom – a standard of accommodation that has long since disappeared from the North Sea. McNair had already taken the precaution of informing the Chief Immigration Officer at Harwich that Hersch would henceforth be frequently passing through that port and requesting for Hersch the same consideration that had been shown to him in his frequent travels to Holland. All aid was promptly forthcoming.

From the Hook it was only a half-hour's drive to The Hague. Hersch's destination there was the Wittebrug Hotel, in its heyday one of the grand hotels of Europe but which closed in 1972, at which a number of the judges had taken up semi-permanent residence. McNair had lived there and, on the morning of Hersch's and Rachel's early arrival, the McNairs waited to greet them, to have breakfast with them and to introduce them to the other resident judges. The McNairs then left The Hague for their home in England.[8]

In common with the other judges of the Court there resident, Hersch enjoyed the benefit of two comfortable adjoining rooms. But his lodging failed him in one major respect: he found it difficult to sleep at night on account of the noise – even when given a room on an internal courtyard. But eventually he managed to settle down, although his nights were not

---

[7] Another consequence of his election was that he had to resign as a member of the French–Swiss Conciliation Commission, a position deemed incompatible with membership of the Court because in certain circumstances the Court might have to hear an appeal from a decision of the Commission. McNair was in due course appointed to fill the vacancy.

[8] McNair lived on from 1955 to 1975. During these twenty years, he remained active in the field of international law – as an adviser, an arbitrator and an international judge. He became a peer and occasionally spoke in the House of Lords.

as restful as they should have been. Full board was provided. It was not good for him. The food in the hotel was first-class and the service was over-generous. Hersch was not a greedy man, but the daily temptation to eat too much was irresistible and undoubtedly contributed to the onset of the heart attack that he had in October 1959. Nor was it the hotel food alone that was the only problem. Occasionally, when for professional reasons I had to be in The Hague, I stayed in the same hotel and we would usually go for a walk together through the woods near the hotel in the direction of the Caserne (military barracks) in the Alkemadelaan, about a mile away. At its gates there was a barrow at which we could buy Dutch herrings, the sort that are eaten by holding them by the tail and gradually lowering them into one's mouth. We both had a weakness for this delicacy and would usually have one or perhaps two, and sometimes even also a croquette or meatball, before returning to the hotel. There we would sit down with Rachel to an excellent five-course dinner served by an agreeable and attentive waiter who always invited us to have second helpings. In these conditions willpower was bound to fail.

HL to EL, 4 February 1955
It is very fitting – and a cause of great pleasure to me – that I should write to you my first letter written at my desk in my new room in the Court's building. The room has a lovely view over the garden of the Peace Palace. I feel a bit dizzy from the excitements and the sleeplessness of the journey but – for reasons which you will understand – rather elated.

What would really fill you with envy is the quantity and variety of stationery on my desk!

On 6 February 1955, Hersch attended his first private meeting of the judges, and on 10 February he was formally admitted as a judge at an open session of the Court in the Great Hall of the Peace Palace, making the declaration required by the Statute and the Rules as follows:

I solemnly declare that I will perform my duties and exercise my powers as a judge honourably, faithfully, impartially and conscientiously.

For this, as for every other formal sitting, he wore the traditional Court robes: black silk gown stretching from collar to ankles, buttoning down the front and completely covering all that was worn underneath (a concealment which has often permitted some judges to wear very relaxed clothes to Court). A white shirt with a turn down collar was worn but instead of a tie, a 'jabot' or bib made of Brussels lace was tied round the collar and hung down for about six inches in front of the gown.

After the Court usher had in loud tones announced the impending entry of the judges – 'La Cour' he called – and the audience had risen, the judges proceeded with measured steps into the Hall in a pre-established order in which the most junior judges flanked each end of the row and the President sat in the centre. As the most junior judge on this occasion, Hersch's place was at the left hand end of the row (facing the body of the Hall).

Hersch rapidly made friends with his fellow judges, more warmly with some than with others. The Court consists of judges who each come from a different country with different social, cultural and legal backgrounds. Sometimes the political tensions between them became more than superficial.[9] At the time when Hersch reached the Court the other judges were (in order of seniority – a matter to which at that time greater importance was attached than it would be today): Green H. Hackworth (United States), a former Legal Adviser of the State Department, as President; Abdel Hamid Badawi (Egypt) as Vice-President; José Guerrero (El Salvador); Jules Basdevant (France); Bohdan Winiarski (Poland); Milovan Zoricic (Yugoslavia); Helge Klaestad (Norway); John E. Read (Canada); Hsu Mo (China); Enrique Armand-Ugon (Uruguay); Feodor Kojevnikov (Soviet Union); Sir Muhammad Zafrulla Khan (Pakistan); Moreno Quintana (Argentina); and Roberto Cordova (Mexico). The Registrar of the Court, its principal administrative officer, was Mr Lopez Olivan (Spain), a former diplomat of impressive bearing and sympathetic manner.

Of these, a number were significantly older than the others and had been members of the PCIJ since 1930 followed by nine years on the ICJ: Guerrero was 78; Winiarski was 71; Basdevant was 77 and had been elected to the ICJ in 1946. Though relationships with them were not strained, they were hardly relaxed, not only because of the differences in ages but also because of the intrusion, as the more senior judges might have seen it, into the Court's work of one whose knowledge of international law and standing in the field could be seen as competing with theirs. However, Hersch was seemingly able on the whole to overcome such resentment at his arrival as there might have been amongst his older established colleagues.

The Court had, by that time, developed a procedure for the hearing of cases. The judges were, of course, expected to have studied the written pleadings before the hearings began. Most of them had done so to a greater or lesser extent. Some, by contrast, would rely mainly on what

---

[9] Especially during the *Aerial Incident* case: see pp. 410–11 below.

was said in the oral hearings (and in the daily verbatim transcripts) to guide them to the principal issues. There was then, and remains now,[10] a tendency for parties in their oral arguments to repeat the main essentials of their written cases; so this approach on the part of some of the judges, though seemingly unsatisfactory, may not always have been so in the result.

The practice was that before the hearings opened the judges would meet in private to discuss the case. At this meeting, they would indicate whether there were any questions that they were considering asking; similar meetings were held each day before the commencement of the sitting. This practice reflected the fact that the proceedings were under the close control of the President – something which discouraged or even precluded judges from posing impromptu questions to the parties and which, in fact though not in form, required a judge who might be considering posing a question first to rehearse it with the other judges and, in effect, to secure their approval that the question might be asked. The question having thus been aired in private, the President would at the close of the session say that Judge so-and-so had a question that he would like to put to one or both of the parties and would then invite the judge to speak. There was no obligation on the parties to answer the question immediately and most parties would defer their answers until their next opportunity to speak or, sometimes, with the Court's permission, to a date after the close of the hearings. Giving the parties an opportunity to defer their answers is not really open to criticism as in international proceedings a State is bound by the answers given on its behalf; so its representatives require time to consider the questions and, perhaps, to take instructions from their governments.

The system was thus very different from the more spontaneous exchanges of views that characterise hearings in the English courts. The justification advanced in the ICJ for inhibiting the asking of questions by judges was concern that judges should not, by the questions they pose, give the parties any indication of the way in which their minds are moving and thus suggest some particular outcome to the case. This is not a cogent consideration because in common law jurisdictions it is always understood, or should be understood, that a question put by a judge in the course of argument is entirely without prejudice to his eventual decision. More relevant is the consideration that, with a bench of fifteen

---

[10] Notwithstanding Practice Direction VI, which gives direction to parties to assist them in observing Article 60(1) of the Rules of Court, which states that a degree of brevity in oral pleadings is required.

judges, uncontrolled asking of questions might seriously interrupt the flow of the proceedings.

Although Hersch's previous exposure to ICJ practice had been limited, he was familiar with the common law approach, which in any event suited his temperament. One drawback to this inability to ask questions freely was that it could lead in certain cases to situations in which a judge, and Hersch was such a one, might subsequently deal with a point, even attaching critical importance to it, that had not been argued by the parties and on which no question had been put to them. This appears to have happened in the *Norwegian Loans* case,[11] of which fuller mention will be made in the proceeding pages.

In February 1955, the Court had on its docket six contentious cases (i.e. cases instituted by one State against another) and two requests for advisory opinions made by international organisations. In the previous seven years of its existence, the Court had decided fifteen contentious cases and given eight advisory opinions. So it could be said that at that time it was not particularly hard pressed. Since then, it has become much busier. For example, in the period 2005–8, it decided ten contentious cases and gave one advisory opinion.

The difficulty for Hersch was that, despite his keenness to become immediately involved in the Court's judicial work, he was precluded from participating in the case then being considered by the Court, the *Nottebohm (Liechtenstein v. Guatemala)* case, because, prior to his election, he had given advice to the Government of Liechtenstein and had had a hand in the preparation of its Memorial.[12]

Not being involved in the deliberations of the Court, Hersch was free to spend some leisure time with Paul Guggenheim, the Swiss professor of international law at the University of Geneva, who was the *ad hoc* judge appointed by Liechtenstein for the case. The Court's decision came as a great surprise to Hersch. The central element of the Court's decision was that Nottebohm who, having been a German national by birth, shortly after the outbreak of the Second World War, had acquired Liechtenstein nationality by naturalisation. This had the effect in German law of terminating his German nationality. However, the Court took the view that at the time of the naturalisation there was no 'genuine' or substantial link between Nottebohm and Liechtenstein and, therefore, that the Liechtenstein nationality could not be invoked against the defendant State,

---

[11] *Case of Certain Norwegian Loans (France v. Norway)*, ICJ Reports 1957, p. 9; 24 *ILR* 782.
[12] Hersch had, through McNair, sought a ruling from the President as to whether he should sit in the case. The reply was in the negative.

Guatemala. An approach of this kind had not been foreseen by Hersch when, prior to the institution of proceedings, he had advised Liechtenstein on the prospects of the case. And Hersch cannot be validly criticised for not having anticipated the Court's approach. Although the concept of the genuine link was known in the law of nationality, it had not until that time been invoked except in cases where the dual nationality of the individual required a choice to be made between the two nationalities. The concept had never been applied to the assessment of the validity of a naturalisation without the complication of dual nationality. But the interesting thing is that, novel though the Court's approach was, the insistence on the genuine link struck a chord that was soon reflected in the provisions relating to the nationality of ships embodied in the 1956 Convention on the Law of the High Seas and, later, in the 1982 UN Convention on the Law of the Sea.[13] The decision was also a severe blow to Guggenheim, who filed a dissenting opinion. A few days after the judgment, Guggenheim wrote to Hersch in the following terms:

I take this opportunity to tell you how touched I was, as was my wife, by your friendship, your active sympathy and your kindness towards me. I know that I was not always easy to put up with, the painful hardship having made me sometimes rather nervy and perhaps even insufferable ...

I will never forget, besides your moral support, the conversations that I had with Judges Klaestad and Read. I consider Klaestad as a very great judge and great man and I hope that you will often have the opportunity of actively collaborating with this fine person. The affection of my old friend Lopez-Olivan also made my task much easier.[14]

As had been the case since his election, Hersch remained busy dealing with administrative matters relating to the future editorship of the *BYIL* and arrangements for securing the continuity of the appearance of the *AD* (or *International Law Reports* as it was soon to become). It was quite quickly decided that the editorship of the *BYIL* should pass to Professor Humphrey Waldock at Oxford. Hersch concluded his role with the publication of Volume 31. In appreciation of his editorship, the Royal Institute of International Affairs, under whose auspices the series was published, presented to Hersch a beautiful leather-bound copy of Volume 30.

The *AD* was retained by Hersch under his sole editorship, though he received assistance from a number of contributors who included, notably, Richard Baxter of Harvard Law School and Stephen Schwebel, both of

---

[13] Article 91(1).   [14] Translation from French by the author.

whom in due course became judges of the ICJ. Largely due to Schwebel's initiative, and after extensive correspondence, the Ford Foundation, to Hersch's great relief, made a grant to support the series for a period of five years. Hersch was also heavily involved (though not formally) in the selection of his successor as Whewell Professor. Initially he had thought of Wilfred Jenks, then the Legal Adviser of the International Labour Office and a prolific author whose published work ranged over the whole of the law of peace, international organisation and dispute settlement. But Wilfred felt a very strong commitment to the ILO and declined to stand for election. As he said in a letter written to Hersch on 10 November 1954:

The decisive consideration is, if you will allow me so to put it, one of public duty and international public spirit by which I have felt bound. Apart from Jane,[15] the only people with whom I have discussed the matter at all are the two people with whom I had a special obligation to discuss it – Morse, as Director-General, and Phelan, as the acknowledged elder statesman of the ILO. I need hardly say that both discussions took place in the strictest confidence. Without wishing to influence me unduly in a vital personal decision, they both expressed strongly the view that they regard it as of substantial public importance that I should remain here, and I feel that I have an obligation to respond to that appeal and cannot, consistently with the proper discharge of duties arising from past years, leave my present post on my own initiative at a time as difficult, but as potentially fruitful, as that through which we are now passing.

Hersch thereupon moved his support to R. Y. ('Robbie') Jennings, a younger man, a Fellow and Senior Tutor of Jesus College, Cambridge, and a lecturer on international law in the Faculty, but with much less in the way of publications. Told of the consideration being given to Jenks, Jennings replied, with customary modesty, that 'if beaten by Jenks, he [Jennings] will be the first to say that he was beaten by a better man!' On 18 February 1955, Jennings was elected to the Whewell Chair and immediately wrote to inform Hersch and thank him:

I hasten to let you know; and to say also how very grateful I am for all you have done for me in this matter. I don't mean only in the last few weeks, but your constant encouragement and sympathy extending over many years, without which I would certainly have given up the unequal struggle and allowed myself to become just an administrator.[16]

---

[15] His wife.

[16] He had been offered and declined one of the highest administrative posts in the university, that of Secretary-General of the Faculties. Jennings remained as Whewell Professor till 1982 and was then elected to the ICJ where, eventually, he became President in 1991.

But Hersch was not the sort of man to allow all his time to be spent on matters of this kind. He was reluctant to sit in his room appearing to do nothing except read the pleadings in other pending cases. So, after a short break at home in England, which included attendance at the dinner of the Benchers of Gray's Inn in honour of McNair on his return from The Hague, Hersch began the preparation of a memorandum on the revision of the Statute of the Court. The Statute is an integral part of the UN Charter and the basic constitutional document of the Court. Hersch was, therefore, somewhat bold to embark on a task that was fraught with complications, both legal and political. Nonetheless, he did so and on 1 September 1955 produced a substantial preliminary memorandum of some seventy printed pages that was circulated to the other members of the Court.[17] He had intended to follow this with a final report, but on 12 December he wrote to Rachel that:

The work on the Final Report has proved too troublesome – and dangerous – in view of the generally unhelpful nature of the observations. I am giving it up. I do not want to create the impression that I am hurrying or bossing any one.

The President, Judge Hackworth, wrote to Hersch on 4 January 1956, saying:

I think you are correct in concluding that on the basis of observations received you are not in a position to prepare a [final] report. I imagine that it will eventually fall to your lot to do the work but you will be in a much better position to do it after a discussion by the Court. For this latter purpose you have supplied the Court with an abundance of useful material.

If the judges had read the report, they would have found that one of its most interesting and original items was the discussion of what Hersch described as:

the faculty of States to render inoperative, by way of a particular reservation, the express provision of paragraph 6 of Article 36 which lays down that in the event of a dispute as to whether the Court has jurisdiction the matter shall be settled by the decision of the Court.

The reservation to which he was referring was one made originally by the United States and subsequently largely adopted by Pakistan, France, Mexico and Liberia, reserving to themselves the right to determine

---

[17] When permission was sought from the Court after HL's death to publish the report, it was given on condition that it should not be represented as an official document of the Court. Text reprinted in *Collected Papers*, Vol. 5, pp. 112–83.

whether the dispute was one essentially within their domestic jurisdiction. If they so determined, that would deprive the Court of jurisdiction. Hersch suggested that:

> there is room for the view that declarations thus formulated are contrary to an express provision of the Statute.[18]

This passage anticipated the point that he later made publicly in his separate Opinion in the *Norwegian Loans* case.[19]

In this, as in the many comments on other provisions in the Statute, Hersch expressed himself in a reserved and cautious manner. The phrase 'there is room for the view' appears repeatedly in introducing suggestions for improvement. In this manner, he approached problems connected with the method of election to the Court, the jurisdiction of the Court (especially the question of the extent to which, if at all, it should be made compulsory), the legal force of indications of interim measures of protection, the position of *ad hoc* judges, access to the Court by persons other than States, and the organisation and functioning of the Court.

Although the report contains numerous constructive suggestions for improvement of the Court, it is not in any way an unrealistic document. Hersch was fully aware of the political difficulties involved, not only in persuading his colleagues in the Court to accept his views, but also in securing any modification of the Statute of the Court by the UN even if the Court's members were able collectively to propose any changes. Article 92 of the UN Charter provides that the Statute is 'an integral part of the present Charter'. Consequently, any amendment to the Statute could only be made by the same complicated process as is required for amendment of the Charter itself. There is no record of the report ever having been discussed in detail by the Court. This is a pity, as is the fact that it has received so little academic or professional attention since it was first published in 2002.[20] Nonetheless, it must be borne in mind that a number of problems associated with the operation of the Court have been dealt with by improvements in the Court's Rules that it has itself made, particularly during the last years of the twentieth century and the opening years of the twenty-first, as well as by its own decisions, notably in favour of the binding force of interim measures of protection.

---

[18] *Collected Papers*, Vol. 5, pp. 144–5.   [19] See p. 402 below.
[20] 'The Revision of the Statute of the International Court of Justice' (2002) 1 *The Law and Practice of International Courts and Tribunals* 55–128.

Once the *Nottebohm* case, in which Hersch could not join, was decided on 6 April 1955, he was free to rejoin the mainstream of the Court's judicial work and to become involved in its current cases.

In all, during the five years of his active judicial tenure, Hersch participated in nine cases and advisory opinions. He joined the majority decision in two of these. In three he gave a separate opinion of his own. In one case, he was the prime mover in the delivery of a joint separate opinion, and in three cases he dissented.

From the beginning of his real judicial activity, it is clear that Hersch had his own concept of the role of a judge of the Court, reflecting the ideas he put forward in *The Function of Law*. A judge was not limited to deciding a case on the narrowest possible grounds; rather, each case was seen as an opportunity to expound the relevant law, even beyond the limits strictly required by the needs of the case. He saw the function of the judge as being to expound principles and clarify the law. He did not see the scope of a judicial decision on any particular issue as limited by the arguments advanced by the parties. This would involve, in those cases where he did not find it appropriate to join with the majority, delivering either a separate opinion (which agreed in its conclusion with the Court's decision) or a dissenting opinion (which involved a vote against the stance adopted by the Court).

The first example of his approach was in the Advisory Opinion on *Voting Procedure on Questions Relating to Reports and Petitions Concerning the Territory of South West Africa*.[21] This was the first of two Opinions[22] relating to South West Africa in which Hersch was able to go beyond the seemingly 'technical' – indeed abstruse – nature of the question before the Court to focus on the real issue: the persistent flouting by South Africa, the administering power in South West Africa, of resolutions of the United Nations. To put his views in these cases into context, it is helpful to give a brief account of the historical background.

After the defeat of Germany in the First World War, administration of its colonies had been entrusted to several of the Allied powers under the League of Nations mandate system. For South West Africa, the designated mandate was South Africa. After the Second World War, South Africa, contending that the League of Nations mandate had lapsed, attempted simply to absorb South West Africa into its own national territory. The UN refused to permit this and sought the Court's Opinion on the former mandated territory's international status. In its Advisory

---

[21] ICJ Reports 1955, p. 67; 22 *ILR* 651.
[22] See also the *Hearings of Petitioners* Advisory Opinion, p. 394 below.

Opinion on the *International Status of South-West Africa*,[23] given during the time of Hersch's predecessor, the Court ruled that the League mandate was still in being and that the League's supervisory functions had passed to the General Assembly. However, South Africa refused to accept the Opinion or to cooperate with the committee established by the General Assembly to exercise its supervisory powers.

The question put to the Court in the *Voting Procedure* case was whether it was correct to interpret the Court's earlier Opinion on the territory's international status as requiring the General Assembly to treat questions relating to reports and petitions concerning South West Africa as 'important questions' for the purpose of voting under Article 18(2) of the UN Charter.

The request for an opinion having been made by the General Assembly in December 1954 and the written statements of interested States having been completed by 10 March 1955, Hersch was able to give detailed consideration to the matter. As the Court's opinion was delivered on 7 June 1955, barely four months after Hersch became a judge, his participation in the deliberations of the Court in this matter, to which the preparation of his own opinion must be added, taking place at the same time as he was engaged on the report on the revision of the Statute of the Court, must have meant that he was working under heavy pressure. Nonetheless, he produced, as his first contribution to the jurisprudence of the Court, a highly principled and detailed opinion in support of his agreement with the unanimous decision of the Court. He said:

In my view it is essential, having regard both to the circumstances of the case and to the obligations of the judicial function of the Court in general, that its opinion should contain an answer to the legal issues relevant to the case, especially when relied upon by the Members of the General Assembly, including South Africa.[24]

And later he said:

Clearly, in order to reply to [the] question, the Court is bound in the course of its reasoning to consider and to answer a variety of legal questions. This is the very essence of its judicial function which makes it possible for it to render judgments and opinions which carry conviction and clarify the law.[25]

This is not the place to summarise Hersch's Opinion, but it contains some general statements of law sufficiently important to justify being recalled.

---

[23] ICJ Reports 1950, p. 128.   [24] *Ibid.*, p. 91.   [25] *Ibid.*, pp. 92–3.

Discussing the legal effect of resolutions of the General Assembly, to which South Africa had denied legal effect, he observed:

An Administering State may not only be acting illegally by declining to act upon a recommendation or series of recommendations on the same subject. But in doing so it acts at its peril when a point is reached where the cumulative effect of the persistent disregard of the articulate opinion of the Organisation is such as to fasten the conviction that the State in question has become guilty of disloyalty to the principles and purposes of the Charter. Thus an Administering State which consistently sets itself above the solemnly and repeatedly expressed judgment of the Organisation, in particular in proportion as that judgment approximates to unanimity, may find that it has overstepped the imperceptible line between impropriety and illegality, between discretion and arbitrariness, between the exercise of the legal right to disregard the recommendation and the abuse of that right, and that it has exposed itself to consequences legitimately following as a legal sanction.[26]

How the other – and especially the more senior – members of the Court must have felt about being taught elementary lessons in judicial craftsmanship by a younger newcomer is anybody's guess. But Hersch seems to have been able to carry it off, to have earned the respect of his colleagues and to have remained on good terms with them. Even so, the strain must have been great. And the question must be asked whether he would have been so confident in his views about the effect of a series of General Assembly resolutions if he could have foreseen the subsequent direction in which such resolutions would run.

Others outside the Court approved highly of the Opinion. Fitzmaurice, the Legal Adviser of the Foreign Office, wrote within a few days:

[Y]our separate Opinion of course stands out head and shoulders above the others' and the Court's. It is the only one that attempts to deal comprehensively or conscientiously with the issues in the matter, and its intrinsic quality is infinitely higher. You must have put a great deal of work, and much hard thinking – and perhaps some heart-searching – into it. I am delighted you have felt able to take the line you did in your introductory remarks on pp. 90–93 – because, as you know, some of us have felt troubled at the way the Court has often seemed to ignore or shade important issues, or to dismiss them in a sentence or two – and by its tendency to reach its decisions by some earlier oblique path which, while making the conclusion clear, often left the exact grounds on which it was based and the wider implications in considerable obscurity... I congratulate you on a piece of work of most outstanding excellence. It will receive a great deal of attention, and will I predict be widely and constantly

---

[26] *Ibid.*, p. 120.

cited – and I think certain passages may well come to take on the character of classic *dicta*.

Amongst Hersch's papers was a copy of a decision – that McNair had sent him – of the Court adopted in May 1953 when McNair was President:

> That individual opinions, whether dissenting or concurring, should be distributed to Members of the Court as soon as practicable after they have been examined by the Drafting Committee, and in any case before the beginning of the second reading of the Judgment or Advisory Opinion.

McNair had added in handwriting:

> Please see that this is not overlooked as it required some effort to get it adopted. The Court had got into the habit of giving the draft Judgment a second reading and voting upon it without having read the individual opinions, which is fundamentally wrong.

Having read it, Hersch returned it to McNair in May 1955 with the following note appended:

> You can bring a horse to the water, but you cannot make him drink it. You can send them the individual opinions but you cannot make them read them!

Soon after the Opinion was completed, Hersch suffered some sort of illness, but was sufficiently recovered to be present at the reading of the Court's Opinion on 7 June 1955.

The work of the Court is not, and at that time was not, limited to the cases and requests for advisory opinions in respect of which it was, or would be, exercising substantive jurisdiction. In addition, a number of cases were brought before the Court with seemingly insufficient jurisdictional basis. These nonetheless required private consideration by the Court before they were removed from the Court's list. The cases commenced in May 1955 by the United Kingdom against Argentina and Chile in respect of competing claims to Antarctica had to be reviewed before being struck off in March 1956; likewise an application by the United States made in March 1955 against Czechoslovakia in respect of an aerial incident on 10 March 1953 was removed from the Court's list on 14 March 1956. Hersch would have had to participate in the Court's deliberations on these matters.

There was a good deal of correspondence with Schwebel who was keen to participate in the Court's work as a 'clerk' to Hersch. This position would have been similar to that of a clerk to a judge in the United States, providing the judge with research assistance and drafts of judgments. Hersch was sympathetic to the idea but sensed that it would not be well received by his colleagues, all of whom came from countries where this concept was unfamiliar. Moreover, they all attached great importance to the confidentiality of the deliberations of the Court, which they felt would be compromised if clerks were to be present. Hersch reluctantly concluded that the idea could not be pursued. It was not until some fifty years later, with an injection of funds from wealthy American law schools and a general alteration in the temperament of the Court, that the idea was resurrected.

Sometime in 1955, Jenks asked Hersch for his comments on the draft of an article on 'Craftsmanship in International Law', which was published in the *AJIL* in 1956.[27] In the original draft, the opening section on 'Craftsmanship and Scholarship', Jenks had included a number of pages with rather elaborate guidance as to the kind of reading that an international lawyer should do to equip himself for 'craftsmanship'. Hersch was strongly critical of this feature.

HL to C. W. Jenks, 2 September 1955
It is no use giving you my reactions unless I am frank. Now I am rather critical of the first part of the article, say, up to p. 63. I think that part is pretentious and not very helpful – except perhaps as a bibliographical guide. What is the use of telling the international lawyer that if he wishes to be a good craftsman – you do not define it – he ought to reacquaint himself with the literature in the field of history, legal philosophy, political science etc., as enumerated in the first part of your article? Take, for instance, the historical literature. You and I are quite good 'craftsmen' in international law, but I have not read more than 10% of that literature; you have perhaps read, say, 20%. To give all that advice to budding international lawyers is either to give them an inferiority complex (for no one can hope to read all that) or to make them shrug their shoulders and to say that all these bibliographies are no more than an exhibition of learning. There would be much in that reproach. I think Americans are specially liable to some showmanship of bibliographies; it is not desirable to encourage them in that.

My advice is to cut that part drastically and certainly to eliminate the long bibliographies... I hope you will forgive this reaction even if you do not agree. I may be a bit tired for I have sent off today to the Court a product of four months work – my Provisional Report on the Revision of the Institute.

Hersch left The Hague whenever his Court work permitted. He returned to England several times in 1955. One of the high points was the attendance by Rachel and himself at the dinner given at the Mansion House

---

[27] (1956) 50 *AJIL* 32–60.

on 13 July 1955 by the Lord Mayor of London in honour of Her Majesty's judges. He was also concerned about arrangements for my marriage in the same month. Even so, he and Rachel managed to take a number of holidays, in August in Hove, in September in Cannes, and over the Christmas period in Menton.

Earlier in the year there had been some correspondence between Fitzmaurice and Hersch about the question of a knighthood. Fitzmaurice explained that in official circles there was reluctance to give an honour to British subjects while serving with international organisations or tribunals. However, this difficulty was eventually overcome and in November 1955 there arrived a letter from Downing Street indicating an intention to confer a knighthood on Hersch in the forthcoming New Year's Honours List. After the publication of the list on 1 January 1956 there immediately followed a cascade of more than 260 congratulatory messages, ranging from one from the Lord Chancellor to one from Rachel's Cambridge dressmaker. The correspondence which has survived contains only a few of Hersch's letters of thanks, sufficient to indicate that he would have replied to each letter of congratulation – a pretty onerous task, but one that must have given him the pleasure associated with reading and acknowledging the widespread praise that he received.

In his letter of congratulations of 5 January 1956, Fitzmaurice wrote:

I am sure I need not tell you that these congratulations are in no way tempered by any part I myself may have played in the matter. Someone has got to initiate these things, and it is my business to do so in this particular field. On the other hand, unless such proposals are intrinsically meritorious, they have no chance at all of getting very far. The existence of certain possible obstacles in your case makes the result a very high tribute to you personally, and I hope you will so regard it. You are fully entitled to do so.

I am sorry it did not take the form of an Order,[28] but these are usually only awarded for something in the nature of actual services more specifically to the State or Government rather than for such things as general distinction or eminence in any field of learning. In view of a certain difficulty in your case which you know about, any implication of 'services rendered' had to be avoided, and would, of course, have been quite incorrect in fact.

Towards the end of January 1956, Hersch and Rachel left France, Hersch to go to The Hague and Rachel back to the house in Cambridge, which

---

[28] By this, Fitzmaurice was referring to the fact that the knighthood was a simple 'Knight Bachelor' as opposed to being, for example, a KCMG (Knight Commander of the Order of St Michael and St George) or a KBE (Knight Commander of the Order of the British Empire).

was approaching the conclusion of its extensive refurbishment. Hersch soon returned to Cambridge so as to be able to attend his investiture by the Queen at Buckingham Palace on 14 February.

In The Hague, Hersch had occasionally found life 'wearisome'. The Court had been engaged in extended deliberations on the *South West Africa Voting Procedure* case.

There are meetings in the morning and in the afternoon till nearly 7pm. For me they are specially disagreeable for I do not see eye to eye with the rest. However, I am slowly – but not quickly enough – learning to keep my temper.

There is one comfort. I have had the first draft out of my exposé in the South Africa case. I have still to work on it, but the worst is over.

Rachel urged him to be patient.

The exposé here referred to was no doubt the basis of the extensive separate Opinion that he wrote in the *Voting Procedure* case,[29] in which the Court's Opinion was given on 1 June 1956. The question that had been asked of the Court by the General Assembly was the following:

Is it consistent with the Advisory Opinion of the International Court of Justice of 11 July 1950 for the Committee on South West Africa . . . to grant oral hearings to petitioners on matters relating to the Territory of South West Africa?

On the face of it, this was a somewhat anodyne matter, involving no more than a technical interpretation of the supervisory powers of the Council of the League of Nations (which, in accordance with the Court's Opinion of 1950, had passed to the General Assembly) in respect of a mandated territory, and the corresponding obligations on the Mandatory power. The underlying reality was South Africa's persistent refusal to recognise the Court's decision on South West Africa's legal status, or to cooperate with the General Assembly in regard to its duties as a Mandatory power in respect of the submission of reports and the transmittal of written petitions.[30]

The view of the majority of eight judges was that: (i) the League would have had the power to grant oral hearings in order to render its supervisory function more effective, but had never had occasion to use it; (ii) there was nothing in the 1950 Opinion to prevent the General Assembly exercising powers which the League had possessed but had not yet used; (iii) in the present circumstances, the Committee was 'working without the assistance of the Mandatory [hearings] . . . [which] might

[29] ICJ Reports 1956, p. 23; 23 *ILR* 38.   [30] See pp. 388 *et seq.* above.

enable it to be in a better position to judge the merits of petitions'. Only at the close of its argument, and in relation to a minor point concerning a necessary change in the procedure for the receipt of written petitions by the Committee as a result of South Africa's attitude, does the majority refer in terms to the Mandatory power's 'lack of cooperation' and 'refusal to assist'.

Though being in general agreement with the Opinion of the majority, Hersch had some reservation with regard to the scope of, and the reasons given in, the operative part of the Opinion. This was not a question simply to be answered in the abstract, but one arising out of a specific situation, namely, South Africa's 'persistent attitude of non-cooperation', which he refers to some twenty-five times in the course of his Opinion. The Opinion, supported by a wide range of authorities, covers an impressive amount of ground: the Court's powers in relation to requests for Advisory Opinions; the powers of the Council of the League – and of the General Assembly, its successor in this regard – in relation to the Mandatory power; the merits of oral hearings versus written submissions; the proper approach to interpretation of Court decisions, and, by extension, to treaties in general, in particular where a party is failing to perform its obligations. What stands out is his meticulous and even-handed approach – demonstrating clearly how a judge can make a decision that is ultimately 'political' while remaining above reproach in terms of his interpretation and application of the law.

A number of *dicta* from the Opinion are worth citing. For example, on the Court's approach to requests for advisory opinions:

It is a matter of common experience that a mere affirmation or a mere denial of a question does not necessarily result in a close approximation to truth. The previous practice of the Court supplies authority for the proposition that the Court enjoys considerable latitude in constructing the question put to it or in formulating its answer in such a manner as to make its advisory function effective and useful.[31]

On dealing with the political or legislative issues inherent in an interpretative decision:

Neither can [the Court] avoid its judicial duty by declaring that only a political or legislative body is competent to resolve the conflict which has arisen, as the result of the action of a party, between the overriding purpose of the instrument and its individual provisions and limitations. To resolve that conflict, in the light of the instrument as a whole, is an essential function of a judicial tribunal.[32]

---

[31] ICJ Reports 1956, p. 18.

And again:

Reluctance to encroach upon the province of the legislature is a proper manifestation of judicial caution. If exaggerated, it may amount to unwillingness to
fulfil a task which is within the orbit of the functions of the Court as defined by
its Statute. The Court cannot properly be concerned with the political effects
of its decisions. But it is important, as a matter of international public policy,
to bear in mind the indirect consequences of any pronouncement which, by
giving a purely literal interpretation of the Opinion of 11 July 1950, would have
rendered it impotent in face of obstruction by one party.[33]

A minority of five judges, Badawi (Egypt), Basdevant (France), Hsu Mo
(China), Armand-Ugon (Uruguay) and Moreno Quintana (Argentina),
answered the question in the negative, on the ground that, since the
League has never permitted oral hearings, the Assembly could not do
so. Any question relating to the effect of South Africa's conduct was
'political' and hence outside the Court's purview.

    Hersch added to his Court burdens by engaging in correspondence
with Humphrey Waldock who had by then taken over the editorship of
the *BYIL*. On 17 March 1956, he wrote: 'The lot of the Editor is not a
happy one.' Referring to the reaction of one distressed would-be author,
he said:

I have offended more highly placed people . . . However, one has to pay a price
for maintaining the standard of the Year Book.

There was quite a lot of social activity – lunches and dinners with other
judges and at various embassies. But care had to be exercised that one
was not seen to be too close to a country involved in litigation. In March
1956, Hersch was invited to dinner at the British Embassy to meet the
British Attorney-General. As he wrote to Rachel:

I told them that I will reply later and also will they tell me whether I shall be
the only judge there. They just telephoned and said I would be the only judge.
So I declined for reasons which you will understand. I had previously consulted
Hackworth [the President of the Court] and he said that it would be all right to
accept, but his reasoning rather supplied an argument for not accepting. I have
no doubt in the matter.

Before coming to another example of Hersch's individual approach,
mention should be made of his participation in the Advisory Opinion on
Judgments of the Administrative Tribunal of the International Labour Organization.[34]

---

[32] *Ibid.*, p. 45.   [33] *Ibid.*, p. 57.   [34] ICJ Reports 1956, p. 77; 23 *ILR* 518.

The Court was asked by the Executive Board of UNESCO whether the decisions of the ILO Administrative Tribunal in four cases brought by employees of UNESCO before that Tribunal were within the competence of the Tribunal and whether the decisions given by it were valid. On the face of the Court's Opinion holding that the Tribunal decisions were valid, Hersch was but one of the nine judges who formed the majority. He did not append a separate Opinion. But there appears amongst his papers a lengthy document that appears to be a draft of the Opinion and, because a number of pages in the draft correspond with some pages in the Opinion, it would appear that Hersch was a member of the drafting committee. The composition of that committee, and the manner of its working, being normally confidential, it is not permissible to go further in reflecting his approach. Suffice it to say that this entered into some detail regarding the law of international organisation that was not reflected in the final text. The Opinion was sought in November 1955 and was rendered some eleven months later on 23 October 1956. So a considerable part of that period must have been taken up with this case. Nothing in the rest of Hersch's papers sheds any light on how he felt about the case, or how it may have affected his relations with his colleagues.

As this case had been preceded by the Court's Advisory Opinion on the *South West Africa Voting Procedure* case, delivered on 1 June 1956, in which Hersch gave a substantial separate Opinion, the work on the *ILO Administrative Tribunal* case was most probably fitted into the months from June to November 1956 in addition to his other activities during that period.

At this time, Jenks was the *rapporteur* of the Commission of the Institut de Droit International on the compulsory jurisdiction of the ICJ. He prepared an elaborate report, of which he sent a draft to Hersch for comment.

HL to C. W. Jenks, 20 December 1956

I think the time has come for me to express a view on your Report to the Institute on Compulsory Jurisdiction. In my view it is one of the most valuable things which you have written. There is nothing there which I would suggest should be omitted. I mention this because you may be pressed by some people to make it shorter in order to make it 'more readable'. This, I think, would be a mistake. I have no patience with people saying that an article or Report is 'too long'. Length is a matter relative to the contents. A Report of three pages may be too long if it contains nothing. And a Report of two hundred pages may *not* be too long. Yours is not. It is full of meat – by way of both information and positive suggestions. What is specially impressive is the way in which you outline the questions which might be considered. Your positive suggestions are certainly moderate – so much so that I do not think that you ought to spoil their effect by calling them 'realistic' and by patting yourself on the back by saying that your solution is 'pragmatic'. It would please me no end if you omitted every attempt at boastful descriptions of this kind. Of course, every one thinks that he is a realist and a pragmatic fellow. But he need not say it. By saying it he implies that others are utopian dreamers.

I attach special importance to what you say in para. 75. I fully agree with you. The cases which are likely to come before the Court are of limited importance – so limited that the idea of their being limited by a full Court of 15 Judges is almost incongruous . . . I think that this report of the matter is a material factor in the situation. It discourages Governments.

The second major factor is, of course, what you say in para. 67 in the matter of predictability. This refers not only to judicial 'innovators' and judicial legislation. It refers also to judicial method and the question of the completeness of judicial pronouncements – completeness not from the point of view of the duty to clarify and develop international law (although this is not a negligible matter) but from the point of view of answering all the contentions of the properties (or most of them) and explaining with all necessary details, tone, clarity and cohesion the reasons for the pronouncement. All this is a factor in relation to certainty and predictability.

I do not say that these two major factors are the most important elements in the situation. But they are important. The same applies to the manner in which reservations have so considerably undermined the authority of the Optional Clause. (You will have noticed that the next case before the Court – France v. Norway – is one in which the plaintiff State invokes the jurisdiction of the Court on the basis of an acceptance of the Optional Clause with the qualified reservation of domestic jurisdiction – a subject on which I ought not to say anything.)

You may be told that it may be a mistake to discuss all these matters in such detail seeing that such discussion may tend to give an exaggerated impression of the inactivity of the Court and lower its authority. I do not think that this is a valid objection.

I am also of the view that you are right in suggesting various additional ways for changing the jurisdiction of the Court. This is so even if such jurisdictional clauses remain a dead letter. Even if not invoked, they tend to foster an atmosphere of legality.

So good luck to you in completing the Report and sticking to your guns.

With the *ILO Administrative Tribunal* case disposed of, the Court was able to adjourn for several months pending the completion of the written pleadings in the *Norwegian Loans* case. Hersch spent most of this period in Cambridge completing the revision of his 1935 book on *The Development of International Law by the Permanent Court of International Justice*. He had been working on it on and off for about three years. By 1957, it had grown into a substantial treatise to which he thought of giving the name *International Judicial Process*. In January 1957, Hersch was on holiday with McNair in Sidmouth. He wrote to Jenks about this and other matters on which he was working.

HL to C. W. Jenks, 28 February 1957

I have postponed, for the time being, the idea of publishing my Collected Papers. One reason was that this would have required two volumes of about 700 pages each. It would be a work which would not sell as easily as a treatise, and I quite imagined that I would have to give a subsidy of about £1,500 or more. I have not felt like that. However, I may revert to the idea.

Speaking of my own work, you may recall that I mentioned to you last year what was intended to be the second edition of The Development of International Law by the Permanent Court of International Justice. I worked on that for about three years. I completed the thing last month. It grew into a substantial treatise to which I intended to give the name 'International Judicial Process'. As I mentioned to you the book was in many ways critical, both of the substance of the pronouncements of the Court and of its methods. That critical part makes up about one fifth of the book. As you will also recall I had serious doubts about the feasibility of its publication. I consulted Arnold; he is definitely against it. Robbie Jennings is in favour. However, I think that in this matter I must follow Arnold's view. In case you are interested I enclose the Preface and the Table of Contents. Kindly return them soon. Please treat the matter as strictly confidential. I am laying the whole thing into cold storage for the time being.

I can now think of many other pressing literary matters. I have simultaneous requests for new editions of Recognition, Human Rights and the Function of Law in the International Community – not to mention Private Law Analogies on which I started some time ago. All this is in addition to the promise which I have given to the publishers to prepare new editions of both volumes of Oppenheim.

I had to postpone all that in the last five or six months because I have my hands full with the International Law Reports. The volumes for 1951 and 1952 will be published at the end of April. You can imagine the amount of donkey work involved in that. At the same time I am in the last stages of preparing the material for the volumes for 1953 and 1954 which I hope to hand over to the printers by the end of April. I am getting rather weary of the International Law Reports. But, frankly, I do not see on the horizon anyone able – or willing – to take over part of the burden.

I had some conversations recently with Stevens about a projected encyclopaedia of international law. They want me to think about it and I have been doing some thinking in the matter. The project is so vast and the difficulties so formidable that I do not think anything will come out of it. My idea was that if one could have a modern re-statement of international law, centrally planned in some such way as, for instance, Acton's Cambridge Modern History was planned, there would be some attraction in the matter. The decisive difficulty would be to find ten or twelve persons of obvious ability able to write these volumes. You could not, these days, expect people to engage in such work unless they were very properly paid. As I said, nothing will probably come of it. But I thought that the writer of the articles on the Scope of Modern International Law and, without much encouragement from me, on Draftsmanship, would be interested.

Jenks replied:

C. W. Jenks to HL, 3 April 1957

I enclose, with apologies for my delay in returning it, the Preface and Table of Contents of your book on *The International Judicial Process*. I feel quite clear that McNair's advice is right and that you really have no alternative but to leave it in abeyance for the time being. Happily it will not suffer with the passage of time and can be published at some appropriate future date either in its present form or with any revision which you then think desirable. I have found the Table of Contents alone most stimulating; it gives a very clear picture of how far you have gone beyond the 1934 volume.

Hersch took the matter further:

HL to C. W. Jenks, 7 April 1957

As to my own book – I am now considering the feasibility of eliminating the critical parts. This would leave intact about four fifths of the book. I am beginning to realise that the critical parts can never be published – certainly not [until][35] after I have ceased to be Judge.

The book was eventually published in 1958.[36]

In his letter to Jenks of 7 April, Hersch mentioned other items on which he was working:

---

[35] The manuscript of the letter does not contain the word 'until'. But, as the sentence reads rather strangely without it, I have ventured to insert it.

[36] There is a curious discrepancy about the dates. Although the correspondence on this matter indicates uncertainty as to whether and when the book should be published, the preface to the volume is dated 'January 1, 1957'. It seems unlikely that Hersch would have been seeking the views of both McNair and Jenks as if the question of publication were as yet unresolved, while at the same time carrying forward with Stevens & Sons' plans for publication. The date on the preface should probably be 1 January 1958.

I have completed a rather comprehensive article entitled 'Some Observations on the Prohibition of Non Liquet and the Completeness of the Law' and intended for Verzijl's[37] volume on the occasion of his seventieth birthday.[38] The volumes for the International Law Reports for 1953 and 1954 are going to the printer at the end of this month. Those for 1951 and 1952 are due to appear in May.

It had in the meantime been submitted to the President of the ICJ and some other judges for their imprimatur.

HL to C. W. Jenks, 27 July 1957

I am writing to thank you for sending me your book on the International Protection of Trade Union Freedom. I am very glad to have it for all kinds of reasons. It is much more than a merely informative book. It is in the best tradition – your tradition – in showing that an official position need not prevent a scholar from making contributions of value.

C. W. Jenks to HL, 5 August 1957

Thank you for your note of 27 July. As always, you are too kind. I am now in the frame of mind of not feeling certain whether the book is really worth the effort which it involved. A great deal will depend on how many people take the trouble to read between the lines and to see how far-reaching some of the wider implications of our experience could be. For this one must allow time and have patience.

Having received a copy of *The Development of International Law by the International Court*, Jenks wrote as follows:

C. W. Jenks to HL, 28 March 1958

Matters have finally been brought to a head by the arrival yesterday of 'The Development of International Law by the International Court of Justice'. I am most grateful to you for sending me a copy. It is, of course, quite untrue that I have found nothing new in it. I spent a couple of hours last night dipping into it extensively with growing enjoyment as I read. I have always regarded the earlier version as being one of your best books and now that the intervening years have made it possible to convert what was necessarily originally an impressionist sketch into a full-length survey the result is most impressive. I do not think the book has lost anything essential by the omissions which the obligation of restraint has imposed upon you. I appreciate that the omissions probably cover

---

[37] Jan Hendrik Willem Verzijl (1888–1987), Professor of International Law at Utrecht University, 1919–38, and Professor at the University of Amsterdam (a position from which he was dismissed when the Germans occupied the Netherlands). After the war, he returned to Utrecht University.
[38] The volume, *Symbolae Verzijl*, was presented to him on the occasion of his seventieth birthday. It contained twenty-nine essays, twenty-two in English and seven in French, written by well-known international jurists.

some of the best and most original writing in the book but its essential strength and value seem to me to remain completely unimpaired.

HL to C. W. Jenks, 9 April 1958

Thank you very much for what you say about my book. In a sense I have found it the most difficult of all that I have written but, in the aggregate, I think that it was worth while and that it will count to my credit on the day of judgment. I shall be particularly happy if it achieves some of the objects at which I was aiming, in particular if it acts as an encouragement to make the pronouncements of the Court to fulfil their part in the development of international law and, secondly, if it shows to the student of international law and the general reader the necessity of trying to understand the work of the Court not from the point of view of rigid rules but of more general tendencies and considerations forming part of the judicial function. Also, I am beginning to think that the omissions may have strengthened the book by making it more balanced. It is all too easy to criticise.

The Court's return in April 1957 to deal with the *Norwegian Loans* case provided the occasion for the third example of Hersch's individual approach in his separate Opinion of the *Norwegian Loans* case.[39] This case was commenced by France against Norway in July 1955, in respect of the latter's default on certain international loans that it had contracted. As in every case before the Court, it was necessary for the plaintiff to identify some act by which the defendant had accepted the jurisdiction of the Court. France relied on Norway's declaration accepting the compulsory jurisdiction of the Court which contained, as was permitted, a requirement of reciprocity. Thus, to be satisfied as to the existence of the necessary jurisdictional link, the Court had to be assured that it possessed jurisdiction under the French as well as the Norwegian declarations.

Norway contested the jurisdiction of the Court on the ground principally that the French nationals on whose behalf the proceedings had been brought had not exhausted the local remedies available to them in the Norwegian courts, as required by customary international law. The Court accepted this argument and upheld the Norwegian objection. Though Hersch reached the same conclusion as the majority, he did not join in its judgment but, adopting a significantly different approach, delivered a major separate Opinion of his own running to thirty-two pages.[40] Although his views have been criticised, the closely and elaborately reasoned argument stands as a model of judicial reasoning.

---

[39] ICJ Reports 1957, p. 9.   [40] *Ibid.*, pp. 34–66.

In an opening section of seven pages,[41] Hersch expressed in his own terms the rule relating to local remedies and the grounds on which he found that its requirements had not been satisfied. On this, therefore, he was in line with the Court's thinking and no further indication of his own views was required. Nonetheless, he then went on to consider an aspect of the case that had not been touched on by either party but which he believed raised a point of fundamental principle. As just indicated, France, as plaintiff, had to be in a position to establish that it, as well as the defendant, had accepted the Court's jurisdiction. In this case, the basis of such a demonstration by France, if the issue had been raised by Norway, would have been France's own declaration. This document, however, contained a number of reservations or exceptions, as is permissible, of which one excluded the Court's jurisdiction in any case brought against France relating to its national security 'as determined by itself. The effect of this, read literally, would be to reserve to France the right, even after a case had been started against it, to determine that it affected its national security, and thus to withdraw the case from the Court's jurisdiction. For Hersch, it seemed quite contrary to principle that a State, having seemingly accepted an obligation with one hand, should retain the right to empty it of content with the other. He drew attention to the violation of the Court's Statute involved in such an approach. He also invoked general principles of law derived from French law and the common law. He concluded that the French reservation was invalid. Even more, he found that it could not be severed from the declaration of which it formed part, on the ground that France would never have made the declaration if it could not have attached to it the offending reservation. In consequence, as the reservation was void, so was the declaration. This meant that France had not accepted the Court's jurisdiction at all and was, therefore, not in a position itself to sue any other State that had. On this ground, Hersch held that the Court did not have jurisdiction.

Hersch was almost alone in the Court in developing this line of reasoning – a line that had not been advanced by Norway, which had not been the subject of any French response and which had not been put to the parties either by the Court or by Hersch as a matter requiring consideration. For some, Hersch's approach was open to criticism on this ground alone. Others have found it difficult to accept either the basic concept of the invalidity of a self-judging reservation (or, as Hersch called it, an 'automatic reservation') or of, as in this case, the impossibility

---

[41] *Ibid.*, pp. 34–41.

of severing it from the declaration of which it formed part. Moreover, the rest of the Court, with the exception of Judge Guerrero,[42] had by its silence in the matter implicitly rejected the approach or, at the very least, had not taken the opportunity of associating itself with this rejection of the validity of the French declaration.

There were at that time seven other States that had included comparable reservations in their declaration accepting the Court's jurisdiction. Some of these States in due course withdrew the offending clause. However, it remained part of the United States declaration under the Optional Clause until the whole of its declaration was withdrawn in the wake of the Court's judgment upholding jurisdiction in *Military and Paramilitary Activities in and Against Nicaragua*.

The issue reappeared within two years in the *Interhandel* case between Switzerland and the United States.[43] This related to the treatment in the United States during the Second World War of assets belonging to Swiss nationals. As the basis of the Court's jurisdiction, Switzerland relied on the United States declaration. This, however, contained an automatic reservation, which the United States then invoked. The Court accepted the United States determination as effective to deprive it of jurisdiction without even discussing the possibility that it might be invalid. This led Hersch to file a dissent in which, repeating the argument already developed in the *Norwegian Loans* case, he held that the United States reservation was void and hence that the whole declaration of which it formed part was void. He therefore found that the United States had not consented to the Court's jurisdiction and that the Swiss action must fail.[44]

On this occasion, however, Hersch's approach received support from some other, though not a majority of, members of the Court, for example Judge Sir Percy Spender[45] and, in part, Judges Klaestad[46] and Armand-Ugon.[47]

Apart from his rejection of the validity of 'automatic reservations', Hersch was able in his remaining years to make some important contributions to substantive international law.

In November 1957, he was able to join the majority in the rejection of preliminary objections brought by India against the proceedings

---

[42] ICJ Reports 1957, p. 69.

[43] In his dissenting Opinion at the interim measures stage of the case, Hersch briefly reaffirmed the views that he had expressed in the *Norwegian Loans* case but considered that the issue did not arise at that stage of the case. ICJ Reports 1957, p. 120.

[44] ICJ Reports 1959, pp. 95–122.

[45] *Ibid.*, pp. 56–7.   [46] *Ibid.*, pp. 76–8.

[47] *Ibid.*, pp. 93 and 94. Subsequently, Hersch's views were cited – though with some qualification – by Judge Schwebel in his dissenting Opinion in the case between Nicaragua and the United States on *Military and Paramilitary Activities*. See ICJ Reports 1986, pp. 600 and 609–11.

commenced by Portugal[48] claiming a *Right of Passage over Indian Territory*, a relic of the period when Portugal had been a major colonial power in Asia, and concerning the former's right of passage to and between two small enclaves still held by it within Indian territory. India raised six preliminary objections.

First, it contended that Portugal's condition in its declaration, reserving 'the right to exclude from the scope of the present Declaration at any time during its validity any given category of disputes by notifying the Secretary-General of the United Nations', was incompatible with the object and purpose of the Optional Clause, with the result that the declaration was invalid.

The second and fourth objections related to the shortness of the period (three days in late December) between the filing of Portugal's declaration and its application instituting proceedings, thus effectively precluding India, in breach of the condition of reciprocity, from exercising its right to exclude the dispute from the Court's jurisdiction.

The third objection, relating to the absence of prior negotiations, primarily a question of fact rather than law, need not concern us here.

The fifth objection was based on the reservation in India's declaration excluding from the Court's jurisdiction disputes which, under international law, fell exclusively within Indian domestic jurisdiction.

Finally, India contended that the dispute was based on matters that had arisen prior to 5 February 1930, the starting date for the operation of its declaration.

By substantial majorities, the Court rejected the first four objections and joined the fifth and sixth to the consideration of the merits. In relation to the first objection, it held that any exercise by Portugal of its right to exclude a particular category of dispute could apply only to future disputes; the Court's jurisdiction in respect of prior disputes would continue to exist. Hence, it could not be said that the reservation deprived the declaration of all substance. Nor was it in breach of the condition of reciprocity. In effect, any State was entitled at any time unilaterally to terminate its declaration in whole or in part. Portugal's reservation was simply a particular expression of that right.

As to the second and fourth objections, the Court rejected India's further argument as to lack of reciprocity based on the contention that temporal considerations had denied it the opportunity to exercise its own right to exclude particular categories of dispute, holding that '[a] State

---

[48] ICJ Reports 1957, p. 125.

accepting the jurisdiction of the Court must expect that an Application may be filed against it by a new declarant State on the same day on which that State deposits its Acceptance'.

Given the secrecy surrounding the Court's deliberations (even the names of the members who sit with the President on each drafting committee are strictly confidential), it cannot be known what Hersch had to say on the subject, and to what extent his views may have influenced the wording of the judgment. It is, however, surely significant that, by contrast with his stance in the previous two cases, he was evidently not opposed to reservations as such. A State could at any time exclude the Court's jurisdiction in respect of any or all categories of dispute – *for the future*. What it could not do was to give itself power to exclude disputes *ab initio* on what amounted to entirely subjective grounds – the 'automatic' or 'self-judging' reservation.

Hersch must likewise have accepted, in relation to the rejection of the second and fourth reservations, that it was open to one State to 'ambush' another in the timing of the filing of its acceptance of the Court's jurisdiction. Thus, notwithstanding his academic background, he was clearly aware of, and accepted the realities of, the rough-and-tumble of the practice of international justice – at least insofar as it accorded with the Court's natural tendency to seek to extend, rather than limit, its own jurisdiction.

In 1958, Hersch delivered a concurring opinion in the case between the Netherlands and Sweden concerning the *Application of the Convention of 1902 Governing the Guardianship of Infants*.[49] This case is of special interest because of its position at the interface of private and public international law. It concerned a young girl, Elisabeth Boll, of mixed parentage – child of a Dutch father, but born in Sweden and living there with her mother. When her mother died, her father obtained a guardianship order from the Dutch courts, who applied the Hague Convention on the Guardianship of Infants of 1902, under which the matter was governed by the child's national law which, through her father, was Dutch.

Meanwhile, the deceased mother's Swedish father had obtained a custody order from the Swedish courts on the basis of Swedish domestic child protection legislation. These courts maintained that, since the objectives of the relevant statute, the 1924 Law on Protective Upbringing – namely, the interests of society in the protection of children – were essentially matters of public law, whereas the Convention

---

[49] ICJ Reports 1958, p. 55.

was concerned with private rights of guardianship, their refusal to implement the Dutch court's order was not in breach of the Convention.

In its judgment, the ICJ basically endorsed the view of the Swedish
courts. Hence, Sweden was not in breach of its obligations under the
Convention and the Dutch action failed.

What is interesting about Hersch's concurring Opinion is the way he
goes beyond the superficial approach taken by the judgment to get to
the real heart of the matter.

First, he made the general point in relation to treaty law, not developed
in the judgment, that a State cannot evade its treaty obligations simply
by reference to the stated objectives of legislation or its other actions that
potentially breach the treaty. What counts is the objective nature of the
legislation in light of the terms of the treaty. In this regard, the following
passages are worthy of note:

> If a State enacts and applies legislation which, in effect, renders the treaty
> wholly or partly inoperative, can such legislation be deemed not to constitute
> a violation of the treaty for the reason that the legislation in question covers
> a subject-matter different from that covered by the treaty, that it is concerned
> with a different institution, and that it pursues a different purpose? I have
> considerable difficulty in answering that question in the affirmative.[50]

And again:

> When a State concludes a treaty it is entitled to expect that that treaty will
> not be mutilated or destroyed by legislative or other measures which pursue
> a different object but which, in effect, render impossible the operation of the
> treaty or part thereof...
>
> A State is not entitled to cut down its treaty obligations in relation to one
> institution by enacting in the sphere of another institution provisions whose
> effect is such as to frustrate the operation of a crucial aspect of the treaty... Once
> we begin to base the interpretation of treaties on conceptual distinctions between
> actually conflicting legal rules lying on different planes and for that reason not
> being, somehow, inconsistent, it may be difficult, to set a limit to the effects of
> these operations in the sphere of logic and classification.[51]

Finally:

> It is part of the firmly established jurisprudence of this Court that with regard
> to national laws bearing upon treaty obligations what matters is not the letter
> of the law but its actual effect.[52]

---

[50] *Ibid.*, p. 80.   [51] *Ibid.*, pp. 81 and 83.   [52] *Ibid.*, p. 86.

Meanwhile, he gives short shrift to the private/public law distinction principally relied on by the judgment:

The view has been put forward that there can be no conflict between a Convention on Guardianship and the Law on Protective Upbringing for the reason that . . . the Convention is an institution of private law, . . . while the Law on Protection Upbringing . . . [is] in the sphere of public law seeing that [it is] concerned with the interests of society.

[I]t is clear that the distinction between the protection of the child and the protection of society is artificial . . . All social laws are, in the last resort, laws for the protection of individuals; all laws for the protection of individuals are, in a true sense, social laws. There is an element of unreality in making these two aspects of the purpose of the State the starting-point for drawing legal consequences of practical import.[53]

For Hersch, the principal interest in the case lay in the role of *ordre public* or public policy in the interpretation of private-law treaties and it is to that issue that the remaining thirteen pages of his twenty-three-page Opinion are devoted. He examines the concept at length. While at one point accepting its criticisms, in particular the comparison with 'the vagueness of the law of nature',[54] he nonetheless characterises it as 'a general principle of law of most, if not all, civilized States'.[55] The point is, however, not to determine whether there is a conflict between the Guardianship Convention and *ordre public* and, if so, which should apply, but to decide whether, explicitly or implicitly, the Convention prohibits reliance on it.

The protection of children was clearly a matter of public policy, and Sweden had indeed said as much in its pleadings. Hersch could find nothing in the Convention or in its *travaux préparatoires* to prevent Sweden from applying public policy to override its treaty obligations. Hence, Sweden was not in breach of the Convention and the Dutch claim must fail – the same result as that reached by the majority, but by a different, intellectually more rigorous, route.

During 1958, while performing his duties as a judge, Hersch found time to prepare, together with Humphrey Waldock, a volume of Brierly's collected papers to mark his departure from the Chichele Chair of International Law and Diplomacy at Oxford. Initially, Hersch was asked to prepare a substantive article for the *BYIL* but he declined, finding it too difficult to assess Brierly in a satisfactory way. Hersch only changed his mind after Waldock suggested that Hersch should instead write a

---

[53] *Ibid.*, pp. 83 and 85.   [54] *Ibid.*, p. 94.   [55] *Ibid.*

short, descriptive introduction to a collection of Brierly's papers that was also to be printed in the *BYIL*.

HL to C. W. Jenks, 31 May 1956

I have undertaken to write an article about Brierly for the BY – a piece of work which I am finding more difficult than I expected.

It has been said that about half of the resulting paper congratulates Brierly for qualities and opinions that were, in fact, Hersch's own.[56] Hersch pointed out that one of Brierly's notable achievements was that he identified problems but did not find solutions:

There is one feature of Brierly's work which pertains to the domain of method rather than of substance, but which can nevertheless properly be regarded as being in the nature of a distinct contribution to the science of international law. That contribution lay not so much in the solutions which he propounded – for he often admitted, or implied, that there was no solution or no easy solution – as in the way in which he pointed to the difficulties involved and, after apparently propounding an answer to them, proceeded to develop the theme of the deceptiveness and the insufficiency of the answer thus given. It would almost appear that what weighed with him was not the result of the search, but the search itself; that he was content to be an exponent of difficulties and not a provider of solutions; and that it did not matter to him that in fact he left the problem unresolved.[57]

In the spring of that same year, 1958, Hersch's book on *The Development of International Law by the International Court* eventually appeared (he had dated the preface as early as 1 January 1957). In Hersch's copy to Philip Jessup, he wrote:

I gave some anxious thought to the matter before I decided to send it to the publishers. There is little, if anything, in it that will be new to you. It would have been a more exciting book if I had not considered myself bound by certain obligations of restraint. Constrained by the desire to say nothing which could justifiably be construed as being criticism of the Court. However, I came to the conclusion that the book may be of some use inasmuch as it gives a picture of the activity of the Court from its inception against the background of some of the main problems of the judicial function and inasmuch as it raises some general questions of judicial technique. As such, it may strengthen confidence in the Court. One of my main concerns was to bring home, to all concerned,

---

[56] Koskenniemi, 'Hersch Lauterpacht (1897–1960)', in *Jurists Uprooted: German-Speaking Emigré Lawyers in Twentieth-Century Britain*, ed. Beatson and Zimmerman (Oxford: Oxford University Press, 2004), p. 630. See also: 'Brierly's Contribution to International Law', reprinted in *Collected Papers*, Vol. 2, p. 446.

[57] *Ibid.*

the importance of the problem outlined on pages 37–42 and 395–400. I do not know whether you will agree.

In the first group of pages referred to, Hersch emphasised the need for the fullest possible completeness of judicial reasoning so as to reduce the risk of judicial partiality. For the second group, he identified the element of judicial discretion and spoke of it as being 'circumscribed by the duty to apply the existing law and that it moves within the orbit of the tendencies, enshrined in precedent, whose operation forms the principal theme of this book'.[58] Jessup replied on 23 October 1958, saying, 'without reservation', that he fully shared Hersch's point of view in all of the questions covered there.[59]

In the following year, 1959, Hersch participated in a joint dissenting Opinion with Judges Wellington Koo and Sir Percy Spender, probably playing the leading part in its formulation, in the *Case Concerning the Aerial Incident of July 27, 1955* between Israel and Bulgaria.

The dissenting Opinion began by recalling that the terms of Article 36(5) of the Statute of the ICJ required the application to the ICJ of declarations accepting the compulsory jurisdiction of the PCIJ provided (1) that the declarant State must become a party to the Statute of the ICJ and (2) that its declaration must be 'still in force'. The dissenting Opinion then went on to note that to these two express conditions the judgment of the Court had added two further conditions: (1) that the declarant State must have participated in the San Francisco Conference and (2) that it must have become a party to the Statute of the ICJ prior to the date of the dissolution of the PCIJ. As neither of these two additional conditions had been met by Bulgaria, the Court held that Article 36(5) did not serve to give the Court jurisdiction. The dissenting Opinion rejected the Court's additional conditions on two grounds: that the interpretation is contrary to the clear terms of Article 36(5) and that the interpretation is contrary to the material purpose of that provision.

As to the first ground, the Opinion demonstrated that, at the San Francisco Conference, it was intended that the ICJ was to be in substance a continuation of the PCIJ and that the purpose of Article 36(5) was to provide for the continuing validity of existing adherence to the PCIJ Optional Clause. The words 'which are still in force' could only have been intended to exclude some fourteen declarations made under the Statute of the PCIJ that by their terms had already expired before 1945.

---

[58] *The Development of International Law by the International Court*, London: Stevens & Sons Ltd, 1958), p. 399.
[59] Philip Jessup to HL, 23 October 1958 (Jessup Archive).

The phrase in its ordinary connotation refers to the element of the expiration of time, not to termination as the result of an extraneous event such as the dissolution of the PCIJ.

There then followed a close examination of the object of Article 36(5). The attachment of the declaration under the Statute of the PCIJ to the new Court was considered essential. The dissolution of the PCIJ was precisely the situation envisaged by the framers of the Statute of the ICJ as a reason for the adoption of Article 36(5). The governing principle underlying Article 36(5) is that of automatic succession of the ICJ in respect of engagements undertaken by reference to the Statute of the PCIJ.

The Opinion then dealt at length with a number of other detailed arguments that had been raised in favour of Bulgaria, doing so largely by reference to the proceedings of the San Francisco Conference. Towards the end of the Opinion, however, consideration was given to whether Article 36(5) could be applied consistently with the requirement of reasonableness. The Opinion took the view that the test of reasonableness must itself be applied in a reasonable way and not by reference to contingencies which are in themselves of a manifestly exaggerated character. It distinguished between reasonableness applied, on the one hand, to a substantive claim that causes unfair hardship and, on the other, to a case where the issue was whether the principal juridical organ of the UN should adjudicate upon a controversy by reference to international law.

Some years after Hersch died, a comparable problem of interpretation arose in the *Barcelona Traction* case[60] where one issue was whether Article 37 of the Statute of the ICJ had preserved the jurisdictional provision in a 1927 treaty between Belgium and Spain.[61] Spain contended that the jurisdictional clause failed because Spain was not an original member of the UN and that the continuity provision of Article 37 was therefore inoperative. The Court rejected this contention, asserting that Article 37 should be distinguished from Article 36(5), but nonetheless implicitly abandoned its approach in the *Aerial Incident* case. The position was made plain in the observations of the two surviving judges who had participated in the joint dissenting Opinion with Hersch in 1959. (The only other surviving judges were Winiarski, Badawi and Spiropoulous.) Thus, the President, Judge Sir Percy Spender, said:

[60] Preliminary Objections, Judgment of 24 July 1964, ICJ Reports 1964, p. 6; 46 *ILR* 2.
[61] Statute of the International Court of Justice, Article 37: 'Whenever a treaty or convention in force provides for reference of a matter to a tribunal to have been instituted by the League of Nations, or to the Permanent Court of International Justice, the matter shall, as between the parties to the present Statute, be referred to the International Court of Justice.'

Whilst the text of Article 37 of the Court's Statute is quite different to that of Article 36(5), which was the subject of examination in *Israel* v. *Bulgaria*, and its terms are, in my view, so clear as to admit of no doubt as to their meaning, it is difficult to discern any decisive distinction in principle between Article 36(5) and Article 37 in relation to the cardinal question raised by the second Preliminary Objection.

For my part, for reasons which appear in the Joint Dissenting Opinion in *Israel* v. *Bulgaria*, to which I continue to adhere, I would, apart from other considerations referred to in the Court's Judgment, be compelled to reject this Preliminary Objection.[62]

Likewise, the Vice-President, Judge Wellington Koo, said:

The Judgment in referring to the reliance of the Respondent upon the decision of the Court in the *Israel* v. *Bulgaria* case in support of the second Preliminary Objection points out a number of differences between that case and the present one. In so far as this is done for the purpose of making an independent approach to the instant case on its merits, it can be easily understood. But, as I look at it, calling attention to these differences does not imply, nor do they themselves justify an implication of, any justification of the decision in the former case, concerning which my views remain the same as stated in the Joint Dissenting Opinion appended to the Judgment in that case.[63]

Hersch's last participation in the Court's work was in the *Case Concerning Sovereignty over Certain Frontier Land* between Belgium and the Netherlands.[64] The disputed 'parcels' of land were tiny enclaves claimed by Belgium, lying a few kilometres across the frontier with the Netherlands. The dispute had crystallised in 1839, the year of the treaty between the Netherlands and Belgium formalising the latter's independence, and each side's claims rested on copies of documents of disputed authenticity surviving from that period. The Netherlands supported its documentary claims with the fact that it had exercised unchallenged administrative authority over the enclaves throughout the relevant period.

By ten votes to four, primarily on the basis of a detailed examination of the disputed documents, the Court found in favour of Belgium. Along with three of his colleagues, Hersch once again dissented. One can imagine that he must have had little enthusiasm for the detailed textual analysis that underpinned the judgment. His view was essentially a commonsense one: the documents were uncertain and contained unresolved discrepancies; hence they could not be relied on by either side. What

[62] ICJ Reports 1964 p. 47; 46 *ILR* 58. [63] ICJ Reports 1964, p. 49; 46 *ILR* 62.
[64] ICJ Reports 1959, p. 209; 27 *ILR* 62.

was certain was the fact of the exercise of unchallenged administrative activity by the Netherlands.

Since the documents in the case could not be relied on in favour of either party, it followed that the burden on the Netherlands to establish a prescriptive right of sovereignty by virtue of the unopposed exercise of administrative authority was lower than it would have been had that exercise taken place in face of a clear treaty right on Belgium's part.

[T]here is no room here for applying the exacting rules of prescription in relation to a title acquired by a clear and unequivocal treaty; there is no such treaty . . . the fact that local conditions have necessitated the normal and unchallenged exercise of Netherlands administrative activity provides an additional reason why, in the absence of clear provisions of a treaty, there is no necessity to disturb the existing state of affairs and to perpetuate a geographical anomaly.[65]

During 1959, Hersch was active in encouraging Schwebel and Baxter that in appointing a new member of the Permanent Court of Arbitration, they would consult the American academic world, including the American Society of International Law and the American Arbitration Association. In doing so, they were able to garner support to nominate, and later appoint, Jessup to the Court. Schwebel recalls that Hersch's 'letter was more than influential . . . it was the decisive stimulus' in the matter.

In October 1959, shortly after returning to The Hague following the summer recess, Hersch suffered a heart attack. He was not hospitalised but remained in his room at the Wittebrug where Rachel, with the hotel facilities to support her, cared for him. As he was anxious to see his granddaughter, Deborah, then six months old, I took her over to The Hague on the night boat. She arrived there gurgling and happy, not having been changed in the eighteen hours since she left home. She was, nonetheless, an acceptable sight in her grandfather's eyes.

Conscious as we now are of the relationship between the consumption of excessive amounts of fat and the build-up of cholesterol leading to heart disease, Hersch's illness does not come as a surprise. But Hersch was unaware of the risks that he was running by the kind of life that he was leading: sedentary, with too much eating of heavy and fatty food, only slightly palliated by not particularly energetic daily walks.

Stress was no doubt a further factor. The Court is a collegiate body and reaches its decisions collectively, the judges deliberating together for many hours, if not in plenary session then in the drafting committee, preparing decisions. Hersch would have participated in the plenary

---

[65] ICJ Reports 1959, pp. 231–2; 27 *ILR* 80.

meetings and, at any rate in one of those cases in which he was not dissenting or filing a separate opinion, he was a member of the drafting committee. However, he was not really a committee man, as his experiences as a member of the British team in the Nuremberg trials and the *Corfu Channel* and *Anglo-Iranian Oil Company* cases had already shown. He was an excellent lone draftsman, as demonstrated by his preparation of the drafts of the legal arguments for Sir Hartley Shawcross, the chief British prosecutor at Nuremberg, or the draft of the legal part of the British memorial in the *Anglo-Iranian* case. But he did not accept comfortably what he saw as the presumption of others who might question his drafts in areas of law, or in modes of presentation, where he felt that his knowledge and experience exceeded theirs. The fact that he was not involved in the merits stage of the *Corfu Channel* case, having participated in the jurisdictional phase, may be attributable to recognition by Sir Eric Beckett, then Legal Adviser of the Foreign Office, of this limitation on Hersch's ability to cooperate. Or it may have been that Hersch made it pretty obvious that Beckett's habit of frenetic working late into the night did not suit him. Or it may simply have been because the merits stage was mainly concerned with facts with which Hersch would have been largely unfamiliar.

The extent to which he was engaged in other matters, additional to the work of the Court, is shown in a letter he wrote to Philip Jessup on 2 February 1958:

I have been busy on various things including the seeing through the press of my book on *The Development of International Law by the International Court* . . . ; the preparation of the 1955 volume of the *International Law Reports*; collecting material and doing some writing on the new editions of Oppenheim and *Function of Law*; and last but not least, doing some reading on the Court cases. Its calendar has been rather upset by the postponement of the *Interhandel* case. I hope that the time may come when the court will be more master of its timetable than at present so that it can avoid prolonged periods of inactivity as well as periods of congestion . . . the contingency [of the *Interhandel* case] may begin in the autumn and last quite a while.

So anticipation of the forthcoming resumption of the judicial year, added to the degenerative effect of his mode of life, could well have served to trigger the heart attack.

Nonetheless, on 15 February 1960, while convalescing, Hersch sent McNair some lengthy observations concerning a proposal that McNair had passed on to him on 2 February. McNair's letter cannot be found, but the gist of it can be gathered from Hersch's reply:

I think it important that an authoritative Committee appointed either by one of the great Foundations or by the Institute of International Law or by the Secretary-General of the UN should investigate and report on the causes of the absence of effective jurisdiction and activity of the ICJ and the possible means to improve the situation. It is not, even now, generally realized how nominal is the activity of the Court. The fact that in the last three years the Court has sat for six or seven months in the year has tended to obscure the true position. Most of the judgments of the Court in the last five years have been concerned with pleas to its jurisdiction – more specifically, with finding that the Court has no jurisdiction. With minor exceptions, the few substantive judgments and advisory opinions have been concerned with somewhat insignificant and artificial issues. To mention a recent example, the two phases of the recent *Passage* case have occupied the Court for nearly a year. But, as appears from the published proceedings, the contest between the Parties has become academic. Portugal has agreed that the Court would be entitled to say that, in the circumstances, there is no right of passage. Moreover, even those nominal sources of the jurisdiction of the Court show signs of drying up.

At the same time I feel that the type of question which the promoters of the project have in mind and which are outlined on p. 2 of your letter do not go to the root of the matter, that some of them create the impression of being uninformed, and that if they were to remain the principal object of the enquiry the latter would do harm by failing to cope with the real causes of the *malaise* and by creating, indirectly, the impression that all is well – or beyond any attempt at reform – with regard to the essential aspects of the situation. There is, for instance, little purpose in trying to shorten the duration of the proceedings at a period when the inflated prolixity of the oral pleadings and the slowness of the internal procedure of the Court give appearance – at least – of *some* activity and prevent the Court from disintegrating on account of sitting only for two months in the year. Undoubtedly, there is room for improvements – such as the occasional division of the Court into Chambers of 8 or 9 members. But, these changes are insignificant in relation to the major issue. They are in any case of academic importance at a time when the activity of the Court is nominal. I must also confess that I do not quite follow the meaning of some of the questions, for instance, the desirability of securing stronger majorities (although with regard to that particular question I can imagine that a wise leadership of the Court, instead of putting itself at the head of an impatient and steam-rolling majority, might do a great deal to base the judgment or opinion on the available common agreement – which is possible in many cases. However, this is hardly a matter for a Report.)

The true plight of the Court – of which public opinion, legal and other, ought to be made conscious – stems from other causes which are at the root of the absence both of true compulsory and voluntary jurisdiction. I know that you and I are in agreement as to what these causes are. The main and decisive factor is the absence of confidence on the part of governments in the impartiality of the Court and the predictability of its judgments and opinions. I am not expressing any opinion whether that lack of confidence is justified. But I am certain that it is the decisive factor in the situation and that it ought to be made the subject of a most exacting, open and authoritative enquiry and report. For it is clear that there is an absence of confidence in the political impartiality of the Court. This, it is alleged by some, is due to the fact that the great majority of the Court is composed of former diplomats, foreign ministers, and legal advisers (though there is at least one legal adviser, known to both of us and who is not on the Court, in relation to whom an objection of this kind is quite absurd). Others rely on the allegation that the attitude of some members is politically determined in advance. There are also other considerations in this connection. Secondly, it is contended that the absence of confidence on the part of Governments is due to the feeling that the majority of the members of the Court do not possess the expert knowledge of the law which they are called to administer. It may or may not help to bring to light the fact that these causes – if they *are* the causes – are due to the Governments themselves: to the method of election adopted; the Statute and above all, to the spirit in which the Statute has been applied in this respect. There are other questions of importance such as, for instance, whether the organization of the Court and its interpretation of the requirement of residence are such as to enable the Court to fulfill its duties in the best interests of justice. But it is the composition of the Court which is regarded by many as the central problem. It is probable that, in the nature of things, that problem can never be satisfactorily solved. But many believe that it can be substantially alleviated. If that is done, the Court may be trusted, in the light of its own experience, to effect the necessary changes in its procedure and organization. But I feel that there would be little value – or that there would be a negative value – in an inquiry and Report which by-pass the central issue or which obscure and minimize it through apologetic parenthesis or indirect interventions.

I realize that a Report concerned with the kind of matters which I consider to be essential might, in the view of some, cause damage to the prestige of the Court. It might be held that one is not entitled to do that unless one is sure that that initial damage will be fully compensated by eventual improvements achieved as the result of the Report. Of course, one cannot be sure that any such result will be achieved. But perhaps there is a duty to try. The more authoritative the committee and the more thorough its work, the greater will be the chance that, provided that the Report is detailed and outspoken, it may achieve something or – perhaps – a great deal.

Now I am convinced that a Committee of a composition which you mention would be perhaps the strongest and the most authoritative committee I could conceive for that purpose.

In my view there is no objection – there is every justification – to former judges serving on that committee. The late Judge Huber was President of the Commission which was asked to report on the organization of the Court and the method of electing its members – questions which I consider to be at the root of the matter.[66] Guerrero, a very cautious man, supported and, in fact, initiated the creation of that Commission. (You may recall that last summer I was anxious 'that the Institute should decide to resume the work of that Commission.' You thought – I think rightly – that if any such initiative were to come from me it would be likely to be misunderstood.) I doubt whether it would be really necessary for former judges, with regard to the matters which I consider to be essential, to draw upon their recollection of what happened in the Salle Bol[67] – except perhaps with regard to the sad impact of pressure of time, at the crucial phases of drafting the judgment or opinion in relation to judges not residing at The Hague. As to the other aspects of the process of formulating the judgment or opinions the published material provides ample material for enquiry and reflection. This applies, for instance, to the fact that – according to some – the present procedure is wholly unsatisfactory in as much as an exorbitant amount of time is devoted to preliminary stages (such as oral proceedings, exchange of views, the written notes – which, including the time required for translations, may consume as much as three weeks) while the decisive and most important stage, namely, that of formulating the judgment, is accomplished at high pressure and its value is adversely affected by collective drafting and amendment. However, it is probable that proposals for reform in the latter sphere can better come from the Court itself – provided that its composition is such as to make it amenable to benefiting from experience; which once more brings us back to the main problem.

There is one apparent difficulty – I do not think it is a real difficulty – which may militate against participation of former judges in a committee of this kind. Any report on what I consider to be the major issues must contain a measure of criticism of the method of election to the Court and its composition. Unless the Report is outspoken in its examination [and] conclusions on the subject, it will avoid the main issue. However, I do not think that that particular consideration is of importance. Any criticism would, essentially, be a criticism of a system and of a method – not persons. Undoubtedly, all this constitutes a certain, at least, apparent difficulty. I am inclined to think that if I were a former judge, and *compos mentis* and able to write I might consider it my duty to use my knowledge and experience in the effort to improve the situation. I could do it without hurting or offending any person.

[66] Hersch is referring here to the Institut de Droit International's Commission on Revisions to the ICJ Statute established at its 1952 Siena meeting on the basis of a resolution presented by J. Gustave Guerrero. Max Huber was appointed President and presented his report to the Institute's 1954 meeting in Aix-en-Provence.

[67] The room in the Peace Palace in which, at that time, the judges conducted their deliberations.

As to your participation in the committee, my view is this: I think that you could be its strongest member, and that your absence – and the mere fact of your absence – would weaken it. On the other hand, I understand the reasons why you wish to cut down your commitments – and this would be a very exacting commitment. Having suffered severely from overdoing things, I ought not to urge others to do the same . . .

If the committee were to materialize – and if you wanted me to do it – I could ask for the Court's permission to put at your disposal the large Report on the Revision of the Statute which I prepared for the Court three years ago.

Though Hersch did not realise it, his effective life as a judge had come to an end. He remained in the hotel in The Hague for some weeks until pronounced fit enough to travel abroad for a long convalescence. He and Rachel went to Israel at the invitation of Rachel's sister, Leah. Her house was in Herzliah Pituah, an outlying northern suburb of Tel Aviv, just a few minutes from the sea. In normal circumstances, the change would have done Hersch some good, and his health certainly improved there. But, as the stay lengthened, he became increasingly uncomfortable as a guest. So, after a few weeks, he and Rachel moved to a nearby hotel overlooking the sea. In March 1960, he felt ready to return to the Court. He had, in the meantime, been persuaded to take the lease of a flat in The Hague in an apartment block in the Anna Paulownastraat, right opposite the Peace Palace with a splendid view towards that building. Soon afterwards, on consulting a local doctor about some bowel problem, he was advised to return immediately to England to seek medical treatment. On 4 May, he saw Lord Moran, the most prominent physician then in England, who advised him to take the advice of Mr Naunton Morgan, a specialist in such problems. Morgan advised immediate surgery. On 7 May, Hersch entered the London Clinic to prepare for an operation on the following day, Sunday.

The Saturday was a brilliant summer's day and, before going into the Clinic, he, Rachel and I strolled in Regent's Park, which was close by. It did not cross my mind that anything could go wrong the next day. We saw him into his room and at about 8pm left him. He must have been very apprehensive and not at all confident about the operation. A sign of his anxiety was that he had taken with him his prayer shawl or 'tallith', which men of the Jewish faith wear in the synagogue and in which they are traditionally buried. He also spent some time giving me certain instructions in the event that he did not survive the operation. Though seemingly outwardly calm, he took pains to conceal his worry from Rachel and me. He really should have been given something to calm him, but it was a Saturday evening and no one appeared then to show any concern.

The operation was scheduled for 10am on Sunday morning, 8 May. Hersch's doctor from Cambridge, Dr Edward Bevan, came down to attend. Rachel and I waited in his room for his return from the operation, which was expected to be at 12 noon. The period of waiting grew longer and longer until eventually Dr Bevan came in to tell us that Hersch had died on the operating table after a further heart attack following the operation. No explanation was given nor, in the agony of the moment, did we ask why no cardiac specialist was available to attempt resuscitation. But, perhaps it was better that there was not. The exploratory operation, we were told, had revealed an advanced cancer of the bowel of which secondaries had already spread to the liver and were inoperable. He would at best have had but a few more months to live in increasing agony of body and mind.

His funeral took place in the synagogue in Thompson's Lane, Cambridge, on 11 May 1960. The small synagogue was packed. At the service, Wilfred Jenks, one of Hersch's closest friends, delivered the following eulogy:

We are gathered today, in sadness and humility but with a deep and legitimate pride, to pay our parting tribute to one whom we have all loved, respected and admired – to a warm and staunch friend, a fine scholar, a fearless judge, one of the greatest international lawyers not only of our own but of any time.

A few brief days ago Hersch Lauterpacht was still with us. Now he belongs to the ages and we remain awhile to pay reverent tribute to the richness of his immortality.

We who are privileged to be counted among his friends know how warm and constant was his friendship, how intense was his passion for righteousness, how steadfast was his personal and public courage, how lightly the weight of his learning lay upon him, and how fundamental was the simplicity and earnestness of his humility.

He leaves behind him her who shaped the hopes, labours and difficulties of the young and unknown scholar venturing in what was then a strange land, who shared his early triumphs, who shared his burden of personal sorrow during the years of endurance of his people and his family, who shared in every stage of his successive achievements as scholar, counsellor and judge, and who shared the anxieties and suffering of these last months, weeks and days. He leaves behind also that deepest source of a father's pride, a son worthily pursuing his father's ideal and vocation. To Rachel and to Eli we all extend our deepest and heartfelt sympathy, and our fervent prayers for them and theirs.

Hersch Lauterpacht leaves in Cambridge, in London, in Geneva, at The Hague, in the United States, in Israel, and indeed throughout the world, a great company of teachers, colleagues, students and friends to whose lives he has given new dimensions and to whom his whole life will always remain an abiding inspiration.

The richness of his intellectual achievement in itself affords an inspiration few lives can offer.

For over thirty years he adapted constantly to a succession of revolutionary changes the most comprehensive treatment of the law of nations available to the student in English, or perhaps in any language. His has been the main burden of garnering from all over the world the wealth of international and national decisions which are progressively transforming the law from formless custom into a firmly established body of authoritative judicial precedent. Any one of his five great books would have established the reputation, and might have exhausted the intellectual vitality, of a scholar of high distinction, and his countless occasional writings illumine and enlarge the law.

Hersch Lauterpacht acknowledged, in the things of the mind, under Grotius, two great masters, Hans Kelsen and Arnold McNair, and his own work represents the confluence of speculative philosophy with the abiding vitality of the common law. Therein lies its richness, its strength, and its assurance of immortality.

Of the vision and fearlessness which characterized his all-too-brief service as a Judge of the International Court, and the impact which his judgments have already had and will continue to have on the future of the law and the future of international adjudication, others will speak with authority elsewhere.

Yet exacting as were his standards of scholarship and intellectual integrity, lofty as was his vision of the judicial office, staunch as was his friendship, devoted as was his affection, it is not solely, or perhaps even primarily, as a scholar, judge and friend that he would have wished to be remembered or that we would wish to remember him. He brought to everything he undertook the moral horizon and stature of the great prophets of his race. He leaves with us, as an imperishable bequest to all who inherit his spirit, a sense of moral purpose, of moral earnestness and moral urgency which represents the supreme need of our troubled age and world. His belief that the State exists for man and not man for the State, that the moral law applies in the same manner to public as to private conduct, that the use of force for the protection of private interests is alien to, whereas the judicial process is an expression of, the moral nature of man, that right is ultimately the only right, and that the protection of human freedom and human dignity are the only legitimate purpose of law and government, was not an academic conviction but a consuming fire – a fire which has consumed.

Hersch Lauterpacht will be remembered in generations to come as one of those who lit a beacon such as will never be extinguished until the human race has learned to do justice and to love mercy and to walk humbly with its God in a righteous commonwealth built on the brotherhood of man.[68]

He was interred in the Jewish section of the cemetery in Newmarket Road, Cambridge. His grave is covered by a granite block, on which appear these words:

Hersch Lauterpacht
Knight Queen's Counsel
Fellow of the British Academy
Whewell Professor of International Law at the
University of Cambridge
Judge of the International Court of Justice
16 August 1897–8 May 1960
He loved truth
Did justice and righteousness
And taught the peoples statutes and judgment

When Rachel died some twenty-nine years later, she was laid to rest next to him.

On 9 May the President of the ICJ wrote to the British Ambassador in The Hague:

The news of the death of Judge Sir Hersch Lauterpacht has come as a great shock and has been received by all his colleagues with profound grief.

I now have the honour to convey to the Government of the United Kingdom, through Your Excellency, the sincere sympathy of the International Court of Justice.

Judge Sir Hersch Lauterpacht had achieved world eminence in the field of international law before his election to membership of the Court. In the years, so tragically few, in which he has been our colleague, we have had an opportunity of adding to our respect for his learning an appreciation of his wholehearted devotion to the ideal of the settlement of international disputes by judicial processes and his unremitting labour in the cause of the development of international law, his contribution to which will long survive him.

In the hearts and minds of all of us who had the privilege of working with him, he will be remembered not least for his qualities of warm humanity, kindness and consideration.

---

[68] (1959) 33 *BYIL* ix–xi.

The International Law Commission, of which Hersch had been a member for two sessions (1953 and 1954), observed one minute's silence in Hersch's memory, ten tributes were paid to him and the meeting adjourned early.[69]

Obituaries appeared in many newspapers and periodicals worldwide.[70]

---

[69] Twelfth Session, 535th meeting, 9 May 1960.   [70] See the list in Appendix 3, below.

EPILOGUE: THE MAN

By way of conclusion of this account of the life of Hersch Lauterpacht, it seems appropriate to recall briefly his principal characteristics.

HIS PERSONALITY

Hersch was brought up in an orthodox but not extreme Jewish family. He was imbued with a Jewish spirit that was not expressed in purely local terms. He absorbed in the family home a strong feeling of Zionism in its earliest form – a belief in the importance of the establishment of a Jewish National Home in the land of Israel that had for so long played a central part in Jewish history. It could not then be foreseen that the fulfilment of this ideal would in due course lead to the sad contentions that have marked the development of Israel and its relations with its neighbours since its establishment as a State in 1948. For Hersch, Zionism was a pure ideal to be pursued on the basis of historical knowledge, education and restraint.

He absorbed from his parents the ritual of the orthodox Jewish faith without being inclined to follow it in any detail. His attendance at synagogue was limited to the high holy days of the New Year and the Day of Atonement. When, many years later, he became a professor at Cambridge, he would go to the students' synagogue on such occasions in academic dress, wearing a gown and a mortar board, and would occupy a seat in the front row as befitted his status. At home, he would celebrate the Passover in traditional style, chanting the Hagadah (order of service for Passover) with the rhythm and intonation of his father before him and which still rings in my ears even though I cannot repeat it. He never denied his Jewishness but at the same time he did not make an open display of it. He joined in community matters but never sought a public position as a community leader. He regarded with silent contempt any attempt at concealment of Jewishness, as happened with a number of Jewish refugees who came to England in the 1930s, though he would have kept his views to himself and was even friendly with a number of them.

He was a man of remarkable intellectual energy. As the friends of his youth testified, he achieved leadership amongst them by his ability to organise, to speak, to memorise and to exercise tact and discretion. Although no one has spoken of any special physical strength on his part, his willingness to stand up to the anti-Semitism and oppression in Lwów evidenced a degree of physical courage. This kind of display, appropriate in Lwów and perhaps to some extent in Vienna was not required after he came to England. Instead, his physical vigour was reflected in the intensity of his commitment to his work. He pushed himself very hard, not only in his early days in London when he was trying to prove his worth at the LSE but also later on, for example in the resilience with which he managed his arduous lecture tour in the United States in 1940 and his assistance to the US Attorney-General in 1941–2. There were times, indeed, when he simply ran out of steam and had to take brief holidays.

He had a talent for making and keeping friends from his earliest Polish days, through his time in Vienna, and extending into his period at the LSE and Cambridge. And he achieved this without boastfulness or arrogance. If he had a weakness, it was that he did not suffer fools gladly and would become impatient with those who disagreed with him unless they stood on the firmest grounds. Yet he did not show this and would rather withdraw from the fray than have a confrontation. This restraint, however, did not extend to disagreements on points of law or where he felt that he was not being treated with proper respect.

His friendship with McNair is especially noteworthy. He clearly earned McNair's respect and liking at a very early stage in their relationship. McNair quickly appreciated not only Hersch's range of knowledge but also his willingness to place it at McNair's disposal – such as in his early years in England when he provided McNair with research assistance – though of course he must have learned a lot too from McNair's style, both personal and literary, as would anyone who has occasion to study the style of McNair's letters to him.

Hersch was a warm, welcoming and hospitable person. The correspondence is replete with mention of his welcoming visitors – often his colleagues and students – to lunch or tea at Cranmer Road. Tea was normally at about 4.30pm, often featuring in the Cambridge days a sponge cake from Fitzbillies. Though the cake shop still exists, the sponge, alas, has disappeared from its list of products. Little of this could have been achieved, however, without the caring and diligent support of Rachel. Children loved him; he would often dispense sweets which he carried in his pocket.

There can be no doubt that, even though he did not proclaim his distress, he felt deeply the loss of his parents, his brother and his sister in the Holocaust in Poland. He remained an intensely family man. His concern about money matters in times of difficulty was largely directed to ensuring that there was enough to support Rachel and me. He was vigorous in seeking to control the lives of his wife and son. When Rachel was alone in New York in 1941–3, his letters were full of advice, indeed instruction, verging on command, to her as to what to do to survive. And, as for his son, the wartime letters are an illuminating guide to how a young man should be trained. Though it was not an approach that would go down with children of a later generation, it never occurred to the son then to question or resent what he was told to do.

METHOD OF WORK

Hersch was a poor sleeper and relied constantly on sleeping pills to help him obtain a good night's rest. Because he slept so lightly, all movement in the house after he had gone to bed was forbidden; once woken, he had great difficulty in getting back to sleep.

One consequence of his sleeplessness was that he was, in general, an early riser. He would get up at about 7am and, dressed in sloppy clothes, not what he would wear when he went out, he would make himself some tea and go immediately to his study where he would work for an hour or more before breakfast. When working, he would often play classical music quietly on the wireless or gramophone. His taste ran to the older classics, especially Vivaldi, Bach, Mozart, Beethoven and Brahms. He had, indeed, at one time begun to learn to play the piano, but later on he only very occasionally touched the keyboard.

When living in Walm Lane, in Cricklewood, London, his study was at the back of the house, facing northwest over the garden. The two long sides of the room were covered with bookshelves which had been provided by the LSE. He wrote at a simple pine pedestal desk not more than four feet wide and about two and a half feet deep, varnished black. When he moved house to Cambridge in 1938, a year after he took up the Whewell Chair of International Law (he had spent the first year of his appointment living in Trinity while looking for a house; he eventually bought McNair's house, 6 Cranmer Road), his study was again at the back of the house, facing north towards the garden and the university rugby ground. The pine desk was replaced by a much grander mahogany one. Often, he would stand, somewhat precariously, on the brick wall separating the garden from the rugby ground to watch at least part of the match being played by the university team, usually on a Saturday afternoon. Friends would occasionally be asked to join him. But he was not knowledgeable about the game or really interested in it – in contrast to his neighbour, Professor Winton Thomas, the Regius Professor of Hebrew, who had in his earlier days played rugby for Wales.

The study was really the core of his life. He would spend most of his waking hours there except when eating meals, mostly done in the kitchen, save in those periods when there was resident domestic help in the house. Then, the dining room would be used. The timing of meals was exact – usually 1pm for lunch (1.20pm on Tuesdays and Thursdays in term time when he lectured from 12 noon to 1pm and then walked home) and 7pm for supper. He was very insistent on punctuality and would expect to be summoned to meals by the sound of a brass gong. Not much time would be spent eating except when guests were being entertained.

After breakfast, he would continue to work in the study in casual clothes, not dressing till just before he had to go out or receive a visitor. Most of his time was spent in research and writing. But, on his lecture days, he would spend two hours or so in preparation, then dress, and leave for the Squire Law Library shortly after 11am, unless he had arranged to see a research student there at some earlier time. He always walked to and from the Law School. He did not possess a bicycle or ever show an inclination to use one, though he once demonstrated that he knew how to ride. In those days, the use of motor cars was rare. He had bought one, a second-hand 1935 Standard saloon, for £90 in 1937. Although he succeeded in passing his driving test, he was never a confident driver, believing that 50 mph was the highest speed at which a car could safely be driven and imposing that limit on anyone else driving his car.

His lectures were very polished performances. In his early years at the LSE, he wrote out his lectures, which were typed by his most loyal secretary, Miss Gladys Bloch (later to become Mrs Bernard Lyons). Her friendship with the family was nobly demonstrated by her taking me each year, for a number of years, to a pantomime at Christmas. By the time that Hersch began to lecture at Cambridge, his mastery of the subject and his facility for speaking were such that he required no more in the way of notes than a single sheet of paper on which he had jotted down a few key headings. The presentation of his lectures, always including a humorous touch to lighten their substantive content, was widely admired and even attracted non-lawyers. But, for all the seeming ease of delivery, their presentation involved for him considerable stress and physical effort, so much so that he would perspire freely and have to change his shirt before starting for home.

His dress at lectures was always immaculate – a dark suit, white shirt and starched collar. When walking to the Law School he would invariably wear a black homburg hat and, if it was cold, an overcoat, and carry a briefcase. At the lecture itself, he wore his Doctor's black silk gown.

The nature and scope of international law in his most active days was such that the books and periodicals he had in his own library were mostly sufficient for research. Only occasionally would he look up material in the Squire Law Library. By reason of his editorship of *Oppenheim* and, later, of the *British Year Book of International Law*, he received complimentary copies of many books. Also, as editor of the *Annual Digest and Reports of Public International Law Cases* he was in constant touch with a number of foreign contributors and had unique access to the growing jurisprudence of international law. Nonetheless, as a member of the Committee of the Squire Law Library, he was active in trying within the limited library budget to ensure that its holdings were kept up to date.

When preparing an article he would compose a very rough outline, placing a few introductory words to each section at the head of separate sheets of paper. He would produce a first manuscript draft which would be typed by Mrs Lyons or, after he moved to Cambridge, by the devoted Mrs Jansen. There would then follow one or two further drafts, depending upon the complexity of the topic. He was a stylistic perfectionist and placed great store upon correct grammar and punctuation. His style, though elegant, was not light. It was influenced by his wide reading of English classics, not least by the ornate and rotund language of Lord Macaulay. He never made use of research assistants, except in connection with the *AD*, preferring to write everything himself.

He would seek intermittent relaxation from his research and writing by forays into the garden where on occasion he would dig or weed. As he attached importance to his lawn being free of weeds, lawn seed and a weeding fork were always to hand. He did not actually mow the lawn himself, preferring to contract this out. He also had some help from a part-time gardener who divided his day between waiting at table in Gonville and Caius College and spending a few hours in each of several gardens in the neighbourhood.

In those days, footwear was not as waterproof as it is today and Hersch was always worried about catching a cold if he got wet feet from walking on damp grass. If the lawn had to be crossed in such conditions, he would walk only on his heels, tipping his toes up in a manner aimed at minimising contact with the ground. The result was picturesque, to say the least.

In the garden, his favourite flowers were daffodils, hyacinths, crocuses, lilies of the valley, chrysanthemums, peonies, roses and gladioli. These were regarded as being only for external decoration and were therefore sacrosanct. Only rarely might they be cut for the house. He enjoyed pruning the fruit trees; there were some apples, plums and a particularly delicious variety of greengage.

He enjoyed the company of a black and white cat, Vitzi, inherited from some wartime lodgers in the house. His care for the animal was such that he would during the war often spend time standing in a queue at the butchers to buy food. I can recall no reason why he never got himself a dog, who would have been a great companion to him on his walks.

HIS POLITICS

Once he left Poland, where he had been politically active in the sense of pursing his Zionist interests and organising his contemporaries to resist local anti-Semitism, Hersch had little time for politics. His political interests were limited to the organisation of Jewish students in Vienna and, when he reached England, to the organisation of the World Union of Jewish Students. But, once in England, he did not become involved in domestic politics – heeding in this respect McNair's warning to keep clear of politics. Inevitably, in the left-wing atmosphere of the LSE, he came into friendly contact with Labour Party adherents. However, he did not join a political party. The closest he came to any political activity was the preparation of the Peace Act in 1934,[1] and even then he was insulated from direct Labour Party connection by the League of Nations Union – a non-party body. From time to time in the 1930s and 1940s, he was approached to advise on Zionist Organization matters but, again, was not involved in Zionist politics. And, occasionally, he advised on matters specially affecting Jewish people. At the same time, he was definitely not a Conservative, though he never had occasion to proclaim his views.

By contrast with his passivity in national political matters, he had a profound interest in international politics. His views on, for example, human rights were rooted in the importance that he attached to the limitation of national sovereignty and his belief in the emergence of a peaceful, organised world order based on international law. In his view that all international disputes could be settled on a basis of law he was, perhaps, a bit unrealistic. It is in the nature of inter-State political disputes that many of them involve one or the other party in claiming

---

[1] See p. 72 above.

a change in the law, so that existing law cannot provide a solution. But he was undoubtedly correct in his view that mechanisms, either judicial or conciliatory, should be invoked for the settlement of disputes. Beyond these general views – elaborated in great detail, for example, in *The Function of Law* – international politics did not play a major role in his thinking.

Before I began this biography, I thought that I knew my father fairly well. Up to a point this was true, but it has only been after examining his life in greater detail that I have come to realise the true extent of his remarkable quality. It is to be hoped that the preceding pages have not failed to do appropriate justice to his memory.

APPENDIX I

THE PUBLISHED WRITINGS OF SIR HERSCH LAUTERPACHT

Where publications have been reprinted in the *Collected Papers*, the volume and page number appear next to the citation. The publications are listed in chronological order.

BOOKS

Private Law Sources and Analogies of International Law (with Special Reference to International Arbitration), London: Longmans, Green & Co. Ltd, 1927, xxiii + 326 pp.

The Function of Law in the International Community, Oxford: Clarendon Press, 1933, xxiv + 452 pp.

The Development of International Law by the Permanent Court of International Justice, London: Longmans, Green & Co. Ltd, 1934, ix + 111 pp.

An International Bill of the Rights of Man, New York: Columbia University Press, 1945, x + 230 pp.

Recognition in International Law, Cambridge: Cambridge University Press, 1947, xx + 442 pp.

International Law and Human Rights, London: F. A. Praeger, 1950, xvi + 475 pp.

The Development of International Law by the International Court, London: Stevens & Sons Ltd, 1958, xix + 408 pp.

EDITORIAL PUBLICATIONS

Annual Digest and Reports of Public International Law Cases

Volume number	Volume date	Date of publication
1	1919–22 (with Sir John Fischer Williams)	1932 (Preface, 1 December 1932)
2	1923–4 (with Sir John Fischer Williams)	1933 (Preface, 1 July 1933)

Volume number	Volume date	Date of publication
3	1925–6 (with Dr Arnold D. McNair)	1929 (Preface, 31 May 1929)
4	1927–8 (with Dr Arnold D. McNair)	1931 (Preface, 1 October 1931)
5	1929–30	1935 (Preface, 1 July 1935)
6	1931–2	1938 (Preface, May 1938)
7	1933–4	1940 (Preface, December 1939)
8	1935–7	1941 (Preface, July 1941)
9	1938–40	1942 (Preface, September 1942)
10	1941–2	1945 (Preface, 1 December 1944)
11	1919–42 (supplementary volume)	1947 (Preface, March 1947)
12	1943–5	1949 (Preface, February 1949)
13	1946	1951 (Preface, July 1951)
14	1947	1951 (Preface, August 1951)
15	1948	1953 (Preface, 1 May 1953)
16	1949	1955 (Preface, May 1955)
17	1950	1956 (Preface, March 1956)
18	1951	1957 (Preface, January 1957)
19	1952	1957 (Preface, January 1957)
20	1953	1957 (Preface, August 1957)
21	1954	1957 (Preface, August 1957)
22	1955	1958 (Preface, September 1958)
23	1956	1960 (Preface, October 1959)
24	1957 (completed by E. Lauterpacht)	1961 (Preface, April 1961)

Oppenheim, *International Law*

Volume number	Edition	Date of publication
II	5th	1935 (Preface, 1 June 1935)
I	5th	1937 (Preface, July 1937)
II	6th	1940 (Preface, June 1940)
II	6th revised	1944 (Preface, August 1944)
I	6th	1947 (Preface, October 1946)
I	7th	1948 (Preface, March 1948)
II	7th	1952 (Preface, November 1951)
I	8th	1955 (Preface, 1 October 1954)

British Year Book of International Law

Volume number	Volume date	Date of publication
21	1944	1944
22	1945	1945
23	1946	1946
24	1947	1948
25	1948	1949
26	1949	1950
27	1950	1951
28	1951	1952
29	1952	1953
30	1953	1954
31	1954	1956

'The Law of War on Land', Part III of the *Manual of Military Law* (1958), xxvi + 374 pp.

Brierly, *The Basis of Obligation in International Law and Other Papers* (with C. H. M. Waldock) (1958)

COURSES OF LECTURES DELIVERED AT THE HAGUE ACADEMY OF INTERNATIONAL LAW

'La Théorie des différends non-justiciables en droit international' (1930-IV) 34 *Hague Recueil* 499–653 (*Collected Papers*, Vol. 4, p. 449)

'Les Travaux préparatoires et l'inteprétation des traités' (1934-II) 48 *Hague Recueil* 713–819 (*Collected Papers*, Vol. 4, p. 449)

'Règles générales du droit de la paix' (1937-IV) 62 *Hague Recueil* 99–419 (*Collected Papers*, Vol. 1, p. 179)

'International Protection of Human Rights' (1947-I) 70 *Hague Recueil* 5–107

ARTICLES AND PAPERS

'The Teaching of Law in Vienna' (1923) *Journal of the Society of the Public Teachers in Law* 43–5 (*Collected Papers*, Vol. 5, p. 711)

'Westlake and Present Day International Law' (1925) 5 *Economica* 307–25 (*Collected Papers*, Vol. 2, p. 385)

'The United States and the Permanent Court of International Justice' (1926) *Survey of International Affairs* 80–98 (*Collected Papers*, Vol. 5, p. 380)

'Spinoza and International Law' (1927) 8 *BYIL* 89–107 (*Collected Papers*, Vol. 2, p. 366)

'Revolutionary Activities by Private Persons against Foreign States' (1928) 22 *AJIL* 105–30 (*Collected Papers*, Vol. 3, p. 251)

'Revolutionary Propaganda by Governments' (1928) 13 *Transactions of the Grotius Society* 143 (*Collected Papers*, Vol. 3, p. 279)

'Sukcesja pastw w odiesieniu do zobowiazan prywatnoprawnych' (1928) *Glos Prawa* 5 (trans. 'Succession of States with respect to private law obligations' in 'The Voice of Law', an inter-war legal journal) (*Collected Papers*, Vol. 3, p. 121, English translation)

'The Doctrine of Non-Justiciable Disputes in International Law' (1928) 8 *Economica* 277–317 (*Collected Papers*, Vol. 5, p. 26)

'The Legal Remedy in Case of Excess of Jurisdiction' (1928) 9 *BYIL* 117–20 (*Collected Papers*, Vol. 5, p. 401)

'Decisions of Municipal Courts as a Source of International Law' (1929) 10 *BYIL* 65–95 (*Collected Papers*, Vol. 2, p. 238)

'Dissenting Opinions of National Judges and the Revision of the Statute of the Court' (1930) 11 *BYIL* 182–6 (*Collected Papers*, Vol. 5, p. 184)

'The Absence of an International Legislature and the Compulsory Jurisdiction of International Tribunals' (1930) 11 *BYIL* 134–7 (*Collected Papers*, Vol. 5, p. 201)

'The British Reservations to the Optional Clause' (1930) 10 *Economica* 137–72 (*Collected Papers*, Vol. 5, p. 347)

'The So-Called Anglo-American and Continental Schools of Thought in International Law' (1931) 12 *BYIL* 31–62 (*Collected Papers*, Vol. 2, p. 452)

'Japan and the Covenant' (1932) 3 *Political Quarterly* 174–94 (*Collected Papers*, Vol. 5, p. 409)

'The Nature of International Law and General Jurisprudence' (1932) 12 *Economica* 301–20 (*Collected Papers*, Vol. 2, p. 3)

'Boycott in International Relations' (1933) 14 *BYIL* 125–40 (*Collected Papers*, Vol. 3, p. 297)

'Kelsen's Pure Science of Law' (1933) *Modern Theories of Law* 105–38 (*Collected Papers*, Vol. 2, p. 404)

'"Resort to War" and the Covenant During the Manchurian Dispute' (1934) 28 *AJIL* 43–60 (*Collected Papers*, Vol. 5, p. 444)

'The Pact of Paris and the Budapest Articles of Interpretation' (1934) 20 *Transactions of the Grotius Society* 178–204 (*Collected Papers*, Vol. 5, p. 424)

'Some Observations on Preparatory Work in the Interpretation of Treaties' (1935) 48 *Harvard Law Review* 549–91

'Contracts to Break a Contract' (1936) 52 *LQR* 494–529 (*Collected Papers*, Vol. 4, p. 340)

'International Law after the Covenant', (1936) (10th Series) *Problems of Peace* 37–56 (*Collected Papers*, Vol. 2, p.145)

'Neutrality and Collective Security' (1936) 2 *Politica* 133–55 (*Collected Papers*, Vol. 5, p. 611)

'The Covenant as the "Higher Law"' (1936) 17 *BYIL* 54–65 (*Collected Papers*, Vol. 4, p. 326)

'Peaceful Change – The Legal Aspect', in *Peaceful Change – An International Problem* (ed. C. A. W. Manning) (1937), pp. 135–68 (*Collected Papers*, Vol. 5, p. 7)

'The Credentials of the Abyssinian Delegation to the Seventeenth Assembly of the League of Nations' (1937) 18 *BYIL* 184–6 (*Collected Papers*, Vol. 3, p. 589)

'The Cristina' (1938) 52 *LQR* 339–46 (*Collected Papers*, Vol. 3, p. 374)

'Insurrection et Piraterie' (1939) 20 *Revue Générale de Droit International Public* (Series 3) 513–49

'The Form of Foreign Office Certificates' (1939) 20 *BYIL* 125–8

'Recognition of Insurgents as a De Facto Government' (1939–40) 3 *Modern Law Review* 1–20

'Is International Law a Part of the Law of England?' (1940) 25 *Transactions of the Grotius Society* 51–88 (*Collected Papers*, Vol. 2, p. 537)

'Resurrection of the League' (1941) 12 *Political Quarterly* 121–33 (*Collected Papers*, Vol. 3, p. 592)

'The Principle of Non-Recognition in International Law', in *Legal Problems in the Far Eastern Conflict* (1941), pp. 129–56

'Implied Recognition' (1944) 21 *BYIL* 123–50

'The Law of Nations, the Law of Nature and the Rights of Man' (1944) 29 *Transactions of the Grotius Society* 1–33

'Recognition of States in International Law' (1944) 53 *Yale Law Journal* 385–458

'De Facto Recognition, Withdrawal of Recognition and Conditional Recognition' (1945) 22 *BYIL* 164–90

'The Law of Nature and the Punishment of War Crimes' (1944) 21 *BYIL* 58–95 (*Collected Papers*, Vol. 5, p. 491)

'Recognition of Governments, I' (1945) 45 *Columbia Law Review* 815–64 (*Collected Papers*, Vol. 3, p. 113)

'Recognition of Governments, II' (1946) 46 *Columbia Law Review* 37–68 (*Collected Papers*, Vol. 3, p. 113)

'The Grotian Tradition in International Law' (1946) 23 *BYIL* 1–53 (*Collected Papers*, Vol. 2, p. 307)

'Allegiance, Diplomatic Protection and Criminal Jurisdiction over Aliens' (1947) 9 *CLJ* 330–48 (*Collected Papers*, Vol. 3, p. 221)

'An International Bill of Rights', *The Times*, 26 July 1947 (*Collected Papers*, Vol. 3, p. 407)

'The Subjects of the Law of Nations, I' (1947) 63 *LQR* 438–60 (*Collected Papers*, Vol. 2, p. 487)

'The Subjects of the Law of Nations, II' (1948) 64 *LQR* 97–119 (*Collected Papers*, Vol. 2, p. 487)

'Human Rights', Statement at the Brussels Conference of the International Law Association, Report to the International Law Association, Report of the Forty-Third Conference of the International Law Association, 1948, pp. 29–44

'Human Rights, the Charter of the United Nations, and the International Bill of the Rights of Man', Report to the International Law Association, Report of the Forty-Third Conference of the International Law Association, 1948, pp. 80–138

'The Universal Declaration of Human Rights' (1948) 25 *BYIL* 354–81

'Restrictive Interpretation and the Principle of Effectiveness in the Interpretation of Treaties' (1949) 26 *BYIL* 48–85 (*Collected Papers*, Vol. 3, p. 410)

'Survey of International Law in Relation to the Work of Codification of the International Law Commission', memorandum submitted by the Secretary-General of the United Nations, New York, 1949 (*Collected Papers*, Vol. 1, p. 445)

'The Nationality of Denationalized Persons' (1949) *Jewish Yearbook of International Law* 164–85 (*Collected Papers*, Vol. 3, p. 383)

'Towards an International Bill of Rights', talk given on the Third Programme of the BBC, *The Listener*, Vol. 42, 3 November 1949, pp. 747–8 (*Collected Papers*, Vol. 3, p. 410)

'De l'Interprétation des traités', Rapport et projet de résolutions présentés à l'Institut de Droit International (1950-1) 43 *Annuaire* 366–460 (*Collected Papers*, Vol. 4, pp. 393 and 528)

'Observations on the Report of Professor de la Pradelle' (1950-1) 43 *Annuaire* 42 (*Collected Papers*, Vol. 4, p. 90)

'Recognition of China', *The Times*, 6 January 1950

'Sovereignty over Submarine Areas' (1950) 27 *BYIL* 376–433 (*Collected Papers*, Vol. 3, p. 143)

'The Proposed European Court of Human Rights' (1950) 35 *Transactions of the Grotius Society* 25–47

'Foreword' to Lissitzyn, *The International Court of Justice* (New York, 1951), pp. v–xiv

'The Problem of Jurisdictional Immunities of Foreign States' (1951) 28 *BYIL* 220–72 (*Collected Papers*, Vol. 3, p. 315)

'De l'Interprétation des traités', Observations complémentaires et projet définitif de résolutions, présentés à l'Institut de Droit International (1952-I) 44 *Annuaire* 197–223 (*Collected Papers*, Vol. 4, p. 393)

'Implications of the Norwegian Fisheries Case', *The Times*, 8 January 1952

'The Hague Judgment' (in the Anglo-Iranian Oil Company Case), *The Times*, 30 and 31 July 1952 (*Collected Papers*, Vol. 3, p. 242, and *Collected Papers*, Vol. 5, p. 231, respectively)

'The Problem of the Revision of the Law of War' (1952) 29 *BYIL* 360–82 (*Collected Papers*, Vol. 5, p. 582)

'Law of Treaties', *Yearbook of the International Law Commission* (1953-II) 90–166 (*Collected Papers*, Vol. 4, pp. 101–74, 182–233, 243, 273–388)

'Rules of Warfare in an Unlawful War', in *Law and Politics in the World Community (Essays on Hans Kelsen's Pure Theory and Related Problems in International Law)* (ed. G. A. Lipsky) (1953), pp. 89–113

'The Limits of the Operation of the Laws of War' (1953) 30 *BYIL* 206–43 (*Collected Papers*, Vol. 5, p. 542)

'Law of Treaties', *Yearbook of the International Law Commission* (1954-II) 123–39 (*Collected Papers*, Vol. 4, pp. 174–81, 234–42)

'Some Possible Solutions of the Problem of Reservations to Treaties' (1954) 39 *Transactions of the Grotius Society* 97–118

'The Rose Mary' (1954) 12 *CLJ* 20–2 (*Collected Papers*, Vol. 3, p. 245)

'Codification and Development of International Law' (1955) 49 *AJIL* 16–43 (*Collected Papers*, Vol. 2, p. 269)

'Brierly's Contribution to International Law' (1955–6) 32 *BYIL* 1–19 (*Collected Papers*, Vol. 2, p. 431)

'Some Observations on the Prohibition of "Non Liquet" and the Completeness of the Legal Order' (1958) *Symbolae Verzijl* 196–221 (*Collected Papers*, Vol. 2, p. 213)

'International Law and Colonial Questions, 1870–1914', in *Cambridge History of the British Empire*, Vol. III (1959), pp. 667–701 (with R. Y. Jennings) (*Collected Papers*, Vol. 2, p. 95)

INTERNATIONAL COURT OF JUSTICE, SEPARATE AND DISSENTING OPINIONS

South-West Africa – Voting Procedure, ICJ Reports 1955, p. 67: Separate Opinion, pp. 90–123 (*Collected Papers*, Vol. 3, p. 514)

Admissibility of Hearings of Petitioners by the Committee on South-West Africa, ICJ Reports 1956, p. 23: Separate Opinion, pp. 35–59 (*Collected Papers*, Vol. 3, p. 549)

Application of the Convention of 1902 Governing the Guardianship of Infants, ICJ Reports 1956, p. 55: Separate Opinion, pp. 74–101 (*Collected Papers*, Vol. 4, p. 539)

Case of Certain Norwegian Loans, ICJ Reports 1957, p. 9: Separate Opinion, pp. 34–66 (*Collected Papers*, Vol. 5, p. 235)

Interhandel Case (Preliminary Objections), ICJ Reports 1959, p. 6; Dissenting Opinion, pp. 95–122 (*Collected Papers*, Vol. 5, p. 276)

Aerial Incident Case of July 27, 1955, ICJ Reports 1959, p. 127: Joint Dissenting Opinion (with Judge Wellington Koo and Sir Percy Spender), pp. 156–94 (*Collected Papers*, Vol. 5, p. 306)

Sovereignty over Certain Frontier Land, ICJ Reports 1959, p. 209; Declaration, pp. 230–2 (*Collected Papers*, Vol. 3, p. 207)

BOOK REVIEWS

Die Abänderung völkerrechtsgemässen Landesrechts, grundsätzliche Untersuchungen zum Englischen, Amerikanischen, Deutschen und Oesterreichischen Recht (1927), G. A. Wells: (1928) BYIL 210–11

Die Fortbildung der internationalen Schiedsgerichtsbarkeit seit dem Weltrieg, besonders durch den Locarno-Pakt (1927), P. Kaufmann; *Die Fortbildung der internationalen Schiedsgerichtsbarkeit seit dem Weltrieg* (1927), H. W. Thieme; and *Der völkerrechtliche Garantievertrag, insbesondere seit der Entstehung des Genfer Völkerbundes* (1927), O. Bussman: (1928) BYIL 197–8

Die völkerrechtliche Haftung des Staates, inbesondere bei Handlungen Privater (1927), K. Strupp: (1928) BYIL 209–10

Die völkerrechtliche Option (1925–8), J. L. Kunz: (1928) BYIL 199–200

Les effets des transformations des États sur leurs dettes publiques et autres obligations financières (1927), A. N. Sack: (1928) 10 *Journal of Comparative Legislation* (3rd series) 164–7

Théorie de la Société des Nations (1927), R. Redslob: (1928) BYIL 206–7

Die elsass-lothringische Staatsangehörigkeitsregelung und das Völkerrecht. Eine rechtsvergleichende Studie der Problem der Staatsangehörigkeitsregelung bei Gebietsveränderungen (1929), W. Schätzel; *Der Lausanner Vertrag und der griechisch-türkische Bevölkerungsaustausch* (1929), G. Streit; and *Russland und Westeuropa (Russlands historische Sonderentwicklung in der europäischen Völkergemeinschaft)* (1928): (1929) 10 *BYIL* 284–6

Das Wesen des Völkerrechts und Kritik der Völkerrechtsleugner (1930), G. A. Walz: (1930) 11 *BYIL* 262–3

The Present Juridical Status of the British Dominions in International Law, P. J. Noel Baker: (1930) 30 *Economica* 330–3

Die zwangsweise Durchsetzung im Völkerrecht (1930), H. van Bardeleben: (1931) 12 *BYIL* 212

Internationale Rechtspflege, ihr Wesen und ihre Grenzen, Hans Morgenthau: (1931) 12 *BYIL* 229–30

Lehrbuch des Völkerrechts (1930), A. Hold-Ferneck: (1931) 12 *BYIL* 220–1

Das Verhältnis der französischen Bundnisvertrage zum Volkerbundpakt und zum Pakt von Locarno (1932), F. Krämer: (1933) 14 *BYIL* 221–2

Die Voraussetzungen für die Andwendung von Völkerbund-zwangsmassnahmen (1931), M. Rottger: (1933) 14 *BYIL* 222–3

Einstweilige Verfüngen des Weltgerichtshofs, ihr Wesen und ihre Grenzen (1932), H. G. Niemeyer: (1933) 14 *BYIL* 222

Lehrbuch des Völkerrechts (1932), A. Hold-Ferneck: (1933) 14 *BYIL* 211

Verträge in Gunsten und in Lasten Dritter im Volkerrecht (1932), C. H. Winkler: (1933) 14 *BYIL* 223

De Jure Belli Libri Tres (2 vols., 1933), ed. J. B. Scott, trans. J. C. Rolfe: (1934) 50 *LQR* 425–6

Der Internationale Richter (1934), V. V. Bruns: (1935) 16 *BYIL* 217

Neutralization, Befriedung, Entmilitarisierung (1933), K. Strupp: (1934) 15 *BYIL* 215

Kriegsrecht und Neutralitätsrecht (1935), J. L. Kunz: (1936) 17 *BYIL* 228–9

Geschichte des Völkerrechts (1936), A. Wegner: (1937) 18 *BYIL* 245

La Rappresentanza nel Diritto Internazionale (1936), A. P. Sereni: (1937) 18 *BYIL* 245

Gebietshoheit über die B und C Mandate (1937), W. Gaupp: (1938) 19 *BYIL* 272

Völkerrecht (1937), A. von Verdoss: (1938) 19 *BYIL* 285–6

International Legislation, Vol. 4 (1937), ed. M. O. Hudson: (1939) 20 *BYIL* 178–9

International Responsibility of States for Denial of Justice (1939), A. V. Freeman: (1939) 55 *LQR* 591–3

A Collection of Neutrality Laws, Regulations and Treaties of Various Countries (1939), ed. F. Deák and P. C. Jessup: (1941) 7 *CLJ* 428

Control of Aliens in the British Commonwealth of Nations (1940), C. F. Fraser: (1941) 7 *CLJ* 427

Diplomatic Correspondence of the United States: Mexico (1937), ed. W. R. Manning: (1941) 7 *CLJ* 181

Diplomatic Correspondence of the United States: Spain (1939), ed. W. R. Manning: (1941) 7 *CLJ* 303

Diplomatic Correspondence of the United States: Texas and Venezuela (1939), ed. W. R. Manning: (1941) 7 *CLJ* 429

Law, the State and the International Community (2 vols., 1939), J. B. Scott: (1941) 7 *CLJ* 428–9

Le règlement conventionnel des conséquences de remuniements territoriaux. Considérations suggérées par l'expérience de Haute-Silesie (1940), G. Kaekembeeck: (1941) 7 *CLJ* 430

The English Navigation Laws. A Seventeenth Century Experiment in Social Engineering (1939), L. A. Harper: (1941) 7 *CLJ* 430

Diplomatic Correspondence of the United States: Canadian Relations, 1784–1860, ed. W. R. Manning: (1942) 8 *CLJ* 229

Protection of Coastal Fisheries in International Law (1942), S. A. Riesenfeld: (1942) 8 *CLJ* 229

The Conference of Ambassadors (Paris 1920–31) (1942), G. P. Pink: (1942) 8 *CLJ* 223

Digest of International Law (3 vols., 1940–2), G. H. Hackworth: (1943) 6 *Modern Law Review* 251–2

Legal Effects of War (2nd ed., 1944), A. D. McNair: (1944) 21 *BYIL* 253–4

The International Law of the Sea (1943), P. A. Higgins and C. J. Colombos: (1943) 8 *CLJ* 334

A Study of War (2 vols., 1942), Q. Wright: (1944) 21 *BYIL* 265–6

Diplomatic Correspondence of the United States: Canadian Relations, 1784–1860 (3 vols, 1940–3), ed. W. R. Manning: (1944) 21 *BYIL* 245–6

International Economic Law of Occupation (1942), E. H. Feilchenfeld: (1944) 60 *LQR* 95

International Law and Totalitarian Lawlessness (1943), G. Schwarzenberger: (1944) 21 *BYIL* 261

The British Commonwealth at War (1943), ed. W. Y. Elliott and H. D. Hall: (1944) 21 *BYIL* 237–8

The International Law of the Sea (1943), A. P. Higgins and C. J. Colombos: (1944) 21 *BYIL* 241–2

Trading with the Enemy in World War II (1943), M. Domke: (1944) 21 *BYIL* 237

Were the Minorities Treaties a Failure?, J. R. Robinson, O. Karbach, M. Laserson, N. Robinson and M. Vichniac: (1944) 21 *BYIL* 259–60

Axis Rule in Occupied Europe (1944), R. Lemkin: (1945) 9 *CLJ* 140

Digest of International Law (7 vols., 1940–4), G. H. Hackworth: (1945) 22 *BYIL* 310–1

Headquarters of International Institutions: A Study of Their Location and Status (1945), C. W. Jenks: (1945) 22 *BYIL* 312–3

Justice and World Society (1945), C. Stapleton: (1945) 9 *CLJ* 135–6

Prisoners of War: A Study in Development of International Law (1942), W. S. Flory: (1945) 9 *CLJ* 134–5

The Czechoslovak Cause: An Account of the Problems of International Law in Relation to Czechoslovakia (1944), E. Taborsky: (1945) 9 *CLJ* 140–1

A Guide to the Practice of International Conferences (1945), V. D. Pastuhov: (1946) 9 *CLJ* 255

Essential Human Rights. A Symposium (1946), ed. W. D. Lewis and J. R. Ellinston: (1946) 23 *BYIL* 497

International Law (1946), G. Schwarzenberger: (1946) 9 *CLJ* 258–9

International Law Chiefly as Interpreted and Applied by the United States (2nd edn, 3 vols., 1945), C. C. Hyde: (1946) 23 *BYIL* 505–7

Le Préambule de la Charte base idéologique de l'ONU (1946), A. Salomon: (1946) 23 *BYIL* 518

League of Nations and National Minorities: An Experiment (1946), P. de Azcarate: (1946) 9 *CLJ* 264–5

Lehrbuch des Völkerrechts. Unter Berücksichtigung der internationalen und schweizerischen Praxis (1947), P. Guggenheim: (1946) 23 *BYIL* 502–3

Military Occupation and the Rule of Law (1944), E. Fraenkel: (1946) 9 *CLJ* 256

Political Reconstruction, Karl Lowenstein: (1946) 23 *BYIL* 510–1

The International Secretariat: A Great Experiment in International Administration (1945), E. K. Ranshofen-Werthheimer: (1946) 9 *CLJ* 265

The Pure Theory of Law (1945), W. Ebenstein: (1946) 9 *CLJ* 256–7

Modern Law of Nations, an Introduction (1947), P. Jessup: (1947) 24 *BYIL* 502–5

The Collected Papers of John Bassett Moore (1944): (1947) 9 *CLJ* 394

Legal Effects of War (3rd edn, 1948), A. D. McNair: (1948) 25 *BYIL* 487–8

Allgemeine Lehren de Staatsangehörigkeitsrecht (1947), A. N. Makarov: (1949) 10 *CLJ* 339–40

Federal Protection of Civil Rights – Quest for a Sword (1947), R. K. Carr; and *A Study of Judicial Review in Virginia 1789–1928* (1947), M. V. Nelson: (1949) 10 *CLJ* 337–9

Historical Survey of the Question of International Criminal Jurisdiction (1948), *Ways and Means of Making the Evidence of Customary International Law More Readily Available* (1949), *Survey of International Law in Relation to the*

Work of Codification of the International Law Commission (1949), *Preparatory Study Concerning a Draft Declaration of the Rights and Duties of States* (1948), *The Charter and Judgment of the Nuremberg Tribunal: History and Analysis* (1949), *Report of the International Law Commission Covering Its First Session from 12 April to 9 June 1949*, all published by the United States: (1949) 26 *BYIL* 530–1

International Law (3rd revised edn, 1948), C. G. Fenwick: (1949) 26 *BYIL* 540–1

Interpretations of Modern Legal Philosophies: Essays in Honour of Roscoe Pound (1947), ed. P. Sayre: (1949) 10 *CLJ* 285–7

La Technique et les principes du droit public. Études en l'honneur de Georges Scelle (2 vols., 1950), Librarie générale de droit et de jurisprudence: (1949) 26 *BYIL* 548–50

Prisoners of War: A Symposium (1948), Institute of World Policy: (1949) 10 *CLJ* 336–7

Rediscovery of Justice (1947), F. R. Bienenfeld: (1949) 10 *CLJ* 299

Reports of International Arbitral Awards (3 vols., 1948–9), United Nations: (1949) 26 *BYIL* 543–4

Systematic Survey of Treaties for the Pacific Settlement of International Disputes, 1928–48 (1949), Secretariat of the United Nations: (1949) 26 *BYIL* 551–2

Yearbook of Human Rights for 1947 (1949), United Nations: (1949) 26 *BYIL* 555–6

Law and Peace (1950), E. D. Dickenson: (1950) 27 *BYIL* 487–8

Law of the United Nations (1950), H. Kelsen: (1950) 27 *BYIL* 489–90

Völkerrecht (2nd revised edn, 1950), A. Verdoss: (1950) 27 *BYIL* 512

Law and Society in the Relations of States (1951), P. E. Corbett: (1951) 28 *BYIL* 424–5

The American Mind: An Interpretation of American Thought and Character since the 1880s (1950), H. S. Commager: (1951) 11 *CLJ* 136–7

The Law of Nations. Cases, Documents and Notes (2nd edn), ed. H. W. Briggs: (1951) 28 *BYIL* 419–20

Traité de droit international public (2 vols., 1951), M. Sibert: (1951) 28 *BYIL* 438–9

History of the Second World War, Vol. 1, *The Economic Blockade* (1952), W. N. Medlicott: (1952) 29 *BYIL* 514–5

Year Book of the United Nations, 1951, Department of Public Information, United Nations, and *Year Book on Human Rights, 1951* (1952), United Nations: (1952) 29 *BYIL* 489

Documents and Speeches on British Commonwealth Affairs, 1931–1952 (2 vols., 1953): (1953) 30 *BYIL* 564–5

The International Law Standard in Treaties of the United States (1953), R. Wilson: (1953) 30 *BYIL* 567–8

European Year Book (1955), ed. B. Landheer and A. H. Robertson: (1954) 31 *BYIL* 485–6

Repertory Practice of the United Nations Organs (1955), Secretariat of the United Nations: (1954) 31 *BYIL* 490–2

The International Court of Justice. An Essay in Political and Legal Theory (1957), S. Rosenne: (1958) 7 *ICLQ* 199–202

BIOGRAPHICAL AND ACADEMIC WRITINGS ON SIR HERSCH LAUTERPACHT

Friedmann, Wolfgang G., 'Sir Hersch Lauterpacht and the International Court' (1959) 45 *Virginia Law Review* 407

Andrassy, J., 'Hersch Lauterpacht, In Memoriam' (1960) 7 *Jugoslovenska Revija za Medunarodno Pravo* 151

Jenks, C. Wilfred, 'Hersch Lauterpacht – The Scholar as Prophet' (1960) 36 *BYIL* 1

Stone, F., 'In Memoriam' (1960) 35 *Tulane Law Review* 1

'Hersch Lauterpacht', 10 *ICLQ* 1 (1961) (tributes by Kelsen, McNair, Barquin, Verzijl, Jessup, Fitzmaurice, Baxter, Klaestad); McNair and Kelsen's tributes are republished in (1997) 8 *EJIL*

Baxter, R., and Jessup, P., 'Contribution of Sir Hersch Lauterpacht to the Development of International Law' (1961) 55 *AJIL* 97–103

Bentwich, N., *Studies in Public International Law in Memory of Sir Hersch Lauterpacht*, ed. N. Feinberg (Faculty of Law, Hebrew University, Jerusalem, 1961)

Fitzmaurice, Gerald, 'Hersch Lauterpacht – The Scholar as Judge – Part I' (1961) 37 *BYIL* 1

Guggenheim, P., 'Sir Hersch Lauterpacht (1897–1960)' (1961-II) 49 *Annuaire* 529

Rosenne, Shabtai, 'Sir Hersch Lauterpacht's Concept of the Task of the International Judge' (1961) 55 *AJIL* 825

Fitzmaurice, Gerald, 'Hersch Lauterpacht – The Scholar as Judge – Part II' (1962) 38 *BYIL* 1

Yoran, E., 'Sir Hersch Lauterpacht' (1962) 18 *Hapraklit* 376

Fitzmaurice, Gerald, 'Hersch Lauterpacht – The Scholar as Judge – Part III' (1963) 39 *BYIL* 133

McNair, A., 'Hersch Lauterpacht 1897–1960', in *Proceedings of the British Academy*, Vol. 47 (London: Oxford University Press, 1963), pp. 871–85

Feinberg, N., 'Hersch Lauterpacht – Jurist and Thinker' (1968) 3 *Israel Law Review* 333–42

Fitzmaurice, Gerald, 'Hersch Lauterpacht and His Attitude to the Judicial Function' (1979) 50 *BYIL* 1

Stone, Dorothy, 'Sir Hersch Lauterpacht: Teacher, Writer and Judge – A Presidential Address, 29 July 1982' (1981–2) 28 *Jewish Historical Society of England Papers* 102

Friedlander, Robert A., 'Lauterpacht, Hersch', in Warran F. Kuehl (ed.), *Biographical Dictionary of Internationalists* (Westport, CT: Greenwood Press, 1983), p. 422

Herzog, Chaim, 'Sir Hersch Lauterpacht: An Appraisal' (1997) 8 *EJIL* 299

Jennings, Robert, 'Hersch Lauterpacht: A Personal Recollection' (1997) 8 *EJIL* 301

Kelsen, Hans, 'Tributes to Sir Hersch Lauterpacht' (1997) 8 *EJIL* 309

Koskenniemi, Martti, 'Lauterpacht: The Victorian Tradition in International Law' (1997) 8 *EJIL* 215

Lauterpacht, Elihu Sir, 'Hersch Lauterpacht: 1897–1960' (1997) 8 *EJIL* 313

Schwebel, Stephen M., 'Hersch Lauterpacht: Fragments for a Portrait' (1997) 8 *EJIL* 305

Scobbie, Iain G. M., 'The Theorist as Judge: Hersch Lauterpacht's Concept of the International Judicial Function' (1997) 8 *EJIL* 264

Koskenniemi, Martti, 'Lauterpacht: The Victoria Tradition in International Law', in *The Gentle Civilizer of Nations: The Rise and Fall of International Law 1870–1960* (Cambridge: Cambridge University Press, 2001), pp. 353–412

Koskenniemi, Martti, 'Hersch Lauterpacht and the Development of International Criminal Law' (2004) 2 *Journal of International Criminal Justice* 810–25

Simpson, Brian, 'Hersch Lauterpacht and the Genesis of the Age of Human Rights' (2004) 120 *LQR* 49

Apple, James G., 'Leading Figures in International Law: Sir Hersch Lauterpacht (1897–1960)' (2006) 1(5) *International Judicial Monitor*, available at www.judicialmonitor.org/archive_1206/leadingfigures.html

Carty, Anthony, 'Hersch Lauterpacht: A Powerful Eastern European Figure in International Law', in Lauri Mälksoo *et al.*, (2008) *Baltic Yearbook of International Law* 83–111

Koskenniemi, Martti, 'The Function of Law in the International Community: 75 Years After', Keynote Paper, Opening Plenary

Session at the Lauterpacht Centre for International Law 25th Anniversary Symposium, Cambridge, 11–12 July 2008

Nishi, Taira, 'Hersch Lauterpacht as a Positivist. Understood in the Context of Methodological Argument' (2008) *Kansai University Review of Law and Politics* 29

Vrdoljak, Ana Filipa, 'Human Rights and Genocide: The Work of Lauterpacht and Lemkin in Modern International Law' (2009) 20 *EJIL* 1163–94

APPENDIX 3

OBITUARIES OF SIR HERSCH LAUTERPACHT

C. J. Hamson, 'Lauterpacht, Sir Hersch (1897–1960)', *Oxford Dictionary of National Biography, 1951–1960* (1971)

9 May 1960, 'Tribute to the Memory of Sir Hersch Lauterpacht', *Yearbook of the International Law Commission*, Vol. 1 (New York: United Nations, 1960), pp. 51–2

9 May 1960, Anonymous, *Daily Telegraph*

10 May 1960, Anonymous, *International Herald Tribune*

10 May 1960, Anonymous, *The Guardian*

10 May 1960, Anonymous, 'Sir Hersch Lauterpacht: International Law', *The Times*

11 May 1960, Lord Chorley, *The Times*

11 May 1960, Professor L. J. Harris, brief address at the funeral, unpublished

11 May 1960, Wilfred Jenks, funeral address in Cambridge synagogue

12 May 1960, Paul Guggenheim, Swiss newspaper

12 May 1960, Shabtai Rosenne, *Jerusalem Post*, p. 4

13 May 1960, Mrs H. G. Steers, *The Times*, p. 17

13 May 1960, Anonymous, *Jewish Chronicle*

17 May 1960, Lord Chorley, *The Times*, p. 15

19 May 1960, Professor N. Feinberg, *Haaretz*

20 May 1960, Sir Gerald Fitzmaurice, *The Times*, p. 17

24 May 1960, Anonymous, *The Day – New York*

8 June 1960, eulogy by the President of the ICJ in open court

1961, R. R. Baxter, (1961) 10 *ICLQ* 14–16

1961, Paul Guggenheim, 'Sir Hersch Lauterpacht (1987–1960)', (1961–II) 49 *Annuaire de l'Institut de Droit International* 529

January 1961, Professor Norman Bentwich, *Studies in Public International Law in Memory of Sir Hersch Lauterpacht*, ed. N. Feinberg (Faculty of Law, Hebrew University, Jerusalem, 1961)

4 May 1962, Rudolf Levy, *Mitteilungsblatt*, p. 12

1968, Professor N. Feinberg, 'Hersch Lauterpacht – Jurist and Thinker' (1968) 3 *Israel Law Review* 333–42

CHRONOLOGY OF SIGNIFICANT EVENTS IN THE LIFE OF SIR HERSCH LAUTERPACHT

Date	Event
1897, 16 August	Born in Żółkiew, Eastern Galicia
1910	Moved to Lemberg. Attended the Humanist Gymnasium and joined the 'Shahei' (a group of Zionist school pupils).
1913	Elected chairman of the 'Shahei'.
1915–16	Conscripted into the Austrian Army.
1915	Began his legal studies at the University of Lemberg (Lwów), which he continued for eight semesters.
1916	Revived the Zeire Zion movement in Lemberg, and formed the Herzlia Society of Zionist Youth. Later became leader of the Zionist undergraduate association, HAZ.
1917, 26 April	University of Lwów issued a certificate stating that Hersch took an examination in law and history before the Commission for State Examinations of the University.
1917, November	Responsible for arranging a demonstration to celebrate the publication of the Balfour Declaration.
1919	Travelled to Vienna for further study and research.
1920, 7 May	Was issued a passport by the Lemberg Police Directorate.
1920, 10 June	Applied to the Zionist Executive in London for a job.

(cont.)

Date	Event
1921, 13 June	Graduated 'Doctor jur' (University of Vienna).
1921, Autumn	Met Rachel Steinberg ('RS') in Vienna.
1922, July	Applied for a Polish passport.
1922, 15 July	Received degree of 'Doctor rerum politicarum' (University of Vienna).
1922, 18 December	Became engaged to be married to RS (while in Berlin).
1923, 20 March	Married RS in Vienna.
1923, 5 April	Arrived in Grimsby and took up residence in London.
1923	Registered for 1922–3 lectures at the LSE.
	Published 'The Teaching of Law in Vienna' (1923) *Journal of the Society of the Public Teachers in Law* 43–5.
1924 to beginning of 1927	Worked on the preparation of *Private Law Sources*.
1924, July	Accepted as a candidate for the LLD.
1925	Submitted *Private Law Sources* for the LLD. This was approved by the Faculty of Law of the University of London.
	Published 'Westlake and Present Day International Law' (1925) 5 *Economica* 307–25.
1926, 18 March	Joined International Law Association.
1926	Published 'The United States and the Permanent Court of International Justice' (1926) *Survey of International Affairs* 80–98
1926, November	*Private Law Sources* sent to press.
1927, May	*Private Law Sources* published.
1927, after May	Appointed as Assistant Lecturer at the LSE.
1927, July	Delivered a paper to the Grotius Society on 'Revolutionary Propaganda by Governments' (1927) 13 *Transactions of the Grotius Society* 143.
1927, mid to late	'Spinoza and International Law' published in (1927) 8 *BYIL* 89–107

Date	Event
1927, late	Moved to 103 Walm Lane, Cricklewood, London.
1928	Began work on *The Function of Law*.
	'The Doctrine of Non-Justiciable Disputes in International Law' published in (1928) 8 *Economica* 277–317.
	Published 'Sukcesja panstw w odiesienuiu do zobowiazari prywatnoprawnych' (1928) 5 *Glosu Prawa*.
	Published 'Legal Remedy in Case of Excess of Jurisdiction' (1928) 9 *BYIL* 117–20.
	Published 'Revolutionary Activities by Private Persons Against Foreign States' (1928) 22 *AJIL* 105–30.
	Hersch was elected to the LSE's Sociology Club.
1928, 13 July	Birth of his son, Elihu.
1928, November	Joined Gray's Inn.
1929	Began contributing to the *Annual Survey of English Law*.
1929	The 1925–6 volume of the *Annual Digest and Reports of Public International Law Cases* (with Sir Arnold D. McNair) was published (this was the first volume in the series to be published).
	Published 'Decisions of Municipal Courts as a Source of International Law' (1929) 10 *BYIL* 65–95
1930	Delivered 'La Théorie des différends non-justiciables en droit international' at the Hague Academy of International Law ((1930-IV) 34 *Hague Recueil* 499–653).
	Published 'Dissenting Opinions of National Judges and the Revision of the Statute of the Court' (1930) 11 *BYIL* 182–6.
	Published 'British Reservations to the Optional Clause' (1930) 10 *Economica* 137–72.

(cont.)

Date	Event
	Published 'Absence of an International Legislature and the Compulsory Jurisdiction of International Tribunals' (1930) 11 *BYIL* 134–7.
1931, 6 July	Was naturalised as a British subject.
1931	The 1927–8 volume of the *Annual Digest and Reports of Public International Law Cases* (with Sir Arnold D. McNair) was published.
	Published 'The So-Called Anglo-American and Continental Schools of Thought in International Law' (1931) 12 *BYIL* 31–62.
1932	The 1919–22 volume of the *Annual Digest and Reports of Public International Law Cases* (with Sir John Fischer Williams) was published.
	Published 'The Nature of International Law and General Jurisprudence' (1932) 12 *Economica* 301–20.
	Published 'Japan and the Covenant' (1932) 3 *Political Quarterly* 174–94.
1932, December	Provided the International Law Committee of the League of Nations Union with a memorandum on the Equality of States in the League.
1933	*The Function of Law in the International Community* was published.
	Published 'Boycott in International Relations' (1933) 14 *BYIL* 125–40.
1933, January	Accepted invitation to join the International Law Committee of the League of Nations Union.
1933	The 1923–4 volume of the *Annual Digest and Reports of Public International Law Cases* (with Sir John Fischer Williams) was published.
	Published 'Kelsen's Pure Science of Law' (1933) *Modern Theories of Law* 105–38.
1933, October	Prepared a memorandum for the International Law Committee on the question of the definition of 'war'.

Date	Event
1934, January	Delivered five lectures at the Graduate Institute of International Studies at Geneva.
1934	*The Development of International Law by the Permanent Court of International Justice* was published.
	Delivered 'Les Travaux préparatoires et l'interprétation des traités' at the Hague Academy of International Law ((1934-II) 48 *Hague Recueil* 713–819).
	Published 'The Pact of Paris and the Budapest Articles of Interpretation' (1934) 20 *Transactions of the Grotius Society* 178–204.
	Published '"Resort to War" and the Covenant during the Manchurian Dispute' (1934) 28 *AJIL* 43–60.
1935	Promoted to Reader at the LSE.
1935, early	Became editor of Volume II of *Oppenheim's International Law*; published the 5th edition of Volume I and Volume II in 1935.
1935	The 1929–30 volume of the *Annual Digest and Reports of Public International Law Cases* was published.
	Published 'Some Observations on Preparatory Work in the Interpretation of Treaties' (1935) 48 *Harvard Law Review* 549–91.
1936	Called to the Bar.
	Became a member of the Editorial Committee of the *BYIL*.
	Published 'Contract to Break a Contract' (1936) 52 *LQR* 494–529.
	Published 'Neutrality and Collective Security' (1936) 2 *Politica* 133–55.
	Published 'The Covenant as the "Higher Law"' (1936) 17 *BYIL* 54–65.
	Published 'International Law after the Covenant', (1936) (10th Series) *Problems of Peace* 37–56.

(cont.)

Date	Event
1936, Michaelmas	Started part-time teaching at Cambridge University Law Faculty.
1937	Published 'The Legal Aspect', in *Peaceful Change – An International Problem*, ed. C. A. W. Manning (1937), pp. 135–68.
	Published 'The Credentials of the Abyssinian Delegation to the Seventeenth Assembly of the League of Nations' (1937) 18 *BYIL* 184–6.
	Delivered 'Règles générales du droit de la paix' at the Hague Academy of International Law ((1937-IV) 62 *Hague Recueil* 99–419).
1937, Lent Term	Continued Dr McNair's course on State and Diplomatic Immunity at Cambridge.
1937, November	Elected to the Whewell Chair of International Law at Cambridge.
1937, late	Began writing *Recognition in International Law* (published 1947).
1938, 1 January	Officially assumed duties of the Whewell Professor.
1938, June	Bought 6 Cranmer Road, Cambridge, from Arnold McNair.
1938	The 1931–2 volume of the *Annual Digest and Reports of Public International Law Cases* was published.
	Published 'The Cristina' (1938) 52 *LQR* 339–46.
1938, September	Family moved into 6 Cranmer Road.
1939, February	Prepared opinion concerning Article 18 of the Palestine Mandate.
1939	Published 'The Form of Foreign Office Certificates' (1939) 20 *BYIL* 125–8.
	Published 'Insurrection et Piraterie' (1939) (Séries 3) 20 *Revue Générale de Droit International Public* 513–49.
	Published 'Recognition of Insurgents as a De Facto Government' (1939–40) 3 *Modern Law Review* 1–20.

Date	Event
1940–2	Continued work on his draft of *Recognition in International Law.*
1940	Published the sixth edition of Volume II of *Oppenheim's International Law.*
	The 1933–1934 volume of the *Annual Digest and Reports of Public International Law Cases* was published.
	Published 'Is International Law a Part of the Law of England?' (1940) 25 *Transactions of the Grotius Society* 51–88.
1940, June	Joined the Home Guard.
1940, late	Accepted invitation from the Carnegie Endowment for International Peace to give US lecture tour.
1940, 21 September	Left for the US with RL and EL.
1940, 3 October	Arrived in the US.
1940, 4 October	Met with Professor Philip C. Jessup.
1940, 7 October to 9 December	US lecture tour:
	• University of Virginia, Charlottesville, 8–14 October 1940
	• Duke University, Durham, and University of North Carolina, Chapel Hill, 15–23 October 1940
	• Tulane University, New Orleans, 25–31 October 1940
	• University of Kansas, Lawrence, 3–9 November 1940
	• University of Illinois, Urbana, 11–18 November 1940
	• University of Wisconsin, Madison, 21–24 November 1940
	• University of Minnesota, Minneapolis, 25–30 November 1940
	• Cornell University, Ithaca, 4–8 December 1940

(cont.)

Date	Event
	Independently of his engagements as Visiting Carnegie Professor, Hersch delivered lectures at:
	• University of Louisiana
	• University of Chicago
	• University of Michigan
	• Harvard Law School
	• Amherst College
	• Smith College
	• Queens College
1941, 4 January	Sent to the Carnegie Endowment a report on his lecture tour.
1941, early January	In Washington to consult with the US Attorney-General, Robert H. Jackson.
1941, 15 January	Sent memorandum to the US Attorney-General on 'Qualified Neutrality'.
1941, 27–29 January	Arrived back in Cambridge.
1941, 5 February	Reported to Sir Stephen Gaselee at the Foreign Office regarding his US lecture tour.
1941, March	Published a review article for the *Political Quarterly* of Lord Cecil's autobiography, *A Great Experiment*.
1941, 27 May	Delivered paper on 'The Reality of the Law of Nations' at the Royal Institute of International Affairs.
1941	The 1935–7 volume of the *Annual Digest and Reports of Public International Law Cases* was published.
	Published 'The Principle of Non-Recognition in International Law', in *Legal Problems in the Far Eastern Conflict* (1941), pp. 129–56.
	Published 'Resurrection of the League' (1941) 12 *Political Quarterly* 121–33.
1941, 29 July	Left for the US to give lectures at Wellesley College, Massachusetts.
1941, 2 August	Arrived in the US.

Date	Event
1941, 22 September	Began lectures at Wellesley in international law and international relations.
1941, 15 October	Delivered public lectures on 'The Present Position and the Future of the Law of Nations'.
1941, 16–22 October	Travelled to Washington to meet the US Attorney-General, Francis Biddle.
1941, 23 October	Delivered public lectures on 'The Present Position and the Future of the Law of Nations'.
1941, November	Travelled to Washington to meet the Attorney-General in connection with work he was doing for him.
1942, 23 March	Arrived back in England.
1942	The 1938–40 volume of the *Annual Digest and Reports of Public International Law Cases* was published.
1942, 2 December	Delivered lecture to the Grotius Society on 'The Law of Nations, the Law of Nature and the Rights of Man' (1944) 29 *Transactions of the Grotius Society* 1–33.
1942–5	Prepared book on *International Bill of Human Rights*.
1942	Participated in a memorandum on the prosecution of war criminals.
1942, January	Became member of the Inter-Allied Commission on the Punishment of War Crimes.
1942, August	Prepared a paper on the defence of superior orders for the Inter-Allied Commission on the Punishment of War Crimes.
1942, 17 August	Completed his memorandum on Crimes against International Public Order and the Punishment of War Crimes.
1943, May	Gave three public lectures at Cambridge on 'The Law of Nations, the Law of Nature and the Rights of Man'

(cont.)

Date	Event
1943, 26 October	Gave a twenty-minute talk on the BBC Third Programme on human rights.
1944	Became editor of the *BYIL* (remained editor until 1955) and published Volume 21.
	Published the revised sixth edition of Volume II of *Oppenheim's International Law*.
	Published 'The Law of Nations, the Law of Nature and the Rights of Man' (1944) 29 *Transactions of the Grotius Society* 1–33.
	Published 'Implied Recognition' (1944) 21 *BYIL* 123–50.
	Published 'Recognition of States in International Law' (1944) 53 *Yale Law Journal* 385–458.
	Published 'The Law of Nature and the Punishment of War Crimes' (1944) 21 *BYIL* 58–95.
1945	Published Volume 22 of the *BYIL*.
	Became a Fellow of Trinity College, Cambridge.
	Published *An International Bill of the Rights of Man*.
1945, Spring	Sent the 1945 volume of the *BYIL* to press.
1945, 1 and 29 July	Met with Justice Jackson to discuss the Nuremberg indictment.
1945	The 1941–2 volume of the *Annual Digest and Reports of Public International Law Cases* was published.
	Published 'De Facto Recognition, Withdrawal of Recognition and Conditional Recognition' (1945) 22 *BYIL* 164–90.
	Published 'Recognition of Governments, I' (1945) 45 *Columbia Law Review* 815–64.
1945, August to January 1946	Provided Attorney-General Sir Hartley Shawcross with assistance in the prosecution of William Joyce.

Date	Event
1945, August	Appointed to the British War Crimes Executive.
1945, 21 August to 27 May 1946	Prepared drafts of the British Prosecutor's opening and closing speeches at the Nuremberg trial.
1945, 21 August	Met with Sir Hartley Shawcross in connection with the Joyce case and the Nuremberg trial.
1945, 4 September	Drafted a memorandum regarding the William Joyce case for Sir Hartley Shawcross.
1945, 26 September	Attended a meeting of the British War Crimes Executive in London to consider administrative matters.
1945, 1 October	Drafted a second and a third memorandum to assist Sir Hartley Shawcross in the William Joyce case.
1945, 20–23 November	Attended the opening of the Nuremberg trial.
1945, 4 December	Delivered an open lecture in Cambridge on the Nuremberg trial.
1946	Published Volume 23 of the *BYIL*. Published 'Recognition of Governments, II' (1946) 46 *Columbia Law Review* 37–68. Published 'The Grotian Tradition in International Law' (1946) 23 *BYIL* 1–53.
1946, January	Elected a member of the Athenaeum.
1946, January	Visited by Green H. Hackworth, the Legal Adviser of the US State Department.
1946, March	Prepared an opinion on the effect of certain laws issued by the Allied Military Government, regarding 'denationalisation' and the Allied Control Commission in Germany.
1946, March	Learnt that his niece, Inka Gelbard, had survived the Holocaust.
1946, 29 March	Sir Hartley Shawcross requested assistance in the case *R. v. Bottrill, ex parte Kuechenmeister.*

(cont.)

Date	Event
1946, Lent Term	Delivered a lecture on the William Joyce case in Cambridge; subsequently published in (1947) 9 *Cambridge Law Journal* 330–48.
1946, May	Declined an invitation from the Director of the LSE to return to the School as Professor of International Law.
1946, May	Prepared draft closing speech for Sir Hartley Shawcross at Nuremberg.
1946, 29 May	Travelled to Nuremberg to consult with Sir David Maxwell Fyfe.
1946, June	Delivered a thirty-nine-page Opinion in the case of the *Adelaide Star*.
1946, 3 June	Reported to Sir Hartley Shawcross on his meeting with Sir David Maxwell Fyfe.
1946, Autumn	Opinion for the Imperial Continental Gas Association in connection with the nationalisation by France of two utility companies.
1946, Autumn	Asked to advise on the treatment of the property of the Prince of Liechtenstein in Czechoslovakia.
1946, September	Travelled to Nuremberg to hear the final judgment, delivered on 1 October 1946.
1947	Published Volume 24 of the *BYIL*. *Recognition in International Law* published. Published the sixth edition of Volume 1 of *Oppenheim's International Law*. Delivered 'International Protection of Human Rights' at the Hague Academy of International Law ((1947-I) 70 *Hague Recueil* 5–107).
1947, April	Received a request from Sir Hartley Shawcross relating to the effect of the German denationalisation law of 1941.
1947	The 1919–42 Supplementary Volume of the *Annual Digest and Reports of Public International Law Cases* was published.

Date	Event
	Published 'The Subjects of the Law of Nations, I' (1947) 63 *LQR* 438–60.
1947, 15 September	Attended International Law Association meeting in Prague.
1947, October	Provided an opinion on two legal points relating to Palestine.
1948	Published Volume 25 of the *BYIL*.
	Published 'The Subjects of the Law of Nations, II' (1948) 64 *LQR* 97–119.
	Published 'The Universal Declaration of Human Rights' (1948) 25 *BYIL* 354–81.
	'Human Rights, the Charter of the United Nations, and the International Bill of the Rights of Man' published in the *Report of the Forty-Third Conference of the ILA* (1948), pp. 80–113.
	'Human Rights', Statement at the Brussels Conference of the International Law Association is published in the *Report of the Forty-Third Conference of the ILA* (1948), pp. 29–44.
	Published the seventh edition of Volume I of *Oppenheim's International Law*.
	Published 'The Nationality of Denationalized Persons' (1949) *Jewish Yearbook of International Law* 164–85.
1948, February to March	Assisted in the *Corfu Channel* case as part of the British legal team. Left for The Hague in the last week of Lent Term in Cambridge.
1948, March	Received a request to draft a document that could serve as a Declaration of Independence for Israel.
1948, April	Left Cambridge for New York, spending four weeks working in the Legal Department of the UN on the 'Survey of International Law in Relation to the Work of Codification of the International Law Commission'.

(cont.)

459

Date	Event
1948, early June	Received a request for his assistance in connection with a developing dispute between Hyderabad and India. Attended two consultations in London before leaving for the University of Colorado.
1948, June	Sailed to New York en route to Colorado.
1948, June to August	Visiting Professor at the University of Colorado.
1948, June	Produced a second Opinion in the *Adelaide Star* case.
1948, 28 June	Asked to prepare a summary of the arguments for and against the proposition that Hyderabad was a 'State'.
1948, July	Elected a Fellow of the British Academy.
1948, 5 July	Sent a nine-page memorandum dealing with a number of issues in the Hyderabad situation.
1948, 13 July	Sent to London the summary argument on the status of Hyderabad.
1948, 20 July	Replied to a request for advice from Sir Eric Beckett at the Foreign Office on the question of whether recommendations made by the UN Security Council under Chapters VI and VII of the UN Charter are binding on Members of the UN.
1948, 22–26 July	Left Colorado to lecture at the Universities of Michigan and Illinois.
1948, 29 and 30 July and 1 August	Gave further advice regarding the Hyderabad situation.
1948, 20 August	Advised by cable on submitting the Hyderabad situation to the UN Security Council and General Assembly.
1948, 26 August	Arrived back in England.
1948, 27 August	Attended a consultation in connection with the Hyderabad case.
1948, 29–30 August	Travelled to Brussels to attend a meeting of the ILA.

Date	Event
1948, 31 August	Circulated a detailed note regarding the Hyderabad case and the possibility of recourse to the ICJ.
1948, September	In Paris working on the Hyderabad case.
1948, 6 September	Finished a more developed summary of the Hyderabad case.
1948, 21 September	Instructions in the Hyderabad case were concluded.
1949	Published Volume 26 of the *BYIL*.
1949, January	Confined to bed for twelve days with a sinus infection. Later in January, went to Hove for a few days.
1949, 10 February	Concluded 'Survey of International Law in Relation to the Work of Codification of the International Law Commission'.
1949, February	Delivered a paper to the Grotius Society on 'The Proposed European Court of Human Rights' (published in (1950) 35 *Transactions of the Grotius Society* 25–47).
1949, February to June	Advised on dispute between the Kuwait Oil Company and the Sheikh of Kuwait.
1949, April	Appointed King's Counsel.
1949, end of April	Prepared Opinion for the Swiss Government in the *Vitianu* case.
1949, June	The Lord Chancellor, Lord Jowitt, asked Hersch to provide some suggestions for a talk that he was to deliver. Hersch sent the Lord Chancellor a complete draft.
1949	The 1943–5 volume of the *Annual Digest and Reports of Public International Law Cases* was published.
1949, October	Sent a message of congratulation to the Hebrew University on the occasion of the opening of its Faculty of Law.
1949, 5 October	Sent the revision and expansion of his book, *International Law and Human Rights*, to press.

(cont.)

Date	Event
1949, 12 October	Recorded a talk on the BBC Third Programme entitled 'Towards an International Bill of Rights' (published in *The Listener*, 3 November 1949, pp. 747–8).
1949	Published 'Restrictive Interpretation and the Principle of Effectiveness in the Interpretation of Treaties' (1949) 26 *BYIL* 48–85.
1949, October	Consulted by the Kuwait Oil Company with regard to the concession dispute with the Sheikh of Kuwait; produced a draft joint Opinion.
1949, October	Began work as *rapporteur* on the 'Interpretation of Treaties' commission of the Institut de Droit International.
1950	Published Volume 27 of the *BYIL*.
1950, January	Invited to become a member of a British Government Inter-departmental Committee on the law of State and diplomatic immunity. Prepared a substantial memorandum on State immunity.
1950	*International Law and Human Rights* was published.
1950, 6 January	Article published by *The Times* regarding the law relating to recognition.
1950, 8 January	Wrote to the Chinese Ambassador regarding article in *The Times*.
1950, 4 July	Wrote to Beckett at the Foreign Office expanding on the letter published in *The Times*.
1950, late	Contacted Beckett at the Foreign Office regarding the legality of the use of atomic weapons.
1950	Formally retired from the Bar. Published 'The Proposed European Court of Human Rights' (1950) 35 *Transactions of the Grotius Society* 25–47.

Date	Event
	Published 'Sovereignty over Submarine Areas' (1950) 27 *BYIL* 376–433.
	Presented a series of lectures, 'De l'Interprétation des traités, Rapport et project de résolutions', to the Institut de Droit International (1950-I) 43 *Annuaire de l'Institut de Droit International* 366–460.
1951	Published Volume 28 of the *BYIL*.
	The 1946 and 1947 volumes of the *Annual Digest and Reports of Public International Law Cases* were published.
	Published 'The Problem of Jurisdictional Immunities of Foreign States' (1951) 28 *BYIL* 220–72.
	Published a foreword to Lissitzyn, *The International Court of Justice* (1951), pp. v–xiv.
1952	Published Volume 29 of the *BYIL*.
	Presented a series of lectures 'De l'Interprétation des traités, Observations complémentaires et projet définitive de résolutions', to the Institut de Droit International, (1952-1) 44 *Annuaire de l'Institut de Droit International* 197–223.
	Published 'The Problem of the Revision of the Law of War' (1952) 29 *BYIL* 360–82.
	Published the seventh edition of Volume II of *Oppenheim's International Law*.
1953	Published Volume 30 of the *BYIL*.
	Published the 1948 volume of the *Annual Digest and Reports of Public International Law Cases*.
	Published 'The Limits of the Operation of the Laws of War' (1953) 30 *BYIL* 206–43.
	Published 'Rules of Warfare in an Unlawful War' in *Law and Politics in the World Community (Essays on Hans Kelsen's Pure Theory and Related Problems in International Law)*, ed. G. A. Lipsky (1953), pp. 89–113.
	Published 'Law of Treaties' (1953-II) *Yearbook of the International Law Commission* 90–166.
1954	Published report on the 'Law of Treaties' (1954-II) *Yearbook of the International Law Commission* 123–39.

(cont.)

Date	Event
	Published 'Some Possible Solutions of the Problem of Reservations to Treaties' (1954) 39 *Transactions of the Grotius Society* 97–118.
1954, 7 October	Elected a judge of the International Court of Justice.
1954	Published 'The Rose Mary' (1954) 12 *Cambridge Law Journal* 20–2.
1955	Published the eighth edition of Volume 1 of *Oppenheim's International Law*.
1955, 3 February	Travelled to The Hague.
1955, 10 February	Formally admitted as a Judge
1955	Published the 1949 volume of the *Annual Digest and Reports of Public International Law Cases*.
1955, 7 June	Gave his separate Opinion on the *Question of Voting Procedure Relating to Reports and Petitions Concerning the Territory of South West Africa* (ICJ Reports 1955, p. 67: Separate Opinion, pp. 90–123).
1955, 13 July	Attended a dinner given at the Mansion House by the Lord Mayor of London in honour of Her Majesty's judges.
1955, 1 September	Completed substantial memorandum on the revision of the Statute of the Court.
1955	Published 'Codification and Development of International Law' (1955) 49 *AJIL* 16–43. Published 'Brierly's Contribution to International Law' (1955–6) 32 *BYIL* 1–19.
1956	Published Volume 31 of the *BYIL*.
1956, 1 January	Knighted in the New Year's Honours List.
1956, 14 February	Attended investiture by the Queen at Buckingham Palace.
1956, March	Participated in the review of, and the decision to strike off, cases brought by the US against Czechoslovakia in respect of an aerial incident on 10 March 1953 (ICJ Reports 1956, p. 6); and by the United Kingdom against Argentina and Chile in respect of competing claims to Antarctica (ICJ Reports 1956, p. 12).

Date	Event
1956	Published the 1950 volume of the *International Law Reports*.
1956, 1 June	Delivered a separate Opinion on the *Admissibility of Hearings of Petitioners by the Committee on South West Africa* (ICJ Reports 1956, p. 23: Separate Opinion, pp. 35–59).
1956, June to November	Involved in the drafting of the Advisory Opinion on *Judgments of the Administrative Tribunal of the International Labour Organization upon Complaints Made Against UNESCO*, delivered on 23 October 1956 (ICJ Reports 1956, p. 77).
1956	Delivered separate Opinion in *Application of the Convention of 1902 Governing the Guardianship of Infants* (ICJ Reports 1956, p. 55: Separate Opinion, pp. 74–101).
1957	Delivered a thirty-two-page separate Opinion in the *Norwegian Loans* case (ICJ Reports 1957, p. 9: Separate Opinion, pp. 34–66).
	Published the 1951, 1952, 1953 and 1954 volumes of the *International Law Reports*.
	Delivered separate Opinion in the *Case of Certain Norwegian Loans* (ICJ Reports 1957, p. 9: Separate Opinion, pp. 34–66).
1957, November	Concurred in the rejection by the ICJ of preliminary objections brought in the *Case Concerning a Right of Passage over Indian Territory* (ICJ Reports 1957, p. 125).
1958	Published 'The Law of War on Land', being Part III of the *Manual of Military Law*.
	Published 'Some Observations on the Prohibition of "Non Liquet" and the Completeness of the Legal Order', in *Symbolae Verzijl* (1958), pp. 196–221.
	Published Brierly, *The Basis of Obligation in International Law and Other Papers*.

(*cont.*)

Date	Event
	Published *The Development of International Law by the International Court.*
	Published the 1955 volume of the *International Law Reports.*
	Delivered a concurring Opinion in the *Case Concerning the Application of the Convention of 1902 Governing the Guardianship of Infants* (ICJ Reports 1956, p. 55: Separate Opinion, pp. 74–101).
1959	Published 'International Law and Colonial Questions, 1870–1914', in *Cambridge History of the British Empire* (1959), Vol. II, pp. 667–707 (with R. Y. Jennings).
	Delivered a dissenting Opinion in the *Interhandel* case (Preliminary Objections) (ICJ Reports 1959, p. 6: Dissenting Opinion, pp. 95–122).
1959, June	Delivered a joint dissenting Opinion, together with Judge Wellington Koo and Sir Percy Spender, in the *Case Concerning the Aerial Incident of July 27, 1955* (ICJ Reports 1959, p. 127: Joint Dissenting Opinion, pp. 156–94).
1959	Delivered dissenting Opinion in the *Case Concerning Sovereignty over Certain Frontier Land* (ICJ Reports 1959, p. 209: Declaration, pp. 230–2).
1959, October	Suffered a heart attack in The Hague.
1959, October	Travelled to Israel for convalescence.
1960	Published 1956 volume of the *International Law Reports.*
1960, May	Returned to England; saw Lord Moran.
1960, 7 May	Entered the London Clinic to prepare for an operation the following day.
1960, 8 May	Died on the operating table after suffering a further heart attack.
1960, 11 May	Funeral took place in the synagogue in Thompson's Lane in Cambridge.
1961	The 1957 volume of the *International Law Reports* (completed by Sir Eli Lauterpacht) was published.

INDEX

INDEX

Lemberg (Lwów/Lviv) (*cont.*)
  occupation
    German forces (1941–2) 100–1, 175,
      209–11
    Soviet forces (1939–41) 100–1, 175, 209
  Shahei 11, 19, 21–2
Lemberg University
  boycott by Jewish students 23–4
  HL's attendance at 9, 14, 15
    certificate from (26 April 1917) 15
    uncertainty relating to final
      examinations/graduation 15
  numerus clausus/closure to Jews 12–13, 15, 16,
    21
Li-Liang, Yuen 303–4, 306–7, 356, 357
Lissitzyn, Oliver J. 348–9
Logan, Douglas 84, 86
London School of Economics and Political
    Science: *see* LSE; LSE Archives; LSE
    and HL (1923–37)
Longmans
  AD and 68–9
  Annual Digest and 50–1, 57
  bombing and loss of *Oppenheim* stock 146
  Private Law Sources and 47–8
Lothian, Lord (1882–1940) 105, 114, 120
Lourie, Arthur 184
LSE
  ADM and 40–1
  Contributions to International Law and Diplomacy
    series 56, 68–9
  evacuation to Cambridge 102–3
  as Fabian institution 40–1
  Fry Library of International Law 40–1, 45
  grant to *AD* 68–9
  Houghton Street building 40–1
  Institute of International Studies, proposal
    for 47
  international law and 40–1
  staff numbers 40 n. 6
  student numbers 40 n. 6
LSE Archives x, 59 n. 40, 59 n. 41
LSE and HL (1923–37)
  assistant lecturer (1927–33) 57–9
  coaching in international law 40 n. 8
  election as Professor of International Law
    5–6
  HL leaves with regret
  HL's affection for/gift to (1958) 99
  HL's difficulty in paying fees 40
  Lecturer (1933–5) 59
  lectures/lecture notes 59, 426–7
  LLD
    ADM's support 45
    application for (1924)/meeting the
      qualifying requirements 45
    awarded (1925) (*Private Law Sources*) 45
    thoughts of (1922) 32

opens discussion on 'Westlake and
    International Law of Today' (1925) 46
photograph of 1923–4 class *Plate 8*
proving his worth 424
Reader (1935–7) 59
reasons for HL's choice of 38–9, 40–1
research students class
  ADM and HL discuss possible changes
    46–7
  publication of Transactions 47
'Revision of the Laws of War' (lecture, 2
    February 1953) 359
salary 91–2
Sociology Club membership 58
Lwów/Lviv: *see* Lemberg (Lwów/Lviv)
Lyons, Gladys (GL) and Bernard 69, 212, 276,
    426–7
  take EL to pantomime 426–7

MacGibbon, Iain 97
McKinnon Wood, Hugh 128
Mackintosh, James 202
MacLeish, Archibald, Rede Lecture in
    Cambridge ('a poor show') 207
McNair, Arnold Duncan (Lord McNair)
    (ADM)
  career
    Anglo-Iranian Oil Company case
    Aramco case 41–2
    Cambridge Professor of Comparative
      Law (1945–6) 41
    Committee chairmanships 201
    decision not to seek re-election (1954) 373
    European Court of Human Rights
      (President) (1959–65) 41–2
    ICJ: election to (1946) 41, 283; following
      retirement from 379 n. 8; President
      (1952–5) 41; role of separate opinions
      391
    ILA and Grotius Society, hopes for
      improving 179
    international law: development of interest
      in 41; importance of teaching 179
    Liverpool University Vice-Chancellor
      (1937–45) 41, 82
    LSE 40–1
    not an *anima naturaliter philosophica* 41–2, 52
    Opinion on Latin Monetary Union 51
    qualification as solicitor and (1917)
      barrister 41
    Whewell Chair 41, 82
  family 41
    John McNair (son) 194
  photograph of *Plate 8*
  publications
    'Effect of War on Contracts (including
      Frustration)' (Grotius Society,
      September 1941) 179

Lightning Source UK Ltd.
Milton Keynes UK
UKOW050210080213

206004UK00001B/31/P